COMPARATIVE HEALTHCARE LAW

Cavendish
Publishing
Limited

London • Sydney

COMPARATIVE HEALTHCARE LAW

Professor Peter de Cruz, LLB, LLM, PhD
School of Law
Staffordshire University

Routledge
Taylor & Francis Group
LONDON AND NEW YORK

First published 2001 by Cavendish Publishing Limited

2 Park Square, Milton Park, Abingdon, Oxon OX14 4RN
711 Third Avenue, New York, NY 10017, USA

Routledge is an imprint of the Taylor & Francis Group, an informa business

First issued in hardback 2016

British Library Cataloguing in Publication Data

De Cruz, Peter
Comparative healthcare law
1 Public health laws
I Title
344'.04

ISBN 978-1-85941-588-7 (pbk)
ISBN 978-1-138-16307-2 (hbk)

PREFACE

Healthcare law is a subject which has grown over the years from notions of doctor-patient responsibility which originated several centuries ago. Some forms of doctor-patient relationships probably pre-date even medieval times in the era of witch doctors and medicine men in the more remote areas of the world. Towards the end of the 20th century, healthcare law has become a recognisable body of law, many parts of which have been labelled 'medical law' (see Kennedy and Grubb (1998)) which, as Montgomery in his *Health Care Law* explains, might be seen as unduly restricting the subject to the clinical medical context. In contemporary times, as we approach the end of the first year of the new millennium, not just doctors but also other health professionals are responsible for delivering health services to the public and, in Britain, the National Health Service (NHS) continues to be unique in being a government-run body which provides a range of health services to the general population. Today, there are many public health issues which affect and concern either whole communities or the bulk of the population which now require consideration from a legal, medical and ethical point of view.

In the latter part of the 20th century, when faced with medical cases or cases involving healthcare professionals, the English courts have begun to refer to other jurisdictions with increasing frequency to provide persuasive authority for principles which they wish to support and apply. The classic example has been the consistent citation of Justice Cardozo's principle of self-determination in *Schloendorff v New York Hospital* (1914), which is of course not an English case but whose principle has subsequently been affirmed and approved, relatively recently, in English courts. One reason for this reliance on overseas authorities was the relative lack of English common law cases which actually addressed the disputes before the English courts.

It seemed to me that, although there are some excellent books on this subject, one had to search through fragmented parts of texts or have recourse to sources such as international journals if one wished to ascertain the American, Australian, French or German position on a particular topic or leading overseas cases on, for example, abortion. As far as I am aware, there is no other book which contains an eclectic but fairly comprehensive survey of English law relating to issues such as abortion, surrogacy, sterilisation of mentally handicapped persons, human organ donation and transplantation and euthanasia, and the law in other jurisdictions in some detail, except in piecemeal form, or as isolated chapters, in edited collections.

This book intends to begin to fill a gap in the medico-legal literature by considering a range of selected topics in healthcare, *first*, from the English common law perspective, although Irish and Scots law sometimes features, as do other occasional comparative allusions and, *secondly*, from a comparative law perspective which includes, wherever appropriate and available, American law, Australian law, and civil law countries broadly represented by France and Germany. It needs to be emphasised that this book does not attempt to present a fully comprehensive comparative analysis of the various topics, as that would require many more years than this writer has available for research and analysis. Rather, this text surveys some of the *key topics* and cases which have attracted attention by virtue of their universality and commonality. For instance, the ethics and law relating to genetics, research subjects and biomedicine are not really tackled at this juncture, although cases of children born posthumously, such as in the Diane Blood case in the UK, have been included and compared to the Australian equivalent, to illustrate the differences in approach and to a German case involving sperm donation. Surrogacy is discussed from the point of view of the English cases, the famous American case of *Baby M* and the case of *Re Evelyn* in Australia. There is a historical survey of compulsory sterilisation of mentally incapacitated persons, but there is no comparative survey of mental health legislation or mental health cases in the present volume, although case law developments in England and Wales have been noted. For abortion, a global survey has been offered in outline, and for the controversial topic of euthanasia, the Dutch position is examined in some detail. In some ways, this is merely the beginning of an enterprise and I would like to thank Professor Margaret Brazier (Manchester University), for her support and encouragement in this venture; my colleague Dianne Gibbons, Module Leader of the Healthcare law and Ethics course which we teach at Staffordshire University Law School, for her very useful ideas and opinions on various topics, and senior law librarian Alison Pope at our Law School, for obtaining a summary of the recent conjoined twins case very speedily; thanks also go to Staffordshire University Law School for their support in this enterprise; heartfelt thanks are also due to Cavendish Publishing, who have been very understanding of the problems I have encountered in writing this book, resulting in delays at crucial times, but who have nevertheless remained very supportive throughout; most of all, I wish to thank the current Research Associate at Staffordshire University Law School, Joanne Beswick, who provided me with a range of materials with speed and efficiency and provided tremendous research assistance and support throughout. However, the usual caveat applies and I remain solely responsible for any errors that exist herein.

Finally, I wish to dedicate this book first of all to my wife, Lois, who has put up with the many travails of authorship, not least my apparent addiction to the word processor for what seemed interminable months and the ever-growing mounds of folders and books apparently everywhere; and secondly to the memory of my late father, and to my mother, who has never ceased to encourage me enthusiastically in all my endeavours, despite having to cope with all her own recent recurring health problems. She has certainly seen the work of healthcare professionals at first hand in her latest sojourn in an NHS hospital.

The law is stated as at 1 November 2000.

Peter de Cruz
Staffordshire University
December 2000

CONTENTS

Preface *v*

Table of Cases *xv*

Table of Statutes *xxxiii*

Table of Statutory Instruments *xxxvii*

Table of International Legislation *xxxix*

Abbreviations *xlvii*

INTRODUCTION **xlv**

PART I: HEALTHCARE LAW IN ENGLAND AND WALES 1

1 CONSENT TO MEDICAL TREATMENT **3**

INTRODUCTION 3
THE ETHICAL FRAMEWORK 3
INFORMED CONSENT IN ENGLISH LAW 4
CONSENT TO MEDICAL TREATMENT UNDER ENGLISH COMMON LAW 8
CONCLUSIONS ON THE ENGLISH NOTION OF CONSENT TO TREATMENT 43
SELECTIVE BIBLIOGRAPHY 44

2 MEDICAL CONFIDENTIALITY AND HEALTHCARE LAW **47**

INTRODUCTION 47
GUIDANCE IN PROFESSIONAL CODES 49
JUSTIFICATIONS FOR CONFIDENTIALITY 51
CONFIDENTIALITY FOR PEOPLE UNDER 16 53
LEGAL BASES FOR CONFIDENTIALITY? 55
ACCESS TO MEDICAL RECORDS 69
CONFIDENTIALITY, HIV AND AIDS 70
INTERNATIONAL PROTECTION OF PRIVACY RIGHTS? 73
COMMENTS ON CONFIDENTIALITY IN ENGLISH LAW AND UK MEDICAL PRACTICE 73
SELECTIVE BIBLIOGRAPHY 74

3 ABORTION **77**

INTRODUCTION 77
ETHICAL AND PHILOSOPHICAL PRINCIPLES 78
HISTORICAL BACKGROUND 81

ABORTION LAW IN THE UK 83
THE ORIGINS OF LIFE AND EMBRYO RESEARCH 109
CONCLUSIONS 112
SELECTIVE BIBLIOGRAPHY 113

4 CHILDREN AND HEALTHCARE 117

INTRODUCTION 117
FUNCTIONS OF CONSENT 118
CHILDREN'S RIGHTS 132
ACTING IN THE 'BEST INTERESTS OF THE CHILD' 133
INTERNATIONAL PERSPECTIVES 134
THE MEDICAL TREATMENT OF HANDICAPPED BABIES 135
THE EUROPEAN CONVENTION FOR THE PROTECTION OF HUMAN RIGHTS AND FUNDAMENTAL FREEDOMS 138
PARENTAL WISHES, MEDICAL TREATMENT AND DISABLED BABIES 138
CONCLUSIONS 161
SELECTIVE BIBLIOGRAPHY 161

5 ASSISTED REPRODUCTION AND SURROGACY 163

INTRODUCTION 163
LEGAL AND ETHICAL FRAMEWORK 164
SURROGACY 168
COMMENT ON SURROGACY 187
POSTHUMOUS REPRODUCTION FROM SPERM TAKEN FROM A DECEASED DONOR 187
ACCESS TO IVF SERVICES – OPEN TO ALL OR ONLY TO THOSE WITHIN CERTAIN AGE LIMITS? 191
SELECTIVE BIBLIOGRAPHY 194

6 STERILISATION, FERTILITY CONTROL AND THE MENTALLY INCAPACITATED PATIENT 197

INTRODUCTION 197
ETHICAL PRINCIPLES 197
HISTORICAL BACKGROUND 198
CONSENSUAL AND NON-CONSENSUAL STERILISATION 200
STERILISATION IN THE 'BEST INTERESTS' – A SCOTTISH COMPARISON 227
CONCLUSIONS 230
SELECTIVE BIBLIOGRAPHY 231

7 **MEDICAL NEGLIGENCE AND PROFESSIONAL ACCOUNTABILITY** **233**
INTRODUCTION 233
HISTORICAL PERSPECTIVES 233
NEGLIGENCE IN ENGLISH LAW 233
GENERAL PRINCIPLES 234
MEDICAL LITIGATION IN THE UK 266
CONCLUDING COMMENTS ON MEDICAL NEGLIGENCE IN ENGLISH LAW 267
SELECTIVE BIBLIOGRAPHY 268

8 **DONATION AND TRANSPLANTATION OF HUMAN ORGANS** **271**
INTRODUCTION 271
BACKGROUND TO ORGAN TRANSPLANTATION 272
LEGAL PERSPECTIVES 272
KEY ETHICAL ISSUES 273
SALE OF HUMAN ORGANS 273
REMOVAL OF ORGANS, UNLAWFUL ACTS AND CONSENT 275
LIVE DONOR TRANSPLANTATION 277
CHILDREN AS ORGAN DONORS 280
LIVE DONOR TRANSPLANTS – THE HUMAN ORGANS TRANSPLANT ACT 1989 281
TRANSPLANTS BETWEEN UNRELATED PERSONS 282
FETAL TRANSPLANTATION 283
INCOMPETENT ADULTS AS DONORS 283
EFFECTIVE VENTILATION OF PATIENTS CLOSE TO DEATH 284
CADAVERIC TRANSPLANTATION 284
RECENT DEVELOPMENTS 287
REFORMING THE LAW 289
SELECTIVE BIBLIOGRAPHY 289

9 **THE END OF LIFE – EUTHANASIA AND PHYSICIAN-ASSISTED SUICIDE** **291**
INTRODUCTION 291
HISTORICAL LEGAL BACKGROUND TO ASSISTED SUICIDE 291
DEFINITIONS OF EUTHANASIA 292
A RIGHT TO LIFE? 294
A RIGHT TO DIE? 294
THE ANENCEPHALIC BABY AND BRAIN DEATH 298
THE ETHICAL DIMENSION 298
CRIMINAL LIABILITY 299

AUTHORISATION OF NON-TREATMENT 303
ADVANCE DIRECTIVES 315
RECENT DEVELOPMENTS 317
CONCLUSIONS 318
SELECTIVE BIBLIOGRAPHY 318

PART II: COMPARATIVE PERSPECTIVES 321

10 CONSENT TO MEDICAL TREATMENT: EVOLUTION AND DEVELOPMENT OF THE LAW IN NON-UK JURISDICTIONS 323

INTRODUCTION 323
AMERICAN LAW 324
A BRITISH COMPARATIVE EXCURSUS 332
CANADA 333
AUSTRALIA 337
AN AUSTRALIAN-AMERICAN COMPARISON 348
NEW ZEALAND 348
CIVIL LAW COUNTRIES 348
NON-EUROPEAN PERSPECTIVES 352
COMPARATIVE OBSERVATIONS 355
SELECTIVE BIBLIOGRAPHY 356

11 MEDICAL CONFIDENTIALITY AND PROFESSIONAL PRIVILEGE 359

INTRODUCTION 359
COMMON LAW JURISDICTIONS 359
A SCOTTISH LAW EXCURSUS 383
THE EUROPEAN CONVENTION ON HUMAN RIGHTS AND HEALTHCARE LAW 384
SELECTIVE BIBLIOGRAPHY 390

12 THE MEDICAL TREATMENT OF DISABLED NEWBORNS: A COMPARATIVE PERSPECTIVE 391

INTRODUCTION 391
THE ETHICAL FRAMEWORK 391
MEDICAL PRACTICE IN COMMON LAW AND CIVIL LAW COUNTRIES 392
THE ALLOCATION OF SCARCE RESOURCES 409
CONCLUDING OBSERVATIONS 410
SELECTIVE BIBLIOGRAPHY 410

13 ABORTION: A GLOBAL OVERVIEW AND COMPARATIVE STUDY **413**

INTRODUCTION 413
GLOBAL SURVEY 413
COUNTRIES WHICH BAN ABORTION IN ALL CIRCUMSTANCES 416
COMPARATIVE OBSERVATIONS ON THE AMERICAN LAWS ON ABORTION 429
ROE ERA REFORMS 449
COUNTRIES WITH RECENT ABORTION LAW REFORMS 451
EASTERN LEGAL PERSPECTIVES 452
CONCLUDING COMPARATIVE OBSERVATIONS 453
SELECTIVE BIBLIOGRAPHY 454

14 SURROGACY AND REPRODUCTIVE TECHNOLOGY **457**

INTRODUCTION 457
SURROGACY 457
REPRODUCTIVE TECHNOLOGIES: TERMS AND PROCEDURES 459
SURROGATE MOTHERHOOD 459
GESTATIONAL SURROGACY: WHO IS THE 'NATURAL' AND LEGAL MOTHER? 467
COMPARATIVE OBSERVATIONS 467
POSTHUMOUS TAKING AND USE OF SPERM 474
CIVIL LAW COUNTRIES 476
FUTURE DEVELOPMENTS IN THE REPRODUCTION REVOLUTION 486
CONCLUDING COMMENTS ON SURROGACY AND THE REPRODUCTION REVOLUTION 487
SELECTIVE BIBLIOGRAPHY 488

15 STERILISATION OF PERSONS WITH A MENTAL DISABILITY: A COMPARATIVE ANALYSIS **491**

INTRODUCTION 491
HISTORICAL BACKGROUND 491
A CONTEMPORARY OVERVIEW 493
COMPARATIVE OBSERVATIONS ON STERILISATION 522
SELECTIVE BIBLIOGRAPHY 522

16 **MEDICAL MALPRACTICE IN OTHER COMMON LAW AND CIVIL LAW JURISDICTIONS** **525**

INTRODUCTION 525
MEDICAL MALPRACTICE – A PRELIMINARY COMPARATIVE POINT 525
CONTRACTUAL LIABILITY – THE GENERAL POSITION 526
THE 'NON-CONTRACTUAL' COUNTRIES 531
DEGREE OF CARE OWED 532
SCOPE OF THE DUTY OF CARE 532
CRITERION OF PROFESSIONAL NEGLIGENCE 533
EFFECT OF LACK OF CONSENT ON PHYSICIAN'S LIABILITY 533
A COMMON LAW APPROACH 544
A CIVIL LAW APPROACH 545
NO-FAULT COMPENSATION SCHEMES FOR MEDICAL INJURIES 547
SELECTIVE BIBLIOGRAPHY 549

17 **ORGAN DONATION AND ORGAN TRANSPLANTATION: COMPARATIVE PERSPECTIVES** **551**

A GLOBAL PERSPECTIVE 551
ETHICAL PRINCIPLES 552
THE CONTRACTING OUT OR PRESUMED CONSENT POLICY 552
WORLD HEALTH ORGANISATION: PRINCIPLES ON HUMAN ORGAN TRANSPLANTATION 553
CIVIL LAW COUNTRIES 555
COMMON LAW COUNTRIES 571
FAR EASTERN AND ASIAN PERSPECTIVES 589
COMPARATIVE OBSERVATIONS ON ORGAN TRANSPLANTATION 595
SELECTIVE BIBLIOGRAPHY 596

18 **EUTHANASIA, DEATH AND DYING: A COMPARATIVE OVERVIEW** **599**

INTRODUCTION 599
CIVIL LAW COUNTRIES 599
COMPARATIVE OBSERVATIONS 606
FUTURE DECISION MAKING FOR DEATH AND DYING – ADVANCE DIRECTIVES 620
OBSERVATIONS ON REVOCATIONS 625
CONCLUDING COMPARATIVE OBSERVATIONS 625
SELECTIVE BIBLIOGRAPHY 626

19 A COMPARATIVE OVERVIEW OF HEALTHCARE LAW THEMES AND PRINCIPLES 629

COMPARATIVE METHODOLOGY 630
ABORTION 631
CONSENT TO TREATMENT 632
DISCLOSURE OF INFORMATION 633
MEDICAL MALPRACTICE AND THE STANDARD OF CARE 634
CONFIDENTIALITY 635
DOCTOR'S LIABILITY TO PERSONS INFECTED BY HIS PATIENT 636
ASSISTED REPRODUCTION 636
SURROGACY 637
PATERNALISM – MEDICAL OR JUDICIAL? 638
STERILISATION OF PERSONS WITH MENTAL DISABILITIES 639
CHILDREN AND HEALTHCARE 640
TREATMENT OF DISABLED NEWBORNS AND DISABLED CHILDREN 641
PHYSICIAN-ASSISTED SUICIDE, EUTHANASIA AND PVS PATIENTS 642
HUMAN ORGAN TRANSPLANTATION AND DONATION 645
CLONING 647
THE 'BEST INTERESTS' TEST – SLOGAN OR *AD HOC* SOCIAL POLICY? 652
TEENAGERS 653
NON-CONSENSUAL STERILISATION OF INCAPACITATED PATIENTS 653
THE *TONY BLAND* CASE AND 'BEST INTERESTS' 653
ALLOCATION OF SCARCE RESOURCES 654
HUMAN RIGHTS AND MEDICAL TREATMENT 655
MEDICAL ETHICS AND THE LAW IN THE 21ST CENTURY 657
FEMINIST PERSPECTIVES? 660
LAW AND ETHICS IN THE 21ST CENTURY 660
SELECTIVE BIBLIOGRAPHY 662

Index 665

TABLE OF CASES

A

A, Re [1992] 3 Med LR 303 284
A (A Mental Patient: Sterilisation), Re [2000] 1 FLR 549; (2000) The Times, 15 March 218, 219
A (A Minor) (Wardship: Medical Treatment), Re [1992] Fam 11 395
A (Children), Re (2000) *The Times*, 10 October 153–60, 402, 641
A (Male Sterilisation), Re [2000] 1 FLR 549 156
A (Northern Health and Social Services Board v F and G), Re [1991] 2 Med LR 274 102
A v C (1978) 8 Fam Law 170; [1985] FLR 445 . . . . .168, 173
AB v AG of Victoria [1999] Med LR 84 . . . . .474, 475
AB v CD (1851) 14 Sess Cas (second series) 17; (1851) 14 D 177 . . . . .370, 384
AB v CD (1904) 7 F 62 384
AC, Re (1990) 573 A 2d 1235 14
AL v GRH (1975) 325 NE 2d 501 . . . . .495, 496
Adoption Application (Payment for Adoption), Re [1987] 2 FLR 291; [1987] 2 All ER 826 . . . . .176–78, 183
Airedale NHS Trust v Bland [1993] 1 FLR 1026 . . . . .146, 157, 291, 292, 304–13, 316, 318, 324, 408, 614, 643, 653, 657
Alkmaar case (1984) (Netherlands) 603
Alma Mater Association case (1989) Cass Civ 1, 13 December 1989, D990, J273 478
Alperton Rubber v Manning 55
Anderson v Chasney [1949] 4 DLR 71 (Manitoba Ct of Appeal) 538
Ashcroft v Mersey RHA [1983] 2 All ER 245, 251
AG v Able [1984] QB 795 302
AG v Guardian Newspapers (No 2) [1990] AC 109 . . . . .52, 56
AG v Guardian Newspapers [1990] 1 AC 1309 59
AG v Qld, ex rel Kerr v T (1983) 46 ALR 275 97
AG v X [1992] 2 CMLR 277 103
AG's Reference (No 3 of 1994) [1997] 3 All ER 936 . . . . .30, 97, 100, 108
Auckland Area Health Board v AG [1993] 1 NZLR 235 408
Auckland Health Services v L (the Baby L case) [1998] NZFLR 998 407

B

B (A Minor) (Wardship: Medical Treatment), Re [1981] 1 WLR 1421 ....140, 144, 145, 147, 149, 301, 395, 406, 407, 606, 641

B, Re (the Baby Alexandra case) [1982] 3 FLR 117 502

B, Re (the Jeanette case) [1987] 2 All ER 206, HL 39, 91, 92, 117, 197, 198, 200, 201, 204, 205, 211, 213, 214, 222, 227, 229, 230, 501, 509, 516, 640

B (A Minor) (Wardship: Sterilisation), Re [1987] 2 WLR 1025; [1987] 2 FLR 314; [1988] AC 199 ....223, 228, 499

B v Croydon HA [1995] 1 All ER 683 ....35, 37

Baby Cotton case, *see* Re C (A Minor) (Wardship: Surrogacy)—

Baby K, In the matter of (1994) 16 F 3d 590 406

Baby M, Re (1988) 109 NJ 396; (1988) 537 A 2d 1227 ....168, 172, 457, 462, 463, 637

Baby P (An Unborn Child), In the matter of [1995] NZLR 577; [1997] Med LR 143 107

Barker, Re (1998) The Times, 14 October, CA 35, 37

Barnett v Chelsea [1968] 1 All ER 1068 234

Beausoleil v The Sisters of Charity (1964) 53 DLR (2d) 65 334

Billings v Sisters of Mercy of Idaho (1964) 86 Ida 485, 389 536

Blyth v Bloomsbury HA [1993] 4 Med LR 151 ....249, 250

Bolam v Friern Barnet NHC [1957] 1 WLR 582; [1957] 2 All ER 118 ....66, 117, 139, 217, 218, 221, 236, 238–41, 243, 245–47, 249, 250, 255–57, 259, 260, 262–64, 266, 267, 300, 305, 306, 308, 345, 346, 521, 532, 533, 538, 540, 543, 633, 634, 638, 639, 653

Bolitho v City and Hackney HA [1998] AC 232; [1997] 4 All ER 771 ....66, 117, 240, 251, 255, 259–62, 264, 267, 268, 533, 634, 638

Bradshaw v Daniel (1993) 854 SW 2d 865 364

Breen v Williams [1995] 6 Med LR 385 377

Buck v Bell 274 US 200 (1927) 199, 492, 494, 499, 638

Bundesgerichtsoft case (Germany) (1993) BGHZ 124,52 636

Burton v Islington [1992] 3 WLR 655 234

C

C, Re (1990) 5 BMLR 100; [1990] 3 All ER 725 .222
C (A Minor) (Evidence: Confidential Information), Re (1991) 7 BMLR 138 .63,72
C (A Minor) (Medical Treatment), Re [1998] Lloyd's Rep Med 1; [1998] 1 FLR 1 .148
C (A Minor) (Wardship: Medical Treatment), Re [1989] 2 All ER 782 .141, 395
C (A Minor) (Wardship: Surrogacy), Re (Baby Cotton case) [1985] Fam Law 191; [1985] FLR 846 .168, 174, 460, 462, 637
C (Adult: Refusal of Medical Treatment), Re [1994] 1 FLR 31; [1994] 1 WLR 290; [1994] 1 All ER 819; (1993) 143 NLJ 1642 .11, 12, 16, 19, 21, 30–32, 43, 44, 90, 127, 633, 653, 660
C (Detention: Medical Treatment), Re [1997] 2 FLR 180 .123, 133
C (HIV Test), Re [1999] 2 FLR 104 .129, 149
C (Medical Treatment), Re [1998] 1 FLR 1 .148
C v D [1925] 1 DLR 734 .372
C v S [1988] QB 135 .20, 84, 93–95
Canterbury v Spence (1972) 464 2d 772 .245, 248, 328–30, 341, 345, 633
Carter v Carter (1974) 53 DLR (3d) 491 .370
Carver v Hammersmith and Queen Charlotte's Special Health Authority, 25 February 2000, 7 Med Law Monitor 6 .10, 263
Casey v Provan (1984) 11 DLR (4th) 708 .336
Cassidy v Ministry of Health [1951] 2 KB 343 .253
Castell v De Greef (1994) (4) SA 408 .634
Central Manchester Healthcare Trust v (1) Mr and Mrs A; and (2) A Child (by the Official Solicitor, her guardian ad litem) LTL 22/9/00l, *sub nom* Re A (Children) .153–60, 402, 641
Chabot case (1994) Nederlandse Jurisprudentie nr 656; Tijdschrift voor Gezondsrtecht 1994/96, nr 47 .604, 605
Chare née Jullien v France (1991) 71 DR 143 .384
Chatterton v Gerson [1981] QB 432; [1981] 1 All ER 257 .5, 7, 9, 11, 32, 43, 247, 350
Chelliah a/l Manickam v Kerajaan Malaysia (1997) 2 AMR 1856 .634

Chin Keow v Government of Malaysia [1967] WLR 813 241
Clark v MacLennan [1983] 1 All ER 416 .....252, 253
Clarke v Hurst (1992) (4) SA 630 312
Cobbs v Grant (1972) 502 P 2d 1 329
Coco v Clark (AN) (Engineers) Ltd (1969) RPC 41 376
Cody v Fraser (1950) 122 Colo 252; (1950) 222 P 2d 422 326
Cole v Turner (1704) 6 Mod 149 9
Collins v Wilcock [1984] 1 WLR 1172 29
Conservatorship of Valerie N (1985) 40 Cal 3d 143 494
Considine v Camp Hill Hospital (1982) 133 DLR (3d) 11 335
Corn v French (1955) 289 P 2d 173 326
Corrs Pavey v Collector of Customs (1987) 74 ALR 428 375
Craine v Allison (1982) 443 A 2d 558 330
Crawford v Board of Governors of Charing Cross Hospital (1953) The Times, 8 December 239
Cronkwright v Cronkwright (1970) DLR (3a) 168 ONLR 372
Cruzan v Missouri Department of Health (1990) 110 S Ct 2841; (1990) 497 US 261 .....611, 612, 615, 617, 644
Cull v Royal Surrey Hospital and Butler [1943] 1 BM 9
Cunningham v MacNeal Memorial Hospital (1970) 47 Il 12d 443; (1970) 266 NE 2d 897 (Illinois SC) 545
Curran v Bosze (1990) 566 NE 2d 1319 .....280, 281, 587

D

D, Re (the Sotos syndrome case) [1976] 1 All ER 326 .....200–04, 207, 208, 210, 214, 230, 502, 639
D, Re [1987] 1 All ER 20 .....96, 109
D, Re [1998] 1 FLR 411 311
D (A Minor), Re [1976] Fam 185; 1 All ER 326 8
D (A Minor), Re [1987] AC 317, HL 108
D v NSPCC [1977] 1 All ER 589 68
Daniels v Heskin [1952] IR 73 541
Davis v Berry (1914) 216 F 413 494
Davis v Lhim (1983) 335 NW 2d 481 364
Davis v Rodman (1921) 147 Ark 385; (1921) 227 SW 612 .....364, 636

De Freitas v O'Brien [1993] 4 Med LR 481 244
DeGrella v Elston (1993) 858 SW 2d 698 644
Dembie v Dembie (1963) 21 RFL 46 372
Department of Health v JWB and SMB (Marion's case)
(1992) 66 AJLR 300; (1992) 106 ALR 385, Aust HC 229, 504, 507, 510, 512, 513, 639
Dewi v West Midlands RHA (1981) unreported, CA 7
Dick v Bardsley (1983) 46 BCLR 240 337
DiMarco v Lynch Homes – Chester County
(1990) 525 Pa 558 368
Doe v Bolton (1973) 410 US 179 .... 423, 425, 427
Doe v Kelly [1980] FLR (BNA) 3011 .... 457, 461
Donoghue v Stevenson [1932] AC 562 .... 382, 383
Duncan v Cammell Laird [1942] AC 524 67
Duncan v Medical Practitioners' Disciplinary
Committee [1986] 1 NZLR 513 379
Dunleavy v McDevitt and the North Western Health
Board (1992) SC 19 February 541
Dunne v The National Maternity Hospital and Another
(the Dunne case) [1989] IR 91 .... 538–40, 543

E

E (A Minor) (Medical Treatment), Re [1991] 2 FLR 585 .... 215, 518
E (A Minor) (Wardship: Medical Treatment), Re
[1993] 1 FLR 386 .... 124, 126, 133
E (A Minor), Re (1992) 9 BMLR 1 147
Edward Wong Finance Co Ltd v Johnson Stokes and
Master (A Firm) [1984] AC 296; [1984] 2 WLR 1 258
Elizabeth, Re (1989) FLC 92–023 504
Emeh v Kensington and Chelsea Health Authority
[1985] QB 1012 10
Eve, Re (1986) 31 DLR (4th) 1 .... 197, 198, 204–08, 210, 212, 226, 229, 230, 501, 503, 509
Evelyn, Re (1998) 23 Fam LR 53 471

F

F (Adult: Court's Jurisdiction), Re
(2000) The Times, 25 July 41, 43
F (In Utero), Re [1988] Fam 122 ....20, 93, 96, 97, 108
F (Mental Patient: Sterilisation), Re
[1990] 2 AC 1; [1989] 2 FLR 376 ....4, 29, 42, 204, 219, 223, 230, 475, 499, 500, 516
F (Sterilisation: Mental Patient), Re [1989] 2 FLR 276 ....9, 13, 15, 17, 639, 640
F v F (Re F) (1986) Supreme Court of Victoria 407
F v R (1983) 33 SASR 189 (FC) 340, 341, 355, 543, 634
F v West Berkshire HA (Mental Health Act Commissioning Intervening) [1989] 2 All ER 545, *sub nom* Re F (Mental Patient: Sterilisation) [1990] 2 AC 1 228
F v West Berkshire HA (Re F) [1989] 2 All ER 545 ....31, 33, 38, 210, 217, 218, 229, 314, 317
Fairfax (1980) 147 CLR 39 376
Ferguson v Hamilton Civic Hospitals
(1983) 144 DLR (3d) 214 336
Fiori, Re (1995) 652 A 2d 1350 ....613, 614
Fought v Solce [1993] Med LR 256 (Texas Ct of Appeals) 536, 537
Freeman v Home Office (No 2) [1984] QB 524 ....9, 32
Frenchay NHS Trust v S [1994] 2 All ER 403;
[1994] 1 FLR 485, CA 310, 311, 313
Fryer v Pearson and Another (2000) The Times, 4 April 254
Furniss v Fitchett [1958] NZLR 396 381–83

G

G, Re [1995] 2 FCR 46; [1995] 2 FLR 528 ....311, 314
GF, Re [1992] 1 FLR 293 ....39, 518
G (Adult Patient: Publicity), Re [1995] 2 FLR 528 224
Gammill v US (1984) 727 F 2d 950 ....364, 365
Garcia v Santa Rosa Health Corp (1996) 925 SW 2d 372 368
Gillick v Wisbech and West Norfolk AHA
[1985] 3 All ER 402 ....53, 69, 91, 117–28, 133, 134, 161, 505, 638, 640
Gold v Haringey [1987] 2 All ER 888 ....248, 249
Grady, Re (1981) 85 NJ 235 ....497, 498, 499

Gratton v People (1984) 477 NYS 2d 881 .370
Gray v Grunnagle (1966) 223 A 2d 663 .326
Green v Matheson [1989] 3 NZLR 564 .548
Guardianship of Pescomski, Re (1975) 226 NW 2d 180 .587

H

H (Mental Patient: Diagnosis), Re [1993] 4 Med LR 91 .38
H v ACC [1990] NZAR 289 .547
H v Norway (1992) No 17004/90 .656
HG (Specific Issue Order: Sterilisation), Re
[1993] 1 FLR 587 .215
HIV Haemophiliac Litigation, Re (1990) 140 NLJ 1349 .67
Halls v Mitchell [1928] SCR 125; [1928] 2 DLR 97 .370
Halushka v University of Saskatchewan
(1965) 53 DLR (2d) 436 .333
Hamilton v Birmingham RHB (1969) 2 BMJ 456 .9
Hart v Brown (1972) 289 A 2d 386 .280, 586, 587
Hasenai v US (1982) 541 F Supp 999 .364
Hawkins v McGee (1929) 84 NH 114; (1929) 146 A 641 .536
Hayes (Guardianship), Re (1980) 608 P 2d 635 .497, 498, 500
Haynes v Lapeer (1918) 201 Mich 138 .494
Hecht v Superior Court of Los Angeles County
(1993) 20 Cal Rptr 775 .482
Heil v Rankin [2000] Lloyd's Rep Med 203 .267
Herczegfalvy v Austria [1993] 15 ECHR 437 .656
Hofmann v Blackmon (1970) 241 So 2d 752 (Fla App) .364, 636
Houston, Applicant [1997] Med LR 237 .640
Howell v Carpenter (1969) 19 Mich App 233; (1969) 172 NW 2d 549 .536
Hucks v Cole [1993] 4 Med LR 393 .240, 241, 258, 259
Hughes v State of Oklahoma (1994) 868 P 2d 730 .106
Hunter v Hanley (1955) SC 22 .238, 241, 264
Hunter v Mann [1974] 1 QB 766 .50, 57, 377

I

Infant Doe, *see* Weber v Stony Brook Hospital—
Inquiry into the Confidentiality of Health Records in
Ontario, Re (1979) 98 DLR (3d) 704 .370

J

J (A Minor) (Wardship: Medical Treatment), Re
[1990] 3 All ER 780 ....133, 141–46, 148, 395
J (A Minor) (Wardship: Medical Treatment), Re
[1992] 2 FLR 165 ....143, 395
J (Wardship: Medical Treatment), Re [1991] Fam 33;
[1991] 2 WLR 140 ....153, 408
Janaway v Salford AHA [1989] AC 537 89
Jane, Re (1988) 94 Aust FLR 1 ....504, 506
Johnson, Re (1980) 45 NC App 499
Johnson v Calvert (1993) 851 P 2d 776;
[1994] Med LR 239 ....166, 172, 457, 467, 468, 470
Johnson v UK [1998] 2 EHRLR 224 656
Johnstone v Bloomsbury HA [1991] 2 All ER 293 ....237, 238
Jones v Manchester Corporation [1952] 2 All ER 125 238
Jones v Stanko (1928) 118 Ohio St 147; (1928) 160 NE 456 ....364, 636
Joyce v Merton, Sutton and Wandsworth HA
[1996] 7 Med LR 1 259

K

K, W and H, Re [1993] 1 FLR 854 ....122, 133
K (A Minor) (Northern Health and Services Board
v F and G), Re (1991) 2 Med LR 371 102
K and Public Trustee, Re [1985] 3 WWR 204 ....229, 230, 503
Kadijk case (1995) (Netherlands) 605
Kamalam a/p Raman v Eastern Plantation Agency
(Johore) Sdn Bhd Ulu Tiram Estate, Ulu Tiram Johore
(1996) 429 US 922; (1976) 355A 2d 647 ....500, 634
Karen Quinlan case, *see* Re Quinlan—
Kazan v Comstock (1959) 270 F 2d 839 535
Kelly v Hazlett (1976) 75 DLR (3d) 536 333
Kelly v Kelly (1997) The Times, 5 June 436
Kervorkian v Thomson (1997) 947 F Supp 1152 617
Knight v Department of the Army (Texas) (1994) 547
Kozan v Comstock (1959) 270 F 2d 839 535

L

L (An Adult: Non-consensual Treatment), Re
[1997] 1 FLR 609 .13
L (Medical Treatment: Gillick Competence), Re
[1998] Fam Law 591 .124
L and M, Re (Sarah's case)
(1993) 17 Aust FLR 357; (1994) Med LR 94 .510, 512
Law Hospital NHS Trust v Lord Advocate 1996 SLT 848 .312
Lawrence, Petitioner (L v I's Curator *ad litem*)
(1996) 32 BMLR 37; (1996) The Times, 19 March;
[1997] Med LR 325 .227, 229
Lee v South West Thames RHA [1985] 2 All ER 385 .67
Legislative Privilege, In Re (1978) 39 CCC (2d) 226 .373
Lindsay v The Mid-Western Health Board
[1993] 13 ILRM 550, SC .539, 541, 543
Little v Little (1979) 576 SW 2d 493 .587
Lochgelly Iron and Coal Co v M'Mullan [1934] AC 1 .234
Lowns v Woods [1996] Aust Torts Reports 81 .260

M

M (A Minor) (Medical Treatment), Re, LTL 15/7/99 .125
M (A Minor) (Wardship: Sterilisation), Re
[1988] 2 FLR 497 .214
M et Madame V (1992) .528, 529
M, Re, *see* Re Baby M—
MB (Medical Treatment: Caesarean Section), Re
[1997] 2 FLR 426 .6, 13, 18, 21, 25–27, 29, 32,
44, 100, 108, 156, 659
MS v Sweden (1988) 45 BMLR 1; [1999] Med LR 346 .388
MacDonald v York County Hospital Corporation
(1972) 28 DLR (3d) 521 .254
McGhee v National Coal Board [1972] 3 All ER 1008 .252, 253
McPherson v Ellis (1982) 287 SE 2d 892 .330
Male v Hopmans (1967) 64 DLR (2d) 105 .333
Malette v Schulman [1991] 2 Med LR 162 .333
Malone v UK Applications No 8691/79 (1984) .73
Marion (No 2), Re (1994) FLC 92–448 .510

Marriage of Moschetta, Re (1994) 30 Cal Rep 2d 893 . . . . .172, 470
Marriott v West Midlands HA [1999] Lloyd's Rep Med 23 259
Marshall v Curry (1933) 3 DLR 260 7
Maynard v West Midlands RHA
[1981] 1 All ER 635; [1984] 1 WLR 634 . . . . .241, 243, 251, 256, 264
McInernery v MacDonald (1992) 93 DLR (4th) 415 . . . . .374, 379
Merchants National Bank v Trust Co of Fargo
v US (1967) 272 F Supp 409 364
Meyer Estates v Rogers (1991) 78 DLR (4th) 307 337
Moe, Re (1982) 432 NE 2d 712 496
Montreal Tramways Co v Leveille [1993] SCR 246 106
Morgentaler, Smoling and Scott
v The Queen (1988) 44 DLR (4th) 385 . . . . .430, 631

N

Natanson v Kline (1960) 186 KAN 393; (1960) 350 P 2d 1093 327
National Health Service Trust, A v Mrs M; National Health
Service Trust B v Mrs H (2000) LTL, HC 309, 655, 657
National Health Service Trust, A v D (2000) The Times, 19 July 138, 152
Nettleship v Weston [1971] 2 QB 691 237
Norfolk and Norwich v W [1997] 1 FCR 269 . . . . .13, 17, 21, 44
North Carolina Association for Retarded Children
v State of California (1976) 420 F Supp 451 499

O

O'Brien v Komesaroff (1982) 150 CLR 310 376
O'Donovan v The County Council of the
County of Cork [1967] IR 173 538–40
O'Grady v Brown (1983) 654 SW 2d 904 422
Ohio v Akron Centre for Reproductive Health
(1990) 497 US 502 . . . . .423, 427, 429
Open Door Counselling Ltd and Dublin Well Woman
v Ireland (1992) 18 BMLR 1 103

P

P, Re [1992] 1 FLR 321 127

P, Re [1992] 2 FCR 681 127
P (A Minor), Re (1982) 80 LGR 301 91
P (A Minor) (Wardship: Sterilisation), Re [1989] 1 FLR 182 . . . . 214, 215, 223
P (Minors) (Wardship: Surrogacy), Re [1987] 2 FLR 421 . . . . 173, 179
P v P (1994) 120 ALR 545; (1994) 19 Fam Law 1 512
Parham, Re, *see* Parham v JR—
Parham v JR (1979) 442 US 584, *sub nom* Re Parham 500
Parkinson v MacDonald (1987) 40 CCLT 90 337
Parpalaix case (1984) JCP 1984.II.20321 . . . . 481, 482
Paton v British Pregnancy Advisory Service
[1979] QB 276 . . . . 44, 92–94, 96
Paton v UK (1980) 19 DR 244 656
Pearce v United Bristol Healthcare NHS Trust
[1999] Med LR 60 260–63
Penney and Others v East Kent HA
(1999) The Times, 25 November 263
People v Calvo (1982) 432 NE 2d 223 370
Perlmutter v Beth David Hospital
(1954) 308 NY 100; (1954) 123 NE 2d 792 . . . . 544, 545
Pfizer Corpn v Ministry of Health [1965] AC 512 234
Planned Parenthood of Central Missouri
v Danforth (1976) 96 S Ct 2831 423
Planned Parenthood of Southeastern Pennsylvania
v Casey (1992) 505 US 833 . . . . 418, 423, 428, 429, 615
Postma case, Dr (1973) (Netherlands) 602
Practice Direction [1989] 2 FLR 47 222
Practice Direction [1993] 2 FLR 222 . . . . 222, 228–30
Practice Direction [1994] 2 All ER 413 316
Practice Direction [1996] 2 FLR 111 . . . . 223, 230, 314, 521
Practice Direction on PVS [1994] 1 FLR 654 313
Practice Direction on PVS [1996] 4 All ER 766 . . . . 313, 408
Presley v Newport Hospital
(1976) 117 RI 177; (1976) 365 A 2d 748 422
Prince Albert v Strange (1849) 41 ER 1171 55
Prins case, *see* TGR 1995/41—
Procureur Général v Madame X
(1991) Cass Ass Plénière, 31 May 1991, J 417 . . . . 478, 479

Q

Q (Parental Order), Re [1996] 1 FLR 369, HC .182, 183
Quinlan, Re (1976) 429 US 922; (1976) 355 A 2d 647;
(1976) 70 NJ 10; (1976) US 922, *sub nom* Karen Quinlan case .500, 610

R

R, Re [1991] 4 All ER 177 .122, 124, 128
R, Re [1992] 1 FLR 190 .133, 640, 653
R (A Minor) (Blood Transfusion), Re [1993] 2 FLR 757 .147
R v Arthur (1981) 12 BMLR 1 .133, 137, 139, 300, 398, 641
R v Bergmann and Ferguson (1948) 1 BMJ 1008 .85
R v Blaue [1975] 3 All ER 446 .295
R v Bodkin Adams [1957] Crim LR 365 .292–94, 301, 642
R v Bourne [1938] 3 All ER 615; [1939] 1 KB 687 .84–86, 93, 102, 215, 216, 432, 631
R v Bournewood Community and Mental Health
NHS Trust ex p L [1998] Fam Law 592 .39–42, 236, 237
R v Brown [1993] 2 All ER 75 .277
R v Cambridge HA ex p B [1995] WLR 898 .654
R v Clarence (1888) 22 QBD 23 .12
R v Cox (1992) 12 BMLR 38 .292, 299, 642
R v Crozier (1990) The Independent, 11 May;
(1990) The Guardian, 8 May .62
R v Davidson [1969] VR 667 .432, 434
R v Donovan [1934] All ER 207 .276
R v DPP ex p Kebeline [1999] 4 All ER 801 .387
R v Dudley and Stephens (1884) 14 QBD 273 .159
R v Ethical Committee of St Mary's Hospital (Manchester)
ex p Harriott [1988] 1 FLR 512 .191, 192
R v Hallstrom [1986] 2 All ER 306 .34
R v Human Fertilisation and Embryology Authority
ex p Blood [1997] WLR 806 .187–91, 474, 474, 482
R v Johnson (1961) 1 Med Sci & Law 192 .294
R v Le Brun [1992] QB 61 .99
R v Mid-Glamorgan Family Health
Services ex p Martin [1995] 1 All ER 356 .377, 378
R v Newton and Stungo [1958] Crim Law 469 .85

R v Portsmouth NHS Trust ex p Glass [1999] Med LR 125;
[1999] Lloyd's Rep Med 367 .149–51
R v Sheffield HA ex p Seale (1994) 25 BMLR 1 .191–93
R v Sheppard [1981] AC 394 .301
R v Sullivan [1991] 1 SCR 489 .97
R v Tabassum (2000) The Times, 26 May .12
R v Wald (1971) 3 DLR (NSW) 25 .434
R v Wilson [1996] 3 WLR 125, CA .65
R v Wray (1970) 11 DLR (3d) 673 .373
Reibl v Hughes (1980) 114 DLR (3d) 1;
(1980) 2 SCR 894 (Can Sup Ct) .245, 333–37, 355, 538, 633
Reisner v Regents of the University of California
(1995) 37 Cal Rptr 2d 518; (1997) Med LR 250 .366, 368
Richardson, Re (1973) 284 So 2d 185 .587
Rochdale v Choudhary [1997] 1 FCR 274 .13, 16, 44
Roe v Ministry of Health [1954] 2 QB 66 .239
Roe v Wade (1973) 410 US 113 .97, 413, 417–19, 422–30, 449, 452, 453, 631
Rogers v Whittaker [1993] 4 Med LR 79;
(1992) 175 CLR 479 .8, 260, 262, 341–47, 378, 543, 634

S

S, Re (2000) The Times, 26 May, CA .39, 633, 653
S, Re (1989) 98 Aust FLR 41 .504
S (A Minor) (Consent to Medical Treatment), Re
[1994] 2 FLR 1065 .124, 133, 147
S (A Minor) (Medical Treatment), Re [1993] 1 FLR 376 .133, 147
S (Adult; Refusal of Medical Treatment), Re
[1992] 4 All ER 671 .13, 14
S (Sterilisation: Patient's Best Interests), Re
(2000) The Times, 26 May .220
SG (Adult Mental Patient: Abortion) [1991] 2 FLR 329 .38
SPUC v Grogan [1991] 3 CMLR; [1991] IR 593 .103
Salazar v St Vincent Hospital
(1980) 95 NM 150; (1980) 619 P 2d 826 .422
Salgo v Leland Stanford Jr University Board of Trustees
(1957) 154 Cal App 2d 560; (1957) 317 P 2d 170 .8, 324, 326

Saltman Engineering Co Ltd
v Campbell Engineering Co Ltd (1948) 65 RPC 203 376
Schloendorff v Society of New York Hospital
(1914) 105 NE 92; (1914) 211 NY 125 . . . . .8, 325, 326, 338, 617, 632
Scott v St Katherine's Docks Co (1865) 3 H & C 596 542
Sewell v Electrolux (1997) The Times, 7 November 226, 251
Shortland v Northland Health Ltd [1998] 1 NZLR 433 408
Sidaway v Board of Governors of the Bethlem Royal
Hospital and the Maudsley Hospital
[1984] 1 All ER 1018; [1985] AC 871 . . . . .6, 28, 29, 43, 241, 243–50,
257, 261, 262, 340, 341,
345, 351, 355, 539,
543, 633
Simpson, Re (1962) NE 2d 206 495
Skillings v Allen (1919) 143 Minn 323; (1919) 173 NW 663 . . . . .364, 636
Skinner v Oklahoma ex rel Williamson (1942) 316 US 535 . . . . .494, 498
Slater v Baker and Stapleton (1967) 2 Wils KB 358; (1967) 95 ER 860 . . . . .8, 632
Slavutych v Baker (1975) 55 DLR (3d) 373
Smith v Auckland Hospital Board [1964] NZLR 191 348
South Glamorgan CC v W and B [1993] 1 FLR 574 . . . . .123, 133, 653
St George's Healthcare NHS Trust v S, R v Collins and
Others ex p S [1998] 2 FLR 728; (1998) The Times, 8 May 13, 22, 25–31, 34, 100
State v Bouse (1953) 199 Or 676; (1953) 264 P 2d 800 609
State v Feilen (1912) 70 Wash 65 494
State v Horne (1984) 319 SE 2d 703 106
State v Perry (1992) 610 So 2d 746 (Louisiana) 534, 634
Stephens v Avery and Others [1988] 2 All ER 477 . . . . .64, 65
Stewart v Rudner (1957) 349 Mich 459; (1957) 84 NW 2d 816 536
Stinissen case, Jurisprudence nr
1987/50 and Jurisprudentie nr 1990/63 312
Storie v Storie (1945) 80 CLR 597 511
Stratton v Swanlond (2nd Surgeon's case)
(1930) Year Book 48, Edward B, Hilary Term 233
Strunk v Strunk (1969) 445 SW 2d 145 . . . . .278, 587
Stump v Sparkman (1978) 435 US 49 496
Superintendent of Belchertown State School
v Saikewicz (1977) 373 Mass 728 500

Superintendent of Family and Child Services and
Dawson, Re (1983) 145 DLR (3d) 610 407
Surgeon's case (1329) Kiralfy, A Source Book of
English Law, 1957 233
Swindon and Marlborough NHS Trust v S
(1994) The Guardian, December 10 312

T

T, Re [1997] 1 All ER 906 .....117, 131, 133, 137, 299, 406, 641
T (A Minor: Wardship: Medical Treatment), Re
[1997] 1 WLR 242; [1997] 1 All ER 906 .....138, 143, 146–49, 408, 606
T (An Adult) (Consent to Medical Treatment), Re
[1992] 2 FLR 458 .....9, 11, 13, 14, 20, 29
T (An Adult) (Refusal of Medical Treatment), Re
[1992] 4 All ER 649; (1992) 9 BMLR 46 .....6, 316, 317
T v T [1988] 2 WLR 189 .....38, 216, 499
TGR 1989/51, 28 April (Supreme Court, The Netherlands) 396
TGR 1991/28, 11 January (Court of Utrecht) 396
TGR 1995/41, 26 April (district court); TGR 1996/1,
7 November 1995 (Amsterdam Appeal Court),
sub nom the Prins case 399, 606
TGR 1996/2 13 November 1995 (Court of Groningen);
TGR 1996/35, 4 April 1996 (Leeuwaeden Appeal
Court) (the Kadijk case) 399
Tameside and Glossop Acute Services Trust
v CH [1996] 1 FCR 753 .....15–17, 36, 37
Tarasoff et al v The Regents of the University of California
(1976) 17 Cal (3d) 358 .....62, 63, 359, 361–64, 367–70, 376, 381, 635
Teenager, Re A (1989) FLC 92-006; (1989) 94 Aust FLR 181 .....504, 506
Thompson v County Alamede (1980) 614 P 2d 728 364
Tremblay v Daigle (1989) 62 DLR (4th) 634 97

V

Vacco v Quill (1997) 117 S Ct 2293 (US Sup Ct) 614, 616

W

W, Re [1992] 4 All ER 627; [1993] 3 WLR 758 . . . . .118, 120, 121, 123, 128, 133, 640, 653
W (A Minor) (Medical Treatment), Re [1992] 4 All ER 627 280
W (Mental Patient: Sterilisation), Re [1993] 1 FLR 381 . . . . .222, 225
W (Minors) (Surrogacy), Re [1991] 1 FLR 385 180–82
W v Egdell [1990] 1 All ER 835 . . . . .59–62, 359, 635
Wall v Brim (1943) 138 F 2d 478 326
Walsh v Family Planning Services and Others [1992] 1 IR 496 . . . . .539, 543
Ward of Court, In the Matter of [1995] ILRM 401 312
Washington v Glucksberg (1997) 117 S Ct 2258; (1997) 138 L Ed 2d 608, 614, 615
Watterson v Conwell (1952) 258 Ala 180; (1952) 61 So 2d 690 536
Weber v Stony Brook Hospital (the Baby Jane Doe case) (1983) 456 NE 2d 1186, *sub nom* Infant Doe 400, 401, 402, 405, 406
Webster v Reproductive Health Services (1989) 492 US 490 . . . . .418, 423, 427, 429
Wellesley v Duke of Beaufort (1827) 2 Russ 1 203
Wells v Wells [1999] 1 AC 345 267
White v Turner (1981) 120 DLR (3d) 269 . . . . .335, 337
White v Yup (1969) 85 Nev 527; (1969) 458 P 2d 617 422
Whitehouse v Jordan [1981] 1 All ER 267 . . . . .241, 242
Wilkinson v Vesey (1972) 295 A 2d 676 329
Williams v Smith (1921) 190 Ind 526 494
Wilsher v Essex AHA [1986] 3 All ER 801; [1988] 1 All ER 871 . . . . .237, 238, 252
Wilson v Pringle [1987] QB 237 . . . . .38, 43
Winnipeg Child and Family Services v G [1999] Med LR 88 105
Wojcik v Aluminium Co of America (1959) 18 Misc 2d 740; (1959) 183 NYS 2d 351 . . . . .364, 636
Wooding v Little (1982) 24 CCLT 37 370
Wyatt v Wilson (1820) unreported 56, 64

X

X v Y [1988] 2 All ER 648 . . . . .59, 61

Y

Y, Re (1996) 35 BMLR 111 . . . . .279, 283
Yeager v Dunnavan (1946) 26 Wash 2d 559; (1946) 174 P 2d 755 536

Z

Z (A Minor) (Identification: Restriction of Publication), Re [1996] 2 WLR 88 156
Z v Finland (1997) 45 BMLR 107; [1999] Med LR 338 . . . . .73, 385

TABLE OF STATUTES

Abortion Act 1837 83
Abortion Act 1928 83
Abortion Act 1967 . . . . .29, 38, 39, 44, 81, 83, 86–88, 92, 421, 631
  s 1(1) 89
  s 1(1)(a)–(d) 88, 95
  s 4(1), (2) 89
  s 5(1) 88, 93
  s 5(2) 95
Abortion Act 1990 83
Adoption Act 1958—
  s 50 178
Adoption Act 1976—
  s 57 . . . . .171, 178, 477
Age of Legal Capacity (Scotland) Act 1991 53
AIDS (Control) Act 1987 58

Children Act 1989 . . . . . .96, 117, 118, 164, 175, 176, 208, 212, 640
  s 1(1) 127
  s 1(5) 131
  ss 2(7), 3(1), (5), 4 127
  s 8 . . . . .108, 120, 122, 131, 132, 150, 222–24
  s 8(1) 222, 223
  s 10(8) 120
  s 12(1), (2) .127
  s 38(6) 123
  ss 39, 43(8), 44(7), 45(8) 120
  s 100 128
  s 100(3) 143
  Pt IV 108
Children and Young Persons Act 1933—
  s 1 . . . . .129, 301
Child Support Act 1991 164
Contempt of Court Act 1981 224
  s 11 314
Courts and Legal Services Act 1980 332
Criminal Justice Act (Northern Ireland) 1953 102

Data Protection Act 1998 . . . . .69, 70

Family Law Reform Act 1969—
  s 8 .117, 118, 123
  s 8(1) 90

Guardianship of Minors Act 1971—
  s 1 208

Human Fertilisation and Embryology Act 1990 . . . . . .4, 26, 165, 171–73, 185, 188, 190, 421, 460, 631, 632, 637, 648–51
  s 1(1)(a), (b) .648
  s 1(1)(d) 632
  s 3 . . . . .112, 651
  s 3(3)(d) 649, 651
  s 4(1), (b) 189
  s 4(2) 649
  s 12 189
  s 13(5) .166, 191
  s 27 . . . . .166, 182, 467, 470, 478
  s 28 182
  s 28(2), (3), (5) 166
  s 28(6) .166, 190
  s 29 182
  s 30 . . . . .173, 180–83, 186
  s 30(2)–(7) 173
  s 30(7) 184
  s 37 . . . . .88, 95
  s 37(4) 88
  s 38 112
  Sched 2, para 3 . . . . .112, 649
  Sched 2, para 4 649
  Sched 3 .188, 189

Human Organs Transplant
Act 1989 281
ss 1, 2 281
Human Rights Act 1998 . . . . .73, 134, 138, 187, 291, 309, 633, 655, 656, 657, 661
Sched 1 . . . . .153, 655
Human Tissue Act 1961 284–87
s 1(1), (2) 285
Human Tissue Act 1982—
Pt IV 475
Human Tissue Act 1989—
s 7(2) 280
Human Tissue (Northern Ireland) Act 1962 285

Infant Life (Preservation) Act 1929 . . . . .29, 83, 84, 88, 101, 112
s 1(1) 84, 85, 93, 94, 421

Law Reform Act 1969 . . . . . . .87, 120, 121
Lord Ellenborough's Act
1803 . . . . .82, 83, 419

Magna Carta 1217 26
Magna Carta 1257 26
Matrimonial Causes Act 1973 164
Mental Health Act 1959 . . . . . .32, 33, 215
s 34 32
Mental Health Act 1983 . . . . . . .17, 24, 25, 201, 215, 236
s 2 22–25
s 2(2)(a), (b) 24
s 3 . . . . .15, 33, 34, 36, 37, 40
s 6(3) 24
s 8 32
s 12(2) 27

Mental Health Act 1983 (Contd)—
s 17 34
s 20 . . . . .35, 37
s 57 . . . . .15, 33, 34
s 58 . . . . .15, 33, 34
s 62 33
s 63 . . . . .12, 15, 16, 33, 35–37
s 79 60
s 131 40
s 145 12
s 145(1) 35
Pt IV 33

National Health Service (Family Planning) Act 1967 199

Offences Against the Person Act 1861 . . . . .29, 83, 84, 88, 101, 112
s 18 97
s 47 65
s 58 83–85

Prevention of Terrorism (Temporary Provisions) Act 1989 56
s 18 . . . . .50, 58
Public Health (Control of Diseases) Act 1984 58

Road Traffic Act 1988 . . . . .56, 57, 377
s 168 57
s 172 . . . . .50, 57

Suicide Act 1962—
s 2 302
Supreme Court Act 1981—
ss 33, 34 70

Surrogacy Arrangements
Act 1985 . . . . .171, 176, 185, 186, 478, 637
s 1A 172, 173, 176, 460, 470, 478

Surrogacy Arrangements
Act 1985 (Contd)—
s 2 477

TABLE OF STATUTORY INSTRUMENTS

Abortion Regulations 1968 SI 1968/390 93

Access to Health Records (Northern Ireland)
Order 1993 SI 1993/1250 70

Human Organs Transplants (Unrelated Persons)
Regulations 1989 SI 1989/2480—
reg 3 282

Public Health (Control of Diseases) Regulations
1985 SI 1985/434 58

Rules of the Supreme Court—
Ord 80 314

TABLE OF INTERNATIONAL LEGISLATION

Austria

Federal Law No 273,
 1 June 1982 557

Australia

Children (Care and Protection) Act 1987 (NSW)—
 s 20B 514

Consent to Medical and Dental Procedures Act 1985 (SA) 338

Crimes Act 1958 (Vic)—
 s 65 435

Criminal Code (NT) 619
 s 222 375

Euthanasia Laws Act 1997 (Cth) 618, 619

Evidence Act 1958 (Vic)—
 s 28(2) 375
 s 96(2) 375

Evidence Ordinance 1939–72 (NT)—
 s 18(2) 375

Family Law Act 1975—
 s 60D 506, 513
 Pt VII 513

Family Relationships Act 1975 (SA) 471

Family Relationships Act 1988 (SA) 471

Guardianship Act 1987 (NSW) 512

Guardianship Act 1987 (NSW) (Contd)—
 s 33(1) 514
 s 35(1) 513
 ss 37(1), 45(2) 514
 Pt 5 512

Guardianship and Administration Act 1993 (SA)—
 ss 61(2), 62 515
 Pt V 515

Health Administration Act 1982 (NSW) 375

Health Commission Act 1976 (SA) 375

HIV/AIDS Preventive Measures Act 1993 (Tas) 578

Human Tissue Act 1982 (Vic) 572

Human Tissue Act 1983 (NSW) 572

Human Tissue Act 1985 (Tas) 572

Human Tissue and Transplant Act 1982 (WA) 572, 577

Human Tissue Transplant Act 1978 (NT) 572

Infertility (Medical Procedures) Act 1986 (Vic) 471

Infertility Treatment Act 1995 (Vic) 475
 ss 43, 56 475

Mental Health Act 1983 (NSW) 338

Mental Health Act 1986 (Vic) 338

Natural Death Act 1983 (SA) 622
 s 3 622

Natural Death Act 1988 (NT) 623

Northern Territory (Self-Government) Act 1978 (Cth) 618

Rights of the Terminally Ill Act 1995 (NT) 617–19

Surrogacy Contracts Act
1993 (Tas) 471
Surrogate Parenthood Act
1988 (Qld) 471

Transplantation and Anatomy
Act 1978 (ACT) 572
Transplantation and Anatomy
Act 1979 (Qld) 577
Transplantation and Anatomy
Act 1983 (SA) 572

Canada

Charter of Rights and Freedoms—
s 1 431
s 7 ....430, 431
Code of Civil Procedure Stat
Quebec 1969—
c 80 369
Criminal Code—
s 223 431
s 251 ....430, 431

Medical Act s 40 stat
Quebec 1973—
c 46 369

Ontario Medicine Act 374
Ontario Vital Statistics Act 374

Privacy Act RSBC 1979—
c 336, s 1(1) 370
Public Health Act SA 1984—
s 63(1), (3), (5)(b) 371
Quebec Code of Civil Procedure 1965
c 80, s 308 369

Yukon Communicable Diseases
Regulations YT Reg 1961/48
s 5(1) 370
Yukon Communicable Diseases
Regulations YT Reg 1970/46 370
Yukon Territory Public Health
Act RSYT 1986
c 136, Sched I 370

Chile

18 Act No 18.826, 24
August 1989 (Abortion) 416

China

Maternal and Infant Health
Care Law 1994 452

Denmark

Pregnancy Act 1973 449

France

Civil Code—
Art 6 480
Arts 311–9 479
Arts 311–14 479
Arts 319, 341 478
Art 376 479
Art 1128 ....479, 480
Art 1382 525
Criminal Code—
Art 334 477
Art 353(1) 477
Art 353(1)(3) 477
Art 345 477

Decree No 97-704 of
30 May 1997 558

Deontological Code 1995 393

Law of 1901—
Art 3 479

Law No 75-17 of 17 January 1975—
Art L 162-1 438
Art L 162-4 438
Art L 162-12 . . . . .4, 439
Law No 76-1811 of 22 December 1976 (Caillavet Law) 558, 561
Law No 79-1204 of 31 December 1979 438
Law No 94-653 of 29 July 1994 559
Art 10 482
Law No 94-654 of 29 July 1994 559

Napoleonic Penal Code 1810—
Art 317 437

Penal Code 1791 437

Germany

Act for Assistance to Pregnant Women and Families 1992 443–45
Act for the Prevention of Congenitally Defective Future Generations 1933 440

Bavarian Abortion Counselling Act 1996 449
Bundesgesetzblatt No 74 (Transplantation Act) of 5 November 1997 . . . . .561, 562
Pts I, II 561
s 4(1) 563
s 4(2) 563, 564
s 4(3) 564
s 4(4) 563, 564
s 8(1) 564
ss 8(2), (3), 9, 11 565
s 17 . . . . .565, 566
s 18(1), (4) 566
Carership Law 1990 516
Civil Code—
para 680 532
para 8231(1) 546

Federal Embryo Protection Act 1980 486

Grundgesetz 1948—
Art 1(1) 350, 441, 445
Art 2(1) 350, 445
Art 2(2) 441, 445

Non-Contentious Proceedings Law 520

Penal Code 439, 441, 442, 445–48, 606
paras 27, 211, 212 606
para 216 607
para 226 606
Pregnancy Conflict Act 1995 447–49
Pregnant Women's and Families' Aid Amendment Act 1995 . . .445, 447, 448

Women's Aid Act concerning Abortions in Special Cases 1996 448

Greece

Civil Code—
Art 652 533
Art 732 532

India

Corneal Graft Act 1986 (Maharashtra State) 590

Ear Drum and Ear Bones (Authority for Use for Therapeutic Purposes) Act 1982 (Union Territory of Delhi) 590
Kidney Transplantation Act 1983 (Maharashtra State) 590

Medical Termination of
Pregnancy Act 1971 453

Penal Code 590
s 46 590

Registration of Births and Deaths
Act 1969—
s 29(B) 590

Transplantation of
Human Organs Act 1994 590–93

Italy

Civil Code 531
Arts 2229–38 531
Art 2236 532
Code of Professional
Medical Ethics—
Art 32 393
Constitution—
Art 3 394
Art 32 393

Deontological
Medical Code 1998—
Art 14 394

Penal Code—
Arts 50, 328 393

Japan

Civil Code—
Arts 415, 709 531

Luxembourg

Deontological Code 1995—
Art 45 393

Law of 10 August 1992—
Art 7 393

Law of 28 August 1998—
Art 43 393

The Netherlands

Burial Act 1994 601

Penal Code 601, 603, 605
Art 40 ....601, 603
Art 289 601
Art 293 601–03
Art 294 604
Wet op de Orgaandonatie
(Organ Donation Act) 1998 567

New Zealand

Accident Rehabilitation and
Compensation Insurance
Act 1992 548
s 5(5) 548
Children, Young Persons and
their Families Act 1989 107
Crimes Act 1961 107
ss 159, 182 108

Evidence Act 1968—
s 8 379
Evidence Amendment Act 1980 359
ss 32, 33 380

Romania

Decree Law No 1, 26 December
1989 (Abortion) 451

Seychelles

Termination of Pregnancy
Act 1994 451

Singapore

Advance Medical
Directive Act 1996 620–25
s 1 622
s 9 621
s 11 . . . . .622, 624
ss 12, 13 622
ss 14, 16, 17 .621

South Africa

Choice of Termination of
Pregnancy Act 1996 452

Sweden

Abortion Act 1974 450

Insurance Act .389

Law on Transplantation
No 831 of 8 June 1995 . . . . . . .568, 569

Secrecy Act 389

Switzerland

Penal Code—
Arts 114, 115 607

Turkey

Population Planning
Law 1983 . . . . .450, 451

United States of America

California Natural Death
Act 1976 . . . . .622, 624

Death with Dignity Act
1997 (Oregon) 609, 610

Emergency Medical Treatment
and Labour Act 1992 406

Federal Child Abuse
Prevention and
Treatment Act 1974 405
Federal Rules of Evidence 360
r 501 360
Florida State Constitution 617

Model Penal Code 1962 . . . . .421, 608
s 230.3 421

National Organ Transplant
Act 1984 (NOTA) 585, 586
s 301(a), (b) .585
New York Act of 10
December 1828, ch 20,
s 4, 1828 NY Laws 19 608
New York Privilege Statute 1828 359

Pennsylvania Abortion
Control Act 1982 428
Pennsylvania Abortion
Control Act 1988 428
Pennsylvania Abortion
Control Act 1992 428

Rehabilitation Act 1973—
s 504 405

Second Reinstatement of
the Law of Torts—
s 402(a) .544, 545
Social Security Act 422
State Constitution of Missouri 612
Art 1, ss 2, 10 612

Uniform Anatomical Gift
Act 1968 (UAGA) 582–85
Uniform Anatomical Gift
Act 1987 . . . . .584, 585
s 10(a) 584

Uniform Parentage Act
1975 (California) 468
Uniform Rights of the
Terminally Ill Act 1989 . . . . 609, 622, 624, 625
s 4 625
US Constitution 615
14th Amendment 1868 . . . . 608, 612–15, 631
s 251 631

International Conventions

Council of Europe's Convention for the Protection of Human Rights and Dignity of the Human Being with Regard to the Application of Biology and Medicine: Convention on Human Rights and Biomedicine (European Treaty Series/164. 4.4.1997) 323
Art 1(a), (2) 486
Arts 5, 6.1 323
Art 7 486
Art 21 457

EC Treaty—
Art 59 189
Art 60 . . . . 189, 655
European Convention on the Protection of Human Rights and Fundamental Freedoms 134, 138, 656
Art 2 . . . . 138, 153, 294, 309, 655–57
Art 3 . . . . 138, 153, 655, 656
Art 5 656
Art 8 . . . . 73, 93, 359, 384–89, 629, 656
Art 8(1) 386–89
Art 8(2) 93, 386, 387, 389
Art 9 657
Art 12 656
Art 13 387

UN Convention on the Rights of the Child 1989 134

ABBREVIATIONS

AI	artificial insemination
AID	artificial insemination by donor
AIH	artificial insemination by husband
BMA	British Medical Association
CA 1989	Children Act 1989
CCNE	French National Ethical Consultative Committee for the Life and Health Sciences
CMA	Canadian Medical Association
COTS	Childlessness Overcome Through Surrogacy
DGSW	Director General of Social Welfare
DHSS	Department of Health and Social Services
DNR	do not resuscitate
FPA	Family Planning Association
GAL	guardian *ad litem*
GIFT	gamete intrafallopian transfer
GMC	General Medical Council
GMSC	General Medical Scottish Council
GP	general practitioner
HA	health authority
HEA	Human Embryology Authority
HFEA 1990	Human Fertilisation and Embryology Act 1990
HGAC	Human Genetics Advisory Commission
HHS	Department of Health and Human Services

ICNY	Infertility Centre of New York
IVF	*in vitro* fertilisation
MHA 1983	Mental Health Act 1983
NBAC	US National Bioethics Advisory Committee
NHMC	(Australian) National Health and Medical Council
NICE	National Institute for Clinical Excellence
NSF	National Service Framework
NSPCC	National Society for Prevention of Cruelty to Children
OAPA 1861	Offences Against the Person Act 1861
PCR	polynurase chain reaction
PVS	persistent vegetative state
QUALY	quality-adjusted life years
RCGP	Royal College of General Practitioners
RCPCH	Royal College of Paediatrics and Child Health
RDMA	Royal Dutch Medical Association
RLF	retrolental fibroplasia
SHA	Special Health Authority
SIO	Social Insurance Office
UKCC	UK Central Council for Nursing, Miwifery and Health Visiting
UKTSSA	Transplants Support Service Authority
ULTRA	Unrelated Live Transplant Regulatory Authority

INTRODUCTION

BACKGROUND, PRINCIPLES AND THE MAKING OF MEDICAL DECISIONS IN HEALTHCARE LAW

BACKGROUND TO HEALTHCARE LAW

Structure of healthcare provision in the United Kingdom

Britain has a system of State funded and private healthcare provision. The vast majority of patients are treated by the State funded National Health Service (NHS) although the number of patients who have signed up for and are having treatment on a contractual basis with a private physician (as opposed to an NHS doctor) is rising.

Regulation of the National Health Service in the United Kingdom

In the United Kingdom, the responsibility for providing health services, to inpatients and outpatients at general practitioners' surgeries and hospitals and for improving the health of the nation as a whole, lies with the organisation founded by Aneurin Bevan, the Secretary of State for Health of the British Labour Government (elected in 1948). It was known as the National Health Service and was intended to provide free, State run, healthcare for all, a central part of the Welfare State. As *A Guide to the NHS* (1996, NHS Executive) puts it, 'its creation 'represented an international landmark in the provision of healthcare' and the principles on which it is based are the same in 2000 as they were when it was founded in 1948, stated in the guide as:

- provision of comprehensive care;
- the right of everyone in the UK to use it; and
- care is provided according to people's clinical need – not on their ability to pay.

The statutory duty to provide an NHS is imposed upon the Secretary of State for Health by the National Health Service Act 1977 (under ss 1, 3 and 5). The duty to ensure provision of health services lies with the local health authorities, under the auspices of the Department of Health and the NHS Executive.

The NHS is supposed to provide a comprehensive level of care, namely:

> ... *primary care* through family doctors, opticians, dentists and other healthcare professionals; *secondary care* through hospitals and ambulance services; and

tertiary care through specialist hospitals treating particular types of illness such as cancer. At the same time, the NHS works in partnership with local social services departments to provide community care.

The important fact is that almost all these services and facilities are provided free of charge, although Britain's taxpayers are paying for the NHS through at least part of their taxes. However, there are charges for medical prescriptions, which have been steadily increasing, although certain categories of people, such as persons over 60, are exempt. Dental care has to be paid for by everyone except children under 16. Over the years since 1948, the organisation has had to adapt to the needs of a changing population and to create new ways of providing healthcare.

An ICM poll for the Hutton Commission (the results of which were reported in, for example, *The Guardian*, 18 April 2000) suggested that, although two-thirds of the British public polled felt that the NHS needed to be improved quite considerably, the vast majority of those questioned (63%) thought the NHS was the 'most valuable' national institution in the UK, well ahead of Parliament (12%) and the police (11%). The founding principles of the NHS (see above) are what inspire its special place in popular affections. Ninety-six per cent of those polled believed in the right to 'free medical treatment at the time of need', even saying that this right should be enshrined in a Bill of Rights of the UK. No such Bill exists at present, hence, there is no constitutional guarantee to such treatment in English law.

The system that used to exist under the National Health Service and Community Care Act 1990 was in the nature of an 'internal market' within the NHS. GP 'fundholders' and local health authorities had a purchasing role which they operated through bargaining and buying health services from service providers such as the self-governing NHS Trusts which ran the facilities for the public. As of 1 April 1999, GP 'fundholders' have been abolished, the internal market has been replaced by a system called 'integrated care', based on partnership and driven by performance. This new system will form the basis of a 10 year programme to renew and improve the NHS through evolutionary change, rather than organisational upheaval. The health authorities no longer have a purchasing role, this having been replaced by a supervisory and strategic function. The purchasing role has now been given to the newly created 'primary care trust' based on the primary care groups and the primary health practitioners in a particular area who wish to be independent and are capable of being so (see the government White Paper, *The New NHS – Modern, Dependable*, 1997, Department of Health).

Lottery funded Healthy Living Centres

The present Labour Government is in the process of redrawing the legislation on the use of the National Lottery funds for the establishment of Healthy

Living Centres. These will not just be traditional health centres for primary healthcare or screening. They are to be centres or networks of services and advice targeted at vulnerable people within the community with poor health status.

National Institute for Clinical Excellence

A new National Institute for Clinical Excellence (NICE) has been established to promote high quality national guidelines for treatment based on the most up to date scientific evidence.

COMMISSION FOR HEALTH IMPROVEMENT

A new national Commission for Health Improvement will make sure that all parts of the NHS learn from, and are brought up to, the very best standards. This is an independent body for England and Wales, operating at arm's length from government but having statutory functions. Its legislative basis is the Health Act 1999 and it was formally established on 1 November 1999. Its programme of work was due to begin in April 2000. As stipulated in the Health Act, its functions will be to:

- provide national leadership to develop and disseminate clinical governance principles (see below);
- independently scrutinise local clinical governance arrangements to support, promote and deliver high quality services. The Commission will conduct a rolling programme of reviews of clinical governance arrangements visiting every NHS Trust, Primary Care Trust, and health authority every four years;
- review and monitor local and national implementation of national guidelines in the form of the National Service Frameworks (NSFs) and NICE guidance;
- help the NHS identify and tackle serious or persistent clinical problems. The Commission has the capacity for rapid investigation and investigation and intervention to help put these right;
- increasingly take on responsibility for overseeing and assisting with external NHS incident inquiries in England and Wales.
- seek to identify excellence and celebrate and share good practice, thus producing benchmarks.

According to the Department of Health website (www.doh.gov.uk), the work done by the Commission will be based on evidence and will not be 'opinion based'. Their style 'will be developmental not confrontational, fair and open'.

REVISED PATIENTS' CHARTER

There is to be a revised Patients' Charter which will include rights for patients in respect of information, treatment, access to GPs, participation in decisions and confidentiality. The new rights are to be set in the context of patient responsibilities, such as keeping appointments, not knowingly withholding information relevant to diagnosis or treatment, taking good care of one's own well being and not making gratuitous demands on the service.

CLINICAL GOVERNANCE AND HEALTH GOVERNANCE

The government has developed the concept of 'clinical governance', as described in a number of policy papers. This is a 'central unifying concept that draws in ideas of evidence based practice, effectiveness, management responsibility, outcomes and quality (Harrison (1997)). The Government White Paper provides as follows:

> 6.12 Professional and statutory bodies have a vital role in setting and promoting standards, but shifting the focus towards quality will also require practitioners to accept responsibility for developing and maintaining standards within their local NHS organisations. For this reason, the government will require every NHS Trust to embrace the concept of 'clinical governance' so that quality is at the core, both of their responsibilities as organisations and of each of their staff as individual professionals.
>
> A quality organisation will ensure that:
>
> - quality improvement processes (for example, clinical audit) are in place and integrated with the quality programme for the organisation as a whole;
> - leadership skills are developed at clinical team level;
> - evidence based practice is in day to day use with the infrastructure to support it;
> - good practice, ideas and innovations (which have been evaluated) are systematically disseminated within and outside the organisation;
> - clinical risk reduction programmes of a high standard are in place;
> - adverse events are detected, and openly investigated; and the lessons learned promptly applied;
> - lessons for clinical practice are systematically learned from complaints made by patients;

- problems of poor clinical performance are recognised at an early stage and dealt with to prevent harm to patients;
- all professional development programmes reflect the principles of clinical governance;
- the quality of data collected to monitor clinical care is of itself of a high standard.

6.13 This new approach to quality will be explicitly reflected in the responsibilities and management of NHS Trusts. Under the internal market, NHS Trusts' principal statutory duties were financial. The Government will bring forward legislation to give them a new duty for the quality of care. Under these arrangements, Chief Executives will carry ultimate responsibility for assuring the quality of the services provided by their NHS Trust, just as they are already accountable for the proper use of resources.

6.14 Chief Executives will be expected to ensure that there will be appropriate local arrangements to give them and the NHS Trust Board firm assurances that their responsibilities for quality are being met. This might be through the creation of a Board Sub-Committee, led by a named senior consultant, nurse, or other clinical professional, with responsibility for ensuring the internal clinical governance of the organisation.

6.15 These arrangements should build on and strengthen the existing systems of professional self-regulation and the principles of corporate governance, but offer a framework for extending this more systematically into the local clinical community. It is important that these arrangements engage professionals at ward and clinical level. NHS Trust boards will expect to receive monthly reports on quality, in the same way as they now receive financial reports, and to publish an annual report on what they are doing to assure quality. Quality will quite literally be on the agenda of every NHS Trust board [*The New NHS – Modern, Dependable*, 1997, Department of Health].

Recent studies suggest that the NHS entered the 21st century severely underfunded and experiencing increasing criticism from all its stakeholders for not being what it could and should be (see Hutton, W, *New Life for Health*, 2000, Vintage). Certainly, every winter in Britain, media reports abound of bed shortages in hospitals and there is always a plethora of stories about the 'crisis' in the NHS, frequently fuelled by stories of chaotic emergency wards and crammed morgues. The Labour Government, which was elected in May 1997, has responded to criticism by pledging to pour more money into the NHS and promising a new National Plan, which was recently published (see below).

THE NEW NHS NATIONAL PLAN FOR BRITAIN'S HEALTH SERVICE 2000–10

The Labour Government published its much heralded National Plan for overhauling the NHS on 27 July 2000. The blueprint for the next 10 years has been drawn up by six committees made up of government ministers, doctors' leaders, patients' groups and other experts. It promises to be the biggest revolution in healthcare since the NHS was founded in 1948. A massive £19 billion boost was announced in the 2000 budget for the next four years. The government wants to bring spending on health up to European Union levels by 2005, but has warned that huge cash injections must be matched by fundamental reform.

A report commissioned by the present Health Secretary, Alan Milburn, highlighted problems of poor management, disillusioned staff, dirty hospitals and massive bureaucracy. The main changes, as widely leaked to the press, include:

- *Waiting lists*: any NHS patient whose operation is cancelled for non-medical reasons will be guaranteed surgery within 28 days, even if it means private treatment. By 2005, 90% of patients will wait less than three months for non-urgent hospital care. No one should wait longer than six months. Special centres dedicated to particular operations such as cataract surgery or hip replacements could work 24 hours a day to cut queues.
- *Doctors*: there will be a large increase in the number of medical school placements and changes in way junior doctors are trained. In the interim, a recruitment drive will target doctors from the USA, Australia and Europe.
- *Nurses*: sizeable increases in the number of nurses are also planned. Nurses will also be given extra powers to prescribe drugs, treat patients in casualty departments and carry out routine surgery.
- *Hospitals*: new standards to clean up filthy wards and hospitals will be set and bosses will have to work to ensure there are enough beds to cope with winter pressures. Hospitals failing to achieve a range of performance targets will be deprived of extra cash.
- *Patients*: the crux of the plan is to make the Health Service more 'consumer friendly' so that every hospital will have a 'patient's champion' – a Patient Advocacy Service and Liaison Service which will handle complaints and have the power to demand action.
- *The elderly*: the national plan will include the Government's long awaited response to the proposal by the Royal Commission on Long Term Care of the Elderly which said that old people should be cared for by the State for free.

THE PRACTICE AND CONTROL OF MEDICAL ETHICS IN THE UNITED KINGDOM

The General Medical Council

The General Medical Council (GMC) is a statutory body, which was established under the Medical Act 1858, and is empowered to govern the training of doctors and the practice of medicine. It keeps the medical register, and its disciplinary committee has the power to suspend or strike a doctor off the register for serious professional misconduct. It does not purport to regulate day to day decisions of doctors but is really an overseeing and disciplinary body charged with maintaining professional standards. The GMC comprises members of the profession and lay members and it occasionally issues ethical guidance on specific matters, especially if they have been the subject of debate. An example of this is where it issued guidance on *Professional Confidence: Treatment of Persons under 16* (1985), in the 1980s, following the House of Lords' ruling in the *Gillick* case [1985] 3 All ER 402. Unfortunately, this advice conflicted with the British Medical Association (BMA) guidance at the time on the question of confidentiality. (For a contemporary discussion on *Gillick* at the time, see de Cruz (1987.)) However, there is far more unanimity nowadays between the BMA and the GMC on guidance documents.

The Professional Societies

The medical royal colleges have issued various ethical guidelines jointly and separately. The Royal College of Nursing is the equivalent of the BMA and also issues guidance, but it has tended to concentrate mainly on pay and employment conditions rather than on ethical issues.

The British Medical Association (BMA) is the organisation to which most doctors belong. It has been a registered trade union since 1974 and has been influential in formulating medical ethics for many years. It has a Central Ethical Committee and issues a *Handbook of Medical Ethics* which is updated from time to time, although the earlier versions were often mainly concerned with fees and etiquette. In certain controversial areas, such as withdrawal of treatment in cases of patients in a persistent vegetative state, and human organ donation, it has issued detailed and wide ranging ethical guidelines, even referring to the law in other jurisdictions. The key difference between the GMC and the BMA is that the BMA has no powers to enforce any breach of ethics, whereas the GMC has. The BMA has also been active in advising and giving evidence to bodies such as Royal Commissions and the GMC.

Terminology: medical law, healthcare law and medical ethics

Terminology comes and goes, and it is worth reflecting that many of the labels now firmly attached to a given corpus of law, such as 'contract law' and 'tort', originated in the 19th century, having been labelled by the pioneering academics of the time. Thus, while 'healthcare law' has become a more popular (some might say 'populist') term within the last 10 years or so of the 20th century, 'medical law' is arguably still a recognisable area of law, which was described by Professor Ian Kennedy in a lecture given in 1983 as a 'discrete area of law' despite not being 'marked out or accepted as having its own territory' (see Kennedy, I, 'The emerging problems of medicine, technology and the law', in *The Cambridge Lectures* (1985)). Kennedy went on to define medical law as 'a discrete area, concerned with the interactions between doctors and patients and the organisation of healthcare' (Kennedy, *Treat Me Right* (1988), Chapter 1). As he pointed out then, which still remains true today, medical law draws upon and is seen as a development of tort law, family law, contract law and public law. 'Medical ethics', however, are closely linked with philosophy, and have been described by Professor Dunstan as 'the obligations of a moral nature which govern the practice of medicine' (Dunstan *et al* (1981)). Medical Ethics have also been described as 'the analysis of choices in medicine' (Veatch, *Medical Ethics* (1989)). However, doctors are not the only professionals who deal with the health of people and the delivery of healthcare in the UK is the responsibility of the National Health Service. The term 'healthcare law', which has become somewhat more popular particularly in nursing circles over the last decade or so, is therefore wider and, as defined by Montgomery, 'not only embraces the practice of medicine but also that of the non-medical healthcare professionals, the administration of health services and the law's role in maintaining public health' (Montgomery (1997)).

Hence, the term 'medical ethics' can cover not only choices made by doctors, but those made by other healthcare professionals such as nurses, pharmacists and healthcare administrators.

LEGAL AND ETHICAL FRAMEWORKS IN WESTERN SOCIETIES

Evolution of medical ethics

The origins of very early medicine and medical ethics remain shrouded in antiquity and our knowledge of early tribes and civilisations suggest that the witch-doctor probably utilised natural remedies from the environment and then the supernatural to explain curing the sick, and this role eventually moved to the priests of organised religion who would probably have called on the 'Gods' and the spirit world! The Gods were always perceived as the arbiters of good and evil and so, even at this early stage, medicine men were already an elite group, but Mason and McCall Smith (1994) argue that the advantage of being a somewhat closed community meant that these high priests of medicine could learn from each other and could appreciate the advantages of organisation and codification. This also meant that they could teach, and by virtue of their privileged position, attract the very highest calibre of students so 'Medicine thus developed both priestly and secular practitioners while still preserving the image of superiority' (Mason and McCall Smith (1994)). Research suggests that organised medicine first began in the Middle East, in Egypt, where Imhotep, the father figure of medicine, and the 'archetypal combination of physician, priest and court official' practised (see Beasley (1982)). The Papyri discovered in the nineteenth century show that Egyptian medicine was comparatively advanced as early as the second millennium BC (Castiglioni (1947)).

Remarkably, as Mason and McCall Smith (1994) record, several features of this very early organisation of medicine seem far ahead of its time and must now be viewed with admiration in relation to modern structures in medical organisation:

- there appears to be a well-developed concept of a national health service;
- rigid rules were established for experimental treatment: for instance, no culpability followed from failure to cure so long as standard textbooks were followed;
- severe penalties were threatened for breach of the instructions because the rationale was very few men would be expected to know better than the best specialists who had gone before;
- the notion of specialisation was deeply ingrained;
- medical treatment remained the practice of the priest caste.

In Babylonian medical practice, the extension of surgical practice into lay hands continued apace and it is from here that the first known legal code – the Code of Hammurabi (c 1900BC) – originated. This contained traces of medical ethics and had rules on a system of payment based on results and, to some extent, on the ability to pay and on the status of the patient. There were also very severe penalties prescribed for negligent failure.

Greek medicine and the origins of ethical codes

Historically, medicine has had its own code of ethics for around two and a half thousand years originating, it is widely believed, from a group of physicians in ancient Greece, which produced the works of Hippocrates, dating from probably around the late fourth century BC (see the evidence gathered by Edelstein which suggest that this is the most likely date: Edelstein, 'The Hippocratic Oath: text, translation and interpretation', in *Ancient Medicine: Selected Papers of Ludwig Edelstein* (Temkin and Temkin (eds) (1967)) from which the Hippocratic Oath originates and which, despite several modifications, remains the *fons et origo* of modern codes of medical ethics in Western society. The exact origin of the Oath remains uncertain, as some of the doctrines it contains are not consistent with Greek thought, but are more consonant with the Pythagorean school of thought and as such may well predate the Hippocratic school that was created. In any event, the Oath was certainly being referred to in the 5th century BC and produced a large body of scientific and ethical writing with the leading figure being Hippocrates, who was the leader of a school of physicians, of which there were many in ancient Greece. The Hippocratic Oath indicates a 'prevailing ethos rather than a professorial edict' (Mason and McCall Smith (1994). There is no attempt here to lay down definitive rules on medical etiquette. The Oath lays down guidelines for medical ethics and Mason and McCall Smith paraphrase it thus: 'It implies the need for co-ordinated instruction and registration of doctors' with the need to protect the public 'from the dabbler and the charlatan'; it is clearly stated that the doctor is there for the benefit of his patients – 'to the best of his ability he must do them good and must do nothing which he knows will cause harm'; 'euthanasia and abortion are proscribed'; there is a reference to lithotomy which prohibits mutilating operations (castration), but this has been interpreted by many as indicating limiting such practices to those with the proper expertise; the nature of the doctor-patient relationship is outlined and taking advantage of it is disapproved; it also expresses the doctrine of confidentiality (Mason and McCall Smith (1994)).

The Oath did not become an essential part of ethical teaching until well into the Christian era and it in fact lapsed with the decline of the Greek civilisation and was restored with the evolution of University Medical Schools. A modernised version of the Oath was introduced by the World Medical Association as the Declaration of Geneva which was amended in Sydney in 1968 and it provides the basis of an appendix in the International Code of Medical Ethics.

Writing in 1996, Smith points out that, according to the New York Times, the Hippocratic Oath is rarely studied in medical schools in the USA, and is sworn to by only 6% of medical students (see Smith, C, in McLean (ed), *Death, Dying and the Law* (1996), p 84, fn 34). In addition, Smith points out that, apart from requiring a physician to relieve pain, the Oath also prohibits the giving of deadly drugs; in cases of unrelenting pain, some physicians might not find this an acceptable option to relieve their patients' suffering.

Apart from the Hippocratic Oath, there is the Declaration of Geneva (1947, revised 1968 and 1983), the modern restatement of the Hippocratic Oath, the

World Medical Association's international code of medical ethics (1949, revised 1968 and 1983), the Declaration of Helsinki on human experimentation (1964, revised 1975 and 1983), the Declaration of Oslo on therapeutic abortion (1970, revised 1983), the Declaration of Sydney on death (1968, revised 1983), the Declaration of Tokyo forbidding torture (1975, revised 1983), and several other codes adopted by various countries (some of these are discussed below and in subsequent chapters). However, even more up to date codes, and treaties dealing with biomedicine and biotechnology, have had to be formulated amongst and between countries, and global-focused organisations (like the World Health Organisation) have been very active in promulgating and promoting such codes. The pace of modern technological advancement is so rapid that the old codes have, in many respects, been rendered obsolescent by the development of procedures that were non-existent just 30 or so years ago. General principles require interpretation but, more problematically, there is an underlying conflict between general principles, especially if they are framed in absolute terms. As Phillips and Dawson put it 'it is the conflict between absolute principles, which say that something is inherently right or wrong, and utilitarian principles, which stress the consequences of an action' (Phillips and Dawson (1985), p 8), using the term 'utilitarian', they stress, in a 'lay' sense. So many of the situations that arise in medical ethics require making choices between competing principles and, again, Phillips and Dawson assert that 'the codes tend to fall apart at the seams as soon as they are put under pressure' (Phillips and Dawson (1985), p 7).

Two examples which they cite are abortion and confidentiality (which are discussed in this book in separate chapters, see Chapters 3 and 2, respectively, for the English legal position and Chapters 13 and 11 for a comparative discussion of these topics). Abortion pits the notion of the *absolute principle,* which says that destroying the fetus is inherently wrong and always wrong, against the *utilitarian principle,* which says that the question of what is right will depend on the best results for society at large. As far as confidentiality is concerned, the absolutist would argue that the duty of confidence is sacrosanct and should never be breached under any circumstances. However, the utilitarian would argue that it would depend on the particular situation and its particular circumstances (Phillips and Dawson (1985), pp 10–11). There is, they suggest, the philosophical notion of 'rule utility' which 'allows the absolutists the inherent value of their arguments, but then measures that value against what is best for society at large' and, citing euthanasia, they explain how such an approach would be that one reason why it is wrong to take life in such circumstances is, as they put it: '... once one has breached the principle of the sanctity of life, one is on a dangerous "slippery slope" in which people may be killed for a range of tendentious reasons. In other words, there are powerful utilitarian reasons to demonstrate that the absolutist principle is the right one to apply.' The idea seems to be that it is beneficial to more people if one follows general principles such as keeping promises, respecting freedom and acting justly. However, this is not a panacea, which Phillips and Dawson are at pains to emphasise, because while some notion of conflating or fusing the absolute and the utilitarian might provide some kind of basic structure to solve the problem of which type of principle to apply, 'it does not tell us how to rank those absolute principles in order to get the most beneficial result. For the principles still conflict' (Phillips and Dawson (1985), p 10). They assert that patients might disagree with the doctor's notion of what is for the best, and a society which respects that autonomy would then face a conflict of principles.

Many more examples of conflicting principles can be found, and this book will explore the English law on the area and, where applicable, consider how other jurisdictions have responded to similar conflicts and dilemmas.

Before one is able fully to appreciate the niceties of medical decisions and ethics, however, we must first consider the difficulties in even defining a 'medical decision' because, in the context of a doctor-patient, health professional-patient context, it is not purely a decision made by a medical professional or one that has medical consequences.

MEDICINE, ETHICAL PRINCIPLES AND 'MEDICAL DECISIONS'

What is a 'medical decision'?

Given the rapid advances in technology and medical technology in particular, it is clear that, as Pellegrino and Thomasma say, 'Without the reasonable restraints imposed by philosophical critique, medicine and its practitioners may unintentionally convert science and medical method into a muddled philosophy of human life' (see Pellegrino and Thomasma (1981), pp viii–ix)). As Sheila McLean has pointed out, 'Medicine can ... try to deal with the diseases which most concern us, but it can also absorb social and personal problems into its own unique sphere of influence' (see McLean (1999), p 16). The difficult question of what is really a 'medical decision' is an important one, because there are many situations that now arise in which doctors may be faced with decisions which are not strictly 'medical' ones; for instance, deciding on whether a handicapped newborn baby should be kept alive because of its poor 'quality of life'. If the doctors decide that the baby should not be kept alive with modern technology because it might then have a life as a paralytic, for example, this is arguably not really a 'medical' decision at all, except that it has been made by a medical practitioner. As Kennedy has argued, '[a] decision as to what quality of life is worth living is not ... a medical decision and thus not for doctors alone to make' (Kennedy (1998), p 25). And, he argues, persuasively, that 'failure to examine the question [of what is a medical decision] has resulted in decisions being taken by doctors which may not properly be within the unique or special competence of a doctor *qua* doctor to make' (Kennedy (1998), p 20).

In his Introduction to *Medicine, Ethics and the Law*, Professor Michael Freeman remarked in 1988 that 'Science, in particular but not exclusively bio-technology, has given doctors tools to work miracles, to cause life and to prolong it. The ethical dilemmas to which this gives rise are manifold and intractable'. Significantly, he adds:

> Decision-making cannot be governed by consensus for clearly there is none. There may be agreement on such fundamental principles as the sanctity of life but conflict remains on the content to be attached to such a principle ... The ultimate decision cannot be left to doctors alone. But doctors are expected to provide answers. Lawyers and philosophers can debate the questions involved endlessly, but doctors must take decisions, often there and then [Freeman (1988), p 1].

He stresses that doctors work within the framework of the law, but this 'is itself fraught with problems. Many of the issues thrown up by bio-medical advances elude the ingenuity or the skills of lawyers'. He then endorses the value of looking at other jurisdictions, because 'the problems confronting us in Britain are shared by the medical and legal professions as well as the philosophers of other countries ... where countries have approximately similar cultures and philosophies, we should not ignore the work done in them' (Freeman (1988), p 3).

This is precisely what this present book is attempting to do, and, in some cases, it is looking even further afield to see what countries that are very different from Britain (like Japan), or civil law countries like France and Germany, are doing to cope with certain problems like abortion, human organ shortages for transplantation, physician-assisted suicide (and forms of euthanasia) and non-consensual sterilisation of mentally handicapped persons. In a specialised topic like abortion, we offer a global view of abortion laws grouped according to grounds for abortion and list countries which do not allow abortion under any circumstances. We frequently discuss the medico-legal decisions that have been and are being taken in these difficult medico-legal situations in their comparative context where, for instance, a similar situation has arisen in another jurisdiction. But Michael Freeman reminds us that 'ideology is cloaked by framing solutions as inevitable consequences of unquestioned and supposed unproblematic legal institutions' and that 'it would be idle to pretend that philosophers have answers to questions' [such as 'should we permit involuntary sterilisation, is research upon human embryos morally justifiable ... should we allow assisted reproduction?].

In her book, *Old Law, New Medicine* (1999), Professor Sheila McLean argues that, despite the fact that the law might have been expected to make 'disinterested' decisions in areas like the good functioning of the individual and the State and the control of health and in matters of life and death, 'both our [that is, Western] society and our law seem happy to pass the burden of decision-making on many moral (or at least clinical) matters to the clinician (whether or not the clinician actually wants to accept this load). Decisions about who should live and who should die are perhaps the starkest of choices which are value-laden and complex' (McLean (1999), p 17). She also submits that, while doctors are 'uniquely qualified to reach a medical prognosis', the 'outcome of that prognosis is a matter which has moral, ethical, social and political consequences which doctors' training and technical knowledge in no way equip them to address, far less to answer' (McLean (1999), pp 18–19).

ETHICAL PRINCIPLES

The question of ethical questions

In a stimulating article written in 1985, Leon Kass argues that there are many possible ways of thinking about ethical questions:

> For some people, ethical issues are immediately matters of right and wrong, of purity and sin, of good and evil. For others, the critical terms are benefits and harms, risks and promises, gains and costs. Some will focus on so-called rights of individuals or groups (for example, a right to life or childbirth); still others will emphasise so-called goods for society and its members, such as the advancement of knowledge and the prevention and cure of disease [Kass, 'The meaning of life – in the laboratory', in *Toward a More Natural Science: Biology and Human Affairs* (1985), Chapter 4].

If one may paraphrase a famous expression of English law in relation to the notion of wardship, the 'golden threads' that run through the various medico-legal problems that this book examines, are notions of: *autonomy, consent, paternalism, beneficence* (doing good), *non-maleficence* (not doing any harm), *respect for persons, preserving life, the sanctity of life* and the *quality of life* and *justice.* these concepts have derived from long established tenets or principles of religious origin of various faiths such as Roman Catholicism, Protestantism, Judaism and Islam. Some of the concepts which we shall revisit are utilitarianism and 'deontological' ethics. It is important to bear in mind that, despite variations on a theme, nearly all the medico-legal dilemmas that have arisen from abortion, confidentiality, involuntary sterilisation, embryo research, surrogacy, children and medical treatment, through to organ transplantation and physician-assisted suicide, involve the balancing of principles that conflict with each other.

Autonomy and consent

In an essay published in 1985, Raanan Gillon contrasted the conflict between:

> ... the desire to do what is considered to be in the best interests of the patient and a desire to do what the patient says he wants ... Ultimately, the conflict is between, on the one hand, beneficence, the principle that one should do good and/or non-maleficence, the principle that one should not do harm (the Hippocratic principle *primum non nocere*); and on the other hand, the principle that one should respect people's autonomy [see Gillon in Lockwood (1985), p 111].

This encapsulates the classic conflict in many medico-legal situations. For example, a woman patient might refuse a blood transfusion or a Caesarean section which is required to save her unborn fetus or her own life, on religious grounds, but the healthcare professionals might decide that, in the light of her particular state of mind, for example, she is so terrified by a needle phobia that she lacks the capacity to decide whether to consent or not at that stage (for example, to be able to weigh in the balance the risks and benefits of the proposed treatment) and, therefore, proceed to give her a transfusion and save her life or a Caesarean section which saves both herself and her unborn fetus. Several cases have, in fact, been decided in this way by the English courts, especially since 1996, dealing with these kinds of situations, and the English Court of Appeal has now reiterated the right of the adult of sound mind to decide for herself on the medical treatment she will or will not receive, including these sorts of cases (see *Re MB* (1997), discussed at length in Chapter 1). This may be described as the right of self-determination or autonomy. However, although this principle has been unequivocally reaffirmed by the judiciary, there is clearly scope for discretion in certain circumstances (see Chapter 4). So what *is* the 'principle' of autonomy?

Definitions of autonomy

Ranaan Gillon in *Philosophical Medical Ethics* (1986) defines autonomy (p 60) as 'the capacity to think, decide, and act (on the basis of such thought and decision) freely and independently'. Writing in Lockwood's edited collection *Moral Dilemmas in Modern Medicine* (1985), he distinguished the *concept* of autonomy from the *principle* of autonomy, which he describes as 'the moral requirement to respect other people's autonomy'. The definition contained at the end of this edited collection reiterates this definition and adds: '... to allow [people] to make their own decisions.' Hence, in his opinion, respect for autonomy is 'the moral principle that people should have their autonomy respected to the extent that such respect is consistent with respect for the autonomy of others. Part of what such respect for autonomy implies, in practical terms, is not interfering with people without their consent.' In other articles, Gillon is again precise in referring to the principle of 'respect for autonomy' rather than simply the principle of autonomy (see, for example, Gillon (1989), pp 107, 110). Gillon (1986) also describes three aspects of autonomy: of thought, of will, and of action, and argues that the principle of respect for autonomy is intended to safeguard these three types of autonomy in all persons, except that limits to an individual's autonomy are necessary when it encroaches on someone else's autonomy.

Similarly, Campbell (1991) also writes (p 101) about the 'centrality of autonomy' as a principle and qualifies the word 'autonomy' by saying he means 'respect for the autonomy of patients', which indicates he is referring to the principle to which Gillon has referred.

However, other commentators do not make this distinction; McLean describes autonomy as 'rights to self-determination' (McLean (1999), p 60), which is the preferred phrase of lawyers, and Phillips and Dawson (1985) simply state (p 12) that the principle of autonomy 'means that individuals should be permitted personal liberty to determine their own actions'.

Harris describes autonomy as 'critical self-determination in which the agent strives to make decisions which are as little marred by defects in reason, information or control as she can make them' (Harris (1985), p 212).

Clearly, if one respects another person's autonomy, one will also observe another principle which is to have *respect for persons*. However, this principle has arguably been extended to respect for persons even after (and perhaps especially after) their death, because of the special significance given to a person's expressed wishes while alive or as contained in a will, not to deal with his body in a particular way, or, as in ancient civilisations, because of the special regard accorded to corpses in general. This might explain why, across the world, there is a plethora of legislative rules stretching from France to Sweden to the USA to Australia, which carefully regulate when human organ donation may or may not take place (see Chapter 17).

Justifications for autonomy

Gillon (1986) also identifies the two classic justifications for the principle of respect for autonomy:

(a) the Kantian argument that the nature of rational beings recognised that they were bound by a 'supreme moral law' whereby rational beings were 'ends in themselves' and recognised the autonomy of other such beings;
(b) the Utilitarian argument of John Stuart Mill, who argued that autonomy was an essential part of utilitarianism because autonomy was an essential part of the flourishing of the human subject.

Campbell, commenting on Gillon, argues that providing a justification for autonomy based on Mill's creates other ambiguities, because there will always be scope for argument over what constitutes the good of society. Pertinently, he points out that: 'In particular, we can ask whether an emphasis on individual liberty, even when defined in Kantian fashion, as autonomy of the will, can of itself necessarily ensure a just and compassionate society' (Campbell (1991), p 104).

Utilitarianism

The basic premise behind this philosophy is 'the greatest good for the greatest number', strongly promoted by the philosopher John Stuart Mill and Jeremy Bentham, amongst others. It judges the value of an action in terms of its consequences. The utilitarian appears to wish to maximise the happiness and welfare of the greatest number and it is usually contrasted with deontological theories, which are duty based (actions carried out because of duty or obligation) and the opposite of teleological theories, which are consequences based or consequentialist. Thus, teleological theories are promoted by the utilitarians. There are, of course, several difficulties with utilitarian theories, such as who decides what is good, how do we quantify well being, how does one calculate the 'greatest number'? As Johnson puts it: 'Is this an average well being or a maximum?' As he points out, 'if medical care is spread too thinly, no one will benefit, so the greatest good conflicts with the greatest number' (Johnson (1991), p 45).

Deontological theories

'The concept of rights and duties is classified as deontological theory' (Johnson (1990), pp 4–5), and he also reminds us that 'Deontological theory is usually associated with ethics that have a religious basis' (Johnson (1990), p 5). The word comes from 'deon' which means 'duty' in Greek.

'Deontological' is defined in Lockwood's edited collection (Lockwood (1985), p 242) as:

> That form of moral theory or moral reasoning which assesses the rightness or wrongness of actions not, or not merely, on the basis of their likely or possible consequences, but on the basic of their intrinsic character, as according with, or running contrary to, some specific duty, such as the duty to keep one's promises, or to tell the truth, or to respect the rights of others.

MEDICAL PATERNALISM

The word paternalism means, literally, to act as a father would towards his children. In the medical context, this is usually applied to the case where the healthcare professional acts against the wishes of the patient, but on the basis of wishing to promote the patient's 'best interests'. Paternalism has been defined by Thomasma as 'acting for the good of others in the absence of their consent, or even against their wishes' (Thomasma (1992), p 12). Fairburn has said that 'paternalism is most often defined in terms of one person's acting in what she takes to be another person's best interests even when that other might wish to act otherwise' (Fairburn (1991), p 123). Fairburn discusses suicide and its moral connotations and, in that context, argues that paternalism and, therefore, intervention may be justified in certain circumstances, namely:

(a) where the individual in question is badly informed;

(b) where the individual in question is lacking in rationality;

(c) where the individual in question is going to die unless we intervene, but where it seems likely that his intention is something other than to bring about his death;

(d) where the person's autonomy interests are best served by intervention [see Fairburn (1991), p 124].

The question might be asked whether medical paternalism remains part of English law, and it is clear from cases dealing with sterilisation of mentally handicapped persons, children with anorexia and, indeed, even in the last few years of the 20th century, for pregnant women who appeared to refuse Caesarean sections, that it is very much in evidence as far as the English judiciary is concerned. Yet, in a lecture delivered after the *Sidaway* decision, in which he had been on the bench in the Lords, Lord Scarman could say that 'Medical paternalism is no longer acceptable as a matter of English law; that has gone' (see Scarman (1986), p 697). With respect, as the cases mentioned above indicate, medical paternalism, supported by judicial paternalism, has continued to thrive in the second half of the 20th century. However, judicial pronouncements by the Court of Appeal in 1997 in *Re MB* can be read as an attempt by the courts to curb medical paternalism for certain situations involving refusal of Caesarean sections.

DOING GOOD, NOT DOING HARM AND THE DOCTRINE OF DOUBLE EFFECT

This is based on the principle of 'above all, do no harm', and these two principles are probably the essence of what people might come to expect from doctors. The problem is that there may be cases when one might have to perform an action which may lead to an evil, although this is the result of doing something which is *prima facie* good – like prescribing pain killers to someone in dire pain – but which, either because of the need to increase the dosage, or because of the patient's condition, leads to a 'bad' result, which might be a premature death. This is the Catholic *doctrine of double effect*, whereby acts done with the intention of doing good result in unintended, or unforeseen and secondary, bad effects. The principle is that one is responsible for the intended results of one's actions rather than any consequences that may follow from the actions as long as those consequences were not intended. This doctrine was developed by Thomas Aquinas, who formulated a concept whereby it is morally acceptable to cause or permit evil in the pursuit of doing good. As we shall see in the chapter on the end of life (Chapter 9), this doctrine usually arises in cases of dying patients, and, according to the doctrine, provided it can be proved that the doctor administered the pain killing drugs primarily to relieve the patient's suffering and not to cause that patient's death, he is morally and legally blameless. As far as the law is concerned, there has been a conflict of approaches in the case law, but *R v Cox* (1992) 12 BMLR 38 appears to have resolved any contradictory judicial pronouncements. The words of Devlin J in *R v Adams* [1957] Crim LR 773, where he said that 'The doctor is entitled to relieve pain and suffering even if the measures he takes may incidentally shorten life', were approved by Lord Goff in the *Bland* case when he said: '[It is] the established rule that a doctor may, when caring for a patient, who is, for example, dying of cancer, lawfully administer painkilling drugs despite the fact that he knows that an incidental effect of that application will be to abbreviate the patient's life ... Such a decision may properly be made as part of the care of the living patient, in his best interests; and, on this basis, the treatment will be lawful' (see *Airedale NHS Trust v Bland* [1993] 1 All ER 868).

PRESERVING LIFE

Various ethical codes stress the doctor's obligation to respect life, but they do not require doctors to preserve life at all costs. The distinction is often drawn between actively killing a patient and letting that patient die. The former is regarded as unlawful and morally unacceptable, and the latter is regarded, in certain circumstances, as 'acting in the best interests of the patient'. The duty or obligation to preserve life may, in practice, conflict with another principle, to respect a patient's autonomy, if, for example, the patient has specifically asked the doctor to end his life. Hence, if the doctor does not accede to the patient's request, it may be argued that the doctor is overriding the right of the patient to decide what should be done with his body, but the patient cannot expect the doctor to break the law. If the patient is in great pain, and wishes the doctor merely to alleviate this pain, but the doctor knows that to prescribe an increasing amount of pain killing drugs would kill the patient, what is the doctor to do? If the doctor refuses to prescribe the drugs, is that acting in the patient's best interests, especially when the patient says he only wants relief from his pain? As often cited in the context of euthanasia, in the famous couplet from Arthur Clough, the approach is: 'Thou shalt not kill, but needs't not strive officiously to keep alive' (Clough, A, 'The last decalogue', cited in Glover (1977), p 92). The acts and omissions doctrine may be considered briefly at this point.

THE 'ACTS AND OMISSIONS' DOCTRINE

As described by Gillon (1986), this acts and omissions doctrine is where 'actions that result in some undesirable consequences are always morally worse than inactions, or failures to act, that have the same consequence'. It is worth noting that Roman Catholic philosophers, theologians and secular philosophers have strenuously rejected this acts and omissions doctrine on three grounds, which are discussed by Gillon thus: first, 'an omission by definition is not simply an inaction but a morally culpable inaction'; secondly, the Roman Catholics claim that 'not only does outcome matter when a moral judgment is made on a person's actions. But so too are preceding consideration, including pre-existing moral obligations and the understanding and intention with which the person acted'; thirdly, 'certain sorts of action and inaction are absolutely forbidden, in particular, intentional killing of an innocent person, including bringing about death by omission, is absolutely forbidden' (Gillon (1986), pp 129–30).

The English courts appear to have resolved the question of 'physician-assisted suicide', as the Americans call it, by requiring proof that the physician acted solely to relieve the patient's pain and suffering (for example, in prescribing pain killing medication) in order to exonerate the physician's actions if the patient ultimately died from taking the prescribed medication (see Chapter 9).

SANCTITY OF LIFE, RESPECT FOR HUMAN LIFE AND QUALITY OF LIFE

The 'sacredness' of life

The Declaration of Geneva speaks of the 'utmost respect for human life', and some would argue that *all* life is sacred (both human and non-human) on purely religious grounds, for example, because all life comes from God, the ultimate sacred being. However, the phrase and concept is complex enough even if we confine ourselves to *human* life. In his famous book, *Life's Dominion*, Professor Ronald Dworkin discusses his notion of what 'sacredness' of human life may mean; he also ponders what the notion of 'intrinsically valuable' might mean, and suggests that a thing might be considered 'sacred' or 'valuable' by association, because of its history, because of intrinsic value, respect for God as the divine creator, or because of the wonder at natural and human creation. In a memorable passage, he says 'The life of a single human organism commands respect and protection ... no matter in what form or shape, because of the complex creative investment it represents and because of our wonder at the divine or evolutionary processes that produce new lives from old ones' (Dworkin (1994), p 84).

Arguments about the sanctity of life, as opposed to the 'quality of life', tend to surface in the context of the proposed sterilisation of mentally handicapped persons, or in cases which require decisions about whether to save the life of a severely disabled newborn child, or to such a child who has a poor prognosis of life expectancy, be allowed to die 'with dignity' (see Chapter 5).

So how does one judge the 'quality of life' of a person? Can this ever be a fruitful exercise? Is it even possible to do so with any consistency or rational justification?

Sanctity of life v quality of life

In the early 1980s, two English cases on handicapped babies led Professor Glanville Williams to say that if he were suddenly told by a wicked fairy that he was about to be transformed into a Down's syndrome baby and asked whether he would want to die immediately, he would say 'yes'. This suggested the fallacy, as McLean says, 'that we could take our own life experiences and translate them into someone else's reality' (McLean (1999), p 118). Thus, the *quality of life* approach focuses on whether a particular patient has the capacity or potential to live a 'normal' life, that is, experience all the five senses, and the life experiences that a 'normal' person would. In the case of a handicapped newborn, of course, such a child would never have known what a 'normal' life would be like, so it would be simply fallacious to impose a 'normal' person's life or developmental experiences on such a person and assume that this person would reject life on the basis that it would have a very poor 'quality of life'.

In *The Value of Life*, Professor John Harris argues that:

> ... the ultimate question for medical ethics ... is simply: what makes human life valuable and, in particular, what makes it more valuable than other forms of life? ... When we ask [this question] we are trying to identify those features, whatever they are, which both incline us and entitle us to value ourselves and one another and which license our belief that we are more valuable (and not just to ourselves) than animals, fish or plants ... It is important to realise that it is the capacity to value one's own life (and those of others) that is crucial ... [Harris, J, *The Value of Life*, 1985, Routledge & Kegan Paul].

According to Harris, therefore, embryos, newborn babies and the severely handicapped would not have lives that were 'valuable' by his criterion. Indeed, if we look at the English court cases involving severely handicapped newborns, the courts have appeared to have moved from a 'qualified' sanctity of life position to a quality of life position with the proviso that only lives which, if prolonged by artificial means or technology, were going to be 'demonstrably awful' could be seen as not worth preserving and should be 'allowed to die' with decency and dignity. Indeed, in *Re T* (1997), a case involving a toddler who needed a liver transplant, but was not given authorisation by the court to have the operation because his parents objected, a senior judge of the Court of Appeal (Butler-Sloss LJ) said that it 'was *not* the function of the [English] court to preserve life at all costs' (see Chapter 5 for a detailed discussion of *Re T* (1997)). However, post-*Re T* cases appear to have endorsed the 'qualified' sanctity of life principle again and were not guided by parental wishes.

In the 'real world', as McLean reminds us, 'An absolute commitment to the sanctity of all life is absent in every community. Whether through laws about self-defence, engagement in war, the imposition of the death penalty or our failure to save everyday life that could be saved, we already concede that lives may be balanced and some may be lost' (McLean (1999), p 118).

The notion of justice and QUALYs

Another principle contained in the Hippocratic Oath is the importance of the doctor's duty towards the individual patient. Phillips and Dawson (1991) caution (p 16) that, 'taken to extremes, this is a socially irresponsible philosophy, since the community is composed of many patients in which care for some may impinge upon the quality of care for others'. Basically, in a society of limited resources, the 'principle of distributive justice, under which those in greatest need have their needs met first ... conflicts with the principle of autonomy, under which every individual is entitled to an equal share of the healthcare provided by the community. If services have to be rationed, how equal can the share-out be?' (Phillips and Dawson (1991)). It is in the context of allocation of scarce resources that difficulties have arisen as to how to mete out distributive justice, and it is in that difficult area where 'hard choices' (Calabresi) have to be made and where the economic notion of QUALYs (Quality Adjusted Life Years) has been utilised. This allows some calculation to be made of evaluating healthcare outcomes according to a generic scale by asking (a) to what extent and for how long will a particular treatment improve the quality of a patient's life, and (b) how much will that treatment cost? As Lockwood explains, 'What economists who favour the QUALY approach do ... is to take a checklist of health factors that are likely to affect the perceived quality of life of normal people, and assign weightings to them' because 'the assumption is that there is some rational way of trading off length of life against quality of life, so that one could say, for example, that three years of life with some degree of discomfort, loss of mobility or whatever was worth two years of normal life'. As he also points out, there is 'an inescapable element of arbitrariness here, both in the choice of factors to be taken into account and in the relative weightings that are attached to them which ... would differ markedly from patient to patient' (Lockwood, in Bell and Mendus (1988), pp 36–37).

CLINICAL GUIDELINES AND PROTOCOLS

Both the British Medical Association and the General Medical Council have issued guidelines over the years. Only the GMC has any power to discipline doctors and, therefore, to enforce the observance of these guidelines. The legal status of guidelines and protocols has, to date, never been definitively clarified by the English courts, hence their precise status must remain in doubt at this time. However, there is a school of thought that believes that such guidelines represent best practice and, certainly, in the case of child law, the famous Cleveland Guidelines (which were a series of points laid down in an inquiry report to assist the preferred approach to interviewing children suspected of having been abused) of 1988, the English courts have actually cited them as examples of best practice, although they were not contained in any legally binding document or statute, statutory instrument, regulation or judicially decided case. The USA Institute of Medicine defines 'clinical guidelines' as 'systematically developed statements to assist practitioner and patient decisions about appropriate healthcare for specific clinical circumstances' (Gordon (1995), p 3; cited by Salako (1998), p 65). Some researchers have said that the origin of these guidelines may be traced to the Egyptian Eber Papyrus, the Hippocratic Corpus and the aphorisms of Osler, where numerous attempts were made to put into written form the ways that the contemporary medical knowledge should be applied in terms of successive behavioural actions (see Klazinga (1995), p 11, cited by Salako (1998)).

Protocols have been defined by Goldfield *et al* as follows: 'Protocols are outlines, diagrams, or flow charts that describe each step in a process of clinical diagnosis and treatment. They show recommended alternatives and actions at each point of decision making. They may, at times, overlap with administrative flow charts. You can use them both to analyse patterns of care and to plan improvements.' Guidelines as such have been referred to as 'cookbook medicine' (Goldfield *et al*, section 6.14) and 'demeaning', 'deskilling' and 'professionally mediocre' by Gordon and Christensen (1995), p 7). Be that as it may, it would appear that at least the healthcare professions have some sort of yardstick of 'best practice' to which to conform in everyday practice and it is only at the highest levels, that is, when a 'standard practice' is under scrutiny in litigation, that the most eminent and experienced consultants and specialists are called upon to express an expert opinion. Under the *Bolam* rule, as interpreted by the English courts, though not actually stated as such in the case itself, all that needs to be established in a given case is that there is one body of opinion that would support the procedure that was carried out, regardless of whether there is also another body of reputable opinion that would not. As we shall see in the chapter on Medical Negligence, the *Bolam* case still prevails, but perhaps it might not always be unquestioningly followed as a result of the *Bolitho* decision (on which, see Chapter 7 for a detailed analysis).

OTHER CODIFICATIONS ON MEDICAL ETHICS

Three schools of thought may be identified as containing collections of principles which deal with the health professional's duty. Indeed, religious groups have long formulated principles dealing with ethics which, *inter alia,* deal with decisions relating to medicine. Roman Catholic scholars and theologians have, since at least the middle ages, written and preached on morals and ethics, and medical ethical principles based on Christian ethical precepts. Papal edicts on abortion, contraception and sexual ethics are well known and, occasionally, misunderstood by the general public. They also have strong doctrinal views on other medical issues such as the treatment of critically and terminally ill patients, and the means that should be expended in saving patients who have poor prospects of immediate survival. One of the lesser known tenets of the Catholic Church is the doctrine justifying *withholding* 'extraordinary' treatment, because the Church recognises that extraordinary means to prolong life may be inappropriate. Although the Church does not sanction euthanasia, it accepts that using extraordinary means might be inappropriate in the case of trying to resuscitate a patient who has no chance of surviving very long. It has employed the principle of proportionalism and the question that it asks here is: would the proposed treatment, with its accompanying pain, discomfort and risk be proportionate to the benefit that is likely to be obtained?

The other famous concept developed by Catholic thought is the *doctrine of double effect* (discussed, above). The doctrine is applied in medical ethics to justify a case where a doctor operates on a pregnant woman with a cancerous uterus, for example, with no wish to harm the fetus, but as a result of his action, fetal death may unintentionally occur. The doctor is not responsible, because she would have saved the fetus if she could have done so, but the crucial point, it is said, is that the doctor had no intention of harming the fetus.

Judaism

Judaism has a long tradition of laws that provide Jewish views on matters such as abortion, autopsy and circumcision, and it has had a significant influence on medical ethics throughout history, through Christianity and in its own right. Jews believe that God created an ordered world and plays an active part in influencing the way the universe operates. God has made his values, his Divine Will and precepts known through the Ten Commandments and also through the many edicts contained in the words of the Prophets. Doing good reflects God's nature. God's laws are for the benefit of mankind. A Hebrew physician's oath dates from the seventh century and contains prohibitions on causing death, on performing an abortion (for an adulterous wife), and revealing confidences. This oath was referred to as the Oath of Asaf, and was administered by a teacher to his students (Etziony (1973), pp 24–26, cited in Veatch (1989), p 14). Similarly, the prayer of Yehudi Halevi, a Judeo-Spanish philosopher and physician dating from the 11th or 12th century, makes it clear that it is God, not the physician, who heals. Orthodox scholars of the Talmud hold that life is sacred and to be preserved until the time when the patient is moribund (Bleich (1979), pp 33–35, cited by Veatch (1989), p 13). There is also a specific exhortation to show mercy to the poor and needy and a warning to avoid sorcery, magic and witchcraft. Apparently, the best-known Jewish document is prayer attributed to the 12th century Jewish physician, Moses Maimonides, but which Veatch suggests 'probably dates from 18th century Germany' (Veatch (1989), p 14). It condemns 'thirst for profit' and ambition for renown and admiration. Obviously, these and more recent writings provide different frameworks for medical ethics than the professionally formulated codes.

Jewish thinking also believes that each person has an immortal soul which represents his true worth and never dies even after death. It believes that it is very important to live a good life, because God will punish or reward us according to how we live. Observance of customs and traditions is therefore very important to Jews.

Medical ethics in non-Western cultures

In non-Western cultures, or at least cultures outside the Anglo-American West, cultures rooted in the Islamic tradition, China, Japan, India and African cultures and sub-cultures have their own views on medical ethics, either based on the Koran or the major philosophical ethical systems of the broader cultural traditions. The Egyptian papyri of the second millennium BC also contain some indication of medical ethics. In China, it is believed that medical ethics were not established until around the 7th century.

However, we look first at medical ethics in Islam.

Medical ethics in Islam

People of the Islamic tradition have a history of views on medical ethics which are based on Qur'anic teaching, since the Qur'an is the prime authority in Islam and the fundamental source of Islamic teaching. In modern times, the Oath of the Islamic Medical Association of the USA and Canada contains a strong prohibition on killing, similar to that of Jewish thought. Islamic physicians are committed to the virtues of 'strength', 'fortitude', 'wisdom', and 'understanding'. They are to be honest, modest, merciful, and objective. There is a strong commitment to serving mankind, 'poor or rich, wise or illiterate, Muslim or non-Muslim, black or white' (see Veatch (1989), p 17).

Rispler-Chaim (1989) argues that Islamic medical ethics constitute a field in their own right and have practical relevance to contemporary Muslims. He states that, although some issues that Islamic medical ethics deal with are typical for Islam and pertain primarily to Muslims, others are common to most religions. These include the legitimacy of abortions, organ transplants, artificial insemination, cosmetic surgery and doctor-patient relationships. However, the main characteristics of Islamic medical ethics are:

(a) there is a constant attempt to base modern medical treatments in the classical sources of Islamic law;

(b) the problems raised are pertinent predominantly to Muslims, or derive directly from the commandments of Islamic law;

(c) when Islamic law and the State law on certain medical ethics are contradictory, the fatwa is issued to mediate. The fatwa in this context is a legal opinion often expressed in a question/answer format;

(d) Islamic medical ethics are often inseparable from social and political issues.

Abdel-Haleem (1993) discusses various medico-legal topics in relation to Islamic ethics and reports, *inter alia*, as follows:

Abortion

(a) Abortion from 120 days onwards is illegal; hence, from this point, neither the parents nor a third person has the right to bring about abortion and if they do, they face the religious responsibility in the hereafter, financial responsibility for compensation according to Islamic norms and modern legal liability. So 120 days is seen as the beginning of obvious life. But abortion after 120 days is permissible if it is for the safety of the mother. The High Council for Islamic Legal Opinions in Kuwait issued a statement on 29 September 1984 that abortion may be done with the consent of the two parents before the completion of 40 days from conception; after 40 days and before 120, it may not be done except if the continuation of the pregnancy would cause grievous harm to the woman which she cannot bear or would continue after birth; or if it is certain that the fetus will be born with severe deformation or physical or mental deficiency, neither of which can be cured. It also stated that, except in urgent circumstances, abortion must be done in a government hospital and after 40 days it can only be done by a decision of three specialist doctors, one of whom at least must be a specialist in gynaecology and obstetrics, and the decision must be agreed by two trustworthy Muslim doctors.

(b) A fetus has a legal identity (even if it is 'incomplete') separate from its mother and if the mother commits premeditated murder on someone and has to be executed, this sentence cannot be carried out before the birth.

(c) Although the fetus does not have a full legal identity, it acquires four rights: (1) lineage; (2) entitlement to a proper share in the inheritance from close relations; (3) wills can be made in its name; (4) trusts can also be made in its name but there can be no liabilities of any kind brought against it.

Euthanasia

There is no mention as such of euthanasia, but life is sacred under Islamic law and suicide as such is prohibited. Terminating the life of those who have reached old age is even more abhorrent in Islamic ethical and social thinking.

Turning off life-support systems

Before the 'death of the brain' occurs, doctors are not allowed to disconnect life support systems from one patient to use it for another in the same condition and, generally, are under the obligation to keep such systems connected to patients who require them to protect their lives rather than to merely prolong their lives.

Artificial insemination

This is likened to the sexual approach to a woman in error (that is, not by her husband) and indicates that early Muslim jurists were aware of indirect impregnation. Deliberate insemination with the 'seed of a stranger' is equated with adultery and is a sin punishable by death according to Islamic law.

Chinese medical ethics

Veatch informs us that 'Chinese medical ethics are closely integrated with ancient Confucian, Buddhist and Taoist teaching, but there are no definitive religious texts as there are in Hindu and Muslim thought. Instead, there are compendia of codes or rules of conduct compiled by many Confucian medical scholars and critics of the classical Confucian position' (Veatch (1989), p 132). Lee writes that medical ethics in China were not established until the 7th century. Sun Ssu-miao (581–673 AD), the 'father of medicine' in China, first discussed the duties of a physician to his patients and to the public in his book *The Thousand Golden Remedies*. This was similar in certain respects to the Hippocratic Oath (see Lee, in Veatch (1989), pp 132–39).

Ancient Chinese ethics laid great store on the virtue of charity and the value of gratuitous service to the poor. Lee also writes that, in the Ming Dynasty, many physicians discussed and wrote about questions of medical ethics, including Hsu Chun-fu who, in 1556, compiled a section on medical ethics under the heading 'The medical way', and Kung Hsin wrote a 'maxim' for the 'good physician' who was exhorted to read widely, be highly skilled in the arts of his profession, having in his mind adequate treatments which he could adapt to different conditions. His main concern should be to relieve suffering among all classes. He 'revives the dying and restores them to health' (Lee, in Veatch (1989)).

It was Kung Hsin's son, Kung Ting Hsien, who then set 10 requirements for physicians in 1558, which were very similar to the maxim paraphrased above. About 30 years later, Chen Shih-kung, in his book *An Orthodox Manual of Surgery*, stated 10 commandments and 10 requirements for physicians which form the most comprehensive statement on medical ethics in China. It included: the duties of a physician to his patients (including professional secrecy, responsibility, deportment and compensation). It also mentioned the importance of advancement of medical knowledge as well as the rules for social intercourse.

Japanese medical ethics

The more traditional Japanese medical ethics derive from Buddhist thought and indigenous Shinto tradition. One example of a Japanese code of medical ethics comes from the Ri-shu school of medical practice dating from about the 16th century. This code, the *Seventeen Rules of Enjuin*, has several similarities with the Hippocratic Oath, including secrecy and a strong commitment to serving the patient. The physician is obliged to protect against disclosing any secrets he learns during his medical education. Instructions are also given to make sure that his books are returned to the school upon his death (Veatch (1989), p 19). Veatch comments that this view contrasts with the ethics of Protestantism, which 'places great emphasis on entrusting the texts to the lay person and to secular liberalism, which insists that lay persons should be reasonably informed about the nature of the treatments and the consequences' (Veatch (1989), p 140).

HEALTHCARE PROVISION IN NON-UK COUNTRIES

Common law and civil law countries

Unlike the UK, there is no health service comparable to the NHS in other countries, but rather, there are private medical schemes, and medical schemes run and funded on a regional basis or particular geographical zones.

In France, with its archetypal public/private divide, there is a clear division between State run hospitals and private hospitals and the implications for liability for injuries suffered through the medical negligence of doctors has been that for State employed doctors, only those acts which indicated a complete lack of responsibility so as to constitute 'gross' fault would be actionable by their patients. However, this is now being modified by recent case law developments. On the other hand, the duties of medical practitioners in private practice derive from contract, namely, the contract between the doctor and his or her patient. The standard of care is 'reasonable care', in return for which the patient pays the doctor's fees. In other words, there are two standards of care in countries like France, depending on whether the patient is being treated by a State employed physician or a doctor in private practice (see, further, Chapter 16).

It may be argued that, if a patient is paying for every single aspect of her medical treatment, from the medication to every individual swab in an operating theatre, there seems to be a consumerist principle which dictates that, if you are having to pay for what you are getting, you are entitled to receive a full and frank explanation of the treatment that is being proposed, in every detail. This might explain, in part, the informed consent doctrine that operates in American jurisdictions with full rigour as opposed to the less fully developed doctrine of consent utilised in England and Wales. At present, the USA is seriously considering a system which would be a variation of the NHS in Britain.

A comparative law methodology

A consensus on comparative methodology, namely, how to compare different legal systems in a 'meaningful' way, so that the comparisons are not merely superficial or misleading as a result of the inevitable variables within each jurisdiction, is not easy to find. The legendary pioneers of comparative law such as Pollock, Gutteridge, Rabel, Kahn-Freund and Rene David had a lot of wisdom to impart on why comparisons should be undertaken, but did not really formulate any detailed blueprint on comparative methodology. They certainly emphasised that 'comparative law' was not a subject like contract or criminal law, with a core content, but rather a method of study which, to be meaningful, did not merely make comparisons between legal cultures or systems, but studied the relationship between those systems in the context of their historical development. In the 1970s, Professors Zweigert and Kotz were the first of the great comparatists to enunciate some sort of criteria for undertaking a comparison of legal systems, listing (a) their historical background and development of that system; (b) their characteristic (typical) mode of thought in legal matters; (c) their distinctive institutions; (d) the types of legal sources those systems acknowledge and their treatment of those sources; and (e) their ideology; and they have not seen fit to change their approach, even by the end of the 20th century (see Zweigert, K and Kotz, H, *An Introduction to Comparative Law*, 1998, OUP). However, it is also possible and, indeed, useful to examine and compare certain aspects of different legal systems to glean insights which would then place the 'home' jurisdiction into perspective. This is because it can become far too easy to assume that one's own medical system or particular rules governing medical law are the only ways of dealing with health situations. Complacency and insularity can so easily breed stagnation and become enemies of progress. Hence, a knowledge of how other jurisdictions and/or cultures cope with similar health problems provides a broader and more informed basis for appraisal of one's own system. Of course, all comparatists must be very wary of cultural, economic, political, historical and religious factors that have usually shaped a particular jurisdiction's approach to a given problem or situation. These differentiating factors will then form the basis of the initial comparison. Of course, once the comparison has been made, the analysis should then commence, by synthesising and unravelling the various concepts so as to place them within their historical, economic, political, cultural and social context. In essence, therefore, this book seeks to examine key topics and activities within healthcare law as they operate in various common law and civil law jurisdictions, within their unique context and environment, in an attempt to better understand their evolution and rationale and to appraise their validity within a medico-legal and ethical framework.

Some key differences between common law and civil law jurisdictions

A cardinal principle for the comparatist to bear in mind is that common law countries/jurisdictions are generally guided by their judicial decisions (or case law) and the judicial decisions which have interpreted their statutes and secondary legislation, whereas civil law countries such as on the European continent have been, and are generally, governed by their statutes and legislation as contained in their comprehensive codes. Hence, it should be noted that, at least in strict theory, but not always in practice, common law jurisdictions like the UK, Australia, New Zealand and the USA (although to a lesser extent in the latter) have developed and are usually guided in their case law, or the decisions of their courts, and adhere to a system of precedent which generally requires courts to be bound by previous decisions on the same kinds of cases, either on the facts of the case or in relation to the principles of the case. A lower court is generally 'bound' (that is, obliged) to follow the decisions of a higher court, and certainly the decisions of the appellate courts at the top of the hierarchy of courts would usually be followed. Of course, cases may be 'distinguished' and, therefore, not followed on the basis of their facts (which might have been significantly different) or law (the principle capable of equally valid but opposing interpretations), or both.

However, no such doctrine of binding precedent exists in civil law countries, where the first port of call is usually to consult one of their codes, which are typically detailed, authoritative, comprehensive, exhaustive collections of general clauses and legal principles with examples of their application given after each statement of principle. There is often a general Code which contains books or divisions entitled 'Of Persons', 'Of Property and Different Kinds of Ownership' and 'Of the Different Ways of Acquiring property' and these books are further divided into titles, such as 'Enjoyment and Loss of Civil Rights', 'Marriage', 'Divorce' and so on, to describe the segments that follow. As in France, most civil law countries also have other comprehensive codes dealing with civil procedure, criminal procedure, commerce and a penal code. Hence, a lawyer in a civil law country, when seeking to clarify a point of law, would consult the codes and legislation, whereas her common law counterpart would consult the judicial decisions as contained in textbooks or in the authoritative and long established collections of law reports of cases such as the All England Law Reports or Weekly Law Reports.

This is not to say that common law countries such as the USA do not have codes. Indeed, extensive codes have been compiled in common law jurisdictions such as the USA, mainly for procedure, but by no means exclusively, since some contain substantive law as well. In terms of sheer volume, the USA has more codified laws than any other country, but the key difference is that a common law code is generally based on pre-existing law and seeks to consolidate and/or clarify this, whereas a civil law code is *prima facie* and *per se* meant to be authoritative, definitive and comprehensive. Cases are, however, acquiring greater usage in courts in civil law countries, particularly in certain German courts and, to a lesser extent, in French courts, where it would have to be a line of consistent decisions before a French judge would be allowed to at least take notice of it. However, although Art 5 of the French Civil Code states that judges are forbidden, when giving judgment in the cases before them, to lay down general rules of conduct amounting to a regulation, a century of experience has led to French academic writers (jurists) to concede that judges are, in fact, making law from time to time, particularly in 'gap-filling' cases, where no codified rule exists. However, the French courts would only acknowledge that a case is illustrative of a broader general principle as contained in a Code, not a binding authority on that court.

These differences have implications for the speed of law reform and must feature in any assessment of the evolution and future development of healthcare law in the various jurisdictions. In other words, if a particular jurisdiction finds there are good reasons to reform an area of law and medical ethics and there is sufficient support for the changes, it would be much speedier changing the law via a comprehensive, authoritative code than waiting for a particular case to come to court in order to resolve it, which might still leave the law in an uncertain state because of the special facts of a given case. But, legislation has not been the usual common law procedure for law reform, although this is gradually changing. A crucial difference between a civil law country's code and a common law country's code is that there is usually far more scope for judicial interpretation of the provisions in the latter. On the other hand, there is a growing tendency for case law to determine the speed of legal changes in Germany, because the practice has been developing that German judges in the lower courts devote a great deal of attention to the decision to the Federal Constitutional Court and the supreme courts. On the other hand, international treaties such as the European Convention on Human Rights or the Council of Europe's Convention on Human Rights and Biomedicine set out broad principles, and the more countries that ratify these instruments, the more international the applicability of such universal principles will be. (For more detailed analysis and discussion of the operation of common law and civil law systems, see, generally, de Cruz, P, *Comparative Law in a Changing World*, 2nd edn, 1999, Cavendish Publishing.)

A basis for comparison – common ethical concepts

In the light of the foregoing discussion, it is now possible to embark on our journey through the medico-legal dilemmas that make up nearly all the topics discussed in this book. At the outset, from the complex history of consent on both sides of the Atlantic and abroad, to confidentiality, abortion, involuntary sterilisation of mentally handicapped children and adults, and to organ transplantation, death, dying and euthanasia, the recurrent themes of autonomy, respect for persons, paternalism, doing good and not doing harm, the sanctity of life v the quality of life conflicts, and notions of 'best interests' will be ever-present.

Human rights have once more returned to the forefront, as a result of the entering into force of the Human Rights Act 1998 in England and Wales in October 2000. At this international/European level, at least, the commonality of ethical/moral principles between several countries has begun to grow apace. In this respect, knowledge of what other jurisdictions do when faced with common medico-legal situations will be extremely instructive and, perhaps, even critical, for tribunals, when faced with cases which, quite often, will involve matters of life and death.

SELECTIVE BIBLIOGRAPHY

On medical ethics

Abdel Haleem, MAS, 'Medical ethics in Islam', in Grubb, A (ed), *Choices and Decisions in Health Care*, 1993, Wiley

Bleich, J, 'The obligation to heal in the Judaic tradition: a comparative analysis', in Rosner, F and Bleich, J (eds), *Jewish Bioethics*, 1979, Sanhedrin

Campbell, A, 'Dependency revisited: the limits of autonomy in medical ethics', in Brazier, M and Lobjoit, M (eds), *Protecting the Vulnerable: Autonomy and Consent in Healthcare*, 1991, Routledge

Duncan, A, Dunstan, G and Welbourn, R, *Dictionary of Medical Ethics*, 1981, Darton, Longman and Todd

Dworkin, R, *Life's Dominion*, 1994, HarperCollins

Etziony, M, *The Physician's Creed: An Anthology of Medical Prayers, Oaths and Codes of Ethics Written and Recited by Medical Practitioners Through the Ages*, 1973, Thomas

Fairburn, G, 'Suicide and justified paternalism', in Brazier, M and Lobjoit, M (eds), *Protecting the Vulnerable, Autonomy and Consent in Healthcare*, 1991, Routledge

Gillon, R, 'Autonomy and consent', in Lockwood, M (ed), *Moral Dilemmas in Modern Medicine*, 1985, Wiley, Chapter 5

Gillon, R, *Philosophical Medical Ethics*, 1985, Wiley

Gillon, R, 'Ethics in a college health service', in Dunstan, G and Shinebourne, E (eds), *Doctors' Decisions: Ethical Conflicts in Medical Practice*, 1989, OUP

Gillon, R, 'Teaching medical ethics: impressions from the USA', in Byrne, T (ed), *Medicine, Medical Ethics and the Value of Life*, 1990, Wiley

Glover, J, *Causing Death and Saving Lives*, 1977, Penguin

Harris, J, *The Value of Life*, 1985, Routledge

Johnson, AG, *Pathways in Medical Ethics*, 1990, Edward Arnold

Lee, T, 'Medical ethics in ancient China', in Veatch, R (ed), *Cross-Cultural Perspectives in Medical Ethics*, 1989, Jones and Bartlett

Mason, JK and McCall Smith, R, *Law and Medical Ethics*, 4th edn, 1994, Butterworths. See, also, 5th edn, 1999

Pellegrino, ED and Thomasma, DC, *A Philosophical Study of Medical Practice*, 1981, OUP

Phillips, M and Dawson, J, *Doctors' Dilemmas*, 1985, Harvester

Rispler-Chaim, V, 'Islamic medical ethics in the 20th century' (1989) 15 JME 203

Thomasma, DC, 'Models of the doctor-patient relationship and the ethics committee: Part 1' (1992) 1 Cambridge Quarterly of Healthcare Ethics 11

Veatch, R, *Cross-Cultural Perspectives in Medical Ethics*, 1989, Jones and Bartlett

On law and ethics

de Cruz, SP, 'Parents, doctors and children: the *Gillick* case and beyond' (1987) JSWL 93

Freeman, MDA, 'Introduction: legal and philosophical frameworks for medical decision making', in Freeman, MDA (ed), *Medicine, Ethics and the Law*, 1987, Stevens

Kennedy, I, 'What is a medical decision?', in Kennedy, I (ed), *Treat Me Right*, 1988, OUP

McLean, S, *Old Law, New Medicine*, 1999, Pandora

Montgomery, J, *Healthcare Law*, 1997, OUP

Salako, S, *Life Issues and the Law. Essays in Medical Law and Ethics*, 1998, Pentaxion

Scarman (Lord), 'Consent, communication and responsibility' (1986) 79 Jo of the Royal Society of Medicine 697

Sheldon, S and Thomson, M, 'Health care law and feminism: a developing relationship', in Sheldon, S and Thomson, M (eds), *Feminist Perspectives on Health Care Law*, 1998, Cavendish Publishing

On medicine and medical practice

Beasley, AW, 'The origins of orthopaedics' (1982) 75 J Royal Soc Med 648

Castiglioni, A, *A History of Medicine*, Krunbhaar, EB (trans and ed), 1947, Knopf

Gordon, C, 'Practice guidelines and healthcare telematics: towards an alliance', in Gordon, C and Christensen, JP (eds), *Health Telematics for Clinical Guidelines and Protocols*, 1995, IOS

Goldfield, N *et al*, *Measuring and Managing Health Care Quality: Proceedings, Techniques and Protocols*, 1994, Maryland, Vol 2, section 6:1

Klazinga, N, 'Clinical guidelines bridging evidence based medicine and health services reform: A European perspective', in Deighan, M and Hitch, S (eds), *Clinical Effectiveness from Guidelines to Cost-Effective Practice*, 1995, Earlybrave

Lockwood, M, 'Quality of life and resource allocation', in Bell, JM and Mendus, S (eds), *Philosophy and Medical Welfare*, 1988, CUP

Lockwood, M (ed), *Moral Dilemmas in Modern Medicine*, 1985, OUP

On comparative law generally

de Cruz, P, *Comparative Law in a Changing World*, 2nd edn, 1999, Cavendish Publishing

Harrison, D, *The NHS Structure and Key NHS Reforms since May 1997*, www.nwlhpu-preston.demon.co.uk

Zweigert, K and Kotz, H, *An Introduction to Comparative Law*, 4th edn, 1998, Cavendish Publishing

PART I

HEALTHCARE LAW IN ENGLAND AND WALES

CHAPTER 1

CONSENT TO MEDICAL TREATMENT

INTRODUCTION

In the *Report of the Select Committee of Medical Ethics* (1994), para 40 states:

> Alongside the principle that human life is of special value, the principle is widely held that an individual should have some measure of autonomy to make choices about his or her life. Such autonomy has become important in relation to medical treatment, as the relationship between doctor and patient has changed to one of partnership. As the law stands, medical treatment may be given to competent adult patients only with their informed consent, unless in an emergency.

While there is a circular entitled *A Guide to Consent for Examination or Treatment*, and guidance issued by the BMA to doctors, the notion of consent is by no means straightforward in its scope or application. This chapter concentrates on consent to treatment in English law, examining its history and the general principles, consent and the pregnant patient, and consent issues for the mentally incapacitated adult (the comparative survey is contained in Chapter 10, which deals with the origins of the notion of consent in American law and other non-English jurisdictions).

THE ETHICAL FRAMEWORK

The notion or principle of consent to medical treatment is often stated to be the prerequisite to treatment of adults of sound mind and is generally regarded as a fundamental principle in medical treatment. Consent is necessary, in law, as a defence to an action in battery or negligence and is sometimes described as the 'doctrine' of informed consent, but as we shall see shortly, this notion more accurately describes the *American* rather than English version of consent to medical treatment. Of course, the requirement of consent can have several functions. For instance, Professor Margaret Brazier (1991) has argued that: (a) requiring consent affirms and safeguards the patient's autonomy; (b) consent makes manifest respect for persons; (c) informed participation in healthcare may assist and enhance the quality of that care; (d) requiring consent from patients and research subjects operates as a means of regulating medical practice and research and of preventing abuses. Hence, the need for consent serves several functions: first, to promote individual autonomy; secondly, to encourage rational decision making, both of which derive from the basic principle of the right to self-determination, which has been reaffirmed by the English courts. Lord Donaldson MR stated, in 1989: 'The ability of the ordinary adult to exercise a free choice in deciding whether to accept or refuse medical treatment and to choose between treatments is not to be dismissed as desirable but inessential. It is a crucial factor in relation to all medical treatment' (see *In Re F (Mental Patient: Sterilisation)* [1990] 2 AC 1). This is now contained in the Human Rights Act 1998 (Art 2, the 'right to life', whereby there is a positive obligation to give life-sustaining treatment – because there is no derogation to the principle that 'everyone's right to life shall be protected by law' – and Art 8, which protects the patient's right to personal autonomy or the right to physical and bodily integrity (the 'right to respect for private and family life')). Finally, the rules on consent (for example, consent has to be 'real' to be meaningful) were intended to impose on health professionals 'an obligation to make appropriate disclosure of relevant information to the patient, so that the exercise of autonomy was meaningful' (McLean, S, *Consent and the Law: Review of the Current Provisions in the Human Fertilisation and Embryology Act 1990 for the UK Health Ministers*, 1997, HMSO). Hence, as we see in the following discussion, any touching without consent is *prima facie* against the law, rendering the perpetrator liable to an action for assault. It is clear, however, that the underlying ethical principle is *self-determination*, and this is complemented by the principle of *respect for persons*.

INFORMED CONSENT IN ENGLISH LAW

In order to determine the status of the notion/doctrine/concept of informed consent, one would do well to echo the words of Gerald Robertson, writing in 1981, when he wrote that any writer attempting to examine the status of the 'doctrine' (*sic*) of informed consent in English law 'must do so with a considerable degree of caution' (Robertson (1981), p 112). Although Robertson was writing nearly 20 years ago, a commentator writing in the Journal of Medical Ethics, published in 2000, in the context of medical ethics and biomedical ethics, could still justifiably remark that this notion of consent is 'relatively new' and, in historical terms, 'there is no reference to the concept in Egyptian, Greek or Roman medicine' (Habiba (2000), p 183). Moreover, in a leading textbook on law and medical ethics, the eminent authors observe that consent is 'a doctrine which lies surprisingly uneasily in the medico-legal ambience of the United Kingdom' (Mason and McCall Smith (1999), p 245).

But what does 'informed consent' actually mean in English law? As Professor Michael Jones puts it, '[t]here are many different conceptions of what this involves' (Jones (1999), p 103). We need to be aware that the term has been called a 'misnomer', in so far as it describes a doctor's duties rather than the patient's reaction (which is the view of Tan Keng Feng (1987)), and 'tautologous' (Mason and McCall Smith (1999), p 278), because, they argue, 'to be ethically and legally acceptable, "consent" must always be "informed" and consequently, they argue that the first element of the phrase is redundant (Mason and McCall Smith (1999), p 278). Professors Kennedy and Grubb have argued that the term 'informed consent' is 'not synonymous with valid consent' because it gives only a partial view, and because the requirement that consent be 'informed' is only one of the ingredients of a valid consent (although it is a very important one): see Kennedy and Grubb (1994), p 151).

In a paper published in 1999, Professor Michael Jones lists six weaknesses of the English law of informed consent (Jones (1999), pp 105–08):

(a) He argues there is no English law of informed consent; conceptually, consent in law is a defence to the tort of battery, and battery requires a touching of the patient, a direct application of force. Consequently, any situation where the treatment does not involve a touching, such as self-administered medication provided on prescription, cannot be governed by principles of consent, though the requirement for information disclosure within the context of a negligence claim based on a duty to inform the patient about the risks associated with the medication, still applies.

(b) Where there has been a failure to obtain appropriate consent, the courts are extremely reluctant to contemplate claims based in battery, which is an intentional tort.

(c) The law's guidance, such as it is, is both *ad hoc* and *post hoc*; it can never be a comprehensive framework, unlike the guidance provided by the medical profession itself, which can be more specific and more likely to be acted upon by doctors.

(d) The law is not widely known and probably even less well understood by the medical profession.

(e) Obtaining consent may become too formalistic if viewed purely as a medico-legal requirement, as a means of protecting doctors from litigation, yet the requirement for consent is presented in this way by some judges.

(f) The law of informed consent does not work, at least as a remedy for breach of the 'rules' on information disclosure.

In addition to these points, it bears reiterating that commentators such as Michael Jones have argued that: 'Technically, English law does not have a concept of informed consent except in the very limited form accepted in *Chatterton v Gerson* [1981] QB 432, where the patient only needs to be informed "in broad terms of the nature of the procedure which is intended"' (Jones, 1999). With respect, it depends on what Professor Jones means when he uses the term 'concept'. If he is using the term as a synonym for doctrine, then there can be little argument. But, the term concept can also be used as a *notion* or *idea* and the notion or idea of informed consent, at least with a core of meaning, certainly *does* exist in English law. The fact that it is applied *ad hoc* and *post hoc* does not diminish its basic content or nullify its existence as a concept which, at the very least, is a basic requirement. Surely, the very nature of the term and the inevitability of the variability of the medical context must make it a concept that adapts to the particular set of circumstances. Indeed, English case law illustrates that there are fairly well established sets of rules which govern the English version of informed consent, which we examine below. Hence, one needs to define one's terms and be wary of judicial pronouncements such as those of Dunn LJ when he said, in *Sidaway*, 'The concept of informed consent forms no part of English law' (*Sidaway v Board of Governors of the Bethlem Royal Hospital* [1984] 1 All ER 1018, p 1030); here, he was almost certainly referring to the subjective patient (American-derived) approach – judging what needs to be disclosed by what the individual patient would have needed to know rather than by an objective standard of disclosure. Again, Lord Donaldson's statement in *Re T*, when he said 'English law does not accept the transatlantic concept of informed consent' (see *Re T (Adult) (Refusal of Medical Treatment)* [1992] 4 All ER 649, p 663; [1992] 9 BMLR 46, p 61), has to be read with the caveat that he was probably referring to some form of the American 'doctrine' which conforms to some 'subjective' standard that would vary from patient to patient; yet, the majority of the American jurisdictions appear to adhere to the 'professional standard' of disclosure, which is an objective standard which would look more to the 'reasonable' patient's standards.

As far as English courts were concerned, in the 1997 case of *Re MB* [1997] 2 FLR 426, the English Court of Appeal unequivocally reaffirmed the English principle of autonomy and self-determination, albeit in the context of the Caesarean section cases (discussed below, p 13 *et seq*). This suggests that patients should have the right to decide for themselves, yet the English cases suggest that it is still the *medical profession* which decides how much a patient should be told in order to make a decision as to whether to consent to a particular medical procedure or treatment (following the *Bolam* principle as it has come to be interpreted in the vast majority of cases in England and Wales), and the English judiciary have, up to *Re MB*, and in cases involving children under 16, or those considered lacking legal capacity to decide for themselves, have applied their standard of welfare to authorise medical treatment even in the face of refusal of such treatment (see discussion on p 13 in this chapter and Chapter 4). On a comparative note, in jurisdictions such as the USA, Australia and Canada, there is a concept of informed consent which looks to what the reasonable patient, in the plaintiff's position, would consider significant enough to warrant disclosure in order to make a sufficiently informed decision on treatment (the 'prudent patient' approach). This, therefore, focuses on the needs of the patient, rather than on what the doctor considers the patient needs to know.

Legal consequences of proceeding without consent

Prima facie, any touching of another without consent amounts to a civil assault/battery or trespass to the person. The patient may, therefore, sue for damages for the battery which is committed if non-consensual treatment is carried out. However, a claim may also lie under the tort of negligence. An action for battery arises when the plaintiff has been physically touched by the defendant without the defendant's consent, express or implied, to such touching. In an action for battery, there is no need to establish loss as a result of the touching, so long as the plaintiff can establish that the defendant wrongfully touched him. Hence, where there is no consent whatever to the physical contact, a civil action for battery would be appropriate.

However, if the patient has given consent to treatment, and an unexpected injury is sustained, the question of how much information should have been disclosed arises and the legal position is that provided the patient has been informed in broad terms of the risks of the treatment, then any action for injury suffered by the plaintiff based on failure to disclose risks of treatment will lie in negligence. This was the effect of *Chatterton v Gerson* [1981] 1 All ER 257, a case dealing with battery.

Therefore, an action in negligence would have to establish that the defendant wrongfully touched him and that the negligence of the defendant in treating him resulted in the injury for which damages are sought. There might often have been consent to a specific procedure, but not to the particular procedure which caused the injury. The treatment must be related to the consent to specific treatment and must not exceed what is necessary for the patient's survival. The illustrative English case is *Devi v West Midlands RHA* (1981), CA transcript 491, where the surgeon, believing it was in the patient's best interests, removed her uterus when all the patient had consented to was the repair of a perforation in her uterus. The court found the case for a battery proved. The parallel non-English example is usually provided by the Canadian case of *Marshall v Curry* (1933) 3 DLR 260, where the plaintiff's testicle was removed by a surgeon in the course of performing a hernia operation. The doctor's case, which the court accepted, was that the removal was essential to a successful operation, because the testis was diseased, and non-removal would have endangered the patient's life. The court also accepted that the removal of the testicle was necessary and could not have been deferred to a later date.

CONSENT TO MEDICAL TREATMENT UNDER ENGLISH COMMON LAW

Historical background – American roots

It is often assumed that it is a well established principle in English law that consent (in the sense of assent or agreement) needs to be obtained before an adult, mentally competent patient can be lawfully treated by a doctor or health professional. Indeed, it is a commonplace that textbooks on medical law, family law and tort law often begin expositions of the law relating to consent with a reference or quotation from the 1914 American case decided by Cardozo J wherein he said: 'Every human being of adult years and sound mind has a right to determine what shall be done with his own body ...' (see *Schloendorff v Society of New York Hospital*, 105 NE 92 9 (NY, 1914)). This case is often seen as heralding the development of the doctrine of 'informed consent' in the USA, although the seeds of the doctrine properly so called were sown in the USA from around 1957 in *Salgo v Leland Stanford Jr University Board of Trustees*, 154 Cal App 2d 560, 317 P 2d 170 (1957) (for a full discussion of the American developments, see Chapter 10 of this book). But, as far as the English rules on judicial precedent are concerned, *Schloendorff* is an American case and is, therefore, not binding on English courts and remains only of 'persuasive' authority, although it is still cited frequently in many textbooks on English medical law. So, how has the notion or version of 'informed consent' to medical treatment become part of English law?

The notion of informed consent may be traced as far back as the 18th century, to *Slater v Baker and Stapleton* (1967) 2 Wils KB 358; 95 ER 860, but it may be somewhat sweeping to say that a full blown 'doctrine' was in place by then.

Historically, however, English courts have tended to approve statements of principle of this nature made by judges in other common law jurisdictions such as the USA (in *Schloendorff v Society of New York Hospital* 105 NE 92 9 (NY, 1914)) and Australia (see *Rogers v Whittaker* [1993] 4 Med LR 79). The central point is that a doctrine (in the sense of a well developed theory), of consent, or informed consent, is well established in American jurisprudence, but was implicitly borrowed by English courts and only started to develop in England and Wales in the 1980s (see Robertson, G, 'Informed consent to medical treatment' (1981) 97 LQR 102). Before the 1980s, the term 'informed consent' appears to have been used in only one reported case in England in 1976, *Re D (A Minor)* [1976] Fam 185; 1 All ER 326. Yet, the principle that a doctor must obtain consent from his adult patient of sound mind, before undertaking treatment involving physical contact with the patient, is seen as a logical extension of the law of trespass to the person, wherein it was said: 'the least touching of another in anger is a battery' (*Cole v Turner* (1704) 6 Mod 149, giving rise to an action for damages for trespass to the person). Similarly, other cases have indicated the application of this principle (see *Cull v Royal Surrey Hospital and Butler* [1943] 1 BMJ 1195 and *Hamilton v Birmingham RHB* [1969] 2 BMJ 456).

In recent cases, English appeal judges have begun to be more explicit in their statements about general rules relating to consent to treatment, as in the case of *Re F (Sterilisation: Mental Patient)* [1989] 2 FLR 276, p 284E and *Re T (An Adult) (Consent to Medical Treatment)* [1992] 2 FLR 458, where Lord Donaldson MR declared: 'An adult patient who ... suffers from no mental incapacity has an absolute right to choose whether to consent to medical treatment, to refuse it or to choose one rather than another of the treatments being offered.'

The 'rules' of consent to treatment

Must consent be 'real'?

English law has also established that, in order for the consent to be valid it must be: free from fraud, misrepresentation, duress or coercion; and 'real', meaning the patient must know what he or she is consenting to.

The level of information required

The question then arises: how much should the patient be told in order to give a valid consent? In other words, how informed should the consent be? The doctor's duty under English law appears to be merely to explain 'in broad terms the nature of the procedure which is intended' (*Chatterton v Gerson* [1981] QB 432). This means only that the 'nature and purpose' of the proposed treatment must be understood by the patient since, in the leading English case, it was said that 'once the patient is informed in broad terms of the nature of the procedure which is intended, and gives her consent, that consent is real': see *Chatterton v Gerson* [1981] QB 432, p 442B–C. So long as this is done, no battery will be committed (see, also, *Freeman v Home Office (No 2)* [1984] QB 524, p 556). As one commentator rightly says, 'the terms "real" and "nature" are at least as vague as the term "informed"' (Skegg (1999), p 142).

Sufficient information must be provided to a patient about an antenatal test for consent to be valid

In a recent decision dealing with an antenatal test, the Court of Appeal had to decide on the sufficiency of the information provided.

The Carver *case (2000)*

In the case of *Carver v Hammersmith and Queen Charlotte's Special Health Authority*, decided on 25 February 2000 (see (2000) 7 Med Law Monitor 6), a High Court judge decided that insufficient information had been provided to a patient about an antenatal test.

The case involved a claim for damages for the wrongful birth of the claimant's Down's syndrome child in 1989. The claimant had worked with handicapped children and was determined not to have a handicapped child herself, so when she became pregnant, requested an amniocentesis at the defendant's hospital, but was refused this test under the hospital's policy. However, she agreed to undergo the 'Bart's test', developed at St Bartholomew's Hospital. She believed that this test, like amniocentesis, would determine whether or not her fetus had Down's syndrome or spina bifida, but this belief was mistaken. In fact, the baby was born with Down's syndrome even though the test did not reveal this, and the claimant argued that, if she had known this, she would have terminated the pregnancy. The fact that she did not do so was the result of the defendant's negligence through the failure of its senior house officer to inform her that the 'Bart's test' was not, like amniocentesis, a diagnostic test, but only a screening test, and that it would fail to detect one in three Down's syndrome fetuses.

Nelson J considered that the issues on liability turned on what advice had been given to the claimant by the defendant's doctor, and whether, if she had received correct advice, the claimant would have insisted on having an amniocentesis. Finally, if an amniocentesis showed that the baby she was carrying had Down's syndrome, whether she would have terminated her pregnancy.

It was held that the entitlement of the claimant to damages in respect of costs of bringing up a seriously disabled child went to quantum, and not liability – *Emeh v Kensington and Chelsea Health Authority* [1985] QB 1012 applied.

On the issue of liability, the judge was satisfied that the claimant and her partner had made a clear decision not to have a handicapped child and to do all that was necessary in order to ensure that that did not happen. He found that she was determined to have an amniocentesis when she went to the defendant's hospital for her antenatal clinic appointment, and was so determined that, if she were not offered one there, she intended to have the test privately.

Nelson J concluded that the claimant was fully aware of the risks of undergoing an amniocentesis, but such was her determination not to have a handicapped child that she was prepared to take the risk of losing a healthy baby, and if she discovered that she was carrying a handicapped child, to have the pregnancy terminated. The learned judge concluded that the defendant's doctor did not tell the claimant that the 'Bart's test' did not detect one in three Down's syndrome babies, and that the explanation given by him of the test generally was not provided in such terms as could reasonably have made clear to her the fact that the test was not diagnostic. Consequently, the claimant left the consultation with the clear, albeit mistaken view that the 'Bart's test' would determine whether or not she had a handicapped child.

On the issue of causation, the learned judge found that, if the claimant had been told that the test was not diagnostic, or had been told that it did not detect one in three Down's syndrome babies, she would not have used the 'Bart's test', but would again have requested the amniocentesis. If that had not been available on the NHS, she would have undergone the test privately. Had she then discovered that the baby had Down's syndrome, she would then have terminated the pregnancy.

The judge concluded that the defendant doctor's failure to advise the claimant correctly constituted a breach of duty.

Level of understanding and legal capacity

It is also the general rule that, as far as any possible liability for battery is concerned, the patient need only be told the nature of the treatment 'in broad terms'. This comes from the leading case of *Chatterton v Gerson* [1981] QB 432. However, the more recent case of *Re C* suggests that the question of whether the patient has the capacity to give consent is more demanding (see *Re C (Adult: Refusal of Medical Treatment)* [1994] 1 WLR 290; [1994] 1 All ER 819; (1993) 143 NLJ 1642).

Re C *(1993): the schizophrenic/amputated leg case*

This case involved a paranoid schizophrenic male, C, who was aged 68 and had spent many years at Broadmoor prison, where he was when he suffered an injury to his foot. He appeared to develop gangrene in his foot and amputation was suggested, which he refused. He said he would rather die with two legs than live with one. On removal of the patient to a general hospital, the consultant said the patient's chance of survival if the limb was not amputated below the knee was around 15%. An application for an injunction restraining the hospital from carrying out the operation without his express consent was lodged with the court on C's behalf.

Thorpe J held that C was entitled to refuse the treatment, even if this meant he would die. He cited with approval Lord Donaldson's *dictum* in *Re T* [1992] 2 FLR 458, which declared that, *prima facie*, every adult has the right and capacity to accept or refuse medical treatment. This might be rebutted by evidence of incapacity, but the onus must be discharged by those seeking to override the patient's choice. When capacity is challenged, its sufficiency must be determined by asking whether the capacity of the patient has been so reduced by his chronic mental illness that he did not sufficiently understand the nature, purpose and effects of the proposed medical treatment. This depends on whether the patient has been able to comprehend and retain the information, has believed it and been able to weigh it in the balance with other considerations when making his choice.

Comment

Although C was a prisoner (and therefore a detained patient) and a schizophrenic in a special hospital, the court did not mention s 63 of the Mental Health Act 1983 (MHA), presumably because, although that provision allows the imposition of treatment on patients *without* requiring their consent, the intention is to impose 'medical treatment' (widely defined under s 145 of the MHA as *including* nursing and care, habilitation and rehabilitation) for a *mental* disorder. The court later said that C's gangrene was entirely unconnected with the mental disorder that he was already suffering from. Hence, any treatment they might wish to carry out on the patient's foot would not be treatment for his *mental* condition. As Kennedy and Grubb put it, 's 63 provides a defence to a battery' in these sorts of situations (see Kennedy and Grubb (2000), p 890), but the treatment nevertheless still has to be in the patient's best interests.

Re C affirms the adult patient's right to self-determination or respect for patient autonomy, but there are several aspects of the so called three-part test (which was derived from a psychiatrist who gave evidence) which are still vague and open to different and, therefore, inconsistent and uncertain interpretations. It appears to be up to the medical staff to decide whether the patient has understood the treatment information; a patient who did not comprehend sufficiently the information that the medical staff gave him could not exercise his right of free choice in the matter. As a postscript, it should be noted that the patient here did not, in fact, die from the gangrene, and the alternative conservative treatment he was given proved successful.

Consent must be 'real' or genuine

Another rule of consent in English law is that, in order for the consent to be valid, it must be 'real', meaning that the patient must know what it is he or she is consenting to. This means that the 'nature and purpose' of the proposed treatment must be understood by the patient. In *R v Tabassum* (2000) *The Times*, 26 May, the Court of Appeal, citing the leading case of *R v Clarence* (1888) 22 QBD 23, again emphasised that, if patients consented to being touched for purposes of medical examination, their consent was only legally valid (and therefore genuine or 'real') if they assumed the touching was for medical purposes only. Here, the women only consented to the touching through deceit to the nature, but not the quality of the act. In the absence of genuine consent, the defendant would be guilty of indecent assault.

Consent and the pregnant patient

A cluster of recent cases, culminating in a Court of Appeal ruling in *Re MB* [1997] 2 FLR 426; (1997) 8 Med LR 217, has highlighted the apparent ethical dilemma between a mother's rights and fetal rights. The appellate court reviewed the case law and gives clear guidance on whether there are circumstances where it is lawful for doctors to perform a Caesarean section even though the patient concerned has refused to consent to the operation. Subsequent to that case, the Court of Appeal decided the *Collins* case (*St George's Healthcare NHS Trust v S, R v Collins and Others ex p S* [1998] 2 FLR 728; (1998) *The Times*, 8 May).

It is only in recent cases that English appeal judges have begun to be more explicit in their statements about any general rule relating to consent to treatment, as in the case of *Re F (Sterilisation: Mental Patient)* [1989] 2 FLR 276, p 284E and *Re T (An Adult) (Consent to Medical Treatment)* [1992] 2 FLR 458, when Lord Donaldson MR declared that 'An adult patient who ... suffers from no mental incapacity has an absolute right to choose whether to consent to medical treatment, to refuse it or to choose one rather than another of the treatments being offered.' Yet his Lordship then added, *obiter*: 'The only possible qualification is a case in which the choice may lead to the death of a viable fetus.' Serious doubts have now been cast on the correctness of this statement in *Re MB*. It is, therefore, apparent that the English law on consent to medical treatment of mentally capable adults is by no means as easily applicable as might have been assumed.

In the context of Caesarean sections, obstetricians have tended to argue that the life of the unborn child is paramount and other commentators have reiterated that it is up to a pregnant woman to decide on the kind of medical treatment she should receive. Despite the pungent academic criticism stirred up by the earlier case of *Re S (Adult: Refusal of Medical Treatment)* [1992] 4 All ER 671, a High Court judge in the Family Division granted two separate orders permitting NHS Trusts to perform Caesarean sections despite the absence of consent from the patients involved, in *Norfolk and Norwich v W* [1997] 1 FCR 269 and *Rochdale v Choudhary* [1997] 1 FCR 274. In *Re L (An Adult: Non-consensual Treatment)* [1997] 1 FLR 609, a Family Division judge also ruled that a Caesarean section could be performed lawfully despite the patient's objection if that patient lacked the competence to make a rational decision.

What have *Re MB* and the *Collins* case decided in the light of previous key cases? Let us first examine the earlier cases on Caesarean sections and then consider the guidelines enunciated in both these highly significant appellate cases and evaluate the legal position relating to consent to Caesarean sections in the context of autonomy and judicial paternalism.

The earlier Caesarean section cases

Re S (Adult: Refusal of Medical Treatment) *[1992] 4 All ER 671*

In this Family Division case, the 30 year old patient (a 'born-again Christian') was in labour with her third pregnancy, having been admitted to hospital with ruptured membranes and six days overdue beyond the expected date of birth of her unborn child. The medical staff recommended a Caesarean section operation, which they regarded as vital as her medical condition was regarded as 'desperately serious', as was the situation of her unborn child, who was in a 'transverse lie' position with the elbow projecting through the cervix and the head on the right side. The health authority asked Sir Stephen Brown P for a declaration to authorise the doctors to perform a Caesarean section (which they argued was warranted in the vital interests of the patient and the unborn child) when S refused consent to the operation on religious grounds, a decision which was supported by her husband.

The application was received at 1.30 pm, the hearing commenced shortly before 2 pm and the learned President made the declaration which was sought at 2.18 pm. The desperate nature of the application was emphasised and the Court of Appeal case of *Re T* was cited as 'having left the matter open' on the issue of authorising an operation despite the patient's refusal, and the court took comfort in the fact that there was no English authority directly in point. In addition, the American case of *Re AC* (1990) 573 A 2d 1235, p 1240, which, while not binding, was cited as a case which suggested that an American court would also be likely to grant a declaration in these circumstances. American authorities are, of course, persuasive in the absence of clear English authorities; in any event, this was clearly dealt with as an emergency situation.

Comment

Somewhat ironically, the American case of *Re AC*, which was cited to the court to support authorisation despite the patient's refusal of consent, had been reheard *en banc* and the Court of Appeals had, in fact, *reversed* its previous order on the grounds that there had not been a proper finding of fact whether the patient was competent, or, if she was not, how 'substituted judgment' was to be applied. But the court did hold that the decision of a competent patient or substituted judgment should prevail, even if surgery was refused, in virtually all cases unless there were 'truly extraordinary or compelling reasons to override them' by taking account, for example, of the State's interest in protecting life. Consequently, the case did not provide a clear cut authority to support authorisation of treatment in the face of refusal of consent.

The Tameside *case*

The 41 year old patient in this case (*Tameside and Glossop Acute Services Trust v CH* [1996] 1 FCR 753) was a paranoid schizophrenic who was detained in a psychiatric ward of a hospital under s 3 of the MHA 1983. The patient had a psychotic and deluded belief that her own doctors were malicious and that they intended to harm the child. The patient was in the 38th week of pregnancy and the medical staff were concerned that the fetus was not growing properly because it was not being provided with nourishment by the placenta. Obstetric intervention was considered necessary to prevent stillbirth. She had a history of refusing to co-operate with antenatal care in the early stages of her pregnancy and there was a fear that she might continue to do so, despite the fact she had, in fact, consented to an induced birth. On the basis of the patient's refusal of consent to a Caesarean, the Trust therefore applied to the court for a declaration that it would be lawful to treat the patient in whatever way that might be necessary in order to save the fetus, including a Caesarean section without her consent if this was considered necessary. The court, therefore, required a way to override the woman's refusal of consent and Wall J therefore made an order under s 63 of the MHA 1983, which does not require the patient's consent in certain cases and, in effect, justified delivery by Caesarean as constituting 'medical treatment' of her mental disorder.

Section 63 of the MHA 1983 reads:

> Treatment not requiring consent
>
> 63 The consent of a patient shall not be required for any medical treatment given to him for the mental disorder from which he is suffering, not being treatment falling within s 57 or 58 above, if the treatment is given by or under the direction of the responsible medical officer.

In view of the woman's mental condition, however, the court, in any event, found the patient lacked the capacity to consent to or refuse medical treatment concerning the management of her pregnancy.

The learned judge nevertheless stated that it was an assault to perform invasive treatment without the patient's consent and that a mentally competent patient has an absolute right to refuse treatment for any reason, rational or irrational, or for no reason at all, even where that decision will lead to her own death. However, where the patient is incompetent, treatment should be given in accordance with the principles enunciated in *Re F* [1989] 2 FLR 276, namely, that it is lawful to provide treatment which is in the patient's best interests, such as that which is necessary to save the life or preserve or prevent deterioration of the physical and mental health of a patient.

He followed the test of mental competence to make decisions as laid down in *Re C (Adult: Refusal of Medical Treatment)* [1994] 1 WLR 290, namely, the ability to:

(a) comprehend and retain treatment information;

(b) believe such information;

(c) weigh such information in the balance to make a choice.

This was the test put forward by a psychiatrist's analysis of the decision making process and is also similar to the criteria recommended by the English Law Commission (1995) in their *Report on Mental Incapacity*. On the facts, the patient in this case failed the *Re C* criteria, yet mental competence is not required under s 63. Utilisation of s 63, therefore, appears to have been made *ex abundanti cautela*, so that even if some other court might consider the woman to be competent to make a decision, imposition of s 63 did not, in any case, require consent, so no liability in battery could exist for the doctor.

The Rochdale *Case [1997] 1 FCR 274*

This application concerned Mrs C. She objected to Caesarean section because she had had a previous pregnancy terminated by Caesarean section. At approximately 4.30 pm, the consultant obstetrician treating Mrs C contacted a solicitor because, in his opinion, the patient's uterus was rupturing and unless he was able to deliver the baby by Caesarean within an hour, both child and mother would die. Johnson J was already hearing another emergency Caesarean case (the *Norfolk* case, below) but he regarded the present facts as sufficiently urgent for him to consider this case immediately. In a two minute hearing, the judge heard that the patient's objection to Caesarean section was that she had previously been delivered in this way and had suffered backache and pain around the resulting scar. She told the consultant that she would rather die than have another Caesarean section. The consultant asked the patient what would happen to her first born child after she was dead and the patient replied that her own mother would look after her. The Trust's solicitor sought an urgent psychiatric opinion as to the patient's competence because there were only 15 minutes or so remaining for the operation to be carried out successfully. The only information the judge had as to her competence came from her consultant obstetrician. Her view was that the patient's mental capacity was not in question and that she seemed to him to be fully competent.

Given the extremely short time available for consideration, Johnson J applied the test of legal competence laid down by Wall J in *Tameside* (see above, p 15) and found that, although Mrs C was not suffering from a mental disorder, she lacked the mental competence to make a decision because she was incapable of weighing up the considerations that were involved and could not weigh up even considerations of the most trivial kind. Thus, he found her incapable of comprehending, retaining and weighing up the information she had been given, particularly because she was 'in the throes of labour with all that is involved in terms of pain and emotional stress'.

The declaration sought was, therefore, granted by Johnson J.

The Norfolk *case [1997] 1 FCR 269*

The patient, Miss W, aged 32, arrived at the Accident and Emergency department of the hospital at 9 am, in the last stage of the pregnancy, apparently without having had any antenatal treatment. She was fully dilated and physically ready to deliver her baby. However, she denied she was even pregnant. She had a history of psychiatric treatment and had had three previous pregnancies, all terminated by Caesarean section. The consultant obstetrician sought authority to terminate the patient's labour by forceps delivery and, if necessary, by Caesarean section. Otherwise, there were two risks to the patient: (a) if the fetus was not delivered, it would suffocate within the patient; (b) the patient's old Caesarean scars would reopen, with a consequent risk to the life of the fetus and the health of the patient. A consultant psychiatrist interviewed the patient and formed the view that she was not suffering from a mental disorder within the meaning of the MHA 1983, but was unable to say whether she was capable of comprehending and retaining information about the proposed treatment, nor whether she was capable of believing information given to her about the treatment. However, he took the view that she was not able to balance the information given to her.

In the *Tameside* case (above, p 15), Wall J had specifically left open the question whether the court had the power at common law to authorise the use of reasonable force as a necessary incidence of treatment or whether the power was limited to cases which fell within s 63 of the MHA 1983. That section reads:

> ... the consent of a patient shall not be required for any medical treatment to him for the mental disorder from which he is suffering ... if the treatment is given by or under the direction of the responsible medical officer.

Johnson J held that, in these circumstances, the court *had* the power at common law to authorise the use of reasonable force. He applied Lord Goff's principle in *Re F* [1989] 2 FLR 276, p 284E, namely, that there must be a necessity to act and 'the action taken must be such as a reasonable person would in all the circumstances take, acting in the best interest of the assisted person'.

Accordingly, he ruled that, although the patient was not suffering from a mental disorder, she lacked the mental competence to make a decision about the treatment that was proposed because she was incapable of weighing up the considerations that were involved. Termination of labour would be in the best interests of the patient. It would end the stress and the pain of her labour, avoid the likelihood of damage to her physical health which might have potentially life-threatening consequences, and it would avoid her having any feeling of guilt were she, by her refusal of consent, to cause the death of the fetus. The situation was one where 'there was a necessity to act'.

Johnson J stressed that the patient was called upon to make a decision about whether to have a Caesarean 'at a time of acute emotional stress and physical pain in the ordinary course of labour' which was made even more difficult because of 'her particular mental history'. He also emphasised that his main attention was focused on the patient's interests, not the interests of the fetus, yet he also declared that 'the reality was that the fetus was a fully formed child, capable of normal life if it could only be delivered from the mother'.

Recent cases

Re MB *[1997] 2 FLR 426 (the* Needle phobia *case)*

In this Court of Appeal case, Miss MB, aged 23, first attended an antenatal clinic when she was 33 weeks pregnant. Then and later, she refused to allow blood samples to be taken because of her fear of needles. When she was 40 weeks pregnant, it was discovered that the fetus was in the partial breech position. The risk to the unborn child was assessed at 50%, although there was little physical danger to the mother. However, it was explained to the patient that vaginal delivery would pose a serious risk of death or brain damage to the baby. It was recommended that delivery should be by Caesarean section. Miss MB agreed to have a Caesarean section and was admitted to hospital, where she and her partner agreed to the operation and signed a consent form. However, when successive attempts were made to carry out the operation, she panicked at the last moment because of her needle phobia and withdrew her consent. Finally, when the patient was in labour and not responding to the midwife or the consultant and had again consented to and then refused to agree to the anaesthesia, the health authority eventually obtained a declaration from the High Court that it would be lawful for the consultant gynaecologist to operate on her, using reasonable force if necessary. The declaration was granted at 9.55 pm and, 65 minutes later, the Court of Appeal heard the appeal. It dismissed the patient's appeal from that order in the early hours of the next morning, reserving its reasons. On the following morning the patient co-operated in the operation and was delivered of a healthy baby boy.

The Court of Appeal judgment

The Court of Appeal (Butler-Sloss, Saville and Ward LJJ) reviewed the law on this difficult question and provided guidance for future cases involving refusal of surgery and guidance concerning Caesarean section cases. Butler-Sloss LJ gave the judgment, with which the other appeal judges concurred.

General principles

(a) In general, it was a criminal and tortious assault to perform physically invasive medical treatment, however minimal the invasion might be, without the patient's consent;

(b) a mentally competent patient had an absolute right to refuse to consent to medical treatment, even where that decision may lead to his or her own death;

(c) the only situation in which it was lawful for the doctors to intervene was if it was believed that the adult patient lacked the capacity to decide, the treatment was a necessity and did no more than was required in best interests of the patient;

(d) the court did not have the jurisdiction to take into account the interests of the unborn child at risk from the refusal of a competent mother to consent to medical intervention;

(e) in an emergency situation, treatment could be given even if no consent had been obtained, so long as the treatment was essential and achieved the minimum that was required in the patient's interests.

On the facts of the case, the court found:

(a) Miss MB did consent to the Caesarean section;

(b) she accepted the incision of the surgeon's scalpel, but not the anaesthetist's needle; and

(c) she could not bring herself to accept the Caesarean section because her fear of needles dominated her thinking to the extent that she could think of nothing else.

Consent to Caesarean section

On Caesarean sections, her Ladyship noted that all the recent decisions dealt with urgent or extreme situations, the evidence was limited in scope and the mother had not always been represented in the proceedings. Indeed, in all but one of the recent cases, it had been held that the woman concerned did not have the mental capacity to make the decision. In the present case, the evidence of the obstetrician and the consultant psychiatrist was that the patient could not bring herself to undergo the Caesarean section she desired because a panic fear of needles dominated everything and, at the critical point, she was not capable of making a decision at all. On that basis, it was clear that she was, at the time, suffering from an impairment of her mental functioning which disabled her, and was temporarily incompetent. The tests in *Re C* (above, p 11) were applied. Furthermore, since the mother and father wanted the child to be born alive and the mother was in favour of the operation, subject only to her needle phobia, and was likely to suffer long term danger if the child was born handicapped or dead, medical intervention in this case *was* in the patient's best interests, with the use of force if necessary for it to be carried out. In these circumstances, the judge had been justified in granting the declaration sought.

The court opined that an 'irrational' decision was one which was 'so outrageous that no sensible person could have arrived at it', but panic, indecisiveness and irrationality did not necessarily amount to incompetence. However, these factors might be evidence of incompetence and the gravity of the consequences of the decision was commensurate with the level of competence required to make the decision. A person would lack the capacity to make a decision if rendered unable to do so by some impairment or disturbance of mental functioning. Capacity might be eroded by shock, fatigue, confusion, pain or the effect of drugs, but only if the ability to decide is absent as a result.

The court added that panic induced by fear could influence a woman's decision. However, the evidence needed to be scrutinised with great care in every case because, in some circumstances, the fear of surgery can be rational, but in others, fear could paralyse the will entirely, thus destroying capacity. That was the position in the present case, and the woman was found to be incapable of making a decision at all.

On the earlier cases, the Appeal Court observed that, although some of them had been decided on the issue of lack of consent to Caesarean section, the mothers involved were subsequently very glad that the operation had been performed successfully. However, the court also emphasised that, however desirable a successful outcome might be, and however important it was for a child to be born alive, this consideration was *not strictly relevant*. Hence, while doctors could lawfully attempt to persuade a woman to undergo medical treatment, if that attempt proved unsuccessful there would be no further steps which could be taken, even though the mother might regret her decision if her child died or was born handicapped.

Accordingly, the only situation in which medical intervention against a woman's wishes was justified was where an adult patient lacked the capacity to make the decision. The court rejected the submission that it should weigh in the balance the rights of the unborn child. Although the *dictum* of Lord Donaldson in *Re T (An Adult) (Consent to Medical Intervention)* [1993] 2 FLR 458 supported that submission, there were many other decisions denying any rights to the fetus 'which were more persuasive'. These were cases applicable by analogy, for instance, *C v S* [1988] QB 135 and *Re F (In Utero)* [1988] Fam

122. In effect, the fetus: 'up to the moment of birth did not have any separate interests capable of being taken into account when a court had to consider an application for a declaration in respect of a Caesarean section operation. The court did not have the jurisdiction to declare that such medical intervention was lawful to protect the interests of the unborn child even at the point of death.'

Comment on *Re MB*

Several important points may be gleaned from *Re MB*:

(a) consent remains a necessary prerequisite to medical treatment for adult patients of legally sound mind; consent was, of course, eventually obtained from the patient in *Re MB*;

(b) the interests of the unborn fetus would not normally take precedence over those of its mother unless she was incapable of making a reasoned choice regarding her medical treatment by reason of an impairment of mental functioning caused by a variety of factors of which the court gave examples;

(c) the unborn fetus does not have a legal status until it is born. Otherwise, an interested party could seek to obtain court orders to curtail the lifestyle of the mother or even prevent her from having a legal abortion on the basis of protecting the rights of the unborn fetus;

(d) the court approved the *Re C* ([1994] 1 FLR 31) test (comprehension and retention of the information, believing such information and being able to weigh it in the balance to make a reasoned choice), but the difficulty remains of ascertaining the circumstances in which the patient would pass this test. For instance, Johnson J in the *Norfolk* case (above, p 17) cited the case of the woman 'in the throes of labour' with all that that implied in terms of trauma and emotional stress. Is this now a new 'exception' to the general principle and does it indicate that such a woman (perhaps this would include most women in labour!) is, *ipso facto*, incapable of making a rational choice when in the thrall of such a situation?

(e) The procedure for such cases was clearly elucidated, the main guidelines being: (1) the court is unlikely to entertain an application unless the capacity of the person to give or refuse consent is in issue; (2) for the time being, doctors ought to seek a ruling from the High Court on the issue of competence; (3) those in charge should identify a potential problem as early as possible so the patient and the hospital can obtain medical advice and in non-emergency cases, for the case to be brought before the court before it becomes an emergency and wherever possible, for the court to hear oral evidence, if appropriate; (4) the hearing should be *inter partes*; (5) the mother should be represented in all cases, unless, exceptionally, she does not wish to be. If unconscious, she should have a guardian *ad litem*.

In practice, not all the procedural steps, such as bringing the case to the attention of the court at an early stage, will be possible or indeed practicable in some cases and there remain the problems associated with conflicting evidence or statements as to the patient's religious beliefs or true wishes.

The Collins *case* (St George's Healthcare NHS Trust v S, R v Collins ex p S *[1998] 2 FLR 528)*

Facts

On 25 April 1996, S, a single 29 year old woman, sought to register as a new patient at a local NHS practice in London. This was the first time she had consulted a GP; she was approximately 36 weeks pregnant but had not sought antenatal care. An examination of S revealed that she had severe pre-eclampsia, severe oedema extending to her abdomen and proteinnuria. She was told that her condition risked the life of both herself and her unborn fetus. She was also advised that she therefore needed urgent attention, and the only treatment was medication, bedrest and admission to hospital for an induced delivery. Treatment and medication would aim to reduce high blood pressure, but if the fetus is viable, an early delivery is usually indicated, either by induced labour or by Caesarean section. Without this treatment, her health and life and the health and life of her baby were in real danger. The GP was of the opinion that she was depressed and this was also the opinion of two other doctors who later examined her. She had recently separated from the father of the child and said that she did not want the child and would give it to the father once it had been born. She fully understood the potential risks, but rejected the advice. She wanted her baby to be born naturally, that is, by natural vaginal delivery and refused to be admitted to hospital. An approved social worker, Louize Collins, and two doctors, Dr Chill and Dr Jeffreys, saw her. S had also been examined by the duty psychiatrist. They repeated the advice, but she adamantly refused to accept it. An application was therefore made under s 2 of the MHA 1983 by Louize Collins for her admission to Springfield Hospital 'for assessment'. The two doctors signed the necessary written recommendations. That evening, 25 April, Ms S was admitted to Springfield Hospital against her will, on the same day that she had turned up at the surgery.

Section 2 of the MHA 1983 states:

> An application for admission for assessment may be made in respect of a patient on the grounds that (a) she is suffering from mental disorder of a nature or degree which warrants the detention of the patient in hospital for assessment (or for assessment followed by medical treatment) for at least a limited period; and (b) he ought to be so detained in the interests of his own health or safety or with a view to the protection of other persons.

As the court commented later, the phrase 'other persons', which was on the form completed by the doctors, could only have referred to the fetus carried by S.

Later that evening, shortly before midnight, again against her will, she was transferred to St George's Hospital. She continued to refuse consent to treatment, so an application was made *ex parte* to Hogg J on behalf of the hospital. She was told, incorrectly, that labour had commenced, that S had been in labour for 24 hours, and that her life and the life of the fetus were in danger, that 'every minute counted and this was a matter of life and death'. It remains unclear how this information was presented in this manner since S was not in labour at the time and, in fact, had recorded her objections in an articulate letter which she wrote while at Springfield Hospital. Hogg J granted a declaration which, in summary terms, dispensed with S's consent to treatment. Later that evening, medical procedures were carried out and at 10 pm, S was safely delivered by Caesarean section of a baby girl. When she recovered, S developed strong feelings of revulsion towards the baby and, at first, rejected the child. Fortunately, she has since bonded with the child and is reportedly now looking after her quite happily.

On 2 May, S's compulsory detention under the MHA was terminated. During the period when she was a patient, no specific treatment for mental disorder or mental illness was prescribed.

Ms S, a 30 year old veterinary nurse, appealed against an *ex parte* decision of Hogg J sitting in Chambers on 26 April 1997, in which it had been decided that the consent of Ms S to a Caesarean section could be dispensed with. The Court of Appeal was also asked to consider granting relief by way of judicial review against a social worker, Louize Collins, Pathfinder Mental Health Services Trust, and St George's Healthcare NHS Trust as Ms S had been admitted to and detained in hospital for assessment under s 2 of the MHA 1983. Judicial review was being asked, therefore, of the application to Hogg J itself, the medical procedures which culminated in the birth, and her return to and treatment at Springfield Hospital.

The Court of Appeal judgment

Judge LJ gave the judgment of the Court of Appeal. The court concluded that virtually every stage in the medical and legal procedures could be criticised. The view of the court was that, even when a person's life depended upon receiving particular medical treatment, as long as that person is an adult of sound mind, he or she has the right to refuse such treatment. This view reflected the ethical principles of the autonomy of the individual and the right to self-determination, and was supported by case law. In their Lordships' opinion, although pregnancy increased the responsibilities which a woman had, it did not diminish her right to refuse medical treatment, as long as she was of sound mind. Nevertheless, the Court of Appeal thought it appropriate to consider the position of the fetus, and Judge LJ stated that, although an unborn child was human and was protected by law in some instances, it was not a separate person from its mother, and its need for medical treatment or assistance did not prevail over the rights of the mother. She could not, therefore, be forced to submit to treatment against her will, even if her life and that of the fetus depended upon her receiving such treatment, and even if her decision might appear to be morally repugnant.

The mother's compulsory detention

On the question of S's compulsory detention under the MHA 1983, the court took the view that the Act could not be deployed in order to detain a person, even if her thinking appeared bizarre and irrational, and contrary to that of the vast majority of people in the community. Even if compulsory detention were justified, it could only be used to force a person to have treatment for mental disorder. Any compulsory medical treatment unconnected with medical disorder was contrary to law and could not be justified, unless the patient's capacity to consent to such treatment was diminished. This was a matter which required consideration in the light of all the available evidence in each case.

Application of the Mental Health Act 1983

With regard to the application of s 2 of the 1983 Act in the instant case, the Court of Appeal decided that the cumulative grounds for compulsory admission set out in s 2(2)(a) had not been established, and although the grounds specified in s 2(2)(b) might well have been satisfied, they had to be considered in the light of the cumulative grounds which preceded them. The compulsory admission of S to hospital was, therefore, unlawful. However, s 6(3) of the Act operated to allow Springfield Hospital to escape liability for unlawfully accepting Ms S as a patient, because the documentation would have given the authorities there the impression that the application for admission had been made correctly.

Was admission to St George's Hospital's lawful?

The admission to St George's Hospital was unlawful, as was S's period of detention there. Although this was admitted, and was due to an administrative oversight, the Court of Appeal concluded that it should not be dismissed as a technicality, since the truth was that S would have been entitled to an application for habeas corpus and to her immediate release from hospital. Her admission to St George's and her subsequent detention for treatment had therefore been unlawful.

Proceedings before Hogg J

These were described as 'extraordinary and unfortunate', and the court made it clear that declaratory relief should not be sought on an interim basis without proper investigation of the evidence on both sides. Nor should an order be made on an *ex parte* application, especially if it has implications for a person's autonomy. In the case of S, the order had been made on an *ex parte* application in proceedings which had not then been instituted by a summons, and without the knowledge of S or any attempt to inform her solicitor. There had been no evidence presented either orally or by affidavit on behalf of S, and there had been no provision for S to apply to have the order varied or discharged. She was, therefore, entitled to have the order to subject her to have surgery against her will set aside. The order to have S transferred back to Springfield Hospital and her final period of compulsory detention there was also unlawful, as was her discharge from there, which was based upon the original unlawful s 2 application.

Main principles in *Collins*

The Court of Appeal affirmed that:

(a) a mentally competent adult woman has the right to refuse a Caesarean section, even if it means that she and her unborn fetus are in danger of dying as a result of this decision;

(b) the MHA 1983 cannot be deployed to achieve the detention of an individual against her will merely because her thinking process is unusual, even if apparently bizarre and irrational and contrary to the views of the overwhelming majority of the community at large.

Comments on the *Collins* case

(a) There are major criticisms of the way in which the initial case was handled which emerge as a result of the clear misinterpretation of the procedural requirements. S suffered serious infringements of her liberty as a result of what the Court of Appeal called 'extraordinary and unfortunate' proceedings. The Court of Appeal basically restated some of the elementary points about declaratory relief stated in *Re MB*. Both cases now illustrate that the Court of Appeal takes a strong line on the need to observe the correct procedural steps in cases involving treatment without consent. The first instance hearing in the *Collins* case took place before the guidance handed down in *Re MB* by the Court of Appeal.

(b) The MHA 1983 should never be used as a means of detaining people in order to force them to have medical treatment to which they do not consent, unless the criteria set out in s 2 of the Act are met. Even then, only treatment for mental illness or disability is permissible, unless the patient lacks capacity to consent to other forms of treatment unrelated to mental illness and that treatment is in the patient's best interests.

(c) The *Collins* case confirms that the fetus is unprotected by law in these kinds of situations. Although the fetus is regarded as human and is protected by the law in certain ways, as described in *Re MB*, the fetus is not a being which is separate from its mother, and as such, its need for medical care and assistance cannot prevail over that of the mother. It would seem that the problem here is that it is impossible to achieve a compromise between fetal and maternal rights. The court forced to choose between mother and fetus will now decide in favour of the autonomy of the mother. Thus, the fetus, which has no status in law, has no legal protection in these sorts of situations.

(d) This approach is logical in the light of the law on abortion, but becomes more difficult to justify the closer the fetus is to term and it may be argued that logic might give way to emotional response when the obstinate refusal of medical assistance by the mother means probable death or serious injury to the fetus.

(e) The case starkly illustrates the contradictory approach taken by English law to the unborn, especially when one considers that the Human Fertilisation and Embryology Act 1990 focuses on the welfare of the child to be born as a result of fertility treatment.

(f) The Court of Appeal said that: 'in the present case there was no conflict between the interests of the mother and the fetus: no one was faced with the awful dilemma of deciding on one form of treatment which risked one of their lives in order to save the other. Medically, the procedures to be adopted to preserve the mother and her unborn child did not involve a preference for one rather than the other. The crucial issue can be identified by expressing the problem in different ways: for example, if all life is sacred, why is a mother entitled to refuse to undergo treatment if this would preserve the life of the fetus without damaging her own?'

(g) On the quantum of damages, this matter might well be settled out of court, but the recent Court of Appeal guidance suggests that moderation is to be exercised.

The Court of Appeal even referred to the 1217 and 1257 Magna Carta versions at one stage to provide authority for the proposition that no adult person should be detained unlawfully except by order of the law!

Postscript to the Collins *case: new guidelines*

After giving judgment on the *Collins* case, in a case relating to treatment without a pregnant woman's consent, the Court of Appeal received further written submissions from counsel who had taken soundings from the midwives, nursing and medical professions and from patients' organisations, and issued new guidelines, superseding those given in the original judgments in *St George's Healthcare NHS Trust v S (No 2)* and *R v Collins and Others ex p S (No 2)* [1998] Fam Law 662:

(a) In principle, a patient may remain competent notwithstanding detention under the MHA 1983.

(b) If the patient is competent and refuses consent to treatment, an application to the High Court for a declaration is pointless. In such a situation, the advice given to the patient should be recorded and the hospital authorities should seek unequivocal assurances from the patient, recorded in writing, that the refusal represents an informed decision, that is, she understands the nature of and reasons for the proposed treatment, and the risks and likely prognosis involved in the decision to refuse or accept it. If the patient is unwilling to sign a written indication of this refusal, this should also be recorded in writing. Such a written indication is merely a record for evidential purposes and is not to be regarded as a disclaimer.

(c) If a patient is incapable of giving or refusing consent, whether in the long term or temporarily (for example, due to unconsciousness), the patient must be cared for according to the authority's judgment of the patient's best interests. Where the patient has given an advance directive before becoming incapable, treatment and care should normally be subject to the advance directive. But if there is a reason to doubt its reliability (for example, because it may sensibly be thought not to apply to the circumstances which have arisen), then an application for a declaration may be made.

(d) The authority should identify as soon as possible whether there is concern about a patient's competence to consent to or refuse treatment.

(e) If the patient's capacity is seriously in doubt, it should be assessed as a matter of priority. In serious or complex cases, the issue should be examined by an independent psychiatrist, ideally one approved under s 12(2) of the MHA 1983. If there remains doubt, and the seriousness or complexity of the issues in the cases may require the involvement of the court, the psychiatrist should consider whether the patient is incapable of managing her property or affairs. If so, she may be unable to instruct a solicitor and will require a guardian ad litem in any court proceedings. The authority should seek legal advice as quickly as possible, and if a declaration is sought, should inform the patient's solicitors immediately, who should, if practicable, have a proper opportunity to take instructions and apply for legal aid where necessary. Potential witnesses for the authority should be made aware of the criteria laid down in *Re MB (Medical Treatment)* [1997] 2 FLR 426 and the present case, together with any guidelines from the Department of Health and the British Medical Association.

(f) If the patient is unable to instruct solicitors or is believed to be incapable of doing so, the authority or its legal advisers must notify the Official Solicitor and invite him to act as guardian *ad litem*.

(g) The hearing before the judge should be *inter partes*. A declaration granted *ex parte* will not be binding on the patient. The Official Solicitor may be called upon to assist an *amicus curiae* even where the patient is capable of instructing her own solicitor.

(h) Information presented to the judge must be accurate and complete. It should include the reasons for the proposed treatment, the risks involved if it is carried out or not, and any alternative treatment, and the reason, if ascertainable, for the patient's refusal. The judge will need sufficient information to reach an informed conclusion about the patient's capacity and the issue of best interests if it arises.

(i) The precise terms of any order should be recorded and approved by the judge before these are transmitted to the authority. The patient should be accurately informed of the precise terms.

(j) Applications for emergency orders from the High Court made without first issuing and serving the relevant applications and evidence in support have a duty to comply with the procedural requirements (and to pay the court fees) as soon as possible after the urgency hearing.

(k) There may be occasions when the situation facing the authority is so urgent and the consequences so desperate that it is impracticable to attempt to comply with these guidelines, which should be approached for what they are, that is, guidelines. Where delay may itself cause serious damage to the patient's health, or put her life at risk, then formulaic compliance with these guidelines would be inappropriate.

Comment on the revised *Collins* guidelines

It appears that, if the patient is expected to be given as much information as the judge in relation to the consequences of consent or refusal, this might sometimes require going beyond the usual practice accepted by a responsible body of medical opinion, since the position appears to be that a doctor would only be expected to give further information to a patient if the patient asks questions (*Sidaway v Board of Governors of Bethlem Royal Hospital and the Maudsley Hospital* [1985] AC 871). The court's comment that an *ex parte* declaration would be ineffective to bind the patient does seem to be somewhat incongruous in cases of extreme urgency, where a decision needs to be made 'in a matter of minutes', and yet the health authority could still be open to a charge of criminal and/or tortious assault if it is later accepted by the courts that the woman had refused her consent to the operation.

Further analysis of Re MB *and the* Collins *case*

The Court of Appeal in *Re MB* and the *Collins* case was courageous in attempting to lay down guidelines in this controversial area of law, medical ethics, morality and human and constitutional rights. Yet, what is the legal position in marginal cases? True, the appellate court has reiterated the general principle that all adults of sound mind have the absolute right to choose whether to consent to medical treatment, to refuse it or to choose one or the other of the treatments being offered. However, these principles have been stated as the law since at least *Collins v Wilcock* [1984] 1 WLR 1172 (cited with approval in *Re F (Mental Patient: Sterilisation)* [1990] 2 AC 1) and at least in general terms in the *Sidaway* case [1985] AC 871 and *obiter* in *Re T (Adult: Consent to Medical Treatment)* [1992] 2 FLR 458. In *Re MB*, the Court of Appeal concluded that none of the earlier cases lent support to the proposition that the court should take into account the interests of the unborn child at risk from the refusal of a competent mother to consent to medical intervention. Butler-Sloss LJ therefore stated:

> The law is ... clear that a competent woman who has the capacity to decide may, for religious reasons, other reasons, or for no reasons at all, choose not to have medical intervention, even though the consequence might be the death or serious handicap of the child she bears or her own death.

This was stated after a review of the earlier case law, which suggested that an unborn fetus might be protected by the law both at common law and, indeed, by statutes such as the Offences Against the Person Act 1861, which makes it an offence to procure an abortion and the Infant (Life Preservation) Act 1929, which makes it a criminal offence for the intentional destruction of a child, capable of being born alive, before it has an existence independent of its mother.

Her Ladyship then observed:

> ... it might seem illogical that a child capable of being born alive is protected by the criminal law from intentional destruction and by the Abortion Act from termination otherwise than as permitted by the Act, but is not protected from the (irrational) decision of a competent mother not to avert the risk of death [but] this appears to be the present state of the law.

The *Collins* case could be perceived as confirming the stark dilemma between maternal rights and fetal rights. Yet, is it always necessary to see such decisions in these polemical terms? Katherine O'Donovan has argued (SPTL lecture, 1999, Leeds) that it might be more constructive and positive to see these Caesarean cases as those in which the rules of natural justice ought to be applied. Thus, a woman in this situation should be given the right to express her views on the principle of *audi alteram partem*. However, the difficulty is that, in all these cases, with the exception of the *Collins* case, there was very little time to make a considered judgment either on the part of the woman or the court. *Collins* might well be regarded as unexceptional in view of the law on abortion, but as the fetus approaches full term, it might well become more difficult to accept that the unborn fetus should receive no legal protection or indeed warrant no special consideration.

The court in *Collins* appeared to confirm that the principle of the sanctity of life should be subordinate to that of self-determinism or patient autonomy; that the MHA should not be used to justify admission, detention and treatment of individuals unless its conditions have been fulfilled. Pregnant women may not necessarily be held to be temporarily incompetent in certain circumstances, as courts have declared in previous cases, but the test of competence is that laid down in *Re C* ([1994] 1 FLR 31) (comprehension and retention of the information the patient is given, believing the information *and* the capacity to weigh and balance the information and to make a reasoned choice).

As for the status of the unborn fetus before birth, the court also referred to *AG's Reference (No 3 of 1994)* [1997] 3 All ER 936, where the House of Lords disagreed with the Court of Appeal, which had said that the fetus should be treated as an integral part of the mother in the same way as any other part of her body, such as her foot or arm. The House of Lords' view (*per* Lord Mustill, p 428) is that the mother and the fetus are two distinct organisms living symbiotically, not a single organism with two aspects. The fetus is a unique organism, and the Court of Appeal in the present case confirmed that the interests of the fetus cannot be disregarded.

Yet, as Margaret Brazier puts it (Brazier (1997), p 280):

> English law recognises no general authority to compel pregnant women to act to protect the health of their children-to-be. Fetus never equals child in theory. Yet at the very threshold of transformation from dependent fetus to independent living infant, the law and medicine may covertly combine to prevent a healthy fetus suffering harm where any aspect of maternal behaviour can be seized upon as evidence of her inability to make an independent judgment.

Should Parliament legislate in this case? The problems relating to assessment of a patient's mental condition and true wishes and feelings on Caesarean sections would remain. In a recent article (see Thorpe (Judge), 'The Caesarean section debate' [1997] Fam Law 663), Thorpe J emphasised that the applications for Caesarean section are confined to judges of the Family Division who are dedicated to upholding child welfare and the equal preservation of the mother and unborn fetus and that, at some level, the expert evidence would influence the judicial outcome of the case. He added, 'what is consistent in principle may not be practical in application'. Many of these cases were heard either in minutes or within a matter of hours so that it was simply impossible to give full and considered attention to the legal and ethical issues raised by the particular case. While *Re MB* and *Collins* take a step in the direction of greater recognition of autonomy, it would be unduly optimistic to expect professionals to anticipate all potential problems in every case. Further, as *Collins* confirms, the judicial approach to 'irrational' and *ipso facto* 'incompetent' decisions suggests that the courts may still find considerable scope for refusal of consent to be ignored and for paternalism to reign supreme, especially in cases where the woman is required to make a decision while in the 'throes of labour'. On the other hand, have we also now reached the stage where saving a woman for the sake of her unborn fetus can never be seen as acting 'in her best interests' unless it is with her consent? No doubt, health professionals and the courts will continue to grapple with the continuing tension between upholding a patient's autonomy and respecting the principle of the sanctity of life.

Consent and the mentally incapacitated patient

There will always be people who, for one reason or another, will be *incapable* of deciding whether they should have medical treatment either because they are:

(a) temporarily incompetent; or

(b) permanently incompetent through disease or trauma or as a result of mental handicap or illness;

(c) those who have not yet reached maturity;

(d) those suffering from dementia and those who are incompetent because of mental impairment or injury.

In legal parlance, such persons lack the 'capacity' to make competent decisions with regard to medical treatment.

The test of legal capacity

Broadly, this is said to be the ability to understand the nature and purpose of the proposed care and to be able to weigh the risks of that treatment, as stated by the House of Lords in *F v West Berkshire HA* [1989] 2 All ER 545. Yet, the leading case containing a comprehensive definition of capacity is only a first instance case from the High Court, namely, *Re C (Adult: Refusal of Treatment)* [1994] 1 FLR 31; [1994] 1 WLR 290; [1994] 1 All ER 819, although it has been approved by an appellate court (see *Re MB*).

To avoid being liable in battery, all the *doctor* needs to do is to explain the nature and purpose of the treatment in broad terms (*Chatterton v Gerson*). Once the patient is informed in broad terms of the treatment, the consent then given is 'real' in law. But, the requirements are more exacting for determining whether the *patient* had capacity to consent, as seen in *Re C*, which, as we have seen, required the patient to comprehend and retain the necessary information, believe the information and be able to weigh the information, and balance the risks and needs in order to reach a decision.

It is worth noting that *Freeman v Home Office (No 2)* [1984] QB 524 ruled that whether or not consent had been given by a patient was a question of fact in every case. It should be noted, further, that a valid consent can also be withdrawn.

Can anyone consent on behalf of an incompetent adult?

On the question of consent by incompetent adults, the current legal position, as established by a combination of factors and case law, therefore is: no one can consent to medical treatment on behalf of an incompetent adult. This is because the *parens patriae* jurisdiction of the court was revoked (inadvertently) in 1960; thus, once a patient is over the age of 18, English law has no provision for proxy consent (that is, on behalf of a patient) where the patient is unable to consent for themselves. However, the courts may validate the actions taken by a health care professional *ex post facto*, by means of a declaration, provided they were carried out in the patient's best interests.

Patients who may be treated under the Mental Health Act 1983

Historical background

Before 1983, the governing legislation was the MHA 1959, and s 34 of that Act allowed a guardian to be appointed to care for a mentally handicapped adult and to consent to treatment on behalf of that patient in the same way a parent often does for a child. Section 8 of the MHA 1983 restricts the powers of a guardian so that he may no longer consent to such treatment on behalf of such a person. In any event, the guardian was not used very much.

If there is some doubt or dispute over a child's capacity to consent, that child can be made a ward of court – that is, placed under the wardship jurisdiction of the court. Thereafter, no important decision may be taken regarding that child without the consent of the court, until the court says so, or the child reaches 18. But this is not possible for an adult. The *parens patriae* jurisdiction of the court which once enabled courts to decide such treatment for incompetent adults was removed by the MHA 1959. This is because the ancient *parens patriae* jurisdiction of the courts in England and Wales, which dates from the 13th century, and originally held by the English monarch, eventually passed to the High Court, the prerogative being passed to the Lord Chancellor by means of the Sign Manual, which was a regnal order authorising the Officer to exercise the jurisdiction on behalf of the Sovereign. As a result of the passing of the MHA 1959, all legislative provisions dealing with incapable adults were revoked so that the power to treat adults suffering from mental illness was contained in a single statutory enactment. This meant that the Sign Manual was also revoked so that it was removed completely from the common law, through the enactment of the MHA 1959. Thus, as the law stands, once a mentally incompetent person is over 18, no court can decide on that person's medical care, unless it falls within the provisions of the mental health legislation. But the courts can manage property issues relating to such an adult patient.

Thus, as Margaret Brazier (1992) points out, the mentally incompetent patient is in legal limbo, because no one can decide on medical treatment for such persons.

The courts (in cases like *F v Berkshire*) have proceeded on the basis that, if a decision/procedure has been undertaken in that patient's best interests, as judged by responsible medical opinion, then a declaration may be sought to confirm that decision *ex post facto*.

However, Pt IV of the MHA 1983 does contain some provisions dealing with persons *detained* under the Act. The Act allows treatment of such people without their consent. Such patients can be given most forms of medical treatment without their consent. But, only a small percentage of patients are detained under the Act – most cases fall outside their scope.

Section 3 of the MHA 1983 lays down criteria for their detention.

The scope of s 63

Section 63 states that the consent of the patient is not required for any medical disorder from which he is suffering, provided it is not treatment falling under s 57 or s 58 (these sections are discussed below).

Section 62 is supposed to be used only to authorise treatment for mental disorder, not physical illness as such. But, the courts have taken a broad interpretation of mental disorder and have authorised enforced tube feeding of a patient compulsorily detained for a psychopathic disorder the symptoms of which included depression and compulsion for self-harm. The section only applies to detained patients, not voluntary patients.

Under s 58, some treatments (including electroconvulsive therapy – ECT) can only be given to detained patients either with their consent *or* on the basis of an independent medical opinion which certifies that such a patient is capable of consenting, has consented and the treatment will be beneficial (see s 58).

Under s 57, other treatments (including psycho-surgery) can usually only be given with the patient's consent *and* on the basis of a second medical opinion which certifies that the patient is capable of consenting, and has consented, and that the treatment will be beneficial. There must also be two non-medical witnesses who have also been appointed for the purpose. This section also applies to informal patients, that is, those being treated on a voluntary basis.

Detention in hospital and consent

It is important to bear in mind that, in principle, a person may remain competent *notwithstanding detention* under the MHA 1983 (see the *Collins* case, discussed above, p 25). Further, the MHA 1983 cannot be used to authorise treatment of a mentally disordered person who withholds his consent *unless* he is detained in hospital or has first been detained and been given leave of absence under s 17. The case of *R v Hallstrom* is a case in point.

***R v Hallstrom* [1986] 2 All ER 306**

This High Court case involved two chronic paranoid schizophrenics who had been admitted to hospital several times. It decided several points:

(a) There is no power under the 1983 Act to give treatment to a mentally disordered person who withholds his consent unless he is detained in hospital or has first been detained and been given leave of absence under s 17.

(b) Unless clear statutory authority to the contrary exists, no one is to be detained in hospital or to undergo medical treatment or even to submit himself to a medical examination without his consent. This is as true of a mentally disordered person as of anyone else.

(c) Section 3 (which lists criteria for detention for treatment) only covers those whose mental condition was believed to require a period of in-patient treatment.

(d) It was unlawful to recall to hospital a patient on indefinite leave of absence when the intention was to prevent him from being on leave of absence for six months continuously; s 17 only empowered the medical officer to recall the patient when it was necessary for the patient's health or safety or for the protection of other persons and, therefore, the purported recall of the patient in this case would have been unlawful even if he had been 'liable to be detained'.

It was stated, *per curiam*, that there is a difference between being 'detained' in a hospital and being *liable* to be detained. Someone on leave of absence *from* a hospital cannot be regarded as detained *in* a hospital. But the *Barker* case, decided by the Court of Appeal, says the detention *can* be renewed, pursuant to s 20.

B v Croydon HA [1995] 1 All ER 683

This involved a 24 year old patient suffering from borderline psychopathic disorder with a compulsion to self-harm. She cut and burned herself several times and was admitted to hospital for assessment where her mental disorder was diagnosed. She was later compulsorily detained, and then refused to eat as a means of inflicting harm on herself and only accepted food under threat of feeding by nasogastric tube. The plaintiff 's case was that the forced feeding was unlawful.

The issue here was: was tube feeding 'treatment given to her for the mental disorder'?

The first instance court held that the patient's application for an injunction to restrain the force feeding could not be granted because the nasogastric feeding was treatment for the mental disorder and, therefore, because of s 63, did not require her consent.

The Court of Appeal agreed with this and held that the term 'medical treatment' included a wide range of acts 'ancillary to the core treatment' so that nasal feeding *was* a form of medical treatment designed to alleviate the symptoms of mental disorder and, therefore, fell within the scope of s 63. The refusal of food and drink was the product of the patient's mental disorder and so the tube feeding could be seen as treating her mental condition, which was therefore lawful and legally permissible *even without the patient's consent.* Relieving symptoms is just as much a part of treatment as relieving the underlying cause.

Comment

This appears to be a disturbing case which appears to widen the range of procedures which may be administered without the patient's consent. It is notable that the first instance court found that the patient did have the capacity to refuse medical treatment, but the Court of Appeal questioned this. It was accepted that, because of the patient's condition, it would not have been lawful to detain her unless her condition was treatable. However, not every act could be said to form part of the treatment as defined under s 145(1) (whereunder 'medical treatment' includes 'nursing ... care, habilitation and rehabilitation under medical supervision'). In practical terms, some form of restraint might foreseeably be exercised in order to keep a disruptive patient quiet and make life more peaceful for the other patients within proximity. Yet, if the patient in this case was able to object to the nasal feeding, she might well have possessed sufficient capacity to refuse medical treatment, but the whole point of patients who are compulsorily detained under the Act is that their consent is dispensed with and this wide definition of treatment appears to justify non-consensual treatment which does not alleviate the mental disorder of the patient. The Code of Practice (para 15.4) strongly suggests that, despite s 63, the consent of the patient to treatment for the mental disorder should at least be sought in the first instance.

We have, of course, already considered a case where 'treatment' was given a wide meaning in circumstances where the court believed the a statutory justification was required in order to override a refusal of consent in order to save the life of the mother and the unborn fetus. This was the *Tameside* case (see, also, discussion, above, p 13).

Caesarean section constituting 'medical treatment' for mental disorder?

The *Tameside* case (*Tameside and Glossop Acute Services v CH* [1996] 1 FLR 762)

The woman, aged 41, had suffered from paranoid schizophrenia since 1983, and was detained in hospital under s 3 of the 1983 Act, where it was discovered that she was pregnant. The doctors felt the patient had no capacity to consent or refuse treatment concerning her pregnancy. The woman was resisting treatment in the delusional belief that the treatment and advice given by the consultant obstetrician and the psychiatrist dealing with her case was malicious and harmful to the child. The hospital sought a declaration authorising treatment, to perform a Caesarean section if necessary.

Wall J made the declaration sought under s 63 because the evidence indicated that the patient lacked the capacity to consent or to refuse medical treatment in relation to the management of her pregnancy, justifying delivery by Caesarean if necessary, which the court held could constitute 'medical treatment' for her mental disorder.

Comment

The court in *Tameside* held that the Caesarean section performed on a schizophrenic pregnant patient could be 'treatment' of her mental disorder within the meaning of s 63 of the MHA 1983. This is a somewhat curious decision in terms of the court's usage of s 63, not least because the Code of Practice advises that treatment for physical disorder cannot be given under this section unless 'it can reasonably be said that the physical disorder is a symptom or underlying cause of the mental disorder'. *Tameside* falls outside this situation because it could not be said that the woman's pregnancy was a 'symptom or underlying cause' of her schizophrenia.

However, the woman's doctor presented the court with a stark choice, as Bartlett and Sandland put it: 'between a psychotic patient and a dead child on the one hand and a mentally healthy mother and child on the other' (Bartlett and Sandland (2000), p 222). It is, therefore, unsurprising that the judge preferred the second option and adopted the 'holistic' approach of the *Croydon* case (see *B v Croydon HA* [1995] 1 All ER 683, discussed above, p 34) so that he could argue that, if the proposed treatment was administered (which was the Caesarean section), it would be beneficial to the mental health of the patient. The court said that it would not be stretching language to say that 'achievement of a successful outcome of the pregnancy is a necessary part of the overall treatment of her mental disorder'. Consequently, Wall J held that the treatment fell within s 63.

It is, of course, questionable whether the fact that the baby is born safely will somehow result in the mother recovering from her long standing mental problems, although there is no doubt that facilitating the birth (if it can be called that) and ensuring the survival of both herself and her baby would be beneficial to her mental health. As Widdett and Thomson suggest, the case seems to illustrate the pull of a particular, normative, ideology of femininity (see Widdett and Thomson (1997)).

Re Barker (1998) *The Times*, 14 October, CA

This case disapproved of the interpretation of the court in the *Hallstrom* case with regard to the possible meaning of 'detained' under the MHA.

The Court of Appeal held (*inter alia*) that:

> A patient who was detained under s 3 of the MHA 1983 could have her detention renewed pursuant to s 20 of the MHA even though, at the time of renewal, she had been granted lengthy leave of absence from the hospital where she was detained and only returned periodically for her progress to be monitored.

Incompetent patients not covered by the MHA 1983

In an emergency, medical staff may rely on a defence of necessity. What is the situation where a patient suffers from a disability which renders them permanently incapable of giving consent?

The legal basis for discussing this issue is *T v T* [1988] 2 WLR 189, wherein Wood J held that doctors could lawfully proceed with an abortion and sterilisation of a severely handicapped 19 year old girl. As he put it: 'In these exceptional circumstances where there is no provision in law for consent to be given and, therefore, no one can give consent, and where the patient is suffering from such mental abnormality as never to be able to give such consent, a medical practitioner is justified in taking such steps as good medical practice demands.'

This case was approved and followed in *F v West Berkshire HA* [1989] 2 All ER 545, which disapproved of the *Wilson v Pringle* 'hostile intent' test (see [1987] QB 237) which basically said that battery could only be established if there was 'hostile intent' on the part of the defendant.

After *F*'s case came a series of decisions and a Practice Note to clarify the position and, since then, several other such Practice Notes were issued, until 1996, which is the current Practice Note.

In the case of abortions, there is no need for declarations from the court: *Re SG (Adult Mental Patient: Abortion)* [1991] 2 FLR 329. It was stated by the court here that regulation by the Abortion Act 1967 provided adequate safeguards; however, the present writer submits that this is at least questionable as far as this incapacitated adult patient was concerned.

Comment

For sterilisations, court approval *is* usually required. For abortions, one might have thought court approval should normally be required as well but *Re SG* (above) suggests otherwise.

Other cases

Re H (Mental Patient: Diagnosis) *[1993] 4 Med LR 91*

The court in this case ruled on an application as to whether relatively intrusive diagnosis procedures could be performed on an incapacitated patient, on the basis of *F v West Berkshire HA* [1989] 2 All ER 545 and held that it could, as long as treatment was in the patient's 'best interests'.

Re GF *[1992] 1 FLR 293*

Here, the woman suffered from severe menstrual bleeding. A hysterectomy was performed, with the court saying there was no need for a declaration, as it was a 'therapeutic' sterilisation.

Comment

As Stauch *et al* (1998) point out, the provisions of the Abortion Act 1967 are *not* an adequate safeguard for a mentally incapacitated woman. As they say: 'There is something highly distasteful about forcing [an incompetent woman] to submit to an abortion' (p 219). Ironically, the very therapeutic/non-therapeutic distinction so summarily dismissed by Lord Hailsham in *Re B* (the *Jeanette* case) [1987] 2 All ER 206, on the basis that the patient would not be able to understand the nature of the sterilisation, has now been resurrected to justify invasive treatment, either on the basis that it was purely to deal with menstruation problems or to authorise an abortion because it is now seen as 'therapeutic'. There have to be the same safeguards for an abortion as exist for a proposed sterilisation.

The recent case of *Re S* (2000) *The Times*, 26 May (discussed in Chapter 6) is indicative of the appeal court not authorising an operation that is invasive – a hysterectomy – on a mentally incompetent 28 year old woman; an intra-uterine device was preferred as less invasive.

The position seems to be that non-invasive contraception would be the preferred option rather than surgery, such as hysterectomy. However, if contraception proves unsuccessful, the question of abortion would become a serious alternative and this is not necessarily adequately safeguarded under the Abortion Act 1967. Some might well hope that, in future cases, the courts might take the view that an abortion would have to be the last resort or the *only* option (as opposed to a less invasive procedure such as insertion of an intra-uterine device) before an English court would approve it for a mentally incapable woman. The question of what is genuinely in the best interests of such persons remains a contentious issue.

Court's supervisory jurisdiction over incapable adults at risk of harm: can the doctrine of necessity co-exist with the statutory regime?

The leading case in the area is the House of Lords' decision in the *Bournewood* case.

The Bournewood *case (*R v Bournewood Community and Mental Health NHS Trust ex p L*) [1998] Fam Law 592*

This case involved L, a 48 year old autistic man, who was profoundly mentally retarded and unable to speak. He had always been incapable of consenting to medical treatment. He had no sense of danger and a history of self-harming behaviour. In 1994, he was discharged from the hospital in which he had lived for over 30 years, and went to stay with paid carers, Mr and Mrs E. L was not finally discharged from hospital and the relevant Trust remained responsible for his care and treatment. He attended a day centre.

In July 1997, while at the day centre, he became agitated and began to harm himself, hitting his head and banging it against the wall. The carers could not be contacted, and he was sedated and taken to hospital. The consultant considered that he should be admitted as an in-patient, and, since he appeared to be compliant, he was admitted informally under s 131 of the MHA 1983, and not compulsorily.

The carers began proceedings in L's name against the Trust for judicial review of the decision to detain him, a writ of habeas corpus, and damages for false imprisonment and assault. The action was dismissed at first instance, but the Court of Appeal allowed the appeal.

The Trust appealed with leave of the Court of Appeal to the House of Lords. The Secretary of State for Health, the Mental Health Act Commission and the Registered Nursing Homes Association were granted leave to intervene in the appeal.

In the meantime, the Trust committed L compulsorily under s 3 of the 1983 Act. In November 1997, he applied for discharge from the hospital, and he was discharged in December 1997.

The House of Lords allowed the appeal and held:

(a) patients admitted under s 131 may be classed as either voluntary patients, if they have capacity to consent and give their consent to admission, or as informal patients who, though lacking capacity to consent, do not object to admission;

(b) the treatment and care of such informal patients who lack the capacity to consent can be justified on the basis of the common law doctrine of necessity;

(c) the re-admission of L to the hospital did not constitute the tort of false imprisonment because he was not kept in a locked ward and, since he had made no attempt to leave, he had not actually been deprived of his liberty;

(d) all the steps taken had in fact been taken in the best interests of L and, in so far as they might otherwise have constituted an invasion of his civil rights, had been justified on the basis of the common law doctrine of necessity.

Lords Nolan and Steyn considered that L had been 'detained', but regarded such detention as justifiable under the doctrine of necessity. However, Lord Steyn drew attention to the consequences of their decision. The main problem is that the decision leaves compliant, incapacitated patients without the safeguards enshrined in the MHA 1983.

Effect of the judgment

This case exposed the failure of the mental health system to protect some of the most vulnerable members of society. At present, compulsorily detained patients' cases are reviewed by mental health review tribunals. The effect of the judgment is that mentally incapacitated patients can be treated when they lack capacity without the protection of review by an independent body which is afforded to compulsorily detained patients. The Mental Health Commission, which has responsibility for the oversight of the care of patients in hospitals, gave evidence that, on any given day, there would be 22,000 patients in hospital in the same position as Mr L. During a year, a further 48,000 persons can expect to be admitted. To avoid similar actions to that brought by Mr L means hospitals would have to go for wholesale sectioning of hitherto 'voluntary' patients. The consequences for Mental Health Trusts, in having to assess every patient, might be an administrative nightmare.

Re F – Bournewood *followed*

In a case heard by the Court of Appeal in June 2000, the principle was affirmed that the court has jurisdiction to supervise an incapable adult who is at risk of harm on the basis of the doctrine of necessity, which was affirmed in the *Bournewood* case.

Re F (Adult: Court's Jurisdiction) *(2000)* The Times, *25 July*

Facts

In this case, T, aged 18, was said to have the intellectual age of a five to eight year old child. The local authority sought to invoke the inherent jurisdiction of the court under the doctrine of necessity in order to: (a) direct where T lived; and (b) to restrict and supervise her contact with her natural family, principally her mother. The mother contended that, the doctrine of necessity having been ousted by the decision not to extend the former *parens patriae* jurisdiction which had lapsed in 1959, the courts were unable to fill the gap caused by statutory amendments.

The Court of Appeal (*per* Dame Butler-Sloss P) said that it was accepted for the purposes of the appeal that the local authority's allegations as to the mother's care of T, who was mentally incapacitated, were correct, and that T lacked capacity to make decisions as to her future. The Court of Appeal had already held that T did not come within the guardianship provisions of the MHA 1983, nor did wardship apply to her after the age of 18.

While there was a limited jurisdiction to make declarations in medical cases on issues capable of resolution at the time of hearing, it did not extend to cases where the effect would be coercive over a long period without limit of time and without a clear view of future requirements for that person. The local authority, supported by the Official Solicitor, submitted that the doctrine (of necessity) operated on a day to day basis in making ordinary decisions for the care and protection of an incapable adult as recognised in *R v Bournewood Community and Mental Health NHS Trust ex p L* [1999] AC 458.

In the instant case, it was necessary for a decision to be made as to where T should live and, in the absence of agreement, that decision required the intervention of the court.

Her Ladyship had no doubt that there was a serious justiciable issue which did require a decision by the court. Mental health legislation did not cover the day to day affairs of the mentally incapacitated adult and both *In Re F (Mental Patient: Sterilisation)* [1990] AC 1 and *Bournewood* have recognised that the doctrine of necessity might properly be invoked side by side with the statutory regime.

The jurisdiction of the High Court to grant relief by way of declaration was, therefore, not excluded by the MHA 1983. A declaration was, in many ways, a flexible remedy, able to meet a variety of situations. In the present conflict, where serious questions hung over the future care of T if returned to her mother, there was no practicable alternative to intervention by the court.

It was essential that T's best interests should be considered by the High Court and that there was no impediment to the judge hearing the substantive issues involved in the case.

Sedley LJ also concurred saying that, in the absence of any statutory inhibition where, as here, a strong case of necessity was made out, the court could, by declaring what was in the person's best interests, sanction not only the provision of care, but also the use of such moral or physical restrictions as might be needed to keep them out of harm's way; nor did such a conclusion conflict with the European Convention for the Protection of Human Rights and Fundamental Freedoms.

Thorpe LJ delivered a concurring judgment.

Comment

The principle currently adopted by the courts, therefore, appears to be that if an adult patient lacks the capacity to consent, and no one can strictly consent on her behalf, it is still possible, by invoking the doctrine of necessity and the best interests of the patient approach, to exercise supervisory control over such a patient on a day to day basis, to safeguard that patient's welfare, care and protection.

CONCLUSIONS ON THE ENGLISH NOTION OF CONSENT TO TREATMENT

In retrospect, it can be seen that there is no 'doctrine' as such of informed consent in the sense of a full blown, highly developed doctrine which requires practically full disclosure on nearly every occasion. On the contrary, all that a medical practitioner needs to do in England and Wales is to comply with the *Chatterton v Gerson* test – the patient usually needs only to be informed in broad terms about the proposed treatment or medical procedure and it is up to the doctor to decide how much a patient needs to know in order to come to a decision on proposed medical treatment. *Sidaway's* case only appeared to say that if a patient asked a question, it should be answered truthfully, but not a great deal more was clarified. So, there is no clarity about how much information a patient is supposed to receive about proposed medical treatment.

The meaning of 'incompetence' and 'incompetent patients'

According to *Chatterton v Gerson*, the patient needs only to be told in broad terms the 'nature and purpose of the proposed treatment' so that any consent subsequently given will be 'real' and will exclude battery. It could be argued that this is a pro-doctor stance, and the courts wish to avoid any stigma that may attach to a doctor or health professional being found liable in battery. A case like *Wilson v Pringle* [1987] QB 237 was initially used to protect doctors further from actions based on any unauthorised touching, by requiring battery to exist only if there had been 'hostile intent'. This has now been doubted because of Lord Goff's comments in *Re F*. On the other hand, as far as the level of capacity to consent is concerned, in *Re C* it was said that the assessment of capacity necessitated a *three stage test*. This, *inter alia*, appears to require the patient to 'believe' the information. This is arguably flawed, since it is very difficult in evidentiary terms to establish whether the patient actually understood the information; surely, the test should be whether, at the material time, the patient was *capable* of understanding the information provided to her. Yet, *Re C* remains the test, now approved by other English courts, including the appellate courts. There seems to be a significant difference between a patient not understanding because she is not given all the relevant information and one who is *incapable of understanding the information*, no matter how much she was told; in the latter case here, the patient is truly incompetent in the legal sense.

As far as the Caesarean cases are concerned, the court sometimes had very little time to decide, as in the *Norfolk* and *Rochdale* cases. It was literally 'a matter of minutes' for the court to decide. Controversially, in the *Rochdale* case, the court suggested that a woman might be 'incompetent' if in the throes of labour, the implication being that she was, therefore, irrational and incapable of satisfying the *Re C* tests; yet, C himself was not behaving in a rational manner. Admittedly, *Re MB* attempted to redress the balance, and the appellate court there stated that it should not matter if the patient was being irrational in refusing treatment. Clearly, the Court of Appeal has reaffirmed the need to respect a patient's autonomy and this, as ever, has to be balanced by a court against the need to protect the patient from harm or even death. It remains to be seen, despite *Re MB*, whether the courts will revert to some form of 'throes of labour' exception or the 'best interests' approach to justify authorisation of treatment such as a Caesarean section if this is perceived as necessary to save a woman and an unborn fetus. Despite the various judicial statements affirming the non-legal status of the fetus, (confirming *Paton*) the fetus clearly has been a consideration for the courts in several cases where there has been some doubt as to the rationality of the mother. As far as authorisation of an abortion on a mentally incompetent woman is concerned, there should be the same safeguards and monitoring as exists for proposed sterilisations. The Abortion Act 1967 does not appear to contain adequate safeguards. It remains to be seen how the English courts will deal with these sorts of cases in the early years of the 21st century, particularly with human rights legislation now more readily available and, at least currently, more visible.

SELECTIVE BIBLIOGRAPHY

Bartlett, P and Sandland, R, *Mental Health Law: Policy and Practice*, 2000, Blackstone

Brazier, M, 'Patient autonomy and consent to treatment: the role of the law?' (1987) 7 LS 149

Brazier, M, 'Competence, consent and proxy consents', in Brazier, M and Lobjoit, M (eds), *Protecting the Vulnerable: Autonomy and Consent in Health Care*, 1991, Routledge, p 34 *et seq*

Brazier, M, *Medicine, Patients and the Law*, 1992, Penguin

Brazier, M, 'Parental responsibilities, fetal welfare and children's health', in Bridge, C (ed), *Essays in Honour of Peter Bromley*, 1997, Butterworths, p 180 de Cruz, P, 'Caesarean sections, consent and the courts' [1998] 10 Practitioners' Child Law Bulletin 8

Faulder, C, *Whose Body is It? The Troubling Issue of Informed Consent*, 1985, Virago

Gillon, R, *Philosophical Medical Ethics*, 1986, Wiley, Chapter 18

Habiba, MA, 'Examining consent within the patient-doctor relationship' (2000) 26 JME 183

Jones, MA, 'Informed consent and other fairy stories' (1999) 10 Med L Rev 103

Kennedy, I and Grubb, A, *Medical Law: Text with Materials*, 2nd edn, 1994, Butterworths. See, also, 3rd edn, 2000, Chapter 5

Kennedy, I and Grubb, A (eds), *Principles of Medical Law*, 1998, OUP, Chapters 3 and 4

Kirby, MD, 'Informed consent: what does it mean?' (1983) 9 JME 69

Kluge, E-H, 'When Caesarean section operations imposed by a court are justified' (1988) 14 JME 206

Mason, JK and McCall Smith, RA, *Law and Medical Ethics*, 5th edn, 1999, Butterworths, Chapter 10

McHale, J and Fox, M, *Health Care Law: Text and Materials*, 1997, Sweet & Maxwell, Chapter 6

Robertson, G, 'Informed consent to medical treatment' (1981) 97 LQR 102

Scarman (Lord), 'Law and medical practice', in Byrne, P (ed), *Medicine in Contemporary Society*, 1987, King Edward's Hospital Fund for London, King's College Studies

Skegg, PDG, 'English medical law and "informed consent": an Antipodean assessment and alternative' (1999) 9 Med L Rev 135

Stauch, M and Wheat, K, with Tingle, J, *Sourcebook on Medical Law*, 1998, Cavendish Publishing, Chapter 3

Tan, KF, 'Failure of medical advice: trespass or negligence?' (1987) 7 LS 149

Teff, H, 'Consent to medical procedures, paternalism, self-determination or therapeutic alliance?' (1985) 101 LQR 432

Thorpe (Judge), 'The Caesarean section debate' [1997] Fam Law 663

Widdett, C and Thomson, M, 'Justifying treatment and other stories' (1997) 5 FLS 84

Young, P, *The Law of Consent*, 1986, LBC

CHAPTER 2

MEDICAL CONFIDENTIALITY AND HEALTHCARE LAW

INTRODUCTION

Confidentiality is often said to be the cornerstone of good medical practice. There is a long standing tradition of confidentiality among healthcare professionals which has been an integral part of a code for many centuries. For doctors, it is contained in the Hippocratic Oath which dates from around 500BC, from the Greek philosopher/medic Hippocrates. That part of the Hippocratic Oath states:

> All that may come to my knowledge in the exercise of my profession or not in connection with it, or in daily commerce with men, which ought not to be spoken abroad, I will not divulge abroad and will never reveal.

The International Code of Medical Ethics also states:

> A doctor shall preserve absolute secrecy on all he knows about his patients because of the confidence entrusted in him.

Similarly, the Declaration of Geneva declares:

> I will respect the secrets that have been confided in me, even after the patient has died.

The undertaking to preserve confidentiality *even after death* is significant and the well known controversy in the 1960s that ensued when Sir Winston Churchill's doctor, Lord Moran, published details about him illustrates the depth of feeling that revelation even (or, perhaps, especially) after death, can arouse. The book's publication provoked critical comment from fellow members of the medical profession and the same furore occurred in 1983 when the British Medical Journal published graphic details about General Wingate's death in an obituary which the GMC regarded as a breach of confidence.

As we enter the 21st century, however, many questions relating to preserving the confidentiality of patients or, indeed, of doctors can no longer be resolved by simply referring to these codes, but require careful, rational consideration appropriate to rapidly changing conditions. In fact, as Brody reminds us, 'The historical basis of confidentiality can ... be misleading' (Brody (1989), p 83), because there is now a network of doctors, nurses and other healthcare professionals involved in care; there is also a need for patient records to which many people must have access, as part of the care 'team' and the need to communicate information to insurance companies or new employers; and there is the computerisation of records. No wonder there is a need for an analysis of 'what it is, why it is basic to the physician relationship, as well as a sense of its limits' (Brody (1989), p 83).

The British Medical Association (BMA) declares that the queries on confidentiality and disclosure form the bulk of inquiries that it receives from BMA members. Hence, while doctors and other healthcare professionals are well aware of their traditional duty of confidence and the need to protect confidentiality, increasingly complex dilemmas now arise which are not easily dealt with by simply citing or relying upon a code. Nevertheless, confidentiality remains an important part of the GMC's Blue Book and the UKCC's Code of Conduct.

In 1985, John Havard, then Secretary of the BMA, asserted that 'The most important distinguishing feature of a profession is the existence of a set of ethical principles regulating the conduct of the professional towards the patient or client, transcending his own moral, religious or political views and applying throughout the whole range of professional practice ... The justification for medical confidentiality is that if it is not observed, patients will be reluctant to disclose and doctors will be reluctant to record. The patient may even be reluctant to seek medical advice at all' (Havard (1985), p 8). These words are as true today as they were then. In order for a doctor properly to advise a patient, the doctor may well be given confidential information that the patient does not wish to be disclosed to a third party. These facts will have different implications and their relative importance and sensitivity will vary across different branches of medicine. The duty is certainly *not absolute* and the exceptions to confidentiality are discussed below. In more pragmatic terms, there are often countervailing or conflicting moral or legal considerations which override a duty of confidentiality. For instance, can a *private interest* in maintaining confidentiality be outweighed by a *public interest* in safety, for example, where certain doctors are HIV positive but their patients have not been informed of this in a clinical situation where they may be in danger of contracting the disease? What is the position if a patient discloses to a doctor, in the course of a consultation, that he intends to kill another of that doctor's patients? Would the duty of confidentiality still apply? This chapter will examine what English law and professional medical guidance has had to say on these sorts of dilemmas. In particular, we shall look at cases where the medical information is of extreme sensitivity. If a doctor or healthcare professional breaches the patient's confidence, at the very least, there will be censure from his professional body, which in the case of doctors, will be the GMC.

Definition

The BMA defines confidentiality as:

> The principle of keeping secure and secret from others, information given by or about an individual in the course of a professional relationship.

But, general guidance cannot supply definitive solutions to all problems or all situations that might arise in the course of a doctor-patient relationship. As with most matters relating to law and ethics, rules on confidentiality need to keep abreast of current developments, and the rapidity of technological change. Interpretations may and will often change as a sign of the times and changing values and situations. Genetic testing and new communications technology present fresh challenges to the duty of confidentiality.

Some examples of where a duty arises

Some examples of where a duty arises are between doctor and patient; priest and penitent; solicitor and client, and banker and customer.

Two main issues have tended to arise within the healthcare professional-patient relationship:

(a) disclosure to third parties, including other doctors, nurses, clerical staff, relatives, the employer, police, and the media;

(b) subject access: the right of the individual to obtain access to their own records/information. The latest developments in this area are discussed below.

GUIDANCE IN PROFESSIONAL CODES

The BMA Guidance

The BMA has no disciplinary authority, but operates as a trade union for doctors. Consequently, its advice provides a background to the GMC's instructions. In essence, the BMA Guidance is a comprehensive survey of the general principles and exceptions, which we shall be considering throughout this chapter.

We turn now, however, to the GMC Guidance.

The General Medical Council (GMC) Guidance

Subject to eight exceptions, the GMC imposes a strict duty on registered medical practitioners to refrain from disclosing voluntarily to any third party information about a patient which he has learnt directly or indirectly in his professional capacity. The exceptions under the Guidance where the doctor may properly breach confidentiality are:

(a) Disclosure within teams – where there are medical teams of doctors, nurses and other healthcare professionals, and sometimes people from outside the healthcare professions. To provide the patients with the best possible care, it is essential to pass confidential information between members of the team. The Guidance also mentions the case of emergencies where it is not possible to obtain a patient's consent but also stresses that a patient's request not to share certain information with other team members must be respected.

(b) Disclosure to employers and insurance companies.

(c) Disclosure where the patient or his/her legal advisor gives consent.

(d) Disclosure without the patient's consent, but which is 'in the patient's medical interest' where it is impossible to seek the patient's consent, so that information may be given to a close relative; these cover cases where the patient is incapable of giving consent to treatment because of immaturity, illness or mental incapacity.

(e) When, in the opinion of the doctor, disclosure to someone other than a relative would be in the best interests of the patient, the doctor must make every effort to get the patient's consent, but if this is not obtained and he believes that disclosure is in the patient's best interests, then he may go ahead and disclose; examples are where there is suspicion that the patient is a victim of neglect, physical or sexual abuse, when information should be given to an appropriate responsible person or statutory agency, in order to prevent further harm to the patient; this may also, unusually, require disclosure of the patient's condition to a close relative (for example, if it is terminal) and not to a patient because the doctor thinks the patient might be seriously harmed by the information.

(f) Disclosure in the interests of others in accordance with specific statutory requirements; this covers disclosure of a notifiable disease such as cholera, smallpox or typhus; notification of a termination of pregnancy must be sent within seven days of the abortion to the Chief Medical Officer; information that must be disclosed under s 172 of the Road Traffic Act 1988, but the doctor is only required to provide the patient's name and address and not the clinical details; disclosure to the medical adviser of the Driver and Vehicle Licensing Agency of relevant medical details of a driver who is continuing to drive against medical advice (see *Hunter v Mann*, discussed below, p 57); disclosure is required under s 18 of the Prevention of Terrorism (Temporary Provisions) Act 1989, where disclosure is necessary for the prevention or detection of a serious crime, and must be done as soon as practicable unless there is some 'reasonable excuse', hence the doctor-patient relationship will not be seen as such as excuse.

(g) Disclosure after a patient's death; the general rule is non-disclosure even after death, but the extent of disclosure will depend on the circumstances; factors considered will include whether the information is already public knowledge, and how long has it been since the patient died.

(h) Disclosure of information which is necessary for the purposes of a medical research project approved by a recognised ethical committee.

The UK Central Council of Nursing and Midwifery Code of Practice (1992)

The responsible governing and licensing body for doctors is the GMC. For nurses, it is the UK Central Council for Nursing, Midwifery and Health Visiting (UKCC).

With self-regulatory organisations, there is a long tradition of enunciating rules and regulations for the professions.

The UKCC Code states, *inter alia*, that:

> ... as a registered nurse, midwife or health visitor you are personally accountable for your practice and in the exercise of your professional accountability, must protect all confidential information concerning patients and clients obtained in the course of professional practice and make disclosures only with consent, where required by order of a court and you can justify disclosure in the wider public interest.

JUSTIFICATIONS FOR CONFIDENTIALITY

Various justifications can be found for maintaining a duty of confidentiality as far as the doctor-patient relationship is concerned. Johnson (1990) identifies three: (a) the patient's autonomy – that is, the right of the patient to have his confidences respected by the doctor, so that any information he divulges to the doctor in order for a diagnosis to be made is given on the basis of confidentiality; (b) the doctor's integrity, which is the doctor's undertaking to the patient about what use will be made of the information that has been obtained, so this promise is broken if the information is divulged to a third party without the patient's permission; and (c) the consequences for the future relationship: if confidences are broken, the patient might not pass on vital information to the doctor and this might result in a misdiagnosis or the wrong treatment being given to the patient which could have potentially damaging or even fatal results (see Johnson (1990), pp 74–75).

Ethical justifications

Consequentialist arguments

Gillon (1986) has outlined the justifications for medical confidentiality in philosophical and pragmatic terms:

> The commonest justification [for medical confidentiality] is undoubtedly consequentialist: people's better health, welfare, the general good, and overall happiness are more likely to be attained if doctors are fully informed by their patients, and this is more likely if doctors undertake not to disclose their patients' secrets. Conversely, if patients did not believe that doctors would keep their secrets then either they would not divulge embarrassing but potentially medically important information, thus reducing their chances of getting the best medical care, or they would disclose such information and feel anxious and unhappy at the prospect of their secrets being made known.

Hence, if the doctor is fully informed about the patient's medical history and undertakes not to disclose information received in the course of the consultation/treatment, people's health, welfare, a patient's general good and overall happiness will be more easily attained. Conversely, if patients thought that doctors might disclose private information about their health and related matters, they might be too embarrassed to reveal this information and might, therefore, not disclose potentially vital information which the doctor might need to treat the patient properly; or the patient might reveal the information, but be very anxious that the information could be revealed to third parties at any time.

Utilitarian arguments

Against this is the utilitarian view that will argue that the duty cannot be absolute and can be breached in certain circumstances (the 'greatest good for the greatest number' (Bentham, J, *The Collected Works of Jeremy Bentham*, cited in Hart, HLA, *Essays on Bentham: Studies on Jurisprudence and Political Theory*, 1982, OUP)) The utility of disclosure would have to outweigh the utility of maintaining the secrecy. At common law, the only legal justifications for disclosure are: (a) that the patient has consented; or (b) that it is in the public interest to disclose the information.

As Stauch *et al* put it, 'the utilitarian view is particularly appropriate to confidentiality as it will readily admit that the duty is not absolute and can be breached in certain circumstances' (Stauch *et al* (1998), p 221).

An example of a utilitarian approach may be found in *AG v Guardian Newspapers (No 2)* [1990] AC 109, where Lord Goff said (p 282) that, 'although there is a public interest in preserving confidences which should be preserved and protected by the law, nevertheless, that public interest may be outweighed by some other countervailing public interest which favours disclosure'.

Upholding autonomy and respect for a person's privacy

Yet another justification for preserving confidentiality is to look to the moral principles of autonomy and respect for a person's privacy (used by the deontologists who use the language of duty and morality: see, further, p 47).

The duty of confidentiality is to be maintained even after a patient's death, but it is not entirely clear as to whether there is a strict legal obligation to keep confidences after the death of a patient if the relevant information is in the death certificate, which is a public document, since this information is generally accessible.

In addition, it should be noted that doctors do not enjoy a privilege equivalent to legal professional privilege.

CONFIDENTIALITY FOR PEOPLE UNDER 16

The legal position with regard to healthcare for persons under 16 is considered in detail in the chapter on children and healthcare (see Chapter 5) and is also considered in the chapter on consent (see Chapter 1). Suffice to say for present purposes that, according to the Guidance issued jointly by the BMA, GMSC, HEA, Brook Advisory Centres, FPA and RCGP:

> ... the duty of confidentiality owed to a person under 16 is as great as that owed to any other person. Regardless of whether or not the requested treatment is given, the confidentiality of the consultation should still be respected, unless there are convincing reasons to the contrary;
>
> any competent young person, regardless of age, can independently seek medical advice and give valid consent to medical treatment;
>
> competency is understood in terms of the patient's ability to understand the choices and their consequences, including the nature, purpose, and possible risk of any treatment (or non-treatment).

This has to be read with reference to the leading House of Lords' ruling in the *Gillick* case (*Gillick v Wisbech and W Norfolk AHA* [1985] 3 All ER 402). This case established that people under 16 who are able fully to understand the treatment proposed and its implications are competent to consent to medical treatment regardless of age. Scottish law goes further by recognising certain rights of self-determination of young people. The Age of Legal Capacity (Scotland) Act 1991 assigns various legal rights to people over the age of 12, but, as in England and Wales, there is no minimum age for legal capacity to consent to medical treatment.

The GMC Guidance reiterates that people under 16 are legally able to consent on their own behalf to any surgical, medical or dental procedure or treatment if, in the doctor's opinion, they are capable of understanding the nature and possible consequences of the procedure. Clearly, the more serious the medical procedure proposed, a correspondingly better grasp of the implications is required. Doctors should particularly consider the following issues when consulted by people under 16 for contraceptive services:

> ... whether the patient understands the potential risks and benefits of the treatment and the advice given;
>
> the value of parental support must be discussed. Doctors must encourage young people to inform parents of the consultation and explore the reasons if the patient is unwilling to do so. It is important for persons under 16 seeking contraceptive advice to be aware that, although the doctor is legally obliged to discuss the value of parental support, the doctor will respect their confidentiality;
>
> the doctor should take into account whether the patient is likely to have sexual intercourse without contraception; the doctor should assess whether the patient's physical or mental health or both are likely to suffer if the patient does not receive contraceptive advice or supplies;
>
> the doctor must consider whether the patient's best interests would require the provision of contraceptive advice or methods or both without parental consent.

Under the heading 'Immature patients', the Guidance states:

> The General Medical Council advises that disclosure without consent may be justified where the patient does not have sufficient understanding to appreciate what the advice or treatment being sought may involve, cannot be persuaded to involve an appropriate person in the consultation, and where it would, in the doctor's belief, be essential to the best medical interests of the patient. Thus it is clear that the doctor is not entitled to breach confidentiality unless all these conditions are met. Therefore, even when the doctor considers the young person is too immature to consent to the treatment requested, confidentiality should still be respected concerning the consultation, unless there are very convincing reasons to the contrary.

Under 'Exceptional circumstances', it states:

> Although respect for confidentiality is an essential element of doctor-patient relationships, no patient, adult or minor, has an absolute right to complete confidentiality in all circumstances. Confidentiality must be balanced against society's interests in protecting vulnerable people from serious harm. Thus, in rare cases, for example, a breach of confidentiality may be justified if the patient's silence puts others at risk and the doctor cannot persuade the patient to make a voluntary disclosure.
>
> In exceptional circumstances, the doctor may believe that the young person seeking medical advice on sexual matters is being exploited or abused. The doctor should provide counselling with a view to preparing the patient to

agree, when ready, to confidentiality being relaxed. This task assumes greater urgency if the patient, siblings or other minors continue to be in a situation of risk so that in some cases, the doctor will have to tell the patient that confidentiality cannot be preserved. Disclosure should not be made without first discussing it with the patient whose co-operation is sought. To breach confidentiality without informing the patient and in contradiction of patient refusal may irreparably damage the trust between doctor and patient and may result in denial by the young person that abuse has taken place.

LEGAL BASES FOR CONFIDENTIALITY?

Sources of the legal obligation of confidence

There is some uncertainty as to the legal foundation of the duty of confidentiality or why there is a legal obligation of confidence (Law Commission, *Breach of Confidence* (Law Com No 110, Cmnd 8388, 1981, HMSO)). No less than seven grounds were identified by Wacks (1977) as to the basis of a legal obligation including contract (implied or express), the general duty of care in negligence (in the law of tort) and a special obligation in equity, where equity here refers to the special jurisdiction which grew up as a subdivision of judge-made law and the corpus of law that has accumulated within it. This question has generated a considerable amount of academic debate. As Gurry puts it (1984), p 25):

> The jurisdictional basis of the action for breach of confidence has been a source of lingering uncertainty and controversy. Contract, equity and property have at different times each provided the basis on which the courts have granted relief. In some cases, a mixture of these bases have been relied upon. Thus, in *Alperton Rubber v Manning*, Peterson J referred to the defendant's conduct as 'a breach of trust or confidence, and ... a breach of the implied provision in all contracts of service that the employee will observe the rules of honesty'; and in *Prince Albert v Strange*, the court founded the defendants' liability first on property, secondly on a 'breach of trust, confidence or contract'.

The lack of clarity prompted a Law Commission inquiry which reported in 1981 (see Law Commission No 110, above) but, despite making several recommendations, including a new statutory tort of breach of confidence, so far, nothing has actually been turned into statute.

Breach of confidence

Elements of the action for breach of confidence

The courts readily recognise and enforce obligations of confidence and the obligation generally arises when the requirements, as laid down in cases like *AG v Guardian Newspapers (No 2)* [1990] AC 109, pp 281–82, described by Lord Goff, and in *Wyatt v Wilson* (1820) unreported (referred to in *Prince v Albert* [1849] 41 ER 1171, p 1179), have been satisfied.

Lord Goff (*AG v Guardian Newspapers (No 2)* [1990] AC 109, pp 281–82), stated the three elements which constituted an action for breach of confidence: a duty of confidence arises when (a) confidential information comes to the knowledge of a person; (b) in circumstances where he has notice, or is held to have agreed, that the information is confidential; (c) with the effect that it would be just in all the circumstances that he should be precluded from disclosing the information to others.

He then added that there were three limiting principles:

> ... the principle of confidence only applies to information to the extent that it is confidential (that is, that it is private); once it enters the public domain, it is generally accessible to the public and then, as a general rule, the principle of confidentiality can have no application to it;
>
> it does not apply to useless information or to trivia;
>
> the public interest in preserving confidences may be outweighed by some other countervailing public interest which favours disclosure.

Justifications for breaching confidentiality

As we have seen from the GMC Guidance, there are several justifications for breaching confidentiality, ranging from statutory to public interest reasons. Some of the more common exceptions will now be considered under the following headings:

(a) disclosure with patient's consent;

(b) statutorily permissible breaches of confidentiality:

  (1) Road Traffic Act 1988;

  (2) Prevention of Terrorism (Temporary Provisions) Act 1989;

  (3) healthcare statutes;

(c) disclosure in the public Interest on the basis of:

  (1) protecting the public generally;

(2) protecting the public from crime;

(3) protecting third parties.

On the other side of the coin, we then consider cases where the courts have upheld the duty of confidentiality and, therefore, maintained a prohibition on disclosure to third parties by the doctor, for example, in relation to a patient's sexual conduct.

Disclosure with patient's consent

The patient may certainly give his or her express consent to pass confidential information on to a third party either orally or in writing and this will justify a breach of confidence. On the other hand, the patient may be taken to give implied consent when a patient makes no objection to, for example, the sharing of information. The typical situation is where there is a healthcare team providing care to the patient.

Disclosure allowed by statute

Obligations under the Road Traffic Act 1988 in relation to a doctor's confidentiality came under judicial scrutiny in *Hunter v Mann*.

Hunter v Mann *[1974] 1 QB 766*

Facts

A car, taken without the owner's consent, was involved in an accident. After the accident, both the driver and passenger left the scene and could not be traced. Later that day, a doctor treated a man and a woman for injuries. The woman said they had been involved in a car accident. The police later approached the doctor and asked for the names of those who had been treated. Section 168(3) (now s 172) provided that:

> Where the driver of a vehicle is alleged to be guilty of an offence to which this section applies:
>
> (b) any other person shall be required as aforesaid give any information which is in his power to give and which may lead to the identification of the driver.

The question to be answered by the Divisional Court was whether a doctor who failed to comply with the provision under s 168, in respect of information brought to his knowledge in the course of his professional relationship with a patient, was guilty of an offence under s 168(3). The argument on the part of the doctor was that the relevant words should be given a restricted meaning, so as to exclude confidential information, and those in a special position of confidence, such as doctors.

Judgment

Boreham J stated that the doctor is under a duty not to disclose voluntarily, without the consent of the patient, information which the doctor has gained in his professional capacity. In the present case, it was important to bear in mind the distinction between privilege which is to be claimed in legal proceedings and a contractual duty not to disclose. Privilege refers to a right to withhold from a court or a tribunal exercising judicial function, materials which would otherwise be available in evidence. The contractual duty of confidence exists between banker and customer, doctor and patient and accountant and client. Such a duty is subject to, and overridden by, the duty of any party to that contract to comply with the law of the land. If it is the duty of such a party to a contract, whether at common law or under statute, to disclose in defined circumstances confidential information, then he must do so, and any express contract to the contrary would be illegal and void. In the present case, he saw no ground for saying that a restricted meaning should be given to the words of the statute. Hence, the doctor remains liable under the statute.

It should be noted that there is no general obligation to volunteer information to the police unless a specific statute creates such a duty. It is not usually a crime to stay silent, except in the context of anti-terrorist legislation.

Prevention of Terrorism (Temporary Provisions) Act 1989

Under s 18, it is an offence for any person having information which he believes may be of material assistance in preventing terrorism or apprehending terrorists to fail without reasonable excuse to give that information to the police. Thus, the duty of confidence between doctor and patient is unlikely to be seen as a reasonable excuse for failing to go to the police.

Healthcare statutes

AIDS is not a notifiable disease under the Public Health (Control of Diseases) Act 1984 but, under the AIDS (Control) Act 1987, health authorities must provide reports to the responsible minister. The minister (the Secretary of State for Health) can also order hospitalisation and, if necessary, detention of sufferers under the Public Health (Infectious Diseases) Regulations 1985 SI 1985/434.

Disclosure in the public interest

Apart from the traditional duty of secrecy incorporated into the professional codes of health workers, there is a strong public interest in maintaining confidentiality so that individuals will be encouraged to seek appropriate treatment and share information relevant to it (see BMA Guidance).

As Scott puts it (in Clarke (1990), p xxii):

> The law of confidence, like the law of negligence and the law of nuisance, requires a balance to be struck. The balance will, on both sides, involve public and private interests. The newspapers that wanted to publish extracts from *Spycatcher* had private commercial interest in doing so. But there was also a public interest in freedom of speech. On the other side there was a public interest in the protection of the secrets of the security service (no private interest since the litigant was the Government). In the *Francome* case, the plaintiff had a private interest in maintaining the privacy of his telephone conversations but, ranged on the same side, there was a public interest that private telephone conversations should not be the subject of eavesdropping. On the other side, the *Daily Mirror* could rely, in aid of its own private interest, on the public interest in the disclosure of alleged wrongdoing. These are examples that make the point that every case where the law of confidentiality is invoked requires the judge to strike a balance between competing interests.

What is the public interest?

The concept of 'the public interest' is a well known exceptional situation where the right of an individual to confidentiality as contemplated by statute, case law and professional guidance may be overruled by society's interest in disclosure. It has always been in the nature of an overriding supervening public interest, but there is no universal definition of what it means. It has been discussed in general in cases such as *AG v Guardian Newspapers* [1990] 1 AC 139 (the *Spycatcher* case) and *W v Egdell* [1990] 1 All ER 835. In other words, as with many such cases in medical law, and by virtue of the generality of the concept, each case has to be considered on its own merits, so that precedent plays a smaller part than in other areas of law.

Protecting the public generally

Two contrasting cases illustrate the English courts' approach to the issue of breaching confidence in the interests of protecting the public generally.

X v Y [1988] 2 All ER 648 (the HIV doctors)

A national newspaper acquired and published, in breach of confidence from a health authority employee, details regarding two general practitioners (GPs) who had developed AIDS but were continuing to practise. The health authority sought an injunction to stop further publication of the doctors' and patients' names. The newspaper argued that the public at large, and the doctors' patients in particular, had an interest in knowing that doctors were HIV positive.

Rose J considered the evidence regarding transmission of HIV from doctor to patient where the doctor had received proper counselling about safe practice. He concluded that the risk to patients was negligible and there were greater risks from the possibility that, if they could not rely on confidential treatment, people with AIDS, or who feared they might have AIDS, would not seek medical help.

In granting the injunction, the learned judge remarked that:

> ... preservation of confidentiality is the only way of securing public health; otherwise doctors will be discredited as a source of education, for future individual patients will not come forward if doctors are going to squeal on them. Consequently, confidentiality is vital to secure public as well as private health, for unless those infected come forward they cannot be counselled and self-treatment does not provide the best care ...

Accordingly, the judge prohibited the tabloid newspaper from identifying the two HIV positive doctors.

In contrast, in the *Egdell* case, the Court of Appeal took a different view.

Protecting the public from crime

W v Egdell [1990] 1 All ER 835 (the psychiatrist)

Facts

The patient, W, was a prisoner in a secure hospital, following conviction for the manslaughter and the wounding of two others. He had been ordered to be detained indefinitely in the secure hospital. He could be released only by order of the Home Secretary if he were found to be no longer a danger to public safety. He therefore made an application to a mental health review tribunal with a view to being transferred to a regional unit. This would be a step towards W's discharge. The transfer was not approved by the Home Secretary and W then applied for a conditional discharge. His legal advisers sought the advice of Dr Egdell, an independent psychiatrist, to support his application, but Dr Egdell formed the view that the patient was still dangerous, had a psychopathic personality, no real insight into his condition and a morbid interest in explosives. Unsurprisingly, W's solicitors withdrew their application for his discharge, but did not pass on the report to the tribunal or the hospital where W was detained. W's case was due to be reviewed by the automatic review process (under s 79 of the MHA 1983) and

Dr Egdell asked that a copy of his report be placed in W's hospital file. However, W's solicitors refused, as the report has been commissioned confidentially. Realising that his report would not be included in his notes, Dr Egdell sent a copy of the report to the medical director of W's hospital and a further copy to the Home Office.

W's solicitors obtained an injunction to restrain Dr Egdell from disclosing the contents of the report at the hearing but, unknown to them, disclosure had already taken place. W sued Dr Egdell for breach of confidence, but the court upheld the breach on the grounds of the public interest, that is, the protection of the public from dangerous criminal acts. The patient appealed to the Court of Appeal.

The Court of Appeal judgment

The Court made it absolutely clear that Dr Egdell did owe W a duty of confidence. Bingham LJ opined:

> It has never been doubted that the circumstances here were such as to impose on Dr Egdell a duty of confidence owed to W. He could not lawfully sell the contents of his report to a newspaper ... nor could he discuss the case in a learned article or in his memoirs or in gossiping with friends, unless he took appropriate steps to conceal the identity of W. It is not in issue that a duty of confidence existed. The breach of such a duty is, however, in any case, dependent on the circumstances ... The decided cases establish that (1) that the law recognises an important public interest in maintaining professional duties of confidence, but (2) that the law treats such duties not as absolute, but as liable to be overridden where there is held to be a stronger public interest in disclosure.

Bingham LJ then remarked that 'the critical question was how, on the special facts of the case, the balance should be struck between the public interest in maintaining professional confidences and the public interest in protecting the public against possible violence'. Having reviewed the evidence, he said:

> There is one consideration which, in my judgment ... weighs the balance of public interest decisively in favour of disclosure ... Where a man has committed multiple killings under the disability of serious mental illness, decisions which may lead directly or indirectly to his release from hospital should not be made unless a responsible authority is properly able to make an informed judgment that the risk of repetition is so small as to be acceptable ... Dr Egdell did ... act in accordance with the law and his conduct was ... necessary in the interests of public safety and the prevention of crime.

The implication, therefore, was that, in the exceptional circumstances, with the potential danger to the public still present, the duty could be breached.

Brazier (1992) submits that '*X v Y* and *Egdell* do not mean that a doctor may *never* disclose that a patient has AIDS, or that he may always disclose findings about a patient's health'. As she points out, 'In each case, the powerful interest in maintaining confidentiality must be balanced against the danger ensuing if confidentiality is not breached. Only where there is clear and significant risk of the patient causing harm to others which cannot be abated by any other means may confidence be breached ... For disclosure to be lawful, there must be an overwhelming *public* interest in disclosure' (Brazier (1992), p 55).

W v Egdell was considered (and analogies drawn between the psychiatrists in each case) in the later case of *R v Crozier* (1990) *The Independent*, 11 May; *The Guardian*, 8 May, where the public interest defence in the prevention of crime was also upheld by the Court of Appeal; there, a psychiatrist, instructed by the defendant in an attempted murder case, disclosed his report to the prosecution (which concluded that the defendant was suffering from a psychopathic disorder) when he realised that the defence had not produced it in court, where a sentence of imprisonment of nine years had been passed. As a result, the Crown informed the judge of the contents of the report, and the judge quashed the sentence of imprisonment, making a hospital order instead.

The whole notion of the 'public interest' remains open to interpretation and the cases suggest that the particular situation that comes before the courts would have to be sufficiently serious in terms of the danger posed before the breach of confidence would be justifiable. It would appear that the perceived potential danger would have to be proven and physical harm to a third party would probably need to be the greatest risk. Hence, there does not appear to be any 'right' to disclosure in any spouse (of the other spouse's condition) or in any parent (of the child's intention to seek an abortion).

Disclosure to protect third parties

An American comparison

The duty is not absolute, and respecting confidences at all costs can have dire consequences, as the well known American case of *Tarasoff* illustrates.

Tarasoff (1976) 17 Cal (3d) 358, p 425

In August 1969, the patient, P, was a voluntary outpatient receiving therapy at a hospital in the University of California at Berkeley. The plaintiff's case was that P informed Doctor Moore, his therapist, that he was going to kill an unnamed girl, his former girlfriend, who was readily identifiable as Tatiana Tarasoff, when she returned home from spending the summer in Brazil. The therapist contacted the police, who briefly detained the patient, but released him when he appeared to be rational and he promised not to harm the woman. The therapist's superior directed that no further action be taken to detain P. No further action was taken, and no one warned the victim about the threat. In October 1969, shortly after her return from Brazil, P went to see her at her home and killed her there. Her parents sued the psychologist/therapist, his superior and the university.

The judgment

The court held that there is a duty of care owed by the therapist to the woman murdered by the therapist's patient. The court accepted that there was a balance to be drawn between the public interest in effective treatment of mental illness and the consequent requirement of protecting confidentiality, and the public interest in safety from violent assault. The protective privilege ends where the public peril begins.

We consider the *Tarasoff* case in greater detail in Chapter 11.

Protecting third parties even if no potential crime is threatened

The Court of Appeal also had occasion to consider a case where it was necessary to protect third parties but *not* to prevent a crime. In *Re C (A Minor) (Evidence: Confidential Information)* (1991) 7 BMLR 138, the English Court of Appeal had to deal with a novel point of law which had not been previously decided.

Re C (1991)

This case involved the proposed adoption of a one year old baby. The mother withdrew her consent a day before the adoption hearing. At an adjourned hearing, the adopting parents' solicitor produced an affidavit sworn voluntarily by the mother's GP, containing evidence of her mental condition and fitness to bring up a child. The mother objected to the admissibility of the evidence as it was a breach of medical confidentiality. She was unsuccessful in the lower court and appealed.

The Court of Appeal decision

Sir Stephen Brown, delivering the leading judgment, called this an unusual case and said there was no previous authority directly in point; all the cases which were cited to them were referring to very different situations. Since it involved the adoption of a little child, it was a very serious matter for the child, and a serious decision for the court to have to make when the mother was withholding her consent. The court needed to have all relevant and significant information before it to assist it in making a right decision.

He opined that the case 'rests on its own very special facts' and he had considerable hesitation in concluding that any breach of confidence had taken place. He continued:

> However that may be, in my judgment in this case the doctor was justified in making available her evidence ... I believe that a judge, if carrying out some balancing exercise, would be fully justified in coming down clearly in favour of admitting this evidence. It should also be recognised that the disclosure of the material contained in this affidavit was the subject of a restricted disclosure. It was being made available only to the judge who had to decide the application, and to those who were also bound by the confidentiality of the hearing in chambers. Accordingly, I have no hesitation in reaching the conclusion that the judge was correct to rule that this evidence was admissible and that it should be admitted.

Prohibiting disclosure to third parties

Wyatt v Wilson *(1820) unreported*

An action was taken against George III's physician to stop him publishing his diary which contained information about the King's health and mental instability. The action was upheld.

Information relating to sexual conduct could be subject to legal duty of confidentiality

Stephens v Avery and Others *[1988] 2 All ER 477*

In this case, which was heard in the Chancery Division, the plaintiff and first defendant were close friends who freely discussed matters of a personal and private nature on the express basis that what the plaintiff told the first defendant was secret and disclosed in confidence. The first defendant passed on to the second and third defendants, who were the editor and publishers of a newspaper, details of the plaintiff's sexual conduct, including details of the plaintiff's lesbian relationship with a woman who had been killed by her husband. The plaintiff brought an action against the defendants claiming damages on the grounds that the information was confidential and was knowingly published by the newspaper in breach of the duty of confidence owed by the defendant to the plaintiff. The defendants applied to strike out the claim as disclosing no reasonable cause of action, but the master refused their application. The defendants appealed, contending (a) that information about a person's sexual behaviour outside marriage was not protected by the law relating to confidential information because the behaviour itself was immoral and the discussion of it was mere gossip, and (b) that the relationship between the plaintiff and the first defendant was not such as to give rise to a duty of confidence since it was merely a relationship of friendship and had no special characteristics.

The court held that information relating to sexual conduct (in that case, a lesbian relationship) could be the subject of a legally enforceable duty of confidentiality, if it would be unconscionable for a person who had received information on the express basis that it was confidential subsequently to reveal that information to another.

On the basis of this case, information concerning the sexual conduct of a patient, if imparted to a doctor in circumstances of confidentiality, will be protected, even though it is not strictly medical information as such.

R v Wilson *[1996] 3 WLR 125, CA*

The defendant appealed against his conviction for actual bodily harm under s 47 of the Offences against the Person Act 1861. He had been charged as a result of marking his wife's buttocks with his initials by the use of a hot knife. This was done with her consent, and it appears from the case reports, at her request. The implications from the case appears to be that there was a potential breach of confidentiality here if the police were informed by the doctor who became aware of the marks when he was examining her in the course of a medical examination. The fact that the information was not strictly medical would not entitle the doctor to assert the duty of confidentiality because, first, on the basis of *Stephens v Avery* (above), it has the necessary basis of confidence, and secondly, it was imparted in the circumstances of a medical consultation. The information had to be kept confidential.

Remedy for improper disclosure: defamation action

The action of defamation may also be borne in mind if a doctor's disclosure does take place which causes responsible persons to shun the patient if he or she becomes open to ridicule, hatred or contempt. Clearly, diagnoses of AIDS, venereal disease, alcoholism and, indeed, allegations of child abuse would all be possibly defamatory if they were disclosed to a third party and were subsequently proved to be untrue.

Of course, if what the doctor said is true, this would be a complete defence, and another defence would be qualified privilege if the doctor reasonably believed his statements to be true and he communicated them to a person with a legitimate interest in relevant information, such as the police (for a discussion of AIDS and confidentiality, see below, p 70).

Quasi-legislation

Quasi-law refers to standards to which health professionals are expected to conform contained in documents such as official guidance from non-statutory professional bodies, health service circulars and executive letters, including those which are not legally binding. The various documents have different degrees of legal force, depending on the manner in which they set standards, or their relationship to statute. They are usually influential in practice and are often representative of a responsible body of opinion within the health professions. Of course, whenever there is any query about whether a given medical procedure is negligent, or conforms with the legal and professional standards expected of healthcare professionals, the law looks to whether that medical procedure or practice was 'in accordance with the practice followed by or supported by a responsible body of medical opinion' or the 'standard practice' for that procedure. Consequently, these circulars or guidance documents would offer one form of evidence of what that current standard practice is. Of course, the mere issue of guidelines does not resolve the dilemmas for health professionals, since the guidance may not be representative of widespread consensus. There is now some doubt cast on this general principle as a result of the *Bolitho* case, although healthcare professionals acting in accordance with the practice or procedure followed by a reputable body of opinion will *prima facie* not be negligent in the eyes of the law (see *Bolam v Friern Barnet NHC* [1957] 2 All ER 118). The medical opinion itself, however, has to be 'logical' (see *Bolitho v City and Hackney HA* [1998] AC 232; [1997] 4 All ER 771; see, further, the detailed analysis of *Bolitho* in the chapter on medical negligence, see Chapter 7). The health professional should, however, also 'take reasonable steps to ascertain whether the guidance they are following is the current practice within the profession'.

Hospital reports and confidentiality

Reports prepared in contemplation of litigation are covered by legal privilege

Reports will usually be prepared by hospitals after an incident. If these are merely routine, then they are not *prima facie* covered by legal privilege. However, if such reports are prepared in contemplation of litigation, they might be covered by legal privilege.

Lee v South West Thames RHA *[1985] 2 All ER 385*

In this case, an infant suffered brain damage due to treatment in one of two hospitals. The first was under the control of Hillingdon AHA and the second was under the control of North East Thames AHA. Disclosure of reports compiled by the ambulance crew of SW Thames RHA for the purpose of Hillingdon obtaining legal advice was refused. The court held that they were covered by legal professional privilege.

The rationale for this decision seems to be that a defendant should be able to obtain evidence without having to disclose the findings of the other party.

Re HIV Haemophiliac Litigation *(1990) 140 NLJ 1349*

This was the case involving a large number of haemophiliacs who had received blood infected with HIV. They sought to bring an action against the Department of Health on the grounds that the Department was negligent in failing to ensure that there was enough blood available for donation in the UK, which necessitated having to obtain blood from the USA. The government refused disclosure of certain documents on the ground that the law did not permit such disclosure. These documents contained briefings for ministers as to whether a policy for self-sufficiency in blood products should be established and what measures should be required for such a policy, planning decisions relating to the Blood Products Laboratory and the decision whether and how to organise the Blood Transfusion Service.

The Court of Appeal held that discovery of the documents was necessary in order for the plaintiffs to make a thorough presentation of their case.

However, reports prepared as part of the organisation's normal administrative routine would not be so covered and, therefore, subject to disclosure.

Confidentiality, informants and public policy

Identity of informant can remain confidential for 'public policy' reasons

Another reason for maintaining confidentiality has been the notion of 'public policy'. The English courts have been prepared to exclude confidential personal information if its exclusion is based on public policy reasons for instance in issues of vital importance to the State (see *Duncan v Cammell Laird* [1942] AC 524). The courts have also used public-policy grounds to justify the exclusion of evidence relating to police sources of information in order to facilitate the investigation of crime. However, the issue of whether information could be kept confidential purely because it was confidential was examined by the House of Lords in *D v NSPCC*.

D v NSPCC *[1977] 1 All ER 589*

In this case, The National Society for the Prevention of Cruelty to Children, a national charity which has the power to bring care proceedings, received a complaint that a child was being maltreated. The society sent one of its inspectors to investigate the complaint and visited the mother at her home; the complaint was found to be false, as the child had been well treated. The mother of the child who, it had been alleged, had been abused by her, brought proceedings in negligence against the NSPCC, following the illness she had suffered (allegedly from shock) from the society inspector's visit. She alleged that the society had failed properly to investigate the complaint made against her and applied for an order that the NSPCC should disclose to her all the documents in its possession relating to the identity of the person who had made the false allegation against her. The society denied negligence and made an application to the court for an order that there should be no discovery of documents which might reveal the identity of the complainant/informant. They argued that, without guaranteed confidentiality of sources, individuals might be discouraged from coming forward. The case went to the House of Lords, who rejected the disclosure application and held that, in the interests of the proper functioning of a body such as the NSPCC, charged with the duty of protecting children against ill-treatment, they should have immunity from disclosure, analogous to the guaranteed anonymity of police informers. Several further points were made by the Law Lords:

(a) there was no public interest in safeguarding confidentiality *per se* in the law of evidence;

(b) however, confidential information may be protected if there is a sufficiently strong public interest in doing so. Lord Hailsham held that there was a public interest that the party able to bring care proceedings should receive information under a cloak of confidentiality. Whether it was the police or the local authority or the NSPCC, they were all entitled to claim protection for the confidentiality of their sources.

Lord Diplock's comment (p 218) is particularly instructive, when he said:

> The private promise of confidentiality must yield to the general public interest that in the administration of justice, truth will out unless by reason of the character of the information or the relationship of the recipient of the information to the informant a more important public interest is served by protecting the information or the identity of the informant in a court of law.

Hence, the case also confirmed the principle of disclosure in the interests of the administration of justice.

As McHale (1993) points out: 'The mere fact that information is confidential is no automatic justification for privilege protection.'

ACCESS TO MEDICAL RECORDS

The implementation of data protection legislation in early 2000 changed patients' statutory rights of access to their health records. This is by virtue of the Data Protection Act 1998. Here are the main points of the legal requirements on doctors as holders of health records (source: BMA Guidance):

- all manual and computerised health records about living people are accessible under the Data Protection Act 1998;
- access must be given equally to all records regardless of when they were made;
- competent patients may apply for access to their own records, or may authorise a third party, such as their lawyer, to do so on their behalf;
- parents have access to their child's records if it is in the child's best interests and not contrary to a competent child's wishes (a competent child would be a '*Gillick* competent' child (see Chapter 5);
- people appointed by a court to manage the affairs of mentally incapacitated adults may have access to information necessary to fulfil their function.

Exemptions

The main exemptions are that information must not be disclosed if it:

- is likely to cause serious physical or mental harm to the patient or another person; or
- relates to a third party who has not given consent for disclosure (where the third party is not a health professional who has cared for the patient).

Copies of the records

Patients are entitled to a copy of their records, that is, a photocopy of paper records or print out of computerised records.

Applications for access to records

There is no legal requirement that prevents doctors from informally showing patients their records or, bearing in mind duties of confidentiality, discussing relevant health issues with carers. The fees charged will depend on the type of record and whether the patient wants copies of the records or just to see them.

Access to records of deceased patients

The Data Protection Act 1998 only covers the records of living patients. If a person has a claim arising from the death of an individual, he or she has a right of access to information in the deceased's records necessary to fulfil that claim. These rights are set out in the Access to Health Records (Northern Ireland) Order 1993. The provisions and fees are slightly different from those in the Data Protection Act.

Supreme Court Act 1981

Sections 33 and 34 of the Supreme Court Act 1981 permit disclosure of documents, both prior to commencement of proceedings, and during the course of those legal proceedings. This is an exception to the principle of confidentiality. The provisions of the Act permit disclosure to the applicant's legal and medical advisers only. Given that doctors are now permitted to show patients their records on an informal basis, there appears to be no legal obstacle to prevent the advisers showing the applicant his medical notes.

CONFIDENTIALITY, HIV AND AIDS

Ethical perspectives

Although AIDS carries with it a damaging stigma, because of its implied sexual connotations and its serious association with drug addiction, it does not automatically follow that disclosure of HIV-seropositivity should be disclosed by a doctor to a third party. The delicate problem here is whether relaxation of the confidentiality rule would lead to a failure to seek advice and treatment and thus to the spread of the disease, or whether the imposition of absolute secrecy would deny others the opportunity to avoid the risk of exposure to infection. Should a sexual partner be informed of the risk if the patient declines to inform him or her? There is arguably a potentially dangerous situation if the person known to be affected is employed in an environment where he might expose others to the virus. The public dimension also enters the equation, so it is not just a case of balancing conflicting private interests. Since AIDS is not a notifiable disease, at least its exemption helps to maintain confidentiality. Arguably, mandatory notifiability would inhibit people from undergoing testing and, in any event, HIV is transmitted in very rare circumstances, if at all (see Mason and McCall Smith (1999)).

The GMC has advised doctors that patients should be persuaded of the need for their GPs to be informed of the diagnosis of HIV-seropositivity, but states that the patient's wishes should be respected if consent to disclosure is refused. The exception will be where the doctor believes that a failure to pass on this information exposes other health staff to serious risk. In any event, the doctor must be prepared to justify such action.

For clarity, the GMC Guidance is reproduced here.

GMC Guidance

The General Medical Council (GMC) has issued specific guidance on serious communicable diseases.

Informing other healthcare professionals

If you diagnose a patient as having a serious communicable disease, you should explain to the patient:

- the nature of the disease and its medical, social and occupational implications, as appropriate;
- ways of protecting others from infection;
- the importance of giving the professionals who will be providing care information which they need to know about the patient's disease or condition. In particular, you must make sure the patient understands that general practitioners cannot provide adequate clinical management and care without knowledge of their patients' conditions.

If patients still refuse to allow other healthcare workers to be informed, you must respect the patients' wishes except where you judge that failure to disclose the information would put a healthcare worker or other patient at serious risk of death or serious harm. Such situations may arise, for example, when dealing with violent patients with severe mental illness or disability. If you are in doubt about whether disclosure is appropriate, you should seek advice from an experienced colleague. You should inform patients before disclosing information. Such occasions are likely to arise rarely and you must be prepared to justify a decision to disclose information against a patient's wishes.

Disclosures to others

You must disclose information about serious communicable diseases in accordance with the law. For example, the appropriate authority must be informed where a notifiable disease is diagnosed. Where a communicable disease has contributed to the cause of death, this must be recorded on the death certificate. You should also pass information about serious communicable diseases to the relevant authorities for the purpose of disease control and surveillance.

As the GMC booklet makes clear, a patient's death does not, of itself, release a doctor from the obligation to maintain confidentiality. But, in some circumstances, disclosures can be justified because they protect other people from serious harm or because they are required by law.

Giving information to close contacts

You may disclose information about a patient, whether living or dead, in order to protect a person from risk of death or serious harm. For example, you may disclose information as to a known sexual contact of a patient with HIV where you have reason to think that the patient has not informed that person, and cannot be persuaded to do so. In such circumstances, you should tell the patient before you make the disclosure, and you must be prepared to justify a decision to disclose information.

You must not disclose information to others, for example, relatives, who have not been, and are not, at risk of infection.

This Guidance, which does *not* have the force of law, suggests that, if there is a serious and identifiable risk to a specific individual, and this might include a spouse or sexual partner, then disclosure appears to be permitted. The case of *Re C (A Minor) (Evidence: Confidential Information)* (1991) 7 BMLR 138 provides some authority for arguing that, in the case of the spouse or partner who is also a patient of the doctor, they may be given confidential information by the doctor without committing a breach of the duty (see above).

On the litigation front, it is perhaps arguable that a patient would have a *prima facie* cause of action against a doctor who warned his or her spouse or other sexual partner of their potential risk. Mason and McCall Smith (1999) believe it is unlikely that a court would award damages to such a plaintiff, and the argument that disclosure was necessary to protect others from a possibly fatal risk will certainly carry a great deal of weight, and may well counterbalance the two private interests.

As far as prisons are concerned, we have an environment which many might consider ideal for the spread of the condition and the consequences of disclosure of a positive status could be disastrous for the individual concerned. Consequently, while a policy of confidentiality is the norm, it is difficult, if not impossible, to maintain so long as positivity is seen to be synonymous with segregation, the provision of separate utensils and similar 'safety' measures, and there has, therefore, been some limited breaching of confidentiality in accordance with a 'need to know' policy on the part of staff (see Groves, T, 'Prison policies on HIV under review' (1991) 303 BMJ 1354).

However, the possibility of disclosure discourages voluntary testing and counselling and also prohibits effective public health measures. Apparently, according to Gore and Bird (1993), it has been shown that a guarantee of confidentiality has led to a marked increase in identified positive subjects (see Gore, S and Bird, A, 'No escape: HIV transmissions in jail' (1993) 307 BMJ 147).

INTERNATIONAL PROTECTION OF PRIVACY RIGHTS?

It is possible to argue that the principle of confidentiality would come under the broader notion of privacy that operates in jurisdictions like the USA. However, English law does not recognise any explicit right to privacy. Nevertheless, Art 8 of the European Convention on Human Rights (ECHR) has been interpreted by the European Court of Human Rights as affording protection to individual privacy (see *Malone v UK* Applications No 8691/79) (1984)). Article 8 of the ECHR provides:

1 Everyone has the right to respect for his private and family life, his home and correspondence.

2 There shall be no interference by a public authority with the exercise of this right except in accordance with the law and is necessary in a democratic society in the interests of national security, public safety or the economic well being of the country, for the prevention of disorder or crime, for the protection of health or morals, or for the protection of the rights and freedom of others.

On the comparative front, for the leading case on Art 8 and medical confidentiality, see *Z v Finland* (see Chapter 11).

From 2 October 2000, the European Convention became part of English law by virtue of the Human Rights Act 1998, which entered into force on that day.

COMMENTS ON CONFIDENTIALITY IN ENGLISH LAW AND UK MEDICAL PRACTICE

Confidentiality remains a cornerstone concept, without which the doctor-patient relationship could never function smoothly and effectively, with the trust reposed in the doctor by the patient being the cement that binds the relationship. Patients must feel that, in the general course of events, and in the overwhelming majority of cases, they may disclose the most private medical conditions without fear of disclosure or publicity, which would also ensure they had the best possible chance of curing or alleviating their medical problems. However, the emergence of AIDS as a stigmatising illness has made it extremely difficult for healthcare professionals to know what to do in the 'best interests' of their patients, particularly if that patient's partner is at risk. However, the law and the medical profession do recognise several exceptions to the duty of confidence and there is now a human rights dimension. Balancing the public interest in the preservation of confidentiality against the public duty to protect members of the public who may foreseeably be injured or harmed by non-disclosure of information relating to the patient remains a delicate and difficult exercise for doctors and other healthcare professionals.

SELECTIVE BIBLIOGRAPHY

BMA, *Confidentiality and Disclosure of Health Information*, 1999, BMA

Brazier, M, *Medicine, Patients and the Law*, 2nd edn, 1992, Penguin, Chapter 3

Brody, H, 'The physician/patient relationship', in Veatch, R (ed), *Medical Ethics*, 2nd edn, 1997, Chapter 4

Davies, M, *Textbook on Medical Law*, 1998, Blackstone, Chapter 2

Gillon, R, 'AIDS and medical confidentiality' (1987) 294 BMJ 1657

GMC, *Confidentiality: Guidance from the General Medical Council*, 1995, GMC

Gurry, F, *In Breach of Confidence*, 1984, Clarendon

Harris, J, *The Value of Life*, 1985, Routledge and Kegan Paul, Chapter 11

Havard, J, 'Medical confidence' (1985) 11 JME 8

Johnson, AG, *Pathways in Medical Ethics*, 1990, Edward Arnold, Chapter 9

Kennedy, I and Grubb, A, *Medical Law: Text with Materials*, 2nd edn, 1994, Butterworths, Chapter 9. See, also, 3rd edn, 2000

Kennedy, I and Grubb, A, *Principles of Medical Law*, 1998, OUP

Mason, JK and McCall Smith, RA, *Law and Medical Ethics*, 5th edn, 1999, Butterworths, Chapter 8

McHale, JV, 'Doctors with AIDS: dilemmas of confidentiality' (1988) 4 Professional Negligence 76

McHale, JV, *Medical Confidentiality and Legal Privilege*, 1993, Routledge

McConnell, T, 'Confidentiality and the law' (1994) 20 JME 47

Jones, M, 'Medical confidentiality and the public interest' (1990) 6 Professional Negligence 16

Scott, R, 'Introduction', in Clarke, L (ed), *Confidentiality and the Law*, 1990, LLP

Stauch, M and Wheat, K with Tingle, J, *Sourcebook on Medical Law*, 1998, Cavendish Publishing, Chapter 5

Thompson, 'The nature of confidentiality' (1979) 5 JME 57

Wacks, R, 'Breach of confidence and the protection of privacy' (1977) 127 NLJ 328

CHAPTER 3

ABORTION

Abortion raises the most fundamental issue of all: the nature of life and death.
[Edwin Kenyon, *The Dilemma of Abortion*, 1986, Faber & Faber.]

INTRODUCTION

The view that 'abortion or pregnancy termination is one of the most controversial moral, social and legal issues in contemporary Western society', as a writer has expressed in an article written in the early 1990s, is still accurate as we enter the 21st century. Abortion transcends moral, political, religious, legal, medical and psychological boundaries. It is, moreover, not a problem confined to Western societies and, to the parties involved, may seem, at the time, the most controversial and problematic situation that a woman may face. It has been practised, however, to a lesser or greater extent, in all societies since prehistoric times (see Lane Committee, *Report on the Working of the Abortion Act*, Cmd 5579, 1974, HMSO, Appendix to Section A). Abortion has been called 'the most intractable and most prominent of family issues' by Gilbert Steiner (see Steiner (1981), p 51). It has certainly been the subject of vigorous debate and controversy in countries like the USA and, far less so, in Britain. Indeed, it remains a subject of heated debate and not inconsiderable moral outrage in the USA where the latest incidents at abortion clinics and centres demonstrate the continuing depth of feeling and passion that this subject arouses in people, such as the so called pro-life groups. As Linda Clarke has put it (Clarke (1990), p 155):

> Abortion continues to arouse passionate feelings and disagreements between those who believe that the fetus should be accorded the status of a human being (and thus its destruction be prohibited by law) and those who believe that the individual woman should have the choice to terminate her pregnancy if she chooses, and that she should be able to terminate her pregnancy if she chooses, and that she should be able to do so freely and legally up to term.

The clear evidence that the law has been used, and continues to be used, is that the number of terminations carried out in England and Wales reached a peak in 1990 when almost 187,000 abortions were performed. The comparable figure for Scotland was 11,978, amounting to 10.9 for every 1,000 women. We shall conduct a global overview of the abortion laws in various countries in Part II of this book (see Chapter 13). However, this chapter looks briefly at the history of abortion law, especially in England, examines its many ramifications and looks at the leading cases that continue to make it a much-vexed question. We also survey the Irish position, looking at both Northern Ireland and the Irish Republic, and their stance on abortion. At the outset, we begin by listing some of the fundamental philosophical and ethical issues posed by abortion.

ETHICAL AND PHILOSOPHICAL PRINCIPLES

The main issues that have surrounded abortion, on which there has been considerable debate and a fairly voluminous literature are: whether the fetus is a 'person' (if so, at which point in the pregnancy?), whether it has a right to life and legally protected interests, whether a woman has a right to decide what happens in and to her body, whether there is some ethical link between abortion and infanticide, and whether there is any point after conception where it is possible to draw the line beyond which killing is not permissible. Philosophical discussions of the ethics of abortion have a pedigree traceable as least as far back as Aristotle. Over the years, various stages in human development have been claimed as a threshold, after which an embryo is supposed to have a protected status. To name some of these: conception, implantation, the moment when the fetus becomes (judging from its form) recognisably human and 'ensoulment' or animation takes place, quickening, 57 days from conception if one follows the brain life criteria, the capacity to experience pain, viability, the moment of actual consciousness or self-consciousness, the potential to become conscious and self-conscious, and finally, birth itself (see Schlegel (1997), p 56).

Professor Dworkin says that the abortion debate should be about the sacredness of human life rather than about personhood or rights. He argues that the deliberate extinction of human life at any stage is an offence against the sanctity of individual life, 'a kind of cosmic shame' and 'intrinsically a bad thing'. Basically, Dworkin equates sacred with 'inviolable'.

In more specific and practical terms, abortion may involve a consideration of whether the mother or father has the ultimate right to decide to terminate to terminate a pregnancy, whether the fetus itself has any 'right' to be born, and determining the criterion for deciding when a fetus is capable of being born alive within the meaning of the law. In this writer's view, abortion is not a purely medical issue, but one that must also be evaluated by the legal and ethical rules of any given society. Nevertheless, it is the state of medical knowledge that informs and sometimes determines the legal regulation of cases involving an abortion.

Moral stances on abortion

The British Medical Association (BMA) has published a detailed guide to the moral, ethical and legal perspectives on abortion (see *The Law and Ethics of Abortion: BMA Views*, March 1997, rev December 1999). Key extracts from this are reproduced in the following section.

According to the BMA guide, there are at least three stances that people have taken of abortion: (a) pro-abortion; (b) anti-abortion; and (c) that abortion is acceptable in some circumstances.

Arguments used in support of abortion

(1) Abortion is not wrong in itself and need not involve undesirable consequences.

This argument does not recognise fetal rights or that the fetus is a person.

(2) According to some, abortion is a matter of a woman's right to exercise control over her own body. Moralists who judge actions by their consequences alone could argue that abortion is equivalent to a deliberate failure to conceive a child and, since contraception is widely available, abortion should be too. Some think that even if the fetus is a person, its rights are very limited and do not weigh significantly against the interests of people who have already been born, such as parents or existing children of the family. The interests of society at large might outweigh any right accorded to the fetus in some circumstances, such as if, for example, overpopulation or famine threatened that society. In such cases, abortion might be seen as moving from a neutral act to one which should be encouraged.

(3) The overriding principle, some argue, is that it is the woman's right to choose what happens to her body. This use of the language of 'choice' conveys approval regardless of the type of pressures the individual faces and any constraints on her freedom to make a genuine choice.

Arguments against abortion

(1) Abortion is wrong in any circumstances because it fails to recognise the rights of the fetus or because it challenges the notion of the sanctity of all human life.

(2) Permitting abortion diminishes the respect society feels for other vulnerable humans, possibly leading to their involuntary euthanasia.

(3) Abortion is seen as killing in the same sense as the murder of any other person because an embryo, from the moment of conception, is a human being with full moral status. Those taking this view cannot accept that women should be allowed to obtain abortion without legal repercussions,

however difficult the lives of those women or their existing families are made as a result.

Such views may be based on religious or moral convictions that each human life has unassailable intrinsic value, which is not diminished by any impairment or suffering that may be involved for the individual living that life. It is also argued that abortion treats humans merely as a means to an end, in that abortion can be seen as a discarding of a fetus in which the pregnant woman no longer has any interest. Many worry that the availability of abortion on grounds of fetal abnormality encourages prejudice towards any person with a handicap and insidiously creates the impression that the only valuable people are those who conform to some ill defined stereotype of 'normality'.

Some people who oppose abortion in general concede that it may be justifiable in very exceptional cases where it is the result of rape or the consequence of exploitation of a young girl or mentally incompetent woman. Risk to the mother's life may be another justifiable exception, but only where abortion is the only option. It would thus not be seen as justifiable to abort a fetus if the life of both fetus and mother could be saved by any other solution.

Arguments used to support abortion in certain circumstances

Many people argue that abortion may be justified in a greater number of circumstances than those conceded by anti-abortionists, but that it would be undesirable to allow abortion on demand. To do so might incur undesirable effects, such as encouraging irresponsible attitudes to contraception. It could also lead to a devaluation of the lives of viable fetuses and trivialise the potential psychological effects of abortion on women and on health professionals.

These types of arguments are based on the premise that the embryo starts off without rights, although having a special status from conception in view of its potential for development, and that it acquires rights and status throughout its development. The notion of developing fetal rights and practical factors, such as the possible distress to the pregnant woman, nurses, doctors or other children in the family, gives rise to the view that early abortion is more acceptable than late abortion.

Some people support this position on pragmatic grounds, believing that abortions will always be sought by women who are desperate and that it is better for society to provide abortion services which are safe and which can be monitored and regulated, rather than allow 'backstreet' practices.

The BMA view on abortion

In the 1970s and 1980s, the BMA approved policy statements supporting the 1967 Abortion Act as a 'practical and humane piece of legislation' and calling for its expansion to Northern Ireland. The BMA does not consider abortion to be unethical, but as with any act having profound moral implications, the justifications must be commensurate with the consequences. The BMA's advice to its members is to act within the boundaries of the law and of their own conscience. Patients are, however, entitled to receive objective medical advice regardless of their doctor's personal views for or against abortion. Furthermore, a doctor could be sued for damages if, because of a failure to refer, a delay is caused which results in the woman being unable to obtain a termination.

Fetal pain

The BMA Guidance states that whether, and at what stage, a fetus feels pain has been a matter of much recent debate and past practice has been partly influenced by Department of Health advice. Interpretation of the evidence on fetal pain is conflicting with some arguing that the fetus has the potential to feel pain at 10 weeks' gestation, others arguing that it is unlikely to feel pain before 26 weeks' gestation and still others arguing for some unspecified gestational period in between.

There is clearly a need for further research to provide more conclusive evidence about the experiences and sensations of the fetus *in utero*. In the meantime, the BMA recommends that, when carrying out any surgical procedures (whether an abortion or a therapeutic intervention) on the fetus *in utero*, due consideration must be given to appropriate measures for minimising the risk of pain. This should include an assessment of the most recent evidence available. Even if there is no incontrovertible evidence that fetuses feel pain, the use of pain relief, when carrying out invasive procedures, may help to relieve the anxiety of the parents and of health professionals.

HISTORICAL BACKGROUND

The Roman Catholic Church has traditionally opposed abortion, but its view of what constitutes abortion has changed over time. Pence (1990) claims that, in the 12th century, abortions began to be distinguished from homicides by differentiating 'unformed' from 'formed' fetuses. Thomas Aquinas wrote that God 'ensouled' the latter (that is, when the soul entered the fetus) if male, at 40 days, and if female, at 80 days. This became known as the point of 'quickening' – when the woman first feels the stirring of the fetus inside her.

Significantly, it was claimed that killing early male, but not female, embryos was, therefore, sinful and killing an embryo before 40 days was 'neither abortion nor murder' (see Pence (1990), p 115). So sexism was in evidence even (or especially) then! B Dickens, in *Abortion and the Law* (1966, McGibbon & K) claims that, in the 13th century, ecclesiastical authorities were debating whether counselling an abortion or providing poison or using violence on the pregnant woman would be homicide. In the mid-19th century, the Popes denounced abortions in strongly absolutist terms and, during this period, religion felt very threatened by science. One response from Pope Pius IX was to declare that his edicts and those of other Popes were 'infallible'; he also encouraged the worship of the Virgin Mary and, *inter alia*, emphasised miracles, such as the well known 'visions' at Fatima (see Johnson (1983)). It was around this time, when medical biology revealed the small beginnings of human life, that the Catholic view was promulgated that personhood begins at conception.

During 1,300 years of Christian rule, abortion was rarely conceptualised as murder, even after the time the fetus 'quickened', or kicked in the mother's womb. During those centuries, personhood was not considered to begin at conception, but at some later time, such as ensoulment, quickening, animation or viability. Hence, the view among some Christians that personhood begins at conception is only about 150 years old. Exceptions were made for ectopic pregnancies and for cancerous uteruses (where uterus and fetus had to be removed together). In both cases, the 'doctrine of double effect' was used to allow physicians to save the mother 'because it was said that an action having two effects, one good and the other harmful, was morally permissible if (a) the action was good in itself or not evil; (b) if the good followed as immediately from the cause as the evil effect; (c) only the good effect was intended and (d) there was a proportionately grave cause for performing the action as for allowing the evil effect' (Pence (1990), pp 115–16).

In 17th century European law, aborting a quickened fetus was not indictable. The English 1803 Act (Lord Ellenborough's Act) made abortion a felony punishable by death. America followed the English common law from the 17th to the 19th centuries, making abortion before quickening only a misdemeanour, or legal for therapeutic reasons if recommended by two physicians. It was only after the Civil War in America that most States made abortion illegal, with stiff penalties and firm cut off points.

The doctrine of double effect became well known in the early part of the 20th century whenever physicians confronted problems with abortions. The maternal v fetal conflicts required impossibly difficult decisions to be made as to whose life to save. The doctrine seemed to require that a physician must intend only the repair of the uterus, and not the death of the fetus.

ABORTION LAW IN THE UK

England

History of abortion in England

In the view of one writer, 'English law has stumbled, through a series of criminalising and decriminalising provisions, into a period of liberalised abortion' (Terry (1990), p 76). The same writer says that, in the context of abortion and the legal protection afforded to the fetus, English law is 'dominated by unanswered questions' and 'difficult decision making with regard to abortion has been abdicated to the medical profession'. According to Keown, 'whether the common law prohibited the destruction of unborn life has been, and remains, a controversial question' (see Keown (1988), p 3).

In the period before the first statutory prohibition of the offence, there is reasonably strong evidence that abortion was already punishable in the royal courts, but it was largely dealt with by the ecclesiastical courts. However, the common law gradually seemed to move to a position where it distinguished between abortion before and after 'quickening'. This position was reflected in 1803, when Lord Ellenborough's Act of 1803 made abortion a crime punishable by death, but continued to use quickening as the defining moment, providing for lesser penalties up to this point. So 'quickening' remained significant.

However, the 1803 Act also made those acts a felony even for women who had not reached the stage of 'quickening' or 'animation'. In those cases, the death penalty was replaced by either transportation (for up to 14 years) or the offender was 'fined, imprisoned, set in and upon the Pillor [or] privately whipped' (Act of 1803 (43 Geo III c 58).

The 1803 Act was substantially re-enacted in the 1928 Act, whereby in cases where the child had not quickened, transportation was retained, but imprisonment reduced to a maximum of three years. Flogging was restricted to males.

The next development was particularly significant – the passing of an 1837 Act which abolished the quickening distinction and reduced the penalties to transportation or up to three years' punishment.

This Act was, in turn, replaced by the Offences Against the Person Act (OAPA) 1861, in which the fundamental law is still contained, although it has to be read with the Abortion Act 1967 (as amended in 1990) and the Infant Life (Preservation) Act 1929.

Under the OAPA 1861, s 58 makes it an offence to procure or attempt to procure a miscarriage by a third party, self-induced miscarriage, or using an instrument to do so. The word 'abortion' only appears in the marginal notes to the sections. The OAPA was passed to protect the mother from any self-help she might undertake since termination of pregnancy was far more hazardous in the mid-1860s than at present.

The Infant Life (Preservation) Act 1929 stipulated that if a fetus is 'capable of being born alive' then it cannot be killed in the mother's womb, that is, *in utero*. This Act therefore created the offence of child destruction – the killing of a child 'capable of being born alive' before it was capable of having an existence independent of its mother.

Section 1 of the 1929 Act states:

> 1(1) Subject as hereinafter in this section provided, any person who, with the intent to destroy the life of a child capable of being born alive, by a wilful act causes a child to die before it has an existence independent of its mother, shall be guilty of a felony ...

One criterion of determining whether a child is capable of being born alive is where the baby can breathe for a few hours through its lungs unaided, without deriving any of its living or power of living through the connection to its mother; having independent pulmonary ability, which was confirmed in *C v S* (1987) (see below, p 93). The exception is that no person should be convicted of this offence if he acted in good faith for the purpose only of preserving the life of the mother. This 1929 Act was enacted to deal with the gap left by OAPA. The 1929 Act also introduced the legal presumption that a fetus which had achieved 28 weeks' gestation was capable of being born alive. As Mason stresses, 'it did not imply the converse – that is, that a fetus of less than 28 weeks' gestation was *not* capable of being born alive' (Mason (1990), p 46). A second purpose of the Act was to legalise the operation of craniotomy – the deliberate crushing of the fetal skull in the mother's pelvis, inevitably causing fetal death. This was widely practised to save the life of the pregnant woman before Caesarean section became commonplace.

At common law, there was already some protection offered to doctors, as illustrated in the seminal case of *R v Bourne* [1939] 1 KB 687, where it was declared that 'no person ought to be convicted under s 58 of the OAPA unless the jury are satisfied that the act was not done in good faith for the purpose only of preserving the life of the mother'. This case was the impetus to reform the law.

R v Bourne *[1939] 3 All ER 615*

The surgeon, a man of impeccable reputation within his profession, notified the authorities that he intended terminating the pregnancy of a girl of 15, who had been raped by a group of soldiers under particularly unpleasant and violent circumstances. The girl's parents had given their consent to the operation. He was charged under s 58 of the OAPA 1861. He defended himself on grounds of good medical practice, and that the words 'unlawfully', as found in the OAPA 1861, did not apply to therapeutic abortions, and asserted that the girl's mental and physical health might have suffered had the pregnancy continued.

Macnaghten J linked the 1861 and 1929 statutes and ruled that the burden rested on the Crown to satisfy the jury that the defendant did not procure the miscarriage of the girl for the purpose of preserving her life. He effectively chose to apply the 1929 Act to any termination in good faith by a registered medical practitioner, observing that:

> ... the word 'unlawfully' [in s 58 of the 1961 Act] is not a meaningless word. I think it imports the meaning expressed by the proviso in s 1(1) of the Infant Life (Preservation) Act 1929 and that s 58 of the Offences Against the Person Act 1861 must be read as if the words making it an offence to use an instrument with intent to procure a miscarriage were qualified by a similar proviso. In this case, therefore, my direction to you in law is this – that the burden rests on the Crown to satisfy you beyond reasonable doubt that the defendant did not procure the miscarriage of the girl in good faith for the purpose only of preserving her life.

In his summing up, the judge addressed the meaning of 'preserving the life of the mother', and told the jury that they should take a broad view of this phrase. He further instructed them:

> [The law] permits the termination of pregnancy for the purpose of preserving the life of the mother ... those words ought to be construed in a reasonable sense, and, if the doctor is of opinion ... that the probable consequence of the pregnancy will be to make a woman a physical or mental wreck, the jury are entitled to take the view that the doctor ... is operating for the purpose of preserving the life of the mother.

Macnaghten J accepted the defendant's defence and, in view of the circumstances in *Bourne*, it is not surprising that the defendant was acquitted.

In 1948, in *R v Bergmann and Ferguson* [1948] 1 Brit Med J 1008, the *Bourne* approach was further clarified. The judge there held that it was not relevant whether Dr Ferguson (the psychiatrist who had certified the need for termination) held a correct opinion as to the existence of such grounds for termination, as long as it was *honestly* held. This therapeutic abortion approach was further strengthened in *R v Newton and Stungo* [1958] Crim Law 469, where the doctor's defence was that the mental condition of his patient had necessitated termination. The defendant had not further treated or supervised the patient after the termination and she died of renal failure as a result. Although the defendant was convicted, Ashworth J's instruction (p 1008) is certainly worth recording:

> Use of an instrument is unlawful unless the use is made in good faith for the purpose of preserving the life or health of the woman. When I say health I mean not only her physical health but also her mental health. But I must

emphasise that the burden of proof that it was not used in good faith is on the Crown.

Hence, as long as the doctor acted in good faith, therapeutic abortion was legal. Keown (1988) points out that even before *Bourne*, doctors were performing therapeutic abortions according to criteria established by themselves (such as on the ground of mental disorder, to prevent transmission of hereditary disease or to avert mental breakdown, to preserve the mother's life or to defuse the threat of suicide). Thus, provided these doctors abided by professional ethics, there was little danger of prosecution. It should be remembered that *Bourne* was no exception to this, since he actively encouraged his prosecution (see Keown (1988), pp 70–78).

Terry (1987) therefore remarks that:

> ... from relatively early times, the English law of abortion has displayed two noteworthy characteristics: (i) it has never dealt with the question whether there are any abortion 'rights'. Rather, the English position has been that abortions (although that specific term seldom has been used) are generally illegal, but criminal sanctions will not lie against certain people in certain situations; and (ii) the exceptions from criminal sanction that have been created depend, *de lege*, upon medical criteria and involve the application of medical discretion.

Indeed, Terry argues that, even in its advanced decriminalised state, the 1967 Act, despite being replete with detailed criteria and regulatory standards, 'permits a physician considerable latitude when he is of the opinion, formed in good faith, that the termination is immediately necessary to save the life or to prevent grave permanent injury'. He observes that an important side effect of this 'medicalisation of abortion law is that it has tended to keep abortion issues out of the English courts' (Terry (1987), p 79).

The modern English abortion law – the liberalising of abortion?

According to Mason (1990), 'the legal and medical professions in the UK co-existed in a state of watchful neutrality following the *Bourne* decision'. Mason surmises: 'There is no doubt that large numbers of therapeutic abortions were performed but these were undertaken, in the main, at specialised centres and by relatively courageous staff.' In the 15 years preceding the Abortion Act 1967, there were five parliamentary initiatives aimed at reform and, indeed, shortly after the *Bourne* decision in 1939, a government committee, the Birkett Committee, was set up to examine the abortion issue. The committee basically proposed a codification of Macnaghten J's summing up in *Bourne*, but this was effectively ignored for nearly 30 years until 27 April 1968 when the Abortion Act 1967 came into force at last. As Sheldon (1994) points out, 'The combination of a climate of social reform with very restrictive legislation (and wide variations in medical interpretation of it) formed the backdrop to the introduction of the 1967 Abortion Act' (Sheldon (1994), p 10).

The factors which appeared to contribute to the 1967 abortion reform 'whose time had come' (as described by Madeleine Simms of the Abortion Law Reform Association) are many and various. They include, as discussed by Sheldon (1994):

(a) strong campaigning by women's groups;

(b) pressure exerted by medical groups;

(c) concern at the widespread flouting of the law.

However, there is no doubt that the 1967 Act is a product of the *Zeitgeist* of the 1960s. Sheldon calls it 'permissive', not least because it 'decreased repressive criminal controls and facilitated a greater degree of individual (especially female) autonomy in sexual and reproductive matters' (Sheldon (1994), p 2). However, Sheldon goes on to remind us that this was the time when the Labour Party, voted into power in 1964 and having obtained a larger majority in 1966, embarked on a substantial programme of social reform. This included:

- the voting age was lowered to 18 (in 1969);
- divorce was made easier (in 1969 – through the Law Reform Act 1969);
- access to contraception was facilitated;
- the death penalty was largely abolished (1965–69);
- there was a more liberal attitude taken towards censorship of plays (1968);
- homosexuality was decriminalised, albeit in very restricted circumstances (1967).

Christine Davies (in *Permissive Britain: Social Change in the Sixties and Seventies*, 1975, Pitman) assesses such measures as indicating a new and more permissive Britain. Abortion reform was a central piece of these social reform measures. Margaret Brazier (1992) recounts how reports in the press of bizarre stories of attempted abortions by girls as young as 13, who were prosecuted in 1927 for attempting to induce an abortion on themselves by taking laxative tablets and sitting in a hot bath, built up public pressure and exposed the uncertainty surrounding the extent of the doctor's position if he attempted to save the mother's life in preference to the unborn child. Illegal abortion flourished and several thousand women were admitted to hospital for treatment after 'backstreet' abortions. In her opinion, the 1967 Act was introduced 'to bring uniformity into the law, to clarify the law for the doctors, and to stem the misery and injury resulting from unhygienic, risky illegal abortions' (Brazier (1992), p 290).

The current position provides for the abortion decision to be made by the pregnant woman but, as a matter of law, her decision is subject to professional medical discretion and no 'right' to abortion is recognised.

A jurisdictional point on abortion laws in the UK

It is particularly pertinent in a book of this nature to be clear that, while the UK consists of Great Britain and Northern Ireland, the Abortion Act 1967 does not apply to Northern Ireland. Furthermore, Scotland has its own legal system which differs in form and substance and, indeed, in its legal foundations, from that of England and Wales. Neither the OAPA 1861 nor the Infant Life (Preservation) Act 1929 applied to Scotland and, in the Scottish jurisdiction, many statutes are of very little importance because of the common law in Scotland. However, as a result of the implementation of s 37 of the Human Fertilisation and Embryology Act (HFEA) 1990, the law and practice of abortion in Scotland is now the same as in England.

The Abortion Act 1967 (as amended by the HFEA 1990)

The Abortion Act 1967 was amended by the HFEA 1990 and the amended 1967 Act now provides that no offence will be committed where a pregnancy is terminated by a registered medical practitioner in circumstances where two such practitioners have formed an opinion in good faith that one of the following conditions is in existence:

(a) that the pregnancy has not exceeded 24 weeks and that continuance would involve risk, greater than if the pregnancy were terminated, of injury to the physical or mental health of the pregnant woman or any existing children of her family – s 1(1)(a);

(b) that the termination is deemed to be necessary to prevent grave permanent injury to the physical or mental health of the pregnant woman – s 1(1)(b);

(c) that continuance of the pregnancy would involve risk to the life of the woman, greater than if the pregnancy were terminated – s 1(1)(c);

(d) that there is a substantial risk that the child if born would suffer from such severe physical or mental abnormalities as to be seriously handicapped – s 1(1)(d).

The fourth ground has provoked criticism from various quarters in Britain.

Section 5(1) of the 1967 Act – before its amendment by the 1990 Act – provided:

> 5(1) Nothing in this Act shall affect the provisions of the Infant Life (Preservation) Act 1929 (protecting the life of a viable fetus).

A further amendment made to extend lawful termination was subsequently brought about by s 37(4) of the 1990 Act, which amends s 5(1) of the 1967 Act to read:

> No offence under the Infant Life (Preservation) Act 1929 shall be committed by a registered medical practitioner who terminates a pregnancy in accordance with the provisions of this Act.

Hence, this uncouples carrying out an abortion from the possible commission of the offence of child destruction under the 1929 Act, so that a registered medical practitioner may carry out an abortion within the parameters of the 1967 Act (as amended) without worrying about a possible breach of the 1929 Act.

Conscientious objection

Section 4(1) of the 1967 Act provides that '... no person shall be under any duty, whether by contract or by any statutory or other legal requirement, to participate in any treatment authorised by this Act to which he has a conscientious objection'.

Section 4(2) states that 'Nothing in sub-s (1) of this section shall affect any duty to participate in treatment which is necessary to save the life or to prevent grave permanent injury to the physical or mental health of a pregnant woman'.

Sub-section (2) is clearly aimed at preventing a doctor from relying on s 4(1) if his services are required in an emergency situation. But the question was: who could rely on it, and how far could the phrase 'participate in any treatment' extend to persons who were not directly involved in performing or 'assisting' in the abortion?

This provision was examined and tested in the *Janaway* case, which went all the way to the House of Lords.

Janaway v Salford AHA [1989] AC 537

The plaintiff, who was a Roman Catholic, lost her job working as a secretary/receptionist for the defendant health authority after refusing to type a letter of referral in respect of an abortion patient. She brought an action for unfair dismissal on the ground that her refusal was protected under s 4(1) of the Abortion Act 1967.

The key issue was what was the true construction of the words in s 4(1) on the meaning of 'participate in any treatment authorised by this Act'.

The Court of Appeal (by a majority) accepted the main thrust of the appellant's argument to the effect that s 1(1) and s 4(1) are co-extensive, but decided against her on the ground that her intention in typing a letter of referral would not be to assist in procuring an abortion, but merely to carry out the obligations of her employment. In their view, the typing of such a letter by the applicant would not be a criminal offence in the absence of s 1(1). However, both Nolan and Balcombe LJJ preferred to accept the health authority's argument that the word 'participate' in s 4(1) did not import the whole concept of principal and accessory residing in the criminal law, but referred to taking part in treatment administered in a hospital in accordance with s 1(3) for the purpose of terminating a pregnancy.

The case went to the House of Lords, who agreed with Nolan and Balcombe LJJ's points of view. In essence, they gave 'participate in any treatment' its ordinary meaning, which was participation in the medical process of abortion, and the plaintiff was not involved in this process.

Consent to abortion: Re C

As far as consent to an abortion by the competent adult is concerned, the three stage requirements in *Re C* (1993) (see *Re C (Adult: Refusal of Treatment)* (1993) 15 BNLR 77; [1994] 1 All ER 819), as laid down by Thorpe J, apply. Thus, the patient (a) has to take in and retain treatment information; (b) to believe it, and (c) to be able to weigh that information, balancing risks and needs.

Abortion by minors and 'rights' to abort

In the UK, a girl aged between 16 and 18 *prima facie* has the right to consent to medical treatment under s 8(1) of the Family Law Reform Act 1969 or under the common law in Scotland. Hence, no question of parental consent arises for this age group. However, an issue that could arise with regard to a girl aged 16 but under 18 is where there might be some question as to her incapacity.

The DHSS memorandum in 1980

For girls under 16, on the question of whether such a girl had the right to seek an abortion without her parents giving their consent beforehand, the saga began in 1980 when the Department of Health issued a revised memorandum of guidance with regard to the provision of contraceptive substances and appliances to those under 16. There had already been public concern voiced regarding the earlier 1974 version. The 1980 circular stated, *inter alia*:

> The Department would ... hope that in any case where a doctor or other professional worker is approached by a person under the age of 16 for advice on these matters, the doctor, or other professional, will always seek to persuade the child to involve the parent or guardian (or other person *in loco parentis*) at the earliest stage of consultation, and will proceed from the assumption that it would be most unusual to provide advice about contraception without parental consent ...
>
> The Department realises that, in ... exceptional cases, the nature of any counselling must be a matter for the doctor or other professional worker concerned and that the decision whether or not to prescribe contraception must be for the clinical judgment of the doctor.

The Gillick *case*

In *Gillick*, a Roman Catholic mother of five daughters (who were under 16 years old) sought a declaration to the effect that this circular was unlawful and that no contraceptive or abortion services should be supplied by the NHS to her daughters without her consent. Mrs Gillick lost her case in the first instance court, won it by a unanimous decision in the Court of Appeal and then lost it on a majority judgment in the House of Lords (3:2) where the House of Lords held that a girl under 16 did not, for that reason alone, lack legal capacity to consent to medical advice and treatment relating to contraception. It was a question of fact in any given case whether such a person had the capacity to consent. Thus, a doctor who gave contraceptive advice and treatment within the framework of the Guidance (on which Lord Fraser based his set of requirements – see Chapter 5), intending to act in the best interests of the child, would not commit a criminal offence (for a detailed discussion of the judgments in the *Gillick* case at the time of the judgments, see de Cruz (1987) and see, also, Chapter 5).

Re P *(1982) 80 LGR 301*

In the only relevant reported British case, *Re P (A Minor)* (1982) 80 LGR 301, a 13 year old girl, who had been convicted of theft in 1979, had been committed to the care of the local authority. The following year, she gave birth to a child and they were put into a 'mother and child unit'. The court spoke of her in complimentary terms, but said that 'the tragedy of it is that, having put her criminal record behind her, she seems unable to stop getting pregnant, and cannot thereby put her current life into proper perspective'. When she was 15 years and two months old, in 1981, she became pregnant again. She was still under age and her father, for religious and moral reasons, refused consent to an abortion, and the girl disagreed with this decision.

The court held that, even though the local authority was *in loco parentis* under the current statute, it was appropriate in a case like this to involve the court through wardship proceedings. The court authorised termination and the fitting of an internal contraceptive, which the girl had also requested.

Comment

This case indicates that the courts are still prepared to override a girl's parents if they believe that the ultimate decision will be in her best interests. In any event, at that time, English authority was clear that parental wishes would usually be considered, but were not determinative of any issue before the court. Around this time, cases dealing with severely handicapped babies had been decided by the English courts, and the Court of Appeal decision in *Re B*

(1981), dealing with a Down's syndrome baby, is indicative of the English court's approach.

The GMC Guidance

The latest GMC Guidance stresses that, if a doctor considers that a patient is incapable of giving consent because of immaturity, he or she may disclose relevant information to an appropriate person or authority if it is essential to do so in the patient's medical interests. This is subject to that patient being told of the intention to disclose. The Guidance follows Lord Fraser's guidelines in emphasising that the judgment of whether the patient is capable of giving or withholding consent to treatment or disclosure must be based on an assessment of their ability to appreciate what the treatment or advice being sought may involve, and not solely on their age (GMC Guidance, *Confidentiality*, 1995).

Spousal consent

The Abortion Act 1967 (the 1967 Act) is silent on the question of spousal or paternal consent, although a written spousal consent provision was the subject of a defeated amendment to the 1967 Act while it was in committee (see Lyon and Bennett (1979)). However, the question was resolved in the *Paton* case (1979), which is discussed below.

Preventing an abortion

The 1967 Act does not say anything about who, if anyone, has a right of veto over an intended abortion. For instance, can the father of the unborn child prevent an abortion?

***Paton v British Pregnancy Advisory Service* [1979] QB 276**

In this case, the plaintiff sought an injunction restraining his wife from having an abortion under the 1967 Act. The wife had obtained the required certificates from two doctors that she satisfied one of the statutory grounds, but the plaintiff alleged that she was acting in bad faith. As a starting point, the plaintiff needed to establish that he had *locus standi* to bring his action, either in his own right or as 'next friend' of the fetus. In the High Court, the late Sir George Baker, President of the Family Division, said: 'The husband ... has no legal right enforceable at law or in equity to stop his wife from having this abortion or to stop the doctors from carrying out the abortion.'

The plaintiff subsequently lost his case before the European Commission on Human Rights, when he argued that his right to family life under Art 8 of the European Convention on Human Rights had been infringed. The Commission pointed out that Art 8(2) limits that right in so far as necessary to protect the rights of another person – the pregnant woman (on the question of the status of the fetus, see other comments in *Paton* and *Re F (In Utero)* (below, p 96)).

C v S [1988] QB 135

The background facts to the case are sketchy. It appears that the plaintiff, a 23 year old Oxford male postgraduate who was single, and the woman, a 21 year old Oxford student, also single, met in Oxford in 1986, and sex took place shortly after their relationship began. She became pregnant, and the couple's relationship eventually deteriorated. A doctor prescribed a pill to her, which was believed to have terminated her pregnancy, but which did not. She also took anti-depressant drugs and had two X-rays for a chest infection, one of which was without a protective shield. The fact that she was still pregnant became apparent only after she had a body scan. The woman then obtained medical approval to have an abortion. Two doctors signed the necessary certificate as required by the terms of the Abortion Regulations 1968 SI 1968/390) and the termination was arranged for 23 February 1987.

The plaintiff sought, as first plaintiff, on his own behalf and as the next friend and father of the second plaintiff, a fetus which was 18 to 21 weeks *en ventre sa mere*, an injunction to restrain the defendant from terminating the pregnancy. At the same time, the plaintiff sought an injunction to restrain the health authority from carrying out the abortion, even though all the relevant conditions of the Abortion Act 1967 had been fulfilled.

The application for an injunction was based on the ground that the fetus was 'a child capable of being born alive' within the meaning of s 1(1) of the Infant Life (Preservation) Act 1929 (the 1929 Act), as specifically preserved by s 5(1) of the Abortion Act 1967. The relevant provisions, as we have seen, created the criminal offence of child destruction. Hence, the plaintiff was seeking to enforce the criminal law, in order to prevent the abortion from being carried out. Case law has also suggested that no distinction should be drawn between a threat to life, and a threat to health. This appears to be the effect of *R v Bourne* (1938), discussed above.

The key issues

The central issue was whether the fetus, which was between 18 and 21 weeks *en ventre sa mere*, was 'capable of being born alive' within the terms of the 1929 Act. Two further issues were: (a) whether the father had the right to be heard on the application of this nature; and (b) whether a fetus was a legal person capable of suing its mother, through its father as next friend, in order to prevent its mother from terminating her pregnancy.

The High Court hearing

Heilbron J, sitting in the Queen's Bench Division of the High Court, heard the case in private, and accepted medical evidence as to the stage of development the fetus would normally be expected to have reached. The expert medical evidence suggested that the cardiac muscle of the fetus would be contracting, that primitive blood circulation and physical movements would be demonstrated by the fetus, but that, if delivered by hysterotomy, such a fetus would *never* be able to breathe either naturally or with artificial assistance (emphasis added). Consequently, having subsequently decided to give her judgment in open court, Heilbron J held, following Sir George Baker in *Paton*, that the applicant potential father had no legal standing to ask for an injunction and that she was satisfied that a potential offence, under the 1929 Act in respect of child destruction, had not been proved. She then proceeded to dismiss the application of the potential father.

The applicant appealed to the Court of Appeal.

The Court of Appeal held that a fetus of between 18 and 21 weeks which showed signs of primitive movement and blood circulation, but which, if delivered by hysterotomy, would never be capable of breathing either naturally or artificially, was not a 'a child capable of being born alive' within the meaning of s 1(1) of the 1929 Act. The Court of Appeal therefore ruled that abortion of the fetus would not constitute an offence of child destruction under the 1929 Act. Accordingly, regardless of the *locus standi* (legal standing), the plaintiffs were not entitled to an injunction to prevent an abortion from being carried out. A subsequent appeal to the Appeal Committee of the House of Lords was also dismissed (for a full discussion of the various judgments, see de Cruz, SP [1987] Fam Law 319).

C v S – making legal history

C v S [1987] Fam Law 987 is believed to have made legal history for the extraordinary speed with which it progressed from the High Court to the Court of Appeal and then to the Law Lords. The application for an injunction to stop the abortion was lodged on Tuesday, the High Court (before Heilbron J) delivered its judgment on the following Monday, and as it was being read, Heilbron J's handwritten notes were taken page by page to the Court of Appeal, where a three man court began hearing the matter almost immediately. The Court of Appeal then delivered its judgment the following day, and this was being considered in a matter of hours by an emergency appeal committee comprising three Law Lords. On the same day, the Law Lords' committee declared that they unanimously agreed with the decision of the Court of Appeal and refused to grant any further leave to appeal. The reason for the swiftness of the judicial process was that the fetus was said to be between 18 and 21 weeks old and the longer the case took to be resolved, the closer it would be to the stage of gestation when a legal abortion could not be performed. In addition, the Oxford Area Health Authority had refused to carry out the operation without knowing the views of the House of Lords. This attitude was strongly criticised by the Court of Appeal, which pointed out that, since they heard 1,000 appeals a year, of which only 50 went to the House of Lords, the area health authority's attitude might allow the first plaintiff to achieve by delaying tactics what he could not obtain by law. In any event, all appeal stages of this case were completed in approximately 72 hours.

'Capable of being born alive' – *Bolam* in *C v S*?

In the High Court, the affidavits of eminent obstetricians indicated the wide difference in their interpretation of the phrase 'capable of being born alive'. One expert opinion (from a Mr Norris) was that an unborn fetus of 18 weeks, were it to be delivered, would be live born. The other expert's view was that such a fetus would be unable to breathe and unable to breathe even if placed on a ventilator. The latter view (from a Professor Newton) was that 'born alive' was synonymous with viability or having a chance of survival. Hence, his interpretation of a live child was one that was living and breathing by reason of its unaided breathing through its lungs, without deriving any of its living or power of living through any connection with its mother. Faced with opposing views, Heilbron J decided that there was a body of 'eminent medical opinion' that found Mr Norris's view unacceptable.

Selective reduction of multiple pregnancy

A new s 5(2) of the 1967 Act (as inserted by s 37 of the HFEA 1990) allows for selective reduction, providing one of the grounds in s 1(1)(a)–(d) in the Abortion Act are met. In other words, selective reductions can take place either on the ground of fetal abnormality or because the multiple pregnancy creates the amount of risk to the mother for s 1(1)(a), (b) or (c) to be satisfied.

Abortion pill

The pill RU486 – mifepristone and mifegyne – impairs the womb's ability to hold on to an egg.

It will be lawful to prescribe this if one of the grounds in the Abortion Act are met. This pill has been described as 'a medical advance of the same magnitude as the contraceptive pill' ((1991) *Sunday Times Magazine*, 6 January). Three visits are required to administer RU486. At the first, the drug is given in tablet form and the woman is sent home. Forty-eight hours later, the woman should return to be given a pessary containing prostaglandin to complete the process. Within 4–6 hours, the woman would then be expected to have a heavy period which expels the fertilised egg. The third visit is a check up and, if the drug has failed, a surgical operation is performed. Although not available in the USA until now, it was announced in September 2000 that RU486 may well be made available in years to come, including availability in the USA.

Protection for the unborn fetus

The rights and status of the fetus

The argument that the fetus has a right to be protected was further considered in *Re F (In Utero)*.

Re F (In Utero) [1988] Fam 122

In this case, the local authority claimed that an unborn child should be made a ward of court to protect it from injury, because its 36 year old nomadic mother had a reputation for somewhat aberrant behaviour and had a history of psychiatric problems. She had absconded from the residential care home in which she lived when she was 38 weeks pregnant.

In the Court of Appeal, May LJ held that the court had no jurisdiction to entertain the application, and agreed with the comments of Sir George Baker P in the *Paton* case. He also agreed with the lower court judge that to accept that wardship jurisdiction existed in this case and yet to apply the principle that it is the interest of the child which is to be predominant 'is bound to create conflict between the existing legal interests of the mother and those of the unborn child, and that it is most undesirable that this should occur'.

It is at least of historical interest to note that in *Re D* (or the *Berkshire* case) [1987] 1 All ER 20, which was decided on pre-1989 Children Act legislation, the House of Lords dealt with the issue of whether it was possible to protect an unborn fetus.

Legal status of the unborn child – a common law overview

The basic approach of common law countries as far as unborn children are concerned is not to confer rights upon them as legal 'persons'. In English law, an unborn child is clearly not a 'child' or 'person' in law (*Re F (In Utero)* [1988] 2 All ER 193. This is also the position in Australia (*AG v Qld ex rel Kerr v T* (1983) 46 ALR 275) (Australian High Court), Canada (*Tremblay v Daigle* (1989) 62 DLR (4th) 634 (Can Sup Ct) and *R v Sullivan* [1991] 1 SCR 489 (Can Sup Ct)) and, of course, the USA (*Roe v Wade* (1973) 410 US 113 (US Sup Ct)).

England

AG's Reference (No 3 of 1994) – policing pregnancy or protecting the fetus?

This case appeared to be a straightforward case of grievous bodily harm, except that the harm that was caused was to the unborn fetus of the woman who was attacked and it raised questions about whether murder may be committed on an unborn fetus, which has no legal personality in English law.

Some commentators regard this case as of 'major significance as to judicial attitudes to fetal status' (Mason and McCall Smith (1999), p 126).

AG's Reference (No 3 of 1994) [1997] 3 WLR 421

In this case, a man stabbed his pregnant girlfriend in the abdomen, causing her to be admitted to hospital with numerous stab wounds, including one to her left abdomen which penetrated her uterus. She was admitted to hospital, a cut to the wall of the uterus was discovered and surgically repaired, and the mother was prescribed a course of indomethacin to prevent the onset of premature labour. The doctors believed (mistakenly) that the fetus had not been harmed, and discharged her from hospital. Approximately two weeks later, she suddenly went into labour and gave birth to a daughter at 26 weeks' gestation. Following the birth, it became evident that the baby was two weeks older than previously thought when the attack occurred and that the knife had, contrary to the earlier diagnosis, penetrated the fetus itself, cutting through the left side of her abdomen. As a result of the prematurity of the child, she was perceived as having a 50% chance of survival. However, despite intensive neonatal care, including several surgical operations, the baby died after 120 days.

Prior to the birth, the man admitted wounding his girlfriend with intent to cause grievous bodily harm (under s 18 of the OAPA 1861) and was sentenced to four years' imprisonment. Following the death of his child, he was also charged with the child's murder. The first instance court held that there was evidence upon which a reasonable jury could conclude that the causal link between the wounding and the death could be established. Even if the facts and inferences suggested by the Crown were established, they could not result in a conviction for either murder or manslaughter and, thus, it was directed that the respondent be acquitted. The man was therefore acquitted on this second charge.

Two points were referred to the Court of Appeal by the Attorney General:

(a) whether the crimes of murder or manslaughter can be committed where unlawful injury is deliberately inflicted on a child *in utero* or to a mother carrying a child *in utero*; and where the child is subsequently born alive, enjoys an existence independent of the mother, thereafter dies and the injuries inflicted while *in utero* either caused or made a substantial contribution to the death;

(b) whether the fact that the death of the child is caused solely as a consequence of direct injury to the *mother* rather than as a consequence of direct injury to the fetus can negative any liability for murder or manslaughter in those circumstances.

The Court of Appeal considered the two elements of the *actus reus* of murder: the *unlawfulness of the act* and the necessity of the person killed being to be a *person in being*. On the first element, the court held, somewhat unusually, that, legally, the fetus is regarded as part of the mother until it has a separate existence from her; hence, to 'cause injury to the fetus is just as unlawful as any assault upon any other part of the mother'.

On the second element, it was necessary to consider the point at which a fetus becomes a person in being. Basing his opinion on several common law decisions, Lord Taylor CJ accepted that 'to cause the death of a fetus in the womb cannot be murder'. Yet, despite the court's acceptance that 'when the respondent stabbed his girlfriend, the child was not a person in being', it held that there was 'no requirement that the person who dies needs to be a person in being at the time that the act causing the death is perpetrated'. This conclusion was reached by reliance on a number of pre-1957 cases, and acceptance of the Crown's submission that those cases correctly represented the law and remained unchanged by the Homicide Act 1957.

Lord Justice Taylor CJ also observed that:

> An intention to cause serious bodily injury to the fetus is an intention to cause serious bodily injury to a part of the mother just as an intention to injure her arm or her leg would be so viewed.

Despite the obvious flaw in the reasoning, that a body part like an arm or leg is not able to develop into a human being, this merely indicates the transferred malice idea – an intention to cause serious harm to the fetus is deemed an intention to cause serious harm to the mother.

It is important to note that the comments of the Court of Appeal judgment indicate that the judgment was not intended as a step toward the recognition of a fetal right to life.

On appeal to the House of Lords, the Law Lords made it clear that a charge of murder could not be founded on the circumstances of the case, and that the Court of Appeal approach was wholly unfounded in fact. However, the charge of manslaughter could be upheld.

The view of Taylor CJ that a fetus was an integral part of its mother was rejected by Lord Mustill (with whom the other Law Lords agreed). Lord Mustill emphasised that the maternal-fetal relationship was one of 'bond, not of identity'. The fetus was neither a 'person' nor an adjunct of its mother, but it was simply a unique organism. As Lord Mustill put it: '... the fetus was an organism *sui generis* lacking at this stage the entire range of characteristics both of the mother to which it is physically linked and of the complete human being which it will later become.' Thus, the criminal law did not recognise violence to the fetus as an offence against a person, unless it was subsequently born alive, as it was not a person in being.

The conviction for unlawful act manslaughter was, as mentioned above, upheld. The reasons the Law Lords gave for this were: the act was done intentionally, was unlawful, was also dangerous in that it was likely to cause harm to somebody, and that act caused death. In the instant case, as Lord Hope explained, 'the stabbing of the mother was an unlawful and dangerous act and if the boyfriend had the *mens rea* which was required for him to be convicted of an assault on the child's mother, he also had the *mens rea* for unlawful act manslaughter' (see Fovargue and Miola (1998), p 280).

Following the decision in *R v Le Brun* [1992] QB 61, p 68, Lord Hope held that the act which caused the death and the mental state which is required for manslaughter do not need to coincide in time. It was, therefore, immaterial that the child was not alive when her mother was stabbed. He rejected submissions that, since the fetus was not a living person at the time of the unlawful act, manslaughter could not be committed, and emphasised that the 'dangerous' act was determined by what all sober and reasonable people would recognise was dangerous towards persons who were alive when the danger manifested itself. A particularly illuminating comment from his Lordship was:

> For the fetus ... it is not sensible to say that it cannot ever be harmed, or that nothing can be done to it which can be dangerous. Once it is born it is exposed, like all other living persons, to the risk of injury. It may also carry with it the effects of things done to it before birth which, after birth, may prove to be harmful. It would seem not to be unreasonable, therefore, on public policy grounds, to regard the child in this case, when she became a living person, as within the scope of the *mens rea* which [the defendant] had when he stabbed her mother before she was born.

Comment on *AG's Reference (No 3) of 1994*

Fovargue and Miola (1998) argue that a synthesis of this case with the 'Caesarean section cases' (see Chapter 1) indicates that 'there is no consistency or balance between the interests of the fetus and those of the pregnant woman', despite the affirmation by the Court of Appeal in *St George's* case (or the *Collins* case) [1998] 3 All ER 673 of the fact that an unborn child is not a person until born, for legal purposes. The fact remains that the English appellate courts have also held that the pregnant woman is not *per se* entitled to put at risk the healthy viable fetus she is carrying (for example, see the comments by Judge LJ in the *Collins* case, p 686). Indeed, the House of Lords' judgment in the *AG's Reference* case 'opens the door for criminal liability to ensue when the subject of an unlawful act is a fetus. The danger is that, even though the fetus has no theoretical legal personality, this assumption will be, and has been, eroded in the minds of the courts.' Hence, Fovargue and Miola argue further that 'it is the future application of the decision which is one of the most worrying aspects of the case'. This is because, for instance, the rejection of murder but the endorsement of unlawful act manslaughter by the House of Lords 'leaves open the question of maternal liability for children born addicted to illegal drugs because of their mother's ingestion of such drugs whilst pregnant' (Fovargue and Miola (1998), p 293). They would go so far as to argue that the general tone of even cases like *Re MB* [1997] Med LR 217, *Collins* and *AG's Reference* is (a) they have indicated the courts' willingness to intervene in childbirth decisions in order to save the life of the fetus and this indicates how the courts may determine the extent of maternal liability and autonomy; and (b) they combine to indicate that 'the balance between maternal autonomy and fetal welfare has undergone a drastic change'. They conclude that, 'by further personalising the fetus, the House of Lords in the *AG's Reference* case legitimise the ethics of the Caesarean section cases and provide an opportunity for the development of judicial policing of pregnancy'.

Some common law comparisons

Abortion in the Irish context

In the corresponding chapter to this in Part II (Chapter 13), a worldwide overview of abortion is presented, although considerable discussion focuses on the position in the USA as well as France and Germany. However, it may be helpful to the reader interested in the 'British' position to note the legal position on abortion in Northern Ireland and the Republic of Ireland.

It is well known that Irish women have, for many years, sought access to abortion in the UK and organisations and individuals in Ireland have sought to facilitate this by arranging travel facilities and advance appointments at abortion clinics there. In the absence of legislation, the judges have ruled that the availability of the operation in other jurisdictions cannot be translated into positive action to assist women wishing to use that facility. The numbers of Irish women travelling to Britain to obtain an abortion continues to grow. In 1983, Ireland adopted in its constitution a total ban on abortion and an explicit recognition of the right to life of the fetus (Eighth Amendment). This amendment to the basic law reinforces an existing statutory prohibition on abortion.

The Irish legal system

The legal systems of Northern Ireland and the Irish Republic derive from the English common law which came with the Norman invasion at the end of the 12th century. Following a turbulent history of struggle and conflict, English rule eventually survived until the achievement of independence at the beginning of the 20th century. Southern Ireland became a dominion within the British Commonwealth in 1922 and, in 1937, a new constitution was adopted, which formed part of the process of political and constitutional development which strived for full severance of all links with mainland Britain. The Republic of Ireland became an independent republic in 1948. An important constitutional point is that, under the 1937 Constitution, there is an affirmation of the ultimate authority of God and of the people, not the supremacy of the (British) Parliament. Consequently, if parliament enacts a law which is inconsistent with the constitution, the judges can declare it void, which amounts to a judicial review power similar to the American doctrine exercised by the US Supreme Court, and not the English version of judicial review, which is merely a judicial power to review the procedural impropriety of administrative decisions and merely remits the case for a rehearing or a fresh exercise of the decision making process which must then be conducted in a manner that is neither unreasonable, irrational nor illegal. The Irish Constitution may only be amended by a referendum of the people.

Northern Ireland

In Northern Ireland, the OAPA 1861 remains the governing law. The English Abortion Act 1967 has *not* been extended to, and therefore does not apply to Northern Ireland. Under the OAPA 1861, it is an offence to 'procure a miscarriage ... unlawfully'. The fetus is protected from the time of conception by the OAPA 1861; and the 1929 Infant Life Preservation Act protects the child in the process of being born. The offence of child destruction is committed when one destroys the life of a child capable of being born alive unless this was done in good faith for the purpose only of preserving the life of the mother. This legislation only applies upon proof that the woman was pregnant for a period of 28 weeks. In practice, abortions on clear medical grounds are carried out in Northern Ireland without prosecution.

However, the law in Northern Ireland has been modified by some significant court decisions. In *Re K (A Minor) (Northern Health and Social Services Board v F and G)* (1991) 2 Med L Rev 371, it was held that the law lay in the OAPA 1861 as modified by the charge to the jury in the *Bourne* case and consequently the court authorised the termination of a 13 week pregnancy in a severely handicapped ward of court. In *Re A (Northern Health and Social Services Board v F and G)* (1991) 2 Med L Rev 274, the court again used the *Bourne* reasoning to apply s 25 of the Criminal Justice Act (NI) to the OAPA 1861 and authorised an abortion for a handicapped woman on the basis that it was in her best interests.

The effect of Irish case law is that the doctor's act is lawful where the continuance of the pregnancy would affect the mental or physical health of the mother. However, the adverse effect must be a 'real and serious one' and it will always be a question of 'fact and degree' whether the perceived effect of non-termination is sufficiently grave to warrant terminating the unborn child.

As far as statistics are concerned, 1,573 women from Northern Ireland and 4,894 from the Irish Republic obtained terminations in England and Wales in 1996 (see Mason and McCall Smith (1999), p 119).

The Republic of Ireland

Abortion remains illegal in the Irish Republic under Art 40.3.3 of the constitution (see, also, below on the Eighth Amendment). The vast majority of the population are Roman Catholic and over 90% of the population remain affiliated. The Roman Catholic Church, therefore, continues to wield a considerable influence on the Republic socially, politically and culturally, so that there are also restrictions on the availability of contraception, and there is a constitutional ban on divorce.

The 'pro-life amendment'

In 1983, on 8 September, the people of Ireland amended the constitution to protect the rights of the unborn child. This became the Eighth Amendment to the constitution and guaranteed the right to life of the unborn. The amendment inserted this guarantee in the context of Art 40.3 of the constitution. This article is fundamental to the scheme of the basic law by guaranteeing to the citizen particular human rights, such as the right to life and property, and reserving to the judges the right to identify and protect such other human rights as emerge from the natural order and which are consistent with the fundamental aim of the constitution in promoting the freedom and dignity of the individual citizen within a society based on just and Christian laws. The full article, with the Eighth Amendment, now reads:

1 The State guarantees in its laws, to respect, and, as far as practicable, by its laws, to defend and vindicate the personal rights of the citizen.

2 The State shall, in particular, by its laws protect as best it may from unjust attack and, in the case of injustice done, vindicate the life, person, good name, and property rights of every citizen.

3 The State acknowledges the right to life of the unborn and, with regard to the equal right to life of the mother, guarantees in its laws to respect, and, as far as practicable, by its laws to defend and vindicate that right.

This amendment was adopted by a majority of two to one, but in a comparatively low turnout of 54% (*Irish Times*, 9 September 1983). There was stronger support for the amendment in rural areas.

A series of cases in the early 1990s has appeared to both confirm and undermine the general prohibition on abortion and access to abortion services and information. For instance, the Court of Justice of the European Communities upheld the right of the State to prohibit the dissemination of abortion information in *SPUC v Grogan* [1991] 3 CMLR 849; [1991] IR 593. However, this appeared to be countered in the European Court of Human Rights in *Open Door Counselling Ltd and Dublin Well Woman v Ireland* (1992) 18 BMLR 1.

In *AG v X* [1992] 2 CMLR 277, the Irish Supreme Court held that the Irish Constitution did allow abortion where it was established as a matter of probability that there was a real and substantial risk to the life of the pregnant woman which could be avoided by termination of pregnancy. In the case itself, X was a 14 year old girl who had regularly visited a school friend. Her friend's father had, almost two years previously, begun to molest her sexually. In December 1991, she was raped, and in late January 1992, she told her parents what she had been subjected to. The family doctor confirmed her pregnancy. Her parents decided that a termination of pregnancy should be obtained in England and requested the Garda Siochna (the police) to send a representative to the abortion clinic so that a DNA test could later be proved to have been performed on the aborted fetus with a view to proving paternity should the accused agree to give a blood sample. They were advised that such evidence would not be admissible because of the circumstances in which it would have to be obtained. In early February, X and her parents travelled to England and arrangements were made for an abortion to take place. Meanwhile, the Attorney General had applied to the High Court and Costello J had granted an injunction to the effect that the operation should not take place. On returning from London, X had developed suicidal tendencies. The parents decided to challenge the injunction. Evidence was given by a clinical psychologist that the girl had become capable of suicide and, further, that the psychological damage to her of carrying the child would be considerable.

The main issue for discussion, on which the High Court and the Supreme Court sharply differed, was whether the Eighth Amendment allowed for abortion in limited circumstances where the mother's life had been put at risk for psychological reasons resulting from pregnancy. It was argued that if this risk arose from the psychological burden of pregnancy, it was as real as a physical risk where a termination could be lawful. Costello J disagreed, saying that this was a case where the risk to the mother's life comes from herself, and the court was being asked not to make an order because if it did, the mother might take her own life. In this sort of situation, involving a young girl in a highly distressing and deeply disturbing situation, the court has a duty to protect her life not just from the actions of others, but from the actions she may herself perform. He was convinced that there was a real and imminent danger to the life of the unborn and that if the court did not step in and protect it by means of an order, its life would be terminated. The court also accepted that there was a risk that the defendant might take her own life, but this risk 'was of a different order of magnitude than the one certainty that that the life of the unborn would be terminated if the order were not made'. He felt strengthened in his view by the fact that the girl had the love, care and support of loving parents to help her in the difficult months ahead and decided that, having regard to the rights of the mother, 'the court's duty to protect the life of the unborn requires it to make the order sought'. The abortion was therefore *not* authorised.

There were several expressions of concern after this judgment; protests were heard from various quarters after this decision, with even public demonstrations outside the Irish Parliament, and it appeared that a shift in public opinion had taken place in the public as to whether abortion should be allowed in limited circumstances. An opinion poll confirmed this change in public attitudes.

The State offered to pay the costs of an appeal, which was eventually allowed by a 4:1 majority, that abortion could be justified where it was established as a matter of probability that there was a real and substantial risk to the life, as distinct from the health, of the mother, which could only be avoided by a termination of her pregnancy, and by a 3:2 majority, that the court could grant an injunction to restrain travel from the jurisdiction for the purpose of obtaining an abortion in another State but that having regard to the difficulty of enforcement, the court had a discretion as to whether to exercise that power.

In November, a referendum was held which confirmed the Irish people's preference for access to information and travel, but a proposal to liberalise the basic law was defeated for mainly procedural reasons.

Canada and New Zealand

Canada and New Zealand also provide useful comparative illustrations of how some other common law jurisdictions have responded to situations where the mother may pose a threat to the life or well being of her unborn fetus.

Canada

The Canadian equivalent of this case occurred in *Winnipeg Child and Family Services v G* [1999] Med LR 88. In this 1997 case, which reached the Canadian Supreme Court, the subject of the application was a solvent addict who had continued her habit into pregnancy. She had already given birth to two children who suffered from chemical addiction and were developmentally handicapped wards of the plaintiff agency. Concern for her unborn child led them to apply for an order under the Mental Health Act 1987 committing her to a place of safety and requiring her to refrain from the consumption of intoxicants during the course of the pregnancy.

The trial judge made an order on the basis of the mother's mental illness, but doubted his jurisdiction to do so solely for the protection of the unborn child.

The Court of Appeal of Manitoba allowed an appeal on the basis that there was insufficient evidence of mental incompetence and noted that any such order must be for the mother's benefit, any incidental advantage to an unborn child being fortuitous. Since a fetus had no legal personality, neither *parens patriae* nor an injunction to restrain tortious conduct could be invoked for its protection. Before the appeal to the Supreme Court of Canada was heard, the child was born.

The Supreme Court considered the issues relating to the justification, if any, for the detention and compulsory treatment of a pregnant woman in order to protect her unborn child from potentially harmful conduct.

The court (by 7:2) upheld the decision of the Manitoba Court of Appeal and dismissed the appeal, and held:

(a) The unborn child is not presently recognised as a legal person possessing rights. Any interests it may have remain inchoate and incomplete until birth.

(b) Major revisions of the law, with profound legal, social and moral ramifications, exceed the incremental law making powers of the courts and are best left to the elected legislature. It is therefore inappropriate for the courts to overturn the rule that rights accrue only at birth, to recognise a general fetal right to sue its mother for pre-natal injuries for lifestyle choice or to recognise an injunctive remedy for involuntary confinement in such cases as proposed by the appellants.

Dissenting judgments

Major and Sopinka JJ (dissenting) remarked that, while it may be preferable for the legislature to act, the court may properly extend the law since the assumptions on which the former law were based have been rendered outdated and indefensible by developments in obstetric and fetal medicine. The rule that rights accrue at birth was born of evidentiary convenience in an era when it was considered impossible to determine with accuracy whether a woman was pregnant prior to 'quickening'. They referred to a number of cases, criminal and civil, in other jurisdictions, which have recognised that the rule is incompatible with current fetal monitoring and micro-surgical techniques (*Hughes v State of Oklahoma* (1994) 868 P 2d 730 and *State v Horne* (1984) 319 SE 2d 703). Canadian cases were also cited for another jurisdiction, which questioned the validity of the rule in pre-natal injuries – *Montreal Tramways Co v Leveille* [1933] SCR 246. In the light of this, the *parens patriae* jurisdiction, which exists for the stated purpose of protecting the interests of those unable to protect themselves, must be invoked 'to protect the particularly vulnerable fetus'.

(c) Such extensions of the law have the potential to create an adversarial relationship between mother and fetus, which might well exacerbate any perceived risk, as well as posing a threat to basic human rights, including the right to bodily integrity and the right to equality, privacy, and dignity. Furthermore, the deterrent value of such legislation is 'questionable' and may lead to greater numbers of women avoiding antenatal care, thereby exposing the unborn to still greater danger.

Dissenting judgments

Major and Sopinka JJ (dissenting) opined that since exercise of the *parens patriae* jurisdiction will necessarily involve an overriding of some maternal rights, the threshold for intervention must be high, the remedy granted must be the least intrusive option and comprehensively procedural safeguards must be adopted. They then stressed that 'autonomy is widely recognised as subject to interference where others are endangered and this should, in accordance with the principle of fundamental fairness, apply to pregnant women who have decided to carry their pregnancy to term and who are engaging in activity which, on the balance of probabilities, will cause serious and irreparable harm to the fetus'. The learned judges pointed out that these matters must be established at a hearing prior to any restriction on the mother's liberty. The option to terminate the pregnancy will remain unaffected since it is the decision to give birth which generates correlative and enforceable responsibilities.

New Zealand

A Family Court in New Zealand was faced with a case which suggested that an unborn fetus required protection from its mother. In *In the matter of Baby P (An Unborn Child)* [1995] NZLR 577; [1997] Med LR 143, Baby P's mother was a 15 year old girl who remained deeply attached to her father despite the fact that he had previously attacked her and had threatened to kidnap and kill the baby. The birth was expected within the next few weeks. The mother was already under the custody of the Director General of Social Welfare (DGSW) and concern for the welfare of the unborn child prompted the DGSW to apply to the court for a declaration that she was in need of care and protection. The question arose whether the fetus was a 'child' within the meaning of the Children, Young Persons and Their Families Act 1989 and, therefore, able to benefit from the protective jurisdiction of the court.

The court (Inglis QC) granted the declaration and held:

(a) Baby P was at a stage of development when he would be capable of living independently of his mother and there would be little difference between his present stage of development and that which he would attain immediately after the birth. There was no indication of any legislative intent to restrict the application of the protective jurisdiction to children who have already been born. Assistance could also be derived from the Crimes Act 1961 which protects the unborn child of at least 20 weeks' gestation, whether or not it is capable of being born alive. It was unnecessary to decide whether the 1989 Act should also be taken to apply to a fetus at a much earlier stage of gestation.

(b) Overseas authority to the effect that an unborn child has no legal personality unless and until born alive simply illustrates the different approach that may be taken in other jurisdictions. The question of the legal status of the fetus need not be conflated with the issue of whether it is a human being entitled to the protection of the law.

(c) In the instant case, there was little, if any, conflict between the interests of the mother and the unborn child.

In his commentary on this case, Grubb remarks that the case reaches a 'unique result in the common law world' (Grubb (1997), p 144). This is because the judge interpreted the New Zealand *child protection* legislation to cover an unborn child. There was no judicial view expressed on the earliest point in the development of the fetus when the provisions of the Act would apply. In effect, the court relied on the protection afforded by ss 182 and 159 of the Crimes Act 1961 and concluded that the word 'child' should include 'at least an unborn child which has achieved a state of development where it could survive independently of the mother'. Grubb argues that 'this equates roughly to a viable fetus'. As in England, however, it is a crime to destroy an unborn child or fetus prior to birth, subject to the laws allowing termination of pregnancies. It is also a crime to bring about the death of a child after its birth by pre-natal conduct (see *AG's Reference (No 3 of 1994)* [1996] 2 All ER 10). Consequently, it was not really crucial to decide, as the judge in this case seemed to think, whether the unborn child was a legal person (which he agreed it was not) and whether it was a 'human being entitled to protection'.

However, because English law does not regard an unborn fetus as a 'child' or 'person' in law, it is not possible to ward a fetus (according to *Re F (In Utero)*) or for a fetus to be made subject to the court's inherent jurisdiction or a s 8 order under the English Children Act 1989. On a comparative point, Grubb argues that English child protection legislation would be inapplicable to protect an unborn child under the current English law (Pt IV of the Children Act 1989). However, under previous English legislation, it was possible to regard the mother's conduct as a basis for State intervention (see de Cruz (1987); and Fortin, J, 'Legal protection for the unborn child' (1988) 51 Mod LR 54 and *Re D (A Minor)* [1987] AC 317, HL). On the other hand, the present writer submits that is was arguable that, should a similar situation arise where there is potential danger to an unborn fetus, an emergency protection order could be applied for under the English Children Act 1989. However, the English Court of Appeal (*per* Butler-Sloss LJ) in *Re MB (Caesarean Section)* [1997] 2 FLR 426, made it clear that 'the court does not have the jurisdiction to declare that ... medical intervention is lawful to protect the interests of the unborn child even at the point of birth'.

Grubb (1997) (p 145) also emphasises that 'the policy of English law is not to interfere coercively in a mother's conduct during pregnancy'. He argues that it might deter mothers from seeking help for fear of being the subject of coercive measures, thereby causing even more harm to unborn children. It is not possible to draw a clear line between 'acceptable' and 'unacceptable' behaviour and it is 'undesirable' for the law to be used to force competent individuals to submit to interference with their bodily integrity.

Comment

The New Zealand court is certainly attempting to be innovative in seeking to protect the unborn child by using child protection legislation. However, it was surely a lacuna in English law (pre-Children Act 1989) when its legislation seemed unable, on the face of it, to deal with a situation like the pre-Children

Act case of *Re D* [1987] 1 All ER 20 where the child was born to drug-addicted parents, and was found to be suffering from drug withdrawal symptoms which required six weeks of intensive care to 'dry out' and attracted the attention of the social services who, commendably, did all their power to rescue the unborn fetus from its plight. One way round the situation, if it were to occur in England today, would be to argue that, if the child's parents were drug addicts, they would pose 'significant harm' to the child and therefore justify an emergency protection order, followed by a care order, under the Children Act 1989, in order to protect the child's longer term future or even to preserve its life. The dilemma must lie between respecting the mother's autonomy and freedom to live her own life, and the need or desire to protect the fetus, where circumstances are such that the child protection authorities feel that the fetus clearly needs protection.

THE ORIGINS OF LIFE AND EMBRYO RESEARCH

Embryo research

Experimentation on embryos has proved to be a contentious issue. Some have argued that embryo research is justified by scientific advances such as the development of new contraceptive techniques, more effective IVF procedures and a greater understanding of miscarriages, providing a better understanding of genetic defects and diseases. Indeed, the argument has been that there are no particular ethical difficulties in embryo research because an embryo is simply a clump of cells with no special status and therefore requires no special protection under the law.

On the other hand, it has been argued that research is unjustifiable because the embryo is a human being or, at least, a potential human being. Embryo research has been seen as sinister, and some have argued that this is the start of the slippery slope towards unjustifiable manipulation of the human race. Some feminists have argued that embryo research should be opposed because it is an exploitation of procreative activity, destroys women's physical integrity, or undermines women's struggle for control of their own reproduction.

A key issue in the debate on embryo research is: at what point does the human life come into existence? There are various points during the development of the fetus that are considered to be significant – the moment of fertilisation, viability, quickening, development of the primitive streak, implantation. Legally, birth has been regarded as being significant. But, the argument runs that, from the moment of fertilisation, the fetus is arguably a unique genetic entity.

Another point at which an embryo has been said to become a unique genetic entity is at another stage of development, such as after 8–10 weeks after conception, when brain activity is detected.

However, it is the appearance of the line known as *the primitive streak* (at around 14 days) on which the Warnock Committee focused as the crucial transformation between molecular matter and potential human being. Scientists called this molecular matter the 'pre-embryo'. Writers such as Braude and Johnson have argued that the primitive streak is important for three reasons:

(a) it is the time at which the precursor cells for the basic body tissues are laid down in the correct relative position;

(b) it is the first time at which the embryonic disc has a front and back, left and right and top and bottom;

(c) it is likely that this is the last stage at which twinning of the conceptus can occur, the number of embryos being determined by the number of primitive streaks that develop.

These assertions and the value judgments which flow from them have been balanced against arguments such as the sanctity of all human life from the beginning of fertilisation. The fact that many conceptuses are spontaneously lost before implantation in the uterus does not, as some would argue, deal with the question of the sanctity of life. The fact that nature is so prodigal does not mean that humans should act in the same way with the products of their creation.

Until the 14th day, cells are pluripotential – that is, it is not known whether they will develop into a hydatiform mole; into twins; into one embryo; or degenerate into nothing. Arguments have been made about cell commitment being a gradual process: the 'I'm in there somewhere' argument: although it is, initially, not possible to identify one individual human being in the pluripotential cells, it is sufficient to be able to argue that, in due course, an identifiable individual will emerge from the cluster.

In a memorable passage in the House of Lords debates, the Archbishop of York, John Hapgood, said:

> By and large a biological approach to life is rooted in gradualism ... The same is true in the development of individual lives. They begin with chemistry and they reach their fulfilment in mystery.

The philosophical debate

The philosophical debate has centred on the question: 'is this a human being?' The questions that have been much debated are: how do we go about identifying a human being? Is it a matter of criteria, or of how we feel it is right to treat such a human entity?

It is clear from information emanating from the Nazi regime that some people thought it right to experiment on human beings and even to destroy them, in the supposed name of medical science.

Let us look, then, at some arguments for and against embryo research.

Arguments against embryo research

(a) It is morally wrong, because embryos are human and can be seen as having the same status as a child or adult by virtue of their potential for human life. The right to life is considered to be a fundamental human right and the taking of human life is always abhorrent.

(b) If it is accepted that they are human, then just like a child or adult, it is unethical to carry out research on them which may result in harm or death.

(c) Consent cannot be obtained from the human embryo, so to carry out research without this consent would be ethically unacceptable as it usually is for any other human being.

(d) Potential for the mad scientist to create hybrids, or carry out selective breeding or eugenic selection.

Arguments for embryo research

(a) A human embryo cannot be thought of as a person; merely a clump of cells which, unless it implants in a human uterine environment, has no potential for development. There is, therefore, no reason to afford these cells special protection. However, the more generally held position is that, although the human embryo should be accorded some measure of respect beyond other animal subjects, that respect should not be absolute and may be weighed against the benefits resulting from research carried out using human embryos.

(b) Sometimes, there is no substitute for using human embryos when studying disorders only occurring in humans, such as Down's syndrome, or research into the processes of human fertilisation, or perhaps into the specific effects of drugs or toxic substances on human tissue.

It is not possible to prove the arguments either way, or to pinpoint the moment of ensoulment.

The report of the Committee of Inquiry into Human Fertilisation and Embryology (the Warnock Report) was published in 1984. Their remit was 'To consider recent and potential developments in medicine and science related to human fertilisation and embryology; to consider what policies and safeguards should be applied, including considerations of the social, ethical and legal implications of these developments; and to make recommendations'. They recommended that embryo research should continue, but subject to regulation. Many of their recommendations were incorporated into the HFEA 1990.

Embryo research is permitted if a research licence is obtained from the Human Fertilisation and Embryology Authority. The research licence allows for the creation and use of *in vitro* embryos for certain specified projects. It is a criminal offence punishable for up to two years in prison to bring about the creation of an embryo (outside the human body) or to keep or use an embryo except in pursuance of a licence. Paragraph 3 of Sched 2 to the Act sets out the type of projects for which these licences may be granted:

(a) the promotion of advances in the treatment of infertility;

(b) increasing knowledge about the causes of congenital disease;

(c) increasing knowledge about the causes of miscarriage;

(d) developing more effective contraception techniques;

(e) developing methods of detecting the presence or absence of gene or chromosome abnormalities before the implantation of an embryo.

Section 3 of the Act defines the parameters of activity allowed in relation to embryos. The authority may not authorise the use or retention of a live human embryo after the appearance of the primitive streak – not later than 14 days after the mixing of the gametes. This does not apply to cases where the embryo has been frozen. The Act also provides a right of conscientious objection in s 38. Certain other activities are prohibited, for example, cloning, placing of a human embryo in an animal and vice versa.

CONCLUSIONS

Abortion in English law has now reached the stage where it appears to be accepted by a majority of the population, although its modern origins stem from the 'swinging 60s', where it was, arguably, part of the liberalising movement and mood of the times. However, apart from some sporadic attempts to curb its scope, it has endured into the 21st century, with a reduced time limit and with a controversial fetal handicap ground which carries no time limit.

Abortion remains illegal under Irish law. In Northern Ireland, the fetus is protected from the time of conception by the OAPA 1861; and the 1929 Infant Life Preservation Act protects the child in the process of being born. The offence of child destruction is committed when one destroys the life of a child capable of being born alive unless this was done in good faith for the purpose only of preserving the life of the mother. This legislation only applies upon proof that the woman was pregnant for a period of 28 weeks. In practice, abortions on clear medical grounds are carried out in Northern Ireland without prosecution.

In the Irish Republic, the abortion law has undergone something of a challenge via some highly publicised cases, but the basic position appears to be that abortion is still illegal under the Irish Constitution. However, a series of cases in the early 1990s has appeared to both confirm and undermine the general prohibition on abortion and access to abortion services and information. The case law indicates that Irish women have no general right to travel abroad and obtain an abortion, but it may be permitted if it is proved that there is a 'real and substantial risk' to the life of the mother.

Strong historical and religious reasons currently militate against a wholesale reform of the law in Ireland, but some might argue that more humane elements have begun to seep into the law so as to allow abortion in tightly circumscribed conditions. There is also a growing recognition and desire for more personal autonomy, and it may well be that the law will continue to be eroded until there are at least limited rights to abortion under the constitution or in statutory form, the existence of which will not depend on judicial discretion. Maintaining the delicate balance between religious conviction, tradition, protection of the fetus and recognition of some rights of self-determination and autonomy remains an ongoing challenge in Ireland.

SELECTIVE BIBLIOGRAPHY

Arras, JD and Steinbock, B, *Ethical Issues in Modern Medicine*, 1997, Mayfield

Bentil, JK, 'US and Anglo-Australian decisions on a husband's right to prevent abortion' [1990] Law and Justice 68

Bowles, and Bell, 'Abortion on demand or request: is it legal?' (1980) LSG, 24 September

Brazier, M, *Medicine, Patients and the Law*, 1992, Penguin

Brazier, M, 'Embryos' "rights", abortion and research' [1988] CLP 9

BMA, *Abortion, Law and Ethics*, 1999, www.bma.org.uk

Cohen, M, Nagel, T and Scanlon, T (eds), *The Rights and Wrongs of Abortion*, 1974, Princeton UP

Clarke, L, 'Abortion: a rights issue?', in Lee, R and Morgan, D (eds), *Birthrights*, 1990, Routledge

de Cruz, SP, 'Abortion, *C v S* and the law' (1987) 17 Fam Law 319

de Cruz, SP, 'Parents, doctors and children: the *Gillick* case and beyond' [1987] JSWL 93

Douglas, G, *Law, Fertility and Reproduction*, 1991, Sweet & Maxwell

Dworkin, R, *Life's Dominion*, 1993, HarperCollins

Fortin, J, 'Legal protection for the unborn child' (1988) 51 MLR 54

Fovargue, S and Miola, J, 'Policing pregnancy: implications of *Attorney General's Reference (No 3 of 1994)*' (1998) 9 Med L Rev 265

Gillon, R, 'Human embryos and the argument from potential' (1991)17 JME 59

Glazebrook, PR, 'Capable of being, but no right to be, born alive?' [1991] CLJ 241

Glover, J, *Causing Death and Saving Lives*, 1971, Penguin

Grubb, A, 'The new law of abortion: clarification or ambiguity' [1991] Crim LR 659

Harpwood, V, *Legal Issues in Obstetrics*, 1993, Dartmouth

Harris, J, 'Embryos and hedgehogs: on the moral status of the embryo', in Dyson, A and Harris, J (eds), *Experiments on Embryos*, 1990, Routledge

Hoggett, B, 'The Abortion Act 1967' [1968] Crim LR 608

Johnson, P, 'Faith, reason and unreason, 1648–1870', in *A History of Christianity*, 1983, Atheneum

Kennedy, I, 'A husband, a wife and an abortion', in Kennedy, I, *Treat me Right*, 1988, OUP

Kennedy, I and Grubb, A (eds), *Principles of Medical Law*, 1998, Butterworths

Keown, J, *Abortion, Doctors and the Law: Some Aspects of the Legal Regulation of Abortion in England from 1803–1982*, 1988, CUP

Lovenduski, J, 'Parliament, pressure groups, networks and the women's movement: the politics of abortion law reform in Britain (1967–83)', in Lovenduski, J and Outshoorn, J (eds), *The New Politics of Abortion*, 1986, Sage

Lyon, C and Bennett, G, 'Abortion: whose decision?' (1979) 9 Fam Law 935

Mason, K, 'Abortion and the Law', in McLean, S (ed), *Legal Issues in Human Reproduction*, 1990, Dartmouth

Mason, JK and McCall Smith, RA, *Law and Medical Ethics*, 5th edn, 1999, Butterworths, Chapter 5

Montgomery, J, 'Rights, restraints and pragmatism' (1991) 54 MLR 524

Morgan, D, 'Abortion: the unexamined ground' [1990] Crim LR 687

Pence, G, *Classic Cases in Medical Ethics*, 1990, McGraw-Hill

Seal, V, *Whose Choice?*, 1990, Fortress

Sheldon, S, 'Who is the mother to make the judgment? Constructions of woman in UK abortion law' (1993) 1 FLS 3

Sheldon, S, 'The British Abortion Act 1967: a permissive reform?' (1994) EUI Working Paper LAW No 94/2, European University Institute, Florence

Schlegel, C, 'Landmark in German abortion law: the German 1995 compromise compared with English law' (1997) 11 IJ Law, Policy and the Family 36

Terry, N, 'England', in Frankowski, S and Cole, G (eds), *Abortion and Protection of the Fetus*, 1987, Nijhoff

Williams, G, *The Sanctity of Life and the Criminal Law*, 1958, Faber & Faber

CHAPTER 4

CHILDREN AND HEALTHCARE

INTRODUCTION

The medical treatment and care of children should be carried out in accordance with the general professional standards which all the cases we have already considered have laid down, as stated more than 40 years ago in *Bolam*, namely, in accordance with a responsible body of medical opinion; although a particular procedure might be challenged if it is not necessarily 'logical' (*Bolitho*), and the courts have consistently said all treatment should always be in the 'best interests' of the child. This is a concept that takes its content from the nature of the cases it governs. A 'child' or 'minor' in English law is a person who has been born and is under 18 years of age. *Prima facie*, and historically, children have been regarded as coming within the category of those who are legally incompetent to give consent, being unable, at least in the early years of their life, to decide on what medical treatment they should have, until they reach 16. The guiding principle for older children under 16, since 1985, has been and is the so called *Gillick* principle, whereby a minor of 'sufficient age and understanding' (a phrase open to interpretation) is *prima facie* entitled to make her own decisions and give valid consent in relation to medical treatment. This is contained in various provisions of the English Children Act 1989, in force since 14 October 1991. *Prima facie*, the consent of a child who is 16 is effective under s 8 of the Family Law Reform Act 1969.

However, there are several difficulties associated with child patients:

(a) very young or younger patients cannot usually decide on their medical treatment for themselves, that is, exercise autonomous choice and give their consent, so parents or their caretakers would *usually* have to decide for them, especially when they are very young and give proxy consent;

(b) 'consent' as a pragmatic and legal concept presents special issues for child patients;

(c) what are the limits of parental choice (*Re B*) and parental opinion (*Re T*)?

(d) the issue may arise of whose consent should be effective where there is disagreement over what is in the child's best interests: the parents', the courts, the local authority if the child is in care, or the 'mature' child who claims to be '*Gillick* competent'?

(e) despite s 8 of the Family Law Reform Act 1969, case law suggests that a child's refusal of consent may sometimes be overridden, even if she is aged 16 or 17. Is this ethically justifiable?

FUNCTIONS OF CONSENT

Lord Donaldson in *Re W* [1992] 4 All ER 627 appeared to identify two functions of consent:

(a) the legal function: to provide a justification for care;

(b) the clinical function: to secure the patient's trust and co-operation.

Clearly, without such consent, the crime of battery would be committed and any healthcare professional who touched their patient would also be liable in tort for trespass to the person.

When can a child consent?

Although a child is a person who has been born (as opposed to a fetus *in utero*), but under the age of 18, consent to treatment of a child aged 16 is as effective as if she or he were an adult, under s 8 of the Family Law Reform Act 1969. 'Treatment' includes diagnosis and procedures such as the administration of anaesthetics which are ancillary to treatment (the *Gillick* case and *Gillick* statutory provisions in the Children Act 1989: see below). Case law in the mid 1980s and 1990s has established the concept of '*Gillick* competence': a level of maturity, as ascertained by a court, possessed by a child 'of sufficient age and understanding' to make its own decisions. Lord Donaldson MR in *Re W* mentioned the 'flak jacket' of consent to protect healthcare professionals from any liability for assault or battery.

Gillick v West Norfolk and Wisbech AHA and the DHSS
[1985] 3 All ER 402; [1986] FLR 224

This was undoubtedly the *cause célèbre* of the 1980s; it dominated the headlines for some time in Britain and was seen as heralding a new era in children's rights, and was also hailed as a landmark case in delineating some parameters of a parent's responsibility. It has led to statutory recognition of children's right to refuse consent to a medical assessment or examination, in the Children Act 1989 (see de Cruz (1987) J Social Welfare Law 93 for an early commentary; Parkinson P [1986] 16 Fam Law 12).

The Gillick *case*

Under a DHSS guidance (1980), it was stated that, although parents should normally be involved in cases of children under 16, in exceptional cases, it was for a doctor to prescribe contraception without informing the parents of that child's request for contraceptive advice or treatment. Mrs Gillick had several daughters under that age and sought a declaration that the guidance gave unlawful advice which adversely affected parental rights and duties. She lost the first hearing in the High Court. When she appealed, she won a unanimous decision in the Court of Appeal, with all three appeal court judges supporting her claim, but ultimately lost 3:2 in the House of Lords.

Lord Fraser formulated five criteria for doctors contemplating whether to provide such an under-age girl with contraceptive advice and treatment without reference to her parents.

He stressed that the doctor should *always* seek to persuade the girl to tell her parents or to agree to the doctor informing her parents. However, if the girl still refused to agree to either of these suggestions, the doctor could give advice and treatment provided that, in the doctor's opinion, the following conditions were satisfied:

(a) that the girl understands the advice;

(b) that the doctor cannot persuade her to inform her parents or to allow the doctor to inform her parents that she is seeking contraceptive advice;

(c) that she is very likely to begin or to continue having sexual intercourse with or without contraceptive treatment;

(d) that unless she receives contraceptive advice or treatment, her physical or mental health or both are likely to suffer;

(e) that it is in the best interests of the child for the doctor to give her contraceptive advice and treatment or both without parental consent.

Put another way, the doctor would be expected to preserve the confidentiality of the consultation *provided* the preceding conditions were satisfied; arguably, the other side of the coin would be that, if these conditions were *not* fulfilled, the doctor would be entitled to breach the duty of confidentiality and inform the parents.

Under (a), there is some scope for interpreting the level of understanding – how deep should it be? Should it cover psychological and emotional implications of the treatment? Should she be able to understand the impact on the family? Lord Scarman's judgment provides some indication of the answers to these queries.

In his judgment, Lord Scarman spoke of the parental right to determine medical treatment which terminated when the child below the age of 16 achieved 'sufficient understanding and intelligence' to be able to understand fully what was being proposed. He also expected the girl to understand: moral and family questions relating to the treatment, especially the girl's relationship with her parents; long term problems associated with the impact of a pregnancy and its termination; risks to health of sexual intercourse at her age. It has to be said that this appears to require an extremely deep and perceptive understanding of the consequences of the proposed (contraceptive) treatment, which, it is submitted, is arguably more demanding than that possessed by most adults who decide to use contraception.

Lords Templeman and Brandon dissented from the majority judicial opinion and Lord Templeman memorably said: 'There are many things a girl under 16 needs to practise but sex is not one of them.'

'Gillick' *provisions in the Children Act 1989*

Several provisions have now been included in the Children Act 1989 which are a clear recognition of the *Gillick* case. The provisions are:

- ss 43(8); 44(7), which give the child the right to refuse to submit to medical assessment or examination;
- s 39, whereby the child may apply for discharge of care orders;
- s 45(8), which gives the child the right to challenge Emergency Protection Orders;
- s 10(8), which gives the child the right to apply to court for leave to apply for a s 8 order dealing with specific issues.

In the aftermath of the *Gillick* case, some commentators believed that the case was a harbinger of children's rights, but in the 1990s (see the post-*Gillick* cases), the courts ruled in a number of cases that a child's refusal of consent could be overridden by the courts in certain circumstances, and this applies even to those girls aged 16 as well. In medico-legal terms, a strong tendency towards judicial paternalism was emerging and has continued to manifest itself in the 1990s and in the early 21st century.

*Post-*Gillick *cases*

Re W *[1992] 4 All ER 627; [1993] 1 FLR 1; [1992] 3 WLR 758*

In this case, W, an anorexic 16 year old, wished to remain in the specialist adolescent unit rather than move to a clinic specialising in eating disorders. Lord Donaldson MR said that s 8 of the Law Reform Act 1969 'conclusively presumed' that a 16 or 17 year old was competent, but the section did *not* confer an absolute right on a child to *refuse* treatment. In other words, the presumption could be rebutted if a child, although 16 or 17, suffered from a mental disability which affected her understanding and capacity to give a valid consent to surgical, medical or dental treatment. In the case itself, since it was a peculiarity of anorexia nervosa to create a wish not to be cured, or only to be cured if and when the patient decides to cure herself, which may be too late, it was doubtful whether the first instance judge had been correct in concluding that W possessed sufficient understanding to make an informed decision.

In view of the deterioration in W's condition and the likelihood of suffering permanent damage to her brain and reproductive organs, 'the point had been clearly reached when the court should be prepared, in W's own interests, to overrule her refusal to consent to treatment'. It accordingly ordered that she be treated by the appropriate hospital.

In effect, the court held that neither s 8 nor the *Gillick* principle gave the child of 16 an absolute right to veto medical treatment. Hence, where the 16 year old child was seen to be suffering from a mental illness which affected her ability to give a valid consent, the court could overrule the child's wishes. However, the court also held that a 16 year old minor's consent cannot be overridden even by those with parental responsibility for the minor. Again, a *Gillick* competent minor (that is, one who might be under-age, but found to possess the necessary maturity and understanding) also has a right to consent to medical treatment which cannot be overridden by those with parental responsibility. Nevertheless, this consent can also be overridden by the court.

Thus, somewhat confusingly, the Court of Appeal also said that, despite having the right to consent, the child had no right to refuse treatment and that both parents and the court can override even a competent child's refusal of treatment.

Comment

Hence, the legal position, after *Re W*, seems to be that:

- Children aged 16 have the statutory right to consent to surgical, medical or dental treatment by virtue of s 8 of the Law Reform Act 1969. Such consent cannot be overridden by those with parental responsibility for the minor but it *can* be overridden by the *court*. The statutory right does not extend to consent to the donation of blood or organs.
- Consent to treatment of a minor is analogous to a legal 'flak jacket' which protects a doctor from litigation for trespass to the person (battery) regardless of whether consent has been obtained from a minor over 16, or a '*Gillick* competent' child under that age or from another person having responsibilities including a right to consent to treatment of the minor (that is, usually, a parent or someone with parental responsibility).
- A practitioner will be liable to a minor of any age in negligence if he fails to advise with reasonable skill and care and to have due regard to the best interests of the patient.
- No minor of whatever age can refuse consent to treatment when consent has been given by someone with parental responsibility or a court. In other words, both parents and the courts can override a minor's refusal to consent in certain circumstances, even where the minor is competent to

make such a refusal of consent. Nevertheless, such a refusal is a very important consideration in making a clinical judgment and for parents and the court in deciding whether themselves to give consent.

The court's approach seems to be to seek to protect such children from doing (potentially life threatening) harm to themselves especially if this results in death or permanent damage.

Re K, W and H *[1993] 1 FLR 854*

This case involved applications from three youngsters, two aged 15, and one nearly 15, who were receiving psychiatric treatment at an adolescent unit at St Andrew's Hospital. In November 1991, the Northampton Area Health Authority set up an inquiry into practices at this unit. Children were only admitted to the unit if their parents or the local authority having care of them consented in writing to the regime adopted by the unit, including the emergency use of medication. In 1991, three adolescents who had received treatment in the unit made a complaint as to the treatment they had received at the unit. All three children had been admitted to the unit because of their highly disturbed behaviour and each had been making commendable progress since admission. The committee's report included a recommendation that, in cases where there was doubt about a child patient's consent, the hospital was advised to seek s 8 orders under the Children Act 1989, if there was doubt as to a child patient's consent. Two of the children had received tranquilising drugs and had shown progress since then.

In all three cases, there had been full parental co-operation and consent to the treatment regime.

Thorpe J held that, having read the reports:

(a) The applications under s 8 of the Children Act 1989 were misconceived and unnecessary. The decision of the Court of Appeal in *Re R* [1991] 4 All ER 177 made it plain that a child of *Gillick* competence could consent to treatment but that, if he or she declined to do so, consent could be given by someone else who has parental rights or responsibilities.

(b) Where more than one person has power to consent, only a refusal of all having that power will create a veto.

(c) None of the three children in this case was *Gillick* competent. Even if they had been, it was manifest that their refusal of consent would not have exposed the doctor at the unit to the risk of civil or criminal proceedings if he had proceeded to administer medication in an emergency and in the face of such refusal, since in each instance he had parental consent.

South Glamorgan CC v W and B *[1993] 1 FLR 574*

This involved a 15 year old girl who suffered from severe psychiatric disturbance since the age of 7. She had received virtually no schooling since the age of 11, had been seen by five child psychiatrists and had been the subject of 22 court appearances. She was approaching the end of her first year as a recluse in a room in her home. She was verbally abusive to her family and effectively controlled them, dictating who could enter her room or cook her meals, and threatening suicide or harm to herself if they failed to comply with her demands. One of the child psychiatrists who had seen her recommended she be removed to an adolescent unit, where she had previously received psychiatric assessment and treatment, as she was clearly beyond control. But nothing was done to remove her at that point. However, when a psychiatrist stated that her behaviour was likely to 'seriously impair her mental health in the future and limit her ability to function reasonably', the local authority eventually applied for care proceedings, essentially asking for the court's consent to assessment and treatment and removal from her home. Her mother supported the application, but her father did not.

Douglas Brown J considered the evidence very carefully and the views of everyone concerned, paying particular attention to the medical evidence and to the views of the experienced social worker and guardian *ad litem*. He noted all the precedents in the field such as *Re W* and Lord Donaldson MR's comments therein, and the result of the balancing exercise he conducted was that the court should give leave to the local authority to do what they asked. He was not prepared to recommend secure accommodation for the girl, but noted that, although the unit she was going to was not such a unit, a doctor's report suggested that the hospital authorities would not let the girl leave unaccompanied. It was therefore imperative that clear permission was given by the court for this to be enforced.

Professor Christina Lyon argues that the reasoning of this case is less justifiable than the reasoning in *Re W* (see p 120). She points out that, in the earlier case, the relevant statutory provision – s 8 of the Family Law Reform Act 1969 – was unclear, but the Children Act 1989 provisions, especially s 38(6), are very clear indeed. As she puts it, the judgment 'conveys to children the message that they cannot trust that the clearly expressed 'rights' given by Parliament will be safe in the hands of the judges' (see Lyon (1994), p 87).

Re C (Detention: Medical Treatment) *[1997] 2 FLR 180*

This case dealt with an anorexic 16 year old girl who had a history of persistent absconding; she refused to eat to the extent that her weight became dangerously low. The court authorised detention for feeding, although she had refused this treatment. It needs to be pointed out that although this case made the headlines because of the compulsory detention element, Wall J stressed that it was unlikely that detention would, in fact, be enforced, but confirmed that this was within the court's powers if necessary (see de Cruz (1999) 62 MLR 595 for a more detailed account of this case.)

Re L (Medical Treatment: Gillick Competence) *[1998] Fam Law 591*

Here, a 14 year old girl accidentally suffered very serious burns. She needed a blood transfusion to save her life and without it a horrible death would have ensued. The girl was a staunch Jehovah's Witness who had signed a 'no blood card' in which she expressed her wish not to receive a transfusion if she suffered injury. The surgeon had not given her full details of the horrible consequences of failure to receive treatment on the ground that it would have been too distressing to her.

The NHS Trust applied for a declaration that surgical intervention including blood transfusion was lawful.

Sir Stephen Brown P held that:

(a) the girl was not *Gillick* competent in respect of the proposed treatment. She had led a sheltered life in the context of her family and their religious community. Her limited experience of life necessarily limited her understanding of matters as grave as her situation. It had been appropriate to withhold from her details of the likely manner of death which would have been necessary to the making of the decision;

(b) the proposed treatment was not only in her best interests, but vital to her survival.

The court also said, *per curiam*, that treatment would also have been declared to have been lawful even if the patient had been found to be *Gillick* competent.

Several points may be made about this judgment. To begin with, it appears to suggest that the determination of *Gillick* competence does not depend simply on the cognitive powers and maturity of the child in question, but also on the seriousness of the decision to be taken. Further, the court appears to have followed the Lord Donaldson MR line of argument in *Re R*, that the court can override the '*Gillick* competent' child's refusal to receive treatment which is in her best interests. Of course, the court follows previous decisions such as *Re E (A Minor) (Wardship: Medical Treatment)* [1993] 1 FLR 386 and *Re S (A Minor) (Consent to Medical Treatment)* [1994] 2 FLR 1065, where Jehovah's Witness adolescents aged 15 were held not to be *Gillick* competent. Both these cases are notable for the courts' emphasis that the child was unable to appreciate the consequences of not receiving the proposed treatment.

Child's refusal of treatment overridden in heart transplant case

Re M – the heart transplant case: *Re M (A Minor) (Medical Treatment)*, Lawtel, LTL 15/7/99

In 1999, in a controversial case involving an afflicted teenager, a High Court judge ordered that the child be treated, despite her refusal of treatment.

Facts

The patient, M, aged 15 and a half, had been perfectly fit and well until about three months previously, had developed heart failure in May 1999, her condition deteriorated and, by 29 June 1999, her doctors' opinion was that a heart transplant was the only course. Their opinion was that the transplant was required within the next few days, otherwise her condition would have deteriorated to the extent that she would not have been well enough to undergo the operation. No other medical option was available. The situation was now that she now had only one week, or thereabouts, to live. Her parents had already consented for her to undergo a heart transplant operation. On learning that her only chance of survival was the operation to which they had agreed, M refused her consent.

The High Court judge who was to hear the case, Johnson J, insisted that M should speak to a solicitor to explain her views. M stated that 'she would rather die than have the transplant and have someone else's heart' and that she did not wish to take medication for the rest of her life. She said that she did not wish to die, but that the idea of being different from other people and living with someone else's heart made her feel very depressed. On hearing her views, the Official Solicitor believed that M was too overwhelmed at the discovery of her fatal illness and the seriousness of her situation to make an informed decision. He recommended that the surgery should take place, and the judge accepted this recommendation on the basis that the surgeons should act in accordance with their clinical judgment. He sanctioned the surgery and ordered that it be carried out.

Johnson J let it be known that he considered that the 'imposition of a heart transplant on a young woman who objected seemed to be very serious.' However, he held:

(a) the power to override M's refusal was undoubted;

(b) the court was very conscious of the great gravity of the decision which it was being asked to make in overriding M's wishes;

(c) nevertheless, whatever the risks, both in short and long term, of authorising the operation against M's wishes, such risks had to be matched against the certainty of M's death if the operation was not carried out;

(d) consequently, it seemed to the court that seeking to achieve what was best for M required, on balance, for the court to give authority for the operation.

Comment

So the trend continues. The English courts continue to adopt a paternalistic approach when it comes to teenagers who are either afflicted with cyclical psychotic illness or are in danger of imminent death, as with anorexia or because of serious heart problems that could ensue when no food has been consumed for a certain length of time. There does not appear to be a 'right to die' as far as these teenagers are concerned but, as usual, the courts rationalise their decisions on the basis of acting in the 'best interests' of the children concerned, which, of course, is the same rationale for authorising sterilisations of mentally incapacitated adults or teenagers. In potentially life threatening situations, there is also no autonomous 'right to refuse' treatment for the older child, despite the *Gillick* principle, because the courts have held that even a *Gillick* competent child can have her refusal to consent overridden (by courts and parents) if the court believes that this approach would better protect the child and certainly, on the facts of the cases themselves, to preserve those children's lives.

When is no consent needed?

Cases of 'necessity' have been identified. For instance, Lord Templeman (in *Gillick*) mentioned cases of urgency, abandonment and child abuse cases. Apart from patently obvious cases, there is some uncertainty in knowing when to proceed without consent. It would arguably be justifiable to do so pending taking further action such as contacting social services. In blood transfusion cases, the courts have so far not seen fit to abide by the wishes of teenagers who have refused consent when the possible outcome of complying with those wishes might be imminent death: see, for example, *Re E (A Minor)* (1992) 9 BMLR 1, where Ward J was prepared to override the refusal by the 15 year old boy's parents who were devout Jehovah's Witnesses, and sanction a life saving transfusion where the boy was suffering from leukaemia.

The general position

When presented with a child of 16, the health professional may presume capacity to consent to treatment, but this may be rebutted if the child is then found not to be, in fact, competent under the law (under the *Re C* tests, which require comprehension, retention and belief in the information being given as well as the ability to weight the pros and cons of treatment (see [1994] 1 All ER

819). For children under 16, if it involves something other than treatment, then an assessment of the child's maturity must be undertaken, but it remains unclear what the criteria might be. Ultimately, at least as far as the Court of Appeal is concerned, the 'best interests test' will be cited, as interpreted, to justify the court's opinion and the court remains the ultimate arbiter: see *Re P* [1992] 2 FCR 681 and *Re P* [1992] 1 FLR 321.

Parental consent

In order to deal with this aspect of consent, it is necessary to ask: who is a parent? Under the current law, it is any person with 'parental responsibility' (PR): s 3(1) of the Children Act (CA) 1989. In addition, the following points should be noted:

(a) married parents and all mothers have PR 'automatically';

(b) unmarried fathers do not have PR; they have to make an application under s 4 of the CA 1989. Alternatively, they may enter into a parental responsibility agreement with the child's mother or may make an application to court that the child reside with the unmarried father: s 12(1) of the CA 1989.

    In addition, if a person has care of a child (that is, the physical care) but no PR, it is permissible to do what is 'reasonable in all the circumstances of the case for the purpose of safeguarding or promoting the welfare of the child': s 3(5) of the CA 1989 (for example, foster parents).

Under s 12(2) of the CA 1989, a person acquires PR for the duration of the residence order. Note that, under s 1(1) of the CA 1989, the general rule is that the child's welfare is the paramount consideration in any matters involving the child's welfare and upbringing.

What if parents disagree amongst themselves?

Under s 2(7) of the CA 1989, one parent can act independently of the other, but is it safe to assume that a 'responsible body of medical opinion' would support a hospital acting without consulting both parents, if they were both available, but in dispute? The matter is unresolved. Under the law, doctors can probably proceed on the basis of one parent's consent or the mature child's consent, but the problem would arise if the doctor's disregard of a child's refusal was something no responsible practitioner would have disregarded, as judged by experts in the medical profession, that is, following *Bolam*.

Under the wardship jurisdiction, it is possible to make a child a ward of court, and what this means is that once a wardship order is made and remains in force, nothing can be done unless the court gives its consent to major matters such as education, health and immigration. Since the implementation of the CA 1989, a distinction has been drawn between inherent jurisdiction and wardship jurisdiction. The wardship jurisdiction overlaps with the court's powers under its inherent jurisdiction, but it is part of the larger powers within the inherent jurisdiction.

Thus, the court has powers under its inherent jurisdiction. A local authority may apply for a specific issue order to deal with a disputed sterilisation proposal. Wardship still exists as an order, although not as a means of appeal against an earlier order that was refused by the court. There is clearly a wide range of powers available. Supervision by the court is also sometimes ordered. There was a curbing of the use of wardship under the Children Act legislation, apparently because the local authorities seemed to use wardship excessively and as a means of appeal when their earlier applications to place a child in care failed. Under s 100 of the CA 1989, leave (court permission) is required before a local authority may be granted a wardship application. The best interests of the child 'test', as perceived and interpreted by the court, will be applied in every case.

What if parents disagree with an older child?

According to the *Gillick* case (1985) and comments from Lord Scarman, parents lose the right to consent on their child's behalf once they become *Gillick* competent. Lord Donaldson did not agree with this in *Re R* [1991] 4 All ER 177, which was a Court of Appeal decision involving a cyclically psychotic child whose medication was causing her nausea. The question arose as to whether she was '*Gillick* competent'. Lord Donaldson, in *Re W*, opined that parents do not lose the right to consent on behalf of their child when their child becomes competent to make a decision. This meant that doctors could get the consent they needed from either the child or the parents. Hence, as Montgomery points out: 'The effect of this is where a doctor believes that treatment is appropriate but a child refuses to accept their advice, then the doctor can approach the parent. So long as one of the parents can be persuaded to agree, then treatment will be lawful' (see Montgomery, J, 'Consent to health care for children' (1993) 5 J Child L 117, p 121).

The limits of parental consent

Under s 1 of the Children and Young Persons Act 1933, there is criminal liability for cruelty to persons under 16 which includes assault, neglect, ill treatment, abandonment, and exposure of the child to unnecessary suffering or injury to health.

Parental consent and medical treatment of their children

Parental refusal of consent and the child of an HIV positive mother

The case of *Re C (HIV Test)* illustrates the English courts' ruling that parental wishes are not usually determinative of a case involving medical treatment of a child. Here, the English Court of Appeal was faced with a situation where it had to consider the reasonableness or otherwise of parental refusal to agree to medical treatment of their child in *Re C (HIV Test)* [1999] 2 FLR 1004; and here, once the child had been born, the local authority was able to apply for a specific issue order under the CA 1989.

Facts

A baby girl, C, was born to a mother who first tested positive in 1990, but was highly sceptical of generally accepted theories about HIV and AIDS and refused conventional therapy for herself. She preferred to explore complementary therapies and concentrated on healthy eating and keeping fit. The father, who was also strongly opposed to testing the child for HIV testing and any form of medical intervention, had practised for a number of years in the sphere of holistic health care, including massage and reflexology. In July 1998, the mother became pregnant. She rejected the advice offered to pregnant women infected with HIV to take medication in the last weeks of pregnancy, to give birth by unforced Caesarean section and not to breastfeed. In April 1999, the mother had a natural water birth at home and, within a few minutes, began to breastfeed the baby.

The case arose when the baby's physician became aware not only that the mother was breastfeeding the child (despite the risk of transmission of HIV), but that the parents refused even to have their daughter tested for the virus, placing their faith in their healthy lifestyle as the optimal treatment even if the child tested HIV positive. At the age of almost five months, it was considered that the baby had already been exposed to a 20 to 25% risk of having contracted the HIV virus, breastfeeding having contributed to this level of risk.

The local authority, supported by the Official Solicitor acting as the baby's guardian ad litem, applied for a specific issue order under the CA 1989 that the four month old baby born to this HIV positive mother be tested for HIV. The order was granted by Wilson J, who declared that testing should take place, holding that:

(a) the arguments for overriding the wishes of the parents and testing the baby were overwhelming;

(b) if the test was conducted and was positive, firm professional advice could be given to which the afflicted baby was entitled;

(c) if the parents rejected that advice, the court might well order monitoring including further testing and, if the baby went into decline, combination therapy;

(d) if the test was negative, the urgent question would then arise of whether breastfeeding should cease. His Lordship said that, as good parents, they owed it to the baby radically to reconsider their stance on breastfeeding if any test proved negative. However, the court would not order the mother to stop breastfeeding. 'The law could not come between the baby and the breast' (p 1016);

(e) the case is not about the rights of the parents. The baby has rights of her own and the father was incorrect in his contention that the rights of the baby were subsumed within the rights of the parents.

The parents made an application for permission to appeal against Wilson J's decision. It was contended that the judge should not have criticised their strongly held views as to the inadequacy of the orthodox approach to treatment for HIV without evaluating those views and also evaluating the impact upon the parents and the baby of any imposed decision. It was further argued that, in this continuing and developing area of medicine, responsible parents should be entitled to a sphere of parental autonomy with which the courts should intervene.

The Court of Appeal refused the application, and held:

(a) the question whether the child should or should not be tested was a matter relating to the welfare of the child, not to the rights of the parents; and it was clearly not in the child's best interests for either the parents or the health professionals to remain ignorant of the child's state of health;

(b) the test which had been ordered provided a comparatively unintrusive way of determining the child's medical status, enabling all concerned with her future welfare to be better informed as to appropriate avenues of treatment in the event of illness;

(c) the only issue before the judge had been the question of testing the child for information purposes; the more complicated issues relating to medical treatment if the child tested positive, or to the risks associated with breastfeeding if the child tested negative, had not yet arisen;

(d) there was no doubt about the relevant legal principles, and the judge had evaluated the scientific evidence with conspicuous care and weighed in the balance all the competing arguments; there was no prospect of any appeal succeeding.

Comment

This case contrasts with *Re T* [1997] 1 All ER 906 (the liver transplant case) where, somewhat unusually, and in a break with precedent, the Court of Appeal placed considerable weight on parental wishes rather than clinical factors in connection with the issue of authorisation of a liver transplant for a toddler. The general trend in English law, particularly in connection with handicapped newborn children, has been to give consideration to parental wishes but *not* to regard them as determinative of any issue regarding the medical treatment of such children (see below, p 135).

Section 8 orders under the Children Act 1989

These orders were introduced by the CA 1989 in October 1991 and include the following: residence order; contact order; prohibited steps order; specific issue order. The restriction on making such orders is contained in s 1(5) of the CA 1989. These orders are described and explained below (p 132). In matters involving certain aspects of the child's medical treatment, a prohibited steps order may be applied for, depending on the circumstances, in order to either prevent a specific procedure to be carried out on the child except with the court's permission; or a specific issue order may be applied for to request the court to give certain directions in order to resolve any dispute over proposed medical treatment for the child.

CHILDREN'S RIGHTS

Determining the 'best interests of the child'

Who usually decides this? When the child is very young, it is usually the child's family. In the event of a dispute, it will be the courts if the case is taken to them, disagreements often occurring either between parents or between the parents and a third party such as a doctor or some other professional who has been looking after some aspect of the child's life, such as a teacher or educational specialist, or if there is uncertainty over the scope of the court's jurisdiction. If a wardship application is made, then as long as this is in force, no major decision can be made with regard to the child's welfare and upbringing without court approval or until a court hearing has taken place or until 21 days has elapsed from the date of the order.

(a) *Wardship v inherent jurisdiction*

The English courts may consider children cases under their wardship jurisdiction or under their inherent jurisdiction. The court's inherent jurisdiction includes the court's wardship powers. The key difference under the CA 1989 (effective since 14 October 1991) is that local authorities can no longer apply for a wardship order for a child as a matter of course or as a means of appeal if they have had an application for another order refused. Under the CA 1989 they have to show why they are invoking the court's inherent jurisdiction, and must establish that they cannot achieve what they are trying to achieve for the child by using any other available order.

(b) *Under the Children Act 1989*

Section 8 orders:

(1) 'Prohibited steps order': this is an order that no step which could be taken by a parent in meeting his parental responsibility for a child, and which is of a kind specified in the order, shall be taken by any person without the consent of the court.

(2) 'Specific issue order': this is an order giving directions for the purpose of determining a specific question which has arisen, or which may arise, in connection with any aspect of parental responsibility.

ACTING IN THE 'BEST INTERESTS OF THE CHILD'

English courts frequently state that they are acting 'in the best interests of the child', but does this slogan have any core content? By necessity, it is a concept of variable content and indeterminate until formulated and crystallised by a court. Some possible examples of the variable content of this slogan are as follows:

(a) To have the child's welfare and well being promoted/protected: for example, *Re S (A Minor) (Medical Treatment)* [1993] 1 FLR 376. The court said here that 'the test must remain the welfare of the child as the paramount consideration'.

(b) The application of the 'principle' tends to be governed by the specific facts.

   Generally, if the child's life is being threatened by non-treatment, the courts usually authorise treatment in the face of the parental refusal. Cases involving anorexic children are *Re W* (1992) and *Re C (Detention: Medical Treatment)* (1997) (see, also, de Cruz, P (1999) 62 MLR 595). For psychotically disturbed children: *Re R* [1992] 1 FLR 190. For children receiving psychiatric care: *South Glamorgan v W and B* and *Re K, W and H* [1993] 1 FLR 854.

Yet children who refuse treatment (supported by their parents) on religious grounds sometimes have their refusal of treatment overridden 'in their best interests': *Re E (A Minor) (Wardship: Medical Treatment)* [1993] 1 FLR 386 (15 year old leukaemia patient); *Re S (A Minor: Medical Treatment)* [1994] 2 FLR 1065.

(c) Relieving suffering is seen as part of their 'welfare'. This refers to cases involving handicapped newborn children. Here, the sanctity of life principle might sometimes be followed, but not always. Cases in this category are: *R v Arthur*; *Re C*; *Re J*; but not *Re T* (the liver transplant case).

(d) Protecting children from a pregnancy they could not cope with. This might be through sterilisation as in *Re B* (the *Jeanette* case) [1987] 2 All ER 206, HL. One of the objections to sterilisation is that it cannot protect the child from rape or sexual exploitation; it merely removes the visible signs of these abuses.

The *Gillick* case and children's rights

Gillick's case had been seen by some writers as the dawn of a new era of children's rights (see, for example, Eekelaar (1986)) and, as we have seen, several statutory 'rights' are now contained in the CA 1989. However, it would be naïve to assume that the mere statement of rights, even in a statute, means that children will suddenly acquire a range of new rights enforceable in a court of law, particularly when English common law and the CA 1989 allow scope for interpretation of the law in a given situation. Indeed, as we have seen, post-*Gillick*, it has been possible for a court to say that a child does not have the right to refuse certain medical treatment, if the result of following the child's wishes is serious physical or mental injury to the child concerned, or even the possibility of death. The English courts have said that their decision to ignore the child's stated wishes in various cases was made in that child's best interests; or that the child was not of sufficient age or understanding to make a legally valid choice, in other words, was not *Gillick* competent; or that although the child might have been *Gillick* competent from time to time, 'true' *Gillick* competence was achieved once and for all. The reality is that all these cases represent judicial (and sometimes medical) paternalism because the courts pay considerable deference to the views of the doctors in this context, and in most cases, the medical opinion is the determinative element in a court's decision. This continuing deference, reflected in the usual application of the *Bolam* principle, militates against any right of true choice on the part of children, particularly those that have not yet achieved *Gillick* competence but, in life threatening situations, even if they have. If abiding by a child's decision means there is a strong likelihood of that child's death, the courts will simply not grant any right to refuse treatment because, irrespective of which criterion one uses, they believe that they are acting in the best interests of that child.

INTERNATIONAL PERSPECTIVES

The UN Convention on the Rights of the Child

The 1989 United Nations Convention on the Rights of the Child (the Convention) creates in international law a duty upon States to accord children rights on a par with adults. A child is defined as 'every human being up to the age of 18 years', but the wording of the Convention does not address the starting point of childhood, that is, when does childhood begin? So the question remains: is it conception, birth or even somewhere in between? Children's rights are limited, especially in their right to vote, but in international law the Convention is binding on States that ratify it, as the UK did in December 1991. However, it is important to realise that ratification does not make the Convention part of the domestic law – the government would need to enact the relevant legislation, as it did with the Human Rights Act 1998, which incorporated the European Convention on Human Rights in October 2000. The situation is different in the USA, where ratification of international treaties automatically makes them part of federal law, but the USA has not, as yet, ratified the UN Convention on the Rights of the Child.

THE MEDICAL TREATMENT OF HANDICAPPED BABIES

Historical background

In ancient times, in countries like Greece, babies born with severe abnormalities would be left to die in country fields, and in Sparta in ancient Greece, the killing of weak or deformed infants was required. Both the *Republic* of Plato and the *Politics* of Aristotle saw nothing reprehensible about killing defective newborns. Indeed, In his *Politics*, Aristotle is supposed to have declared:

> As to the exposure and rearing of children, let there be a law that no deformed child shall live, but that on the ground of an excess in the number of children, if the established customs of the state forbid this (for in our state population has a limit), no child is to be exposed, but when couples have children in excess, let abortion be procured before sense and life have begun ...

In ancient Greece, infanticide was a widely accepted practice in conformity with the legal standards of the time. Plato, in *The Republic*, is again revealing:

> The proper officers will take the offspring of the good parents to the pen or fold, and there they will deposit them with certain nurses who dwell in a separate quarter, but the offspring of the inferior, or of the better when they chance to be deformed, will be put away in some mysterious, unknown place, as they should be.

Euripides dramatised infanticide in *Medea* by having Medea kill her two sons. As Weir explains: 'Young children, weak children, female children, and especially children regarded as being defective were regularly strangled, drowned, buried in dunghills, "potted" in jars to starve to death, or exposed to the elements (with the belief that the gods had the responsibility of saving exposed infants)' (Weir (1984), p 7). The major determinant of survival for these newborns was the infant's normalcy. The issue of normalcy was so dominant in Greek thinking that infants were denied the benefit of the doubt so much so that infants who appeared normal but were offspring of 'inferior' parents were also sometimes killed.

It is documented history that Romans were also in favour of eliminating babies who were born with severe deformities. Several literary works mention instances of infanticide – Chaucer's *Canterbury Tales*, Dickens' *Oliver Twist* and Chekhov's story *Sleepyhead*, to name but a few.

Tribal societies in various parts of the world, such as the Bedouin tribes of ancient Arabia, the Eskimos, Polynesian tribes, Australian tribes, China and India have all practised infanticide (usually female infanticide) for many centuries (for an account of all these societies and more, see Weir (1984), Chapter 1). The Christian church, during the first three centuries, condemned late term abortion and infanticide and around 300 BC the Roman Emperor Constantine converted to Christianity and banned parental infanticide. The edict he passed led to parents not actively killing defective babies, but merely abandoning them to die of exposure. Christianity condemned abandonment and infanticide and did not establish a foundling hospital until the eighth century in Milan.

During the Middle Ages, the practice grew of wet nurses assisting parents who wanted others to raise their children or wished to be relieved of looking after their children. In the 18th century, in the wake of rapidly expanding populations in Europe, exposure and infanticide appeared to function as birth control. As Pence writes: 'Overpopulation led to more institutionalised abandonment in France, Germany, and England. It appears that well into the 19th century, parents continued to turn unwanted babies over to ... wet nurses' or simply abandoned them to rural baby farms 'where they were often fed gin to die painlessly. So many babies were abandoned during Napoleon's reign that he established Foundling Hospitals, where parents could anonymously deposit a baby on a turntable, spin the wheel and leave. In France in 1833, over a 100,000 babies were abandoned' (Pence (1990), p 137).

Towards the end of the 19th century, campaigns were launched to ban such practices and the Infant Life Protection Society was founded (in 1870) to oppose farms and burial clubs where parents collected from payouts on multiple life insurance policies on dead babies.

It was only in the 1960s that intensive care units were developed to keep premature babies alive who would previously have died. Indeed, the development of small respirator and feeding tubes saved many babies, and also managed to resuscitate babies who were born dying. Using respirators to save the lives of babies born with neurological haemorrhages or lung damage was revolutionary, but also raises ethical problems about allocation of resources (see, further, Chapter 19).

Ethical perspectives

As we have seen, in the context of ethical codes which date back several centuries, and in accordance with the modern practice of medicine, doctors have a *prima facie* commitment to respect and preserve life. Nowhere has this been more evident than at birth and in the early weeks of post-natal life. As Campbell reminds us, 'modern perinatal intensive care, in conjunction with improvements in maternal health and socio-economic circumstances, have led to perinatal and infant death rates that are a fraction of what they were last century' (Campbell (1989), p 52). Some commentators point out that it is only relatively recently that the salvaging of all infants born alive has been seen as a desirable social goal (Silverman (1981)).

Sanctity of human life v quality of life

This area brings into conflict several ethical principles, the most obvious being the notion of the sanctity of human life (preservation of life in all circumstances) and the quality of life. In addition, the distinction between 'killing and letting die or allowing to die' is raised, as is the principle of 'double effect', whereby an action that is intended to do good may be justifiable even though its foreseen or unforeseen result is harmful. These difficult cases have been canvassed in several English cases, such as *R v Arthur* (1981) and a host of cases dealing with handicapped newborns who were born with varying degrees of mental and physical disabilities and deformities.

Several difficult questions have to be faced by doctors in treating these infants. Campbell lists these queries: 'What kinds of infants are likely to survive with severe handicaps? How can we recognise them? Can future "quality of life" be predicted with sufficient accuracy to justify its use as a criterion for life or death decisions, or should all infants routinely be given intensive care and other treatments to prolong their lives to the best of our abilities?' (Campbell (1989), p 52). The list does not end there. He asks, pertinently: 'Can it ever be right to withhold or withdraw treatment in the knowledge that death will result? Should death be hastened to avoid pain or distress when further treatment seems futile?' (Campbell).

Should parents have the final decision on the medical treatment of their children?

The question that has sometimes arisen in the English courts has been the extent to which the wishes of the parents of the child should be taken into account by the court in reaching its decision. By and large, English law has said that this should be considered, but is not determinative. However, the case of *Re T* [1997] 1 All ER 906 appeared to suggest that, in certain circumstances, parental opinion might or should be given considerable weight when the court performs the balancing exercise required in reaching their decisions in these very difficult cases. Decisions about the severely disabled and dying are problematic and have been the subject of continuing debate for many years (Duff and Campbell (1980)) and controversy raged, at least in the academic world, in the late 1990s over the non-approval by the Court of Appeal in *Re T* [1997] 1 WLR 242 (see further discussion, below, p 143) of a liver transplant for an 18 month old boy, because his parents felt he had already been through too much and that they were unable to give him the commitment which he might need in aftercare should he have the transplant, even though the chances of a successful transplant were very good. It will be noted that this was not the classic case of a severely handicapped newborn infant, but the prominence given to parental wishes and certain statements from the Court of Appeal have cast some doubt on the law relating to the medical treatment of handicapped babies.

THE EUROPEAN CONVENTION FOR THE PROTECTION OF HUMAN RIGHTS AND FUNDAMENTAL FREEDOMS

With the coming into force of the Human Rights Act 1998 (the 1998 Act) and consequently the incorporation of the European Convention for the Protection of Human Rights and Fundamental Freedoms (the European Convention) into English law on 2 October 2000, it is more relevant than ever to pose the question of whether any decision to withdraw or withhold medical treatment from handicapped newborn children would be in breach of certain articles of the 1998 Act (such as Art 2, the right to life; and Art 3, the right not to be subjected to inhuman and degrading treatment, including the right to die with dignity). Put another way, would allowing a child to die be against the 1998 Act? A recent case, *A National Health Service Trust v D* (2000) *The Times*, 19 July, suggests that it would not. This case is discussed at p 152.

PARENTAL WISHES, MEDICAL TREATMENT AND DISABLED BABIES

What is in the child's best interests?

Should parents have the ultimate right to decide on what medical treatment is best for their handicapped or seriously ill babies? In the case of very severely handicapped newborns, should parents have the right to decide whether their child lives or dies in certain circumstances?

The Court of Appeal case of *Re T (A Minor: Wardship: Medical Treatment)* [1997] 1 WLR 242 might not have sparked off many media headlines, although it has certainly aroused several academic responses, but unless it is overturned by the Court of Appeal or House of Lords, this decision could mark a watershed in the law relating to selective non-treatment of newborn children who are born with life threatening defects, when the parents of the baby refuse their consent to life saving treatment for the child. Cases decided since 1981 appeared to establish several fairly rigorous criteria which had to be satisfied before a court could authorise non-treatment of a severely handicapped neonate and that parental wishes could never be determinative of the question of whether such a child would continue to receive medical treatment despite its serious physical and/or mental disabilities.

Previous cases on handicapped babies

R v Arthur *(the* Arthur *case) (1981) 12 BMLR 1*

In this case, the child was born with Down's syndrome. At the time, it was thought that there were no further physical complications. However, when told of their child's condition, the parents said they did not want him and the consultant paediatrician, Dr Leonard Arthur, prescribed 'nursing care only' for the child. He also prescribed large doses of dihydocodeine for sedative purposes. The child later died, having survived for 57 hours, and it is believed that members of a pro-life group instigated a police prosecution against Dr Arthur. At the trial, it was established that he was a caring, compassionate doctor and several eminent witnesses testified that he was merely following standard medical practice when he prescribed 'nursing care only'. The question then was whether allowing the baby to die when it developed broncho-pneumonia as a result of the repeated dosages of the pain killing medication, which hospital staff were aware would happen, amounted to murder.

It emerged from evidence given by various healthcare professionals that the words 'nursing care only' meant different things to different health authorities. In some regions, it meant simply providing fluids and basic care, but nothing beyond this; in others, it meant doing everything possible to ensure the baby's survival, from resuscitation techniques to life support machines. Hence, there was no consistent or uniform medical practice applicable to the term 'nursing care only' in all health authorities.

A post-mortem was carried out on the baby which revealed that he did have other physical complications and would have died anyway. The charge was then changed to attempted murder. However, Dr Arthur was acquitted. The court stated that, as long as the doctor was following a standard medical practice, which was supported by 'a responsible body of medical opinion' (in other words, the *Bolam* test), he was not negligent and the court would be very slow in concluding that the doctor was breaking the law.

As the law has operated, the *Bolam* test is satisfied provided there is *one* body of responsible medical opinion which supports the practice in question, regardless of whether there are variations across the country and there may be other health authorities which do *not* support the particular procedure or practice. There was no suggestion in the *Arthur* case that the wishes of the parents would be determinative of the court's decision.

The court held, further, that it would be lawful to treat the baby with sedative drugs and offer no further care if (a) the child was irreversibly or irreparably disabled; and (b) the child had been rejected by its parents. The second part of this ruling has never been the law.

Just before the *Arthur* case was decided, the *Baby Alexandra* case had been decided in the Court of Appeal, yet the court was not referred to it and there is no reference to it in the *Arthur* judgment.

Re B *(1981) (the* Baby Alexandra *case) – the 'demonstrably awful' test*

In 1981, the Court of Appeal decided the case of *Re B (A Minor) (Wardship: Medical Treatment)* [1981] 1 WLR 1421 involving a baby suffering from Down's syndrome who had an intestinal blockage which would have proved fatal in a few days without an operation. The parents opposed the operation, believing that it was in the best interests of the child not to have the operation and to be allowed to die rather than to live as a physically and mentally handicapped person. The medical profession could not predict whether the child would suffer or be happy after the operation. Her life expectancy was estimated at between 20 and 30 years. When one surgeon decided that the wishes of the parents should be respected, the local authority sought an order authorising other surgeons to perform the operation. The court overruled the parents' decision and authorised the operation. It declared that the prognosis must be that the child's life must be so *'demonstrably awful'* that it would not be in its best interests to have the operation. Templeman LJ formulated the 'best interests test' in these terms:

> ... it is a decision which must of course be made in the light of the evidence and views expressed by the parents ... but, at the end of the day, it devolves on this court in this particular instance to decide whether the life of this child is *demonstrably going to be so awful* that in effect the child must be condemned to die, or whether the life of this child is still so imponderable that it would be wrong for her to be condemned to die. There may be cases, I know not, of severe proved damage where the future is so uncertain and where the life of the child is so bound to be full of pain and suffering that the court might be driven to a different conclusion, but in the present case the choice which lies before the court is this: whether to allow an operation to take place which may result in the child living for 20 to 30 years as a mongoloid or whether ... to terminate the life of a mongoloid child because she has an intestinal complaint. [Emphasis added.]

Faced with this choice, the Court of Appeal felt it their duty to decide that 'the child must live'.

Indeed, the court indicated that the question for the court was whether the proposed treatment was in the child's best interests, *not* whether the wishes of the parents should be respected.

The operation went ahead and the child survived for six years.

What would the court's approach be if the child were born with severe impairments and was already dying? *Re C* (1989) dealt with this situation.

Re C *(1989)*

In *Re C (A Minor) (Wardship: Medical Treatment)* [1989] 2 All ER 782, even before baby C's birth, it had been decided by the local authority that her parents would be unable to care for their baby when it was born and it was decided that the baby should be made a ward of court after it was born. C was born prematurely and was found to be hydrocephalic, and in addition to the usual blockage of cerebral spinal fluid within the brain, her brain structure was found to be poorly formed. She had been made a ward of court after two weeks and the court had authorised a surgical operation on her to relieve pressure on her brain. There was no medical dispute that her brain was irreparably damaged at birth and there was no question of brain function being restored. The question remained: what treatment, if any, should be given to the baby? The child was, in fact, dying and Ward J made an order that the hospital authorities be given permission that the child be 'treated to die', but to die with the greatest dignity and the least pain, suffering and distress. The judge himself changed some of this terminology when the Official Solicitor objected to it and appealed to the Court of Appeal.

The Court of Appeal held that the child was to be treated in a manner appropriate to its condition; she had no hope of a happy life; her condition had been terminal even before her birth. The court, in considering as paramount the welfare and best interests of the child, was entitled to approve recommendations designed to ease the baby's suffering rather than prolong its life. The court explained that a baby would be *'irreparably damaged'* if it was *'permanently unable to interact mentally, socially and physically'*. The appeal court also agreed that the original words devised by Ward J could give rise to misunderstanding and made it clear that there could not be authorisation of the taking of the life of such a baby without careful consideration of the best interests of the child. The court's view was to leave it to the paediatric team to decide how to treat the baby. It needs to be remembered that there was a clear consensus about the prognosis and C was certain to die, even if this could be delayed for a short time.

The position with regard to babies who are dying appears to be reasonably clear, but what if the newborn was not in danger of imminent death? In *Re J* (1990), the Appeal Court answered this question.

Re J *(1990)*

In *Re J (A Minor) (Wardship: Medical Treatment)* [1990] 3 All ER 780, the child, Baby J, was born 13 weeks prematurely and weighed two and a half pounds at birth. At that stage, the child was not breathing and was placed on a ventilator. Problems at birth had caused irreversible brain damage. The child suffered from fits, was diagnosed as blind, probably deaf, paralysed and was unlikely ever to learn to speak or to comprehend what was going on around him. Baby J would be unable ever to sit up or hold his head up, but could feel pain. The child was *not* in fact dying, nor on the point of death, but it was estimated that he would probably not survive his late adolescence. There were conflicting views as to what should happen to the child, and he was therefore made a ward of court. In the High Court, Baker J held that, if the baby fell ill again, doctors would be entitled not to carry out life saving treatment. The case went on appeal and in the Court of Appeal, Lord Donaldson MR said that one thing the baby could feel was pain. The doctors all agreed that the child should not be put back on a ventilator, because this might cause even greater brain damage, and might not improve his chances of survival. Lord Donaldson opined that to prolong life is not the sole objective of the court and to require it at the expense of other considerations may not be in the child's best interests. The court accordingly held that it would be in this severely handicapped child's best interests for *non*-resuscitation to be authorised if he fell critically ill again, in view of the hazardous nature of reventilation and risk of further deterioration. Baby J could be kept alive indefinitely, but having assessed his *quality of life* if kept alive, the court opined that the task of determining what was in a child's best interests was a balancing exercise.

The court therefore further held that, where a ward of court suffered from physical disabilities so grave that his life would, from his point of view, be so intolerable if he were to continue living that he would choose to die if he were in a position to make a sound judgment, the court could direct that treatment without which death would ensue from natural causes need not be given to the ward to prolong his life, even though he was not on the point of death or dying. However, the court could never sanction positive steps to terminate the life of a person.

Comment

The first thing to note about this case is that the child, although severely brain damaged, quadriplegic and placed on a ventilator, was *not* actually in danger of *imminent* death and could be expected to survive into his teens. However, his 'quality of life' was seen as very poor, and he could feel pain. Hence, the English Court of Appeal applied the '*quality of life principle*' and even mentioned a 'substituted judgment' approach in treating severely handicapped babies. This is redolent of the Glanville Williams approach to preferring death to a life as a disabled person and it remains flawed, since it is impossible to imagine, from a normal person's point of view, what a disabled person would choose in these circumstances, since a disabled person would have never known what not being disabled or being normal is like. *A fortiori*, this applies to a baby who is totally dependent on its carer and will not have many experiences that an adult making the choice associates with the normal pleasures or sensations of life. On the other hand, it is very difficult not to feel wholehearted sympathy for the persons having to care for a disabled child and the court is, arguably, having great regard for the child's parents when it decides not to employ extraordinary means to sustain a severely handicapped baby's life, and to allow that baby to die with dignity. In a later *Re J (A Minor) (Wardship: Medical Treatment)* [1992] 2 FLR 165, medical staff considered it inappropriate to attempt to save the life of a 16 month old brain damaged child with invasive intensive care if he suffered a life-threatening relapse. His mother sought and obtained an order that treatment should be given to prolong his life. The court immediately stayed the order, which was later upheld on appeal. The medical profession will therefore not be required to carry out treatment against their clinical judgment, irrespective of parental demands; parental consent is required but there is no parental right to demand treatment in these cases.

So far, all these cases involved severely handicapped newborns and up to this point, parental wishes were not determinative of the final decision. How would the courts deal with a child who was not as seriously or irreversibly handicapped but where there was a very high rate of success in performing a transplant operation? What if the parents *objected* to further treatment for their child, on the basis that they wished to spare the child further distress, pain or trauma?

The case of *Re T* (1997) answered some of these queries, at least based on its particular set of circumstances.

Re T *(1997) (the liver transplant case)*

Facts

In *Re T (Wardship: Medical Treatment)* [1997] 1 WLR 242, the baby, T, was born in April 1995 suffering from biliary atresia, a life threatening liver defect, and an operation when he was three and a half weeks old was unsuccessful. Without transplantation he would not live beyond the age of two to two and a half. The unanimous medical opinion was that prospects of success of a transplant were good (apparently an 80–90% success rate) and it was in the baby's best interests to undergo the operation when a donor became available. The parents were both healthcare professionals, experienced in the care of sick children, and had jobs in a distant Commonwealth country. They did not wish T to undergo transplant surgery and refused their consent to an operation should a liver become available. The mother's relationship with the consultant paediatricians was strained because the surgeons did not accept the mother's reasons for refusing consent. They were prepared to proceed with the operation without the mother's consent if the court gave its consent. The doctors, therefore, referred the matter to the relevant local authority of the mother's area which applied to the High Court to exercise its inherent jurisdiction with respect to the child under s 100(3) of the CA 1989. The application was granted; the Official Solicitor was appointed guardian ad litem of the child, and he instructed a consultant surgeon.

The court had to consider whether it should overrule the decision of the parents and give consent to the operation.

The High Court decision

When the case came before Connell J, he directed the mother, who had left the jurisdiction with T, to return within 21 days so that T could be returned to the jurisdiction to be assessed for transplant surgery. He based his decision on the medical evidence and on the rationale that the mother's refusal to accept the unanimous advice of the doctors 'was not the conduct of a reasonable parent'. The mother appealed to the Court of Appeal.

The Court of Appeal judgments

The Court of Appeal (Butler-Sloss, Waite and Roche LJJ) allowed the appeal and held that, when an application was made to the court under its inherent jurisdiction, the welfare of the child was the paramount consideration, and although a parent's consent or refusal of consent was an important consideration to weigh in the balancing exercise, it was for the court to decide the matter, and in so doing it might overrule the decision of a reasonable parent.

Reasonableness of the mother not determinative of the issue

Butler-Sloss LJ conceded that Connell J had made a 'careful, comprehensive and sensitive judgment' but that he had erred in that he did not weigh in the balance reasons against the treatment which might be held by a reasonable parent on much broader grounds than the clinical assessment of the likely success of the proposed treatment. In her Ladyship's view, the lower court judge did not give sufficient thought to the fact that the mother had focused on the present peaceful life of the baby without the pain, stress and upset of the intrusive surgery against the future with the operation and treatment taking place. She believed Connell J was incorrect in deeming the mother unreasonable in her assessment of the broader perspective of whether the operation should be carried out. In any event, she considered the 'reasonableness' or otherwise of the mother was *not* the primary issue and 'the mother and baby were one for the purpose of this unusual case'. Parental wishes were merely one consideration to be taken into account in the balancing exercise that had to be carried out in determining the child's best interests. Treatment could not, therefore, be authorised purely on the basis that the mother was being unreasonable.

Her Ladyship considered the line of cases dating back to 1981 (*Re B; Re J* (above, pp 140–41)) and concluded:

> From the decisions to which I have been referred which bind this court, it is clear that when an application under the inherent jurisdiction is made to the court the welfare of the child is the paramount consideration. The consent or refusal of the parents is an important consideration to weigh in the balancing

> exercise to be carried out by the judge. In that context, the extent to which the court will have regard to the view of the parent will depend upon the court's assessment of that view.

She cited Lord Donaldson's *dictum* in *Re J* (above), which stressed that there was a very strong presumption in favour of a course of action which will prolong life, but he then added that it was not irrebuttable and that:

> ... account has to be taken of the pain and suffering and quality of life which the child will experience if life is prolonged ... Account has to be taken of the pain and suffering of the treatment itself ... there will be cases in which ... it is not in the interests of the child to subject it to treatment which will cause increased suffering and produce no commensurate benefit, giving the fullest weight to the child's and mankind's, desire to survive.

Her Ladyship placed great weight upon 'one of the most unusual facts of the case', which was the 'enormous significance of the close attachment between the mother and baby'. Consequently, the decision of the court to consent to the operation jointly affects the mother and son and it also affects the father. In other words, 'the welfare of the child depends upon his mother'. She therefore opined that Connell J's exercise of his discretion was flawed and was satisfied that it could not stand. She also placed great weight on the evidence of one of the consultant surgeons which emphasised the requirements both of the consent of the parents and a 'total commitment by the caring parent to the proposed treatment'.

Significantly, her Ladyship distinguished the case of an intestinal obstruction of the Down's syndrome baby (such as *Re B* (1981)) which could be cured by a simple operation, from the present case, which required complicated surgery and many years of special care from the mother. Even greater significance was placed on the evidence of the consultant, which expressed the view that 'the decision of a loving, caring mother should be respected'.

Further, the prospect of forcing the 'devoted mother' of this young baby to the consequences of this invasive surgery led her to the conclusion, 'after much anxious deliberation', that 'it is not in the best interests of the child' to give consent to the operation and require him to return to England for the purpose of undergoing liver transplantation. She believed that the best interests of the child required that his future treatment be left in the hands of his devoted parents.

Waite LJ agreed with Butler-Sloss LJ and stated at the outset that 'the law's insistence that the welfare of the child shall be paramount is easily stated and universally applauded but the present case illustrates, poignantly and dramatically, the difficulties that are encountered when trying to put it into practice'. He considered the parents' refusal of consent to the operation to be partly instinctive and partly practical, based on their own awareness of the procedures involved. It had 'sufficient cogency' to have led one of the principal medical experts in the field of this operation to say that his team would decline to operate without his mother's committed support. He did not think that this was a suitable occasion to talk of rights, whether of the child, parent or of the courts. He also agreed that Connell J's approach of assessing whether the mother's approach was reasonable led him to make an error of law.

He stressed that all these cases depend on their own facts and render generalisations wholly out of place. When it comes to assessment of the demands of the child patient's welfare, the starting point – and the finishing point, too – must be the judge's own independent assessment of the balance of advantage or disadvantage of the particular medical step under consideration.

Roche LJ agreed with the other two judges. He opined that, if the parents in a liver transplant case are devoted and responsible and have the best interests of the children in mind, their views are to be taken into account and accorded weight and respect by the court when reaching its decision. In addition, the views of the parents have a clinical significance because, in the absence of parental belief that a transplant is the right procedure for the child, the prospects of a successful outcome are diminished. He then referred to *Fact Sheet No 10*, published by the Children's Liver Disease Foundation, which had been given to the mother in this case, in which the sentence appears: 'If the family choose not to proceed with the transplantation once they are acquainted with the facts, this decision is respected.' He believed that the child currently had a 'happy and secure life', albeit short, and thus it would not be in his best interests to have his present life disrupted and having his mother return to this country with him to endure the operation in question, with all its distress and uncertainties.

Comment on Re T

Re T clearly breaks with precedent, since previous cases dating back to 1981 had enunciated that the question for the court in deciding whether an operation should be performed in these kinds of cases was whether the operation would be in the best interests of the child and *not* whether the wishes of the parent should be respected. Secondly, *Re T* appeared to give a highly unusual amount of emphasis on the parental/mother's opinion that was expressed in this case, rather than on the unanimous medical opinion which estimated 80–90% success rate for the liver transplant operation. Thirdly, the court affirmed that the sanctity of life was not an absolute principle. This was in reliance on Lord Donaldson's *dictum* in *Re J* (above) and this was, of course, recognised in the *Tony Bland* case (*Airedale NHS Trust v Bland* [1993] 1 FLR 1026). Fourthly, the court took into account 'non-clinical' factors such as the circumstances of the case, the views of the parents and the doctors (one of whom had placed enormous importance on the need for maternal commitment). The court appeared to regard the mother, who was a healthcare professional, as loving, devoted and caring, considering the benefits and risks of the operation, the life expectancy, the effect on the mother of having to look after the child and having to leave the father who was abroad and/or the father having to give up his job abroad to return to the UK.

In addition, the doctors had also been reluctant to perform the operation when the parents had refused their consent. In the past, the courts have consistently overruled parental opposition (see, in addition to the cases cited at the opening of this chapter, *Re S (A Minor) (Consent to Medical Treatment)* [1994] 2 FLR 1065; *Re E (A Minor)* (1992) 9 BMLR 1; *Re S (A Minor) (Medical Treatment)* [1993] 1 FLR 376; *Re R (A Minor) (Blood Transfusion)* [1993] 2 FLR 757).

Parental opposition in *Re T* led to the operation not being authorised. Yet, all the Lord Justices made it clear that the reasonableness or otherwise of the parental opinion was *not* relevant and that a judicial assessment of it by the lower court judge was an error in law.

Conclusions on Re T

The Court of Appeal appeared unduly swayed by the fact that the parents were healthcare professionals themselves and could (arguably) have a better understanding of the procedures involved. They felt it was more compassionate for the child, who was an otherwise happy baby, not to have invasive surgery, and appeared devoted in every other respect, and this appeared to tip the balance against the child having the operation. Yet the person to come off worst of all here, especially in the longer term, is the child. Was the appeal court really justified in not giving greater weight to the unanimous medical prognosis that the operation would save this child and that its chances of success were very high indeed? This case is further flawed by the fact that the child was not encephalic, did not have a short life expectancy or any other severely disabling defects which might have weighed against an operation being carried out. If the parents were not prepared to be inconvenienced by having to return to the UK, give up jobs, and devote their time to caring for their baby, the local authority could make alternative arrangements, and even explore adoption by people who would be prepared to look after the child. Using the *Re B* guideline, surely the life of the child in *Re T* was not going to be so 'demonstrably awful' that it would not be in his best interests to have the operation. On the other hand, in the view of the parents, particularly in the light of all the medical procedures he had already undergone, perhaps yet another operation would subject the child to considerable distress and they seemed to believe that he had already undergone enough trauma in his life.

A final comment on *Re T* is that the courts have confirmed that the sanctity of human life is not an absolute principle but that, even if the child might survive an operation, the force of parental opposition might sometimes carry so much weight that it would override what might truly be in the child's best interests. In that respect, *Re T* is tragic and deeply worrying.

*Post-*Re T*: clinical factors again determinative?*

A case decided after *Re T* is *Re C (Medical Treatment)* [1998] 1 FLR 1, where, despite parental opposition, the court authorised the withdrawal of ventilation from a severely disabled baby who was dying.

Re C *(1998)*

In this case, *Re C (A Minor) (Medical Treatment)* [1998] Lloyd's Rep Med 1, the 16 month old baby was suffering from spinal muscular atrophy, type 1 (SMA) and was dependent on intermittent positive pressure ventilation. The doctors treating her were of the opinion that her condition fell into the 'no chance' situation defined in *Withholding or Withdrawing Lifesaving Treatment in Children: A Framework for Practice*, published by the Royal College of Paediatrics and Child Health (RCP) in September 1997. Accordingly, they wished to withdraw ventilator support and allow her to die with palliative care in the event of cardiac arrest. Her parents, who were orthodox Jews, felt unable to consent to this course of action and insisted that she be reventilated should she suffer respiratory relapse. Despite her emaciated and deteriorating condition, C did appear to recognise her parents and smile when they visited her. Her doctors refused to accede to their wishes, maintaining that further treatment would cause her increasing distress, could cause medical complications and was futile, as her life expectancy was unlikely to extend beyond 18 months. The hospital authority applied to the High Court for the declaration approving their care management plan. The Official Solicitor appeared as *amicus curiae*.

The court held that: (a) C's condition was a 'no chance' situation as defined in the RCP guidelines, since she suffered from 'such severe disease that life sustaining treatment simply delays death without significant alleviation of suffering'. At p 10, para 2.2.2 of that document, SMA type 1 was cited as a progressive condition in which ventilator care might reasonably be withheld; (b) the order would give leave to treat C, as advised by her doctors, to ease her suffering and permit her life to end peacefully and with dignity, such treatment being in C's best interests; (c) the court would not make an order which would, directly or indirectly, require a doctor to treat a child in a manner contrary to his clinical judgment: *Re J* [1990] 3 All ER 789 followed.

Comment

This case appeared to follow the previous line of authority in that parental opposition was not a determinative factor and the fact that the child's parents were Orthodox Jews whose religion forbade them to sanction any action shortening life. The balancing exercise was applied and, although the parents wished their child to live as long as possible, the court's view was that further treatment would subject the baby to more suffering without commensurate benefit. However, the child's parents were simply adopting the sanctity of life approach rather than any 'best interests' principle, and wanted their daughter to carry on living regardless of her quality of life. The court in this case did, however, consider predominantly *clinical* factors. This also seemed to be the approach in *Re C (HIV Test)* [1999] 2 FLR 1004, where the parents refused to consent to an HIV test for their four month old baby whose mother was HIV positive and was breastfeeding the baby, but the test was nevertheless authorised by the Court of Appeal. The court emphasised that the main criterion was the welfare of the child and at this stage, the HIV test was for information purposes only. Post-*Re T*, therefore, the *Re B* (1981) line of precedent (where parents' views are not determinative) appears to be the preferred judicial approach but, as ever, in this field, the particular circumstances of a case will determine the eventual decision and courts will distinguish precedents where they believe this will be in the child's best interests.

The David Glass *case (*R v Portsmouth NHS Trust ex p Glass *[1999] Med LR 125; [1999] Lloyd's Rep Med 367*

David Glass was born prematurely, at 30 weeks' gestation, on 23 July 1986 in Portsmouth, because he had hydrocephalus, where fluid accumulates on the brain. He also had cerebral palsy and epilepsy. Carol Glass was told her son would not survive. After 55 minutes he was still alive and was seen by a doctor from the special baby care unit. Initially, he was artificially ventilated, but the treatment was stopped and his mother was again told he would not survive. He continued, however, to breathe unaided. Six months later, after his mother had contacted the Association for Spina Bifida and Hydrocephalus, she saw a consultant, Mr Forest, at Carshalton Hospital. He recommended treatment by creating a shunt to drain off the fluid, which happened three months later. In 1998, David's breathing became noisy. He was admitted to hospital and treated with steroids in preparation for an endoscopy. On his way to the operating theatre, his mother was asked to sign a consent form for tonsillectomy. Following the operation, he had four convulsions and was treated with a tranquilliser. He was placed on a life support machine, and suffered from pneumonia and blood poisoning caused by three types of bacteria. He was tube-fed with pre-digested food, which gave him severe diarrhoea, and he was given oral antibiotics. He was discharged, but had to be re-admitted as his pneumonia had not cleared. The medical team wanted to give him diamorphine and allow him to die, but his mother refused, with the support of a solicitor. Over the next month or two, he spent a lot of time in and out of hospital. In October 1998, diamorphine was again suggested, and the mother refused, but the Chief Executive of the hospital endorsed the treatment and the police advised against his mother taking him home. David was treated with a subcutaneous diamorphine drip and was given no food or fluids. He was made the subject of a DNR (do not resuscitate) directive. When he deteriorated, turned blue and virtually stopped breathing, his mother and relatives physically intervened, removed the drip and stimulated him by rubbing, and smelling salts, and he improved. Violent incidents between members of the child's family and two doctors followed, resulting in civil and criminal proceedings being commenced. David was discharged and sent home under police escort, to be treated by his GP. The GP gave him a morphine antagonist, intravenous antibiotics and oxygen, and changed the liquid food. By March 1999, he was feeding again without the tube. Carol Glass went to court to establish the right to an assurance that, should David be re-admitted, he would not be given diamorphine. When she was told it was not in David's interest to keep him alive, and they wished to let him die without distress or pain, she applied for judicial review, making complaints as to the Trust's treatment of David.

The judge dismissed the application, holding that the instant case was not susceptible to judicial review, and that it was not appropriate to grant relief, since it would be difficult to frame any declaration in meaningful terms in a hypothetical situation, so as not to unnecessarily restrict proper treatment by the doctors in an ongoing and developing matter. The applicant (Carol Glass) applied for leave to appeal from that decision.

The Court of Appeal (Lord Woolf MR, Butler-Sloss and Robert Walker LJJ) held that leave to appeal would be refused because:

(a) judicial review was always regarded as a procedure of last resort. In the Family Division there were orders which could be made which dealt specifically with situations such as that before the judge;

(b) a specific issue order could be made under s 8 of the CA 1989, or a declaration in the best interests of the child, or the child could be made a ward of court;

(c) there were advantages and disadvantages to each of those procedures and to judicial review. It should be emphasised that, particularly in cases involving children, the last thing the court should be concerned about was whether the right procedure had been used;

(d) the court had sufficient powers to ensure that the right course would be pursued and a judge of one division could sit as a judge of another division if necessary;

(e) the important concern of the court was to ensure that what was determined was in the best interests of the child. In the instant case, the dilemma facing the court in deciding whether or not it should embark on an appeal was that the considerations which might arise in relation to the child, and to other children with similar disabilities, were almost infinite.

> For the court to act in anticipation in that area to try and produce clarity where currently there was none would be a task fraught with danger.

Comment on the *Glass* case

It needs to be noted that, in this tragic case, both the first instance judge and the Court of Appeal said that they had no jurisdiction by way of judicial review over this type of case and suggested that these matters should henceforth be channelled through the Family Division. If this is the more appropriate forum, then practitioners and parents should take note, but it remains to be seen whether a Family Division judge would necessarily take a different view of the case and be prepared to make an order that could maintain a disabled child whose prognosis for survival was not hopeful. The existing case law (which we have reviewed above) suggests that the portents for this happening are not encouraging.

Allocation of scarce resources

The treatment of handicapped newborns has also given rise to debates about whether it is economically defensible, in an environment of scarce resources, to maintain babies whose chances of life are exceedingly poor rather than using resources to treat persons needing renal dialysis, for example.

The use of QUALYs – quality-adjusted life years – has provoked much debate in the last decade or so about whether this device could assist in decision making over the allocation of healthcare resources. As Fletcher *et al* (1995) explain:

> Using this system, one year of life expectancy counts as one, one year of unhealthy life expectancy counts as less than one and being dead counts as 0. The exact value is lower the worse the quality of life the person has, but it is possible to have a negative score, that is, less than 0, if the person's quality of life is considered to be worse than dead. Healthcare is considered to be beneficial if, as a result, positive QUALYs are generated but healthcare is considered to be efficient if the cost per QUALY is as low as possible.

Alan Williams, the health economist who formulated the system, claims that the system 'incorporates both life expectancy and quality of life, and ... reflects the values and ethics of the community served'. The principle of using QUALYs is based on the assumption that 'if a rational individual was given the choice, that person would prefer to live a shorter life with a minimum amount of suffering and disability as opposed to living for a longer period of time, but with severe disability and suffering'. QUALYs appear to be useful in making decisions about which choice of treatments will be the most beneficial to an individual, but using QUALYs to decide which patients to treat and not to treat 'does not appear to provide the ideal system that its creator suggests and therefore there is no particular reason to favour its use over any other system of allocating resources' (Fletcher *et al* (1995), p 97) (see, also, p 117).

Treating handicapped infants in the 21st century

It did not take long for another case of a handicapped child to reach the English courts in the new millennium and again the parents were opposed to the proposed non-treatment of their baby. On 12 July 2000, the Family Division of the High Court ruled that doctors should not prolong the life of a boy aged 19 months, suffering from irreversible lung disease, rejecting a plea from the child's parents. This was reported a week later as *A National Health Service v D.*

A National Health Service Trust v D *(2000)* The Times, *19 July*

The baby was aged 19 months at the time of the hearing. He had, since birth, suffered a severe, chronic, irreversible and worsening lung disease giving him a very short life expectation, coupled with heart failure, renal and liver dysfunction, with a background of severe developmental delay. As a result of his latest hospitalisation at the end of June with a fever, and although he had recovered from that episode and was now back at home, the issues had arisen whether it would be in his best interests to put him on an artificial ventilator, whether manual or mechanical, and to subject him to all the processes of intensive care if, at some future time, he suffered respiratory and/or cardiac failure or arrest.

The NHS Trust sought a declaration that in the event of future respiratory and/or cardiac failure or arrest suffered by the baby, the Trust should have leave to administer such treatment as excluded resuscitation through artificial ventilation, but which provided full palliative care to ease his suffering and to permit his life to end peacefully and with dignity. They argued that the application was being made at this stage because a decision as to whether to provide artificial ventilation in a paediatric intensive care unit might well need to be taken as a matter of urgency. The parents insisted that everything should be done to save the child and, when the doctors disagreed, the NHS Trust made the baby a ward of court.

Cazalet J noted that the NHS Trust, the applicants in this case, were supported by a very strong body of medical opinion, and maintained that in view of the baby's extremely poor health and the poor prognosis, it was not in his best interests to undergo resuscitation. Furthermore, as his doctors had pointed out, palliative drug treatment had resolved that condition. On the other hand, the child's 'very loving and committed parents', whose care of him was exemplary, strongly opposed the application as being premature. The judge ruled that four general principles applied to this sort of situation:

(a) it was clearly established that, in cases where urgent medical action needed to be taken, the paramount consideration was the welfare of the child, which of course involved careful consideration of the parents' views, but those views could not be allowed to override the court's view of the child's best interests. A doctor had testified in court that there was no treatment available to reverse the lung disease and that the child was unlikely to live for more than a few weeks;

(b) the court's high respect for the sanctity of human life imposed a strong presumption in favour of taking all steps capable of preserving it, save in exceptional circumstances;

(c) the court was concerned only with the circumstances in which steps should be taken to prolong life; indeed, following *Re J (Wardship: Medical Treatment)* [1991] 2 WLR 140 'there was no question of approving, even in the case of the most horrendous disability, a course aimed at terminating life or accelerating death';

(d) there was no question of the court directing treatment which a doctor was not prepared to give, or which was contrary to a doctor's clinical judgment.

In the present case, while the body of medical opinion was clear that artificial ventilation was an intrusive and painful process which could bring no lasting benefit to the child, or change his ever-worsening lung condition, the doctors had made it plain that as and when a decision had to be taken at any future stage as to what treatment he should undergo, his condition would be fully reassessed at that time, to include the possibility of artificial ventilation. The order of the court would reflect the necessity of that full re-assessment. From the child's standpoint, weighing any possible very limited short term extension to his short lifespan against the increased pain and suffering caused by the processes of intensive care and artificial ventilation, the learned judge considered that full palliative treatment as advocated by the paediatricians in the declaration as sought was in the child's best interests and would allow him to die with dignity.

Turning to consider the human rights issue, the court also said that on that basis (that is, applying the best interests test and allowing the child to die with dignity) there was no breach of Art 2 (the right to life) or Art 3 (the right not to be subjected to inhuman or degrading treatment, including the right to die with dignity) of the European Convention for the Protection of Human Rights and Fundamental Freedoms: see Sched 1 to the Human Rights Act 1998. The Human Rights Act 1998 came into force on 2 October 2000.

A declaration was accordingly granted, subject to a direction that there should be leave to continue to treat the baby without artificial ventilation, unless such a course seemed inappropriate to the doctor in charge of the child.

Reaction to the ruling

The parents of the child were reportedly 'deeply upset' by the court's decision to refuse their son resuscitation and condemned the unnamed London NHS Trust which had brought the case. The case only reached the courts after the baby had spent nearly eight months in hospital and was handed over to his parents, and had thereafter spent most of his time with them. However, he still had to have a 24 hour oxygen supply and expert support as well as frequent trips to the hospital. The child needed intensive care at Great Ormond Street Hospital because of respiratory failure in February and was taken to hospital again in June when his parents were told the child was very ill. Ironically, it seemed that healthcare workers then said that the child had now recovered from his fever, and had shown signs of improvement back home and signs of vocabulary, and could indicate pleasure and displeasure. However, the judge's view appeared to be that the parents had become unduly optimistic and the child would remain totally dependent and unable to feed himself or to communicate for such life as was left to him.

On the public front, SOS – Patients in Danger, an anti-euthanasia group, strongly criticised the judgment, saying it should be reversed, and that a 'monstrous precedent' had been created which 'should be reversed immediately for the protection of all vulnerable patients whose lives are now even more at risk from doctors who kill and then hide behind the medical profession's code of secrecy' ((2000) *The Times*, 19 July). Gerald Wright QC, a patron of Alert, another anti-euthanasia group, said he was astonished that the judge should make a ruling of this kind which sets a dangerous precedent because it is all too easy for doctors to say that there is no point fighting at all. He pointed out that there are many cases where the prospects for future life are despaired of and then events contradict the prognosis.

Clearly, the controversy over the medical treatment (or non-treatment) of disabled or very sick young children will continue to exercise the courts from time to time.

The conjoined twins case in Britain 2000

Separating conjoined twins in 2000

'Handicapped newborns' is certainly a description that would fit conjoined ('Siamese') twins who are born connected at the head or abdomen. In Britain, conjoined twins, given the false names Jodie (J) and Mary (M), were born at St Mary's Hospital, Manchester on 8 August 2000, joined at their lower abdomens. One twin, J, was alert, with a heart and lungs, the other, M, did not possess these organs, and was reliant on the other for life. Their parents are devout Roman Catholics from abroad (the Maltese island of Gozo), who came to Britain seeking medical advice and treatment, with the help of the two governments. They believed that separating them was 'not God's will' and wanted nature to take its course, even if that meant the loss of both children.

In an unprecedented legal action, the English courts were asked to decide whether to sanction an operation to separate the month-old twins, which could save Jodie, but mean the killing of Mary.

Medical experts at Manchester said that a failure to operate would mean that both children were likely to die within three to six months. Separation of the twins would, according to the medical experts, mean that one twin would die immediately but the other might survive, although her medical condition would need careful monitoring.

At the High Court in London on 25 August, Johnson J gave surgeons authorisation to separate the girls. Five days later, on 30 August, an appeal was lodged by solicitors acting on behalf of the parents.

The Court of Appeal considered this desperately difficult case and among the questions to be considered was: would separation of the twins amount to murder of one of them (assuming the medical prognosis is correct, and separation resulted in the imminent death of one of them)?

On 22 September, at 2.15 pm, the Court of Appeal announced its decision, which was to confirm the earlier lower court ruling which was to authorise the separation of the twins, who were then six weeks old. The court's opinions were contained in a 130 page judgment.

It was believed that the parents were considering lodging an appeal to the House of Lords immediately as the twins were slowly deteriorating and their chances of survival were diminishing by the day. However, this never materialised.

Summaries of the two judgments (from Lawtel) follow.

Central Manchester Healthcare Trust v (1) Mr and Mrs A; and (2) A Child (by the Official Solicitor, her guardian *ad litem*) *LTL 22/9/00 (*Re A*)*

The facts are broadly as stated above.

The lower court judgment (Johnson J)

The court held:

(a) In any matter relating to the future of a child, the interests of that individual child, whether it be J or M, were paramount; see Art 3(1) of the UN Convention on the Rights of the Child 1989.

(b) Great weight was attached to the wishes of the parents (see *Z (A Minor) (Identification: Restriction of Publication)* [1996] 2 WLR 88. However, the interests of M herself had to be the focus. Those interests were not limited to her best medical interests, but encompassed medical, emotional, and all other welfare issues (*Re MB (Caesarean Section)* [1997] 2 FLR 426 and *Re A (Male Sterilisation)* [2000] 1 FLR 549 considered).

(c) It was necessary for the court to consider the options that were available. Those options were elective separation, semi-urgent or urgent separation, or permanent union. If the decision was made for permanent union, death was likely to ensue for both, probably within a period of between three and six months.

(d) M's state was pitiable. She was fed by tube with little likelihood of being fed otherwise. She was possibly blind, with no significant heart or lung functions and probably had deteriorating brain function. It was clear that her condition would never improve during the few months she had to live if M and J were not separated. Further, there was no way of establishing whether M was in pain or not. She was unable to cry and, as J developed and tried to crawl and sit up, M would surely be in pain.

(e) Accordingly, weighing up those circumstances, the few months of M's life, if not separated from J, would simply be worth nothing to her, they would be hurtful. To prolong M's life for those few months was very seriously to her disadvantage.

(f) The surgery proposed by the hospital had not only an inevitability for M, but also created, at best, the chance for J of a life that had social and emotional problems over and above those problems that could be medically cured. However, the court's focus was on M and what was best for her.

(g) The proposed separation, and its consequences, represented the best interest for M. However, that interest could only be achieved if the surgery was lawful. If the operation was properly regarded as a positive act, then it could not be lawful and could not be made lawful. Where the decision was made that a life may be terminated, that termination could only be following the withdrawal of treatment (*Airedale NHS Trust v Bland* [1992] AC 789 considered).

(h) What was proposed, and what would cause M's death, was the interruption or withdrawal of the supply of blood which M received from J. This was an analogy with the situation in which the court authorised the withholding of food and hydration. This was not a positive act and was lawful. J's blood supply circulated from, and returned to, her heart by her own circulation system, independent of the supply and return for M. The operation proposed was lawful because it represented the withdrawal of M's blood supply. The consequence for M was one that most certainly did not represent the primary objective of the operation.

Accordingly, authority for the operation to separate was granted.

Five days later, an appeal was lodged with the Court of Appeal by the parents' solicitors.

The parents appealed on the grounds that Johnson J erred in holding the operation was (a) in M's best interests; (b) in J's best interests; and (c) in any event, lawful.

On the hearing of the appeal, the court received written submissions from the Archbishop of Westminster and the pro-Life Alliance in addition to the oral submissions of the parties.

Court of Appeal judgment

The Court of Appeal (Ward, Brooke and Robert Walker LJJ) held:

Ward LJ

(a) On the medical aspects of the case, Johnson J was correct in concluding that this was an appropriate case in which to override the objections of the parents.

(b) Assessing the best interests of J in line with family law principles, Johnson J was also plainly right to conclude that the operation would be in J's best interests. However, in the realm of family law, he had been wrong to find that M's life would be worth nothing to her. The sanctity of life doctrine was so enshrined as a fundamental principle of law and commanded such respect from the law that it had to be accepted that each life had inherent value in itself, however grave the impairment of some of the body's functions might be. M's life, desperate as it was, still had its own ineliminable value and dignity.

(c) From that starting point, Johnson J had then gone on to ask whether the course of action proposed was one which could be characterised as not continuing to provide M with treatment which would prolong her life. The answer to that had to be no. M was not receiving treatment (or any substantial treatment) at the time of the application or appeal. What was under consideration was the active invasion of M's body for the purposes of the separation. That would not prolong her life; rather, it would terminate it. With respect to Johnson J, he had asked the wrong question. The question was not: was it in M's best interests that the hospital should continue to provide her with treatment which will prolong her life? The case was not about providing that kind of treatment. What was proposed demanded that the question be framed in terms of: was it in M's best interests that an operation be performed to separate her from J when the certain consequence of that operation was that she would die? There was only one answer to that question: no, that was not in her best interests. It followed that the Johnson J approach was fatally flawed and his assessment of M's best interests fell with it.

(d) It therefore fell to the Court of Appeal to make its own assessment of the respective best interests of J and M. As to that, there was no doubt at all that the scales came down heavily in J's favour. The best interests of the twins was to give the chance of life to the child whose actual bodily condition was capable of accepting the chance to her advantage, even if that had to be at the cost of the sacrifice of the life which was so unnaturally supported. The least detrimental choice, balancing the interests of M against J and J against M, was to permit the operation to be performed.

(e) It followed that the question which was crucial to the outcome of the appeal was whether or not the operation could be lawfully performed under the criminal law. The reality was that M was killing J. That provided the legal justification for the doctors coming to J's defence and removing the threat of fetal harm to her presented by M. The availability of such a plea of quasi-self defence, modified to meet the quite exceptional circumstances which nature had inflicted on the twins, made intervention by the doctors lawful.

Brooke LJ

(a) As to the criminal law aspects of the case, four issues arose:

   (1) Was M a human being in the eyes of the law? The answer was yes.

   (2) Would the proposed operation amount to the positive act of killing M? The answer was yes.

   (3) Would the doctors be held to have the intention of killing M, however little they desired that outcome? The answer was again yes. The doctrine of double effect, which permitted a doctor, acting in good faith, to administer pain killing drugs to a dying patient, had no relevance to this case.

   (4) Would the killing be unlawful? The answer to this was no.

(b) As to the latter, although necessity had been denied as being capable in law of amounting to a defence to murder in *R v Dudley and Stephens* (1884) 14 QBD 273, that denial had been based upon two policy objections: (1) who was to be the judge of this sort of necessity? By what measure is the comparative value of lives to be measured? (2) To permit such a defence would mark an absolute divorce of law from morality. In the present case, as to (1), M's brain, heart and lungs were, for all practical purposes, useless, such that she was already 'designated for death'. This was not a case in which both children had the chance of living. As to (2), although there were those who believed most sincerely that it would be an immoral act to save J if this would involve ending M's life before its brief allotted span was complete, there were also those who believed with equal sincerity that it would be immoral not to save J if there were a good prospect that she might live a happy, fulfilled life if the operation were performed. The court was not equipped to choose between these competing philosophies. All that a court could say was that it was not at all obvious that this was the sort of clear cut situation, leading to a divorce of law from morality, which was of such concern in 1884.

(c) There were three necessary requirements for the application of the doctrine of necessity: (1) The act was needed to avoid inevitable and irreparable evil; and (2) no more should be done than was reasonably necessary for the purpose to be achieved; and (3) the evil inflicted was not to be disproportionate to the evil avoided. Given that the principles of modern family law pointed irresistibly to the conclusion that the interests of J had to be preferred to the interests of M, all these requirements were satisfied in this case.

Robert Walker LJ

(a) The feelings of the parents were entitled to great respect, especially so far as they were based on religious convictions. But, the court could not escape the responsibility of deciding the matter to the best of its judgment as to the twins' best interests.

(b) Johnson J erred in law in equating the proposed surgical operation with the discontinuance of medical treatment (as by disconnecting a lung machine). Therefore, the Court of Appeal had to form its own view.

(c) M had a right to life under both the common law of England and under the European Convention on Human Rights 1950. It would be unlawful to kill M intentionally, that is, by undertaking an operation with the prime purpose of killing her.

(d) But, J also had a right to life. Every human being's right to life carried with it, as an intrinsic part of it, rights of bodily integrity and autonomy – the right to have one's own body whole and intact and (on reaching an age of understanding) to take decisions about one's own body.

(e) By a rare and tragic mischance, M and J had both been deprived of the bodily integrity and autonomy which was their natural right. There was a strong presumption that an operation to separate them would be in the best interests of each of them. In this case, the purpose of the operation would be to separate the twins and so give J a reasonably good prospect of a long and reasonably normal life. M's death would not be the purpose of the operation, although it would be its inevitable consequence. The operation would give her, even in death, bodily integrity as a human being. She would die, not because she was intentionally killed, but because her own body could not sustain her life. Continued life, whether long or short, would hold nothing for M except possible pain and discomfort, if indeed she could feel anything at all. The proposed operation would therefore be in the best interests of each of the twins. The decision did not require the court to value one life above another. The proposed operation would not be unlawful. It would involve the positive act of invasive surgery and M's death would be foreseen as an inevitable consequence of an operation which was intended, and was necessary, to save J's life. But, M's death would not be the purpose or intention of the surgery and she would die because tragically, her body, on its own, was not, and never had been viable.

The appeal was therefore dismissed.

Comment on Re A *(the conjoined twins case)*

In this sort of case, even the wisdom of Solomon might not be sufficient to satisfy all creeds and all needs and would certainly not be sufficient to save both children. A Roman Catholic hospice offered the twins' parents its facilities should they have desired to leave with both twins. There was also the possibility of approaching the European Court of Human Rights on another appeal, but time was running out. After the operation, J would need years of reconstructive surgery to build a vagina and anus, and might never be able to walk. As Ward LJ put it, 'M lives on borrowed time, all of it borrowed from her sister and is fated for early death.' Despite the tragic circumstances of the case, the operation would save a life where, without judicial or medical intervention, two lives would be lost.

On 28 September 2000, it was announced in the British media by the parents' lawyers that, contrary to the expectations of many, they would not be appealing against the decision. The operation to separate the twins was carried out and the prognosis for the surviving twin appears to be good, although her condition continues to be monitored (see (2000) *The Times*, 10 October).

CONCLUSIONS

The explicit promotion of the principle of the paramountcy of the child's welfare has been the outstanding achievement of the English common law over the last decade, a principle which, although statutorily introduced since 1925 in the guardianship of minors legislation, has received judicial approval and endorsement fairly consistently even before the enactment of the CA 1989 in October 1991. The principle of '*Gillick* competence' is arguably the groundbreaking concept of the mid 1980s and 1990s although the case law, dealing mostly with children suffering from psychotic illness of some description, could be said to represent a 'retreat from *Gillick*' in that courts have opted to override a parental refusal or a refusal of treatment by the child where to abide by the refusal would be life threatening to the child concerned. There is certainly ample evidence of judicial paternalism, but not much evidence of explicit judicial recognition of a mature child's right of self-determination or autonomy, unlike, for instance the Scottish position in *Houston, Applicant* [1997] Med LR 237, where the court was prepared to respect the 15 year old's wishes. Ultimately, however, in cases where there were life threatening consequences for the minors involved, the English courts have preferred, as they see it, to err on the side of caution and opt for the preservation of the child's life.

SELECTIVE BIBLIOGRAPHY

Bainham, A, 'The judge and the competent minor' (1992) 108 LQR 194

Brazier, M and Bridge, C, 'Coercion or caring? Analysing adolescent autonomy' (1996) 16 LS 84

Bridgeman, J, 'Old enough to know best?' (1993) 13 LS 69

Davies, M, *Textbook on Medical Law*, 1998, Blackstone, Chapters 6 and 14

de Cruz, P, 'Adolescent autonomy, detention for medical treatment and *Re C*' (1999) 62 MLR 595

de Cruz, P and McNaughton, D, *By What Right? Studies in Medicine, Ethics and the Law*, 1987, Penrhos

Douglas, G, 'The retreat from *Gillick*' (1992) 55 MLR 570

Eekelaar, J, 'The emergence of children's rights' (1986) 6 OJLS 161

Fletcher, N, Holt, S, Brazier, M and Harris, J (eds), *Ethics, Law and Nursing*, 1995, Manchester UP

Murphy, J, 'W(h)ither adolescent autonomy?' (1992) 6 J Social Welfare and Fam Law 529

Lyon, C, 'Whatever happened to the child's right to refuse?' [1994] J Child Law 84

Mason, JK and McCall Smith, RA, *Law and Medical Ethics*, 5th edn, 1999, Butterworths, Chapters 10 and 15

Montgomery, J, *Healthcare Law*, 1997, OUP, Chapter 12

McHale, J and Fox, M, *Healthcare Law: Text and Materials*, 1997, Sweet & Maxwell, Chapter 7

Raphael, DD, 'Handicapped infants: medical ethics and the law' (1988) 14 JME 5

Weir, R, *Selective Nontreatment of Handicapped Newborns*, 1984, OUP

Articles on *Re T* (1997)/handicapped newborns

Campbell, A, 'Some ethical issues in neonatal care', in Dunstan, G and Shinebourne, E (eds), *Doctors' Decisions*, 1989, OUP

de Cruz, P, 'Parental wishes, medical treatment and defective newborn babies: what is in the child's best interests?' [1998] 11 Practitioners' Child Law Bulletin 80

Davies, M, 'Selective non-treatment of the newborn: in whose best interests? In whose judgment?' (1998) 49 NILQ 82

Duff, R and Campbell, A, 'Moral and ethical dliemmas: seven years into the debate about human ambiguity' (1980) 447 *Annals*, American Academy of Political and Social Science, pp 19–28

Loughrey, J, 'Medical treatment – the status of parental opinion' [1998] 18 Fam Law 146

Michalowski, S, 'Is it in the best interests of a child to have a life-saving liver transplantation?' (1997) 9 Child and Fam LQ 179

Michalowski, S, Fox, M and McHale, J, 'In whose best interests?' (1997) 60 MLR 700

Pence, GE, 'The Baby Jane Doe case', in *Classic Cases in Medical Ethics*, 1990, McGraw-Hill

CHAPTER 5

ASSISTED REPRODUCTION AND SURROGACY

INTRODUCTION

Over the past 16 years or so, there has been an acceleration of the amount of discussion in the UK of various medical and scientific techniques which have been called modern reproductive techniques or 'reproductive technologies'. These generally refer to artificial reproductive methods or reproductive methods which intervene in human reproduction. These include artificial insemination using a husband's sperm, that is, injecting a woman with the husband's sperm (AIH); artificial insemination using semen from a donor (AID); ova and sperm mixed together in a drop of fluid and placed back in the fallopian tube (GIFT); *in vitro* fertilisation – fertilisation effected 'in water' outside the body, where, just before ovulation, an egg is collected from the ovary and placed in a laboratory glass (a petri-dish) and semen is added to it so that, if fertilisation occurs, it is returned to the uterus where it may implant and then develop as normal (IVF). Embryo donation and surrogacy also come within this umbrella of 'reproductive technologies'. Surrogacy is a short form for 'surrogate motherhood' (defined and discussed below). Yet, although we tend to think of these kinds of practices as being of modern vintage, there is evidence to suggest that the first recorded AIH took place in 1866 (see Home, E, *Philosophical Transactions of the Royal Society of London*, 1866, Vol 18, pp 157–78; and Hard, AD, 'Artificial impregnation' in *Medical World*, 1909, pp 163–65, cited by Cuisine in 'Legal issues in human reproduction', in McLean, S (ed), *Legal Issues in Human Reproduction*, 1990, Dartmouth) and the broad practice of surrogacy is frequently cited as dating from Biblical times. In more modern times, however, the origin of the growing modern public debate, awareness and discussion of these phenomena might be more readily traced to July 1978, when Louise Brown became the world's first test-tube baby, sparking off a decade of intense speculation and anticipation about reproductive technologies. Louse Brown's birth was seen as heralding a 'new era in making babies' (Singer and Wells (1984), Preface). Of course, other affluent societies, such as the USA, Australia and several Western European countries, have also been debating the legal, social, political and moral implications of these so called 'new technologies'.

This chapter looks briefly at the British legal position on assisted reproduction and its techniques and then examines the law relating to the practice of surrogacy or surrogate motherhood, through a survey of the leading cases and seminal reports on the area, as a basis for subsequent comparison with developments in overseas jurisdictions such as the USA, France and Australia in the corresponding chapter in Part II: Chapter 14.

LEGAL AND ETHICAL FRAMEWORK

The question of who is a 'parent' in law is of some importance, particularly in the modern context of the 'new' reproductive technology. There are different types of parenthood.

Types of parenthood

Biological parenthood would be based on mothers and the mere fact of birth. For a father, biological paternity is not a sufficient condition to exercising legal rights and duties of parenthood.

Social parenthood

This would include adoption and the 'child of the family' formula: creating links between spouse and non-biological children 'treated' by that spouse as children of the family. This has been the case with certain family law legislation in the UK, such as the Matrimonial Causes Act 1973.

Presumptions based on marriage

Several 'presumptions' were created in English law to enforce the social policies of the time, which base the 'legitimacy' of a child on the fact of the marriage of its parents at the time of its birth or even subsequently. Hence:

- at common law, a child born to a married woman is presumed to be the child of the woman's husband;
- a child may also be legitimated by the subsequent marriage of its parents;
- rebuttal of the presumption by a standard of proof higher than balance of probabilities but lower than the criminal standard of 'beyond reasonable doubt';

Parenthood is the underlying principle for ascertaining who has parental responsibility under the Children Act (CA) 1989. Parenthood is also used to ascribe liability for child support under the Child Support Act 1991.

Assisted reproduction and the Human Fertilisation and Embryology Act 1990

In this area, spurred on by radical developments in reproductive technology, such as *in vitro* fertilisation (IVF) and artificial insemination by donor (AID), the British Parliament enacted the Human Fertilisation and Embryology Act (HFEA) 1990, which statutorily lays down certain key principles which are as notable for statements of social policy as for legal rules which currently govern this burgeoning area of healthcare law. The HFEA 1990 was passed, in the words of Morgan and Lee (1991), summarising John Hannam MP, as a response to the perceived need for legislation 'to regulate research on embryos, to protect the integrity of reproductive medicine and to protect scientists and clinicians from legal action and sanction'. In addition, they stress, 'some people feared unregulated embryo research, being prepared to support work in specific areas such as infertility and genetic disease, but uneasy at the thought of reproductive technology taking more sinister directions such as genetic interference with the embryo' (Morgan and Lee (1991), p 22). The HFEA 1990 was preceded by the setting up of the Warnock Committee in 1982 which was followed by the publication of the Warnock Report (*Report of the Committee of Inquiry into Fertilisation and Embryology*, subsequently republished with an introduction by Dame Mary Warnock, the chair, as *A Question of Life*, 1985, Blackwell) in 1984. The HFEA 1990 was described in April 1990 by the then Secretary for Health, Kenneth Clarke, as one of the most significant measures of its kind to be brought before Parliament in the last 20 years.

The Human Fertilisation and Embryology Authority (HFEA): a licensing authority

One of the HFEA 1990's highly significant innovations was to establish a licensing authority – the Human Fertilisation and Embryology Authority (HFEA) – to monitor and control research and the provision of infertility services. It also intended to ensure that there was substantial lay representation on the Authority. It replaced the former Voluntary (later Interim) Licensing Authority, which had operated since the publication of the Warnock Report. Its principal function is to license and monitor, through a licensing system, any research and treatment which involves the creation, keeping and using of human embryos outside the body, or the storage or donation of human eggs and sperm.

The Authority also has to maintain a register of information about gamete and embryo donors and children born as a result of such treatment. It provides advice to the Health Secretary on developments concerning infertility services and embryology and the formulation of a Code of Practice.

Status provisions

The mother

> Section 27(1) of the HFEA 1990: The mother who is carrying or has carried a child as a result of the placing in her of an embryo or of sperm and eggs, and no other woman, is to be treated as the mother of the child.

This section should be read with s 13(5) of the HFEA 1990, under which a woman may not be provided with treatment services unless 'account has been taken of the welfare of any child who may be born as a result of the treatment (including the need of that child for a father)'.

Comparative comment on s 27

It may be noted, for comparative purposes, that the English legislative provision is the exact opposite of the position in California, although this is by no means the position in other American States. In *Johnson v Calvert* (1993), the Californian Supreme Court held that no parental rights attached to a surrogate mother and that the surrogate had merely facilitated the procreation of the commissioning couple's child. We return to this case in detail in Chapter 14, when we review the non-English jurisdictional approaches.

The father

> Section 28(2) of the HFEA 1990: a husband whose wife receives donated sperm or an embryo created from donated sperm, shall be treated as the father of any resulting child, unless it is shown that he did not consent.

A man who is not married to the mother and is not the genetic father may be regarded as the child's legal father *if* treatment services were provided *for the man and woman together* by a person to whom a licence applies: s 28(3) of the HFEA 1990. This provision does not apply to so called DIY treatment, where an officially recognised fertility clinic is mot used.

Non-recognition of the status of 'father'

Where a child is conceived using genetic material from a man who has already died, it is provided by s 28(6) that that man will not be recognised in law as the child's father. As the law currently stands, the child born would be regarded as non-marital, unless the mother had remarried, in which case s 28(5) of the HFEA 1990 would apply to legitimate the child. Otherwise, such children remain legally fatherless. However, the government announced in August 2000 that it intends to change the law so that, in these circumstances, the deceased father's name may be inserted on the Birth Register.

This will affect the status of the child of Diane Blood (on which case, see below, p 187 *et seq*).

Reproductive technologies: some terms and procedures

(a) AID: artificial insemination by donor – insemination of the woman (usually married) by a donor because the husband has (1) defective semen; (2) a hereditary disease likely to be transmitted to his children; or (3) an abnormal sperm which may cause spontaneous abortion; (4) where a single woman wants a child but is unwilling to conceive by conventional means.

(b) AIH: artificial insemination by husband – using husband's semen to inseminate the wife:

Artificial insemination

Artificial insemination (AI) is a technique whereby a man's semen is mechanically introduced into a woman's vagina with the intention that conception will take place. Apparently, the first recorded human artificial insemination took place in 1790, when John Hunter, a British doctor, succeeded in carrying out an artificial insemination of a linen draper's wife with her husband's seed. The husband was suffering from a disability which made normal intercourse impossible. According to accounts, normal pregnancy and delivery took place (see Finegold, W, *Artificial Insemination,* 1964, Charles C Thomas, pp 5–9, cited in Liu (1991), pp 8–9).

The first recorded successful human insemination by donor (AID) was performed in 1884 in Jefferson Medical College in the USA, which was only revealed in 1909 in a letter written by Addison Davis Hard which was published in an American journal. According to Hard, the operation was performed under anaesthetic and neither the wife nor husband was informed. The husband was said to be sterile. However, the wife became pregnant and a son was born, with the secret operation only being publicised when the son was 25. AIH is the least controversial of the available artificial techniques as there is no ambiguity with the resulting child's legal status and the issue of parenthood is not in question.

In the UK, the issue of artificial insemination was discussed in the 1930s and in 1945, the Archbishop of Canterbury set up a Commission to inquire into the development of AI; however, the report that followed not only criticised it, but recommended it be made a criminal offence. Nothing actually transpired on the legislative front and AID continued to be performed on a small scale. By 1970, public opinion had changed. By 1979, the practice was widespread and the Royal College of Obstetricians and Gynaecologists even published an information booklet extolling its virtues. There are a number of medical centres performing it in the UK and it has become an acceptable practice in Britain (see Liu (1991), Chapter 2).

(c) IVF: *in vitro* fertilisation

This refers to the creation of an embryo outside the human body and the child thus born may be related to both, one or *neither* of its 'parents' (that is, the carrying mother and her partner or husband).

(d) GIFT: gamete intrafallopian transfer

This refers to insertion in the womb of eggs, sperm or both for fertilisation to take place in the womb rather than outside it.

SURROGACY

Surrogacy is another method of 'assisted reproduction' and, although not a distinct artificial reproductive technique, is a specialised situation where, unlike its practice in ancient times, artificial reproduction techniques are nowadays frequently applied. They replace conception by natural means and hence a surrogate-produced child may have several genetic links. Although the practice of surrogacy (as the second oldest profession), or surrogate motherhood, dates back several centuries, as a modern phenomenon, it started to be reported only sporadically in the late 1970s, with the first reported English case reaching the courts in 1978 (*A v C* (1978) 8 Fam Law 170; fully reported in [1985] FLR 445), but this was not properly reported or publicised at that time. It then suddenly burst into prominence in the 1980s with the *Baby Cotton* case. The other non-English case which caused a sensation in the USA and, indeed, in most of the Western world, was the case of *Baby M* (*In Re M*), a surrogacy case involving Mary Beth Whitehead, who went from villain to victim within the space of two years (the *Baby M* case is discussed in detail in Chapter 14).

Surrogate motherhood

A surrogate mother is a woman who fulfils the role of another woman by having a child for her. Surrogate motherhood is 'any situation where one mother carries a child for another with the intention that the child should be handed over after birth' (Warnock Committee, 1984).

Another definition that has been suggested is 'any situation where there is an arranged separation of the genetic, gestational and social components of motherhood' (Roberts (1986)).

Two situations have arisen: (a) a woman who is infertile, and her husband's sperm is then used to artificially inseminate another woman who will carry the child to term; (b) a woman who is fertile but cannot carry the child to term, so the ovum is removed and fertilised *in vitro* by her husband's sperm.

Full and partial surrogacy

The most common current form of surrogacy is 'partial surrogacy', where the carrying woman is fertilised with the commissioning man's sperm either as a result of sexual intercourse or assisted insemination. Full surrogacy, however, is where the commissioning couple provide both sperm and ovum so that the child is genetically entirely theirs, although carried by another woman. This necessarily involves the technique known as *in vitro* fertilisation (IVF) (McHale and Fox (1997), p 635). Full surrogacy may therefore be regarded as a form of womb leasing (Douglas (1991), p 141).

Surrogacy appears to retain some level of popularity in the UK, but nothing like the levels prevalent in the USA, yet the numbers of surrogacy arrangements have increased in the UK (see the Brazier Report (1998), para 6.22; discussed below, pp 184–85). Professor Margaret Brazier remarks that there are several attractions which surrogacy still possesses: (a) its success rate in establishing pregnancy, whether by *in vitro* fertilisation (IVF) or artificial insemination are high; (b) while the law (in the UK) currently limits payments to reasonable expenses in theory, in practice, expenses of £10,000 or so involve at least some covert payment for services (see Brazier (1999), p 350, where she cites the Brazier Report (para 5.2–5.9)). On the other hand, the Warnock Report of 1984 rejected all forms of surrogacy by a majority of 16:14. The more recent Brazier Report (1998) adopts a more conciliatory line in some respects, but nevertheless recommends tougher controls on surrogacy, a stronger policing of the types of 'reasonable expenses' that surrogates are paid and much clearer guidelines on what expenses should be allowable.

Ethical and moral issues in surrogacy

Two prominent writers on medical law highlight certain key characteristics of surrogacy which bring into question its morality and ethical turpitude. First, it is the inclusion of a third party to procreation; secondly, surrogacy can be viewed as 'being one way of exploiting women for the benefit of men'; but thirdly, the alternative view is to see the 'outlawing of the practice as outright paternalism which denies a woman a chance to use her body as she pleases' (Mason and McCall Smith (1999), p 85).

Several ethical questions may be posed with respect to surrogacy:

(a) Is the arrangement exploitative of the surrogate mother?

(b) Is the welfare of the child paramount (in the child's best interests) in such arrangements? Should it not be?

(c) Is the law restrictive of procreative choice?

(d) Is this the commercialisation of childbearing?

(e) Is the baby being treated as a commodity rather than as a person of intrinsic value?

Arguments for and against surrogacy

Surrogacy is now frequently seen as useful if the woman is unable to bear a child because of severe pelvic disease or because she has had a hysterectomy or because she has a medical condition such as kidney or heart disease and pregnancy may seriously threaten her life or health.

In the pre-legislative phase, the debate centred around two main issues: (a) should the surrogacy contract be permitted – that is, should a couple be even allowed to enter into such agreements? (b) If permitted, should the agreement be enforceable by either side? (see Douglas (1991), p 146). The pros and cons of surrogacy have been canvassed by several commentators, but will be briefly revisited here to place the ensuing discussion into ethical and social perspective.

Arguments in favour of surrogacy

(a) The autonomy of the parties should be respected: the commissioning couple and surrogate mother should have the freedom to choose which arrangements to enter into; legislation would limit procreative choice. This may be called the 'liberty argument'.

(b) The bodily autonomy of the surrogate mother should be respected.

(c) Surrogacy supports traditional models of the family and of women by enabling the commissioning couple to constitute themselves into a more 'traditional' or 'real' family with a child. It also transforms the commissioning woman from her less valued role in society to become a 'mother' which may be argued is of a more acceptable or favoured status.

(d) Surrogacy relieves (what is for some) the 'burden' of childlessness; if women have had repeated miscarriages, or suffer from conditions which make pregnancy dangerous, surrogacy may be the only hope of having a child (from the Glover Report (1989)).

Objections to surrogacy

(a) The practice of surrogacy is 'exploitative'; it has been said that it 'advantages men' or the rich or leads to a sub-class of underprivileged women; it treats women's wombs as a purely commercial vehicle.

The argument has been made that surrogacy heralds the onset of total male control because it emphasises 'providing the father with a genetic heir and frequently detailed supervision of the surrogate's behaviour and life-style while carrying "his" child' (Douglas (1991), p 147, citing the chapter by Ince, S, in Arditti, R *et al*, *Test Tube Women*, 1984, Pandora).

(b) It undermines the traditional institution of marriage.

(c) It commodifies children, that is, it degrades children by treating them as if they were mere commodities and causes psychological problems for children and psychological harm.

(d) It has the potential to obscure the recognition of children as full persons, entitled to respect as such; confuses children who were not produced by surrogacy who have to live with the surrogacy-produced child as part of their family.

In addition to these arguments, the so called *slippery slope argument* (if we allow this, it will open the door to far worse things and then where will it all end?) has been used, but the counter-arguments to it are equally well known: it is possible to use this argument against any practice that is capable of misuse; the fact that it has been misused does not mean that you should automatically condemn it; dangers are always there, but one cannot prove that they will necessarily materialise; the worst consequences are not inevitable and can be guarded against.

Various commissions of inquiry have expressed their opposition to surrogacy; Warnock, M, *The Warnock Report*; republished as *A Question of Life*, 1985, Blackwell; Waller, *Report on the Disposition of Embryos Produced by In Vitro Fertilisation*, 1984, para 4.17, 1984, Victoria, Australia; Demack, *Special Committee Appointed by the Queensland Government to Enquire into the Law relating to Artificial Insemination, In Vitro Fertilisation and Other Related Matters*, 1984, Queensland, Australia; and, as Freeman (1991) puts it, there have been 'swingeing attacks on the concept' by Corea, *The Mother Machine*, 1985, Harper and Row, Duelli-Klein (cited in Corea), Radin (1987), Dworkin, *Right-Wing Women*, 1983; Prigee, and other feminists (such as Arditti *et al*, *Test Tube Women*, 1984; Arditti, although the feminist response has not been notable for any consensus of opinion (see Zipper and Sevenhuijsen in Stanworth, M, *Reproductive Technologies*, 1987, Polity). Other critical, but somewhat more balanced views have been declared by Capron (1987) and Morgan (1985), and indeed by Freeman (1991) himself.

Legal regulation of surrogacy

The practice of surrogacy is now regulated by the HFEA 1990 and the Surrogacy Arrangements Act 1985. The law prohibits the payment of money for the adoption of a child under s 57 of the Adoption Act 1976. The cases on surrogacy indicate very firmly that the court's decision will be governed by the notion of the 'best interests' of the child and the English courts, at any rate, adopt a theory that it is important to maintain the birth mother's relationship with the child, wherever this is required, in the child's best interests.

Non-enforceability of surrogacy arrangement in English law

The HFEA 1990 has inserted a new section into the Surrogacy Arrangements Act 1985:

> Section 1A: No surrogacy arrangement is enforceable by or against the person making it.

This applies irrespective of whether the child was created by sexual intercourse, artificial insemination or IVF.

Legality and enforceability of the surrogacy agreement: the American approach

It is instructive at this point to refer to the famous case of *Baby M* (*Re Baby M* (1988) 109 NJ 396). This case is discussed in detail in Chapter 14, but is cited at this point to emphasise that, in the lower court hearing there, the New Jersey court held the surrogate arrangement to be valid and appeared to signify American law's approval of such contracts. Judge Sorkow applied the 'best interests of the child' principle so that the biological father should have custody of the child and his wife was allowed to adopt the child. The surrogate's parental rights were terminated. On appeal, the New Jersey Supreme Court unanimously held that the surrogate arrangement was void and against public policy. It overturned the lower court's termination of the surrogate mother's parental rights and rescinded the adoption order of the father's wife. The surrogate was given visitation rights.

In *Johnson v Calvert* (1993) P 2d 776, the California court contrastingly held that surrogate contracts did not violate any public policy as to adoption, yet in the case of *In Re Marriage of Moschetta* (1994) 30 Cal Rep 2d 893, in different circumstances, the California appeals court was able to say that the surrogate mother was both the genetic and gestational mother and should be regarded as such.

(Further discussion of *Baby M* and other American cases is to be found in Chapter 14.)

How many possible parents might a surrogate-produced child have?

Five possible parents: commissioning parents; sperm donor; ovum donor; surrogate mother who bears the child. In this connection, it is instructive to refer to s 30 of the HFEA 1990, as far as married couples are concerned. Their application to be treated as the child's parents will be approved provided one of the spouses is the child's genetic parent and various conditions have been satisfied; hence, the requirements of s 30(2)–(7) must be complied with, for example, that the child's home has been with the applicant husband and wife (this is discussed below).

Section 30 is of no relevance if a surrogate mother changes her mind and is not willing to hand over the baby. As we have already noted, the law clearly states, under s 1A of the Surrogacy Arrangements Act 1985 (as inserted by the HFEA 1990), that a surrogate contract is not enforceable.

What can go wrong with a surrogacy arrangement?

At least four things (as suggested by Singer and Wells (1984), pp 119–20):

(a) the surrogate mother might indulge in drug or alcohol abuse;

(b) she might attempt to extort payment, or additional payment beyond any agreed fee, from the commissioning couple;

(c) she might decide, despite contracting to give the baby away upon birth, not to hand over the child once it has been born;

(d) the commissioning couple might decide they do not wish to accept the baby once it has been born because it has been born with a physical or mental handicap or because they believe it is not their genetic child.

The third possibility actually happened in *Re P* (the twins case), where the court had to decide whether to allow the surrogate mother to keep the baby she had carried and given birth to, although the child had been produced through the sperm of the commissioning father and the surrogate's ovum.

We turn then to the English cases on surrogacy.

The English cases on surrogacy

A v C *(1978) 8 Fam Law 170*

There was an unmarried couple in which the woman, who had children from a previous relationship, was unable to have any further children. Her partner,

A, had a very strong desire to raise his own biological child. They found a woman, C, who agreed, for a sum of £500, to be artificially inseminated using the semen of A. C, the surrogate, changed her mind during pregnancy and wished to keep the child and forgo the money. After the birth of the child, the natural (biological) father started wardship proceedings to obtain custody of the child.

In the High Court, Comyn J described the contract as 'pernicious' and declared that he held the agreement between the parties to be 'against public policy. None of them can rely on it in any way or enforce the agreement in this way. I need only to give one of many grounds for saying this namely that this was a purported contract for the sale and purchase of a child'. Access (as it was then called) was granted to the father. C, the mother, was given care and control of the child, but the child remained a ward of court until majority or further order. The mother appealed.

On appeal, Ormrod LJ described the contract as a 'quite bizarre and unnatural agreement' as well as calling the arrangement a 'sordid little bargain'. Cumming-Bruce LJ called it a 'kind of baby-farming operation of a wholly distasteful and lamentable kind'. The appeal court refused to grant access to the father, justifying this decision as being 'in the best interests of the child'.

The first reported British commercial surrogacy case of the 1980s: the Baby Cotton saga

In the mid-1980s, the birth of Baby C in January 1985, produced by a British mother for a childless American couple, using the husband's seminal fluid, as a result of a commercial surrogacy arrangement, aroused considerable interest from the British media. The agreement was to pay £13,000 for the 'service' that the surrogate mother performed. This was the fee paid to an American organisation, the National Centre for Surrogate Parenting, £6,500 to be paid over to the mother.

Re C (A Minor) (Wardship: Surrogacy) *(the* Baby Cotton *case)*
[1985] Fam Law 191; [1985] FLR 846

Facts

The plaintiffs, Mr and Mrs A, were an American couple, of Asiatic origin, in their 30s. They had been married for several years and dearly wanted a child, but the wife had a genital defect and was consequently unable to bear a child. The couple had thought of adoption, but because of American laws, they would only be able to adopt a child who would be nearly five years old. As a result, in 1983, Mr A entered into a contract whereby he arranged for and paid the National Centre for Surrogate Parenting to find a surrogate mother to bear his child in Britain. He then came to England to provide the seminal fluid for artificial insemination, which subsequently took place. Mr A and the surrogate mother, Kim Cotton, never met and Mr A then returned to America. The insemination was successful and the mother conceived. The mother agreed, via the agency, to hand over the child at birth, amidst much media interest and attempts to find their identity. Mr and Mrs A arrived in England for the birth. The child was born in a hospital on 4 January 1985 and, a few hours after the birth, the mother voluntarily left the child in the care of the hospital until the child could be collected by the plaintiffs. The local authority applied for, and was granted, a place of safety order (under legislation that is now abolished by the Children Act 1989, as of 14 November 1991). Two academics, Professor Michael Freeman and John Hall, questioned the legality of such proceedings and Mr Hall appeared to have suggested that wardship was the more appropriate action. It might be noticed that the child was, in fact, already in a hospital, which qualifies as a 'place of safety'. The husband, Mr A, commenced wardship proceedings and asked that care and control of the child be committed to him and his wife. The matter came before the judge on 8 and 11 January. At a private hearing, Latey J granted a wardship order and gave the local authority time to make inquiries before the matter was restored to the list.

Judgment

The case was heard by Latey J, who reviewed the facts and declared that, first and foremost, at the heart of the wardship jurisdiction was what was in the best interests of the child concerned. The commercial aspects of the ethical, moral and social implications regarding the methods used to produce the child were not relevant to the decision as to what was now best for the child. The court also observed that, having made full inquiries, Mr A was confirmed as the baby's father and he and his wife wanted her. The baby's mother did not. Mr and Mrs A were both highly qualified professional people, with a house in the country and another in a town. Materially, they would be able to give the baby a very good upbringing. But, far more importantly, they are both 'excellently equipped to meet the baby's emotional needs'; he found ample evidence to show that they were 'most warm, caring, sensible people, as well as highly intelligent. When the time comes to answer the child's questions, they will be able to do so with professional advice if they feel they need it'. The learned judge thought that 'looking at the child's well being, physical and emotional' there was no one better to have her care.

It was in the child's best interests to be committed to their care and control. Accordingly, care and control were granted to the plaintiffs with leave to take the child out of the jurisdiction. The wardship was continued until further order and there would be a specific order that there would be no disclosure or publicity which might lead to the identification of the plaintiffs.

Comment on the *Baby Cotton* Case

This case saw a new application for the wardship jurisdiction. It should be noted that part of the wardship order also allowed the couple to take the child out of the jurisdiction, although in theory the child can be recalled to England as long as it is under 18. However, for all intents and purposes, and in the light of the practical realities of the situation, this wardship order served as a form of adoption without the formalities of adoption and without the legal severance of all ties with the biological mother, the surrogate mother. Under the CA 1989 regime, in effect since October 1991, the 'inherent jurisdiction of the court' is more likely to be used to deal with matters involving local authorities, but the wardship jurisdiction appears, in some measure, to have survived the 1989 Children Act reforms.

The Surrogacy Arrangements Act 1985

The immense volume of publicity which the *Baby Cotton* case attracted eventually led to the UK becoming the first country to enact surrogacy legislation when it passed the Surrogacy Arrangements Act 1985 (the 1985 Act), whose main aim is to abolish commercial surrogacy. It applies to arrangements that are being made before a woman becomes pregnant with a view to the child being handed over to be brought up by someone else. The Act does not apply to agreements made after a woman has become pregnant. Where the process of reproduction has been assisted, the relevant time is when the embryos or gametes were placed in the woman's body. Since s 1A of the 1985 Act renders surrogacy contracts unenforceable, disputes over the upbringing of children must be resolved according to the general law on status (see discussion above, p 166, in the opening section of this chapter). The 1985 Act makes it an offence to negotiate a surrogate arrangement 'on a commercial basis' or to compile information with a view to doing so. But, the Act does not cover cases where the only payment is to, or for the benefit of, the surrogate mother. It also provides that the surrogate mother and the commissioning parents cannot be guilty of the offence. The policy behind this is so that the child's upbringing will not be tainted with illegality, but there are potential problems in the context of adoption if money changes hands here for any reason, since the law bans payments for the adoption of a child whom it is intended to adopt. However, the English courts have given some guidance on dealing with this situation (see, further, *Re Adoption Application*, below).

It is also an offence to advertise the fact that someone is willing to be a surrogate mother, negotiate a surrogate agreement or is looking for someone to act as one. Both the advertiser and the publisher of the newspaper or other medium will be guilty of the offence. No exception is made in this context for a surrogate mother or commissioning parents.

Surrogacy, adoption and reasonable payment of expenses

In the late 1980s, the case of *Re Adoption Application* was heard, the first of two surrogacy cases which were decided on the same day. This case dealt with adoption and surrogacy, and clarified the law on the legality of 'reasonable expenses', the interpretation that the English courts might place on this phrase, and the relationship between moneys handed over as reasonable expenses and monetary payments which were prohibited if made as part of payment for a proposed adoption of a baby (for an account of these two cases in the context of the late 1980s, see de Cruz (1988), from which some of the following discussion derives).

Re Adoption Application (Payment for Adoption)
[1987] 2 FLR 291; [1987] 2 All ER 826

Facts

The applicants, Mr and Mrs A, were a childless couple who applied to adopt a child then aged two years and four months, who was conceived as a result of sexual intercourse between the surrogate mother and Mr A in pursuance of a surrogacy arrangement between the applicants and the surrogate mother. The agreement was entered into because Mrs A, in her mid-30s, was infertile. The applicants had been unsuccessful in their attempts to adopt a child both in Britain and abroad. The surrogate was a happily married woman with two children. She enjoyed pregnancy and having learnt about surrogacy appeared genuinely to want to help childless couples. The applicants answered the surrogate's magazine advertisement and they entered into a surrogate arrangement. This was therefore no 'love affair' but a 'partial surrogacy', whereby the surrogate mother is also the genetic mother of the child. In the words of Latey J, it was 'physical congress with the sole purpose of procreating a child'. It was agreed that the applicants pay the mother (who was in full time employment) £10,000 to compensate her for her loss of earnings, expenses in connection with the pregnancy and for emotional and physical factors. The surrogate and Mr A had intercourse on a few occasions, but this stopped as soon as conception occurred. The applicants paid the surrogate mother £1,000 a few months later and a further £4,000 when the baby was born. The surrogate refused to take the remaining £5,000, saying she had not entered the agreement for commercial reasons, would have handed the child over anyway and had made financial gains from the sale of a book she had co-written describing her surrogacy experiences.

When the child was born, Mrs A was present and Mr A joined them almost immediately. Two days later, mother and child went to the applicants' home and the four spent a week together before the mother returned to her home, leaving the child with the applicants. The child remained with the applicants for over two years and, indeed, thrived in their care, and the applicants now applied for an adoption order.

Judgment

Latey J considered the legal questions before the court: (a) whether, in the circumstances, an adoption order would be legally permissible – specifically, had there been 'payment or reward for adoption'?; and (b), if so, could the court authorise payments retrospectively; and (c) would an adoption order be a correct exercise of the court's discretion?

Was there payment or reward for adoption?

The court's view was that, on the facts of the case, it was only after the baby was born that any of the parties began to think of adoption. Accordingly, no payment or reward had been made within the meaning of the legislation (s 50 of the Adoption Act 1958, now s 57 of the Adoption Act 1976).

Could they authorise payments retrospectively?

The court had to interpret s 50 of the Adoption Act 1958, which prohibited payment for adoption but provided that prohibited payments do not include 'any payment or reward authorised by the court'. The difficult point in the present case was that the payment had already been made, so the next question was: could the court give retrospective approval of payments or had it to be given before the payment was made? The learned judge's view was that to penalise every payment, no matter how modest or 'innocently made', would be Draconian and, on a consideration of all the evidence in this case, the court had a discretion whether or not to authorise payments, and such authorisation could be given retrospectively.

Was adoption absolutely prohibited in all surrogacy cases?

Hence, the question then was whether adoption could be allowed in this case. The court gave great weight to the full and balanced reports from the doctor, the health visitor and the guardian *ad litem* (GAL), which confirmed that the child remained happy and contented while in the care of the applicants; the GAL's report stressed the dangers of making any order short of adoption, since this would heighten the anxieties of the adoptive parents that the child might be removed and this might have a 'corrosive' effect on their feelings for the child. Even if the payments had been prohibited, the court was prepared to authorise them and to make an adoption order.

Paying the surrogate mother for her 'services'

The Chair of the Surrogacy Review, Professor Margaret Brazier, reveals that in evidence to the Surrogacy Review (see below, p 184) set up by the Labour government in October 1997, 'a number of distinguished philosophers, lawyers and doctors argued that the law should be altered to allow reasonable remuneration to the surrogate for her services' (Brazier (1999), p 350). She also says that the largest voluntary organisation involved in surrogacy in Britain, Childlessness Overcome Through Surrogacy (COTS), strongly advocated payments for surrogates and 'all the advocates of payments suggest, probably rightly, that a ban on payments would be likely to reduce the available pool of surrogate mothers' (Brazier (1999)). In view of one of the objections to surrogacy – treating the whole enterprise like the business of buying and selling a baby like a commodity rather than treating the child like a human being – this has continued to be a controversial aspect although, as Margaret Brazier herself points out, no one really *buys* a child. She argues that the payments made to the surrogate are to cover the 'cost of continuing the cost of the pregnancy and the inevitable expenses following the birth, the cost of clothes, equipment (etc) ... for the baby' (Brazier (1999), p 349). However, from the point of view of the English law of tort, although you cannot legally buy a baby, the law does price babies, because should a tortfeasor kill your baby, you will receive damages (monetary compensation) for bereavement, so 'Tort prices babies' (Brazier (1999)). Consequently, the Brazier Report has made recommendations to deal with this particular aspect of surrogacy or surrogate motherhood (see, further, below, p 185).

Surrogate mother's right to change her mind

The second case, *Re P* (the twins case) dealt with the issue of whether a surrogate mother has the right to change her mind under a surrogacy arrangement and thus, whether she can be compelled to hand over the baby to the commissioning parents. The case appears to be the first case of twins born under a surrogate arrangement.

Re P (Minors) (Wardship: Surrogacy) *[1987] 2 FLR 421*

The commissioning couple, Mr and Mrs B, had no children of their own. The natural mother, Mrs P, offered her services to the couple when she heard they were seeking a surrogate mother to bear Mr B's biological child as Mrs B could not carry a child to term. Payments were supposed to be made to the surrogate in instalments at various stages of the pregnancy and after the birth of the child. The mother's pregnancy was brought about by artificial pregnancy (the father donated sperm which was artificially inseminated into the mother), and she gave birth to twins. About two months before the birth, the mother was assailed by doubts about whether she could bear to hand over the babies to the father and his wife. The couple later visited the surrogate and the twins three days after the birth, and everything seemed on course for the agreement to be carried out. However, having taken the twins home, the surrogate experienced a conflict of emotions and wrote a letter to Mr B, expressing her doubts about going through with the agreement, but saying she would still go through with it. Eventually, having looked after the babies for five months, the surrogate refused to hand over the twins and both parties approached the local authority, which warded the babies and requested the court to make orders as to their future.

The judgment

The court action, before Sir John Arnold, President of the Family Division, was really a matter of custody (as it was called before the coming into force of the CA 1989). The court carried out a balancing exercise and decided that its duty in deciding the case was to have the welfare of the child as its paramount consideration. There were factors on both sides to support their case, but on balance, the mother had a stronger case because the twins had now been looked after by their genetic mother for the first five months of their lives, and apart from having given birth to them, the care had clearly been satisfactory and the babies had bonded with their genetic mother. The learned judge found 'nothing to outweigh the advantages to these children of preserving a link to the mother to whom they are bonded, and who had exercised a satisfactory degree of maternal care'. Significantly, the judge said that it was not important to rule upon the validity of the agreement and any question of rejecting the agreement as being against public policy was not relevant to the present case. The only relevance of this being a surrogate agreement was if the nature of the agreement reflected so adversely on the character and moral outlook of the custodians as to disqualify them both entirely. The court awarded care and control of the babies to their mother. The wardship proceedings were terminated.

Obtaining parental responsibility without adoption: s 30 of the HFEA 1990

In 1990, the case of *Re W (Minors) (Surrogacy)* was reported, which led to a legislative change to the law and indeed caused Parliament to change its view on whether surrogacy should be discouraged at all costs so that in certain circumstances, a couple could acquire parental responsibility without having to go to court to adopt the child.

Re W (Minors) (Surrogacy) *[1991] 1 FLR 385*

Facts

The twins (aged 17 months at the time of the hearing) were born following a surrogacy arrangement. The genetic mother had no womb, but was able to produce eggs which were taken from her medically and fertilised *in vitro* by sperm from her husband. Two resultant embryos were implanted in the host mother, who gave birth to the twins, who then lived with the genetic parents. There was no dispute about that arrangement. The local authority first brought proceedings for various declarations, the purpose of which was to establish the legal parentage of the children. It then took wardship proceedings to give the court wide powers to supervise the children's future. A court order was made imposing injunctive restrictions on the publication of information about the children. Applications were now made to vary the terms of that injunction. The host mother and her husband applied for the prohibition on their identification to be lifted. This was unopposed. The host mother also made an opposed application to identify the hospital at which she gave birth to the wards. The genetic parents applied for the doctor and the hospital giving the IVF treatment to be included within the injunction so that they should not be identified and information should not be solicited from them. That application was supported by the Official Solicitor, but opposed by the host mother and her husband in so far as it related to the identity of the doctor and the premises. They did not oppose the non-solicitation aspect.

Judgment

Scott Baker J reviewed the evidence and observed that, until recently, when the advance of medical science created the possibility of *in vitro* fertilisation, it was not envisaged that the genetic mother could be other than one and the same person. The advent of IVF presented the law with a dilemma: whom should the law regard as the mother? In the case itself, there is no suggestion other than that the genetic parents are wholly admirable parents and that they should have the upbringing of the twins. The learned judge reviewed the imminent enactment of legislation (of s 30) which he thought would enable the court to approve an agreement by all parties that decide these children's future in a practical manner. If the genetic parents succeeded in their application, the twins would be treated in law as being their children.

The court held:

- the welfare and best interests of the children were the first and paramount considerations. Their future lay with the genetic parents and it was necessary to facilitate any steps that cemented their relationship in that household. The terms of an injunction should be no wider than necessary to protect the wards' welfare;

- the local authority's application for, *inter alia*, declarations as to the twins' legal parentage do stand adjourned generally with liberty to restore, upon the undertaking by the genetic parents to make an application for a parental order under the relevant clauses of the HFEA 1990 within 28 days of its becoming law (the law has now been enacted and is in force);
- pending the determination of the court as to the twins' parentage, they would remain wards of court under the care and control of the genetic parents;
- that the prohibition of the publication of the identity of the host mother and her husband be lifted, as this was unlikely to operate to the ward's disadvantage or prejudice their interests; and
- the existing injunction should continue.

Requirements of s 30 of the HFEA 1990

Under s 30 of the HFEA 1990, certain couples may apply for a parental order. This has been available since 1 November 1994. This order was created at a late stage in the House of Commons proceedings on the Bill in response to a well publicised individual case (*Re W* (1991) (above, p 181)) hence, under s 30, qualified people may apply to the court within six months of the child's birth for an order that they shall be treated as the child's parents despite the application of ss 27, 28 and 29. In order to qualify, the applicants must show that: they are over 18; married to each other; at least one must be a genetic parent of the child (even though another woman gave birth); the child is resident with them; those who are otherwise treated by the law as the parents have unconditionally agreed to the making of the order (if they can be found); and that no money has changed hands other than in respect of reasonable expenses unless authorised by the court (see the Brazier Report for their comment on this requirement that it should be 'genuine' expenses). Of course, s 30 will not be available if the child is not living with the applicants, or the applicants are not married to each other, or if the six month period within which to apply has expired. Under current English law, a court may grant residence orders to the couple who have used assisted reproduction techniques to have a child, and the parental order will last, in the absence of a further court order, until the child is 16, but it will not remove the rights of the legal parents. To deal with this and add finality to the situation, many couples will prefer to adopt the child so that the parental responsibility of the legal parents can be terminated.

A few further points may be noted.

The first reported case on s 30 was *Re Q* (1996).

Re Q (Parental Order) *[1996] 1 FLR 369, HC*

The baby, Q, was born in the summer of 1995 as a result of a total surrogacy arrangement. The unmarried surrogate, who received IVF treatment at a licensed clinic, was paid £8,280 to cover her expenses and loss of earnings. The commissioning couple applied for a parental order under s 30.

The judgment

Johnson J was satisfied that the statutory requirements had been complied with, but he highlighted three for special mention. First, the consent of the carrying mother. She was overcome with doubt when the time actually came to give her consent, but she has now done so and, according to the guardian *ad litem*'s report, 'fully understands the effects of a parental order, understanding she loses all parental responsibility, and wishes the order to be made as soon as possible'.

Secondly, the court had to consider whether or not it should authorise payments totalling £8,280 which had been made to the surrogate mother by Mr and Mrs B. Here, the court held that such authorisation could be given retrospectively following the decision of Latey J in *Re Adoption Application (Payment for Adoption)* [1987] Fam 81 (see above, p 177)). The guardian first thought that the payment was rather high, but on further inquiry concluded that the sum was made up of payments to cover clothes, daily trips to the doctor for injections, child care provision of her own children during some of these visits and similar related expenses. A further £5,000 was a payment to compensate Miss A for loss of earnings.

The court agreed with the guardian that the payment was reasonable and authorised it.

Finally, the consultant who had carried out the medical procedures insisted that, in his view and in the view of the hospital, Mr B was to be treated as the father of the child. The guardian told the court that this was a frequent misunderstanding of the legislation and it was for this reason that the court was asked to give a formal ruling. On the court's interpretation of the Act to the circumstances of the case, there was no man who was to be 'treated as the father' and whose consent was necessary to the making of the order. The court in this case, therefore, held that to qualify as a father under s 28 of the HFEA 1990, the man must have an existing relationship with the woman who is receiving treatment, not the commissioning mother.

Comment on *Re Q*

The significant point here was that, although Mr B provided the sperm and had intended to rear the child, his relationship was with the commissioning mother, not the surrogate mother. It also appears that, where the sum paid for 'expenses' is not extortionate, a court will find very little difficulty in authorising payment retrospectively to the surrogate under s 30(7) of the HFEA 1990.

The Brazier Surrogacy Review

In 1997, a committee chaired by Professor Margaret Brazier was established to review the law on surrogacy, particularly in relation to arrangements for payments and regulation (see *Surrogacy. Review for Health Ministers of Current Arrangements for Payments and Regulation. Report of the Review Team*, Cm 4068, 1998, HMSO). This committee reported in 1998 and the Report ('the Brazier Report') was presented to the British Parliament in October 1998.

Events leading to the Surrogacy Review

In the Brazier Report, the events leading up to the Review were summarised.

(a) In 1984, the medical opinion largely opposed professional involvement in surrogacy, but in 1990, the BMA published its report *Surrogacy: Ethical Considerations*, which endorsed a degree of professional assistance in establishing a surrogate pregnancy. In 1996, the BMA updated that report in its book *Changing Conceptions of Motherhood: The Practice of Surrogacy in Britain*, 1996. In that publication, the BMA declared surrogacy to be an 'acceptable option of last resort' in certain cases but stressed that 'the interests of the potential child must be paramount and the risks to the surrogate mother must be kept to the minimum'.

(b) There was also evidence that clinics offering *in vitro* fertilisation (IVF) were becoming more involved in surrogacy arrangements. This contributed to the impression that such arrangements were becoming more frequent.

(c) During 1996 and 1997, a number of cases involving surrogacy arrangements were reported. These cases provoked a substantial, but mixed reaction both from the media and the public and demonstrated some of the ways in which surrogacy was developing. These included a 1997 case involving a couple from abroad who sought a surrogacy arrangement in the UK. The media reported in detail the difficulties that arose in that case, and the breakdown in the relationship between the parties involved. What should have been a private arrangement took on the appearance of a public spectacle and cast doubt on the ability of the current arrangements to meet society's legitimate concerns about such cases (see Editorial (1997) PCLB 70 for an account of this case).

(d) The arrangements for surrogacy in the USA, in particular its commercial nature, also came into the spotlight early in 1997. The director of a US commercial agency visited the UK to recruit commissioning couples who wished to undertake surrogacy arrangements at his agency in the USA. It was reported that the charge to the commissioning couple for this service, including medical and legal expenses and payments to the surrogate mother, amounted to £30,000.

(e) In another case, a full surrogacy arrangement resulted in the birth of triplets. The children were entrusted to the commissioning couple. This was reported almost entirely positively as an example of surrogacy helping those who would otherwise remain childless.

(f) Other stories also surfaced, including a case in the USA of a couple who arranged for a surrogate to carry their daughter's fertilised eggs after her death to enable them to become grandparents. In the UK, more recently, there were reports of a mother carrying a child for her daughter, and of a daughter carrying a child for her mother.

(g) In particular, concerns were expressed about the welfare of the child in such arrangements and the apparently increasingly levels of payment being offered to surrogate mothers – £13,000 was reported in the media in the case involving the couple from abroad (referred to in (c) above) and even higher figures were reported in other cases. This led to suggestions that surrogacy is, in effect, increasingly practised on a commercial basis.

The Brazier Report referred to the Warnock Committee, set up in 1982, which was asked 'to examine the ethical implications of developments in human reproduction generally, including surrogacy'. The committee conduced its deliberations against a background of considerable public concern about the potential consequences of rapidly developing advances in reproductive medicine. The government, in 1984, only partially accepted the broad conclusions of the Warnock Committee in relation to surrogacy arrangements and Parliament implemented certain of its recommendations in the Surrogacy Arrangements Act 1985 and the HFEA 1990. The government took the view then that, because of the legal, ethical and social problems associated with surrogacy arrangements, they should not be encouraged.

The Brazier Surrogacy Report

Recommendations

In essence, it recommended: tougher controls on surrogacy; that surrogates should only be entitled to 'genuine expenses associated with the pregnancy' and that any additional payment should be prohibited to prevent surrogacy arrangements being entered into for financial benefit; legislation should define expenses in broad terms of principle and empower ministers to issue directions on what constitutes reasonable expenses; and the methods by which expenses shall be proven.

In 'Does surrogacy have a future after Brazier?' (1999) 10 Med L Rev 1, Professor Michael Freeman suggests, *inter alia*, that the aftermath of the Brazier Report on Surrogacy might spell a bleak future for surrogacy as it has been practised in this country.

British Medical Association policy on surrogacy

Despite expressing disapproval of surrogacy practices in the UK during part of the 1980s, in the 1990s, the British Medical Association (BMA) appeared to undergo a change of policy and eventually welcomed the British Government's decision to register and regulate agencies involved in surrogacy. The BMA wrote to the Department of Health in 1996, urging it to implement such a move, and the government's subsequent plans appear to mirror many of the proposals previously submitted by the BMA.

According to a statement issued by its Public Affairs Division in its evidence to the Surrogacy Review Team, the BMA were at pains to point out that people could enter into a surrogacy arrangement without being fully aware of the ethical, legal, medical and emotional factors involved. A high percentage of cases did not seek medical advice, with the voluntary agencies being the only source of information. It was, therefore, imperative that agencies were regulated and had the opportunity to develop their expertise in this multi-faceted area and for intending parents to receive the best possible advice on the legal, emotional, financial and medical problems that they may face. On the question of expenses, the BMA's view was that they should not be so high that they would become an inducement and supports any measures which would prevent this happening.

The BMA also suggested in its evidence to the Review Team that using a regulated agency could become one of the criteria for granting a parental order under s 30 of the HFEA 1990, and the Association supports the proposal to make compliance with the proposed Surrogacy Act and Code of Practice mandatory. The BMA intends to make further submissions for the Code of Practice and will suggest that regulated agencies should be permitted to employ professional staff and possibly charge a fee to cover costs, but they would continue to be a strictly non-commercial and non-profit making body.

COMMENT ON SURROGACY

Several questions can be posed in the light of this discussion.

(a) Whose needs are we serving in these cases? Is it the mother's, the commissioning couple's or the child's needs? The cases suggest that the child's needs might be subservient to those of the commissioning parents and even overshadowed by the surrogate's claims.

(b) Should ethics and morals come into the picture? Ultimately, every society needs to decide what its moral values and priorities are in these cases. Baby selling is not a practice that most societies would want to encourage and, indeed, would wish to outlaw.

(c) What is the role of choice? In a democratic society, if it is argued that people have the right to choose the kind of medical assistance they need to deal with their infertility or their need for a child, at which point can it be said that because of the exchange of money for 'services' (especially if reasonable expenses are really exorbitant and amount to placing a value on the surrogate arrangement), the baby becomes a commodity and therefore purely a means to an end rather than an entity of intrinsic value and worth?

(d) Is it morally right to create a situation where it is highly likely that the child will be the centre of moral, ethical and legal controversy? It is submitted that this cannot be desirable or supportable on purely welfare grounds, if the welfare of the child is to be paramount.

The way forward would probably not be through statutory criminalisation. There would be difficulties in policing it, and trying to ensure the practice is not driven underground is one of the reasons for not criminalising it *in toto*. Another argument against a total ban would be that this would constitute an invasion of privacy under the Human Rights Act 1998, but if regulation is the solution, the question that the Brazier Report raises is: should this be centralised or decentralised?

POSTHUMOUS REPRODUCTION FROM SPERM TAKEN FROM A DECEASED DONOR

The orphaned embryo – insemination with an embryo fertilised in vitro: the *Diane Blood* case

In vitro fertilisation was used in somewhat controversial terms in the now famous *Diane Blood* case, where sperm was taken from Diane Blood's husband while he was in a coma and the husband died without ever having given his consent to the sperm donation in any form. After court forays and initial refusals, Mrs Blood eventually managed to have her child, via *in vitro* fertilisation, using her dead husband's semen, at a Belgian clinic. Mr Blood died in 1997.

The Diane Blood *case (*R v Human Fertilisation and Embryology Authority ex p Blood*) [1997] WLR 806*

This was the case of the widow fighting a legal battle to have a baby using her dead husband's sperm, which had been removed from her husband while he lay in a coma. More specifically, this case deals with the posthumous insemination of a woman with an embryo created with the egg collected from the woman and the sperm of the deceased husband, thereby creating a fatherless child. The HFEA is charged by the HFEA 1990 with the task of regulating and licensing fertility treatment and keeping services.

Facts

Diane and Stephen Blood were a childless couple who married in 1991 and were trying to have a baby when the husband contracted bacterial meningitis and fell into a coma in February 1995. Doctors had taken two samples of sperm from Mr Blood at Mrs Blood's request, by electro-ejaculation, despite the fact that he was in a coma and could not give consent. Both samples were kept by the Infertility Research Trust until the resolution of the proceedings instituted by Mrs Blood. On the third day of the husband's coma, he died without having given written consent to the use of his sperm after his death. In 1997, Mrs Blood was nearly 33 years old and had stated in her evidence that she and her husband had decided to try for a family towards the end of 1994 and, although they had not been successful, had not started a course of treatment together before her husband fell seriously ill. Nevertheless, she was sure that, had her husband not been unconscious, he would have agreed both to the removal and storage of the sperm and to her being artificially inseminated after his death.

Mrs Blood wished to be impregnated with her husband's sperm but, in the first instance, the HFEA refused to license the release of the sperm for the procedure to be carried out in the UK or to exercise its discretion to authorise export of the sperm for treatment abroad. The grounds were that the donor had not given written consent for the storage and that it had been taken without his consent or counselling (as required under Sched 3). The HFEA also refused permission for Mr Blood's sperm to be exported to another EU Member State where written permission is not required. Mrs Blood tried to challenge these decisions by means of judicial review.

The High Court judgment

In the High Court, Sir Stephen Brown P said that this was a very hard case which evoked universal sympathy for the applicant. However, he opined that the powers of the court on an application for judicial review were limited and did not extend to making a decision on the fundamental matter in question. He identified the key issues: (a) the right of the applicant to receive treatment in the UK: s 4(1) of the HFEA 1990 provided that no person could store gametes or provide treatment using sperm except in pursuance of a licence. Section 12 provided that a licence would only be granted where the provisions of Sched 3 had been complied with, requiring counselling and continuing written consent of the donor, unless the donor was being treated together with the relevant woman and consent could be inferred from conduct; (b) the right to have overseas treatment: the HFEA had General Directions – a set of guidelines which expressly prohibited such export of gametes for use abroad as Mrs Blood was requesting. The court concluded that the HFEA had not exceeded its discretion in declining to depart from the principles contained in the General Directions. Her application was dismissed, and she appealed to the Court of Appeal.

Court of Appeal judgment

The Court of Appeal held:

(a) it was necessary to apply the law as an amalgam of domestic and EC law because European law was now part of domestic law, at least where it applied directly, as it did to the question of Mrs Blood's treatment abroad;

(b) the storage of the sperm taken from a comatose man without his consent was technically an offence – a criminal assault, but this was an unexplored legal situation, so there could be no criticism of the Infertility Research Trust;

(c) even if the statutory exception in s 4(1)(b) of the HFEA 1990 provides treatment without written consent for a couple together, the exception did not apply to a corpse;

(d) the HFEA had been right to refuse to license the fertilisation of the man's sperm in the UK but, in refusing the wife an export licence, it had not taken into account her right to cross-border treatment under Arts 59 and 60 of the EC Treaty. These provisions created a directly enforceable right to receive medical treatment in another Member State;

(e) if allowed to export the sperm, Mrs Blood could get lawful treatment in Belgium and an export licence in this case would not create an undesirable precedent.

In February 1997, the Authority allowed Mrs Blood to export the sperm to a Belgian clinic for posthumous insemination. On 11 December 1998, Diane Blood gave birth to a son, Liam, conceived using semen from her dead husband. At that time, it is believed that the son would still be regarded as non-marital, and there would be no recognition in law of Diane Blood's parents to be recognised as the child's grandparents.

Post-*Blood* – the review of consent procedures under the HFEA

In the wake of the *Blood* case, there appeared to be considerable public and parliamentary interest in legal and ethical issues surrounding the removal, storage and use of human gametes. Concern was expressed about whether the provisions in the common law and the HFEA 1990 reflected clinical and public opinion. Hence, in 1997, the government commissioned a review (headed by Professor Sheila McLean) of consent procedures under the common law and the HFEA 1990. A report, *Review of the Common Law Provisions Relating to the Removal of Gametes and of the Consent Provisions in the Human Fertilisation and Embryology Act 1990* (1998), was subsequently published in July 1998. The Report recommends that written consent should continue to be required for treatment under the HFEA 1990.

The recommendations also include the following:

(a) the current common law provisions relating to information disclosure and consent to the removal of human gametes should remain;

(b) in cases where there is doubt about removal of gametes, the courts should be asked to determine the question of legality where consent cannot be given in the usual way;

(c) the requirement in the HFEA 1990 for consent to certain treatment provided in writing (for example, for *in vitro* fertilisation and donor insemination) should remain;

(d) the HFEA 1990 should be amended so that there is no discretion vested in the HFEA to permit the export of human gametes which have been removed unlawfully;

(e) gamete providers should take into account the succession rights of children as yet unborn when storing gametes which might be used in fertility treatment at some future date;

(f) consideration should be given to amending s 28(6) of the HFEA 1990 to secure, in the particular circumstances of these cases, the status of any child created after the death of the gamete provider. Arguably, providing such a child with a legal father is of symbolic rather than practical value, but it may be of significance for the child.

Government plans to change the law relating to birth registers

In August 2000, the Department of Health announced that the government intended to change the law relating to birth registers so that the biological father's name could be inserted on the child's birth certificate even though the child was conceived after his death. In other words, in Diane Blood's case, therefore:

- her baby would no longer be regarded as illegitimate;
- women who conceived after their partner died would have the right to have their dead partner's name inserted on the baby's birth certificate;
- Diane Blood's parents can now be officially recognised as the child's grandparents.

Diane Blood was reported in the media as saying she was delighted with the proposed change in the law for all the relatives of her 20 month old child, Liam.

ACCESS TO IVF SERVICES – OPEN TO ALL OR ONLY TO THOSE WITHIN CERTAIN AGE LIMITS?

As far as allowing access to IVF treatment in Britain is concerned, the test of the child's welfare or best interests has been used to limit such access. However, although the basic policy has been to declare the welfare of the child to be paramount, the outcome of one of the well known cases in this area, the *Harriott* case, has been controversial and ended up in court. This case predated the HFEA 1990.

Section 13(5) of the HFEA 1990 provides: 'A woman shall not be provided with treatment services unless account has been taken of the welfare of any child who may be born as a result of the treatment (including the need of that child for a father), and of any child who may be affected by the birth.'

In the 1994 case of *Seale* (*R v Sheffield HA ex p Seale* (1994) 25 BMLR 1, Mrs Seale, aged 36, had been experiencing difficulties in conceiving and had applied to Sheffield Health Authority for IVF treatment. The authority rejected her application. In a letter to her husband, it was stated that, because of competing health priorities, only £200,000 could be allocated to the provision of assisted reproduction services. The applicant applied to the High Court for judicial review of the decision.

The court held that, in view of its limited resources and the lower success rates achieved with older women, the Authority's policy only to treat women below the age of 35 was not irrational.

The authority was not required to provide this sort of service on demand to any individual patient for whom it may work, regardless of financial and other constraints upon the authority. To consider the financial resources available and to decide that the efficiency of the treatment decreased after the woman reached 35, was not *Wednesbury* unreasonable (that is, would not come within the scope of unreasonableness as defined in the *Wednesbury* case).

Refusal of treatment on the grounds of applicant's personal history?

R v Ethical Committee of St Mary's Hospital (Manchester) ex p Harriott *(the* Harriott *case) [1988] 1 FLR 512*

In this case, Mrs Harriott was experiencing difficulties in becoming pregnant and had applied to her local authority's social services department to adopt or foster a child. Her application was turned down because of the applicant's criminal record (which included soliciting for prostitution) and her allegedly poor understanding of the role of a foster parent. She subsequently applied for IVF under the NHS and, once again, her application was refused. She then sought judicial review of the decision to refuse her treatment, alleging that it was reached by the wrong body and that she was not given adequate opportunity to make representation. However, Schiemann J took the view that she had been given an opportunity to make representations against the refusal, so there was no procedural unfairness. The learned judge was prepared to accept that a blanket policy to refuse treatment to 'anyone who was a Jew or coloured' might be illegal, but the hospital's criteria in this case were acceptable and unobjectionable. The plaintiff therefore failed in her application.

Current law on access to treatment

Under the current law, if a heterosexual couple seek treatment with IVF, individual fertility clinics have a discretion who to treat, so long as they act in accordance with the Code of Practice promulgated by the HFEA. Where a couple are refused treatment, reasons must be given, pursuant to para 3.31 of the Code (2nd revision, December 1995). Two main reasons might justify why treatment may be refused: (a) the couple may be medically unsuitable; (b) they may be deemed socially unsuitable as parents. Here, the decision will turn on the potential welfare of any child born as a result of the treatment.

Comment

In 1996, Mrs Seale, aged 38, gave birth to a baby boy as a result of IVF treatment paid for privately by an anonymous business benefactor (see the *Seale* case, above, p 191). The HFEA 1990 does not say that there is an age limit on recipients of IVF treatment. However, age is a factor which may be taken into account by ethics committees when reviewing applications for this treatment. Age limits are included by many clinics and the latest HFEA Code of Practice includes the ages of the parties seeking treatment, and this is linked to 'their likely future ability to look after or provide for a child's needs' (para 3.17 of the HFEA Code of Practice 1995). The IVF unit of St Mary's Hospital stipulates that they will only treat couples where the female is less than 40 and the male is less than 50.

Comment on reproduction technologies and surrogacy in the UK

There is, today in Britain, far more widespread acceptance of surrogacy as a method of assisted reproduction. In the 1970s, an English judge was heard to label a surrogate arrangement as 'pernicious', yet both the tone and the approach had become more conciliatory in the 1980s by the time other surrogacy cases reached the English courts, when the courts were not prepared to enforce a surrogacy arrangement when the surrogate mother had become too emotionally attached to the child and did not wish to hand the child over to the commissioning parents. Another example of the English courts' change of attitude is that they were even prepared to sanction payment by a couple of 'expenses' prior to adopting the child produced by the surrogacy arrangement, being careful to interpret this as money that was *not* handed over *in pursuance of adoption,* which would otherwise be illegal.

Test-tube babies in Europe

In June 2000, it was reported that nearly one child in 80 born in Britain today is a test-tube baby. In Europe, 200,000 treatment cycles a year are being carried out. France has 45,000, Britain 34,000 and Germany more than 28,000 treatment cycles a year. Statistics from 18 countries, compiled for the first time by fertility experts around Europe, revealed that 1.3% of all births in Europe are the result of either the standard test-tube baby technique, IVF or ICSI (where a single sperm is injected into the egg). In Britain, the proportion is 1.2%. Britain has the second highest number of IVF and ICSI children, at 8,727 in the year 1997–98, just below France at 8,762. In Britain, 27.5% of fertilised eggs returned to the womb resulted in live births and France achieved 25.6%. Scandinavia has the lowest incidence of multiple births from the treatment because clinics have agreed that no more than two embryos should be replaced in the womb. Unlike France, where the State will pay for four attempts at IVF, the NHS in Britain will fund only one or two attempts for most couples, and this results in long waiting lists, so that private treatment (which means the couple have to pay for the treatment) is fast becoming the only option.

Margaret Brazier (1999) has remarked (p 191) that 'The most profound change in regulating reproductive medicine since Warnock is ... the dramatically increased role of commerce'. In the post-Warnock era, research has moved from an 'academic' exercise to an enterprise with enormous commercial potential. As Brazier says: 'A fertility "industry" has developed to provide treatment on a profit-making basis both to British citizens and "procreative tourists" escaping more prohibitive regimes elsewhere in Europe. Pressure to pay gamete donors and surrogates continues.'

SELECTIVE BIBLIOGRAPHY

Bainham, A, *Children: The Modern Law*, 1998, Jordan, pp 75, 201 *et seq*

Barton, C and Douglas, G, *Law and Parenthood*, 1995, Butterworths, Chapter 4, esp p 81 *et seq*

Brazier, M, 'Regulating the reproduction business?' (1999) 10 Med L Rev 166

Brazier, M, 'Can you buy children?' (1999) 11 Child and Fam LQ 345

de Cruz, P, 'Surrogacy, fertility and the pricing of parenthood' (editorial) (1997) 10 Practitioners' Child Law Bulletin 70

de Cruz, SP, 'Surrogacy, adoption, and custody: a case study' (1988) 18 Fam Law 100

Dewar, J, *Law and the Family*, 1992, Butterworths, esp pp 82–101

Dickens, B, 'Reproductive technology and the "new" family', in Sutherland, E and McCall Smith, J (eds), *Family Rights*, 1990, Edinburgh UP

Douglas, G and Lowe, N, 'Becoming a parent in English law' (1992) 108 LQR 414

Douglas, G, 'Assisted reproduction and the welfare of the child', in Freeman, M and Hepple, B (eds) [1993] CLP 53

Douglas, G, 'The Human Fertilisation and Embryology Act 1990' [1991] 21 Fam Law 110

Douglas, G, *Law, Fertility and Reproduction*, 1991, Sweet & Maxwell, Chapters 6 and 7

Duddington, J, 'The legal and ethical aspects of human cloning' (1999) Law and Justice 26; 100

Freeman, MDA, 'Is surrogacy exploitative?', in McLean, S (ed), *Legal Issues in Human Reproduction*, 1991, Dartmouth

Freeman, MDA, 'Does surrogacy have a future after Brazier?' (1999) 10 Med L Rev 1

Hayes, M and Williams, C, *Family Law: Principles, Policy and Practice*, 1999, Butterworths, esp pp 18–26

Hibbs, M, 'Surrogacy legislation – time for a change?' [1997] Fam Law 564

Kirby, M, 'Medical technology and new frontiers of family law', in McLean, S (ed), *Legal Issues in Human Reproduction*, 1990, Dartmouth

Liu, A, *Artificial Reproduction and Reproductive Rights*, 1991, Dartmouth

Lowe, N and Douglas, G, *Bromley's Family Law*, 1998, Butterworths, Chapter 8

McHale, J and Fox, M, *Health Care Law: Text and Materials*, 1997, Sweet & Maxwell, Chapter 11.

McLean, S, 'Mothers and others', in Sutherland, E and McCall Smith, J (eds), *Family Rights*, 1990, Edinburgh UP

Morgan, D, 'Who to be or not to be: the surrogacy story' (1986) 49 MLR 358

Morgan, D and Lee, R, *Human Fertilisation and Embryology Act 1990*, 1991, Blackstone, esp Chapter 1

Radin, M, 'Market-inalienability' (1987) 100 Harv L Rev 1928

Roberts, S, 'Warnock and surrogate motherhood: sentiment or argument?', in Byrne, P (ed), *Rights and Wrongs in Medicine*, 1986, King Edward's Hospital Fund for London/OUP

Singer, P and Wells, D, *The Reproduction Revolution: New Ways of Making Babies*, 1984, OUP

Stauch, M and Wheat, K, with Tingle, J, *Sourcebook on Medical Law*, 1998, Cavendish Publishing, Chapter 7

Reports

Brazier, M, Campbell, A and Golombok, S, *Review for Health Ministers of Current Arrangements for Payments and Regulation*, Cm 4068, 1998, HMSO

Glover, J *et al*, *Report to the European Commission on Reproductive Technologies, Fertility and the Family*, 1989, Fourth Estate

Warnock Committee, *Report of the Committee of Inquiry into Human Fertilisation and Embryology*, Cmnd 9314, 1984, HMSO

CHAPTER 6

STERILISATION, FERTILITY CONTROL AND THE MENTALLY INCAPACITATED PATIENT

INTRODUCTION

This chapter deals primarily with the medico-legal issues arising from the medical procedure of sterilisation when it is performed on mentally incompetent patients, usually female (with some rare exceptions), who might be minors or adults, as an act of medical paternalism, where it is claimed by a third party, usually a relative or a healthcare professional, and approved by a court, as being in the 'best interests' of the patient. The chapter concentrates on English law, although reference will be made to the Canadian case of *Re Eve*, in the context of discussing a leading English case (*Re B*), and also focuses on contraceptive sterilisation, where the intention is the permanent removal of reproductive capacity, again as a means of protection from an 'unwanted' pregnancy with which the incompetent or mentally handicapped patient is perceived as being unable to cope. The discussion, therefore, does not dwell on consensual sterilisation when it is opted for as a voluntary and increasingly popular means of contraception by willing and competent adults. A subsequent chapter in Part II examines developments in common law jurisdictions such as the USA and Australia and civil law jurisdictions like Germany (see Chapter 15). This chapter also considers the latest English cases dealing with failed sterilisations, contrasting the approach of the courts to healthy and handicapped offspring produced from such failed procedures.

ETHICAL PRINCIPLES

In this difficult medico-legal area, it is therefore not the nature of the medical procedure which competent adults might voluntarily choose to undergo, but the circumstances in which it is being proposed and on whom it is proposed, that can give rise to ethical issues. For a start, the variable nature of mental handicap raises certain ethical concerns. The patient's autonomy should, as ever, be respected but medical and judicial paternalism has been known to justify sterilisation. The autonomy-paternalism polarisation is highlighted in the controversial sterilisation cases that have come before the English courts. Whose right should it be to decide whether it is ever in the best interests of a mentally handicapped person to be sterilised? How should one decide what is 'in the best interests' of such a patient? If such operations are carried out, do they really show respect for persons – all persons, whether capable of deciding for themselves or not? As Josephine Shaw wrote in 1991:

> Sterilisation challenges the law, since it represents an interference in bodily integrity and reproductive autonomy which, in the absence of the consent of the subject of sterilisation, would be seen in liberal terms as a human rights violation, attracting the sanction of penalties under the law. Where the subject cannot consent, at least in conventional terms, the issue becomes that of balancing personal autonomy – ie, not forcing upon a person something which she has not agreed to – against welfare – ie, not denying access to medicine to a person simply because she cannot consent [Shaw, J, in McVeigh and Wheeler (eds) (1991), p 75].

Nine years on, English law is still grappling with the challenges this topic presents, as our discussion will show.

HISTORICAL BACKGROUND

It was in the Canadian case of *Re Eve* (1986), reported before the controversial case of *Re B* (the *Jeanette* case) [1987] 2 All ER 206 that La Forest J said that 'There are many reasons for approaching an application for sterilisation of a mentally incompetent person with the utmost caution ... the decision involves values in an area where social history clouds our vision and encourages many to perceive the mentally handicapped as somewhat less than human' (see *Re Eve* (1986) 31 DLR (4th) 1, p 39). A hundred years ago, paternalism was predominant. Mentally handicapped people were kept out of the public gaze, in institutions or workhouses. Given the life expectancy of the time, many died in infancy and, for those with disorders such as Down's syndrome, life expectancy was considered to be short. As is discussed in the comparative chapter on sterilisation in Part II (Chapter 15) the mentally handicapped were among those groups who were seen as vulnerable to involuntary sterilisation programmes employed in the earlier part of the 20th century by the USA and, of course, pursued notoriously and vigorously in Nazi Germany. These were people seen as unfit for parenting and come within the category of eugenic sterilisation, where the sterilisation is performed for those who are perceived as having undesirable or unsuitable genes to be allowed to procreate. The eugenics theory is based on Mendelian genetics or the 'laws' of Gregor Mendel. The eugenicists, basing their arguments on Mendel's findings about the hereditability of physical traits, argued that intelligence, personality and even character traits such as dishonesty, criminality and even laziness could be passed on to future generations (see Laughlin, HH, *Eugenic Sterilisation in the United States*, 1922, Psychopathic Laboratory of the Municipal Court of Chicago, p 369). Certain traits were associated with certain racial or national groups. This view served as the basis of Nazi eugenic policies. The view was that defectives were reproducing more quickly than normal people, thus posing a risk to society.

It was in 1907 when Indiana became the first American State to pass a compulsory sterilisation statute, and Washington, Connecticut and Carolina were to follow this lead so that there were something like 28 American States which had passed involuntary sterilisation laws by the 1920s. This was, therefore, the political and social context in which the case of *Buck v Bell* was decided in 1927, where the Virginia sterilisation statute was held to be constitutional, the sterilisation defended by the court was done not as a punishment, but in order to release the girl concerned into the community, and Justice Holmes (otherwise generally known as a humane and great judge) uttered certain opinions which bear repeating if only to illustrate the attitude of the judiciary, at that time, to people like Carrie Bell, who was described in the law report an 'illegitimate feeble-minded child'(a view now discredited) in authorising her sterilisation:

> In order to prevent our being swamped with incompetents, it is better for all the world if instead of waiting to execute degenerate offspring for crime or to let them starve for their imbecility, society can prevent those who are manifestly unfit from continuing their kind. The principle that sustains compulsory vaccination is broad enough to cover cutting the fallopian tubes. Three generations of imbeciles are enough.

Attitudes towards people with mental handicaps have changed over the years, at least to the extent that it has become 'politically incorrect' to be seen to discriminate in any sphere of activity on the basis of a person's mental disability, and several significant cases have been heard since *Buck v Bell* (1927) 274 US 200. There have been several attempts to reverse the decision, since eugenics is considered 'politically incorrect'; since the Second World War, such persons have been increasingly treated primarily as human beings, with their disability being secondary, despite the high number of sterilisations that were carried out under the American schemes. Memorably, however, it is the Nazi sterilisation laws which were created in 1933 which carry the worst taint in history, because of the rationale of these sterilisations coupled with the sheer numbers affected within that infamous period of history. In England, there has been very little discussion of sterilisation, but the few cases that hit the headlines in the 1970s and 1980s aroused moral outrage from interest groups and the media and generally strong criticism from British academics. It is of some historical interest to note that, before 1960, advice given to doctors by the BMA was that sterilisation could only be done lawfully for therapeutic reasons (that is, to improve health): see Myers (1970), Chapter 1. But, by the mid 1960s, the National Health Service (Family Planning) Act 1967 permitted local health authorities to provide family planning services, and subsequent amendments to this Act in 1972, and re-organisation of the health service, eventually reached the current position which allows all main methods of contraception, including male and female sterilisation, to be available under the NHS. As we shall see, the English courts had occasion to discuss the viability of the therapeutic and non-therapeutic distinction in the mid-1970s and the late 1980s, when the House of Lords eventually rejected it as a viable test for authorisation of sterilisation for a mentally handicapped child and opted for the 'best interests' and 'welfare' test (discussed in the Introduction to this book, above). The one tangible outcome for legal practitioners in the 1980s was the issuing of several Practice Directions dealing with the procedure for authorisation of sterilisations, which are discussed in this chapter.

As far as statistics dealing with sterilisation are concerned, the media in the 1970s put forward various figures which do not tally with figures published in the Journal of Medical Ethics (JME) by Sir George Porter. According to the *Sun* newspaper in September 1975, the DHSS (as it then was) believed that, in 1973 and 1974, 11 girls and four boys under 16 had been sterilised, and 29 girls and 34 boys between the ages of 16 and 18. The JME figures were in the region of at least 14 cases on under 16 year olds and another 22 cases on those in the age range 16 to 18. A report in the *Birmingham Evening Mail* in January 1976 stated that a West Midlands leading child psychiatrist had himself recommended 12 adolescents under 16 for sterilisation. In the 1973 case of *Re D* (the *Sotos syndrome* case), there is reference to two sterilisations having been performed in Sheffield. However, in 1987, the Department of Health released figures which indicated that about 90 sterilisations per year are performed on females under 19 in England.

In 1987, an article was published by Dyer in the British Medical Journal in which it was claimed that 'dozens' of mentally disabled minors were being sterilised each year in England and Wales by way of parent/physician decision, in other words, at the request of the parents, who normally request these operations for their offspring and whose opinions are supported by doctors. Figures for adult incompetents are not available. So, the reality is that there is no hard data on the numbers of mentally disabled persons who undergo sterilisation.

CONSENSUAL AND NON-CONSENSUAL STERILISATION

Consensual or voluntary sterilisation has become more popular over the years, but controversy has grown over non-consensual sterilisation of persons who are intellectually disabled, in the wake of a few cases in the 1980s where the 'rights' of such patients appeared to be compromised or even ignored.

Key principles from case law

The key principle that emerges from the case law on non-consensual sterilisation, mainly from *Re D* (in 1976) to *Re B* in 1987 (see [1987] 2 All ER 206), is that the approval of a High Court judge is usually required for any such operation where it is proposed on a mentally disabled patient, and any operation that is performed can only be authorised if it is in the best interests of the patient. This 'best interests', or 'welfare' test, as it is also called, where the 'welfare of the patient is paramount', is the only criterion, and is also the yardstick used to validate *ex post facto* (that is, after the event) any medical procedures carried out by healthcare professionals on mentally disabled adults provided they were administered in those patients' best interests. Mentally handicapped adults, *strictu sensu*, are the only persons legally entitled to decide on their medical treatment, because of the gap in the law left by the legal reforms unwittingly effected by the Mental Health Act 1983. In practical terms, of course, any consent given to medical procedures would have to be proxy consent, given by parents, guardians or other carers.

Several Practice Directions (also called Practice Notes) have been issued by the Official Solicitor, but these have been amended in response to emerging case law, and the other point worth noting is that the latest Practice Direction retains the words 'virtually all cases' when talking about the necessity for court approval and, more ambiguously, 'straightforward cases', which several commentators have pointed out is vague and susceptible to an interpretation that might not always offer sufficient protection to the patient concerned.

It is even more crucial to note that, as things stand in current English law, there is no distinction to be drawn between therapeutic and non-therapeutic sterilisation. The best interests or welfare test is the only guiding principle.

Sterilisation of mentally handicapped minors

Therapeutic and non-therapeutic sterilisation: now a distinction without a difference?

In 1976, in *Re D* [1976] 1 All ER 326, an English High Court judge made a distinction between therapeutic and non-therapeutic sterilisation in the context of the proposed sterilisation of a girl of 11 with Sotos syndrome. In essence, the only sterilisation that the learned judge thought would be permissible would be therapeutic sterilisation where the operation would be required to cure or alleviate a particular medical condition. Just over 10 years later, in the controversial case of *Re B* (the *Jeanette* case), the House of Lords opined that it was 'not helpful' to make a distinction between therapeutic and non-therapeutic sterilisation because the only test that should apply in any case where court approval for sterilisation was whether it would be in the best interests of the patient concerned. The context was the proposed sterilisation of a 17 year old girl with the mental age of four or five who, it was alleged, could not understand the connection between sex and pregnancy and could not cope with pregnancy or looking after a child of her own, but who was in danger of becoming pregnant because, although intellectually disabled, was physically attractive and therefore at risk. In a sense, it no longer matters whether one classifies a proposed sterilisation as therapeutic or non-therapeutic. All that matters is whether, in the opinion of the court, the operation is in the best interests of the person on whom the procedure is proposed.

Non-consensual sterilisation

Mason and McCall Smith, even in the latest edition of their textbook, published in 1999, still call the area of non-consensual sterilisation 'a minefield of powerful objection' (Mason and McCall Smith (1999), p 96). The root problem of this area, as they call it, is the fact that it 'raises starkly the subject of what has been named the basic human right to reproduce' (Mason and McCall Smith (1999), p 97).

Key cases

***Re D* [1976] 1 All ER 326**

This case came before Heilbron J in the Family Division of the English High Court, as a wardship application to decide: (a) whether it was appropriate to continue the wardship proceedings which had been initiated earlier; and (b) whether a proposed application to sterilise the child, D, could be prevented.

Facts

D, a girl aged 11, suffered from a syndrome called Sotos syndrome, characterised by accelerated growth during infancy, epilepsy, general clumsiness, emotional instability, aggressive tendencies and an impairment of mental function. However, although D displayed these various symptoms, she was not as seriously retarded as some children similarly affected. It was not possible to predict her future role in society, but the likelihood was that she would have sufficient capacity to marry. She was sent to an appropriate school, but did not do well, partly because of behavioural problems. When she was 10, she was sent to a school specialising in children with learning difficulties and associated behavioural problems. She then showed marked improvement in her academic skills, social competence and behaviour. Her widowed mother, who was caring, loving and devoted, was worried lest D be seduced and give birth to a baby for whom she would be incapable of caring, and who might also be handicapped; she wanted D to be sterilised. The consultant paediatrician, Mr Gordon, who had been responsible for D's care for several years, and a consultant gynaecologist, recommended a sterilisation operation which was scheduled to be carried out when D was 11 years old. However, other persons concerned with D's welfare objected, particularly the educational psychologist, Mrs Hamidi, who challenged the decision to operate. When Mr Gordon refused to change his mind, she applied to make D a ward of court and the Official Solicitor was appointed as D's guardian *ad litem* at the plaintiff's request.

The key issue was whether it was appropriate to continue D's wardship and whether the operation to sterilise D should be prevented.

The judgment

When the case came before Heilbron J, she decided that, apart from being of great importance to the child, it also raised a matter of principle of considerable importance, and decided to give judgment in open court, which was in itself unusual. As is the practice, of course, reporting of the case could not extend to the identities of the parties being disclosed. Her Ladyship reviewed all the evidence carefully, noting that the assessment of D's condition by the educational psychologist and another consultant paediatrician differed from that of Mr Gordon, the paediatrician who had known D for many years. In the event, Heilbron J refused to sanction the operation. She declared:

> The operation was one which involved the deprivation of a basic human right, ie the right of a woman to reproduce, and therefore, if performed on a woman for therapeutic reasons and without her consent, would be a violation of that right. Since D could not give an informed consent, but there was a strong likelihood would understand the implications of the operation when she reached the age of 18, the case was one in which the courts [*sic*] should exercise its protective powers. Her wardship would accordingly be continued.

Accordingly, the court held that it would not risk the incurring of damage which it could not repair, but would rather prevent the damage being done (this was citing Lord Eldon in *Wellesley's* case) and that the operation could be delayed or prevented if D were to remain a ward of court; accordingly, the court should exercise its protective function in regard to D. It therefore continued her wardship (*Wellesley v Duke of Beaufort* (1827) 2 Russ 1 applied).

The learned judge was in agreement with the consulting doctors' opinion that sterilisation for therapeutic purposes was not entirely within a doctor's clinical judgment. In the words of Heilbron J:

> Their opinion was that a decision to sterilise a child was not entirely within a doctor's clinical judgment, save only when sterilisation was the treatment of choice for some disease, as, for instance, when in order to treat a child and to ensure her direct physical well being, it might be necessary to perform a hysterectomy to remove a malignant uterus. Whilst the side effect of such an

> operation would be to sterilise, the operation would be performed solely for therapeutic purposes. I entirely accept their opinions. I cannot believe, and the evidence does not warrant, the view that a decision to carry out an operation of this nature performed for non-therapeutic purposes on a minor, can be held to be within the doctor's sole clinical judgment.

The court further held that a decision to perform an operation such as that proposed for non-therapeutic purposes on a minor could not be within the doctor's sole clinical judgment; no important step in the life of a ward could be taken without the consent of the court, and a more important step than that proposed could not be imagined; on the evidence, the operation was neither medically indicated nor necessary and would not be in D's interest; accordingly, the operation would be prevented.

Comments on *Re D*

It is clear that Heilbron J was making several points here, but the three that merit particular attention are: (a) there is a basic right that a woman has to reproduce; (b) the decision to sterilise for non-therapeutic purposes did not lie within a doctor's sole clinical judgment; and (c) under the court's *parens patriae* jurisdiction, it had the power to throw a protective net over D in this case in the exercise of its wardship jurisdiction.

Impact of *Re D*

The aftermath of *Re D* was that there were strong reactions from various interest groups and parts of the media, who expressed 'moral outrage' about the decision, adding the cautionary query: how many had slipped through the net that had saved D? The DHSS even produced a discussion paper entitled 'Sterilisation of children under 16 years of age' which has never re-surfaced. However, no Code of Practice or guidance in any official form appeared until after the next decade, in the wake of the House of Lords' cases of *Re B* and *Re F*, when Practice Directions were issued. *Re D*, however, remained the leading English authority for more than 10 years and was even approved by the Canadian Supreme Court in *Re Eve*.

Since *Re D*, the English courts have given permission to perform medical operations under the *parens patriae* jurisdiction. For example, in *Re P (A Minor)* (1982) 82 LGR 301, local authorities invoked the court's wardship jurisdiction to permit an abortion on a 15 year old girl who had previously given birth and was already caring for the first child in facilities provided by the authority. The evidence indicated that the girl was taking good care of the first child, but could not cope with a second, and that the girl consented to the operation. It should be noted that the girl was not mentally retarded. Butler-Sloss J (as she then was) authorised the abortion, despite the girl's father's objection, on the ground that it was in the girl's best interest.

A Canadian parallel: *Re Eve* – the mentally disabled adult patient

In the 10 years before the next seminal English case on sterilisation had reached the English courts, the Supreme Court of Canada decided *Re Eve*, which did not involve a mentally handicapped child, but the court there had to consider the extent of the *parens patriae* jurisdiction over a mentally handicapped adult. The case involved an adult female, 'Eve', aged 24, who was 'mildly to moderately retarded' and suffered from expressive aphasia. While at a school for retarded adults, she met a male student who was also retarded, but not to the same degree as Eve. An application by her mother for the permission to consent to the sterilisation of Eve was eventually rejected by the Canadian Supreme Court, which held, *inter alia*, that the courts should never authorise a non-therapeutic sterilisation of a mentally retarded person under its *parens patriae* jurisdiction (this case is considered in greater detail in Chapter 15).

The Canadian court took several years to deliberate on this case, but they were able to do this because the patient in question was an adult, so there was no urgency in coming to a decision that had to be 'against the clock'. The patient in this case was 24, and not 17, as was first reported in pre-publicity about this case; this is, as we shall see, in stark contrast to the situation that transpired in the subsequent case of *Re B*, to which we now turn.

The leading English case – *Re B* (the *Jeanette* case) [1987] 2 All ER 206

After *Re Eve* had been reported with its categorical rejection of using the *parens patriae* jurisdiction to authorise non-therapeutic sterilisation, the case of *Re B* (the *Jeanette* case) came before the English courts, which went all the way to the House of Lords.

Facts

B, known as 'Jeanette', was a girl of 17, who suffered from a moderate degree of mental handicap, with very limited intellectual development, came before the English courts. She was the second of three children of her parents, and her early home life was very unhappy. She suffered from severe epilepsy, and had become increasingly disturbed as she grew older. Her father had been violent towards her until he finally left the home when she was two. Jeanette's mother looked after her until May 1973, when she was taken into care, at the age of four, by Sunderland Borough Council. She had been in their care ever since, but spent weekends and part of the school holidays with her mother at her mother's home. Her ability to understand speech was limited to that of a six year old and her ability to express herself was that of a two year old child. Her 'mental age' was said to be about five or six. However, she was capable of finding her way round a limited locality, of dressing and bathing herself and had been taught to cope with menstruation.

Physically, Jeanette was a mature young woman of 17 who, latterly, had been observed by the mother and staff of her residential institution as showing signs of sexual awareness, exemplified by provocative approaches to male members of staff and other residents. She had been given a variety of drugs to control her irregular periods, and to relieve the pre-menstrual tension which had caused her to be violent and aggressive, and to control her epileptic fits. However, almost all drugs appeared to have a bad effect upon her, and she also had an aversion to needles. In these circumstances, the mother and various doctors considered it vital that Jeanette should not become pregnant. The council therefore applied by originating summons for Jeanette to be made a ward of court and for leave to be given for her to undergo a sterilisation operation. The mother supported this operation. It was common ground that she did not need the protection of the Mental Health Act 1983. The case first came before Bush J.

The earlier judgments

At the first hearing, *viva voce* evidence was given by the resident social worker at Jeanette's local authority home, and by three medical witnesses, and the judge considered affidavits filed by both sides. Evidence was given that Jeanette could not be placed on any contraceptive regime and that she could never be capable of understanding the causal connection between intercourse and childbirth, the nature of pregnancy or what was involved in delivery of the child. It would also be difficult, in view of the irregularity of her periods, to detect her pregnancy in time to terminate it with the minimum difficulty. If she were to carry a child to full term, it was said that she would be likely to panic, and would probably have to be delivered by Caesarean section, but because of her high pain threshold, would probably pick at the operational wound and tear it open. She was also likely to be 'terrified, distressed and extremely violent' during normal labour. She was said to have no maternal instincts and was unlikely ever to desire or be able to care for a child. In the event, Bush J firmly concluded that the only possible decision for the future welfare of this minor was that the operation should be carried out, since Jeanette would never have the desire to reproduce and that there was therefore no question of depriving her of any basic human right, the nature of which she would never be capable of understanding. The Official Solicitor, as guardian *ad litem*, appealed to the Court of Appeal.

The Court of Appeal: sterilisation only a last resort

The main judgment was delivered by Dillon LJ (with whom Stephen Brown (as he then was) and Nicholls LJJ agreed). He declared that, in view of the handicapped girl's growing sexual awareness, the consequences of her becoming pregnant were 'frightening'. Thus, although he conceded that sterilisation was the deprivation of a basic human right, in Jeanette's case, the loss of that right would mean nothing to her. Stressing Jeanette's inability to link sexual intercourse with the birth of babies, and the fact that that she would be wholly unable to look after a baby, he opined that, if she did become pregnant, the pregnancy would have to be terminated. He went on to say that, in the past, the girl would probably have been strictly institutionalised all her life, but the modern policy of allowing mentally retarded people as much freedom as possible, brought with it a greater risk of intercourse and pregnancy. Her recently observed provocative behaviour was then referred to, as an indication of the potential danger of pregnancy. The issue of long term contraception was considered and, as a result of the various drugs that she was already taking necessitated by her condition, there were only two possible methods: the first was progesterone, which would have to be taken for the rest of her reproductive life, and the second was sterilisation by occlusion of the fallopian tubes, which would be an irreversible procedure.

He then paused to consider *Re D* (above), and the principle it elucidated on the basic human right of a woman to reproduce, which would be violated if sterilisation were performed on her for non-therapeutic reasons, and without her consent. In Dillon LJ's opinion, the element of consent was crucial to this case. Jeanette would never be able to consent to sterilisation, abortion or marriage. Thus, in the present situation, the wardship court had jurisdiction to authorise a sterilisation operation on a ward in the present circumstances, but it was a jurisdiction which should be exercised 'only in the last resort'.

He further observed that there was no question of a natural parent or local authority having the right to seek sterilisation of a minor without first obtaining prior leave of court in wardship proceedings. But, as far as the instant case was concerned, having regard to all the evidence and taking account of the unsuitability of other forms of contraception, despite the irreversible nature of the operation, this was a situation where sterilisation would be permitted, but only because, on its facts, it was a last resort. The appeal was unanimously dismissed.

Impact and criticism of the Court of Appeal decision

The public reaction to this judgment was generally unfavourable, particularly from those responsible for the care and welfare of the mentally handicapped. Among the criticisms expressed were the views that the decision was a rather extreme step to take; that it could make Jeanette even more vulnerable to those who would exercise sexual power without responsibility; that it did not take into account the different rates of development which certain mentally retarded people experienced, to the extent that she may, as she grew older, acquire a better understanding of the link between sex, pregnancy and babies. In any event, the Official Solicitor decided to appeal to the House of Lords, so as to pursue every possible step to safeguard Jeanette's interests. Before the House of Lords hearing took place, the report of the Canadian Supreme Court case of *Re Eve* (above) became available in this country and, although

Canadian cases are not binding on English courts, *Re Eve*'s categorical rejection of the proposed sterilisation of another mentally retarded female for non-therapeutic purposes warranted its inclusion in the Official Solicitor's submissions to the House of Lords.

House of Lords: welfare principle the only criterion

Five Law Lords led by Lord Hailsham, the Lord Chancellor of the time, unanimously rejected the test case appeal by the Official Solicitor acting on behalf of Jeanette, and every one of them stressed that the only issue to be decided in this case was whether sterilisation of this young woman in her particular circumstances would promote her welfare and be in her best interests. In other words, the only permissible approach in the present wardship proceedings was to apply the welfare principle, which was to regard the welfare of the minor as the 'first and paramount consideration' as laid down at the time in s 1 of the Guardianship of Minors Act 1971 (now repealed and replaced by the Children Act). Apart from Lord Brandon, who simply concurred with his legal brethren, all the Law Lords delivered considered judgments which were remarkably similar in their approach to *Jeanette's* case.

In order to resolve the issue, the House had to carry out two main tasks, namely, to carefully review the medical and factual evidence, and to consider what weight should be given to the two cases dealing with two similar situations. Neither *Re D* nor *Re Eve* were binding on the court, of course, the former being only a first instance decision, the latter merely 'persuasive' in English courts. Nevertheless, since these were the only relevant authorities before the court, it was imperative that they were given due consideration. A third, contingency question was whether the wardship court retained jurisdiction once the minor attained majority. If it did, the need to decide the minor's appeal before attainment of majority would not exist.

Legal issues apart, the Law Lords appeared acutely aware that their judgment could be interpreted as an exercise in eugenic sterilisation, to prevent the possible birth of abnormal children. If this was the opinion of the public at large, then it could not be argued that the health of the patient was involved, but that what was really at stake was the alleged health of the unborn generation and the interest of society in its fitness. The Law Lords were at great pains to stress that this case had nothing to do with eugenics and involved no general principle of public policy.

The medical question

The medical evidence was analysed by the four Law Lords who delivered full judgments, but this discussion focuses on Lord Oliver of Aylmerton, who delivered the principal judgment after the most thorough analysis of the medical evidence. Lord Oliver traced the medical, social and institutional history of the girl, pointing out that, when she was received into care at the age of four, she was described as being like a wild animal, and was subsequently moved to a residential institution managed by the council for minor and adult persons suffering from mental handicap. The consultant psychiatrist's report confirmed that she suffered from an abnormality of the brain and that it was not envisaged that she would ever be capable of caring for herself in the community or reach a stage where she could return permanently to her mother's care. The psychiatrist referred to Jeanette's 'provocative approaches' which brought to the attention of male members of staff and other residents of Jeanette's residential home the 'obvious risk of pregnancy and the desirability of taking urgent and effective contraceptive measures'. However, her mental condition did not make it feasible for anyone to discuss contraception with her, and even if she ever understood its need, she could never weigh the merits of different types of contraception or make an informed choice on the matter. He also emphasised that it was common ground that the only alternative to sterilisation was the daily administration of a contraceptive pill supplemented by the drugs she was already being given to control her other conditions. In his view, this measure would encounter the following problems:

(a) it would have to be pursued regularly over the whole of the minor's reproductive life of some 30 years or so;

(b) it involved administering a daily dosage which, on occasion, could be well nigh impossible if Jeanette was in one of her violent moods, as indicated by the social worker most closely connected with her;

(c) the side effects of the drug over the long term were not yet known. The consultant obstetrician and gynaecologist had testified that there was only a 30% to 40% chance of achieving a successful regime, taking into account her other medication. He surmised that an experimental period of 12–18 months might be required.

Lord Oliver therefore postulated the dilemma in this case as deciding between two procedures, one safe, certain but irreversible (as it was in 1987), the other speculative, possibly damaging and requiring discipline over many years from someone of the most limited intellectual capacity. Three factors were crucial in his assessment of the situation: the degree of Jeanette's vulnerability, the urgency of her need for protection, and the impossibility of her ever attaining the capacity to form an informed consent to treatment. He therefore had no doubt that the lower court and the Court of Appeal were correct in their decision, and that sterilisation was the only practicable alternative.

By and large, the other Law Lords endorsed this assessment of Jeanette's particular situation, Lord Hailsham adding that the ward had been found in a comprising position in a bathroom, accentuating what he thought to be the 'significant danger of pregnancy'. Lord Bridge stated that it was clear beyond argument that pregnancy for Jeanette in her mental condition would be an 'unmitigated disaster', so that the only question was how she could best be protected against it.

Lord Templeman set out a list of factors which he thought a court should consider in these sorts of cases. These were similar to those mentioned above, and he broadly stated that a 'risks and consequences' approach should be followed. Thus, the risks and consequences of pregnancy, sterilisation, and alternative precautions against pregnancy should be weighed against each other, as well as examining expert evidence on the history, conditions, circumstances and foreseeable future of Jeanette. Additional evidence should also be obtained by the court in an appropriate case.

The case law question

The House of Lords decided not to follow or be guided by either *Re D* or *Re Eve*, and seemed to be positing two main guiding principles. The first guideline is that there is no 'basic human right', as such, of a woman to reproduce, unless that woman is capable of appreciating its significance. Hence, for example, Lord Hailsham speaks of Jeanette's inability to make the choice whether to have a child or not, as determining whether the right to reproduce would be of any value. This confirmed the approach taken in all the earlier judgments in the case. Hence, although correctly decided on its facts, *Re D* was distinguished on the facts in *Jeanette's* case and on its human rights principle. The second guideline is that English law will not now accept that the decision whether or not to sterilise a mentally incompetent minor should be governed by whether the treatment is 'therapeutic' or 'non-therapeutic'. Thus, as the Lords perceive it, the welfare principle should be the only criterion (the 'primary and paramount consideration') utilised by a wardship court, after considering all the medical evidence and particular facts of the case, in deciding whether sterilisation of a minor should be authorised. The crucial distinction drawn between these two types of treatment in both the English and Canadian precedents is therefore inapplicable, at any rate, in the context of wardship cases on sterilisation of minors, since the House found it to be unhelpful, serving merely to divert attention from the real issue of what was in the ward's best interests.

The jurisdictional question

A related question that arose in the case was whether a residual jurisdiction remained in the High Court after a minor attained majority. This raised the issue of the scope of the *parens patriae* jurisdiction of the High Court. The matter was left unresolved in the case itself, since only Lord Oliver was prepared to say that the *parens patriae* jurisdiction continues into majority, but the implication of the subsequent House of Lords' case of *Re F (F v West Berkshire HA* [1989] 2 All ER 545) is that nobody can decide on behalf of mentally handicapped adults (for reasons discussed in *Re F*, below, p 217), but a doctor can lawfully operate on, or give other treatment to, a mentally incapable adult patient, provided the operation or medical procedure is in that patient's best interests.

Comment on *Re B*

In the aftermath of the *Jeanette* case, and over the years, a fairly large amount of academic literature commenting on its merits and demerits has appeared, some of which are summarised and synthesised in this section. To begin with, an article I published in *Family Law* in 1988 (see de Cruz (1988)) made several points:

(a) On the positive side, it is certainly true that, for the carers of Jeanette, the operation would relieve them of a great deal of their difficult and perhaps often impossibly demanding responsibilities. However, since Jeanette could not even be allowed on the streets unsupervised, because she could not understand traffic, she would certainly need close and constant attention for a great deal of the time. Provided she was indoors, the supervision need not be so intensive or intrusive, once this alarming prospect of pregnancy no longer existed. Yet, given the prospect of sexual exploitation, sterilisation would give no protection against rape or sexual abuse.

(b) Further, the operation would not free her, as Lord Hailsham seemed to imply, from incarceration or give her the liberty to satisfy the sexual desires she was experiencing, when she would certainly experience difficulties in relationships with the opposite sex.

(c) The ruling accentuates Jeanette's vulnerability and, tragically, results in her being treated very differently from 'normal' people, which would undermine all the advances made in the achievements of mental health groups and their efforts to integrate people with mental disabilities into the community at large.

(d) In the light of the medical evidence, it seemed very clear that Jeanette would experience great difficulties in understanding the causal connection between intercourse, pregnancy, and the birth of children. She might also have had additional problems in labour since, from past behaviour, she was likely to rip open any stitches she might have, which might prevent any post-operative scars from healing. Suppose, however, she had appendicitis? Surely, the need to relieve her condition and to preserve her life would involve a great deal of physical pain for which, the reports revealed, she apparently had a high threshold. Nevertheless, this sort of operation would have to be performed with all its attendant risks and trepidations.

(e) With regard to her particular mental condition, the consultant obstetrician did, in fact, suggest a trial period within which to devise an acceptable contraceptive formulation. The chances of success were not very good, but because the Law Lords assumed Jeanette would never improve mentally, an assumption which was arguably premature, no attempt was made to contemplate experimenting with alternative contraceptive regimes. The other highly suspect assumption that runs through the judgments is that she would be having sex at the earliest opportunity in her mixed hostel where she lived. Even with mentally competent girls, mere provocative gestures are not necessarily to be equated with an invitation to have sex. Thus, if one viewed her actions as those of a playful child, it is surely still incumbent on her caretakers to educate her, warn her and protect her as they would any vulnerable child.

(f) On the question of her inability to appreciate the significance of the right to reproduce as somehow justifying the deprivation of this right, it is submitted that, with the greatest respect to the Law Lords, that line of argument is neither logically sound nor morally tenable. The mere fact that a person is unable to appreciate the significance of a particular right does not entitle anyone to deprive him of that right. Indeed, a child's right to be maintained, educated and protected by persons in *loco parentis* does not derive from that child's appreciation of that right, but from the existence of parental duty (and, it might be added, parental responsibility under the UK Children Act 1989, which was not in force at the time this article was published). Equally, Jeanette's basic human rights should exist regardless of her capacity to appreciate them.

Apart from these observations, it was also pointed out that Canadian courts had the opportunity to consider the case of *Re Eve* for nearly seven years, which meant that they had the opportunity to study a very wide range of expert opinions and the exhaustive research of the Canadian Law Commission. In their desire not to be faced with a jurisdictional problem once Jeanette reached 18, the English Law Lords only took 28 days to decide the case, but their assumptions about her future conduct may well have led them to discount other possibilities too readily.

In a chapter published in *Birthrights* (1989), Lee and Morgan make several noteworthy points, some of which are:

(a) They cite the Law Lords' comment that Jeanette would be deprived of no basic rights which she was capable of valuing since, lacking maternal instinct, pregnancy would mean little to her. Lord Hailsham argued that contrary views would be 'wholly to part company with reality'. Yet, they respond that 'to confer rights only on those to be able to enjoy them opens the way for rights to become the exclusive property of the rich and powerful'. They then cite Sheila McLean, who declared that 'by dismissing the impact of the removal of capacities from certain people on the grounds that they may not in any event recognise their worth [is to minimise] the status of reproduction as a human right' (McLean (1986), p 108). As they go on to say: 'It is a small step from here to a more dangerous argument in relation to the mentally handicapped – their liberties generally are dependent upon usages that others consider reasonable or valuable. This is a familiar complaint against any mediation in contemporary reproductive ethics; it characterises the slippery slope or thin end of the wedge argument.'

(b) They stress that the slippery slope argument is always a difficult and contested one to run. Once on the slope, any subsequent distinction between one case and another will disclose unsupportable discrimination; the slipperiness of the slope is disclosed by the fact that once on the slope, any exit point is arbitrary, and this argument is applicable to *Re B*.

(c) They refute Margaret Shone's views, when she suggests that to refuse the non-therapeutic sterilisation of a mentally handicapped woman is to fragment the person. On the contrary, Lee and Morgan say that 'to view the person as a whole, rather than as atomised bits, mandates a wider view of what is at issue than simply reproductive organs'. They argue further that the rejection of the therapeutic and non-therapeutic distinction by Lord Hailsham and the invoking of the welfare principle is a vague predicate and does not meet the arbitrary result objection. It is also possible to challenge the nature of the 'facts' that Lord Bridge refers to. The so called facts are actually 'a series of assessments as to Jeanette's future capacity, and judgments as to the desirability and nature of her environment, the sexual attractions she might form and the consequences flowing from them'.

(d) There is a curious pattern of Jeanette's capabilities, capable in some tasks, but not in others, and nothing explains why her carers are able successfully to manage the regime of medication necessary to control her epilepsy, but would be unable to supervise the use of an oral contraceptive because 'it would not be possible in the light of her swings of mood and considerable physical strength to ensure the administration of the daily dose'.

(e) The Law Lords were also less than convincing in showing an understanding of the capacities of mentally handicapped women, but using the concept of the 'mental age' was arguably dubious as well. The concept is not a static one, and they cite the opinion of Woolrych, who has observed that the use of the 'discredited concept of "mental age" is disturbing, since current experiences indicate learning potential is dependent on the quality and variety of services available in developing an understanding of issues such as the connection between sex and having babies' (Woolrych, quoted in (1987) *Social Work Today*, 11 May, p 3).

> Moreover, the concept of mental age did not shed much light on Jeanette's biological and emotional state as a 17 year old woman.

Professor Michael Freeman has made several criticisms of these cases and, in particular, has expressed the view that these decisions may start us down a slippery slope. In the context of human rights and the right to reproduce he says: 'Once these rights are trumped on the ground that it is for the right-holder's own good, it is but a simple step to argue that a right should also be undermined where to do so is for the good of others or the general good' (Freeman (1987), p 949). In the context of these cases, in another piece, he notes how 'The shift from *Re D* to *Re B* shows how easily "best medical interests" can become "best interests" with the obliteration of the therapeutic/non-therapeutic distinction'. On the question of the slippery slope in these cases, he says, 'The case for an empirical slippery slope is unproven and unprovable but I would not rule it out' (Freeman (1988), p 78).

Cases in the aftermath of *Re B*

In the wake of *Re B*, two further cases of wardship were reported: *Re M (A Minor) (Wardship: Sterilisation)* [1988] 2 FLR 497 and *Re P (A Minor) (Wardship: Sterilisation)* [1989] 1 FLR 182. Sterilisation was approved in both, without any appeals. The crucial point in these two cases is the introduction of the notion of reversibility; medical evidence was given at both hearings to the effect that the proposed operation was reversible in 50–75% of the cases, which was the opinion of the gynaecologist in *Re M*, who said that he regards the operation of sterilisation by occlusion of the Fallopian tubes as more one of contraception than of sterilisation, especially bearing in mind all the emotive feelings that the use of the word 'sterilisation' arouses. This element of reversibility appeared to persuade the judges to authorise the sterilisations because there was no earlier consensus on the weight to be given to the evidence to support the sterilisation.

In *Re P*, the 17 year old woman was said to have the intellectual development of a six year old, and although her intellectual development would never improve, she would, in time, with care and counselling, acquire some 'social skills'; indeed, her communication skills were said to be good and improving. It was accepted that she had some maternal feelings but her 'attractive demeanour and limited intellect' would make her particularly vulnerable to seduction and the risk of pregnancy. Medical opinion differed on whether she would give a fully informed consent to abortion and her mother was afraid she would not agree to one. At the time of the hearing, the girl was not yet at risk of pregnancy because she regarded intercourse as painful, and she might well value the 'right' to reproduce. Nevertheless, Eastham J was prepared to authorise the sterilisation despite the fact that the girl appeared to have some of the characteristics usually said to be absent in mentally handicapped persons. The testimony of an eminent specialist, that there was a 'very high percentage chance of success' of reversing the operation, appears to have swayed the court.

The oddly named 'ethical' practice which Eastham J referred to, in *Re P* [1989] 1 FLR 189, is worth noting. He said:

> The situation today is that the [sterilisation] operation is not irreversible, although it is still the current ethical practice to tell the patient that it is an irreversible operation as part of the information to be given to them when they are giving consent for the operation to be carried out, although if such a patient changes her mind, no doubt it would be explained to her that the more serious reversal operation could be contemplated.

Then there was *Re E (A Minor) (Medical Treatment)* [1991] 2 FLR 585, which was seen as a case of therapeutic sterilisation (discussed above), since the 17 year old woman here suffered from a menstrual condition which could only be cured by a hysterectomy. The court held that as it was an operation required for therapeutic reasons, the parents of a minor were in a position to give valid consent and the consent of the court was not necessary.

In the case of *Re HG (Specific Issue Order: Sterilisation)* [1993] 1 FLR 587, the girl was nearly 18, severely epileptic and had a chromosomal deficiency which meant that she was an infant in terms of abilities. She lived in a school in circumstances where she was likely to be at risk from sexual relationships leading to pregnancy. There was no dispute that pregnancy, which she would not be capable of understanding, would be disastrous for her, and that the contraceptive pill was not suitable because of her epilepsy. The deputy judge (Peter Singer QC) came to the conclusion (p 592) that 'a sufficiently overwhelming case has been established to justify interference with the fundamental right of a woman to bear a child. I am certainly satisfied that it would be cruel to expose T to an unacceptable risk of pregnancy and that that should be obviated by sterilisation in her interests'.

Sterilisation of the mentally handicapped adult

English courts have had some difficulty in coping with applications for sterilisation of mentally handicapped adults, if only because the rather bizarre effect of the replacement of the original *parens patriae* jurisdiction by the Mental Health Act 1959 (now the Mental Health Act 1983), which does not contain any provision under which consent may be given on behalf of the patient to treatment other than that for their mental disorder. The only situation in which it is lawful to give mental treatment without consent *per se*, is usually only in cases of urgency or necessity, where there is, for example, an unconscious patient and there is an *immediate* need for treatment. Of course, 'immediate' does not have to mean that death is necessarily imminent. In *R v*

Bourne, Macnaghten J said that 'the law does not require the doctor to wait until the unfortunate woman is in peril of immediate death' (*R v Bourne* [1939] 1 KB 687, p 693), referring to the fact that if a woman was in need of an abortion to save her life, the sooner the operation was performed, the better. We now consider the main cases in this area.

T v T *[1988] 2 WLR 189*

In *T v T*, in the Family Division of the High Court, Wood J was faced with the problem of dealing with an application to sterilise a mentally handicapped adult woman and to perform an abortion on her, and the question was: on what legal basis could a consent be granted for medical treatment on such an adult where the wardship jurisdiction was not available?

The facts

T was a 19 year old female who was severely mentally handicapped, and an epileptic, with no hope of improvement. Her mother, friends and social workers from the local authority looked after her, but despite this care, T was found to be pregnant and her medical advisers recommended the termination of the pregnancy. The grounds for the termination were that T could not understand the concept of pregnancy or cope with the problems that would be associated with that condition and that she would be incapable of bringing up and caring for the child. Looking to the future, the medical advisers recommended that she be sterilised, as she needed protection from future pregnancy and that, in all the circumstances, that was the only method. Since T could not give consent, the medical advisers were unwilling to perform the operation without the protection of the court. The mother of the girl applied for a declaration that the termination of the pregnancy and the sterilisation of T would not amount to an unlawful act by reason only of the absence of her consent.

The ruling

Wood J held that, in law, there was no one able to consent to these operations, not even the court; and he felt obliged to rely on the doctrine of necessity to declare the proposed operations legal. He also made a plea for a restoration of the court's jurisdiction to grant consent in these sorts of cases.

However, about 19 months later, the Law Lords had the opportunity to consider this matter.

Re F *(1986)*

The facts

In *F v West Berkshire HA* [1989] 2 All ER 545, the woman was aged 36 and severely mentally impaired. She had the verbal capacity of a child aged two and the general mental capacity was of a child aged four or five. Since the age of 14, she had been a voluntary in-patient at a mental hospital controlled by the defendant health authority. She had formed a sexual relationship with a male patient, P. There was medical evidence that, from a psychiatric point of view, it would be disastrous for her to become pregnant and since there were serious objections to all ordinary methods of contraception, either because she would be unable to use them effectively or because of a risk to her physical health, the medical staff in charge of F decided that the best course of action would be for her to be sterilised. Her mother had to act as her next friend because F's disability meant she was incapable of giving a legally valid consent to the operation. F's mother sought a declaration from the court under the Rules of the Court that the absence of F's consent would not make sterilisation of F an unlawful act.

The High Court (Scott Baker J) held that the court had no power to give consent on behalf of F or to dispense with the need for such consent because the *parens patriae* jurisdiction of the court in respect of persons suffering from mental incapacity no longer existed. However, he granted a declaration that the sterilisation of F would not amount to an unlawful act by reason only of the absence of F's consent. The Official Solicitor's appeal to the Court of Appeal was dismissed and he then appealed to the House of Lords, contending that, in the absence of a *parens patriae* jurisdiction, sterilisation of an adult mental patient who was unable to give her consent could never be lawful.

The House of Lords judgment

The House of Lords dismissed the appeal and held that:

(a) the court had no jurisdiction, either by statute or under the *parens patriae* jurisdiction, to give or withhold consent to a sterilisation operation on an adult woman disabled by mental capacity;

(b) the court did have jurisdiction, however, to make a declaration that the proposed operation was lawful on the ground that, in the circumstances, it was in the best interests of the patient;

(c) in determining whether the proposed operation was in the best interests of the patient, the court should apply the established test of what would be accepted as appropriate treatment at the time by a reasonable body of medical opinion skilled in that particular form of treatment (*Bolam* [1957] 2 All ER 118 applied).

The House of Lords also stated, *inter alia*, that at common law, a doctor can lawfully operate on or give treatment to adult patients who are incapable of consenting to his doing so, provided that the operation or treatment is in the best interests of such patients. The operation will be in their best interests only if it is carried out in order either to save their lives or to ensure improvement or prevent deterioration in their physical or mental health.

Their *dicta* also ranged over a large number of topics. Let us look at some of the comments of the Law Lords on the doctrine of necessity and best interests.

Necessity

The notion of the common law powers of a doctor acting out of necessity in an emergency was commented upon by various Law Lords. For instance, Lord Bridge observed that it was 'axiomatic' that:

> ... treatment which is necessary to preserve the life, health or well-being of the patient may lawfully be given without consent. But, if a rigid criterion of necessity were to be applied to determine what is and is not lawful in the treatment of the unconscious and the incompetent, many of those unfortunate enough to be deprived of the capacity to make or communicate rational decisions by accident, illness or unsoundness of mind, might be deprived of treatment which it would be entirely beneficial for them to receive.

Best interests

All the judges in *Re F* agreed that the test for determining whether the decision to operate was taken in the best interests of the patient should be in accordance with the well known *Bolam* test (*Bolam v Friern Hospital Management Committee* [1957] 1 WLR 582), namely, that the doctor must act in accordance with a responsible and competent body of opinion, in relation to that particular area of medical practice and procedure.

Court will decide whether sterilisation is in the best interests of a mentally handicapped male patient

In a recent case, *Re A (Mental Patient: Sterilisation)* (2000) *The Times*, 15 March; [2000] 1 FLR 549, the Court of Appeal had to consider an application to grant a declaration under the court's inherent jurisdiction that it would be lawful to perform a sterilisation operation by way of vasectomy on him despite his inability to consent to the operation. This case is especially noteworthy because it is the first case where the court has been approached to grant sterilisation of a *male* intellectually disabled patient.

Re A *(2000) (the male sterilisation patient)*

In this case, A was a 28 year old male with significant impairment because of Down's syndrome, and had been cared for from birth by his mother who was now in her early sixties. She had provided him with a high degree of care and supervision, but now felt that her age and health highlighted the need to make sensible plans for the future. Her major concern was that if A moved into local authority care, in the absence of an operation to sterilise, he might have a sexual relationship resulting in his fathering a child for whom he was unable to take responsibility. In the lower court, Sumner J refused to grant the declaration authorising sterilisation. The plaintiff, through his mother and litigation friend, appealed.

In the Court of Appeal (Dame Butler-Sloss P, Schiemann and Thorpe LJJ), Dame Butler-Sloss P stressed that in *Re F (Mental Patient: Sterilisation)* [1990] 2 AC 1, the House of Lords had made it quite clear that an operation to sterilise had to be demonstrated to be in the patient's best interests. An application on behalf of a man for sterilisation was not the equivalent of an application in respect of a woman; this was not a matter of equality of the sexes but a balancing exercise on a case by case basis. The court's task was to balance all the relevant factors and to decide what would be in the best interests of the person unable to make his own decision. There was no evidence that having the operation would have any effect on the care that A received, nor would it allow him any greater measure of freedom. If in the future his quality of life were to be demonstrably diminished because he was not sterilised, that would be the time to seek a declaration that sterilisation would be in his best interests.

Thorpe LJ concurred, and said that the evaluation of best interests was akin to a welfare appraisal in that it was necessary to draw up a balance sheet. On one side, it would be the factors of actual benefit, such as the acquisition of foolproof contraception; on the other side, the counter-balancing disbenefits, such as apprehension, risk and discomfort inherent in the operation. At the end of the exercise, it should be possible to strike a balance between the sum of the certain and possible gains against the sum of the certain and possible losses; only if the account were significantly in credit would the conclusion be that the application was in the best interests of the claimant.

Accordingly, the Court of Appeal held that it was for the court to decide whether an operation to sterilise a person unable to give consent was in his best interests and the considerations, which were not all the same in the case of men and women, encompassed medical, emotional and all welfare issues. The court therefore decided that, in the circumstances, sterilisation would *not* be authorised.

Liability for a failed sterilisation

Although a separate chapter examines the question of medical malpractice or medical negligence, and the duty of care, it is pertinent to consider briefly the circumstances under which liability for a failed sterilisation will ever be imposed on a doctor or health authority. The basic principle that exists in English common law is that, provided a *duty of care* has been shown to exist, liability for a failed sterilisation will not be imposed unless it can be established that the failure to achieve contraception was due to medical negligence or to breach of contract rather than to the possibility that conception might still occur after the operation as a result of the vagaries of nature (see Mason and McCall Smith (1999), p 91, and authorities discussed therein).

Court must decide whether treatment is in the patient's best interests: the hysterectomy case – Re S (Sterilisation: Patient's Best Interests) *(2000)* The Times, *26 May*

S, a woman aged 28, had a severe learning disability and was incapable of giving her consent to any medical treatment. She also suffered from a strong fear of hospitals. Her mother wished her to have a hysterectomy, both to end her heavy periods and to eliminate any risk of pregnancy. There was evidence that the periods caused S distress. S was currently cared for by her mother, aged 54, and was kept under close supervision, so there was little risk of pregnancy at present. However, her mother was finding it increasingly difficult to look after S and there was a plan for her to go into sheltered accommodation, where the risk of pregnancy might increase. S's mother sought a declaration that a hysterectomy was in her daughter's best interests and could lawfully be performed. The Official Solicitor opposed the application, arguing that as an alternative, an intra-uterine device called Mirena would significantly reduce S's periods, and provide adequate contraceptive protection. The insertion of the device would be less intrusive than the proposed hysterectomy, but the device would have to be replaced every five to seven years. The mother's objection to the Mirena coil was that it was unlikely to end S's periods and that, because it was not a single procedure, would involve S in regular visits to the hospital throughout her life, causing her repeated distress.

At first instance, Wall J granted the application, making a declaration that a laparoscopic hysterectomy could be lawfully be performed on S; it was in S's best interests that her heavy periods should come to an end, and therefore the subtotal hysterectomy which could have the incidental effect of sterilising S was in her best interests.

On appeal, however, the Court of Appeal held (*per* Butler-Sloss LJ):

(a) The two issues before the judge were whether it was in S's best interests to be sterilised in order to avoid the risk of pregnancy or to undergo therapeutic treatment to eliminate her menstrual periods.

(b) Accepting the submission that the decision of the judge was contrary to the expert evidence, her Ladyship said that the weight of medical evidence supported the less invasive method as the preferred option, at least in the first instance, and that the understandable concerns of a caring mother did not, on the facts, tilt the balance towards major irreversible surgery for therapeutic purposes.

(c) It was a question of proportionality and the remedy proposed was out of proportion, at that stage, to the problem to be solved. Furthermore, a disabled patient has the right not to have drastic surgery imposed upon her unless or until it had been demonstrated to be in her best interests. As the first ground of appeal had been made out, the decision could not be allowed to stand.

(d) The second ground of appeal raised the question as to the correct approach of the court to the best interests of a patient without mental capacity to consent to an operation and of the relevance of the *Bolam* test to that judicial inquiry. The need for the best interests test in such cases had been first recognised in *Re F*, a case which reflected the concern of the House of Lords that declarations should not be made as to the lawfulness of invasive treatment of incapacitated patients unless the treatment proposed passed the test of being demonstrably in the best interests of the patient.

(e) However, it was for the judge, *not* the doctor, to decide whether a treatment was in the best interests of a patient, a decision which would incorporate broader ethical, social and moral considerations than those set out in *Bolam*, with the patient's welfare as the paramount consideration. Once the judge was satisfied that the options were within the range of acceptable opinion among competent and responsible practitioners, the *Bolam* test was irrelevant as to whether the proposed treatment was in S's best interests. The judge was therefore in error in his application of the *Bolam* test to his decision making process and also in offering the mother the alternatives of the hysterectomy or the insertion of the Mirena coil; logically, the best interests test ought to have provided the best answer, not a range of alternative answers.

(f) It would have been within the best interests test to indicate that the less invasive procedure should have been adopted first and that, if it failed, it would have been appropriate to seek a declaration in respect of the proposed surgery.

The main ruling, therefore, was that where a declaration is sought as to the lawfulness of proposed medical treatment for a patient unable to consent for herself, it was for the court to decide whether such treatment was in the patient's best interests.

Thorpe LJ gave a concurring judgment and Mance LJ agreed with both judgments.

The Practice Directions on sterilisation of mentally handicapped persons in England

During the period 1989 to 1996, no less than four sets of Practice Directions were issued by the Official Solicitor in England.

Practice Note *[1989] 2 FLR 47*

Two years after the controversial decision of *Re B*, the Official Solicitor issued a Practice Direction (or Practice Note, as it is sometimes called) [1989] 2 FLR 47 which detailed the Official Solicitor's involvement in sterilisation applications and gave guidance to medical practitioners and parents or guardians on when the Official Solicitor will support an application to sterilise a mentally incompetent person. Of course, a Practice Note or Practice Direction does *not* bind the judges of the Family Division of the High Court. As we have just seen, it is not binding on a Scottish court, either. It is merely a guide as to best practice on a particular area of law. However, the courts did not regard it mandatory to follow the 1989 Practice Direction, and this attitude was revealed in *Re C* (1990) 5 BMLR 100; [1990] 3 All ER 735. The 1989 Note envisaged a two-stage hearing, but in *Re C*, Thorpe J held that not all of the Note should be followed and that, in straightforward or emergency cases, this could be conflated into a one-stage process. Hence, the Official Solicitor had to issue another Practice Direction in 1990.

However, three years later, this had to be amended again. The 1993 Note ([1993] 2 FLR 222) was issued after the coming into force of the Children Act 1989 and thus referred to procedures to be followed if the parties wished to seek a 'specific issue order' under s 8(1) of the Children Act 1989, but the Official Solicitor stated that the procedural and administrative difficulties attendant on s 8 orders were such that the preferred course would be to apply for an order invoking the court's inherent jurisdiction.

In that year, the report of *Re W (Mental Patient: Sterilisation)* [1993] 1 FLR 381 was published and this made the 1993 Note an inaccurate statement of judicial practice. Although Hollis J found that there was little chance that an incompetent woman would become pregnant at the present time or even in the near future, as she was under the constant supervision of her mother, medical experts agreed that her interests would be best served by having the operation done sooner, rather than later. In view of the *Bolam* rule, Hollis J felt he had little option but to grant the declaration.

Yet, the 1993 Practice Note had stated, for example, para 8(2)(b), that there should be evidence that 'the patient is likely to engage in sexual activity, at the present or near future, under circumstances where there is a real danger as opposed to mere chance that pregnancy is likely to result'. The idea behind this appears to be that there had to proof that the risk of pregnancy was probable and not merely possible, before the Official Solicitor would support an application.

However, nothing was done to correct these discrepancies until 1996, when the Practice Note was amended yet again. The new version deleted all references to the s 8 procedure and, in relation to the risk of pregnancy, now states that: '... the court will ... require evidence clearly establishing ... [t]hat there is a need for contraception because the patient is fertile and is sexually active or is likely to engage in sexual activity in the foreseeable future.' Thus, there is simply a need to show some degree of risk because of fertility and sexual activity or simply because of the possibility of future sexual activity. The premise here seems to be that the risk of pregnancy will be presumed if there is risk of sexual activity, but the risk need not be immediate. Hence, even when the mentally incapable person is under the watchful control of her mother, the court might still hold that a sterilisation is in her best interests, as occurred in *Re P (A Minor) (Wardship: Sterilisation)* [1989] 1 FLR 182.

The 1996 Practice Direction

The latest 1996 Practice Direction [1996] 2 FLR 111 replicates several of the previous guidelines. The key clauses are reproduced here.

Practice Note

Official Solicitor: sterilisation

The need for prior sanction of a High Court judge

1 The sterilisation of a minor or a mentally incompetent adult ('the patient') will in virtually all cases require the prior sanction of a High Court judge: *Re B (A Minor) (Wardship: Sterilisation)* [1988] AC 199; [1987] 2 FLR 314; *Re F (Sterilisation: Mental Patient)* [1990] 2 AC 1; [1989] 2 FLR 376.

Applications to court

2 Applications in respect of a minor should be made in the Family Division of the High Court, within proceedings either under the inherent jurisdiction or s 8(1) ('a specific issue order') of the Children Act 1989. In the Official Solicitor's view, the procedural and administrative difficulties attaching to applications under s 8 of the

Children Act 1989 are such that the preferred course is to apply within the inherent jurisdiction.

3 Within the inherent jurisdiction, applicants should seek an order in the following or a broadly similar form:

> It is ordered that there be leave to perform an operation of sterilisation on the minor [X] (method of operation may be specified) ... and to carry out such post-operative treatment and care as may be necessary in her best interests.

4 Applications in respect of an adult should be by way of originating summons in the Family Division of the High Court for an order in the following or a broadly similar form:

> It is declared that the operation of sterilisation proposed to be performed on [X] ... (method of operation) ... being in the existing circumstances in her best interests can lawfully be performed on her despite her inability to consent to it.
>
> It is ordered that in the event of a material change in the existing circumstances occurring before the said operation has been performed any party shall have liberty to apply for such further or other declaration or order as may be just.

The parties

5 The parties or applicant should normally be a parent or one of those responsible for the care of the patient or those intending to carry out the proposed operation. The patient must always be a party and should normally be a defendant (or respondent). In cases in which the patient is a defendant, the patient's guardian *ad litem* should normally be the Official Solicitor. In any case in which the Official Solicitor does not represent the patient, he should be a defendant.

Procedure

6 There will in every case be a hearing before a High Court judge fixed for directions on the first date after the passage of eight weeks from the issue of the originating summons.

7 The case will normally be heard in chambers. If it is heard in open court, the court will usually take steps to preserve the anonymity of the patient and the patient's family by making appropriate orders under the Contempt of Court Act 1981: *Re G (Adult Patient: Publicity)* [1995] 2 FLR 528.

Evidence

8 The purpose of the proceedings is to establish whether or not the proposed sterilisation is in the best interests of the patient. The judge will require to be satisfied that those proposing sterilisation are seeking

it in good faith and that their paramount concern is for the best interests of the patient rather than their own or the public's convenience. The proceedings will normally involve a thorough adversarial investigation of all possible viewpoints and any possible alternatives to sterilisation. Nevertheless, straightforward cases proceeding without dissent may be disposed of at the hearing for directions without oral evidence.

9 The Official Solicitor will in all cases, in whichever capacity he acts, carry out his own investigations, call his own witnesses and take whatever steps appear to him to be necessary in order to ensure that all medical, psychological and social evaluations are conducted and that all relevant matters are canvassed before the court. Expert and other witnesses called in support of the proposed operation will be cross-examined and all reasonable arguments presented against sterilisation. The Official Solicitor will require to meet and interview the patient in private in all cases where he or she is able to express any views (however limited) about the case.

10 The Official Solicitor anticipates that the court will particularly require evidence clearly establishing the following:

Mental capacity

1 That the patient is incapable of making her own decision about sterilisation and is unlikely to develop sufficiently to make an informed judgment about sterilisation in the foreseeable future, having regard to the most up to date medical knowledge in this field. In this connection, it must be borne in mind that:

(i) the fact that a person is legally incompetent for some purposes does not mean that she necessarily lacks the capacity to make a decision about sterilisation; and

(ii) in the case of a minor her youth and potential for development may make it difficult or impossible to make the relevant finding of incapacity.

Risk of pregnancy

2 That there is a need for contraception because the patient is fertile and is sexually active or is likely to engage in sexual activity in the foreseeable future (*Re W (Mental Patient: Sterilisation)* [1993] 1 FLR 381.

Potential psychological damage

3 That the patient is likely if she becomes pregnant or gives birth to experience substantial trauma or psychological damage greater than that resulting from the sterilisation itself.

Alternative methods of contraception

4 That there is no appropriate reversible method of contraception available having regard to the most up to date medical knowledge in this field.

Comment on the 1996 Practice Direction

The reassuring point about this latest Practice Direction is the retention of the opening clause which says that in virtually all cases involving the sterilisation of a minor or mentally incompetent adult, the sanction of a High Court judge will be required. However, after the usual incantations about the 'best interests' of the patient have been made, which are no less than prerequisites, cl 8 still talks about 'straightforward cases proceeding without dissent'. Hence, the word 'urgent' has been deleted from this Practice Direction. Yet, this still begs the question of how one defines 'straightforward cases', or are 'straightforward cases' simply those that proceed 'without dissent'? In the case of a child who is incapable of expressing a view, it would be up to the Official Solicitor to make a case against the proposed sterilisation. In the case of an adult, again, the Official Solicitor would be expected to make an opposing case, if (s)he thinks fit. But when is a case proceeding 'without dissent'? This presumably refers to an absence of objection from either the patient's relative or parent or social worker or carer or doctor. What are the guidelines for deciding the 'best interests of the patient' in such cases? What sort of evidence would have to be adduced to convince the court that this was a 'straightforward case'? The word 'straightforward' remains problematic, ambiguous and somewhat presumptuous. Several comments can also be made about cl 10. In cl 10(1) it is taken as read that the patient lacks the capacity to make an informed decision or to express a view at the time of the hearing, but the difficulty then arises if there is conflicting medical opinion about whether the patient is likely to develop sufficiently to make an informed judgment about sterilisation in the foreseeable future. According to case law (*Sewell v Electrolux* (1997) *The Times*, 7 November), the court must resolve any conflict of expert opinion, but how would or could a judge decide in the marginal cases? As La Forest J put it so bluntly in the Canadian case of *Re Eve* (1986) 31 DLR (4th) 1, p 32:

> Judges are generally ill informed about many of the factors relevant to a wise decision in this difficult area. They generally know little of mental illness, of techniques of contraception or their efficacy. And, however well presented a case may be, it can only partially inform.

Regarding cl 10(2), is it now the accepted (and acceptable) routine practice that, because the mentally incompetent patient is 'fertile and sexually active or is likely to engage in sexual activity in the foreseeable future', this is a defensible justification for authorising sterilisation? Would this not be *Jeanette* Mark 2? Surely this was Jeanette's problem, but the point that the present writer and others made more than 13 years ago is that sterilisation only removes the visible signs of sexual intercourse, but cannot protect a mentally handicapped girl from sexual exploitation or rape. The medical opinion was in conflict in *Jeanette's* case, but the court chose to accept the view that sterilisation was the only course of action left open; time was running out for the court to have the jurisdiction to make a decision, since it would lose its jurisdiction once Jeanette turned 18, which was a matter of weeks away.

STERILISATION IN THE 'BEST INTERESTS' – A SCOTTISH COMPARISON

Non-consensual sterilisation for a mentally incompetent woman in Scotland

Ten years after the *Jeanette* case, Scotland, which is not a common law country despite its proximity to England, had its own case dealing with a mentally handicapped adult woman. In *Lawrence, Petitioner* (also reported as *L v I's Curator ad litem*) [1996] 32 BMLR 37; (1996) *The Times*, 19 March; [1997] Med LR 325, the treatment of menstrual phobias and the proposed sterilisation of an incapax arose for consideration by the Outer House of the Court of Session and is the first reported case of Scottish law relating to this vexed question.

The Lawrence *case (1996)*

Facts

In this case, Ingrid Lawrence was a 32 year old autistic woman who had been prescribed the contraceptive pill since the age of 13. She had never menstruated. Both her mother and gynaecologist considered the suppression of menstruation to be appropriate because of her tendency to be fastidious to the point of obsession, taking two hours to wash her hair and a further two hours to have a bath. Other medical evidence supported this approach, indicating that she would find menstruation very distressing. She had not suffered any side effects while on the pill, but the risks of hypertension, venous thrombosis and carcinoma of the breast assumed greater significance as she approached the age of 35. There was also continued concern to prevent her from becoming pregnant, even though there was no evidence of her having had sexual relations, since she would be unlikely to understand the process of pregnancy or to care for a child. As a result of her autism, she had not developed spontaneous language skills, merely repeating anything that was said to her, and was unable to comprehend abstract concepts. Her gynaecologist recommended a partial or total hysterectomy.

Ingrid's mother presented a petition, seeking appointment as her tutor dative with various powers including, in particular, the power to consent to the surgical sterilisation of the woman in her best interests.

The court appointed a curator ad litem to look after the woman's best interests in the petition and she opposed giving the petitioner the power to consent to the woman's sterilisation. The curator argued that sterilisation was unjustified and inappropriate in the circumstances, since there was no evidence to suggest that the woman had ever had sexual intercourse or was ever likely to do so.

The petitioner argued that, even though the risk of the woman falling pregnant was not high, its devastating consequences were such that it was not a risk that could ever be taken.

The Court of Outer Session held that:

(a) The petition for appointment of the woman's mother as tutor dative should be granted and should include the power to consent to the proposed sterilisation.

(b) The test to be applied was whether the operation was necessary and in the best interests of the patient: *F v West Berkshire HA (Mental Health Act Commissioning Intervening)* [1989] 2 All ER 545, *sub nom Re F (Mental Patient: Sterilisation)* [1990] 2 AC 1; *Re B (A Minor) (Wardship: Sterilisation)* [1987] 2 WLR 1025; [1988] 1 AC 199 followed; and the test was satisfied in the present case.

(c) Ingrid's case was very unusual, since she required not only contraception protection but the avoidance of menstruation. There was no less invasive way to meet these dual needs. Medical evidence was unanimous that there were dangers in continuing the present contraceptive regime for much longer, due to the woman's age and the fact that she had started the combined pill 20 years previously; there were several disadvantages in moving to another contraceptive method such as Norplant, which would require in-depth counselling of the woman which, due to her condition, was impossible to achieve; tubal ligation would not prevent menstruation.

(d) It is not wise to set down precise rules for the resolution of such cases, since each may turn on its own facts: *Practice Note* [1993] 2 FLR 222 relating to the role of the Official Solicitor in sterilisation cases in England considered.

Comment on *Lawrence* and Scottish law

There is no equivalent in English law to the Scottish 'tutor dative', who has the formal supervisory power to give proxy consent; in English law, as we have seen (in *Re F*), no one is entitled to give consent on behalf of a mentally incompetent adult, because of the repeal of the power in the (earlier) Mental Health Act 1958. Hence, the best interests criterion has been utilised in English law. As far as the *Lawrence* case is concerned, Lord Maclean posited two requirements which required to be satisfied before sterilisation could be authorised: (a) the sterilisation must be 'necessary' and (b) in the woman's best interests.

Yet, although it purported to be relying on speeches in *Re F* and in *Re B* (*Jeanette's* case), the House of Lords did not, in fact, use the word 'necessary', but Lord Goff rejected the view of Neil LJ when he defined it as 'that which the general body of medical opinion ... would consider to be in the best interests of the patient'. The House of Lords did mention the concept of necessity in *Re F*, but the *only* test they were propounding in *Re F* and *Re B* was the best interests test.

In his commentary on the *Lawrence* case, Ian Kennedy's interpretation of Lord Maclean's words is that 'unless the sterilisation can be shown to be necessary, it cannot be in the woman's best interests' (Kennedy, I, 'Commentary' [1997] Med LR 327). In other words, it was not sufficient to authorise sterilisation if Ingrid only needed contraception; it was the fact that she also needed to prevent menstruation that justified the sterilisation – because this was a genuine health need. Kennedy (1997) sees this as invoking the therapeutic requirement before a non-consensual sterilisation may be authorised, which, of course, follows the Canadian approach (*Re Eve*), some of the comments in *Marion's case* in Australia, the other Australian case of *Re K and Public Trustee*, where the reason for the hysterectomy being authorised was the seriously retarded girl's 'phobic aversion to blood', and *Re X* (New Zealand), where the onset of menstruation would have had disastrous psychological effects.

The court's comment on the 1993 English Practice Note ([1993] 2 FLR 22), which was mentioned by counsel for the curator *ad litem*, was that the Note was 'no doubt very instructive', but Lord Maclean responded that the Note in this regard 'simply sets out what the Official Solicitor anticipates the presiding judge will normally require by way of evidence'. There was nothing exceptional about this, but his Lordship continued that 'In this jurisdiction [that is, the Scottish jurisdiction], I do not think it is wise or beneficial to set down precise rules for particular situations, simply because these situations will vary so much according to their own facts'. This, *per se*, is reasonable enough, but certainly leaves scope for some judicial discretion. However, the best that can be said about this judgment is that it appeared to favour the seemingly discredited 'therapeutic/non-therapeutic' approach (stressed in the English High Court in *Re D* in 1976) by insisting on the need to prove an actual health need before the sterilisation could be said to be 'necessary', *before* which it could be said to be in the woman's best interests. There appears to be a more protective approach adopted by the Scottish court, since Lord Maclean also talked about the 'desirability of avoiding a major invasive surgical procedure if it can be' and that Ingrid's case was a very unusual case. This suggests that the Scottish court would *not* wish to authorise sterilisation as a matter of course, despite its comments on the English 1993 Practice Note guidance, which, as we have seen, has now been replaced by a new Practice Note in 1996.

CONCLUSIONS

From a comparative point of view, it should be noted that the *ad hoc* approach of English courts may be contrasted with another common law jurisdiction, like Canada, where in *Re K* [1985] 3 WWR 204, Wood J (at first instance) listed several criteria for reaching a decision and in *Re Eve* where, in the provincial Supreme Court, MacDonald J listed 14 criteria (see discussion in Chapter 15). However, apart from the many detailed criticisms of *Re B (Jeanette's* case*)* discussed above, the case of *Re F* remains the leading English case for legally incompetent adults and it will be recalled that the House of Lords said, in that case, that the test as to whether the sterilisation of a woman who was deemed unable to consent was lawful, was whether it was in that woman's best interests. As we have seen, this means only what a court or doctor says the patient's best interests are in any given case and these will be judged, according to *Re F*, if the standard of care of negligence is met, that is, if a responsible body of co-professionals would be prepared to say the practice or procedure in question reflects their own. True, the *Bolitho* case now offers a gloss on the *Bolam* principle, so that a decision has to be justified if it appears 'illogical' or appears to require further justification or clarification. Yet, as David Carson has put it, 'Why is there a need for a best interests test when doctors can be sued if they are negligent? These are people who, by definition, have special difficulties and yet who may have their basic human rights irretrievably reduced without an independent legal review being necessary' (Carson (1989), p 372).

SELECTIVE BIBLIOGRAPHY

Bainham, A, 'Handicapped girls and judicial parents' (1987) 103 LQR 334

Carson, D, 'The sexuality of people with learning difficulties' (1989) JSWL 355

de Cruz, P, 'Sterilisation of mentally handicapped persons: *In re C*' (1990) J Child L 131

de Cruz, SP, 'Sterilization, wardship and human rights' (1988) 18 Fam Law 6

Douglas, G, *Law, Fertility and Reproduction (Modern Legal Studies)*, 1991, Sweet & Maxwell

Dyer, C, 'Decisions from the House of Lords' (1987) 294 BMJ 1219

Fenwick, AJ, '*Re S (Medical Treatment: Adult Sterilisation)*: retrenching on risk – revising the lawful boundaries of sterilisation' (1999) 11 Child and Fam LQ 313

Freeman, MDA, 'For her own good' (1987) LSG 949

Freeman, MDA, Sterilising the mentally handicapped', in *Medicine, Ethics and the Law*, 1988, Stevens

Gillon, R, 'Autonomy and consent', in Lockwood (ed), *Moral Dilemmas in Modern Medicine*, 1985, OUP

Goston, L, 'Consent to treatment: the incapable person' in Dyer, C (ed), *Doctors, Patients and the Law*, 1992, Blackwell

Grubb, A and Pearl, D, 'Sterilisation and the courts' [1987] CLJ 439

Heginbotham, C, 'Sterilizing people with mental handicaps', in McLean, SAM (ed), *Legal Issues in Human Reproduction*, 1990, Dartmouth, p 141

Kingdom, E, 'Consent, coercion and consortium: the sexual politics of sterilisation' (1985) 12 JLS 19

Jacob, I, 'The inherent jurisdiction of the court' [1970] CLP 23

Lee, S, 'From D to B to T: sterilising mentally handicapped teenagers' (1988) JCL 15

Lee, R and Morgan, D, 'A lesser sacrifice? Sterilization and mentally handicapped women', in *Birthrights. Law and Ethics at the Beginning of Life*, 1989, Routledge, p 132

Mason, JK and McCall Smith, RA, *Law and Medical Ethics*, 5th edn, 1999, Butterworths, Chapter 4

McLean, SAM and Campbell, TD, 'Sterilisation', in McLean, SAM (ed), *Legal Issues in Medicine*, 1981, Gower

McLean, SAM, 'The right to reproduce', in Campbell, TD *et al* (eds), *Human Rights: From Rhetoric to Reality*, 1986, Blackwell

McLean, SAM, *Old Law, New Medicine. Medical Ethics and Human Rights*, 1999, Pandora

Norrie, McK K, 'Sterilisation of the mentally disabled in English and Canadian law' (1989) 38 ICLQ 387

Myers, D, *The Human Body and the Law*, 1970, Edinburgh UP

Ogburne, D and Ward, R, 'Sterilization, the mentally incompetent and the courts' (1989) 18 Anglo-Am L Rev 230

Scroggie, F, 'Why do parents want their children sterilised? A broader approach to sterilisation requests' (1989–90) 2 JCL 35

Shaw, J, 'Regulating sexuality: a legislative framework for non-consensual sterilisation', in McVeigh, S and Wheeler, S (eds), *Law, Health and Medical Regulation*, 1991, Dartmouth

Shone, M, 'Mental health – sterilisation of mentally retarded persons' (1987) 66 Can Bar Review 635

Williams, B, 'Which slopes are slippery?', in Lockwood (ed), *Moral Dilemmas in Modern Medicine*, 1985, OUP

CHAPTER 7

MEDICAL NEGLIGENCE AND PROFESSIONAL ACCOUNTABILITY

INTRODUCTION

We now consider the main principles in English law which determine medical negligence, which, *mutatis mutandis,* are the same principles as the negligence principles which operate under the English law of tort. Note, however, that this chapter is not intended to be an exhaustive study of medical negligence, for which there are several excellent treatises, many of which are listed in the bibliography at the end of this chapter. However, as with other chapters in Part I, a brief conspectus of the main principles is provided so that the reader who wishes to consider the position in non-English jurisdictions has a basis for comparison.

HISTORICAL PERSPECTIVES

Early examples of professional liability

The early indications of the imposition of professional liability appear to have been detected in the 1329 case known as the *Surgeon's Case* (cited by Kiralfy, A in *A Source Book of English Law,* 1957, Sweet & Maxwell, p 184) where it was stated that relations between a professional and his client gave rise to certain duties. In the case itself, however, Denom J held that the oculist who treated an eye ailment with herbs and allegedly caused the loss of the eye was not liable because the damage caused was not intentional. In the second *Surgeon's Case* (also known as *Stratton v Swanlond,* Year Book 48, Edward B, Hilary Term, f 6, p 11 cited in Kiralfy, p 185), heard a year later, Cavendish CJ held that a physician who treated a wounded hand with unsatisfactory therapeutic results was liable for not employing due diligence in treating the patient.

NEGLIGENCE IN ENGLISH LAW

Negligence in English law may be described as any conduct that falls short of the standard expected of a person where a duty of care is owed and which causes foreseeable damage to another person. Hence, in order to establish negligence (in the medical context or otherwise): (a) the plaintiff must prove that the defendant owed the plaintiff a duty of care in the particular situation; (b) if this can be proved, did the defendant breach this duty in the sense that he failed to confirm to the standard of care required by the law?; (c) did the plaintiff suffer injury or loss (damage) as a result of the defendant's actions, either directly or as part of a transaction (causation) (see *Lochgelly Iron and Coal Co v M'Mullan* [1934] AC 1 and *Burton v Islington* [1992] 3 WLR 655, *per* Dillon LJ: 'it is now elementary that the tort of negligence involves three factors: a duty of care, breach of that duty and consequent damage')?

Duty of care between doctor and patient

The conventional view in English law is that a duty of care does exist between a healthcare professional and her patient. This is usually the case where patients are in hospital, where the staff are responsible for their care, and in general practice, where doctors have a duty of care to those on their lists. However, as Montgomery points out, 'It is more difficult to ascertain when professionals are responsible for people who are not already their patients', such as victims of accidents, people placed at risk of infection when a patient is discharged from hospital or a woman who goes into labour in a public place (see Montgomery (1997), p 167).

GENERAL PRINCIPLES

Health professionals may be held accountable if there is a complaint to their professional body, that is, the General Medical Council, or the United Kingdom Central Council for Nursing, Midwifery and Health Visiting. There is also a complaints procedure available to a patient, who may complain to a hospital, or Family Health Service Authority (FHSA), or Health Service Commissioner (ombudsman). They could also be liable under the criminal law. Under the civil law, healthcare professionals may also face a malpractice suit. Another general principle is that no civil liability normally arises from a mere omission (see *Barnett v Chelsea* [1968] 1 All ER 1068).

In English common law, the tort (civil wrong) of negligence is a well established cause of action and, together with the law of battery, plays a major part in the arena of healthcare law. This is mainly due to the fact that as a general principle, there is no contractual relationship between doctor and patient (see *Pfizer Corpn v Ministry of Health* [1965] AC 512) except where the patient seeks treatment privately. Even where patients have entered into contracts with their doctors, the courts have decided to impose on the doctor only those obligations which are imposed in tort; in other words, provided a duty of care is established between doctor and patient, then the usual requirements for proving negligence would apply (see, for example,

Negligence in English Law, above, p 233). Thus, the doctor's duty to his NHS patient is in tort and not contract. Hence, if such a doctor is negligent, such medical negligence forms part of the law of tort. On the other hand, if the doctor treating a private patient falls below the standard required of him by the law, that patient may sue him for breach of contract.

Who should be sued?

An action in negligence is normally brought against the health authority as being vicariously liable for the doctor or other health professional's negligence. Direct action against the hospital for the failure of the hospital to provide a competent medical practitioner has not yet been established in English law.

The plaintiff may sue the doctor (that is, the GP) directly if the allegation is made of negligence on the part of the GP. The GP in the UK is solely responsible for the treatment of his patients and the health authority will not be responsible unless it has intervened in the GP's treatment of the patient. All partners in a practice may be liable for the actions of one of their members. The GP will normally be a member of a medical defence society or union, to which he will refer any claim made against him and the society will then advise him and will undertake the defence or settlement of the claim. A GP will be vicariously liable for the negligence of staff employed by him such as nurses, but he will not be responsible for the acts of a *locum tenens* or a deputising doctor.

But, if the GP has referred the case to some other health service employee, the patient may sue that individual, or the health authority (HA), or both in a joint action. In practice, the HA (rather than an individual employee) is usually sued on the grounds of convenience and on the basis of (a) the duty of the hospital to care for its patients; and (b) vicarious liability of an HA for the negligence of its employees. The GP will not be covered by the NHS indemnity which applies to hospital doctors unless a claim arises in respect of work undertaken under an HA contract.

NHS indemnity – arrangements for negligence claims in the NHS, October 1996

There is an NHS indemnity if the healthcare professional (a) was working under a contract of employment and the negligence occurred in the course of that employment; or (b) was not working under a contract of employment but was contracted by an NHS body to provide services to persons to whom that NHS body owes a duty of care; or (c) neither of these, but where the NHS owed a duty of care to the persons injured.

This does not apply to family health service practitioners working under contracts for services, for example, GPs, general dental practitioners, family dentists, pharmacists or optometrists; or other self-employed healthcare professionals, for example, independent midwives; employees of FHS practices; employees of private hospitals, local education authorities or voluntary agencies.

The basic elements to prove for an action in medical negligence

(a) a duty of care was owed to the patient in question;

(b) there was a breach of that duty; and

(c) injury or harm was caused to the patient as a result of that breach.

(Or the question may be asked: did the conduct of the defendant (doctor) amount to a breach of a duty of care which he owed to the injured plaintiff (patient)?)

Are these elements any different from an 'ordinary' action in negligence?

No, but there are particular features in a medical negligence claim:

(a) one of the most difficult tasks is proving causation; that is, that (assuming it was primarily one doctor) the doctor's 'negligence' (that is, conduct which fell below that of a reasonably competent/skilful doctor in that position) *actually caused* the plaintiff's injury;

(b) there is the other possible problem of there being a group who were all possibly responsible parties – GP, consultant, other hospital doctors, nursing staff, etc;

(c) the general approach of judges has been not to readily find doctors/healthcare professionals liable or guilty in negligence, applying the *Bolam* test as the general standard: see *Bolam v Friern Hospital Management Committee* [1957] 2 All ER 118. In other words, in the vast majority of cases, provided the healthcare professional complied with the current standard procedure which would be supported by at least one responsible body of professional opinion, it would be very difficult to prove negligence.

Tort of false imprisonment

The tort of false imprisonment is also relevant as far as the detention of mentally disordered patients are concerned, since such patient's detention must be justifiable under the common law or the Mental Health Act 1983, or it will constitute the tort of false imprisonment (see *Bournewood Community and*

Mental Health NHS Trust ex p L [1998] 3 All ER 289 and see the discussion of mental health and the law in relation to consent in Chapter 1).

Standard of care expected from a doctor

The standard of care expected from a doctor toward his or her NHS patient is that of the reasonably skilled and experienced doctor who has the same expertise in that speciality, with no concessions being made for inexperience (see *Nettleship v Weston* [1971] 2 QB 691; *Wilsher v Essex AHA* [1986] 3 All ER 801).

Two comments may be made about this principle. First, it is, of course, absolutely essential that patients should expect the same degree of care and skill from any healthcare professional who purports to deal with him in a medical relationship, irrespective of whether that healthcare practitioner is a novice or a seasoned professional. To require anything less would be a recipe for disaster and a licence to kill or at least to injure or maim. The situation that Lord Denning had to consider involving the learner driver in the *Nettleship v Weston* case is also one where the same need exists – to protect other potential victims, in this case, road users. Secondly, however, while there may be more opportunity to control a learner driver's speed and general road handling by the instructor, especially in dual control cars, the situation with an inexperienced doctor is surely different, since by definition, a trainee doctor or intern is still in the process of training on the job. While there is no alternative but to allow them to 'practise' on their patients, it seems almost inevitable that mistakes or errors of judgment may be made and the opportunity to supervise or monitor their skill, conduct or expertise is, under the current system, severely limited and far more infrequent and, at best, at arm's length. The traditional culture of the consultant doing the daily rounds in the hospital wards with several inexperienced medical students in tow, who then vie to make the correct diagnosis when asked by the consultant, often does not really prepare these future doctors for diagnosing the many less obvious symptoms which they might later face. The long hours worked by the trainee doctors has also been a long standing matter for debate and, indeed, litigation (see *Johnstone v Bloomsbury HA* [1991] 2 All ER 293), and this, coupled with the 'cramming' required at the end of each year, suggests that, while the grounding is there, in some cases, the basic knowledge may be akin to shifting sands and no substitute for experience. In other words, there should be little surprise when doctors, who are only human, make mistakes, even at a slightly later stage of their careers, because of the speed of expanding medical knowledge and technology, the unrelenting pressure they face as junior doctors and, unfortunately, inexperience.

Usual practice

In *Hunter v Hanley* 1955 SC 22, a Scottish case, which preceded *Bolam* by two years and may well have been the source of the *Bolam* approach, the so called 'customs test' – whereby a defendant's conduct is tested against the normal usage of his profession or calling – was endorsed. There it was said that:

> ... there is a heavy onus on the pursuer (plaintiff) to establish three facts, and without all three his case will fail. First it must be proved that there is a usual and normal practice; secondly, it must be proved that the defender has not adopted that practice; and thirdly (and this is of crucial importance) it must be established that the course the doctor adopted is one which no professional man of ordinary skill would have taken if he had been acting with ordinary care.

Mason and McCall Smith (1999) point out (p 224) that there is a problem with this definition, simple and attractive as it sounds. This is that, if there is 'usual and normal practice', for instance, where are there are guidelines covering a procedure, then the plaintiff and defendant may have recourse to these guidelines or circulars which will be examples of current best practice and compare them with the professional conduct in question in any given case. However, if there is more than one opinion (both being 'expert' or 'authoritative') on a procedure or technique that should be followed, the existence of more than one course of action available to the practitioner means that there is no single 'established custom' or 'usual practice'. The question would then arise: what is the practitioner's liability if she chooses a course of action which *one* responsible body of opinion would reject, but which another would support?

Junior and inexperienced doctors

In the case of *Jones v Manchester Corporation* [1952] 2 All ER 125, the court said that errors due to inexperience are no defence. In the subsequent House of Lords' case of *Wilsher v Essex AHA* [1987] QB 730 (the full facts of which are discussed under Causation, see below, p 252) the Court of Appeal (*per* Glidewell LJ) stated that: '... the law requires the trainee or learner to be judged by the same standard as his more experienced colleagues. If it did not, inexperience would frequently be urged as a defence to an action for professional negligence.' This case subsequently went to the House of Lords on the issue of causation.

On a slightly different point, in *Johnstone v Bloomsbury* [1991] 2 All ER 293, the Court of Appeal recognised the scope for young, overworked doctors bringing actions against health authorities in respect of injury to their health caused by excessive working hours.

Keeping abreast of current developments

The case of *Crawford v Board of Governors of Charing Cross Hospital* (1953) *The Times*, 8 December, is instructive on the question of the extent to which a doctor is expected to keep himself informed of major developments in practice. The lower court found that there had been no breach of duty when an operative procedure was performed resulting in paralysis, which six months previously had been the subject of a report in *The Lancet* suggesting that the procedure was likely to produce such paralysis. However, the Court of Appeal rejected the claim, declaring that doctors cannot be expected to read every article in the medical press. Failure to read a single article, it was said, may be excusable, but disregard of a series of warnings in the medical press could well be evidence of negligence. In the light of the volume and rapidity of development of medical knowledge, technology and techniques, it is unreasonable to expect doctors to be au fait with every possible new development. However, in the light of the 'general competence' of a practitioner, he would be expected to be reasonably up to date and aware of major developments in his field or which would be known by someone in his position.

The *Bolam* test

So what is the standard of care required by the law? According to the leading case of *Bolam v Friern Hospital Management Committee* [1957] 1 WLR 582, p 586, McNair J said:

> The test is the standard of the ordinary skilled man exercising and professing to have that special skill. A man need not possess the highest expert skill; it is well established law that it is sufficient if he exercises the ordinary skill of an ordinary competent man exercising that particular art.

However, English law has made some concessions. For instance, there may be accidents where the law decides that no one will be held liable (see *Roe v Ministry of Health* [1954] 2 QB 66). A crucial and much-quoted phrase in the *Bolam* case deals with the ascertainment of breach, and McNair J declared that a doctor would not be liable in negligence if he acted:

> ... in accordance with a *practice accepted as proper by a responsible body of medical men skilled in that particular area* ... a man is not negligent merely because there is a body of opinion who would take a contrary view. [Emphasis added.]

Over the years, this phrase has become the touchstone for ascertaining whether or not a particular healthcare professional acted negligently in a given situation, in the sense that, so long as it was possible to point to 'a body of medical men' (but not merely one medical practitioner) whose practice was in accordance with the defendant's professional conduct in the situation under litigation, this satisfied the *Bolam* test, even though there could well be other medical groups who would not have followed the same practice as the defendant's. In other words, the standard of care is that which is set by at least one 'responsible' group of medical practitioners.

Yet, there is a line of authority in English law in cases such as *Hucks v Cole*, decided in 1968 (but only reported in 1993), that laid down that, even if there was compliance with accepted practice, this did not necessarily preclude a finding of negligence. These two divergent lines of authority seem to have antecedents which go back over a century (see Howie, RBM, 'The standard of care in medical negligence' [1983] JR 193). Yet the 'classic' statement from McNair J, although uttered in a lower court judgment, appears to have been regarded even by the highest English courts as 'the law' on this area since the 1980s up until, and including, the 1997 House of Lords decision in *Bolitho*, which actually referred to *Hucks v Cole* with approval.

The 'Bolamisation' of medical law

The so called *Bolam* test has led to the 'Bolamisation' of medical law (as stated by Keown in 'The rise and rise of the "*Bolam* test"' [1995] Singapore JLS 342), as its more general interpretation has been applied fairly consistently since about the 1980s.

We turn to the facts of the *Bolam* case, which was decided in 1957.

The Bolam *case [1957] 1 WLR 582*

In this case, the plaintiff, Mr Bolam, was a manic depressive who was given electro-convulsive therapy.

There were dangers associated with this treatment, such as seizures which would cause fractures of the patient's bones, but measures such as restraint and the provision of relaxant drugs would reduce those dangers. However, Mr Bolam was not given any of these measures. Neither was he given any routine warning about the danger of fracture or the availability of relaxants or restraints so that he could choose to have them utilised to reduce the risk of any personal injury he might suffer. Being unaware of these dangers, he did not ask about them and, in the course of his therapy, he suffered very severe fractures of his pelvis. He therefore sued the hospital and, following the judge's direction to the jury, judgment was given for the defendant hospital.

McNair J said:

> [Where] you get a situation which involves the use of some special skill or competence, then the test as to whether there has been negligence or not is not the test of the man on the Clapham omnibus, because he has not got this

> special skill. The test is the standard of the ordinary skilled man exercising and professing to have that special skill.

It is worth noting that McNair J goes on to say that 'A man need not possess the highest expert skill' and that 'it is well established law that it is sufficient if he exercises the ordinary skill of an ordinary competent man exercising that particular art'. He also makes the now famous statement about a doctor not being guilty of negligence if he has acted 'in accordance with a practice accepted as proper by a responsible body of medical men skilled in that particular art'. He then declares: 'Putting it the other way round, a man is not negligent if he is acting in accordance with such a practice, merely because there is a body of opinion who would take a contrary view.'

About 10 years later, the Privy Council in a Malaysian appeal was quite happy to apply the *Bolam* test in *Chin Keow v Government of Malaysia* [1967] WLR 813, making it clear that 'when you get a situation which involves the use of some special skill or competence, then the test as to whether there has been negligence or not is not the test of the man on the top of a Clapham omnibus because he has not got this special skill. The test is the standard of the ordinary skilled man exercising and professing to have that special skill.'

A year later, in 1968, the case of *Hucks v Cole* was decided, but this case was not reported until 1993.

In the leading House of Lords' case of *Sidaway v Board of Governors of the Bethlem Royal Hospital and the Maudsley Hospital* [1984] 1 All ER 1018, the test received a powerful endorsement from Lord Diplock, who praised its ability to bring up to date an ancient common law principle, that it was comprehensive and applied to every aspect of the duty of care owed by a doctor to his patients in the exercise of his healing duties (*per* Lord Diplock in *Sidaway* [1984] AC 871, pp 892–93). Indeed, the *Bolam* test has also been approved in other common law jurisdictions and approved by the Privy Council (see *Chin Keow* (above)), although it has not had the virtually universal acceptance it has enjoyed in English courts until the 1980s. The 'test' was applied to 'treatment' in *Whitehouse v Jordan* [1981] 1 All ER 267 and then to 'diagnosis' in cases like *Maynard v West Midlands RHA* [1981] 1 All ER 635.

Should it matter if the doctor is a specialist?

In the case of *Hunter v Hanley* 1955 SC 200, Lord Bridge makes it clear that the standard will then be the 'standard of the specialist of ordinary skill'. This is also indicated in *Sidaway* (*per* Lord Bridge).

Can an error of clinical judgment ever amount to negligence?

Whitehouse v Jordan [1981] 1 All ER 267

The defendant was in charge of the plaintiff's delivery. It was a high risk pregnancy, and the plaintiff was born with severe and irreparable brain damage, allegedly as a result of the defendant obstetrician's negligence. After the mother had been in labour for 22 hours, the latter had made six attempts at normal delivery using forceps before realising this was impossible. The plaintiff, suing by his mother as next friend, argued that (a) the defendant had been negligent in pulling too hard and too long; and (b) the defendant should have moved more quickly to utilise delivery by Caesarean section.

The trial judge held that, although the decision to perform a trial of forceps was a reasonable one, the defendant had, in fact, pulled too hard and was, therefore, negligent. This finding was reversed in the Court of Appeal, where Lord Denning said that an error of clinical judgment was not negligent (see [1980] 1 All ER 650, p 658).

The case went all the way to the House of Lords, where Lord Denning's views were rejected. In essence, they ruled that an error of clinical judgment could be negligence if it is an error which would not have been made by a reasonably competent professional man acting with ordinary care.

Lord Edmund Davies' comments are instructive:

> To say that a surgeon committed an error of clinical judgment is wholly ambiguous, for, while some errors may be completely consistent with the due exercise of professional skill, other acts or omissions in the course of exercising 'clinical judgment' may be so glaringly below proper standards as to make a finding of negligence inevitable ...[d]octors and surgeons fall into no special category ... If a surgeon fails to measure up to that standard in any respect ('clinical judgment' or otherwise), he has been negligent and should be so adjudged.

Lord Fraser also declared:

> The true position is that an error of judgment may, or may not, be negligent; it depends on the nature of the error. If it is one that would have been made by a reasonably competent professional man professing to have the standard and type of skill that the defendant holds himself out as having, and acting with ordinary care, then it is negligence. If, on the other hand, it is an error that such a man, acting with ordinary care, might have made, then it is not negligence.

In the instant case, the Law Lords held that the defendant had *not* been negligent because there had not, in any case, been sufficient evidence to justify the trial judge's finding of negligence.

Interpretations of the Bolam *test*

The so called *Bolam* test may be interpreted in different ways. As Keown (1995) asks, 'Is the test whether, in the opinion of the court, the doctor exercised reasonable care? Or is it whether the doctor complied with ordinary practice?'. In other words, he asks: is it for the courts to decide what is reasonable care 'albeit in the light of evidence as to professional practice?'. Or is it for the medical profession to set the standard, so that if a practitioner acts in accordance with the accepted practice, he would not be regarded as liable in negligence. The present writer suggests that the many cases dealing with this issue post-*Bolam* appear to have generally favoured the latter interpretation. Another commentator, Michael Jones (1991), argues that the *Bolam* test 'fails to make this important distinction between the ordinary skilled doctor and the reasonably competent doctor, and this has produced some confusion in the cases'. As we have seen, the House of Lords were certainly in favour of the test in the mid-1980s in cases such as *Sidaway*, as they were in *Maynard v West Midlands RHA* [1984] 1 WLR 634.

Maynard v West Midlands *(1984)*

In *Maynard* (1984), the doctors were of the opinion that the plaintiff's condition was either tuberculosis or Hodgkin's disease. Bearing in mind that the latter condition would be fatal without treatment, they decided that, rather than wait for some weeks for the results of a sputum test to confirm tuberculosis, they would perform a diagnostic procedure known as mediastinoscopy to test for Hodgkin's disease. This procedure involved a risk of damage to the recurrent laryngeal nerve and, even though the procedure was performed competently, the risk materialised. The plaintiff alleged that it was negligent of the doctors to perform the procedure rather than await the results of the sputum test, which would have confirmed tuberculosis. The trial judge found for the plaintiff on the basis of preferring the evidence of the expert witness for the plaintiff rather than that of the defendant's expert witness. The Court of Appeal reversed this decision, and this decision was affirmed by the House of Lords. Lord Scarman's interpretation of the *Bolam* test (p 438) was that:

> It is not enough to show that there is a body of competent professional opinion which considers that their[s] was a wrong decision, if there also exists a body of professional opinion, equally competent, which supports the decision as reasonable in the circumstances.

Lord Scarman went even further to clarify that a judge's mere 'preference' for one body of distinguished opinion over another was not sufficient to establish negligence in a doctor whose action had received the 'seal of approval' of those whose opinions the judge did not prefer.

Similarly, in *De Freitas v O'Brien* [1993] 4 Med LR 481, the same judicial line showing deference to the medical profession was again preferred. In *De Freitas*, the plaintiff underwent an operation on her spine. The procedure was one which only a very small number of neurosurgeons (four or five out of 250 countrywide) would consider safe. But the neurosurgeons considered that they had a very high degree of expertise. The surgeon was held to be not negligent, even though the exploratory surgery which had been undertaken carried an unavoidable risk of infection. The only concession the judge was prepared to make here was that the view of a body of medical opinion could be scrutinised by the court.

The Sidaway *case [1985] 1 All ER 643*

Facts

The plaintiff suffered from persistent pain in her neck and shoulders, and was advised by a surgeon employed by the defendant hospital governors to have an operation on her spinal column to relieve the pain. The surgeon warned the plaintiff of the possibility of disturbing a nerve root and the possible consequences of doing so, but did not mention the possibility of damage to the spinal cord, even though he would be operating within three millimetres of it. The risk of damage to the spinal cord was very small (less than 1%), but if the risk materialised, the resulting injury could range from the mild to the very severe. The plaintiff consented to the operation, which was carried out by the surgeon with due care and skill. However, in the course of the operation, the plaintiff suffered injury to her spinal cord which resulted in her being severely disabled.

She brought an action against the hospital governors and the surgeon's estate (the surgeon having died five years before the trial began), claiming damages for personal injury. Being unable to sustain a claim based on negligent performance of the operation, the plaintiff instead contended that the surgeon had been in breach of a duty owed to her to warn her of all possible risks inherent in the operation with the result that she had not been in a position to give an 'informed consent' to the operation.

The trial judge applied the test of whether the surgeon had acted in accordance with accepted medical practice and dismissed the claim.

On appeal, the Court of Appeal upheld the judge, holding that the doctrine of informed consent based on full disclosure of all the facts to the patient was not the appropriate test under English law. The plaintiff appealed to the House of Lords.

The House of Lords held:

(a) (*Per* Lord Diplock, Lord Keith and Lord Bridge, Lord Scarman dissenting): the test of liability in respect of a doctor's duty to warn his patient of risks inherent in treatment recommended by him was the same as the test applicable to diagnosis and treatment, namely, that the doctor was required to act in accordance with a practice accepted at the time as proper by a responsible body of medical opinion. Accordingly, English law did not recognise the doctrine of informed consent. However (*per* Lord Keith and Lord Bridge), although a decision on what risks should be disclosed for the particular patient to make a rational choice whether to undergo the particular treatment recommended by a doctor was primarily a matter of clinical judgment, the disclosure of a particular risk of serious adverse consequences might be so obviously necessary for the patient to make an informed choice that no reasonably prudent doctor would fail to disclose that risk (*Bolam* applied; *Canterbury v Spence* (1972) 464 F 2d 772 not followed; *Reibl v Hughes* (1980) 114 DLR (3d) 1 considered).

(b) (*Per* Lord Templeman): when advising a patient about a proposed or recommended treatment, a doctor was under a duty to provide the patient with the information necessary to enable the patient to make a balanced judgment in deciding whether to submit to that treatment, and that included a requirement to warn the patient of any dangers which were special in kind or magnitude or special to the patient. That duty was, however, subject to the doctor's overriding duty to have regard to the best interests of the patient. Accordingly, it was for the doctor to decide what information should be given to the patient and the terms in which that information should be couched.

(c) Since (*per* Lord Diplock, Lord Keith and Lord Bridge) the surgeon's non-disclosure of the risk of damage to the plaintiff's spinal cord accorded with a practice accepted as proper by a responsible body of neuro-surgical opinion and since (*per* Lord Scarman and Lord Templeman) the plaintiff had not proved on the evidence that the surgeon had been in breach of duty by failing to warn her of that risk, the defendants were not liable to the plaintiff.

The appeal was therefore dismissed. The Appeal Court decision was affirmed.

In the *Sidaway* case, Lord Scarman again enunciated the *Bolam* test thus:

> The *Bolam* principle may be formulated as a rule that a doctor is not negligent if he acts in accordance with a practice accepted at the time as proper by a responsible body of medical opinion even though other doctors adopt a different practice. In short, the law imposes the duty of care, *but the standard of care is a matter of medical judgment*.

As is readily observable, there is a clear deference to 'medical opinion', which is, for the most part, reflected in a range of cases throughout the common law jurisdictions to a greater extent, with the possible exception of one or two jurisdictions such as Australia.

Comment on *Sidaway*

A reading of the speeches in *Sidaway* reveals that the Law Lords were not entirely clear cut or consistent in their opinions on what standard of information disclosure should be adopted and the dissenting opinion of Lord Scarman has been seized upon because of its more transatlantic style approach, and its more pro-patient focus. Ultimately, the majority favoured the *Bolam* test – reasonable professional practice.

Lord Diplock took the approach that the doctor's duty to his patient was 'not subject to dissection into a number of component parts to which different criteria of what satisfy the duty of care apply', such as diagnosis, treatment and advice (including warning of risks): the *Bolam* test applied to disclosure of risks and to diagnosis and treatment and it was 'a principle of English law that was comprehensive and applicable to every aspect of the duty of care owed by a doctor to his patient in the exercise of his healing functions'. He maintained that there was no evidence in the instant case that the patient asked the neuro-surgeon a single question about whether there were any risks involved in undergoing the operation that he was proposing for her, or, if there were, what were the consequences of those risks or the chances of their occurring. Since the neuro-surgeon's omission to mention the risk of damage to the spinal cord was consistent with a practice accepted as proper by a responsible body of medical opinion, the plaintiff failed.

Lord Bridge (with whom Lord Keith agreed) approached the case somewhat differently. He held that the doctor's duty to disclose was to be determined primarily by an application of the *Bolam* test, but that a court might, in certain circumstances, hold a doctor negligent even though he was following a practice of non-disclosure which enjoyed the approval of the profession, as where the risk was 'a substantial risk of grave adverse consequences' (such as a 10% risk of a stroke). He also stated that, when questioned by a patient about risks involved in a particular treatment proposed, the doctor's duty must be 'to answer both truthfully and as fully as the questioner requires'.

Lord Templeman went over the evidence in considerable detail and, without actually mentioning *Bolam*, held that the doctor must decide, bearing in mind the best interests of the patient and the patient's right to information which will enable him to make a balanced judgment, what information should be given to the patient and the terms in which the information should be couched. In his words, 'I do not subscribe to the theory that the patient is entitled to know everything or to the theory that the doctor is entitled to decide everything'. Earlier, he said: 'There is no doubt that a doctor ought to draw the attention of a patient to a danger which may be special in kind or magnitude or special to the patient.'

Lord Scarman, in a much-quoted dissenting speech, adopted the 'prudent patient' standard and rejected the *Bolam* test in relation to the duty to inform. He took the view that whether the doctor was in breach of his duty to inform was to be determined not exclusively by reference to the current state of responsible professional opinion and practice, though both were relevant considerations, but by the court's view of whether the doctor gave the consideration which the law required him to give to the right of the patient to make up his own mind in the light of relevant information whether or not to accept the treatment proposed.

His Lordship's comments on the prudent patient are also worth noting. He opined that:

(a) the law can require the court to ask: what would a reasonably prudent patient think significant if in the situation of this patient?;

(b) the 'prudent patient' test calls for medical evidence; the two critically important medical factors are: the degree of probability of the risk materialising and the seriousness of possible injury if it does; and the character of the risk.

Applying the test to the facts of the case, his Lordship concluded that the risk of damage to the spinal cord was not material.

Lord Scarman also stated:

> English law must recognise a duty of the doctor to warn his patient of risk inherent in the treatment which he is proposing ... The critical limitation is that the duty is confined to material risk. The test of materiality is whether in the circumstances ... the court is satisfied that a reasonable person in the patient's position would be likely to attach significance to the risk.

How much information should be given to the patient?

As we have seen in Chapter 1, English law only requires the doctor to give the broad nature of the treatment to the patient in order for that patient to make a valid decision on whether to consent, but once the patient is informed in such terms, any complaint that the information given was inadequate belongs in negligence (see *Chatterton v Gerson* [1981] QB 432). In other words, the patient's only cause of action would lie in an action for negligence. As we shall see in Part II, this rule applies pretty much to the whole common law world. Of course, the question in every case will be: *was sufficient information given to the patient so that she could make an informed choice*, and the question will always arise as to what was 'sufficient' in the circumstances of the case?

After *Sidaway*, as far as the extent of disclosure to a patient is concerned:

(a) Material risks of a procedure must be disclosed, subject only to 'therapeutic privilege' (see below) which a doctor might be required to justify; according to *Canterbury v Spence*, a risk can be defined as material if a reasonable person in the patient's position, if warned of the risk, would be likely to attach significance to it. It would also be material if the medical practitioner is, or should reasonably be, aware that the particular plaintiff, if warned of the risk, would be likely to attach significance to it.

(b) The therapeutic or professional privilege to withhold information that might be psychologically damaging to the patient was confirmed in *Sidaway*.

(c) There must be particularly good reasons, which the doctor would have to justify, for failing to answer such questions as the patient poses and there may be a strict obligation to do so.

A significant observation by Lords Keith, Bridge and Templeman in *Sidaway* is their statement that: 'When questioned specifically by a patient of apparently sound mind about the risks involved in a particular treatment proposed, the doctor's duty is to answer both truthfully and as fully as the questioner requires.'

Clearly, if the patient asks further questions about the treatment, the doctor is bound to respond to those questions (see *Sidaway v Governors of Bethlem Royal Hospital* [1984] 1 All ER 1018) unless he has grounds for withholding some information because of 'therapeutic privilege', for instance, if it is thought that giving the patient the information would be detrimental to the health of the patient; thus, it may be thought that disclosure would be *more* harmful to the patient than not giving the information in view of the patient's particular emotional or mental state or medical history. Lord Scarman suggested in *Sidaway* that there would have to be a serious threat of psychological damage to the patient.

The test for disclosure of information revisited – Gold v Haringey [1987] 2 All ER 888

The test for disclosure of information laid down in *Sidaway* was examined by the Court of Appeal in *Gold v Haringey* [1987] 2 All ER 888.

Gold v Haringey *(1987)*

In this case, Mrs Gold decided that she wished to have no further children. Her consultant obstetrician suggested that she be sterilised. The operation went ahead, with Mrs Gold's consent, but was not successful. She subsequently became pregnant again. It was found that the plaintiff had been properly informed about the operation, that it was not guaranteed to succeed.

However, Mrs Gold alleged that the consultant had been negligent in failing to discuss the treatment properly. Two mistakes were alleged: first, that the doctor had failed to explain the risk of failure; and secondly, that he had not discussed any alternative method by which steps could be taken to avoid Mrs Gold becoming pregnant by her husband undergoing a vasectomy. All the medical witnesses called said they would have warned Mrs Gold of the risk of failure, but that a sizeable proportion of doctors (estimated at 50%) would *not* have done so at the time when she had the operation (and this would have satisfied *Bolam*). However, the judge at first instance decided that the existence of this substantial body of medical opinion did not resolve the matter, because *Sidaway* only applied to therapeutic procedures, not to non-therapeutic procedures for contraceptive reasons. Mrs Gold was, therefore, awarded £19,000 damages and the HA appealed.

The Court of Appeal allowed the appeal, saying the *Bolam* test applied to non-disclosure even in relation to a non-therapeutic procedure, such as the one that the plaintiff's contraceptive sterilisation. Lloyd LJ (as he then was) remarked that he found the alleged distinction elusive, saying: 'A plastic surgeon carrying out a skin graft is presumably engaged in therapeutic surgery; but what if he is carrying out a face lift, or some other cosmetic operation?' He also thought that drawing such a distinction would be a departure from the principle on which *Bolam* rested, a principle which depended on a man professing skill in a field beyond that possessed by the man on the Clapham omnibus. The giving of contraceptive advice involved such a skill, and it was therefore to be assessed by the *Bolam* test. Stephen Brown LJ (as he then was) agreed that *Bolam*, as interpreted by Lord Diplock in *Sidaway*, should be applied.

Comment

Gold is another 'pro-doctor' case, because the effect of the appeal court deciding that *Bolam* would apply even to non-therapeutic procedures, such as contraceptive sterilisation, means that a doctor can justify his action and not be liable in negligence simply by showing that there was a body of opinion that would have done exactly what he did. In other words, *Bolam* was said to apply even when the plaintiff's health was not at stake. A more pro-doctor stance would be hard to find in these circumstances, yet about five years later, the *Blyth* case suggested that the courts would still support clinical discretion on disclosure even when a trained nurse was asking the questions, but had not asked the right question about the proposed treatment.

Blyth v Bloomsbury *(1993)*

In *Blyth v Bloomsbury HA* [1993] 4 Med LR 151, the plaintiff, a nurse, claimed that she had asked her doctor about the side effects of the contraceptive drug Depo-Provera. At the time, it was generally accepted medical opinion that Depo-Provera was well tolerated, and no significant side effects had been reported. However, the doctor who treated her was aware there might be a problem with irregular bleeding; and that another doctor in the hospital had carried out research (which was contained in the hospital files) which indicated that there may be other side effects. The patient subsequently experienced menstrual irregularity and bleeding. She brought an action for damages, alleging that as she had expressly inquired of the risks inherent in the contraceptive, she should have been told of all the risks known to the hospital at the time.

At first instance, she was awarded £3,500 damages as the judge held she was entitled to receive all the information known to the hospital about the drug.

However, in the Court of Appeal, the judgment in her favour was reversed on the facts because it was found she had not, in fact, requested that particular information.

Comment

This is another case that appears to take the *Bolam* test so far that it will not matter what a doctor tells a patient in response to a general inquiry any more than what he tells her in response to a specific inquiry. At least, that is what Kerr LJ appeared to say. All that the doctor has to do is prove he complied with medical practice or procedure that some other group of doctors would have also carried out in the same way. In contrast to patients in the USA and Canada, who have the right to be informed about material risks before deciding whether to consent to treatment, UK patients have no such right under the application of the *Bolam* test or *Sidaway*.

Causation

The plaintiff must also establish that the defendant's negligence caused the harm in question – namely, that the defendant's act or omission was the actual cause of the damage. The claim will fail unless this can be proven. In these private law cases, causation must be proved on a balance of probabilities, which means that it has to be shown that it is more probable than not that the negligence caused the injury or damage which is the subject of the complaint.

Evidential and causative factors involved in trying to establish medical negligence

The plaintiff has to prove the defendant caused the injury in fact *and* law, and the injury must not be too remote. Proving the negligence caused the plaintiff's injury is a considerably difficult task, compounded by two factors highlighted by Grubb (see Grubb in Markesinis and Deakin (1999), p 289):

(a) 'the aetiology of disease and injury' may be difficult to establish even for experts;

(b) since patients are ill, and the doctor's negligence will usually relate to a failure to cure or alleviate their existing condition, the court is required to ask the hypothetical question: 'what would have happened if there had been no negligence?'

Differences of medical opinion

Medical opinion may be divided on whether the defendant's conduct accorded with medical principle as was illustrated in *Maynard v West Midlands RHA* [1984] 1 WLR 634 and *Ashcroft v Mersey RHA* [1983] 2 All ER 245.

Judge must resolve experts' difference of opinion

What if the experts who are called by either side of the case (for the plaintiff and defendant) radically disagree with each other on crucial points which have a significant bearing on issues of causation in a medical case? In *Sewell v Electrolux Ltd* (1997) *The Times*, 7 November, the Court of Appeal (Hutchison and Thorpe LJJ), in a judgment handed down on 8 October 1997, but reported a month later, decided that a judge hearing a claim for damages for personal injury from an accident at work where the sole issue turned on conflicting expert medical opinion, had to address and resolve that conflict. He could not decide the case without making findings of fact or giving proper reasons, but by relying on the burden of proof. In the case itself, whose facts are not relevant to our present discussion, Hutchison LJ opined that 'There was a clear cut and irreconcilable difference of opinion between the two consultant ... surgeons which it had been for the recorder to resolve'. This approach was followed in the subsequent House of Lords' case of *Bolitho v City of Hackney* (1997) decided a month later (see [1998] AC 232).

Causation and multiple causes

There may also be cases where the injury might have been the result of multiple causes. The question the court would ask here would be: was the defendant's breach of duty a *necessary element* in the chain of causation? For example, did the defendant's conduct expose the plaintiff to an added risk of harm?

In the Scottish case of *McGhee v National Coal Board* [1972] 3 All ER 1008, which went to the House of Lords, an employee of the defendant brought an action alleging that his dermatitis had come about due to the coal board's failure to provide him with proper washing facilities. This meant that he had to cycle home with the brick dust, to which his work unavoidably exposed him, still caked to his skin. Here, there was no doubt that brick dust caused the plaintiff's injury. The difficulty lay in determining whether the 'guilty' dust, which continued to stick to the plaintiff on his journey home, had played any causative role.

The Law Lords asserted that, in this type of case, it was open to a court simply to infer, as a question of fact, that the defendant's breach had materially contributed to the injury.

Lord Wilberforce suggested that, once the plaintiff has shown that the defendant's breach of duty created a risk of harm, the burden of proving that it did not materialise and materially contribute to the harm passed to the defendant. The House of Lords held that, if the defendant's conduct materially contributed to the harm suffered, the court might find that negligence has been proved.

McGhee was approved in *Clark v MacLennan* [1983] 1 All ER 416, in which it was held that, where there was a precaution which could have been taken to avoid the precise injury which occurred, the defendant then had to prove that his failure to take his precaution did not cause the plaintiff's injury.

The Wilsher *case (1988)*

In *Wilsher v Essex AHA* [1988] 1 All ER 871, the difficulty for the plaintiff was that there were five possible causes for the condition with which he was afflicted.

In this case, the plaintiff baby was born prematurely, and found to be suffering from retrolental fibroplasia (RLF), rendering him virtually blind, following treatment in the defendant's post-natal unit. Owing to a breach of duty by hospital staff, the baby had been over-saturated with oxygen in the first weeks of his life. While the child was in the special care baby unit, an inexperienced junior doctor undertook to monitor the oxygen level in the baby's bloodstream. In doing so, he inserted a catheter into a vein rather than an artery by mistake. The senior registrar failed to notice the junior doctor's mistake and, several hours later, when replacing the catheter, made the same mistake himself. However, whilst this might, according to some of the evidence, have caused or contributed to the RLF, there were four other natural conditions, all of which had afflicted the baby, and which equally have had the same effect. There was a low probability that the baby would survive.

The majority of the Court of Appeal found for the plaintiff on causation on the basis of Lord Wilberforce's speech in *McGhee*. The defendant appealed.

Lord Bridge opined that he found no support in any of the speeches in *McGhee* for the view that the burden of proof of causation is reversed and regarded Lord Wilberforce's reasoning as expressing a minority view. The conclusion he drew from *McGhee* is that it laid down 'no new principle of law whatever'. On the contrary, it affirmed the principle that the onus of proving causation lies on the plaintiff. He approved Sir Nicholas Browne-Wilkinson VC's views in the Court of Appeal in the instant case, and affirmed that the occurrence of RLF following a failure to take a necessary precaution to prevent excess oxygen causing RLF provides no evidence and raises no presumption that it was excess oxygen rather than one or more of the four other possible agents which caused or contributed to RLF in this case. He distinguished this from *McGhee*, where there was only one possible candidate (brick dust) which could have caused the dermatitis, and the failure to take a precaution against brick dust causing dermatitis was followed by dermatitis caused by brick dust. A failure to take preventive measures against one of five possible causes is no evidence as to which of those five caused the injury.

Hence, the Law Lords found for the defendant as the plaintiff was unable to show that the defendant's breach of duty had played a causative role in his injury, since it was only one of five possible causes.

Res ipsa loquitur and the establishment of negligence

In some cases, the doctrine, rule or maxim of *res ipsa loquitur* (the thing speaks for itself) has been applied. This doctrine applies in cases where the only inference on the evidence before the court was that there was no other possible explanation for the plaintiff's injury or loss except through the negligence of the defendant (see, for example, *Clark v MacLennan* [1983] 1 All ER 416). An example is where the plaintiff went into hospital to be cured of two stiff fingers and emerged with four stiff fingers, with no plausible explanation being made, as in *Cassidy v Ministry of Health* [1951] 2 KB 343. Again, if there are multiple possible causes of an injury, for example, the plaintiff could plead *res ipsa loquitur* – alleging that the injury could not have happened but for negligence and, therefore, places the onus on the doctor to prove otherwise.

The doctrine has been appropriately invoked if the facts of the case strongly suggest that there is at least an inference of negligence on the defendant's part. The essentials of the doctrine are:

(a) there is no evidence as to how the accident occurred;

(b) the injury has to be of a kind that does not normally happen in the circumstances unless there was negligence;

(c) the defendant is proven to have been in control of or linked to the situation either personally or vicariously.

The burden of proving the negligence remains throughout on the plaintiff and the doctrine may not usually apply in medical negligence cases because of the uncertainties of medical treatment; the judge still has to decide, on a balance of probabilities, in a civil case, whether the defendant was negligent and whether his negligence caused the plaintiff's injury. An illustrative situation is where a patient has been admitted to hospital for treatment of an injured ankle and has left with an amputated leg. The plaintiff is unable to explain what had happened, and neither can the defendant doctor, and the plaintiff has identified the doctor whose negligence must have caused the injury (see *MacDonald v York County Hospital Corporation* [1972] 28 DLR (3d) 521). A recent development is that certain judges might not like the use of the Latin label in cases where the doctrine might be appropriate.

A 21st century negligence case on res ipsa loquitur – Fryer v Pearson *(2000)*

In April 2000, the Court of Appeal case of *Fryer v Pearson and Another* (2000) *The Times*, 4 April, was decided wherein an appeal judge declared that 'people should stop using maxims or doctrines dressed up in Latin, such as *res ipsa loquitur*, which are not readily comprehensible to those for whose benefit they are supposed to exist' (*per* May LJ). The case itself involved an action for damages in negligence, but was not a medical relationship case as such. The facts were that the plaintiff, a gas fitter, was injured while working at the defendant's house. As he knelt on the floor, the point of a sewing needle concealed in the deep pile carpet entered and broke off in his knee, causing him to become so disabled as to be no longer able to work. The trial judge held that the doctrine *res ipsa loquitur* did not apply in the circumstances, and gave judgment for the defendant. Waller LJ said that negligence could be established against the defendants if the only proper inference to be drawn from the evidence was that they had permitted the needle to remain in the carpet, knowing it to be there. On the facts of the case, the court found that no such inference could be drawn and the trial judge correctly ascribed the plaintiff's injury to 'an unfortunate but freak accident'. The plaintiff's appeal was, therefore, unanimously dismissed (May and Roch LJJ concurring with Waller LJ).

The question arises as to whether this case will now set a precedent for cases where there is a close doctor-patient relationship and a duty of care is owed. For instance, if a needle is left in a patient's stomach which could only have got there by being left there in the course of a medical operation or procedure, there seems little doubt that a court, provided the facts were admitted, would conclude that *res ipsa loquitur* applied, although after this case, perhaps the only difference will be that there will be less usage of the term if not of the principle.

The *Bolitho* case – the 'new' *Bolam* or merely a modern 'gloss'?

Towards the end of the 20th century, some 40 years after its pronouncement, some doubt has been cast on the dominance of the so called *Bolam* test by the House of Lords' decision of *Bolitho v City and Hackney HA* [1997] 4 All ER 771; [1998] AC 232.

Bolitho (Administratrix of the Estate of Bolitho (Deceased) v City and Hackney HA [1997] 4 All ER 771; [1998] Lloyd's Rep Med 26

Facts

In December 1983, the plaintiff, Patrick Bolitho, then aged two, underwent an operation to correct a condition of patent ductus arteriosis. On 11 January 1984, he was admitted to St Bartholomew's Hospital suffering from acute croup. The following morning his condition had deteriorated and he was having difficulty in breathing. On 13 January, he appeared to be cyanosed, although he recovered quickly and was discharged on 15 January. The next night, Patrick was restless and was readmitted to hospital the next day. His respiration rate was high, and there was recession in his breathing, which increased during the evening. The following morning he was much better, although he still had reduced air entry on one side. The consultant examined him, but apparently there was nothing in his condition that attracted the consultant's attention.

His breathing then suddenly deteriorated at 12.40 pm and a nurse summoned the paediatric registrar, Dr Horn. The registrar said she would attend as soon as possible, but did not do so, apparently because she was still on afternoon clinic. She had asked her senior houseman to come in her place but she did not do so because her 'bleeper' was not working. Patrick recovered, quickly regaining his colour and energy. At 2.00 pm, Patrick suffered a second episode of breathing difficulties. The doctor was again summoned and failed to attend. Patrick recovered briefly. Unfortunately, at

2.30 pm, he collapsed, his respiratory system failed and he suffered a cardiac arrest resulting in severe brain damage.

Patrick subsequently died and his mother continued proceedings for medical negligence as administratrix of his estate. The essence of the claim was whether the defendant was responsible for the brain damage caused by the cardiac arrest.

The hospital admitted negligence on the part of the registrar, Dr Horn, in failing to attend Patrick or arrange for a suitable deputy to examine the child. It was common ground that intubation so as to provide an airway for oxygen would have ensured that respiratory failure did not lead to cardiac arrest.

The hospital denied liability on the grounds that, even had she attended Patrick, Dr Horn would not have intubated him. To prevent the cardiac arrest which caused his brain damage, Patrick would have to have been intubated prior to 2 pm.

The trial judge accepted Dr Horn's evidence that she would not have intubated Patrick before 2.30 pm.

The plaintiff's case, supported by the opinion of five doctors called on their behalf, was that after the first episode suffered by Patrick, and certainly after the second, he *should* have been intubated.

The plaintiff's five medical experts all testified that the evidence of respiratory distress was such that a respiratory collapse should have been contemplated and Patrick should have been intubated immediately to prevent such a tragedy. The defendants' three medical expert witnesses contended that the evidence suggested that, apart from the two acute episodes of breathing problems, Patrick seemed quite well, and intubation itself was not a risk free process in such a young child. A responsible doctor would not have intubated before 2.30 pm. The trial judge found that the views of the two leading experts, Dr Heaf for the plaintiff and Dr Dinwiddie for the defendants, were diametrically opposed. Both represented a responsible body of professional opinion, espoused by distinguished and truthful experts.

The trial judge therefore found, applying the *Bolam* test, that if Dr Horn had attended and not intubated, she would have demonstrated a proper level of skill and competence according to the standard represented by Dr Dinwiddie's views and that it had not been proved that the admitted breach of duty by the defendants had caused the injury which occurred to Patrick. He placed considerable weight on Lord Scarman's speech in *Maynard's* case, wherein he had emphasised that a judge's preference for one body of distinguished professional opinion to another is not sufficient to establish negligence in a practitioner whose actions have received the seal of approval of those whose opinions were not preferred.

The Court of Appeal upheld the first instance judgment and the plaintiff appealed to the House of Lords.

The House of Lords upheld the decision of the judge and the Court of Appeal that, despite the doctor's negligence in not attending or arranging for a suitable deputy to attend, the claim failed for want of causation. The only substantive speech was by Lord Browne-Wilkinson.

The two issues for the Law Lords to consider were:

(a) did the *Bolam* test have any application in deciding questions of causation; and

(b) does the *Bolam* test require a judge to accept the views of one truthful body of expert professionals?

The Bolam *test and causation*

On this issue, the House of Lords opined that this really involved the determination of two questions, namely: (a) 'what would have happened but for the defendant's negligence?' or in this case: 'what would the doctors have done if they had attended?'; and (b) 'if the doctor(s) would not have intubated, would that have been negligent?'

The Law Lords' view was that the *Bolam* test has no part to play in the first question – on causation – because the factual inquiry is in the realms of hypothesis and the question 'what would have happened?' does not answer the first question of causation. However, the *Bolam* test is central to the second question, 'what would the competent doctor have done?'. To prove her case, the plaintiff would have had to prove that the continuing exercise of proper care would have resulted in intubation.

The Bolam *test and the views of one body of professionals*

Here, Lord Browne-Wilkinson (with whom his brethren agreed) rejected the view that the court is not bound to hold that a defendant doctor escapes liability for negligent treatment or diagnosis just because he leads evidence from a body of experts who are genuinely of the opinion that the defendant's treatment or diagnosis accorded with sound medical practice. Referring to McNair J's opinion in *Bolam*, he said that there it was stated that the practice had to be endorsed as proper by a '*responsible* body of medical men' and had to be a standard of practice recognised as proper by a competent *reasonable* body of opinion'.

Lord Scarman, in *Sidaway*, he said, also referred to a 'respectable' body of professional opinion.

Then, in a crucial passage, he continued ([1997] 4 All ER 771, p 778):

> The use of these adjectives – responsible, reasonable and respectable – all show that the court has to be satisfied that the exponents of the body of opinion relied on can demonstrate that such opinion has *a logical basis*. In particular, in

> cases involving, as they so often do, the weighing of risks against benefits, the judge before accepting a body of opinion as being responsible, reasonable or respectable, will need to be satisfied that, in forming their views, the experts have directed their minds to the question of comparative risks and benefits and have reached a defensible conclusion on the matter. [Emphasis added.]

In support of these views, his Lordship referred to *Hucks v Cole* and the *Edward Wong* case.

In *Hucks v Cole*, decided in 1968, but only reported in 1993 ([1993] 4 Med LR 393), a doctor failed to treat with penicillin a patient who was suffering from septic places on her skin though he knew them to contain organisms capable of leading to puerperal fever. A number of distinguished doctors gave evidence that they would not, in the circumstances, have treated with penicillin. The Court of Appeal found the defendant to have been negligent. Sachs LJ stressed the importance of current professional knowledge to be taken into account, and the fact that other practitioners might have done the same thing as the defendant practitioner is a very weighty matter, but it is not conclusive. 'The court must be vigilant to see whether the reasons given for putting a patient at risk are valid in the light of any well known advance in medical knowledge, or whether they stem from a residual adherence from a residual adherence to out-of-date ideas ...'

Again, in the Privy Council case, *Edward Wong Finance Co Ltd v Johnson Stokes and Master (A Firm)* [1984] AC 296; [1984] 2 WLR 1, which was not a medical case, the defendant's solicitors had conducted the completion of a mortgage transaction in 'Hong Kong style' rather than in the old fashioned English style. Completion in Hong Kong style provides for money to be paid over against an undertaking by the solicitors for the borrowers subsequently to hand over the executed documents. This practice opened the gateway through which a dishonest solicitor for the borrower absconded with the loan money without providing the security documents for such loan. The Privy Council held that, even though completion in Hong Kong style was almost universally adopted in Hong Kong and was therefore in accordance with a body of professional opinion there, the defendant's solicitors were liable for negligence because there was an obvious risk which could have been guarded against. Thus, the body of professional opinion, 'though almost universally held, was not reasonable or respectable'.

His Lordship therefore pointed out that these decisions demonstrated that, in cases of diagnosis and treatment, there are cases where, despite a body of professional opinion sanctioning the defendant's conduct, the defendant can properly be held liable for negligence. However, he also stated (p 779) that, in the 'vast majority of cases', the fact that distinguished experts hold a particular opinion will demonstrate the reasonableness of that opinion. However, he added, 'if in a rare case, it can be demonstrated that the professional opinion is not capable of withstanding logical analysis, the judge is entitled to hold that the body of opinion is not reasonable or responsible'.

His Lordship then declared: '... it will very seldom be right for a judge to reach the conclusion that views genuinely held by a competent medical expert are unreasonable ... It is only where a judge can be satisfied that the body of expert opinion cannot be logically supported at all that such opinion will not provide the bench mark by reference to which the defendant's conduct falls to be assessed.'

On the facts before him, this was not one of those rare cases and there was no basis for dismissing the defendant's expert evidence, particularly that of Dr Dinwiddie, as illogical. Intubation was not a routine, risk free procedure, and would be particularly difficult for children who would remove the tube unless sedated. There appeared to be good reasons for not intubating.

The plaintiff's appeal was dismissed.

Comment on Bolitho

In *Joyce v Merton, Sutton and Wandsworth HA* [1996] 7 Med LR 1, the Court of Appeal had stated that they had the authority to scrutinise expert evidence to determine whether that evidence represented a responsible judgment of good practice. But neither this case, nor *Hucks v Cole* (possibly because it was not reported at the time, although its existence was known), led to a change in the approach to medical malpractice litigation. In *Marriott v West Midlands HA* [1999] Lloyd's Rep Med 23, a case decided by the Court of Appeal after the *Bolitho* case, the judges concluded that the expert opinion advanced in the doctor's favour was not defensible. Hence, the influence of *Bolitho* may already be said to be manifesting itself. However, it is probably somewhat premature, in the absence of more post-*Bolitho* case law, to assess its longer term impact.

Commentators are generally cautious about its short term impact. Brazier and Miola (2000) say *Bolitho* must not be 'oversold', stressing the 'rare' cases where a court might not agree that the defendant doctor's support of expert opinion was justifiable or logical or reasonable in the given circumstances. They also point out that *Bolitho* seeks no more than to restore *Bolam* to its original limits, which the full judgment of McNair J reveals (see Brazier and Miola (2000), p 98). McNair J made it clear, they stress, that negligence is not proven merely because a doctor conforms to one school of thought and practice rather than another and adds: '... that does not mean that a medical man can obstinately and pig-headedly carry on with some old technique if it has proved contrary to what is really substantially the whole of informed medical opinion.'

Teff (1998) argues that '*Bolitho* is noticeably cryptic as to when expert professional opinion might be discounted. Lord Browne-Wilkinson appears somewhat reluctant to engage in the *Bolam* debate'. Teff criticises Lord Browne-Wilkinson's apparent approval of Dillon LJ's application, in *Bolitho*, of the administrative law 'irrationality test', that the reasons for a group of doctors carrying out a particular practice would only fail to stand up to analysis where the court was 'clearly satisfied that the views of that group of doctors were *Wednesbury* unreasonable'. He finds the use of the word 'logic' as the measure of reasonableness curious, 'because judgments of what is reasonable must rest on normative appraisal rather than on conclusions entailed by deductive reasoning'. However, the more 'measured approach' in *Bolitho* 'should reduce the risk of legitimating the lowest common denominator of accepted practice', but submits that it is unclear whether even abolishing *Bolam* altogether would substantially alter outcomes. Causation would continue to play a 'decisive role' in many cases, and the various considerations which have prompted judicial reluctance to set standards for doctors could still be accommodated within the open-textured and elusive nature of current negligence criteria. On a comparative note, Teff cites the Australian case of *Lowns v Woods* [1996] Aust Torts Reports 81, where despite the New South Wales appeal court interpreting *Rogers v Whitaker* as rejecting *Bolam* in matters of diagnosis, treatment and disclosure, nevertheless conceded that, so long as there was conformity to ordinary medical practice in the relevant specialty, the patient continues to bear a heavy forensic burden to disprove reasonable care in the circumstances (Teff (1998), pp 481–82).

Fuller disclosure required – the influence of *Bolitho*?

In the aftermath of the *Bolitho* case, the courts appear to be moving away from the *Bolam* approach towards insisting that doctors give fuller consideration to the autonomy of the patient. This was the approach which appeared to be taken in the *Pearce* case (1999).

The Pearce *case (*Pearce v United Bristol Healthcare NHS Trust*) [1999] Med LR 60*

In this case, Mrs Pearce, the mother of five children, was pregnant. The baby was due on 13 November 1991. On 27 November, Mrs Pearce saw her consultant, an employee of the defendant. She was very concerned that she was 14 days overdue and requested that the baby be induced or delivered by Caesarean section. Having examined her, the consultant explained the risk of inducing labour and that the recovery from a Caesarean section was slower. He advised her that she should proceed to a natural delivery. Mrs Pearce accepted his advice. On 4 December, Mrs Pearce was admitted to hospital and gave birth to a stillborn baby. Mrs Pearce and her husband sued the defendant for damages in negligence. The trial judge dismissed their claim.

On appeal, the plaintiffs argued that the consultant should have advised Mrs Pearce of the increased risk of the baby being stillborn if delivery was delayed beyond 27 November and that, had she known of the risk, she would have insisted on delivery by Caesarean section.

The Court of Appeal (Lord Woolf MR, Roch and Mummery LJJ) dismissed the appeal and held:

(a) In determining what information to provide a patient, a doctor has to have regard to all the relevant circumstances, including the patient's ability to comprehend the information and the physical and emotional state of the patient. Normally, it is a doctor's legal duty to advise a patient of any significant risks which may affect the judgment of a reasonable patient in making a treatment decision (*Sidaway v Governors of the Bethlem Royal Hospital* [1985] 1 AC 871 and *Bolitho v City and Hackney HA* [1997] 4 All ER 771).

(b) The evidence established that the increased risk of stillbirth in delaying delivery of the baby after 27 November was very small, something like one to two in 1,000.

(c) The experts who gave evidence did not consider this risk to be a significant one. Particularly having regard to the first plaintiff's distressed state, this was not a proper case for the court to interfere with the clinical opinion of the expert medical man responsible for treating the patient.

(d) Even if the first plaintiff had been advised of the risk, the inference from the evidence was that she would still have agreed to a natural delivery.

Lord Woolf MR declared that, if a patient asks about a risk, it is the doctor's legal duty to give an honest answer.

Comment on the Pearce *case*

This is the first case which considers the effect of *Bolitho* on information cases. Grubb (1999) believes that the Court of Appeal's approach shows that there is now only *one* legal standard to be followed in *all* cases, whether they deal with treatment, diagnosis or disclosure of information. Based on a synthesis of both House of Lords' decisions (*Sidaway* and *Bolitho*), the Court of Appeal now appears to recognise that the medical profession does not have the prerogative to set the standard of disclosure. Lord Woolf MR seemed to rely on the speeches of the 'majority' in *Sidaway* (Lord Bridge, with whom Lord Keith agreed, and Lord Diplock) and the judgment of Lord Browne-Wilkinson in *Bolitho*. Somewhat surprisingly, even the approach of Lord Templeman in

Sidaway, described by Lord Woolf MR as 'not precisely that of the majority', was said by Lord Woolf MR to 'reflect the law and does not involve taking a different view from the majority'. Grubb (1999) calls this a rather 'creative' interpretation, since 'a composite view of the speeches in *Sidaway*' is problematic' (see, also, Kennedy (1991)).

The approach of the Court of Appeal to the standard of disclosure is to be found in the conclusion of Lord Woolf MR in *Pearce*, when he says: 'If there is a significant risk which would affect the judgment of a reasonable patient, then in the normal course it is the responsibility of a doctor to inform the patient of the significant risk, if the information is needed so that the patient can determine for him or herself as to what course he or she should adopt.'

Hence, the Court of Appeal has actually adopted an approach which is similar to the Australian High Court in *Rogers v Whitaker* (1992) (on which, see Chapter 16), where the court declared the need for a doctor's duty to include the disclosure of all 'material risks', namely, any risk which 'a reasonable person in the patient's position, if warned of the risk would be likely to attach significance to it'. The Australian High Court seemed to require disclosure of risks which the doctor ought reasonably to know would be significant to the 'particular patient'. This is not required by the *Pearce* approach. As Grubb observes, 'The Australian High Court thought it was rejecting *Bolam* while the Court of Appeal applied it, in its new variant form post-*Bolitho*' (Grubb (1999), p 63).

Pearce retains the 'reasonable doctor' test for breach of duty, which is not the North American approach. But the English Court of Appeal and Australian High Court now both appear to be using the same standard because both use the 'reasonable doctor' test and such a person would disclose 'what a reasonable patient would consider significant'. In effect, 'the courts retain overall responsibility for setting the standard of disclosure and it is to the needs of the 'reasonable patient' in the setting of the actual patient that the courts will look' (Grubb (1999)).

On the issue of when a risk would be considered 'significant', Lord Woolf MR does not really cast any light on this, but the implication of the approach and the ruling seems to be that, if the plaintiff asked about the risk, it would have been considered 'significant' and the doctor would have been required to give an honest answer. Grubb (1999), in his Comment on the *Pearce* case, points out that for a risk to require disclosure by a doctor, it merely needs to be one which a 'reasonable patient' would consider *relevant* to, but not necessarily determinative of, the ultimate decision of whether to consent to the operation. For the patient to establish a causal link between the non-disclosure and injury, the risk must be 'one which alone or in combination with other risks, would have led the patient to a different decision' (Grubb (1999), p 64). In *Pearce* itself, Lord Woolf MR thought that the 'very, very small additional risk' of stillbirth, somewhere between one and two in 1,000, was not 'significant', particularly bearing in mind the plaintiff's distressed condition. Consequently, this was not a case where it was proper for the court to interfere with the doctor's clinical judgment.

A further comment that may be made in response to this ruling is that, in practical day to day terms, *Pearce* does nothing to clarify the scope of the doctor's duty in any given case because the doctor will have to weigh all the relevant considerations, including the ability of the patient to comprehend the doctor's diagnosis and accompanying information. However, *Pearce* is significant in that it appears to have again put a gloss on *Bolam* and shifted the weight of responsibility to the *courts* to decide the standard of disclosure; but the clinical judgment of the doctor as to the extent of the disclosure, it is submitted, will not be easily overturned except in the most obvious case.

If they took a leaf out of the French law on medical negligence, the English courts would say that only for 'gross' acts of negligence, where there is blatant non-disclosure of facts which would have made a difference to the patient's ultimate decision whether to consent to the treatment or not, should liability be imposed. Alternatively, allowing for therapeutic privilege, and the fact that disclosure would have been 'harmful' to the plaintiff, perhaps full disclosure of *any* risks, which are 'serious' in that they might result in serious physical or mental or psychological impairment, should be given in *every* case, whenever there is a risk involved in a particular operation. This might not be a feasible option in the context of the time given to appointments to GP consultations in most surgeries and even consultations with specialists, apart from being few and far between (because of the waiting lists), are usually limited in duration. In practical terms, perhaps patients could be encouraged to ask questions if there is any doubt in their minds before consenting to any operation or procedure.

After *Pearce*, the case of *Carver v Hammersmith and Queen Charlotte's Special HA* was decided on 25 February 2000. Here, the health authority was held liable in negligence for the failure of the doctor to explain that the 'Bart's test' for Down's syndrome was not a diagnostic test, unlike amniocentesis, but was only a screening test, which could not detect one in three Down's syndrome fetuses.

Standard of care and negligence in cervical smear test

Penney and Others v East Kent HA (1999)

In *Penney and Others v East Kent HA* (1999) *The Times*, 25 November (see, also, [1999] Med LR 327), the Court of Appeal (Lord Woolf MR, May and Hale LJJ) held that, although the national cervical screening programme could not be expected to identify all abnormal smear tests, a screener who failed to realise that a test contained obvious abnormalities and should be referred for further examination was negligent. Accordingly, a judge was entitled to conclude that a test contained obvious abnormalities despite the fact that there was conflicting expert evidence on that issue.

Facts

The facts of the case were that actions arose out of cervical smears taken from the claimants (Mrs Penney, Mrs Palmer and Mrs Cannon) in 1989, 1990 and 1992 as part of the national cervical screening programme, which had been reported by the primary screeners as being negative. Each of the claimants had gone to develop invasive adenocarcinoma of the cervix. In the lower court, the agreed experts' report had made it clear that cervical screening did not provide a fault-proof test. Even if the manner in which the test was taken and interpreted was exemplary, not all cases of cervical pre-cancer or invasive cancer would be detected. That was especially true of adenocarcinoma, which was more difficult to detect. If screeners detected or suspected that a smear was abnormal, they were required to pass it to a supervisory checker.

National standards published in 1996 indicated that primary screening should detect 85 to 95% of abnormal smears. More recently introduced methods of quality control were intended to reduce false negative reports to 5% or less.

Court of Appeal judgment

The Appeal Court (*per* Lord Woolf MR, who gave the judgment of the court) endorsed the view of the trial judge, who had said that the standard to be applied was that of a reasonably competent screener exercising reasonable care at the time when the screening took place, and he had referred to *Bolam v Friern Hospital Management Committee* [1957] 1 WLR 582; *Maynard v West Midlands Regional HA* [1984] 1 WLR 634, p 638; *Bolitho v City and Hackney HA* [1998] AC 232, p 242; and *Hunter v Hanley* 1955 SLT 213). In this case, the screeners had been exercising skill and judgment in determining what report they should make and, in that respect, the *Bolam* test was generally applicable. However, the fact that two sets of competent experts genuinely held differing opinions as to whether or not, at the relevant date, the screeners could without being negligent have diagnosed the smears as negative did not necessarily provide the solution to the dispute or liability.

There was the qualification identified in *Bolitho* (p 242) that, 'in cases involving ... the weighing of risks against the benefits, the judge ... will need to be satisfied that, in forming their views, the experts have directed their minds to the question of comparative risks and benefits and have reached a defensible conclusion in the matter'. The *Bolam* test had *no* application where what the judge was required to do was to make findings of fact, even where those findings of fact were the subject of conflicting expert evidence.

There were three questions which the judge had been required to answer:

(a) What was to be seen on the slides?

(b) At the relevant time, could a screener exercising reasonable care fail to see what was on the slides?

(c) Could a reasonably competent screener, aware of what a screener exercising reasonable care would observe on the slides, treat the slides as negative?

Since the experts could not agree, the judge had had the unenviable task of deciding as a matter of fact which of the experts were correct as to what the slides showed. The judge then had to answer the second and third question in order to decide whether the screener had been in breach of duty in giving a negative report. Whether the screener was in breach of duty would depend on the training and the amount of knowledge a screener should have had in order properly to perform his or her task at that time and how easy it was to discern what the judge found was on the slide. In relation to Mrs Penney's slide, for example, the judge had concluded that her slide was difficult to interpret even by a consultant pathologist, but the abnormality was there to be seen. If one applied the 'absolute confidence' test, it had to be classified at least as borderline. The health authority had concluded that that reasoning amounted to no more than saying that, if a slide contained features which might be abnormal, then a negative classification should not be given. In relation to Mrs Penney's slide, the court did not accept this criticism. The judge had been basing himself on the difficulty of interpreting that particular slide, and his reasoning was consistent with the statistics which showed that a false negative rate would not be less than 5–15%.

The phrase 'absolute confidence' was no more than shorthand for the approach which all the experts had endorsed. Their report stated that 'The primary screener is encouraged to refer to the checker and pathologist if in any doubt ...'.

The critical question was whether the judge had been entitled to conclude that a reasonably competent cytoscreener would at least have been aware that Mrs Penney's slide was difficult to interpret.

On the judge's findings of fact, that was what the cytoscreener *should* have concluded. There were abnormalities to be seen on the slide, and the reasonably competent cytoscreener could not with confidence have concluded that they were not pre-cancerous. The cytoscreener should then have referred the slide for further examination. The cytoscreener did not do that, either because of lack of training or because of the way in which the slide was examined.

The appeal court held that the judge was entitled to say that he preferred the evidence of the claimant's experts that there were abnormalities on Mrs

Penney's slide, which were there to be seen. Applying the absolute confidence test to those abnormalities, he was entitled to come to that conclusion.

The court also said the judge was entitled to say that the slides relating to Mrs Cannon and Mrs Palmer showed clear abnormalities.

The appeal court held that, applying the *Bolam* test, no reasonably competent screener could report such slides as negative since, adopting the test proposed in the expert evidence, this would only be appropriate where the screener was 'absolutely confident' that the slide fell within the normal range. The judge had been correct to conclude that the evidence of the defendants' experts to the contrary could not stand up to 'logical' analysis since it was inconsistent with the 'absolute confidence' test that they accepted.

Lord Woolf MR also stated that the judge had been wrong to state that the *Bolam* test was inapplicable to the issue of whether the cytoscreeners conduct was 'excusable'.

The Court of Appeal further emphasised:

(a) The judgment only related to the slides which were the subject of the claims. It was crucial that the judge had decided that they contained obvious abnormalities, which meant that their assessment as negative was negligent.

(b) If the abnormalities observable on the slides had been different, the judge's decision could have been different. The case did not decide that negligence by a cytoscreener could be established by showing that someone who had a slide labelled negative unfortunately developed cervical cancer. It was not in dispute that cervical cancer could develop, even though a relatively recent slide had been labelled negative.

(c) The judge had not rejected the approach of the authority's experts. He had found that, because of the observable abnormalities on the slides, they should not have been labelled negative in order to comply with the absolute confidence approach that those experts supported.

Accordingly, the court dismissed the appeal of the defendant authority and upheld the lower court judgment, finding the defendant liable to the plaintiffs in respect of the negligent assessment of their cervical smear tests.

MEDICAL LITIGATION IN THE UK

Audit Commission report

A report by the Audit Commission, from Sir John Bourn, Comptroller and Auditor General, published in April 2000, hit the headlines in the national media when it indicated that much of the recent cash injection into the NHS will be wiped out by defending a spate of litigation against the NHS for medical negligence claims and the cost of paying damages. The report asserts that thousands of patients die or are seriously injured every year as a result of medical errors and that one in every 14 patients suffers an adverse event such as diagnostic error. It states that, in the year 1999–2000, there has been an estimated 36% increase in the cost of outstanding clinical negligence claims. But the estimate is a 'worst case scenario' based on figures suggested by the bodies responsible for dealing with the defence of claims, and thus the final figures may be lower than those suggested. However, not just the number of claims has increased, but also the amount paid in damages, especially in cases involving accident victims who require a substantial amount of future care (see the House of Lords' case of *Wells v Wells* [1999] 1 AC 345). The *Heil v Rankin* case ([2000] Lloyd's Rep Med 203) further suggests that awards of general damages will increase. In addition, there are apparently many claims awaiting settlement on the basis of the outcome of that decision (see (2000) 7 Medical Law Monitor 1, on which this section is based).

CONCLUDING COMMENTS ON MEDICAL NEGLIGENCE IN ENGLISH LAW

Professor Margaret Brazier and Jose Miola (2000) contend that:

> *Bolitho*, recent case law on informed consent, the establishment of the National Institute of Clinical Excellence and the Law Commission's proposals relating to mentally incapacitated patients are just some of the factors which ... will in many cases ensure that the [English] courts no longer blindly accept assertions of good medical practice, but evaluate that practice. Substance will be given to patients' interests in welfare and autonomy. However, such developments should not cause doctors or other health professionals to fear for their professional integrity or independence. Returning the *Bolam* test to its proper limits and appropriate context will be beneficial, rather than detrimental, to medicine and medical litigation. The revolution, if it can be so styled, will be a velvet revolution, not a bloodbath.

How justified is this view? Certainly, the *Bolitho* case itself does not represent a ringing endorsement of the 'de-Bolamisation' of medical law, but it appears to have restored it to its original sphere of applicability rather than being regarded as the all-encompassing test for all situations.

It is arguable that *Bolitho* merely opened the door to some questioning of the basis of the doctor's case that a responsible body of medical opinion would support his actions and that the court in *Bolam* itself had said this over 40 years ago. The other query that may be posed is: what is 'logical' in the context of proposed treatment? It has been argued that the true impetus for reform of the law in this area lies in the increasing use of guidelines and protocols in medicine (see Harpwood (1998), p 184) and that Bolamisation will be diluted by the establishment of the National Institute of Clinical Excellence (NICE), and the frequent guidelines issued by the Royal College of Medicine which reflect good practice and are regularly updated (Brazier and Miola (2000), p 99).

Recent guidelines include guidelines on treatment of women who have had Caesarean sections, treatment of diabetes, epilepsy, asthma and heart disease. Deviation from the plethora of guidelines may amount to *prima facie* evidence of negligence and could have the effect of shifting the burden of proof onto the defendant who would then have to produce good reasons for the deviation (see the Introduction to this book for more discussion on Guidelines).

Despite *Bolitho*, there seems little doubt that, except for the few cases that may raise unique or novel points of law and which get to the appeal courts, which is rare in itself, or to the House of Lords, which is even more unusual, *Bolam* or some variation thereof will continue to be the main guiding principle in English courts, although *Bolitho* suggests that appeal courts will be more prepared to question a particular medical procedure, practice, act or omission which results in injury if it appears it was not one that reflects current practice, is unreasonable in the given circumstances or is simply out of date. The problem of establishing causation, of course, might prove the most difficult hurdle to overcome. One alternative, suggested around 30 years ago by the Pearson Committee, is to introduce no-fault compensation, but even New Zealand, which did so with great enthusiasm, has had to curtail its scheme in the light of the problems it subsequently encountered (see Chapter 16).

SELECTIVE BIBLIOGRAPHY

Brazier, M and Miola, J, 'Bye-bye *Bolam*: a medical litigation revolution?' (2000) 8 Med L Rev 85

Brazier, M, *Medicine, Patients and the Law*, 1992, Penguin, Chapters 6, 7, 9 and 10

Davies, M, *Textbook on Medical Law*, 2nd edn, 1998, Blackstone, Chapters 3 and 4

Dugdale, A and Stanton, K, *Professional Negligence*, 3rd edn, 1998, Butterworths

Foster, C, 'Surgeons sideline *Sidaway*' (1998) 142 SJ 228

Grubb, A, in Markesinis, BS and Deakin, SF (eds), *Tort Law*, 1999, Clarendon, pp 272–96

Harpwood, V, 'Medical negligence: a chink in the armour of the *Bolam* test?' (1998) 64 Medico-legal Jo 179

Howie, RBM, 'The standard of care in medical negligence' [1983] JR 193

Jones, MA, *Medical Negligence*, 1996, Sweet & Maxwell

Jones, MA, 'Arbitration for medical claims in the NHS' [1992] 8 Professional Negligence 142

Kennedy, I, 'Patients, doctors and human rights', in Blackburn, R and Taylor, J (eds), *Human Rights for the 1990s*, 1991, Mansell

Kennedy, I and Grubb, A (eds), *Principles of Medical Law*, 1998, OUP, Chapters 5 and 6

Keown, J, 'Doctor knows best?: the rise and rise of "the *Bolam* test"' [1995] Singapore Jo of Legal Studies 342

Markesinis, BS, 'Litigation mania in England, Germany and the USA: are we so very different?' [1990] CLJ 233

Markesinis, BS and Deakin, SF, *Tort Law*, 1999, Clarendon

Mason, JK and McCall Smith, RA, *Law and Medical Ethics*, 5th edn, 1999, Butterworths, Chapter 9

McHale, J and Fox, M, *Health Care Law Cases and Materials*, Sweet & Maxwell, Chapter 3

McNorrie, McK K, 'Medical negligence: who sets the standard?' (1985) 11 JME 135

Montgomery, J, *Healthcare Law*, 1997, OUP, Chapter 7

Phillips, AF, *Medical Negligence Law: Seeking a Balance*, 1997, Dartmouth

Puxon, M, 'Comment' [1998] Lloyd's Rep Med 35

Scarman (Lord), 'Law and medical practice', in Byrne, P (ed), *Medicine in Contemporary Society*, 1987, OUP

Scott, W, '*Bolam* and *Bolitho*: a new standard of care for doctors?' (1998) 148 NLJ 64

Stauch, M and Wheat, K, with Tingle, J, *Sourcebook on Medical Law*, 1998, Cavendish Publishing, Chapter 6

Symmons, C, 'Developments in Irish medical negligence law in the past ten years: signs of divergence from UK case law?' (1994) 10 Professional Negligence 134

Teff, H, 'The standard of care in medical negligence – moving on from *Bolam*?' (1998) 18 OJLS 473

CHAPTER 8

DONATION AND TRANSPLANTATION OF HUMAN ORGANS

INTRODUCTION

Organ transplantation is the medical procedure whereby living tissue from a human body is removed from that body and transferred to another part of that body or to another person. An example of transferring tissue from one part of the body to another is a skin graft. Where the transfer is from one person to another, the one supplying the tissue is the donor and the one receiving it is the recipient. The intention behind transplantation is to replace a tissue that is no longer able to fulfil its original function efficiently as a result of disease or injury, with one that will. Kidneys, livers, hearts, lungs, pancreas and bone marrow are the kinds of organs and tissues which may all now be transplanted, although there is no guarantee of success. Thus, whole organs like the heart, or cells as in bone marrow may be transplanted. Kidney transplants may be undertaken when both kidneys have ceased to function; this would be as an alternative to dialysis. Liver transplants are performed if there is liver failure, since there is no treatment like dialysis which can take over the liver's function. Liver transplants are not usually performed when there is liver cancer, because the cancer tends to come back to affect the new liver. However, merely transplanting small parts of the liver have proved more successful, particularly for young children and babies. Heart transplants might be performed for people whose hearts are so diseased that they cannot lead a normal life. These people might have symptoms that might not be controllable by surgery or medicines, may well be home-bound and breathless even when at rest. Lung transplants are performed when the person is suffering from cystic fibrosis or emphysema. Such transplants are far less common, because there is a shortage of suitable organs. Usually only one lung needs to be transplanted to enable normality to be restored. If severe lung disease also affects the heart, lung transplantation might be combined with heart transplantation; this is called 'heart-lung transplantation'. The success of transplants over the last two decades has been far more successful than could have been imagined and today, it is the shortage of organs that poses the major problem. This chapter has as its main focus a review of the law and ethics relating to the donation and transplantation of human organs in Britain; it also discusses some recent developments and national guidelines issued in the wake of these developments.

BACKGROUND TO ORGAN TRANSPLANTATION

Historically, the first corneal graft which took place more than a century ago was probably the first example of an organ transplant and in the early years, a shortage of organs could not have been seen as a barrier to progress. In Britain, and, indeed in most of the developed world, there is a shortage of organs for transplantation and the situation appears to be worsening. According to a British Medical Journal article, something like 1,000 patients on waiting lists die each year. The figure worsens each year, but the number of organs available for transplant remains constant. At the end of March 2000, 5,354 people were on the active national transplant list in the UK, but it is widely acknowledged that waiting list numbers do not give an accurate reflection of the actual overall need.

Early in the 20th century, such procedures were still regarded as almost a Hammer House of Horror type of procedure (in the style of the classic horror movies produced by the British film corporation known as Hammer Films). Blood transfusions began to be widely used in the First World War, but although blood is self-replaceable, kidneys, hearts, lungs, pancreases and livers are non-regenerating. Skin grafts, for example, where burns had been suffered, were performed in the 1920s. Bone marrow, skin and blood were usually taken usually from live donors. The first successful kidney transplant reportedly took place in 1954, which was a live donation between identical twins. In 1997 as far as kidney transplants were concerned, it was estimated that 11% of all kidney donations were from live donors.

According to a British Medical Journal article published in June 2000, although 70% of UK people claim to wish to be organ donors if eligible, only 20% actually fill out donor cards (see Carnall (2000) BMJ 1678).

LEGAL PERSPECTIVES

Questions which used to be purely hypothetical have begun to exercise legal academics as they have begun to acquire far more practical significance. The broad question is: what rights, if any does a person have in disposing of their bodies and body parts? Questions flowing from this are: what property rights exist in such tissue? Indeed, in the early 1990s, Dworkin and Kennedy asked: what is the precise legal nature of the transaction when biological materials are supplied to an academic or commercial researcher? (See Dworkin and Kennedy (1995).)

KEY ETHICAL ISSUES

Jonsen (1989) summarises the key ethical and moral issues raised by organ transplantation, namely: (a) it poses serious moral questions about the intrinsic morality of transplantation; (b) the determination of the death of the source of a cadaveric organ; (c) the right of persons to donate their own organs; (d) the selection of recipients for scarce organs and the procurement and allocation of organs as a scarce social resource. Of these, the procurement of organs raises further issues: there is the need for free and informed consent; when does death occur, legally and medically? Death is now based on brainstem death criteria, but used to be based on heart-lung criteria. Consequently, this shift in the test of death has implications for the supply of organs.

SALE OF HUMAN ORGANS

The case for and against permitting sale of human organs

Wilkinson and Gerrard (1996) discuss the arguments for and against permitting a market in organs; some of these arguments are not *prima facie* obvious.

Arguments in favour of organ sale:

(a) it would generate an increased supply of a scarce and life-saving resource as well as providing some much needed income for those who have little else to sell;

(b) persons donating organs should be equated with bomb disposal experts, firefighters and deep sea divers who are paid for dangerous (and sometimes painful) work;

(c) libertarian policies would allow people to dispose of their own body parts in whatever way they wish.

Arguments against organ sale:

(a) the organ seller is subjected to an extremely high level of pain and risk;

(b) the relationship between buyer and seller is likely to be exploitative and might either cause or constitute an unacceptable commodification of the seller and/or her body. They argue that there are two problems with this objection: (1) although organ sale does necessarily involve treating a human body part as a commodity, there is no reason to suppose that this is necessarily exploitative – if the organ seller were wealthy, educated, rational and well informed and were paid £100,000 for her organ – would we really regard it as exploitative?; (2) we permit many practices which are at least as exploitative and 'commodifying' as organ sale (for example, poorly paid labour); hence, while exploitation and commodification are not acceptable, it is not a special problem for organ sale;

(c) organ sale would undermine the practice of free donation; in other words, marketing of organs would deter the public from donating their organs out of altruism. They argue that the mere permissibility of sale should not deter people who wish to donate their organs from doing so; if organ sale led to an increase in the supply of organs, this would more than compensate for the reduced number of free organs; but it is far from clear whether non-related potential donors would donate without payment, anyway;

(d) no one could ever be in a position autonomously to consent to selling an organ such as a kidney, since the process would be so unpleasant or dangerous that only someone who was coerced or manipulated would agree to it. The evils of a person being coerced into selling an organ should be guarded against, but it is not always the case that a person might never be prepared to 'sell' an organ if the price was high and she was in serious financial straits. Perhaps in countries where organ selling is seen as a necessary evil to secure dire financial need, the evil might not lie in the sale itself, but in the fact that someone should be allowed to get into such a position in the first place and feel the need to resort to organ selling to ensure sheer survival.

Has the sale of organs ever been lawful in the UK?

Presumably, it must have been before 1989, otherwise the British government would not have seen the need to pass legislation to prohibit the exchange of money, other than reasonable expenses, for the purpose of organ donation by the living, when it came to light that certain people were being recruited and paid to donate their kidneys (see below, under 'Live donor organ transplants', for further discussion).

The UK Transplants Support Service Authority (UKTSSA)

The UKTSSA was established as a Special Health Authority (SHA) in 1991 to carry out a range of support functions for transplantation, namely:

- allocation;
- information;
- transport;
- servicing Use Advisory Groups;

- maintaining national waiting lists;
- maintaining databases for tracing, audit and research.

After a review carried out in 1998–99, it was recommended that the UKTSSA continue with responsibility for these functions.

The law differentiates between live organ donations and transplantations involving organs from cadavers – dead bodies.

There is also transgenic or xenotransplantation – using other mammals like pigs to be harvested for making organs for transplantation into human beings. Modern molecular biological techniques have already produced transgenic pigs and, while the possibility of a 'pig heart' might be repulsive to some, the broader question is whether it is morally acceptable to rear animals solely for the purpose of substituting human body parts. If such processes could never be available on the NHS, will it be a case of longevity for the rich? As the population of the so called 'aged' increases because of longer life expectancy (one national headline read: 'Today's babies can expect to live for 130 years' (*The Times*, 2000)) there seems to be a greater need to replace diseased organs as well as using transplants to correct birth defects or the onset of cancer.

A new body, the Xenotransplantation Interim Regulatory Authority, has been set up to monitor the situation since a government inquiry chaired by Professor Ian Kennedy took the view in January 1997 that clinical trials involving transgenic transplants should be delayed, because of the unknown risks associated with infectious diseases being passed from animal to human.

Three main ways that transplant organs could become available are (a) through transgenic transplants; (b) through live donor transplants; and (c) through donation from deceased persons (see Dworkin (1970) 33 MLR 353). These kinds of transplant raise a fundamental question in medical law and ethics: the issue of *consent*. As we have seen, any touching of a person, for example, for an operation, without that person's consent is unlawful. Liability could be founded on the criminal or civil law of battery; but, even if a person does consent, there is another principle founded on public policy or paternalism that there may be times when an individual needs to be protected from himself or herself.

REMOVAL OF ORGANS, UNLAWFUL ACTS AND CONSENT

The question is: could the removal of organs from a person for the purpose of organ donation to another person, constitute assault? The answer is yes, if done without the donor's consent.

Is consent the only requirement? What if a donor consents to removal of an organ, but only in return for money?

Unlawful act remains unlawful even if done with consent

R v Donovan is an illuminating case which establishes, *inter alia*, that an act unlawful in itself does not become lawful just because someone who has suffered from it has consented to it.

R v Donovan *[1934] All ER 207*

The facts of *Donovan* are that the appellant was convicted of indecent assault and common assault and sentenced to 18 months' imprisonment with hard labour for indecent assault and six months with hard labour for the common assault. He was given leave to appeal against his conviction.

The appellant appeared to be addicted to a form of sexual perversion. During a series of telephone conversations he made suggestions to the prosecutrix, a 16 year old girl, which suggested that he wished or desired to beat her. She had, however, apparently agreed to meet him at the cinema and they met at Marble Arch in London. His first remark was: 'Where would you like to have your spanking, in Hyde Park or in my garage?' But, the girl maintained that she did not take his remarks seriously. She eventually went with the appellant on the Tube and then to a garage and the alleged offences were committed, apparently for the appellant's own sexual gratification. A married sister of the girl said that she returned home on the night of the alleged incident looking pale and ill and made a complaint consistent with her injuries. A doctor who examined the girl two days later said that there were seven or eight red marks on her body and that they indicated that she had suffered a fairly severe beating. There was no sign of any other injury.

The appellant gave evidence that the girl had acted throughout to make it plain to him that she had consented to all that he did. The girl testified that she went to the garage with full knowledge of the appellant's intentions and without reluctance.

After a review of the law, the Court of Criminal Appeal finally came to the conclusion that there had a been a misdirection to the jury and that the prosecution had not been able to negative consent in this case. The correct question was: were the jury convinced that the blows were intended to cause bodily harm? If not, then they should not convict the accused. The appellant was, accordingly, acquitted on a technicality, but the principles stand!

As enunciated by the Court of Criminal Appeal, they were as follows:

- if an act is unlawful because it is a criminal act, it cannot be rendered lawful because the person to whose detriment it is done consents to it;
- no person can license another to commit a crime – something wrong in itself;
- thus, the prosecution need not prove absence of consent where an act has been wrong in itself. But, there are many acts which are, in themselves,

harmless and lawful and which become unlawful only if they are done without the consent of the person affected: the onus of negativing consent then falls on the prosecution.

Common law does not allow unfettered licence for self-mutilation

Is it possible for a donor to agree to an organ transplant purely for personal pleasure and in order to satisfy some perverted sense of sado-masochism?

R v Brown *[1993] 2 All ER 75*

This case, which went all the way to the House of Lords, involved sado-masochistic acts. The House of Lords held that consensual sado-masochistic homosexual encounters which occasioned actual bodily harm to the victim were held to be assaults occasioning actual bodily harm, notwithstanding that the victim consented to the acts inflicted on him, because public policy required that society be protected by criminal sanctions against a cult of violence which contained the danger of the proselytisation and corruption of young men and the potential for the infliction of serious injury.

A person could, therefore, be convicted for committing sado-masochistic acts even though they were committed in private, and the person on whom the injuries were inflicted consented and no permanent injury was inflicted on the victim.

The principle established here is: the common law does not afford unfettered licence for self-mutilation.

LIVE DONOR TRANSPLANTATION

For live donors, the ethical question is: how far is it permissible to expose one person to harm, to benefit another person?

Ethical issues

A possible conflict between two types of philosophical theories may be found: deontology v consequentialist theory. In deontology, a person's moral worth dictates decisions and it centres on moral imperatives. The principle of 'respect for persons' means that people should not be used as a means to an end. In consequentialist theory, however, utilitarianism is the watchword, which strives to maximise happiness and minimise suffering and proceeds on the notion of attempting to achieve the greatest good for the greatest number.

Professor Gerald Dworkin (1970) suggests four conditions for surgery in general and donor organ removal in particular, to be legal:

(a) the patient must give full, free and informed consent; in some cases, the psychological pressure brought to bear on a family member may be so intense that consent is not freely given;

(b) the operation must be 'therapeutic' – expressly for the donor's benefit. This is difficult to interpret strictly, but what does 'therapeutic' mean? In the case of the donation of one kidney, there is the increased danger of damage to the remaining kidney;

(c) there must be lawful justification;

(d) the operation must be performed by a person with appropriate medical skills.

The second requirement should probably be regarded as an application of the general principle in (c).

Thus, the law will not sanction the removal of organs where the consequence is the death of the donor; if a surgeon proceeds with the operation, he will commit murder or manslaughter.

Position at common law on removal of an organ from a live donor – consent required

If the adult is adult and competent, there must be consent to the removal of an organ.

This follows the general principle that consent is normally required for any medical procedure if the patient is competent and conscious. As far as the incompetent donor is concerned, the key issue is still: will the procedure benefit the defendant?

An American example

Strunk v Strunk *(1969) 445 SW 2d 145*

In this American case, the court authorised a kidney transplant from Jerry, a 27 year old man with a mental age of six, to his 28 year old brother who was suffering from kidney disease, after hearing psychiatric evidence of the 'extremely traumatic effect' that his brother's death would have upon him.

(For further discussion of this and other American cases, see Chapter 17.)

An English example

Re Y *(1996) 35 BMLR 111*

This was a case which appears to have been unique in its involving judicial authorisation of blood tests and bone marrow harvesting from a mentally incapacitated adult to a sibling, based on the best interests test. A donation from a blood relative presented a 40% of recovery for 18 months, whereas a donation from an unrelated donor reduced that chance to around 30%, as the most optimistic percentage.

Facts

Miss Y was 25 years old and had been severely mentally and physically disabled from birth. She had lived in care since she was 10 years old. Her sister, aged 36 (the plaintiff), suffered from a preleukaemic bone marrow disorder, and would suffer myloid leukaemia within three months. The plaintiff sought a declaration that it would be lawful to perform blood tests and possible bone marrow extraction upon Miss Y, despite the latter's inability to consent.

Connell J held that the taking of blood tests and the harvesting of bone marrow from a person who is incapable of giving consent would be assault and illegal *unless* shown to be in the best interests of that person and therefore lawful. The question to ask is whether the evidence shows that it is in the best interests of the defendant for such procedures to take place. The fact that such a process would obviously benefit the plaintiff is not relevant unless, as a result of the intended donor helping the plaintiff in that way, the best interests of the donor would be served.

The court placed importance on several factors:

(a) the intended donor benefits from the visits which she receives from her family and involvement in family events;

(b) there was manifest affection between mother and daughter;

(c) chances of survival of the plaintiff would be greatly reduced if the transplant were not carried out;

(d) chances of survival semi-indefinitely were good if the recipient survived the first six months after the transplant. Without any transplant, the plaintiff's chances of survival were poor and were deteriorating fast.

The question arises as to whether *Re Y*'s approach could support organ donations by incompetent adults and children? This is probably doubtful. Andrew Grubb (1996), for instance, gives several reasons why not:

(a) *Re Y* is an unusual case where there was minimal risk to the donor, that is, if there was a greater risk, the court might not be so willing to think that organ donation was in the best interests of the donor, for example, where there is danger of the remaining kidney becoming diseased or damaged;

(b) evidence of a 'close relationship' (which would be damaged if the donee patient dies) would be required; thus, close relatives with severe mental disabilities or donations from babies appear to be discounted because such persons would not be able to form a mutually close relationship with the donor by virtue of their limited mental condition;

(c) the agreement of the donor as a condition to allowing the donation raises difficulties – this would also exclude the very young or disabled;

(d) the donation would have a psychological benefit to the donor;

(e) these cases fell into a special category that the court should be involved in for advice.

Comment on bone marrow transplantation

As far as point (b) of Grubb's commentary (above) is concerned, it is submitted that it is still possible for a baby or mentally disabled close relative to form a close relationship with the donor, in the sense of a purely physical or affectionate relationship, although an intellectual relationship would not be possible. A mother forms a very close bond with her baby for many months and years before the child is able to respond in more intellectual terms, but should the mother or baby die, their relationship will certainly be damaged.

On a different point, there is no specific legal regulation on bone marrow transplantation. In fact, bone marrow is not covered by the Human Tissue Act 1989 as it does not appear to fit into the definition of s 7(2) of the Act as a 'structured arrangement of tissues which ... cannot be replicated by the body'. Hence, there does not appear to be any legislative guidance on the conditions under which bone marrow may be donated.

CHILDREN AS ORGAN DONORS

On the question of whether children would be permitted to donate organs, the case of *Re W (A Minor) (Medical Treatment)* [1992] 4 All ER 627 gave some indication. The views of Lord Donaldson MR suggest that it is highly unlikely that even *Gillick* competent children would be permitted to donate organs (in the absence of parental consent) if the operation would not actually benefit the minor. Parental consent *per se* would probably be not good enough – the operation would have to be for the child's health or welfare.

Bone marrow donation between siblings is widely practised. In the USA, several cases have authorised bone marrow transplants, even kidney transplants (see *Hart v Brown* (1972) 289 A 2d 386) between seven year old identical twins), but refused permission in the case of *Curran v Bosze* (1990) 566

NE 2d 1319, decided by the Illinois Supreme Court. This case involved twins who were three and a half years old and a 12 year old child from the father's previous marriage. Permission was refused predominantly because it was held that there was insufficient benefit to the donor, but there was also no existing close relationship between donor and recipient.

As far as anencephalic newborns who are terminally ill are concerned, the use of their transplantable organs to save another person has been a highly controversial issue in medical ethics for at least a decade.

LIVE DONOR TRANSPLANTS – THE HUMAN ORGANS TRANSPLANT ACT 1989

Live donor transplantation is governed by the Human Organs Transplant Act 1989.

Background

In the 1980s, a story came to light in England of donors selling kidneys for transplantation into those who had no genetic or other relation to the donor. There were several advertisements inviting Turkish people (among others) to come to England to make such donations. Three doctors who were found to have been involved were found guilty of serious professional misconduct by the GMC. The British Government swiftly passed the Human Organs Transplant Act 1989.

The Human Organ Transplant Act 1989

This Act was passed to stop payments for organs which are then used for transplants; that is, to criminalise and therefore prevent commercial dealings in organs throughout the UK. This Act therefore seeks to criminalise the commercialisation of live donor transplantation. In addition, the Act makes general provision to regulate transplants between living persons and for the creation of a statutory register of organ transplantation. It also covers organs from dead donors and applies restrictions on live donation of non-regenerative organs. Those who are genetically related must provide evidence of the relationship before proceeding.

Section 1 makes it a criminal offence to make or receive payment at any stage for the purpose of organ donation by the living. Legitimate expenses incurred by the donor are excluded.

Section 2 provides that a person is guilty of an offence if they remove an organ from a living person intending it to be transplanted unless the donor is closely genetically related to the recipient. However, donations between non-relatives are permitted with the consent of the Unrelated Live Transplant Regulatory Authority (ULTRA) (see below).

The 1989 Act makes no reference to minors. It does not, however, prohibit human organ donations from minors in principle, and this is also permitted under jurisdictions such as Canada and Australia. In reality, such cases are few and far between. The basic objective of the 1989 Act was, therefore, to stop the exploitation of poor people who could be pressurised into selling parts of their bodies for money. It could be argued that a society which has no symbolic values ascribed to the dead and is prepared to put a price on anything is one whose practices are little short of savagery, but the Act really seemed to aim to outlaw commercialisation of the human body, and was not really attempting to make any moral statement as such.

TRANSPLANTS BETWEEN UNRELATED PERSONS

For transplants between persons who are unrelated, permission can be given by ULTRA, the Unrelated Live Transplant Regulatory Authority, established by the Human Organs Transplants (Unrelated Persons) Regulations of 1989, reg 3, which allows such transplants with full informed consent of the donor.

Before ULTRA approves an application for donation by a living unrelated donor, it must be satisfied that:

(a) no payment has been, or is to be, made;

(b) the person referring the case for consideration is the doctor with clinical responsibility for the donor;

(c) a doctor has explained to the donor the nature of the procedure and the risks involved in the removal of the organ in question;

(d) the donor's consent was not obtained by coercion or the offer of an inducement;

(e) the donor understands that his or her consent can be withdrawn at any time; and

(f) the donor and the recipient have been interviewed separately by a suitably qualified independent person, who is part of the transplant team, and that person is satisfied that the above conditions have been met.

These conditions are equally important, whether the donation is from a relative or from an unrelated donor.

FETAL TRANSPLANTATION

In Sweden, the USA and England, trials using fetal tissue for transplants into the brains of patients with Parkinson's and Huntington's diseases has been carried out.

INCOMPETENT ADULTS AS DONORS

We have already discussed the case of *Re Y* (1996). There is also BMA Guidance on this topic. Under a section headed 'Adults lacking capacity to make decisions', the BMA Guidance states that 'provision must be made for those adults who lack the capacity to make an informed decision about organ donation ... It should not be assumed that all people with learning disabilities are unable to make decisions about these issues, nor should it be assumed that they would not wish to donate organs after their death'. Up to this point, this is perfectly reasonable and, indeed, quite 'politically correct' in its attitude to persons who have learning disabilities. The Guidance continues: 'Information should be provided in a way individual patients are able to understand and to allow them the opportunity to express their own views about organ donation.' However, the Guidance then turns to the position of patients who 'lack all capacity' because they are in a coma or do not have sufficient capacity to make a decision about organ donation. The King's Fund Institute report suggested that adults lacking mental capacity might be considered 'presumed objectors' in a system of presumed consent. Here, the BMA disagrees and again argues that 'those who lack mental capacity should be given the same opportunities to perform altruistic acts and it should not be assumed that they would not wish to donate'. One cannot reasonably disagree with the sentiments of not second-guessing persons lacking mental capacity but, with respect, this is a somewhat strange approach in relation to patients who have *never* had the mental capacity to understand far less complicated matters, let alone human organ donation. The BMA also says that 'there must be established mechanisms for a proxy, or legal representative to opt out of donation on behalf of someone who is not mentally competent to make a personal decision'. What does this mean? The current system in the UK is an opt-in system, so consent is never presumed. Are they suggesting that consent would be presumed because one cannot assume they would not want to donate their organs? With respect, this can have no application to the patient with the mental age of four or five or to the persistent vegetative state (PVS) (see p 303) patient who has never expressed a view on organ donation while competent, before the onset of PVS. It must be equally dubious to assume that mentally incompetent adults would wish to donate organs any more than the rest of the competent adults in the rest of the population.

ELECTIVE VENTILATION OF PATIENTS CLOSE TO DEATH

The BMA Guidance suggests that another way of increasing the number of organs available for donation is by the use of elective ventilation. Elective ventilation involves ventilating a selected group of patients, who are in deep coma and close to death with no possibility of recovery, for a short period (usually only a few hours) before death is confirmed, to preserve their organs for long enough to prepare for their removal after death. In fact, elective ventilation was introduced in Exeter with strict controls in 1988 and this led to a 50% increase in the number of organs suitable for transplantation, but the practice was stopped abruptly in 1994 when the Department of Health declared it unlawful. The law as it stands is that to protect people who are not competent to make decisions for themselves, procedures may only be undertaken which are necessary and are intended to be in the patient's best interests; any other intervention is unlawful.

Having reviewed this issue, the current BMA position is that there are 'too many ethical and practical difficulties for a change in the law to be recommended at the present time'. It declares, however, that if elective ventilation were to be permitted at some future date, 'strict safeguards' would be needed.

CADAVERIC TRANSPLANTATION

Donation and transplantation of organs for therapeutic purposes after one's death

This would be permissible if there were an express request of the donor who is now deceased; or in the absence of such a request, where reasonable inquiry reveals no objection to the same either by the deceased or by his spouse or surviving relatives.

In the UK, the removal of organs from people after their death is covered by the Human Tissue Act 1961 (the 1961 Act) (covering England, Scotland and Wales) and the Human Tissue (Northern Ireland) Act 1962. Once the patient is brainstem dead, transplantation can take place. The current definition of death allows for 'beating heart donors' or 'beating heart cadavers' – patients who are determined to be dead on the basis of brain death criteria (Jones (1999), p 59). The *'irreversible loss of brainstem function'* as a definition of death has been accepted by the English courts (see *Re A* [1992] 3 Med LR 303) and the legal position appears to be that there is no mandatory requirement that a person cannot be declared brain (stem) dead unless there are two sets of tests carried out to establish death. To complicate matters, it may not always be possible even for medical professionals to be always correct when deciding when a person is dead. In a newspaper report published in 1998 (*The Times*, 5 December 1998) it was reported that a baby girl who had been pronounced dead by medical staff at a hospital in Salford, recovered after doctors had spent 20 minutes trying to resuscitate her and had deemed her dead. The baby was lifeless for 42 minutes after her mother had given birth. When the baby was handed to her father, the child gave a gasp, followed by another, and was then taken to the neonatal unit where she was revived by staff after being put on a ventilator.

The major factor behind the political acceptance of brain death as death is the development of transplant medicine (see Jones (1999)). To obtain organs in good condition, the organs have to be removed as soon as possible after death. If brainstem death is equivalent to death, then surgeons can remove organs while the heart is still beating while the organs are still perfused with oxygenated blood. Thus, as far as 'beating heart donors' are concerned, if brain death occurs as a result of severe damage to the brain and not as a result of a failure of other organs, brain death results in cessation of spontaneous respiration, and if oxygenation is maintained by artificial ventilation, the heartbeat can continue for some days. Brainstem death has, therefore, occurred, but the heart may still be beating for a time after that.

What is the position with regard to giving directions as to the disposal of one's dead body being used for organ removal and transplantation for research or therapeutic purposes?

The Human Tissue Act 1961

1(1) If any person, either in writing at any time or orally in the presence of two or more witnesses at the time of his last illness, has expressed a request that his body or any specified part of his body be used after his death for therapeutic purposes or ... research, the person lawfully in possession of his body may, unless he has reason to believe that the request was subsequently withdrawn, authorise the removal of ... the specified part for use in accordance with the request.

1(2) Without prejudice to the foregoing subsection, the person lawfully in possession of the body ... may authorise the removal of any part from the body for use for the said purpose, if, having made such reasonable inquiry as is practicable, he has no reason to believe:

(a) that the deceased had expressed an objection to his body being so dealt with after his death ...; or

(b) that the surviving spouse or any surviving relative of the deceased objects.

It might be necessary to hold an inquest, or a coroner's post-mortem examination, in which case the Act states that organs or tissues may only be removed with the specific authorisation of the coroner.

The coroner has the right to decide whether to order an inquest – the formal hearing to establish the circumstances of death – as a precondition to the post-mortem. If a coroner authorises a post-mortem, the objections of next of kin will not carry any weight in law. However, the coroner's powers only extend to the removal of tissues to ascertain cause of death.

The person 'lawfully in possession' of the body – and it is by no means clear who this person or entity is – 'may', but not 'must', authorise removal of the organ, suggesting there is some scope for discretion.

In Scotland, organs may not be removed in any case where the procurator fiscal has objected to their removal.

Areas of ambiguity

It is widely thought that the 1961 Act is unsatisfactory and in need of reform. The loose wording of the legislation has been called simplistic and ambiguous and has led to difficulties which will inevitably increase with advancements in communication technology.

What is the scope of making 'such reasonable inquiry as may be practicable'? Does this, with modern technology, include using the internet or e-mail to attempt to contact every surviving relative? Should the view of a surviving relative, who might have been estranged from the deceased for many years, have the power to veto the donation of the organ? In the absence of clarifying legislation or regulations, practice has developed on pragmatic lines.

For example, the BMA Guidance asserts that it is generally accepted, though not beyond doubt, that where a patient dies in hospital, the hospital management is 'lawfully in possession of the body' until the executors or relatives ask for the body to be handed to them. When the person dies elsewhere, the person lawfully in possession of the body is considered to be a close relative or long term partner. Again, a pragmatic approach has been taken in interpreting the phrase 'such reasonable inquiry as may be practicable' and in deciding which relatives' views should be sought. The BMA Guidance further explains that, in most cases, this will mean discussing the matter with those relatives who have been in close contact with the deceased in the period leading up to the death. These people will be asked about 'their own views, those of the deceased patient and whether any other relative is likely to object'. Medical and nursing staff will often have been in communication with potential organ donors who will often have spent some time in hospital before their death.

The use of the 'spouse' would exclude the increasing number of couples who live together as long term partners without marrying. Demographic statistics suggest that up to 25% of the population are cohabiting outside marriage and the figure is rising. In practice, long term partners are consulted about donation, but this is another example of where practice has developed in spite of the wording of the legislation. Seeking the consent of relatives has also become standard practice, although the legislation only requires that the person lawfully in possession of the body has made inquiries to ensure that the surviving relatives do not object to the donation.

The Department of Health Guidance 1998 says discussion with one relative will usually be sufficient.

RECENT DEVELOPMENTS

Removal and retention of children's organs at Alder Hey Hospital

Revelations that entire organs were stripped from children who died at Alder Hey Children's Hospital in Merseyside without parental consent provoked angry reactions from relatives of the children and the British Government announced that an inquiry would be held. An inquiry was launched on 3 December 1999 when allegations were made concerning the discovery in a hospital laboratory of 850 organs from babies and more than 2,000 children's hearts which were removed during post mortem examinations, allegedly *without their parents' consent*. The hospital said that the organs were stored without its knowledge.

In March 2000, the internal inquiry into 'organ stripping' from the children who died, for post mortem examination and other purposes at Alder Hey Hospital, found that removal of organs was so common it became standard practice. It said that between 1988 and 1995, the period covered by the inquiry, nearly 3,000 organs were retained. In 587 cases, a full set of organs was kept.

As we have seen, the Human Tissue Act 1961 lays down preconditions which must be observed before the organs and tissues can be removed. Under the 1961 Act, doctors do *not* have the power to decide on their own whether or not to keep organs, unless the patient is a child who has died after a pregnancy lasting less than 24 weeks. In other cases, as the 1961 Act stipulates, the doctor must have made 'reasonable inquiries' to the patient's immediate next of kin to make sure there is no objection, or authorisation from the local coroner. If the pathologist would like to remove organs for any purpose, or those unrelated to establishing the cause of death, such a removal is not covered by the coroner's authorisation. The situation at Alder Hey came to public attention when a parent told an inquiry into paediatric cardiac surgery in Bristol of their distress at finding that organs had been removed from their children before burial. A day after the inquiry had been announced in December 1999, the British Broadcasting Corporation said it had found in a survey it had conducted, that the practice of retaining parts of children's bodies like hearts and brains, is common and widespread: seven of the 10 biggest NHS trusts in England were removing organs or samples from children's bodies without their parents' consent regularly until recently. Alder Hey Hospital has apologised to the families involved for the distress caused.

Royal College of Pathologists: guidelines for retention of tissues and organs

In March 2000, in the light of the public and media interest in organ-retention procedures, and the Alder Hey hospital disclosures, the UK's Royal College of Pathologists issued new guidelines for the retention of tissues and organs at necropsy, which includes a new model consent form that gives relatives the right to agree or refuse permission for organs of the deceased to be used for research, examination or education. The College recommends that hospitals and medical schools must provide training for doctors and other healthcare staff in requesting and obtaining agreement for necropsies and in dealing with relatives' concerns about tissue and organ retention. Doctors must also liaise with pathologists to determine the reasons for retaining tissues, so that relatives can make informed decisions. The College has drafted an information pamphlet for relatives to explain the medical benefits of tissue and organ retention and relatives of the deceased will now be given a copy of the signed consent form.

The College suggests that relatives are given a wide range of necropsy options of the updated consent form, which mow allows relatives to:

- limit the extent of the necropsy;
- agree or disagree to having organs taken for further examination;
- have tissue or organs disposed of lawfully and respectfully by the hospital or taken away for personal burial;
- donate tissue, fluids, or organs for research for an unlimited period.

(Source: Ashraf, H, 'UK necropsy guidelines updated in the wake of organ retention scandals' (2000) *The Lancet*, 25 March.)

Prohibition of discriminatory conditions being attached to organ donations

In February 2000, the government announced that new guidelines are to be introduced preventing conditions being attached by relatives to organ donations following a government inquiry into the NHS organ transplant service, which was commissioned after a transplant co-ordinator agreed to conditions that a dead relative's organs be given to a white person. The government report calls for NHS staff training in race relations; criticises senior staff for allowing the practice of attaching conditions to organ donation;

and condemns the NHS for failing to stop the practice earlier. Conditions imposed by relatives have included: organs only to go to a child; that a smoker does not receive the organs of a non-smoker; and that the organs of a person convicted of driving while under the influence of alcohol, should not to be given to an alcoholic. These last three conditions are, to say the least, somewhat bizarre.

REFORMING THE LAW

The British Medical Association launched a campaign in June 2000 for a 'presumed consent' to organ donation scheme to be implemented in Britain, under which it would be assumed that every patient wished to be a donor unless he or she had registered an objection. The BMA also calls for an overhaul of the current transplant service and a radical revision of its co-ordination and infrastructure. It is concerned that, although waiting lists for transplants grew by 3% between 1998 and 1999, there was no corresponding increase in the number of transplants. A number of possible options may be considered: (a) retain the existing law and increase public education and awareness on the shortage of organs available for transplantation; (b) amend the Human Tissue Act so as to clarify the ambiguous terms; (c) allow the sale of organs from live donors; (d) use the organs of patients in a PVS state; (e) introduce a system of 'contracting out', that is, the law would allow surgeons to assume that they could use a dead person's organs unless they had expressly registered an objection to this. This system exists in various European countries, such as France, Denmark, Austria and Belgium (see Chapter 17). The BMA has also called for the introduction of a 'single, comprehensive piece of legislation covering all aspects of organ donation from both live and cadaveric donors'.

SELECTIVE BIBLIOGRAPHY

BMA Guidance, *Organ Donation in the 21st Century: Time for a Consolidated Approach*, 1999, BMA

Brahams, D, 'Transplantation, the fetus and the law' (1988) 138 NLJ 91

Davies, M, *Textbook on Medical Law*, 2nd edn, 1998, Blackstone, Chapter 16

Dworkin, G and Kennedy, I, 'Human tissue: rights in the body and its parts' [1993] 1 Med LR 291

Dworkin, G, 'The law relating to organs transplantation in England' (1970) 33 MLR 353

Feenan, D, 'A good harvest? *Re Y (Mental Incapacity)*: bone marrow transplants' (1997) 9 CFLQ 305

Fox, M and McHale, J, 'Regulating xenotransplantation' (1997) 147 NLJ 139

Fox, M and McHale, J, 'Xenotransplantation: the ethical and legal ramifications' (1998) 6 Med L Rev 42

Grubb, A, 'Commentary on *Re Y*' (1996) 4 Med L Rev 204

Jones, DA, 'The UK definition of death' (1999) Law and Justice 56

Jonsen, AR, 'Ethical issues in organ transplantation' in Veitch, RM (ed), *Medical Ethics*, 1989, Jones and Bartlett

Lamb, D, *Organ Transplants and Ethics*, 1990, Routledge

Mason, JK and McCall Smith, RA, *Law and Medical Ethics*, 5th edn, 1999, Butterworths, Chapter 14

Mumford, SE, 'Bone marrow donation – the law in context' (1998) 10 CFLQ 135

New, B, Solomon, M, Dingwall, R and McHale, J, *A Question of Give and Take*, 1994, King's Fund Institute

Price and Mackay, 'The trade in human organs' (1991) 141 NLJ 1272

Redmond-Cooper, R, 'Transplants: opting out or in – the implications' (1984) 134 NLJ 648

Stauch, M and Wheat, K, with Tingle, J, *Sourcebook on Medical Law*, 1998, Cavendish Publishing, Chapter 11

Wilkinson, S and Gerrard, E, 'Bodily integrity and the sale of human organs' (1996) 22 JME 334

CHAPTER 9

THE END OF LIFE – EUTHANASIA AND PHYSICIAN-ASSISTED SUICIDE

INTRODUCTION

In the previous chapter, we looked at organ transplantation and one of the issues that we discussed was the problem of defining death (see Chapter 8, p 284). Clearly, there is a need to define death in some way in order to decide, for instance, whether there are any circumstances in which one may lawfully terminate the treatment of someone who has been in a coma, but not legally pronounced dead. Similarly, it needs to be established whether someone is dead before organs may be removed for transplantation. There is still controversy over the definition of death in certain circumstances and for certain purposes. We now look at death in the context of doctors or other health professionals bringing it about in a way that can be interpreted as merciful or compassionate, for example, where a person has been suffering severe pain for some time and the prognosis is that there is no realistic hope of recovery. In these circumstances, it is argued that it is more merciful to relieve that person with the least amount of suffering – hence the notion of mercy killing, sometimes called euthanasia. This chapter focuses primarily on the English law relating to this area, and includes the historical legal background to 'assisted suicide', the ethical issues, definitions of 'euthanasia', leading criminal law cases, advance directives and the landmark House of Lords' decision – the *Tony Bland* case. We also consider the impact, if any, of the implementation of the Human Rights Act 1998 on the *Bland* principle.

HISTORICAL LEGAL BACKGROUND TO ASSISTED SUICIDE

For over 700 years, the Anglo-American common law tradition has punished or otherwise disapproved of both suicide and assisting suicide. The common law is thought to have developed and emerged through the expansion of pre-Norman institutions some time in the 12th century. England adopted the ecclesiastical prohibition on suicide in 673 at the Council of Hereford and this prohibition was affirmed by King Edgar in 967. In the 13th century, Henry de Bracton, one of the first legal treatise writers, observed that 'just as a man may commit felony by slaying another so may he do so by slaying himself'. The real and personal property of one who killed himself to avoid conviction and punishment for a crime was forfeit to the king. However, Bracton observed 'if a man slays himself in weariness of life or because he is unwilling to endure further bodily pain ... [only] his movable goods [were] confiscated'. Hence, 'the principle that suicide of a sane person, for whatever reason, was a punishable felony was ... introduced into English common law'. Other late medieval treatise writers followed and restated Bracton. In 1644, Sir Edward Coke published his Third Institute. Coke considered suicide to be a category of murder and agreed with Bracton that the goods and chattels, but not the lands (for Coke) of a sane suicide were forfeit. Later, Sir William Blackstone, whose Commentaries on the Laws of England not only provided a definitive summary of the common law but was also a primary legal authority for 18th and 19th century American lawyers, referred to suicide as 'self-murder' and 'the pretended heroism, but real cowardice, of the Stoic philosophers, who destroyed themselves to avoid those ills which they had not the fortitude to endure ...'. Blackstone emphasised that 'the law has ranked [suicide] among the highest crimes', although, anticipating later developments, he conceded that there were harsh and shameful punishments imposed for suicide.

Hence, suicide has a long standing antiquity.

People are said to be living longer than in previous generations. In 1999, a British national newspaper (*The Times*) claimed that today's babies might live to 130 years old or so, maybe more! There is growing concern about the quality of life for the dying and the growing proportion of the elderly in the community has also led to increased interest in euthanasia. Another factor has been the increased interest taken by the media in this subject, thus promoting debate and community awareness in the issue. There is the usual concern with the allocation of scarce healthcare resources – should we be spending a lot of money and resources in preserving the life of persons who is no longer enjoy any sort of quality of life, or should these limited resources go into promoting the health of someone who can still enjoy a reasonable quality of life?

Some well known cases in the area of euthanasia are the *Tony Bland case*; *Dr Cox*; *Bodkin Adams* and, recently, the *Dr Harold Shipman* case, the investigation of which, despite his conviction for 15 murders, is still ongoing, with the suspicion that he might have been responsible for another host of murders of many other of his patients.

DEFINITIONS OF EUTHANASIA

The word euthanasia has been used to refer to the deliberate ending of the life of a person suffering from a painful illness, or the means of inducing or bringing about a gentle and easy death; death without suffering. Confusion remains over the various definitions of euthanasia. Davies (1998) suggests it might refer to a positive act which causes death. It could refer to:

(a) a quiet, painless death;

(b) the intentional putting to death of persons with incurable or painful disease;

(c) the act of killing someone painlessly.

Several different categories may be identified; for example, voluntary euthanasia, which is the situation where a life is terminated at the patient's request. There is also non-voluntary euthanasia, a term which has been applied to the termination of life of an incompetent patient.

Involuntary euthanasia connotes ending the life of patient on paternalistic or other grounds while disregarding the wishes of a patient (this is certainly not regarded as lawful, as it overrides the patient's autonomy).

Active and passive euthanasia

Active euthanasia refers to any positive action terminating life. It has been defined as 'the (deliberate) administration of life-shortening substances with the intention to cause death in order to end pain and suffering' (Giesen (1995), p 202). Passive euthanasia refers to shortening of life through an omission to act, which appears to be allowed by English law in certain circumstances. Passive euthanasia refers to conduct such as withholding life support treatment so that 'nature can take its course'. Despite several legislative proposals, active euthanasia is forbidden by law, regardless of whether the patient has consented or not, and constitutes the crime of unlawful homicide (that is, murder or manslaughter) in nearly all major jurisdictions.

Voluntary euthanasia

One such form (called mercy killing) is where somebody, usually a relative, *deliberately* and *specifically* performs some act, such as administering a drug to accelerate death to terminate suffering. This may be described as active, positive or voluntary euthanasia. In law, however, this is still murder and, as Devlin J put it in the *Bodkin Adams* trial: 'If the acts done are intended to kill, it does not matter if a life is cut short by weeks or months, it is just as much murder if it were cut short by years' (see *R v Bodkin Adams* [1957] Crim LR 365). Intention, not motive, is the all-important prerequisite.

Thus, where a physician gives the fatal dose or injection at the request of a competent, terminally ill patient who is in extreme pain, for the sole purpose of alleviating the pain, knowing that continued dosages will kill the patient, this has sometimes been called 'physician-assisted suicide', particularly in overseas jurisdictions, but it is still murder. However, concessions have been made by prosecutors agreeing to accept a lesser plea such as manslaughter, as in *R v Johnson* (1961) 1 Med Sci and Law 192. In the light of the situation which involves the relieving of severe pain of the terminally ill, the court might even accept a plea of diminished responsibility on the grounds of mental abnormality. Stauch *et al* (1998) (p 654) call it a form of 'special dispensation' to the doctor engaged in the palliative care of a terminally ill patient and explain the *Bodkin Adams* case as one where:

> ... provided [the doctor] is exercising *bona fide* clinical judgment in easing the dying process, the law will exceptionally limit its focus to the 'narrow intention' of the doctor, eg, the desire to relieve pain; it is prepared to overlook the fact that, in foreseeing the patient's earlier death, the doctor intends the death in the 'wide' sense sufficient to establish criminal *mens rea* in most other contexts.

A RIGHT TO LIFE?

Medical technology now enables life to be prolonged, but at what point should treatment cease?

Undoubtedly, there is tremendous value placed in our society on human life. The right to life has been much vaunted, but what does it mean? One view is that it is the right not to be intentionally killed.

Article 2 of the European Convention on Human Rights says:

> Everyone's right to life shall be protected by law. No one shall be deprived of his life intentionally save in the execution of a sentence of a court following his conviction of a crime for which this penalty is provided by law.

A RIGHT TO DIE?

Is there a *right to die*? It might depend on the situation. The Hippocratic Oath mentions good faith and the saving of life. This Oath, which is supposed to date from the fourth century BC, only really represented the opinion of a small segment of Greek society; thus, the notion that life is sacred and the principle of the sanctity of human life actually appear to date only from when Christianity became the dominant religion and introduced the principle of the inestimable value of each person's immortal soul.

Kamisar (1995) argues that the 'right to die' is one of those slogans which are 'fuzzy', 'misleading' and 'misunderstood' and could refer to at least four different rights:

(a) the right to reject or to terminate unwanted medical procedures, including life-saving treatment;

(b) the right to commit suicide or, as it is called, the right to 'rational' suicide;

(c) the right to assisted suicide, that is, the right to obtain another's help in committing suicide; and

(d) the right to active voluntary euthanasia, that is, the right to authorise another to kill you intentionally and directly.

Kamisar submits that each of these rights should be kept separate and distinct, but that sometimes they are not (see Kamisar (1995), p 225).

Blood transfusions and Jehovah's Witnesses

In the case of an adult Jehovah's Witness who refuses a blood transfusion because of religious beliefs, even if the adult will die without such a transfusion, the medical establishment has supported such patient's wishes but has occasionally changed its opinion on whether to support such a right based on religious beliefs.

The case of *R v Blaue* [1975] 3 All ER 446 suggests that the medical profession has been known to respect the wishes of an adult Jehovah's Witness not to have a blood transfusion based on religious convictions, despite their apparent reluctance to do the same when it comes to psychotically or cyclically disturbed children who assert the same right to die or adult women who refuse blood transfusions because they are purportedly Jehovah's Witnesses or 'born again Christians' (see Chapter 1 for a discussion of 'Consent and the pregnant patient'). In the *Blaue* case, the patient involved was a girl, aged 18, a Jehovah's Witness, who had been stabbed with a knife and sustained serious loss of blood from a pierced lung. When told she had lost a great quantity of blood and required a transfusion without which she would die, she refused the blood transfusion on the ground of her religious beliefs. She persisted in her refusal, and also acknowledged in writing that she had refused a transfusion. The doctors respected her views and she died the following day. The actual issue before the appeal court was whether the fact that the girl had refused a blood transfusion broke the chain of causation, so that the stabbing by the appellant could not be said to be the operative cause of the girl's death. This argument was rejected by the court.

New guidelines for treatment of Jehovah's Witnesses

In 1999, new guidelines were announced by the Association of Anaesthetists, which represents the majority of anaesthetists in Britain. They declare that adult Jehovah's Witnesses should have the right to choose to die (see *The Times*, 10 March 1999). The guidelines stress that to administer blood to a patient who has steadfastly refused to accept it is 'unlawful, ethically unacceptable and may lead to criminal and/or civil proceedings'. Jehovah's Witnesses were consulted during the drafting of the guidelines and have been advised to carry identification cards in case they are unconscious when the decision has to be made, or to make advance directives or living wills, giving directions for treatment in these circumstances. In return, doctors are asked to take every precaution to avoid blood loss when operating on Jehovah's Witnesses and to consult the senior anaesthetist to determine whether a transfusion would be crucial. The report stresses that doctors should plan treatment of children well in advance, consult parents and allow enough time to apply to the courts if necessary.

Development of the definition of death in English medical law

The cardio-pulmonary criterion of death was used for a considerable time before the 1960s; hence, the irreversible cessation of breathing and heartbeat, of the functioning of the lungs and heart, were seen as constituting the death of the person as a whole (see Jones (1999), p 57). As we have already mentioned, technology in the form of assisted ventilation and heart bypass machines undermined the previous definition. However, it was only in 1976 that the first pronouncement from the British medical establishment on brain death was made in a paper of the Conference of the Royal Medical Colleges entitled 'Diagnosis of brain death', which describes the procedures for the diagnosis of death and asserts that what is required is the irreversible loss of the brain stem (hence brain stem death). But, nowhere in this document is brain death equated with the death of the patient. The document merely suggests that a diagnosis of brain death implies that the patient will certainly not recover, not that the patient is dead already.

In 1979, a second statement was made by the Conference of the Royal Medical Colleges entitled 'Diagnosis of death', which stated: 'Brain death represents the stage at which a patient becomes truly dead' and also that brain death is the point at which 'all functions of the brain have permanently and irreversibly ceased'.

During the 1980s and 1990s, significant medical evidence has contradicted the claim that brain stem death, as diagnosed by UK criteria, is the point at which all functions of the brain have permanently and irreversibly ceased. In an attempt to deal with confusion and uncertainty, a third document was published in 1995 which appeared in the Journal of the Royal College of Physicians, entitled 'Criteria for the diagnosis of brain stem death'. This document stresses that the correct term is 'brain stem death' rather than 'brain death' and even attempts a definition of death which will explain why brain death implies the death of the patient:

> It is suggested that 'irreversible loss of the capacity for consciousness, combined with irreversible loss of the capacity to breathe' should be regarded as the definition of death.

Jones (1999) suggests another definition of death, namely:

> The irreversible cessation of all integrated functioning of the human organism as a whole, mental or physical.

No statutory definition of death in English law

There is no statutory definition in English law: the courts do not appear to be unduly concerned about the definition of death, and approach it as an issue of fact determined by medical evidence.

Previously, death could be signified by the cessation of heartbeat and respiration, and this was easily verified by physical examination. Now, technology can keep people living longer, or at least prolong the point of death. If technology keeps a patient going when his heart continues to beat on the machine but breathing has stopped and the brain has been irreversibly damaged, this can be very distressing to relatives, is bad for morale among the nursing staff, is costly, and might also be depriving someone of access to the life-support machine who might benefit more from it. The rapid development in transplantation programmes led to the need for speedy diagnosis of death, so that once death was established, organs could be quickly removed from the body for transplantation, while they were still 'fresh'. In certain brain stem death cases, there appears to be a cessation of spontaneous respiration and, instead of being followed by cardiac arrest, when supported by artificial ventilation, the heartbeat can continue for days; this will enable organs such as the liver and kidneys to be maintained.

'Brain stem death' refers to the situation when parts of the brain which operate respiration and heartbeat are dead and there is no electrical impulse, that is, irreversible loss of brain stem function. Consciousness or sensate awareness will have decayed. The patient has no capacity to live and will never recover it.

In a recent case reported in the British media in 1999, a young assault victim who was diagnosed brain stem dead is now communicating with carers. The case has reopened the debate on defining death.

Professor Margaret Brazier (1992) argues that, biologically, death is a process and not an event; different organs and systems supporting the continuance of life cease to function successively and at different times.

One needs to distinguish between two cases:

(a) where the life support machine is turned off because it is medically established that the patient is dead; and

(b) where the machine is turned off because, although the patient is still clinically alive, it is thought that no further justification can be found in continuing life support and so the patient ought to be allowed to die. Considerations here are: consent; the quality of life of the patient; the proper use of scarce medical resources.

Doctors should distinguish between their duties to a dying patient and the power to remove organs from such a person once that person is properly declared to be dead.

THE ANENCEPHALIC BABY AND BRAIN DEATH

Here, the child is born lacking most or all of a higher brain and is bound to die, usually in a matter of days or weeks. Such babies could be kept alive never to become conscious or respond to human beings. If other babies are born with intact brains, but defective hearts or kidneys, doctors may want to use organs from the anencephalic baby to save the life of the baby with other defective organs. Thus, that baby must be ventilated, which poses a problem about the point at which he actually dies.

An anencephalic baby's brain stem may remain alive even when it has been ventilated. If brain stem death is inapplicable to such babies, should we accept that the lack of any higher brain function renders the baby as 'born dead'? Does that confuse euthanasia with defining death? The use of anencephalic newborns as sources of transplantable organs is one of the most controversial issues in medical ethics and has been for the last 10 years on both sides of the Atlantic.

Keeping such babies ventilated just to be organ donors might not be ethically defensible because this could be seen as using such babies as a means to an end (albeit helping others) rather than respecting them as ends in themselves. Anencephalic infants are not like other organ donors because it may be said that they are placed on life-support systems solely for the sake of others. As Annas (1987) puts it, 'since anencephalic newborns are not routinely resuscitated, intubated, or placed on ventilators and given other support, we cannot justify these interventions as "treatment" for these infants'.

THE ETHICAL DIMENSION

There are two main ethical components which require consideration in the present context: self-determination and autonomy, the so called 'right to die'. They present difficult questions for resolution by doctors of their role and duty *qua* doctors. They inevitably raise issues of dignity and personhood and even require the interrogation of what is the essence of a human being.

Another way of approaching this question is to consider notions of beneficence and autonomy. As we have seen at the outset of this book, one of the main medical aims is 'beneficence' – doing good to others; hence killing someone may not *per se* be seen as doing someone no harm! However, relief of pain and suffering is the aim of care; therefore relieving pain by putting an end to a patient's misery could be regarded as beneficent.

The second ethical component is autonomy which, in this context, would mean that a person has the right to oppose treatment. The slippery slope argument has also been suggested: that is, euthanasia is the start of the slippery slope – voluntary euthanasia in extreme circumstances will become euthanasia on request (as has happened with abortion). The ever greater fear is that voluntary euthanasia will imperceptibly change to compulsory euthanasia for the handicapped and the elderly.

As the Report of the Select Committee on Medical Ethics 1994 expressed it: 'The prohibition against intentional killing is the cornerstone of law and social relationships which protects each of us impartially, embodying the belief that all of us are equal.'

The sanctity of life argument

As we have already seen, this is the principle that all life is sacred and it would, therefore, be morally wrong to take someone's life by withdrawing treatment of that person; other ways should be found to relieve suffering. As against this, it could be argued that the sanctity of life principle is not absolute and continuance of a life support system, for example, is not in the best interests of that patient.

The law now appears to adopt a *qualified sanctity of life* argument (as labelled by Stauch *et al* (1998)); although life is given tremendous value, the courts might not see it as their function to preserve life in every case (see *Re T* [1997] 1 All ER 906 (the liver transplant case), discussed in Chapter 4).

CRIMINAL LIABILITY

Deliberate termination of the life of a patient

Any deliberate action aiming to end a patient's life, for example, by administering a lethal injection, will lead to a prosecution for murder. English law has never sanctioned 'mercy killing', yet a patient may sometimes be given a high dosage of drugs as part of his medical treatment even if the incidental effect is to hasten that patient's death. The question is: is this murder or a form of euthanasia? All ethical codes reject euthanasia explicitly or implicitly.

R v Cox *(1992) 12 BMLR 38*

Dr Cox was prosecuted for the attempted murder of Lillian Boyes, a 70 year old patient, who was suffering from an incurable and increasingly distressing form of arthritis. She made him promise that he would not let her suffer, and pleaded with him to put her out of her misery. She was suffering from the terminal stages of the condition and her pain could no longer be controlled by taking of further analgesic drugs. He administered an injection of potassium chloride and Mrs Boyes died within minutes. He was charged only with attempted murder on the basis that her death could have been due to her illness, and she might have died at that time even without the poison being administered.

The evidence indicated that the potassium injection could have no pain relieving effect and it appeared to judge and jury that the potassium was the cause of death, but it was not definitively established whether the injection was the operative cause of her death.

The jury convicted Dr Cox of attempted murder and he was sentenced to 12 months' imprisonment, which was suspended. The principle was reiterated that it is unlawful to administer drugs to a patient with the object of bringing about that patient's death, no matter how laudable the motive.

R v Arthur *(1981) 12 BMLR 1*

This was a case involving a newborn baby born with the condition known as Downs' syndrome, but there were, at this stage, no apparent further complications such as intestinal blockage. The consultant paediatrician in charge, Dr Arthur, having been told by the baby's mother that she did not want the child, prescribed 'Nursing care only' on the baby's chart. Now, for this particular health authority, this meant that there would be no extraordinary attempts to revive the baby if it encountered any difficulties. Indeed, the baby was fed with liquids and prescribed a pain relieving drug which eventually produced broncho-pneumonia from which the child died. The doctor was reported to the police (by a member of the nursing staff – it has never been established who) and the doctor was charged with murder.

In the course of the trial, medical evidence showed that the baby did have an intestinal blockage and would have died in any event. The prosecution, therefore, could not prove the cause of death and the charge was reduced to attempted murder.

The basic issue was whether the preparation and endorsement of the treatment by the consultant paediatrician amounted to an attempt to kill. The court ultimately asked whether the doctor had followed a procedure which could be supported by a responsible body of medical opinion – that is, in accordance with the *Bolam* test. The jury thought that he did and, although Farquharson J stressed that any profession cannot set out a code of ethics and say that the law must follow it, the jury unanimously acquitted him. The court stressed that there is no defence in law of mercy killing; active euthanasia is unlawful and punishable by a mandatory life sentence (the *Arthur* case is also discussed in the context of handicapped newborns, on which see Chapter 4).

Comment

The distinction drawn by the judge between acts and omissions does not seem satisfactory and certainly does not accord with the 1981 case of *Re B* (the Down's syndrome baby) (see [1981] 1 WLR 1421, discussed in Chapter 4). On the criminal law front, a doctor in these circumstances cannot be liable under s 1 of the Children and Young Persons Act 1933 for 'wilful neglect' because he would not, in law, be regarded as having 'responsibility for the child', since the section is limited to those having parental responsibility. Under *R v Sheppard* [1981] AC 394, the failure to provide 'adequate medical aid' has to be 'wilful' and 'cause the child unnecessary suffering or injury to health'. Dr Arthur, in his statement to the police, emphasised that the major aim of the healthcare staff looking after the baby in this case was to relieve distress in the child, which appears to have been accepted by the jury.

Administration of pain killing drugs for the purposes of pain relief

R v Bodkin Adams *[1957] Crim LR 773*

In 1957, Dr Bodkin Adams was charged with the murder of an 81 year old patient who had suffered a stroke. It was alleged that he had prescribed and administered such large quantities of drugs (heroin and morphine) that he must have known that the drugs would have killed her.

She was incurably ill, but not terminally ill; she had left Dr Bodkin Adams a chest full of silver and a Rolls Royce. The decision (before Devlin J) introduced the *double effect* principle: if one act has two consequences, one good and one evil, then it may be morally acceptable in certain circumstances. For example, administering drugs to relieve pain, but which would eventually lead to death if administered in large doses. Devlin J declared: 'No doctor, nor any man, no more in the case of a dying man than a healthy, has the right to cut the thread of life,' but Dr Adams was acquitted of murder on the grounds that the ending of life was incidental to the relief of pain, which appeared to be the primary purpose of Dr Adams' actions. As Devlin J put it: 'The doctor is entitled to relieve pain and suffering even if the measures he takes may incidentally shorten life.'

This is a good example of the statement of a general principle (no doctor may shorten anyone else's life) qualified by an exception – the double effect exception.

Assisting suicide

An individual may end his own life, but to assist in suicide amounts to a criminal offence: see s 2(1) of the Suicide Act 1962, which states:

> A person who aids, abets, counsels or procures the suicide of another or an attempt by another to commit suicide, shall be liable on conviction on indictment to imprisonment for a period not exceeding 14 years.

Another form of assisted suicide is where a doctor furnishes the means to a patient who is not dying to kill himself. Hence, a doctor may provide a pill to a patient which the patient then takes, in the full knowledge that it will kill him, but the act of swallowing the pill breaks the chain of causation between the doctor's act of providing the pill and the patient's death. The doctor would then be guilty of an offence under s 2 of the Suicide Act 1961, which deals with criminal liability for aiding, abetting, counselling or procuring the suicide of another.

AG v Able *[1984] QB 795*

In this case, various ways to commit suicide were set out in a booklet entitled *A Guide to Self-Deliverance* produced by the Voluntary Euthanasia Society, which was sold on request to members of the society aged 25 and over. A declaration was sought by the Attorney General that distribution of the booklet constituted an offence under the Suicide Act 1961. In order to find that an offence had been committed, the Voluntary Euthanasia Society must have intended to distribute the booklet to a person who, at the time of the distribution, was known to be contemplating suicide, with the intention to assist and encourage suicide by means of the booklet and that that person was *in fact* so encouraged and assisted.

The court (Woolf J) held that the sale of the booklet could be an offence, but this did not mean that any particular supply automatically constituted an offence. On the evidence before the court, the declaration sought by the Attorney General was refused.

This case is not a satisfactory one in terms of indirectly allowing the promotion of suicide and the requirements laid down are rather difficult to satisfy. It is noteworthy, however, that such booklets are now available in ordinary bookshops and there is no attempt by the Euthanasia Society to sell such literature in any clandestine manner.

At the other end of the spectrum from sanctity of life is the quality of life principle, which states that, basically, life is not intrinsically of value but is made valuable from the life-holder's capacity for enjoying certain pleasurable states of consciousness which we associate with normal day to day sensations of life.

AUTHORISATION OF NON-TREATMENT

The incompetent adult patient

We now look at another tragic and extremely difficult area of medical law and ethics – the treatment of patients in a persistent (now usually termed 'permanent') vegetative state (PVS). This is the condition where the brain expresses no evidence of activity in the cerebral cortex, the cognitive part of the brain. Difficult legal and moral questions are confronted in these sorts of cases because it brings into sharp focus the sanctity of life doctrine – should human life continue to be preserved, even when the patient is likely to continue to be in a comatose state, insensate, and totally unaware of anything going on around him or her, despite the continued functioning of organs such as the lungs and heart? PVS occurs when there is neurological damage to the cerebral hemispheres which govern voluntary action and consciousness so that the patient may be permanently unconscious. Note that such a patient is not brain dead, as this entails the 'irreversible loss of the capacity for consciousness, combined with irreversible loss of the capacity to breathe', which may be identified applying the accepted 'brain stem death criteria' (see Royal College of Physicians 'Criteria for the diagnosis of brain stem death' (1995) 29 J Royal College of Physicians 381).

Royal College of Physicians: definitions of vegetative state

In 1996, the Royal College of Physicians defined the vegetative state as:

> A clinical condition of unawareness of self and environment in which the patient breathes spontaneously, has a stable circulation and shows cycles of eye closure and eye opening which may stimulate sleep and waking. This may be a transient stage in the recovery from coma or it may persist until death.

The continuing vegetative state

When the vegetative state continues for more than four weeks, it becomes increasingly unlikely that the condition is part of a recovery phase from coma and the diagnosis of a continuing vegetative state can be made.

The permanent vegetative state

A patient in a continuing vegetative state will enter a permanent vegetative state when the diagnosis of irreversibility can be established with a high degree of clinical certainty. It is a diagnosis which is not absolute, but based on probabilities. Nevertheless, it may reasonably be made when a patient has been in a continuing vegetative state following head injury for more than 12 months or following other causes of brain damage for more than six months.

The College had set out the criteria for diagnosis of permanent vegetative state in 1995 (see discussion above, p 296). The Report of the College was endorsed by the Conference of Medical Royal Colleges and their Faculties of the United Kingdom.

In 1994, in the USA, pre-dating the College Report, the Report of the Multi-Society Task Force on PVS was published in the New England Journal of Medicine on 26 May 1994. Its findings are similar, and the only difference of substance appears to be that the periods before artificial nutrition and hydration might be discounted are shorter than those recommended by the College.

The Tony Bland *case*

In the early 1990s, arguably the most significant 'right to life' or 'euthanasia' case to reach the House of Lords was the *Tony Bland* case (*Airedale NHS Trust v Bland* [1993] 1 All ER 821). Some press reports suggested that this was a case about withdrawing a life support machine, but the fact is that Tony Bland, the PVS patient, did not need such artificial support. The case dealt with the question of whether it was lawful to withdraw the provision of food and fluid to a patient through a tube knowing that to do so would result in the death of that patient. The House of Lords' eventual decision, to allow the withdrawal of food, has been seen as marking a watershed in the law relating to the lawful withdrawal of medical treatment in relation to insensate patients.

Airedale NHS Trust v Bland *[1993] 1 All ER 821*

Tony Bland, a victim of the Hillsborough football disaster in 1989, which took nearly a hundred lives, lay in a PVS for more than three years. Bland's brain stem was diagnosed as being still alive; however, he had suffered massive and irreversible brain damage. Medical opinion was unanimous that he would never regain any form of awareness, but he was not legally dead, and was being fed by naso-gastric tube. The Trust looking after him applied to the court (with the approval of the parents) that it would be lawful to withhold any further life-prolonging treatment and care, (which included artificial nutrition, hydration and antibiotics), thus allowing him to die.

(In law, *cessation of treatment* is an *omission* and *not* an act; therefore, it would not be a criminal act unless the doctors are under a duty to continue the regime. Since all hope has been abandoned and there is no longer a duty to continue hydration and nourishment, a failure to do so cannot be a criminal offence. The basis for withdrawal of treatment is what amounts to the best interests of the patient. Withdrawal would not be an offence if it was in the patient's best interests.)

On the question of the acceptable course of action, the majority of the court accepted the test laid down in *Bolam v Friern Hospital Management Committee* [1957] 2 All ER 118, whereby it was acceptable medical practice to withdraw medical treatment if a responsible body of medical opinion supported this course of action.

The ethical issue was clearly the applicability or otherwise of the sanctity of life principle.

Issues

(a) Whether continuance of the treatment would, more than three years after the injuries which resulted in PVS, confer any benefit on Tony Bland?

(b) Was there a duty on the doctors to continue to treat the patient in these cases? If so, then it would not be lawful for a doctor who assumed responsibility for the patient to simply give up treating that patient. However, a medical practitioner is under no duty to continue to treat such a patient where a large body of informed and responsible medical opinion believes that no benefit would be conferred by continuance of the treatment.

The House of Lords ruled that it *was* lawful to withdraw artificial nutrition and hydration from a PVS patient because continued intervention would confer no 'benefit' upon the patient and hence was not in his 'best interests'.

The House of Lords therefore held:

(a) the object of medical treatment and care was to benefit the patient, but since a large body of informed and responsible medical opinion was of the view that existence in the PVS was not of benefit to the patient, the principle of sanctity of life, which was not absolute, was not violated by ceasing to give medical treatment and care involving invasive manipulation of the patient's body, to which he had not consented and which conferred no benefit upon him, to a PVS patient who had been in that state for over 3 years;

(b) that the doctors responsible for the patient's treatment were neither under a duty, nor (*per* Lord Browne-Wilkinson) entitled, to continue such medical care;

(c) that since the time had come when the patient had no further interest in being kept alive, the necessity to do so, created by his inability to make a choice, and the justification for the invasive care and treatment had gone;
(d) accordingly, the omission to perform what had previously been a duty would no longer be unlawful.

Tony Bland had no interests, said the Law Lords, because he was in PVS. The life supports were withdrawn and Tony Bland later died as a result of renal failure. In this case, three of the Law Lords assumed that the doctor's purpose in withdrawing Tony Bland's tube-feeding was to end his life. Nevertheless, they ruled that, in the circumstances, it would be lawful to do so.

Analysis of the Tony Bland *judgments*

Can death ever be in a patient's best interests?

Lord Browne-Wilkinson and Lord Lowry opined that, if it could be established that life prolonging treatment was no longer in the incompetent patient's best interests, such treatment would become an unlawful battery. There appeared to be a reluctance to apply *Bolam*, but they did so anyway.

Lord Goff clearly adopted a strong *Bolam* line, saying: 'There is overwhelming evidence that, in the medical profession, artificial feeding is regarded as a form of medical treatment ...' In even stronger terms, he stated that there was an 'established rule' that:

> A doctor may, when caring for a patient who is, for example, caring for a patient who is, for example, dying of cancer, lawfully administer painkilling drugs despite the fact that he knows that an incidental effect of that application will be to abbreviate the patient's life ... Such a decision may properly be made as part of the care of the living patient, in his best interests, and, on this basis, lawful.

Lord Mustill did not support a best interests test. He was not impressed by the acts/omissions dichotomy and declared (p 388) that 'the ethical status of the two courses of action is for all relevant purposes indistinguishable'. Indeed, he said:

> I venture to feel some reservations about the application of the principle of civil liability in negligence laid down in Bolam ... to decisions on 'best interests' in a field dominated by the criminal law. I accept without difficulty that this principle applies to the ascertainment of the medical raw materials such as diagnosis, prognosis and appraisal of the patient's cognitive functions. Beyond this point, however, it may be said that the decision is ethical, not medical, and that there is no reason in logic why on such a decision the opinions of doctors should be decisive. If there had been a possibility that this question might make a difference to the outcome of the appeal I would have wished to consider it further, but since it does not I prefer for the moment to express no opinion on it.

Lord Mustill also expressed the view that the foundations of the courts' unanimous decision were 'morally and intellectually misshapen'.

Comment on Bland

This case undoubtedly marks a watershed in English medical law. Before the *Bland* judgment, it was a felony to intentionally kill a patient either by commission (such as giving a lethal injection) or by omission (such as not taking steps to stop bleeding, omitting to provide insulin for an insulin-dependent diabetic or failing to provide necessary food and water to a patient. In the case itself, Sir Thomas Bingham MR declared that 'It is ... important to be clear from the outset what the case is, and is not, about. It is not about euthanasia, if by that is meant taking of positive action to cause death.' But Lord Goff of Chieveley clearly disagreed, saying:

> To act is to cross the Rubicon which runs between on the one hand the care of the living patient and on the other hand euthanasia – actively causing his death to avoid or to end his suffering ... It is true that the drawing of this distinction may lead to a charge of hypocrisy because it can be asked why, if the doctor, by discontinuing treatment, is entitled in consequence to let his patient die, it should be lawful to put him out of his misery straightaway in a more humane manner by a lethal injunction, rather than let him linger on in pain until he dies.

The nature of the dilemma was summarised by Lord Browne-Wilkinson, who said:

> ... the conclusion that I have reached will appear to some almost irrational. How can it be lawful to allow a patient to die slowly, though painlessly, over a period of weeks from lack of food but unlawful to produce his immediate death by a lethal injection, thereby saving his family from yet another ordeal ...? I find it difficult to find a moral answer to that question. But it is undoubtedly the law ...

His Lordship also said:

> Murder consists of causing the death of another with intent to do so. What is proposed in the present case is to adopt a course with the intention of bringing about Antony Bland's death. As to the element of intention or *mens rea*, in my judgment there can be no real doubt that it is present in this case: the whole purpose of stopping artificial feeding is to bring about the death of Anthony Bland.

In their Commentary on *Bland*, Kennedy and Grubb (1993) say the case is one of major significance in medical law for three reasons: (a) the Law Lords discussed a number of issues of general importance in medical law; and (b) the judges clarified the law in the previously uncertain area of the care of the patient in a persistent vegetative state (PVS); but (c) there remains uncertainty about how the law approaches the withdrawal of care from incompetent patients who are not in a PVS.

The dominance of *Bolam*

Four of the Law Lords regarded the *Bolam* test as a central criterion in determining the doctor's duty, namely, in determining whether to continue treatment would be in the patient's best interests. Yet, as Kennedy and Grubb (1993) point out, the difficulty in using *Bolam* to determine the legality of a doctor's conduct as opposed to its reasonableness was highlighted by Lord Mustill when he observed that *Bolam* should be restricted to 'the ascertainment of the medical raw material such as diagnosis, prognosis and appraisal of the patient's cognitive functions'. It should *not* be used when the decision was ethical, because there was 'no reason in logic why on such a decision the opinions of doctors should be decisive'.

The sanctity of life principle

What about the sanctity of life principle? The court said this is not an absolute principle; it does not in itself provide a complete answer, apply to force feeding prisoners, or justify compelling the keeping alive of patients who are terminally ill, where to do so would merely prolong their suffering. But it forbids the taking of active measures to shorten the life of a terminally ill patient. Although the judges identified *Bland* as a case in which sanctity of human life should yield to self-determination or best interests, no judgment actually attempts to state the content of the principle of the sanctity of human life.

Ordinary and extraordinary care

The judges in *Bland* do not refer to this well known distinction because, presumably, it takes them no further in determining what sort of care ought to be provided.

Acts and omissions

The Law Lords rejected the view that liability attaches only to acts, but never to omissions. On the contrary, they make it clear that there could be liability even for an omission if a prior duty to act existed and was breached.

The Bland *principle and the Human Rights Act 1998*

The question that arises as a result of the implementation of the Human Rights Act 1998 in Britain is whether the *Bland* principle has to be reconsidered, particularly in relation to Art 2 of the Convention. In essence, does the 'right to life' under Art 2 negate the *Bland* principle? According to a recent case, the decision and approach taken in *Bland* is in accordance with Art 2 of the Human Rights Act. In *NHS Trust A v Mrs M; NHS Trust B v Mrs H* (2000) (Lawtel), the High Court (*per* Butler-Sloss P) held that it was not correct to interpret Art 2 of the Convention to mean that a decision to cease treatment in a patient's best interests was intentional deprivation of life. Although the intention in withdrawing artificial nutrition and hydration in PVS cases was to hasten death, the phrase 'deprivation of life' had to import a deliberate act as opposed to an omission by someone acting on behalf of the State resulting in death. Treatment which was no longer in the best interests of a patient would violate that patient's autonomy even though discontinuance would shorten the patient's life. Article 2 of the Convention contained a positive obligation on a State to take adequate and appropriate steps to safeguard life, but where a clinical decision had been made to withhold treatment on the ground that it was not in the patient's best interests, and the clinical decision was in accordance with a respectable body of medical opinion, the State's positive obligation under Art 2 of the Convention was discharged. In the case itself, one patient had been in PVS for over three years, the other for 10 months. The Court granted a declaration that it was lawful for the hospital trusts to withdraw artificial nutrition and hydration from both patients.

The 1999 BMA Guidelines

The BMA's publication, *The Withholding and Withdrawing of Life Prolonging Medical Treatment*, published in 1999, is an illuminating document which is a potentially controversial contribution to the debate on withdrawal of life support. The document accepts the Law Lords' definition in *Bland* that the provision of food and water through a tube is artificial and part of medical treatment. The BMA now appears to accept that the practice of legally withdrawing food and fluid from patients in PVS should not be subject to court review. It also states (p 57):

> Existing guidance from the courts on the withdrawal of artificial nutrition and hydration refers only to patients in persistent vegetative state and the UK courts have not yet considered other cases. Clearly, this situation may change

> over time. If, subsequent to the publication of this guidance, authoritative legal rulings are made, doctors must respect them.

The patients referred to are mentioned in the same chapter:

> The courts have not specified that declarations should not be sought before withholding or withdrawing artificial nutrition and hydration from patients who are not in a persistent vegetative state. Although a body of medical opinion has developed that such action would be appropriate in some cases (such as patients who have suffered a serious stroke or have severe dementia), UK courts have not yet considered such a case.

It therefore appears that the BMA now suggests that the withdrawal of tube-delivered food and water, not only from PVS patients, but also from patients who are not terminally ill, such as those with severe dementia or serious stroke, should not be subject to court review.

John Keown (2000) offers three criticisms of this guidance, and suggests that it is so flawed it should be withdrawn:

(a) the BMA's argument in its latest Guidance that tube feeding is medical treatment rather than basic care is weak;

(b) the reasons given for not treating or tube feeding undermine the BMA's long standing opposition to active euthanasia and active assisted suicide;

(c) the BMA guidance relies heavily on legal precedent at the expense of ethical reasoning.

Expedited hearing – the Frenchay *case*

Bland was followed in *Frenchay Healthcare NHS Trust v S* (1994).

Frenchay NHS Trust *[1994] 2 All ER 403; [1994] 1 FLR 485, CA*

S, a teenager, took a drug overdose in June 1991 and consequently suffered acute brain damage; he was treated in hospital where he was diagnosed by the consultant in charge as being in a persistent vegetative state (PVS). He was fed through a naso-gastric tube in his stomach (a gastrostomy tube). The tube became disconnected and dislodged, probably as a result of his own movement. The consultant surgeon believed that the tube could not be reconnected and thought the only alternative was to insert another tube, but took the view that continued treatment was not in the best interests of the patient.

The hospital sought a court order that it would be lawful not to reinsert the tube.

The first instance judge agreed; the Official Solicitor appealed to the Court of Appeal, and argued for more time to obtain another independent medical report, but the Court of Appeal held:

(a) Although the time scale had been compressed, the appeal should not be allowed simply on the basis that there had not been an opportunity on behalf of S for a full exploration of the facts. Indeed, there would be cases of acute emergency where it would be impossible that doctors should be obliged or able to come to the court and seek a decision.

(b) The evidence of PVS in the case was not as emphatic nor as unanimous as it had been in *Airedale NHS Trust v Bland* [1993] 1 FLR 1026, but the evidence of those doctors who knew him best was convincing.

(c) That it would be lawful not to reinstate the tube, thus agreeing with the doctor, stressing it was in the best interests of the patient and that there was no medical opinion which contradicted the medical opinion of the consultant in this case.

The court agreed to grant a declaration at an expedited hearing.

Are the views of relatives of any significance?

In *Re SG; Re G* [1995] 2 FCR 46; [1995] 2 FLR 528, the patient, after a motorcycle accident, suffered severe head injuries and lay in PVS for three and a half years. Further brain damage was caused by cardiac arrest in hospital. The wife supported the action, but the mother opposed it and wanted treatment to be continued. The court opined that his mother's views were relevant, but could not prevail.

The court therefore authorised the withdrawal of treatment.

One effect of *Bland* is that the courts will have regard to the wishes of spouses and parents, but will not give their wishes a determinative effect. In other words, they will not be given the ultimate right to decide on their relative's treatment.

The principle that has apparently emerged from these PVS decisions is that the final decision on these sorts of PVS cases lies with the *court*, not the relatives of the patient.

Re D

In *Re D* [1998] 1 FLR 411, Sir Stephen Brown P granted a declaration that it would be lawful not to re-attach the feeding tube of a woman who had been in what was described as a 'near PVS' since September 1995. The decision attracted some concern, since it did not appear to satisfy all the Royal College of Physicians' guidelines for the diagnosis of PVS and it coincided with a report in the media of another patient recovering some awareness after ostensibly being in full PVS for nearly eight years. This case, as in the *Frenchay* and *Swindon* cases, was expedited, that is, was decided at an expedited hearing after a problem developed with the patient's feeding tube of its own accord.

Patients cared for at home

Swindon and Marlborough NHS Trust v S *(1994) unreported*

The patient, a woman, had lain in an unresponsive state for two and a half years. She went into a coma after neurosurgery to remove a brain tumour. Her husband and children, who had strong religious faith, did not wish for her feeding tube to be unblocked when a problem arose without warning. They did not wish for her to be kept alive in her totally unresponsive state. Although only notified late on a Friday afternoon, the Official Solicitor was able to instruct an independent expert in rehabilitation to examine the patient, S, and to report to the hearing which took place before Ward J on the afternoon of the Saturday. The judge granted the declaration authorising withdrawal of treatment asked for by the NHS Trust, even though the patient was being cared for by her family at home. To date, this is the only PVS patient to have been in this situation.

Comparative excursus

In 1996, Scotland followed the *Bland* precedent in the Court of Session case of *Law Hospital NHS Trust v Lord Advocate* 1996 SLT 848. Countries that have differed somewhat in the reasoning, but agreed on the outcome, include South Africa (*Clarke v Hurst* (1992) (4) SA 630); the Netherlands (*Stinissen* case, *Jurisprudence nr 1987/50* and *Jurisprudentie nr 1990/63*); Germany (BGH 1 StR 357 (BGB); and Ireland (*In the Matter of a Ward of Court* [1995] ILRM 401 (Irish Sup Ct), where there was a patient 'very nearly in PVS'). For the USA, the Netherlands and the position in other countries, see Chapter 18).

Practice Note on PVS patients

Practice Note

In March 1994, the Official Solicitor issued a *Practice Direction on PVS* [1994] 1 FLR 654 but, on 26 July 1996, another Practice Note was issued, which replaces the previous Note.

Practice Note [1996] 4 All ER 766

Practice Note on Persistent Vegetative State

1 The termination of artificial feeding and hydration for patients in a vegetative state will in virtually all cases require the prior sanction of a High Court judge: *Airedale NHS Trust v Bland* [1993] 1 All ER 821, p 833 and *Frenchay Healthcare NHS Trust v S* [1994] 2 All ER 403.

2 The diagnosis should be made in accordance with the most up to date generally accepted guidelines for the medical profession. A working group of the Royal College of Physicians issued guidance on the diagnosis and management of the permanent vegetative state (PVS) in March 1996. This has been endorsed by the Conference of Medical Royal Colleges. The working group advises that the diagnosis of PVS is not absolute, but based on probabilities. Such a diagnosis may not reasonably be made until the patient has been in a continuing vegetative state following head injury for more than 12 months or following other causes of brain damage for more than six months. Before then, as soon as the patient's condition has stabilised, rehabilitative measures, such as coma arousal programmes, should be instituted (see *Airedale NHS Trust v Bland* (above) [1993] AC 789, pp 870–71, *per* Lord Goff). It is not appropriate to apply to court for permission to terminate artificial feeding and hydration until the condition is judged to be permanent. In many cases, it will be necessary to commission reports based on clinical and other observations of the patient over a period of time.

Applications to court

3 Applications to court should be by originating summons issued in the Family Division of the High Court seeking a declaration ... subject to specific provisions below, the application should follow the procedure laid down for sterilisation cases by the House of Lords in *F v West*

Berkshire HA [1989] 2 All ER 545 and in the Official Solicitor's Practice Note [1996] 2 FLR 111).

4 Applications to court in relation to minors should be made within wardship proceedings ...

5 ... [form of the originating summons]

6 The case will normally be heard in open court. The court will, however, usually take steps to preserve the anonymity of the patient and the patient's family (and, where appropriate, the hospital) by making orders under s 11 of the Contempt of Court Act 1981 ...

The parties

7 The applicant may be either the next of kin or other individual closely connected with the patient or the relevant district health authority/NHS Trust ... the views of the next of kin or of others close to the patient cannot act as veto to an application but they must be taken fully into account by the court (*Re G (Persistent Vegetative State)* [1995] 2 FCR 46).

8 The Official Solicitor should normally be invited to act as guardian ad litem of the patient, who will inevitably be a patient within the meaning of RSC Ord 80 ...

The investigation

9 There should be at least two independent reports on the patient from neurologists or other doctors experienced in assessing disturbances of consciousness. One of these reports will be commissioned by the Official Solicitor. The duties of doctors making the diagnosis are described in the report of the working group of the Royal College of Physicians ... (*inter alia*):

> They should undertake their own assessment separately and should write clearly the details of that assessment and their conclusions in the notes. They must ask medical and other clinical staff and relatives or carers about the reactions and responses of the patient and it is important that the assessors shall take into account the descriptions and comments by relatives, carers and nursing staff who spend most time with the patient ... It is to be emphasised that there is no urgency in making the diagnosis of the permanent vegetative state. If there is any uncertainty in the mind of the assessor then the diagnosis shall not be made and a reassessment undertaken after further time has elapsed. The most important role of the medical practitioner in making the diagnosis is to ensure that the patient is not sentient and, in this

respect, the views of the nursing staff, relatives and carers are of considerable importance and help.

The views of the patient and others

10 The Official Solicitor's representative will normally require to interview the next of kin and others close to the patient as well as seeing the patient and those caring for him. The views of the patient may have been expressed, either in writing or otherwise. The High Court may determine the effect of a purported advance directive as to future medical treatment ... In summary, the patient's previously expressed views, if any, will always be an important component in the decisions of the doctors and of the court, particularly if they are clearly established and were intended to apply to the circumstances which have in fact arisen ...

The slippery slope argument

The major argument that runs through the debate on euthanasia is that, if 'physician-assisted' deaths were allowed, doctors would assist in suicides in more and more dubious circumstances: that is, if the doctor were authorised to carry out so called mercy killings at the request of patients who were temporarily suffering from very low self-esteem, at which point could he decide that the treatment asked for would be in the patient's best interests? Put another way, if one type of case may be lawful at the discretion of the doctor, how far should he be permitted to go? Would this not eventually lead to carrying out non-voluntary euthanasia as it is perceived happens in the Netherlands?

ADVANCE DIRECTIVES

An advance directive is 'a stipulation made by a competent person about the medical treatment he should or should not receive in the event of his becoming incompetent to make or communicate treatment choices' (Hornett (1995)). It can be in the form of a document (usually called a 'living will') which sets out an individual's wishes regarding what measures should or should not be taken in the event of incompetence and the occurrence of medical conditions or precipitating events. In the alternative, an individual may confer an enduring power of attorney by which he appoints an agent to make decisions on his behalf during any future period of incompetence (Hornett (1995)). It may well include a refusal of treatment, but it can also authorise life prolonging treatment, although it cannot require that such treatment be given. In short, such directives could be general or specific, oral or written. Of course, if oral statements uttered in times of stress or anxiety are accepted, there is potential for exploitation and questions of proof may present insuperable difficulties for relatives and, in some cases, may even endanger the life of the patient.

The UK has no legislative framework giving effect to advance directives or defining their scope, but the legal position of the advance directive is that they will probably have legal effect provided they satisfy the requirements laid down in *Re T (Adult: Refusal of Treatment)* [1992] 4 All ER 649; [1993] Fam 95, namely, that it must be 'clearly established' and 'applicable in the circumstances' (of the particular case). Doctors will also have to consider the true scope and basis of the decision expressed and must ask whether the patient has refused consent to the treatment or procedure which it is desired to carry out. Lord Donaldson particularly stressed that 'what really matters is the declaration by the patient of his decision with a full appreciation of the possible consequences, the latter being expressed in the simplest possible terms'.

Several draft living wills have been published by the Terence Higgins Trust in conjunction with King's College, London.

The two key concepts which underpin these devices are: (a) a patient has the right to refuse medical treatment, including life saving and life sustaining treatment, which refusal should be respected and complied with by the patient's doctors and (b) a person can make valid and enforceable treatment decisions in anticipation of incompetence (Hornett, p 298).

Yet, as Mason and McCall Smith rightly say, it is almost impossible to devise an intelligible document which will be unambiguous in all circumstances, with the need, for example, to define 'severe', 'advanced' or 'comparable gravity' (see Mason and McCall Smith (1999), p 433).

Another concern is that the patient has, in the period between making the living will and the onset of the illness or the incapacitating event, changed his mind.

The only official formulation that appears to exist is in a Practice Note [1994] 2 All ER 413 which states:

> The views of the patient may have been previously expressed, either in writing or otherwise. The High Court exercising its inherent jurisdiction may determine the effect of a purported advance directive as to future medical treatment ... In summary, the patient's expressed views, if any, will always be a very important component in the decisions of the doctors and the court.

Two of the Law Lords in the *Bland* case indicated that the advance directive had legal status (*per* Lord Keith and Lord Goff in *Bland* [1993] 1 All ER 821, pp 860, 866; (1992) BMLR 64, p 105. However, their comments were arguably *obiter*.

Davies (1998) argues that, although Lord Keith found support for the potential legitimacy of an advance declaration of refusal of treatment in the cases of *Re F* and *Re T*, there are still questions which will require resolution before it would be possible to decide whether such a directive will apply to or bind those who may be considering treatment in the future (see Davies (1998), p 358). The questions he highlights are:

(a) Was the directive made while the patient was competent?

(b) Was it meant to apply in the situation which has arisen?

(c) Was it an autonomous, freely made decision?

The Law Commission has recommended the development, through legislation, of legally binding anticipatory declarations as to treatment (see *Mentally Incapacitated Adults and Decision Making, Medical Treatment and Research* (No 129) (1993)).

RECENT DEVELOPMENTS

In early to mid-2000, the media reported that several people had expressed anger at the revelation that a 'Do not resuscitate' (DNR)/'not to be resuscitated' directive is frequently written on a patient's case notes without their knowledge and often in code. The BMA has firmly rejected age discrimination, and reaffirms its commitment to good ethical practice by stating that it was working on new guidance regarding the practice of obtaining consent. It may be argued that cardio-pulmonary resuscitation would be an unwarranted intervention in the majority of frail and dying patients and should only be used where cardiac arrest or cessation of respiration is sudden and unexpected or where there is a good chance of success. However, to write a DNR note on patient's notes without their consent may be interpreted as a denial of that patient's right to decide and the patient's right to the highest standards of medical care and arguably is not necessarily in that patient's best interests.

The Prevention of Euthanasia Bill

On 14 April 2000, the British Parliament backed Anne Winterton's Prevention of Euthanasia Bill by 96 votes to 10. This made it four votes short of the total required for the Bill to proceed to the next stage of parliamentary proceedings. It was therefore defeated. The reasons for this defeat are because the present Labour Government and the British Medical Association opposed it and MPs who supported it did not turn up to vote. The Bill stated: 'It shall be unlawful for any person responsible for the care of a patient to withdraw or withhold from the patient medical treatment or sustenance if his purpose or one of his purposes in doing so is to hasten or otherwise cause the death of the patient.'

The BMA held a two day consensus conference on 3 and 4 March 2000, which firmly rejected any attempt to change the law on physician-assisted suicide. The debates will doubtless continue.

CONCLUSIONS

Philosophy and law make a distinction between active killing and killing by omission (often dubbed omitting to act or withdrawing treatment, as opposed to actively intervening to terminate life). But, is there really a moral difference between the two? This must remain highly doubtful. There must, justifiably, be great sympathy with the relatives of PVS patients who have been insensate for long periods of time and with relatives of all patients who are terminally ill. However, in trying to be compassionate to these relatives, we have continually to be guided by individual conscience and it is argued that allowing withdrawal of treatment from those who have suffered strokes or are suffering from dementia is an ominous step down that 'slippery slope'. In any case, while we must not lose sight of our basic humanity and compassion, we must also know when to draw the line and not extend the *Bland* approach to non-PVS patients. Ann Winterton's Bill, or a variation thereof, must be revived, debated and, if deemed acceptable by a majority of MPs, become law.

SELECTIVE BIBLIOGRAPHY

Age Concern Institute of Gerontology, *The Living Will: Consent to Treatment at the End of Life*, 1988, Age Concern

Annas, G, 'From Canada with love: anencephalic newborns as organ donors' (1987) 17 Hastings Centre Report 36

Brazier, M, *Medicine, Patient and the Law*, 1992, Penguin

Davies, M, *Textbook on Medical Law*, 2nd edn, 1998, Blackstone

Finnis, J, '*Bland*: crossing the Rubicon?' (1993) 109 LQR 329

Giesen, D, 'Dilemmas at life's end: a comparative legal perspective', in Keown, J (ed), *Euthanasia Examined*, 1995, CUP

Glover, J, *Causing Death and Saving Lives*, 1988, Penguin

Hart, H, and Honore, T, *Causation in the Law*, 1959, Clarendon

Hornett, S, 'Advance directives: a legal and ethical analysis', in Keown, J (ed), *Euthanasia Examined*, 1995, CUP, p 297

Jennett, B, 'Managing patients in a persistent vegetative state since *Airedale NHS Trust v Bland*', in McLean, SAM (ed), *Death, Dying and the Law*, 1996, Dartmouth

Jones, DA, 'The UK definition of death' (1999) Law & Justice 56

Kennedy, I and Grubb, A, 'Commentary [on *Bland*]' (1993) 4 Med L Rev 360

Kamisar, Y, 'Physician-assisted suicide: the last bridge to active voluntary euthanasia', in Keown, J (ed), *Euthanasia Examined*, 1995, CUP

Keown, J, *Euthanasia Examined*, 1995, CUP

Keown, J, 'Restoring moral and intellectual shape to the law after *Bland*' (1997) 113 LQR 481

Keown, J, 'Beyond *Bland*: a critique of the BMA guidance on withholding and withdrawing medical treatment' (2000) 20 LS 66

Mason, JK and McCall Smith, RA, *Law and Medical Ethics*, 5th edn, 1999, Butterworths

McCall Smith, A, 'Euthanasia: the strengths of the middle ground' (1999) 10 Med L Rev 194

McColl (Lord), 'Medical decision making at the end of life – euthanasia in the 1990s and beyond' (1999) Law & Justice 16

McLean, SAM (ed), *Death, Dying and the Law*, 1996, Dartmouth

Otlowski, 'Active voluntary euthanasia: options for reform' [1994] 2 Med LR 161

Price, D, 'Euthanasia, pain relief and double effect' [1997] 17 LS 323

Stauch, M and Wheat, K, with Tingle, J, *Sourcebook on Medical Law*, 1998, Cavendish Publishing

Wells, C, 'Otherwise kill me: marginal children and ethics at the edges of existence', in Lee, R and Morgan, D (eds), *Birthrights*, 1989, Routledge

Williams, G, *The Sanctity of Life and the Criminal Law*, 1958, Faber & Faber

PART II

COMPARATIVE PERSPECTIVES

CONSENT TO MEDICAL TREATMENT: EVOLUTION AND DEVELOPMENT OF THE LAW IN NON-UK JURISDICTIONS

INTRODUCTION

Despite its relatively new origins, the notion and concept of consent to treatment is now regarded in major Western jurisdictions as an essential requirement in any doctor-patient or healthcare professional-patient interaction. In certain jurisdictions, this concept has been labelled 'informed consent' or 'voluntary consent'. As we have seen, day to day transactions will usually be carried out on the basis of implied consent, in the sense that the mere presence of the patient in the waiting room of a surgery or hospital or clinic, followed by such actions as holding out an arm when an injection is suggested by the healthcare professional dealing with the patient, or by impliedly agreeing to a medical examination by loosening clothing after receiving a request to do so prior to a medical examination, or allowing blood pressure to be taken, or to indicate agreement to a medical procedure, no matter how simple or commonplace, are all actions which the law in most 'developed' jurisdictions would recognise as signifying consent. Studies indicate that '[i]t is accepted in all major jurisdictions that the legally valid consent of the patient is an essential prerequisite to almost all medical treatment and diagnosis' (Giesen (1993)). The importance of the process by which consent is given or withheld was recently reaffirmed in the Council of Europe's Convention for the Protection of Human Rights and Dignity of the Human Being with Regard to the Application of Biology and Medicine: Convention on Human Rights and Biomedicine (European Treaty Series/164, 4.4.1997). This was opened for signature in April 1997 (see McLean, S, *Consent and the Law: Consultation Document*, 1997, HMSO, p 6). The Council of Europe is composed of 40 Member States and promulgates Conventions within its areas of competence to which it expects Member States to subscribe. Article 5 of the Convention states: 'An intervention in the health field may only be carried out after the person concerned has given free and informed consent to it. This person shall beforehand be given appropriate information as to the purpose and nature of the intervention as well as on its consequences and risks. The person concerned may freely withdraw consent at any time.' The Convention also mandates, in Art 6.1, that, subject to specified exceptions: '... an intervention may only be carried out on a person who does not have the capacity to consent, for his or her direct benefit.'

In the earlier part of this book (see Chapter 1), we attempted an excursus into the origins of this multi-faceted concept, noting that the concept itself originates from the USA, although this point is sometimes overlooked when discussing the 'English law' version of consent, and noting that its exact provenance may now be a matter of purely academic interest.

The term 'informed consent' seems to have made its appearance in an appendix to the Nuremberg Code. As Faulder puts it, '[the concept] emerged as a formally stated principle only after the Second World War, following the trial of the Nazi war criminals, most of them doctors, whose appalling experiments on concentration camp inmates in the name of scientific research shocked the world and produced the Nuremberg Code.' The code 'formulates certain basic principles for medical experimentation on human beings', the first of which declares that 'the voluntary consent of the human subject is absolutely essential'.

In this chapter, we look at how the American concept evolved and came to be established, and see how jurisdictions, particularly Canada and Australia, also began to adopt consent as a guiding principle, but have not accepted the English approach in *Bolam*. In passing, we also note developments in countries like Japan, where their Ministry of Health and Welfare has implemented a policy of paying physicians to explain the nature of the patient's medical condition.

AMERICAN LAW

Evolution of the informed consent doctrine

The doctrine of informed consent, at least in an embryonic state, first appeared in American case law in 1957 in *Salgo v Leland Stanford Jr University Board of Trustees* (1957) 317 P 2d 170 (Cal), where the phrase was apparently coined in an *amicus curiae* (friend of the court) brief by the American College of Surgeons to the California Court of Appeals. The facts of the case were that the defendant was Dr Gerbode, an eminent surgeon and professor of surgery at Stanford Medical School. The plaintiff had a history of an eye condition indicating premature ageing and had developed cramping in his legs, which had been treated with drugs. He was referred to the defendant, who found that the plaintiff had blood circulatory problems likely to cause a stroke in the brain or coronary occlusion to the heart vessels. The plaintiff was, therefore, advised to undergo certain investigative procedures in the hospital which would confirm whether an operation for removing or replacing a segment of the aorta, which would improve blood circulation to his leg and prolong his life, was necessary. The plaintiff entered the hospital at the defendant's suggestion, but the defendant did not explain all the various possibilities. A syringe was attached to a needle inserted in his aorta, through which materials were injected which allowed the medical team to take X-rays while the plaintiff was under anaesthetic. The procedure appeared to have been carried out without any incident until the plaintiff awoke the next morning and found his lower extremities paralysed. It was found that this paralysis was permanent. The lower court judge placed the burden of proof on the doctor under the presumption *res ipsa loquitur* (the thing speaks for itself). On appeal, the judgment of *res ipsa loquitur* was reversed, because it was thought that this would hamper the development of medical science. The court stated the doctrine of informed consent:

> A physician violates his duty to his patient and subjects himself to liability if he withholds any facts which are necessary to form the basis of an intelligent consent by the patient to the proposed treatment, and the physician may not minimise known dangers in order to induce his patient's consent; but the patient's mental and emotional condition is important, and in discussing the element of risk a certain amount of discretion must be employed consistent with full disclosure of facts necessary to informed consent.

Thus, the court concluded that the doctor had the duty to disclose to the patient 'any facts which are necessary to form the basis of an intelligent consent by the patient to the proposed treatment'. However, the earlier phrase 'intelligent consent' was later replaced by 'informed consent' in the part of the judgment dealing with therapeutic privilege where the court said that '[i]n discussing the element of risk, a certain amount of discretion must be employed with full disclosure of facts necessary to an informed consent' (see also Mason and McCall Smith (1999), p 277, who cite Silverman (1989) as the source of their account of the historical facts). In the next few years, this concept of consent was extended to include medical treatment generally, to apply to both clinical practice and clinical research, and only gradually became established and 'formalised in a succession of North American legal judgments' (Faulder (1985), p 13). Indeed, the idea of a malpractice legal action or malpractice suit against medical practitioners did not gather any momentum or pose any threat to the medical profession in America until the 1900s (see Healy (1999), p 93) for a number of reasons which Healy expresses thus: (a) 'the tort of trespass had been narrowly defined ... [it] generally required proof of touching that was intentional, hostile, and non-consensual'; (b) there was also 'a strategic decision within the profession to conceal information which might raise questions or elicit suspicion, grounded in the belief that this was more likely to attract the trust and respect of the general public' (Healy (1999), p 94, citing Konald (1962)). Gradually, however, 'a stream of increasingly sophisticated consent-based cases began to test the precise authority of doctors to treat their patients in specific ways' (Healy (1999), p 95), and despite initial reluctance by the courts to demand strict consent, 'the courts continued to emphasise the importance of express authorisation and consent' (Healy (1999)).

In the much-quoted 1914 case of *Schloendorff v Society of New York Hospital* (1914) 105 NE 92, Judge Cardozo uttered his seminal statement that: 'Every human being of adult years and sound mind has a right to determine what should be done with his own body; and a surgeon who performs an operation without his patient's consent, commits an assault for which he is liable in damages' (*Schloendorff v Society of New York Hospital* (1914) 211 NY 125, p 129). This case did not result in a flood of litigation or a change in approach to the issue of consent to treatment, but there were indications of how the law's approach was starting to change. In *Wall v Brim* (1943) 138 F 2d 478, for example, an attempt to assert disclosure rights by arguing that a doctor had misrepresented the nature of the treatment, by failing to direct the patient's attention to certain risks and possible outcomes, succeeded. Hutcheson J compared the giving of consent to the formation of a contract and concluded that 'a surgeon may not perform an operation different in kind from that consented to or to one involving risks and results not contemplated' (*Wall v Brim*). Hence, the courts 'began to insist more and more on the necessity of obtaining the patient's understanding of what was to be consented to' (Healy, p 96, also citing *Corn v French* (1955) 289 P 2d 173). In *Corn v French*, the plaintiff had signed a consent form 'for mastectomy and hemorrhoidectomy' without understanding the meaning of those words. However, at all stages until unconscious, she had insisted that she did not want her breast surgically removed. The doctor did, in fact, remove the breast and Badt J, of the Supreme Court of Nevada, found that the surgical removal had been contrary to the plaintiff's express oral instructions and could not be protected by the fact that the plaintiff had signed the consent form which had agreed to such an operation. In 1957, a celebrated article by Professor McCoid was published which surveyed the range of actions which doctors could now face, observing that the courts had rejected the charge of battery where it had been coupled with a charge of negligent treatment, on the basis that the two were mutually inconsistent, one relying on the lack of authority and the latter relying on the presence of it. He was referring to *Cody v Fraser* (1950) 122 Colo 252; (1950) 222 P 2d 422. A few months after McCoid's article was published, *Salgo v Leland* (above) was decided wherein Bray J, of the California Court of Appeals, held that 'a physician violates his duty to the patient and subjects himself to liability if he withholds any facts which are necessary to form the basis of an intelligent consent by the patient to the proposed treatment'. Although the plaintiff had formulated the claim in negligence, the court held that liability lay in battery with, as Healy points out, 'the important difference' being that 'whereas the well-established duty to explain the basic nature of the operation was absolute', this broader duty to disclose facts 'necessary to an informed consent' was subject to 'a certain amount of discretion' in doctors by which a decision to disclose may be guided by their apprehension of the 'patient's mental and emotional condition' (*Salgo v Leland* (1957) 817 P 2d 170, p 181). The battery analysis continued to develop in other American States (see, for example, *Gray v Grunnagle* (1966) 223 A 2d 663, where O'Brien J memorably observed, p 669, 'Every consent involves a submission; but a mere submission does not necessarily involve consent') and judicial attention was beginning to focus more on negligence as a more flexible forum for determining the scope of medical disclosure. The first landmark decision was made by the Supreme Court of Kansas in *Natanson v Kline* in 1960 ((1960) 186 KAN 393; (1960) 350 P 2d 1093, in which the court, apparently encouraged by the article by Professor McCoid, said:

> Anglo-American law starts with the premise of thorough-going self-determination. It follows that each man is considered to be master of his own body, and he may, if he be of sound mind, expressly prohibit the performance of life-saving surgery, or other medical treatment. A doctor might well believe that an operation or form of treatment is desirable or necessary but the law does not permit him to substitute his own judgment for that of the patient by any form of artifice or deception.

This has been described as 'an adventurous but deeply flawed attempt to forge a definitive test' (Healy (1999), p 98). Healy argues that, although this went some way towards curbing the dominance of expert testimony in disclosure trials, it 'amounted ultimately to a small step for it retained the professional standard test where any degree of relevant disclosure had been made by the defendant' (Healy (1999)). Indeed, Healy suggests that the decision appears to have caused more confusion by 'misapplying battery and negligence terminology throughout its two decisions'. However, in 1963, three years after this decision, the *Natanson* approach was endorsed with qualifications in *Williams v Menehan*, another Kansas case. In that case, the plaintiff suffered severe burns from radiation therapy following a bilateral mastectomy for breast cancer. She sued for non-disclosure of risks. The court declared that the doctor's duty to disclose meant there was a need to make a 'reasonable disclosure to his patient of the nature and probable consequences of the suggested or recommended treatment' and he also had to make 'a knowledgeable disclosure of the dangers within his knowledge which are incident or possible in the treatment he proposes'. However, the judgment also appeared to concede some form of therapeutic privilege when it said that the doctor was not obliged to disclose 'all facts, diagnoses and alternatives or possibilities which might occur to [him]' if there was a danger that this might cause the patient unnecessary anguish. Other States also began to explore the scope of the professional standard, but there was no consistency except that the weight given to expert testimony was being seriously questioned from time to time as a means of determining the breach of the duty to disclose.

By 1966, the notion of 'informed consent' was made a requirement for all State-funded research work, as a result of several allegations that potentially dangerous experiments were being carried out without the consent of the experimental subjects as embodied in the Surgeon General's Memorandum *Clinical Investigation Using Human Subjects* (1966). Thus, this was another form of 'informed consent' applied to a different context from the day to day medical relationship or transaction.

Canterbury v Spence *(1972)*

In 1972, the other landmark case of *Canterbury v Spence* was decided by the District Court (*Canterbury v Spence* (1972) 464 F 2d 772), which fully articulated the doctrine of informed consent. The 19 year old plaintiff was a clerk-typist employed by the Federal Bureau of Investigation and had been suffering shoulder pains; suspecting that this was the result of a ruptured disc, Dr Spence ordered a laminectomy, which entailed surgical removal of the bone arches of the patient's vertebrae to expose his spinal cord. The plaintiff's mother was told that this was 'not any more serious than any other operation' and she signed a consent form. The plaintiff had not been informed by the defendant that paralysis could be expected 'somewhere in the nature of 1%' (see p 778, col 2). Shortly after the operation, as a result of lack of post-operative supervision by the hospital (the second defendant), the plaintiff fell from his bed and, hours later, experienced paralysis from the waist down. His mother signed another consent form and the patient underwent another operation, resulting in some improvement of his muscle tone. When the case came for trial, the plaintiff remained partially paralysed, needed crutches to walk, suffered from urinal incontinence and wore a penile clamp. It was argued on behalf of Dr Spence that 'disclosure of minute risks of complication was not sound medical practice because this could potentially deter patients from undergoing much-needed surgery, and often caused adverse psychological reactions inimical to contemplated treatment' (Healy (1999), p 92).

In the case itself, Robinson J agreed with plaintiff's counsel that the 1% risk of paralysis should have been disclosed and firmly rejected the view that the standard of disclosure ought to be assessed in accordance with professional practice. The view the court took was that it should not be 'shackled' by expert testimony of general disclosure practices within the medical community.

The court stated two important principles. First, it declared:

> We reject the thought that the patient should ask for information before the physician is required to disclose. Caveat emptor is not the norm for the consumer of medical services. Duty to disclose is more than a call to speak merely on the patient's request or merely to answer the patient's questions: it is a duty to volunteer, if necessary, the information the patient needs for intelligent decision.

Indeed, Robinson J thought that there is 'no basis for operation of the special medical standard where the physician's activity does not bring his medical knowledge and skills into play'. On the contrary, the learned judge advocated that the *court* should take responsibility for deciding whether or not a patient has been given enough information to enable him to make an intelligent choice between alternative courses of treatment. Accordingly, the doctor should disclose all risks which might materially affect the patient's decision. In order to determine what was 'material', the court should consider how 'a reasonable person, in what the physician knows or should know to be the patient's position, would be likely to attach significance to the risk or cluster of risks in deciding whether or not to forgo the proposed therapy'.

Secondly, in the context of whether the standard to be used should be the patient's or the doctor's, the court stated that:

> ... to bind the disclosure obligation to medical usage is to arrogate the decision on revelation to the physician alone. Respect for the patient's right to self-determination on particular therapy demands a standard set by law for physicians rather than one which physicians may or may not impose on themselves. The *patient's right of self-decision* shapes the boundaries of the duty to reveal. [Emphasis added.]

While the statement of these principles appears to champion patients' rights to self-determination, the court also identified several 'contradictions arising from the assessment of disclosure standards by reference to medical practices testimonially approved by expert medical witnesses' (Healy (1999)). As Healy puts it:

> These included: (i) the unlikelihood of there being any 'professional consensus on communication of option and risk information' within the medical communities; (ii) the 'myriad of variables' among patients makes each case so different that its omission can rationally be justified only by the effect of its individual circumstances'; (iii) the danger that 'no custom at all may be taken as an affirmative custom to maintain silence'; (iv) the danger that experts 'may state merely their personal opinions as to what they or others would [disclose] under given conditions'; (v) the inevitability that a professional standard would 'arrogate the decision on revelation to the physician alone' [Healy (1999), p 93].

Hence, this case clarified developments and resolved some of the uncertainty that had surrounded the rather slow and often confusing pattern of development relating to informed consent. Healy highlights the two sides of the *Canterbury* decision: the court opted for a reasonable patient test of due disclosure so as not to subject doctors to unreasonable standards, but its notion of material risks was 'clearly intended to exert a pressure on doctors to ascertain what each specific patient might wish to know' (Healy (1999), pp 98–99). *Canterbury v Spence* was followed by two other influential decisions, *Wilkinson v Vesey* (1972) and *Cobbs v Grant* (1972), and the three cases collectively have been called the informed consent trilogy. In *Wilkinson* (1972) 295 A 2d 676, the Rhode Island Supreme Court endorsed a subjective assessment of causation, but was less willing to reduce the weight given to expert medical testimony. In *Cobbs* (1972) 502 P 2d 1, the California Supreme Court accepted the *Canterbury* principle, but had its own caveat by identifying a minimum standard necessary for the obtaining of an informed consent, beyond which the professional standard would apply (see Healy (1999), p 100, fn 38).

Impact of Canterbury v Spence: *legislative responses*

Between 1972 and 1978, 10 jurisdictions followed *Canterbury*. A number of States reacted to the medical malpractice crisis of the mid 1970s by passing legislation, and currently around 37 American States recognise the informed consent claim, but more than half of these impose statutory limits on the action. States such as Arkansas, Idaho and Texas confirmed their courts' retention of the professional standard: see Arkansas Stat Ann #34-2614(b)(1); Idaho Code #39-4304; and Texas Code Ann Title 71 Art 4590I #6.03(a). Georgia, Louisiana and Washington confirmed the judicial adoption of informed consent: see Georgia Stat Ann #88-2906; Louisiana Stat #1299.40(A); and Washington Stat #7.07.050(1)(a). States such as North Carolina actually altered the approaches taken by their courts. In effect, the North Carolina legislature reversed the effect of its own Supreme Court's decision in *McPherson v Ellis* (1982) 287 SE 2d 892, reverting to an objective test of causation, in other words, moving from a subjective patient standard to a professional standard of disclosure: see NC Gen Stat #90-21.13(a)(3); and NC Gen Stat #90-21.13(a)(1). States such as Hawaii, Pennsylvania and New York carefully defined the use of therapeutic privilege. Under the Hawaiian statute, Hawaii Rev Stat #671-3(c), full disclosure of all risks would only be restricted where 'the obtaining of consent is not reasonably feasible under the circumstances without adversely affecting the condition of the patient's health'. Under the New York Public Health Law #2805-d(4)(d), disclosure would have to be restricted where 'the manner and extent of such disclosure could reasonably be expected to adversely and substantially affect the patient's condition'. In the State of Pennsylvania, under Pennsylvania Cons Stat #1301.103, disclosure of all the risks might be withheld where 'furnishing the information in question to the patient would have resulted in a seriously adverse effect on the patient or on the therapeutic process to the material detriment of the patient's health'. States like Texas even delegated to a committee of physicians and lawyers the task of specifying what risks must be disclosed: Tex Rev Civ Stat Ann Art 4590I #6.03(a), 6.04(a), (d) (Vernon Cum Supp 1985). Other States also passed legislation 'to ensure that patients received certain information for designated treatments such as sterilisation, electroconvulsive therapy, breast cancer treatments, and for the administration of certain drugs' (see Healy (1999), p 101). These statutes had no intention of securing financial compensation for patients, but were attempting to secure compliance by doctors so that patients would undergo certain treatments only with full knowledge of the degree of risk involved.

On a point of precedent, despite the undoubted seminal influence of *Canterbury v Spence*, it was nevertheless only a first instance decision of the District Court of Columbia and it was not until 1982 that a superior court of the district of Columbia was given an opportunity to approve and affirm its tenets in *Crain v Allison* (1982) 443 A 2d 558.

By the end of 1999, it appeared that 49 of the 50 United States had informed consent based in *negligence* rather than in battery, or some other alternative action (see Furrow *et al* (1999), p 327, fn 7).

The American Presidential Commission statement on consent

The American Presidential Commission for the Study of Ethical Problems in Medicine (1982)

In its discussion of informed consent, the Commission report contains the following statement:

> The Commission concludes that considerable flexibility should be accorded to patients and professionals to define the terms of their own relationships. The resolution favoured by the Commission is a presumption that certain types of information should be made available to patients and that all patients competent to do so have a right to accept or reject medical interventions affecting them ... In the light of the disparities between the position of the parties, the interaction should, at a minimum, provide the patient with a basis for effective participation in sound decisionmaking [*sic*] ... It will usually consist of discussions between professionals and patient that brings the knowledge, concerns, and perspective of each to the process of seeking agreement on a course of treatment. [President's Commission for the Study of Ethical Problems in Medicine and Biomedical and Behavioral Research, *Making Health Care Decisions*, 1982, Vol 1, p 38.]

The American system of compensation of counsel, costs and litigation

It is useful, at this juncture, to emphasise that, under the American system of compensation of legal counsel, a medical malpractice plaintiff does not bear serious financial risk. If the plaintiff wins the case, the plaintiff collects less than the full value of the judgment since a portion of it goes to pay the fees of the plaintiff's counsel. If the plaintiff loses, only the formal court costs of the action have to be paid. In other words, the plaintiff does not have to pay fees to her own counsel and will not be liable to pay the fees of the successful defendant's counsel either.

What has happened in Britain in this context?

A BRITISH COMPARATIVE EXCURSUS

The British conditional fee

In Britain, in July 1995, the Courts and Legal Services Act 1990 introduced a new method of dealing with legal costs – the conditional fee. This means that lawyers can take on a case on the basis that they will receive no fee if their client loses, but they will be paid more if they win. This may lead to an increase in the number of legal actions against the health authorities, because the potential plaintiffs who cannot afford to pay costs personally and who do not qualify for legal aid can now initiate litigation without paying for it. This is partly offset by the fact that, if they lose, they may have to pay the costs of the defendant.

This resembles the contingency fees which have been identified as the cause of the alleged malpractice crisis in the USA. The argument is that the contingency encourages more plaintiffs to sue and also pushes up the level of damages because juries are aware that a percentage of the award will go to the lawyers. However, the British conditional fee is different from the US version, because payment will not be a proportion of damages received, but be based on the actual costs. There is a far smaller chance of the contingency costs leading to an increase in the level of damages awarded because, in Britain, it is the judges and not the juries who determine the level of damages. Defendants who lose will not be made to pay more because the plaintiff's lawyers are being paid extra under a conditional fee.

NHS to bear costs of hospital litigation

Within the British National Health Service (NHS) (on which see, further, Introduction) an agreement has been reached with the medical profession that the costs of hospital litigation are borne by the NHS trusts. This has been in operation since 1 January 1990. This replaced the previous arrangement under which medical staff were required to carry professional indemnity insurance. General practitioners remain responsible for paying for malpractice liabilities and need to continue to carry insurance. As far as plaintiffs are concerned, legal aid is available to support those people who cannot afford to bring cases and cover their legal costs. However, the existence of legal aid pushes up the overall costs to the NHS of defending medical accident claims (see, also, Chapter 7).

CANADA

In Canada, the development of the doctrine of informed consent has not been simple or straightforward. Prior to the famous case of *Reibl v Hughes* in 1980, the Canadian courts have swung in both directions – for and against the objective and subjective approaches (that is, the professional v the patient's standard) reflected, for instance, in cases like *Male v Hopmans* (1967) 64 DLR (2d) 105 and *Kelly v Hazlett* (1976) 75 DLR (3d) 536. The objective test was applied in cases involving misrepresentation of treatment such as *Halushka v University of Saskatchewan* (1965) 53 DLR (2d) 436, where the patient, a student at the University of Saskatchewan, voluntarily submitted to an experiment, and signed a consent form, to participate, for a fee of $50, in medical research involving a new drug purported to have been used and tested, and which was 'safe', but which, in fact, had neither been used nor tested. The plaintiff suffered cardiac arrest which resulted in permanent brain damage. The Saskatchewan Court of Appeals held that the doctor was liable in battery and negligence, holding that: 'There can be no exceptions to the ordinary requirements of disclosure in the case of research as there may well be in ordinary medical practice ... The subject of medical experimentation [that is, the plaintiff in this case] is entitled to full and frank disclosure of all the facts, probabilities and opinions which a reasonable man might be expected to consider before giving his consent.' Another example of the application of the objective approach can be found in cases where there was no consent to the actual medical operation carried out, but only consent to treatment which was not in fact carried out.

Medical treatment and refusal of consent by patient

In the Court of Appeal in Ontario, in *Malette v Shulman* [1991] 2 Med LR 162, a Jehovah's Witness was brought unconscious, bleeding profusely, with serious injuries sustained in a car accident, to the casualty department of a hospital carrying a card containing the words 'No Blood Transfusion!' and this was held to be an advance instruction not to submit the plaintiff to a blood transfusion. The defendants were liable in damages for ignoring this instruction and carrying out blood transfusions, as the doctors felt she was critically ill to the point where it was vital to maintain her blood volume, in order to preserve her life and health. The learned judge, Robins JA, observed:

> The law does not prohibit a patient from withholding consent to emergency treatment, nor does the law prohibit a doctor from following his patient's instructions ... To transfuse a Jehovah's Witness in the face of her explicit instructions to the contrary would, in my opinion, violate her right to control her own body and show disrespect for the religious values by which she has chosen to live her life ...

This was an example of the subjective test being used. The Canadian courts have also been prepared to use battery as a remedy in cases where there was valid consent given.

In the Quebec case of *Beausoleil v The Sisters of Charity* (1964) 53 DLR (2d) 65, a patient informed the surgeon before she went for surgery for a slipped disc that she did not want a spinal anaesthetic. However, whilst under sedation, she was persuaded by the chief anaesthetist to consent to a spinal anaesthetic. Following the surgery, she was found to be paralysed from the waist down and the court imposed liability on the basis of battery because the consent that had been obtained at the last moment was, in the circumstances, held to be valid, hence the court found another basis of liability.

Reibl v Hughes *(1980)*

The case of *Reibl v Hughes* (1980) 114 DLR (3d) 1 is the leading case in Canada. Here, the Canadian Supreme Court appeared to resolve the previous uncertainty in the law or, at least, the divergent approaches that other Canadian courts had taken, by opting for a negligence cause of action, rather than an action in battery, where there had been a failure to disclose attendant risks. The facts of the case (source: Healy (1999), p 102, fn 51; Darvall (1999), pp 32–33) were that the plaintiff suffered from carotid artery disease and consulted the defendant neurosurgeon about his headaches. The defendant advised an operation on the plaintiff's brain to avoid a threatened stroke. He had discovered a build up of plaque in the left carotid artery of the plaintiff's neck while examining him for possible causes of his hypertension. This was unrelated to the hypertension he was suffering and did not then affect the plaintiff's health. In four to five years' time, there would be a 10% risk of stroke for each additional year the plaintiff would live with this condition. The defendant surgeon was strongly of the opinion that the plaintiff's condition should be operated on as quickly as possible. The plaintiff, who apparently had some difficulties with the English language, nevertheless agreed to have the operation, unaware that corrective surgery had a 10% risk of stroke or death and it seems that the plaintiff did not appreciate that the surgery recommended was to reduce the risk of a future stroke and would not affect his headaches. Having had the operation, the plaintiff suffered a massive stroke, leaving his right side paralysed. He later claimed that he would not have undergone the surgery if the disclosure had been made since, after about a year and a half, he would have been entitled to a lifetime retirement pension from his employers.

The Supreme Court held that the patient ought to have been informed of the specific risks in order to form a balanced judgment in deciding whether or not to submit to the operation. On the question of the battery action, Laskin CJC, giving the judgment for the court, said:

> In my view... a failure to disclose the attendant risks, however serious, should go to negligence rather than to battery. Although such a failure relates to an informed choice of submitting to or refusing recommended and appropriate treatment, it arises as the breach of an anterior duty of due care, comparable in legal obligation to the duty of due care in carrying out the particular treatment to which the patient has consented. It is not a test of the validity of the consent.

The learned judge declared that the battery action should be restricted to cases where the defendant intervenes beyond that to which there was consent. The professional standard approach to disclosure was rejected, because it was felt this would amount to virtually surrendering to the medical profession the right to decide the scope of liability for non-disclosure. Laskin CJC accepted the plaintiff's testimony and held that it was not enough that the doctor told him he would be much better off after the operation. There was no emergency, nor any present neurological deficit. The defendant neurosurgeon should, therefore, have made full disclosure and, in view of the plaintiff's difficulties with the English language, should have made sure that the risks were understood.

On the question of the subjective and objective approaches to disclosure, Laskin CJC proposed an approach which would take account of the reasonable patient in the plaintiff's position.

The impact of Reibl v Hughes *on disclosure and informed consent*

Reibl v Hughes was seen by many as having 'ushered in dramatic revolutionary change' (Healy (1999), p 103) and, indeed, in its immediate aftermath, it certainly influenced cases such as *White v Turner* (1981) 120 DLR (3d) 269, although there the court interpreted the *Reibl* test as not having gone far enough. Linden J opined that it is not enough 'for the court to be convinced that the plaintiff would have refused the treatment if he had been fully informed; the court must also be satisfied that a reasonable patient, in the same position, would have done so'. The General Counsel of the Canadian Medical Protection Association (CMPA) stated in 1981 that '[no] legal event in the last 50 years has so disturbed the practice of medicine as did the decision of the Supreme Court of Canada in *Reibl v Hughes*' (CMPA, Annual Report, 1981, p 39). About four years after the decision, some Canadian cases illustrated that the duty of disclosure might have been more rigorous under the *Reibl* approach than under English law. Professor Dugdale (1984) highlighted the difficulties faced by plaintiffs, using three Canadian cases as illustrations, where the 'reasonable patient' test has been used. In the first, *Considine v Camp Hill Hospital* (1982) 133 DLR (3d) 11, the patient was not warned of the 1% risk of permanent incontinence which could result from a prostate operation. It was not the standard practice of the surgeons involved to warn of such risk because it was rare, and the approach taken was 'not to dwell on death and serious complications'. Clarke J does not expressly state that there was a breach of the duty to disclose a material risk, but Dugdale points out that the tenor of Clarke J's judgment 'suggests' that this was indeed his view. The learned judge remarked that, on the evidence, the patient had not been told the full story with regard to the risk of permanent incontinence and further observed he was 'not impressed by the manner by which (the surgeons) failed to deal with the risk'. In the second case, *Ferguson v Hamilton Civic Hospitals* (1983) 144 DLR (3d) 214, the court (Krever J) was clear that a failure to warn of a 2% risk of a stroke following an arteriogram was a breach of duty. The 'limited risk explanation' that had been given in the case was regarded as being given at an inappropriate time, in this case, while the patient was affected by valium. In the third case, *Casey v Provan* (1984) 11 DLR (4th) 708, the surgeon failed to warn the patient of a 2% risk of injury to his vocal cord resulting from an endarterectomy. The expert evidence showed that 'in the medical profession there is room for differences of opinion and practice' on whether to warn of such a risk. However, Callaghan J held that the loss of the ability to communicate should be treated as a material risk and there was a breach of duty.

Reibl 10 years on – the Robertson survey

Ten years after the *Reibl* decision, Gerald Robertson published an article (see Robertson (1991)) demonstrating the minimal impact of cases like *Reibl v Hughes* on the frequency of success of malpractice claims. Only 11% (13 cases) of the 117 malpractice cases heard since *Reibl* were based solely on the failure to disclose. In 81 of these cases, the plaintiff succeeded where the defendant was held negligent in treatment and in more than half of these (56%), the court dismissed the additional informed consent claim; the claim was also dismissed in 82% of all the cases in which it was made (see Robertson (1991), cited in Healy (1999), p 104). Healy submits that this suggests that, as in a similar American survey, informed consent is best used as an *ancillary* claim, simply appended to the malpractice claim. The studies also suggest that non-disclosure is difficult to establish, even under the *Reibl* approach, which is more favourable toward plaintiffs. It would appear that the element of proof was the biggest obstacle to a successful claim in Canada. Robertson's survey indicates that in 25 of the 45 cases (that is, in 56% of those cases) in which the defendant was held to have negligently withheld disclosure of material information, the plaintiff failed to establish a sufficiently clear causal link between breach of the duty and the loss suffered. As Healy puts it, 'This was due to what appeared to be a working presumption by many Canadian courts that the greater the trust and confidence which a patient displayed in his physician, the less likely it is that a reasonable person in the patient's position would have declined treatment which that physician recommended (see Healy (1999)). Ironically, post-*Reibl* courts have been influenced by expert testimony of clinical experience, despite the scepticism of both the *Reibl* and *White* courts to statistical analogies, so much so that patients appeared to choose to undergo recommended surgery despite being informed of the relevant risks (for instance, in the cases of *Dick v Bardsley* (1983) 46 BCLR 240 and *Meyer Estates v Rogers* (1991) 78 DLR (4th) 307. In *Meyer*, it was held that a risk between one in 40,000 and one in 100,000 of a fatal reaction to a contrast media dye was a material risk which ought to have been disclosed. In some cases, evidence that the plaintiff had been informed of more serious risks than the one which actually materialised was interpreted by the court as inferring that the patient's decision would not have changed if full disclosure had been made, for instance, in *Parkinson v MacDonald* (1987) 40 CCLT 90. On the basis of his findings, Robertson concludes that the *Reibl*-formulated duty to disclose has not resulted in the opening of floodgates for successful medical malpractice claims.

AUSTRALIA

As a common law jurisdiction, one might have expected a comparative study of consent to concentrate on leading Australian cases in this subject area. Leading cases there certainly are, and we shall we examining them. However, as with the USA, Australia has shown great enterprise in reforming the law their forefathers brought with them from England, where this was seen as necessary, urgent or appropriate, and producing several reports which reviewed the law or legislation which reformed the law. The common law style is unmistakable in Australian jurisprudence and legal practice, in matters such as the reliance on case law and precedent and, of course, in the reliance on English legal concepts and antecedents. But as we shall see in subsequent chapters on matters such as abortion, euthanasia and organ transplantation, Australian States have blazed their own trails, pioneered their own concepts and branched out on their own with their individual statutes and regulations in the particularly virgin territory of medical law and medical ethics.

During the 1980s, various Australian inquiries were conducted which indicated patient dissatisfaction with the amount of information received, as well as communication problems between doctors and patients (see *Informed Decisions about Medical Procedures: Report of the Victorian, Australian and New South Wales Law Reform Commissions* (hereafter '*Informed Decisions*'), 1989, p 7). This report builds upon the legal developments which have already taken place in Australia. Its primary aim 'is to generate an input of principles which can be used to guide disclosure practice. The recommended method of doing this is through the use of guidelines formulated by the National Health and Medical Research Council' (Giesen and Hayes (1992), p 108). Once formulated, these guidelines 'will be admissible in evidence and the courts will consider them in deciding whether a doctor has acted reasonably in relation to the provision of information' (*Informed Decisions*, Recommendation 3, pp 1 and 29–30). On the other hand, practitioner submissions to a joint Law Reform Commissions' reference on informed consent suggested a general level of patient satisfaction with the information disclosure. The Commissions noted that, while most doctors acknowledged the importance of providing information to patients, considerable variations in disclosure practices were evident (*Informed Decisions*, Recommendation 3, pp 10–11). Indeed, information disclosure in the clinical relationship context acquired such public significance during the 1980s that three Australian States enacted disclosure legislation relating to specific categories of patients. These are: (a) Consent to Medical and Dental Procedures Act 1985: South Australia (minors); (b) Mental Health Act 1986: Victoria; and (c) Mental Health Act 1983: New South Wales. It was also the subject matter of a joint Law Reform Commissions' reference and the first discussion paper was entitled *Informed Consent to Medical Treatment*. The reference to the American concept of informed consent (whether or not one accepts that there is a uniform concept) is striking, since the American doctrine has not been incorporated into Australian law (see Darvall (1999), p 28). The discussion paper also has a strong link with American judicial pronouncements on informed consent, as the following extract illustrates:

> Our society recognises the general moral notion that all people are autonomous beings who have a right to, and indeed should, make their own decisions. In the field of medical treatment, this means that a competent adult person is entitled to decide what shall be done with his or her own body ... A doctor should therefore give a patient sufficient information for the patient to understand the nature of any proposed treatment, its implications and risks, and the consequences of not taking the treatment. In the light of that information, it is the patient who should decide what treatment, if any, he or she will undertake. This is called an informed consent. [Victorian Law Reform Commission, *Informed Consent to Medical Treatment*, Discussion Paper No 7, 1987].

The resemblance of this paragraph to the famous statement of Justice Cardozo in the 1914 *Schloendorff* case (see discussion on American law, above, p 324 *et seq*) is self-evident. It therefore represents a 'departure from the notion that the profession ought to be the sole arbiter for determining what is in the best interests of patients, and a clear recognition of patient autonomy and a right of self-determination' (Darvall (1999)). However, at the end of the 1980s, in addition to State statutory provision, there were a handful of Australian common law decisions dealing with information decisions which were far more conservative and cautious than might have been expected with regard to the concepts addressed in the first discussion paper referred to above. The reasons for this are not easily discernible, and Darvall suggests that the 'absence of Australian judicial activism ... is due both to the lack of a constitutional Bill of Rights, and a developed rights jurisprudence, such as that which has evolved in America' (Darvall (1999), pp 28–29).

An Australian definition of informed consent?

Few judges have attempted to provide a definition of informed consent, but one notable exception is Justice Michael Kirby (of the High Court of Australia), who has formulated one, while writing extra-judicially (see Kirby (1983), p 69):

> An informed consent is that consent which is obtained after the patient has been adequately instructed about the ratio of risk and benefit involved in the procedure as compared to alternative procedures or no treatment at all.

Skegg (1999) declares (p 140) that this is a useful definition for the following reasons:

(a) It emphasises the need for information about 'the ratio of risk and benefit involved in the procedure as compared to alternative procedures or no treatments at all'. Previously, information about risks and alternatives had not been required because they would not be requirements of the tort of battery or the crime of assault, which have been the usual legal actions which have been associated with consent to legal treatment.

(b) It includes the word 'adequate' in terms of instruction in the sense of providing information, and consent can never be informed unless the person giving it has some information about the 'ratio of risk and benefit involved in the procedure as compared to alternative procedures or no treatment at all'. Another view is that information would only be needed if it was appropriate – cases might be so trivial or so urgent that there is no need for information. Nevertheless, the person who consents may know a great deal about the procedure, so it might not be accurate to say the consent was uninformed.

On the other hand, Skegg believes that Kirby J's definition focuses on cases where consent is given by a patient who does not already possess adequate information about risks and alternatives, whereas there may well be someone other than the patient whose consent is crucial and who should be provided with information about risks and alternatives. Unfortunately, he does not specify *who* these persons might be, and one can only speculate that they might be parents of minors, or relatives, spouses or partners of patients suffering from some form of mental illness which might render them incapable of making a competent decision.

Similarly, there will always be cases where the patient may be already well informed about the procedure, and consent may relate to matters which may not normally be regarded as procedures, such as the taking of pills; further, the persons involved may be research subjects. Overall, Professor Skegg suggests that Kirby J's definition could be reformulated to take account of these observations, but concedes that, in the process, it might 'lose its clarity and succinctness'. Skegg is not unduly concerned about agreeing a precise definition of 'informed consent' because he believes that it is not a key concept in English medical law and all that needs to be done is for English medical lawyers to explain the relationship of the concept or concepts to their own subject matter.

Comments on Skegg's comments on informed consent in English law

With respect, Professor Skegg's comments on the non-centrality of the 'informed consent' concept in English law can only be correct if one takes an extremely narrow, legalistic and somewhat pedantic view. To be sure, if one is equating the term 'informed consent' with an American version of the term, where the prudent patient will decide or the patient has to be fully informed, regardless of the circumstances of the case, then English law certainly would not and has not, so far, endorsed this approach. However, at its most fundamental level, no treatment or interaction between healthcare professional/institution and patient should take place *unless* the nature and purpose of the treatment has been explained to the patient, albeit in general terms, and the patient is given at least a basic outline of the medical procedure being proposed; except in the case of an emergency or where the patient already knows about the procedure or is suffering from a physical or mental disability (or both) (which includes youth or immaturity) which renders the patient unable to understand the nature of the treatment being proposed. However, it is submitted that a precise definition of informed consent is not really necessary in English law because, by its very nature, it has to be *ad hoc* and *post hoc* (as Michael Jones puts it (see Chapter 1)) and merely requires a sufficiently flexible formulation to suit varying sets of circumstances. On a comparative viewpoint, which Skegg is not referring to, the concept and, sometimes, doctrine, of informed consent, does possess a centrality not only in Western European countries, but even in non-Western countries like Japan, where it has already acquired such a special significance that the government believes that patients will be willing to pay for more information so that any treatment they consent to will be more 'informed' (see discussion of Japan, below, p 352 *et seq*).

Australian case law

The leading Australian authority on disclosure standards is *F v R* (1983) 33 SASR 189 (FC), which was decided by the Full Court of the Supreme Court of South Australia two years before *Sidaway* was decided by the House of Lords. Here, a woman who had become pregnant after an unsuccessful tubal ligation brought an action in negligence alleging failure by the medical practitioner to warn her of the failure rate of the procedure. The failure rate was assessed at less than 1% for that particular form of sterilisation. On the point relating to disclosure of medical information on which the patient could then base an opinion and give or refuse consent to treatment, King CJ said that every case concerning medical information involved a conflict of values. The doctor had a duty 'to act in what he conceives to be in the best interests of his patient' and the patient had 'the right ... to control his own life and to have the information necessary to do so'. The learned judge explained that this conflict was the reason for the difference between the English courts, which tended to emphasise the best interests of the patient as the doctor saw it, whereas the American courts, and to a certain extent the Canadian ones, tended to attach greater weight to the principle of patient self-determination. In the learned judge's opinion, the governing criterion in such cases should be 'the right of every human being to make decisions which affect his own life and welfare and to determine the risks he is willing to undertake'.

King CJ, also considered that the amount of information or advice which a careful and responsible doctor would disclose depended upon 'a complex of factors: the nature of the matter to be disclosed; the nature of the treatment; the desire of the patient for information; the temperament and health of the patient; and the general surrounding circumstances' (citing *F v R* (1983) 33 SASR 192, pp 192–93).

Of course, this is the view that was taken by Lord Scarman (whose views were close to being that of a dissenting judge) in the subsequent English case of *Sidaway*.

Rogers v Whitaker *(1992)*

Nearly 10 years after *F v R*, the Australian High Court, in *Rogers v Whitaker* (1992) 67 ALJR 47, faced the conflict between the patient-oriented 'American' rule of informed consent (as in *Canterbury v Spence*) and the doctor-oriented English rule (stated in *Sidaway v Governors of Bethlem Royal Hospital*).

Facts

Mrs Whitaker had developed an extremely rare condition in her left eye. She had been nearly blind in her right eye from an early age as a result of a penetrating injury from a piece of wood. Despite this injury, she had led a normal life, had a happy marriage, raised four children, was employed in several occupations, actively participated in sporting activities and so on. At the age of 47, as she was about to re-enter the paid work force after three years looking after her injured son, she had a routine eye check-up and was referred to Mr Rogers (the consultant) for advice on possible surgery. He advised her that he could operate on her right eye to remove the scar tissue and said that this would improve its appearance. It would also probably restore significant sight to that eye as well as assisting to prevent the development of glaucoma.

The trial judge found that Mrs Whitaker 'incessantly questioned' Mr Rogers as to, amongst other things, the possible complications, 'to the point of irritating him'. Further, she was, to Mr Rogers' knowledge, 'keenly interested in the outcome of the suggested procedures including any complications as far as they affected her eyes'. Mrs Whitaker was so concerned about the possibility of operating on the wrong eye during surgery that this was noted in her medical record. However, despite her misgivings about the surgery generally, and her high sensitivity to the condition of her eyes, after two discussions with Mr Rogers, Mrs Whitaker consented to the surgery. The operation was performed, but not only was it unsuccessful in restoring any vision to the plaintiff's left eye, but she suffered an extremely rare complication of the surgery which was an inflammation in the treated eye which resulted in sympathetic ophthalmia in the left (good) eye. In 18 months, she lost sight in that eye, leaving her virtually blind. The consequence of the blindness was that the plaintiff was forced to give up almost all of the leisure activities in which she had been involved. She was also placed on a steroid programme which caused her to gain over 30 kg and led to the breakdown of her relationship with her husband. She was unable to secure paid employment again and, as Handley JA in the Court of Appeal put it, '[t]here can be no doubt that her blindness has had a devastating effect on her previous way of life' (p 621)

Mrs Whitaker commenced a negligence action against the defendant.

The lower court trial

At the trial, which was conducted without a jury, the evidence presented was that the risk of sympathetic ophthalmia developing after such surgery was estimated at one in 14,000 cases. Mrs Whitaker did not ask Mr Rogers whether the good eye could be affected by such a condition. However, it was found that, apart from incessantly questioning him, Mrs Whitaker was also very interested in ascertaining the outcome of the procedures and highly concerned that unintended injury could befall her good eye during the operation. The trial judge found that 'the diagnosis, the operation, and the post-operative care and treatment of the respondent were carried out without negligence'. The only claim which was supported by the evidence was that Mr Rogers had failed to warn Mrs Whitaker sufficiently of the risk of sympathetic ophthalmia. This was despite the fact that Mr Rogers was aware of the possibility of this condition developing and knew it could render Mrs Whitaker blind, as of course it did. He also knew that the risk was one in 14,000, but that it was slightly higher for persons who had suffered eye trauma in the past. The trial judge's view was that there was no particular reason for not mentioning it and there was no therapeutic reason for failing to mention it; in fact, he considered sympathetic ophthalmia the 'worst possible result' of the surgery. The only reason Mr Rogers could offer for not mentioning it was that it 'did not come to mind'. Tellingly, there was evidence adduced at the trial that showed that a substantial number of ophthalmic surgeons in Australia in 1984 did *not* provide information on sympathetic ophthalmia to patients undergoing surgery in the absence of a specific inquiry about whether eye surgery could affect the sight in the other eye, and Mrs Whitaker had never put such an inquiry to him *in those terms*.

The trial judge also found that Mr Rogers was negligent in failing to warn Mrs Whitaker of the risk of sympathetic ophthalmia and found that this negligence had caused the injury that was being complained of. Had the plaintiff been so warned, she would not have undergone the surgery. She was awarded A$808,564.38. An appeal to the New South Wales Court of Appeal was dismissed and the High Court of Australia dismissed Dr Rogers' further appeal.

The Australian High Court approach

The High Court, having rejected all the grounds of appeal, only considered the question of the substantive principle to be applied in informed consent cases. Should it opt for the patient-oriented theory (what a reasonable patient would want to know and would find material in making a decision about treatment) or the doctor-oriented theory (what information a reasonable doctor would give, which would be provided by all other reasonable doctors)? There was no doubt that the risk of sympathetic ophthalmia would be a material risk to a reasonable person in the position of Mrs Whitaker, so the patient-oriented theory would mean that Mrs Whitaker would win her case. Similarly, there was little doubt that a reasonable ophthalmic surgeon would not have informed Mrs Whitaker of the small risk of sympathetic ophthalmia. In the event, the High Court preferred the trial court and New South Wales Court of Appeal approach to the *Rogers* case rather than the *Bolam* approach of the English courts. It only accepted that medical practice was a useful guide on what should be told to a patient and merely allowed an exception for the so called 'therapeutic privilege' if, for instance, there was 'a particular danger that the provision of all relevant information will harm an unusually nervous, disturbed or volatile patient' (*Rogers v Whitaker* (1992) 67 ALJR 47, p 52). On this issue, Gaudron J felt that this privilege should be confined to cases of emergency or an impaired ability to receive, understand or evaluate such information.

Having pointed out that the physician's duty to diagnose, treat and provide information is part of a 'single comprehensive duty covering all the ways in which a doctor is to exercise his skill and judgment', the five members of the court opined that the single comprehensive duty is that of 'the ordinary skilled person exercising and professing the special skill' of the defendant. Several points emerge from the judgment (as summarised by Chalmers and Schwartz (1993), pp 146–47):

(a) The question is not what general duty of care is applicable to every act of every doctor or every act of every professional. The question is how that duty is to be applied to a doctor's obligation to provide information to a patient.

(b) The question to be posed is: while the duty of a medical practitioner to exercise reasonable care and skill in the provision of professional advice and treatment is a single comprehensive duty ... the factors according to which a court determines a medical practitioner is in breach of the requisite standard of care will vary according to whether it is a case involving diagnosis, treatment or the provision of information or advice; different cases raise varying difficulties which require considerations of different factors.

(c) Australian courts now treat the physician's obligation to provide diagnosis and treatment differently from the physician's obligation to provide advice.

(d) The Australian High Court draws a distinction between its position and the 'American' position and argues that the American phrases such as 'the patient's right of self-determination' and 'informed consent' (which they called 'amorphous') are 'of little assistance in the balancing process that is involved in the determination of whether there has been a breach of the duty of disclosure' and are thus not relevant to the determination of the duty of physicians to disclose information.

On this last point, Chalmers and Schwartz (1993) comment that 'informed consent' is now a well accepted legal term that 'describes an area of law with at least as much precision and honesty as other tort law terms such as 'product liability', 'strict liability' or 'mass torts' and that, while the Australian court's decision to eliminate Americanisms does no harm to the law, it does not do it any good either (see pp 148–49). Further, Chalmers and Schwartz point out that for the court to say that the phrase 'the right of self-determination' is of little assistance is 'inconsistent with its own evaluation of the purpose of the duty of disclosure'. Indeed, the court refers to the 'paramount consideration' that a person is entitled to make his own decisions about his life' ((1992) 67 ALJR 47, p 51) which is, in fact, 'identical' to the 'right of self-determination and is the reason why the court has decided not to let physicians decide the standards for disclosure (Chalmers and Schwartz (1993), p 149).

The principles laid down in Rogers v Whitaker

If one examines the terminology used in *Rogers*, it is clear that, despite its attempts to say that it was not attracted to the American courts, the High Court of Australia laid down a finding in terms which are very identical to the *Canterbury* ruling. The High Court declared (*Rogers v Whitaker* (1992) 67 ALJR 47, p 52) that:

> The law should recognise that a doctor has a duty to warn a patient of a material risk inherent in the proposed treatment; a risk is material if, in the circumstances of the particular case, a reasonable person in the patient's position, if warned of the risk, would be likely to attach significance to it or if the medical practitioner is or should reasonably aware that the particular patient, if warned of the risk, would be likely to attach significance to it.

As Chalmers and Schwartz remark: 'This is an exceptionally broad rule, imposing a duty on health care professionals to provide all information to which a reasonable person in the patient's position would be likely to attach significance – whatever that may mean' (see Chalmers and Schwartz (1993), p 150).

Gaudron J, they further point out, would adopt an even broader principle, requiring the revelation of all information 'that is relevant to a decision or course of action'. She indicated that she would treat the physician's duty to warn patients of risk as she would any other duty to warn.

The High Court goes on to say:

> ... in the field of non-disclosure of risk and the provision of advice and information, the *Bolam* principle has been discarded and, instead, the [Australian] courts have adopted the principle that ... it is for the courts to adjudicate on what is the appropriate standard of care.

This appears to be saying that *Bolam* might apply to diagnosis and treatment, but not to information disclosure. In other words, this amounts to the 'prudent patient' approach of the *Canterbury* ruling, plus some element of therapeutic privilege. Thus, any risks which are 'material' to the prudent patient to assist in making an informed decision, even where the inquiry is general (as it was in the *Rogers* case) would have to be brought to the patient's attention.

*Reasons for the rejection of the English (*Bolam*) approach in* Rogers v Whitaker

There are two sets of reasons for the rejection of the *Bolam* principle in Rogers. The first set of reasons revolves around the facts of *Rogers* (which evoke sympathy for a 'hard-luck story' which warranted some recompense) and the technical and sometimes unsatisfactory aspects of the application of *Bolam* and the divisions in the *Sidaway* case itself. As identified by Chalmers and Schwartz (1993), there are three main reasons: (a) in *Sidaway*, the House of Lords articulated the *Bolam* principle by which a doctor only needs to prove that 'a responsible body of medical opinion' supports the practice or procedure or standard of disclosure he adopted because the standard of care is a matter of medical judgment. However, the court in *Rogers* rejected this because, in *Sidaway*, the Law Lords 'were divided themselves about the way the *Bolam* test should be applied to evaluate the provision of medical advice; three Law Lords would give some authority to the judiciary to find liability for the failure to warn of some risk of a medical procedure even against unrebutted testimony that some otherwise responsible physicians would not have warned the patient of the risk in question'; (b) the High Court pointed out that, although the *Bolam* test has been applied in English courts, it has not been so well accepted in Australia 'even in the sphere of diagnosis and treatment, the heartland of the skilled medical practitioner'; (c) the High Court found the *Bolam* approach inappropriate because it did not attach any significance to the patients' questions to their physicians. As Chalmers and Schwartz put it ((1993), pp 147–48): 'If expert testimony were to show that some reasonable physicians would not answer a question (or answer it dishonestly, for that matter), the *Bolam* test would not impose liability for failure to answer that question (or for answering it dishonestly). Indeed, the facts of *Rogers* itself suggest the unfairness of such a standard.' This is surely a very telling point. In other words, as they explain further, although Mrs Whitaker did not specifically ask about sympathetic ophthalmia, she communicated her concern about her sighted eye to Mr Rogers, the defendant. It would be 'terribly arbitrary and unfair to allow Mr Rogers to ignore her obvious and clearly manifested concern because she did not use the proper magic words when she put her questions' (Chalmers and Schwartz (1993)). The High Court, in *dicta*, say: 'the opinion that the respondent should have been told of the dangers of sympathetic ophthalmia only if she had been sufficiently learned to ask the question seems curious ...' The critical point, though, is that under the English *Bolam* rule, the defendant 'would not have had to answer [Mrs Whitaker's] questions honestly if other members of the ophthalmic surgeon brotherhood would not have done so' (Chalmers and Schwartz (1993)).

The second set of reasons are broader and more cultural and environmentally based. These are eloquently expressed by Kirby J himself, commenting extra-judicially in an article he published in 1995 (Kirby (1995), p 8). First of all, he highlights the different perspectives of the medical practitioner and the patient. In a malpractice case, the basic issue is 'whether a person who has suffered in some way as a result of medical or hospital procedures will be cast upon the genteel poverty of the social security system or be entitled to recover compensatory damages from the medical practitioner's insurance'. Secondly, he stresses that 'times have changed' and the reasons for this are: 'the general advance of education of the population at large and thus of patients; the decline of the awe of professionals and indeed of all in authority; the termination of unquestioning acceptance of professional judgment; the widespread public discussion of matters concerning health, including in the electronic media, and the growing recognition in medical practice of the importance of receiving a full input from the patient so that the whole person is treated, not simply a body part' (Kirby (1995)). Kirby J is remarkably frank in his article and observes (p 7) that some might think that it was 'ridiculous' to suggest that a patient should be warned about a risk as remote as one in 14,000. However, he thinks that others might argue that the case turned on its special facts and a critical factor was 'the insistence by Mrs Whitaker of her concern about her good eye and her anxiety that it should not be harmed'. Somewhat poignantly, he observes that still others might say that 'it was difficult to overcome an intense sympathy for a woman who had merely gone to have her glasses checked and had ended up almost totally blind' (Kirby (1995)).

Reasons for the limited impact of Rogers v Whitaker

It is always difficult to assess the impact of a statute or a case, particularly in the short term, but there appear to be several reasons why *Rogers v Whitaker* will not lead to a spate of informed consent litigation in Australia. According to Chalmers and Schwartz, these are: (a) 'Australia is yet to permit contingency fees in tort litigation; (b) the Australian social safety net assures that those injured in medical accidents do not become impoverished and desperate; and (c) the Australian healthcare system could not afford it' (see Chalmers and Schwartz (1993), p 156).

On the first point, the vast majority of potential medical malpractice plaintiffs cannot take the financial risk that their actions will be unsuccessful. Unlike the American compensation and litigation system (see Chapter 16 on American law), under the Australian scheme for financing litigation, a potential medical malpractice plaintiff faces the burden of paying her own legal counsel fees and if she is unsuccessful, footing the bill for the defendant's counsel as well. Hence, while the successful Australian plaintiff stands to gain as much as her American counterpart, she could also suffer a far more substantial loss and this serves as a deterrent for bringing malpractice actions. On the second point, the Australian social safety net (or social security net) protects Australians who have become disabled, unemployed or otherwise disadvantaged so that there is always State support for these persons and for those who are injured in medical accidents. On the third and final point, Australia spends relatively limited resources on healthcare, hence their courts could not offer a large range of healthcare choices to all Australians. For example, a court could not require a physician to inform patients of a treatment that might not be available to a person in the plaintiff's position or inform patients of a treatment that is only available outside Australia as this might 'bankrupt the system' (Chalmers and Schwartz, p 158). Indeed, it has been pointed out that the same applies to the UK, where 'the narrow rule on informed consent has been attributed to the need to limit the choices available to patients' (see Grubb and Schwartz (1986)).

AN AUSTRALIAN-AMERICAN COMPARISON

One of the significant differences between the Australian and American system is the different kind of arrangements surrounding litigation. In America, as we have seen, the notable features are jury trials, huge contingent fees, the absence of a developed social welfare system and a greater availability of punitive damages (see Markesinis (1990)). This is certainly not the case in Australia or, indeed, in the UK.

NEW ZEALAND

The leading New Zealand case is *Smith v Auckland Hospital Board* [1964] NZLR 191, decided by the New Zealand Court of Appeals, where it was said that a patient has a 'right to decline operative investigation or treatment however unreasonable or foolish this may appear in the eyes of his medical advisers'.

CIVIL LAW COUNTRIES

As a preface to our brief look at the status of informed consent in Western European countries, it should be noted that informed consent is also well developed in European 'civil law' countries (as they are called: see Introduction to this book). Thus, countries such as France, Germany and Switzerland all adhere to the principle and have done so for many years.

France

The law in France is that the individual's interest in one's bodily integrity requires that all medical procedures be justified by the patient's free and clear consent (Cass Civ *1ère*, 11 January 1966, D 1966.266; 29 May 1951, D 1952.53, note R Savatier, s 1953.1.41, note R Nerson; Cass belg *1ère*, 4 October 1973, Pas 1974.1.121; Civ *1ère*, 2 April 1978, JCP 1 R 204). The character of medical treatment, being invasive and sometimes dangerous, reinforces this principle (Cass Civ *1ère*, 5 March 1974, D 1974 1 R 127). The key principle in French law is that a doctor must provide the patient with information which enables him to understand the nature of the proposed treatment and the possible consequences and risks, so as to put the patient in a position to balance the advantages (and disadvantages) of the proposed treatment against the possible consequences of refusal (Cass Civ *1ère*, 21 February 1961, JCP 1961.112129, note R Savatier). Indeed, there is a wealth of authority to support the principle that it is always for the court to decide whether the required standard of disclosure has been met by the doctor: see Cass Civ 29 May 1951, 1951 D 1952.53, note Savatier, s 1953.1.41, note R Nerson; Cass Civ *1ère*, 21 February 1961, JCP 1961.12129, note R Savatier; 11 January 1966, D 1966.266; 17 November 1969, Gaz pal 1979.1.49; 22 September 1981, D 1982 1 R 274, note J Penneau; Cass Req, 28 January 1942, DC 1942.63; Trib Civ Nice, 16 January 1954, D 1954.178 (see Giesen and Hayes (1992), p 111).

Germany

In what used to be called the Federal Republic of Germany, the right to give informed consent to medical treatment has long been recognised, at least since 1894 (see [1925] RGSt 375). In German law, the doctor has a duty of disclosure (*Ärztliche Aufklärungspflicht*). As an important decision of the German Federal Supreme Court stated: 'The sick person who lacks experience in medical matters looks upon the doctor as an adviser and expects of him advice and information ... Proper respect for the patient's right of self-determination will further rather than damage the patient's trust in his doctor ... To respect the patient's own will is to respect his freedom and dignity as a human being.' (BGH, 9 December 9 1958, BGHZ 29, p 46 (53–56).) Professor Josephine Shaw, whose survey (see Shaw (1985)) on informed consent law forms the basis of this section of our discussion, has pointed out that there are several reasons why the German doctor's duty of disclosure offers excellent material for a comparative investigation. First, there are now 'complex and progressive rules governing every aspect of the disclosure process, many of which offer an interesting perspective on how the law has developed and could develop in the United Kingdom'. Secondly, Germany has 'a level of welfare provision roughly the same as that of the UK' (the reader has to remember this was published in 1986), 'and there are a number of similarities in the legal character of the doctor/patient relationship'. She explains that, as in the UK, 'the contractual relationship, which would normally have determined the duties owed by each party, has largely been superseded by a voluntary relationship in which rights and duties arise under the law of tort. Thirdly, the historical background to informed consent in German law where, as a result of the 'medical' experiments carried out in Nazi concentration camps during the Second World War, the Nuremberg Code on permissible medical experiments, formulated as part of the War Crimes Tribunal's judgment, 'represents an unequivocal declaration of support for the principle of informed consent to experiments on human beings. It declares, in Principle 1, the 'voluntary consent of the human subject to be absolutely necessary' and provides that the subject 'should have sufficient knowledge and comprehension of the elements of the subject matter involved so as to enable him to make an understanding and enlightened decision'. The Code was the basis for all subsequent codes on medical experiments, such as the Declaration of Helsinki 1975, and its principles have had 'a profound effect on medical law and ethics both in Germany and elsewhere' (Shaw (1985), p 871).

The Basic Law (*Grundgesetz*) of 1948 provides, in Art 2(1), that: 'Everyone has the right to the free development of his personality' (*Maunz-Durig, Grundgesetz Kommentar*, Art 2, Abs 1, Rz 34), which is further reinforced by Art 1(1), which stipulates that 'the dignity of man is inviolable'. In view of its history, Shaw remarks that 'it is difficult to imagine a stronger basis for a doctrine of informed consent than this historical background and these constitutional provisions' (Shaw (1985)).

Shaw's study reveals that there are 'serious difficulties' in allowing a situation where the generous evidentiary and causal barriers attached to a cause of action allow it to become 'perverted' because informed consent is being used to allow compensation for medical malpractice without proof of fault, because 'the court's sympathy for a plaintiff who might otherwise recover nothing for serious medical injuries might lead to compensation being awarded on the basis of a marginal failure to disclose'.

Disclosure requirements under German law

The basic rule on 'disclosure' in Germany requires the doctor to give details about the diagnosis, the proposed treatment, the alternatives to it, attendant risks and, so far as is possible, prospects for recovery: BGH [1984] NJW 1397, 1398; BGH [1980] NJW 633.

Therapeutic and diagnostic interventions

German law distinguishes between therapeutic and diagnostic interventions. Where an operation is for diagnostic purposes and carries no additional therapeutic benefits, and unless it represents the only treatment available and must be undertaken as a matter of urgency, the doctor may be required to disclose extremely remote risks. In certain situations, an anaesthetist may even be required to disclose the 'general' risks of such operations (such as heart failure) and the potentially serious consequences of such an occurrence. For therapeutic operations, the patient must be informed in broad terms (which echoes *Chatterton v Gerson* in English law). The key question here is the importance of the risk to the patient's own decision (BGH [1984] NJW 1397, 1398) and disclosure must take into account each patient's own circumstances, such as the patient's level of understanding or prior knowledge (BGH [1980] NJW 633), or that this is only the second operation of its kind (OLG Celle [1979] NJW 1251). As in English law, the mere signing of a consent form will not be proof of disclosure, that is, as proof that there was informed consent (BGH VI ZR 11/83 of 8 January 1985).

High risk and low risk cases

If the operation carries a high risk of harmful side effects, the doctor must be more specific in the information given to the patient, 'detailing the types of complications which might occur, the degree of pain, and the prognosis for recovery: BGH [1972] VersR 153. Shaw (1985) points out that 'even a very low risk, perhaps 1:10,000 or 1:20,000, may not be enough to exclude disclosure if the risk is 'typical' of the operation'. However, if the surgeon has performed some 8,000 diagnostic examinations of the same type without one incident of complications during the last three years, this should displace the need for disclosure (BHG [1984] Juristische Zeitung (JZ) 629). The urgency of the treatment could determine the scope of the disclosure required if time is extremely short (BGH [1972] VersR 153), and urgency may itself be something which has to be disclosed (OLG Hamm [1985] VersR 577).

Therapeutic privilege

German courts recognise a defence of 'therapeutic privilege' (Deutsch [1980] NJW 1305, 1306; BGHZ 29,182), but it is somewhat more circumscribed than discretionary. Disclosure must be tailored to the best interests of the patient. It will be unlawful for the doctor to:

- make a crude or thoughtless disclosure which unnecessarily discourages the patient from undertaking the operation (Deutsch [1980] NJW 1395, p 1308);
- disclose so much information that the patient is unable to discern what is really relevant (Mertens, *Munchener Kommentar*, s 823 Rz 422);
- disclose information where the patient will actually suffer injury to body or health as a result;
- withhold information because the doctor claims that the patient could be disturbed or depressed by it, or that the patient might reject the operation if the disclosure were made.

This last point certainly contrasts with Lord Diplock's view in *Sidaway* that 'the only effect that mention of risks can have on the patient's mind, if it has any at all, can be in the direction of deterring the patient from undergoing the treatment which in the expert opinion of the doctor it is in the patient's best interest to undergo' (*Sidaway* [1985] 1 All ER, p 659, *per* Lord Diplock). In addition, the decision not to disclose, and the reasons for it, must be entered in the medical records and unless this is done, there is a presumption that there was a failure to disclose (see Deutsch, *Arztrecht und Arzneimittelrecht*, 1983, p 47, cited in Shaw (1985)).

Two further significant points emerge from German case law, as identified by Shaw: (a) what is relevant is not just what is disclosed, but also how, when and by whom it is disclosed; thus, disclosure cannot be delegated to a junior member of the hospital staff; the emphasis is on achieving the active comprehension of the patient; (b) the doctor's duty is tailored to those of each individual patient as they are, or ought to be, perceived, by the doctor and not, as in Northern America, to the reasonable or prudent patient. The 'prudent patient' test is seen as inadequate in providing sufficient protection for the patient's right of self-determination or to protect the right of the patient to make unreasonable decisions: OLG Stuttgart [1979] NJW 2355. As Deutsch puts it, '[T]he need for, and contents of, the doctor's disclosure are not a matter of medical discretion, but represent an ethical and legal duty' (Deutsch (1983), p 45).

Having examined the German law on informed consent, Shaw's overall conclusion is that '[i]n every respect the German law on informed consent stands head and shoulders above English law in terms of respect for the individual. Doctors are required to give far more information about the treatment and its risks than are their English counterparts, and their obligations are governed by patient-centred standards requiring them to tailor their disclosure to the needs of the individual' (Shaw (1985), p 888). Of course, this echoes the development of the law in the USA, Canada and Australia, but as we have seen, German law appears to go further than the 'American' prudent patient approach. Shaw goes on to observe that, in the German system, 'emphasis is placed on the active comprehension, rather than the passive reception, of knowledge by the patient. The doctor is required to do more than simply conform to abstract norms of conduct' and, even more significantly, 'causation is presumed too unless the doctor can prove a break in the chain', hence 'causation rarely represents an obstacle to German patients'.

NON-EUROPEAN PERSPECTIVES

Japan

Payment for informed consent?

The Japanese Ministry of Health and Welfare, on 8 March 1996, implemented a policy which states that, if the physician explains the treatment plan, the patient's disease, and the planned period of hospitalisation in a written document to the patient at the time of admission, the physician can charge the equivalent of 2,000 yen (US$16.70/£11.80) (see Ministry of Health Public Notification No 21 (*kokuji*) Official Gazette (*Kampo*) 1996 No 50, 8 March: reported by Akabayashi and Fetters (2000), p 212). The official notification also states that 'the diagnosis or disease condition and planned period of hospitalisation should be explained directly to the patient. In circumstances when full disclosure of the diagnosis is not appropriate given the patient's future treatment, partial disclosure is permissible and must be documented on the chart' (Akabayashi and Fetters (2000)). This exception was necessary because 'most Japanese physicians make a decision about whether to disclose a serious diagnosis to the patient on a case-by-case basis' (Akabayashi and Fetters (2000)). If patients are infants or comatose and, consequently, cannot understand an explanation, then a fee cannot be requested. The Official Notification No 21 directs physicians to meet these requirements within seven days of admission in accordance with a written format illustrated in the notification appendix.

Since 1 April 1996, therefore, when the law came into effect, Japanese doctors have been allowed to charge the national health insurance system for explaining the treatment plan in writing to the patient. The charge is called *Nyuuin Chiryou Keikaku Kasan*, literally meaning 'Additional Fee for the Treatment Plan at Admission'. Hence, apart from care of the elderly and hospice/palliative care, Japanese doctors are paid on a fee-for-service basis with uniform, itemised price-setting by the Ministry of Health and Welfare. This scheme enables the hospital director to charge the national health insurance for hospital doctors who have provided this procedure at the time of the patient's admission to the hospital.

In 1997, the Ministry revised the policy, raised the fee by 1,500 yen and prescribed that the explanation process should be made in co-operation between physicians and related professionals, including nurses. The Ministry of Health and Welfare Notification No 29, which was issued on the same day, clarified the new procedural changes: (a) 'the treatment plan should be made in co-operation with physicians, nurses, and related professionals'; (b) 'the diagnosis, the disease condition, the treatment plan, the content and schedule of physical examination and surgery, and the planned period of stay should be explained by the physician'; and (c) 'in the case of a patient who cannot understand the explanation, the fee can be requested if the information is explained to the family' (Akabayashi and Fetters (2000)). Two phrases in the previous notification – 'in the case of patients who could not understand the explanation, the fee could not be requested' and 'the documents used for explanation should be signed by the patient' – were deleted. The new version of the form simply requires the physician's signature at the bottom and, since the document is given to the patient, the patient's signature is not required. This new version of the form also makes it clear that the physician is giving information to the patient and that no symbolic signature of consent from the patient is required.

Another fee that is charged is the Discharge Guidance Fee (*Taiin Shidoryo*), costing about 3,000 yen and assessed at the time of the discharge of the patient, for informing the patient and/or the patient's family about the post-discharge treatment plan and any matters that require attention after the patient's discharge. This process also requires documentation via a standardised form that is signed by the doctor and placed in the patient's file. Akabayashi and Fetters point out that, as of April 1999, official statistics on the use of this new inpatient charge were not available.

As far as the system itself is concerned, Akabayashi and Fetters (2000) express three criticisms:

(a) A physician's explanation of the patient's medical condition and the treatment plan may conceivably lack 'even the most basic elements of informed consent', yet still be sufficient to qualify for payment. The minimum requirement is completion of the explanation form at the time of admission. There may be a risk that mere completion of the form 'will become an end rather than a means for ensuring sufficient patient understanding and opportunity for participation in decision making'.

(b) The policy will increase the burden on nurses who work in an already hectic clinical setting. While the latest policy requires physicians to provide the essential information to patients, it is really the nurses who are involved in the whole process and it might well be the nurses who do most of the job while the physicians merely complete the forms and hand them to the patients with very little doctor-patient dialogue indeed.

(c) They deplore the fact that Japanese physicians might nowadays be so driven by profit that financial incentives are the only mechanism for sufficiently motivating them to engage patients in informed consent discussions. They would argue that informed consent is such a fundamental component of medical care that it should be included in every encounter, and not billed separately. Even more, they submit that informed consent should be 'an integral part of every doctor-patient decision' irrespective of whether a patient pays for the information on which a patient may need to decide whether to consent to a particular medical procedure. They also point out that a separate charge might be construed as meaning that explaining the nature of the illness and treatment and obtaining the patient's informed consent is optional.

On the positive side, the commentators believe that this scheme has two potential benefits for Japanese doctors: first, it provides an opportunity for doctors to benefit financially for time spent communicating with the patient; and secondly, it provides an opportunity for the doctor to nurture anew 'the faltering doctor-patient relationship' which they say has been occurring for years because of the diminishing trust between doctors and patients in Japan. Overall, they believe that 'the onus is now upon Japanese physicians to prove themselves worthy of remuneration for time spent with the patient to communicate in accordance with the precepts of the informed consent doctrine about the patient's illness and treatment options'. However, they also warn that failure to meet the new expectations may even result in abolition of the scheme and lost earnings for the doctors as well as the missed opportunities to nurture the doctor-patient relationship. There are also plans to audit the scheme using cost-benefit analysis, but no details are available at the moment about the operation or date of commencement of this audit. Whatever happens, this novel scheme may well illustrate one country's response to a paid informed consent scheme, even though that country's experiences have to be viewed and assessed against the backdrop of its unique cultural, political, social and economic heritage.

COMPARATIVE OBSERVATIONS

This brief comparative study of the notion of 'informed consent' to medical treatment appears to have revealed that various common law jurisdictions have rejected the American 'professional standard' of disclosure, where it is the doctor who decides what should be disclosed 'in the patient's best interests', and both Canadian and Australian courts have agreed with Laskin CJC in *Reibl*, saying that to adopt it would be 'to hand over to the medical profession the entire question of the scope of the duty of disclosure, including the question whether there has been a breach of that duty' (*Reibl v Hughes* (1980) 2 SCR 894). The so called American doctrine of informed consent requires the doctor to tell the patient all that a prudent patient would require to know in order to make up his mind. The New Zealand approach is that every patient has the right to decide for himself on whether to undergo operative investigation or treatment, even if the patient's decision appears to be unreasonable or foolish to the medical advisers. In France, the law appears to be that the individual interest in one's bodily integrity requires that all medical procedures be justified by the patient's free and clear consent. It is always for the court to decide whether the required standard of disclosure has been met by the doctor – a principle which has been consistently established in French law. German and Swiss law also proceed on the basic premise that the patient has the right to decide what is to be done to his or her body. On the issue of therapeutic privilege, leading civil law countries do not appear to favour it. Thus, patient autonomy is clearly very much alive in leading European countries, as is the right of self-determination and freedom from non-consensual bodily interference, except in cases of necessity or emergency.

On a point of procedure and substantive law, informed consent is based in negligence in Canada (*Reibl*), the UK (*Sidaway*), 49 of the 50 United States and in Australia (*F v R*).

The fact that these cases have not opened the floodgates to a stream of successful medical malpractice suits is attributable to several factors, some cultural (continuing deference to the medical profession), some economic (presence of a social security safety net which serves as a disincentive for litigation, as in Australia) and some purely legal (failure to establish the causal link between the breach of duty and the loss suffered).

On the other hand, we have also seen the novel law that Japan has recently passed which has been called 'paying for informed consent' which, in a sense, encapsulates the classic capitalist system where you (literally) will only get what you pay for, but we have seen that this could enhance the quality of the doctor-patient relationship in Japan or deteriorate into a purely administrative function, with nurses bearing the brunt of the administration and inconvenience. Irrespective of one's view of this scheme, however, there is no doubt that the notion of an informed consent appears to be accorded great significance in Japan and this must be a step towards a greater degree of patient autonomy, and a public that is better informed about the medical treatment that is being proposed for them; and, as with any scheme under which you are paying for the services rendered, the quality of that service has to be of a high standard or the patient-consumer will demand a better standard of care and expertise, failing which the spectre of compensation and litigation will loom. These potential problems usually provide an excellent incentive for a generally excellent standard of service and customer care and the ultimate beneficiary of this has to be the patient-consumer.

SELECTIVE BIBLIOGRAPHY

Akabayashi, A and Fetters, M, 'Paying for informed consent' (2000) 26 JME 212

Chalmers, D and Schwartz, R, '*Rogers v Whitaker* and informed consent in Australia: a fair dinkum duty of disclosure' (1993) 4 Med L Rev 139

Darvall, L, *Medicine, Law and Social Change*, 1999, Dartmouth

Dickens, BM, 'Medical consent legislation in Ontario' (1994) 5 Med L Rev 283

Dugdale, A, 'Diverse reports: Canadian professional negligence cases' (1984) 2 Professional Negligence 108

Faden, R and Beauchamp, T, *A History and Theory of Informed Consent*, 1986, OUP

Faulder, C, *Whose Body is It? The Troubling Issue of Informed Consent*, 1985, Virago

Giesen, D and Hayes, J, 'The patient's right to know – a comparative view' (1992) 21 Anglo-Am L Rev 101

Giesen, D, 'Vindicating the patient's rights: a comparative perspective' (1993) 9 J Contemporary Health, Law and Policy 273

Grubb, A and Schwartz, R, 'Why Britain can't afford informed consent' (1986) 16 Hastings Centre Report 22

Healy, J, *Medical Negligence: Common Law Perspectives (Modern Legal Studies)*, 1999, Sweet & Maxwell, Chapter 4

Kennedy, I and Grubb, A, *Medical Law: Text with Materials*, 3rd edn, 2000, Butterworths

Kirby, M (Justice), 'Informed consent: what does it mean?' (1983) 9 JME 69

Kirby (Justice), 'Patients' rights – why the Australian courts have rejected *Bolam*' (1995) 21 JME 5

Markesinis, B, 'Litigation mania in England, Germany and the USA: are we so very different?' [1990] CLJ 233

Mason, JK and McCall Smith, RA, *Law and Medical Ethics*, 5th edn, 1999, Butterworths

Myers, D, *The Human Body and the Law*, 1971, Edinburgh UP

Robertson, G, 'Informed consent ten years later: the impact of *Reibl v Hughes*' (1991) 70 Canadian Bar Review 424

Rosoffs, A, 'Informed consent in the electronic age' (1999) Am J Law and Medicine 367

Shaw, J, 'Informed consent: a German lesson' (1985) 35 ICLQ 864

Silverman, WA, 'The myth of informed consent: in daily practice and in clinical trials' (1989) 15 JME 6

Skegg, PDG, 'English medical law and 'informed consent': an antipodean assessment and alternative' (1999) 10 Med L Rev 135

Stauch, M and Wheat, K, with Tingle, J, *Sourcebook on Medical Law*, 1998, Cavendish Publishing, Chapter 3

CHAPTER 11

MEDICAL CONFIDENTIALITY AND PROFESSIONAL PRIVILEGE

INTRODUCTION

The notion of medical confidentiality of information or medical professional privilege, as it is sometimes called, the ethical origins of which can be found in the Hippocratic Oath, also operates in jurisdictions other than the UK. Medical confidentiality is absolute in France and Belgium and is contained in their criminal codes. New Zealand has enacted its Evidence Amendment Act 1980 where, subject to minor reservations, privilege is accorded to medical confidence. Medical professional privilege (as it is referred to in the American literature) is particularly significant in the context of the confidentiality of information such as a patient's HIV seropositivity and in cases involving balancing the breaching of confidence on the grounds of an overriding public interest in public safety against the public interest in the maintenance of confidentiality when dealing with potentially dangerous patients, as in the well known American case of *Tarasoff* (1976) 17 Cal (3d) 358 and the English equivalent, *W v Egdell* [1990] 1 All ER 835, which we have already looked at. This chapter discusses developments in American, Canadian, Australian, New Zealand and Scottish jurisdictions, before examining some cases from Scandinavian jurisdictions which brought the issue of confidentiality and the operation of Art 8 of the European Convention of Human Rights to the European Court of Human Rights.

COMMON LAW JURISDICTIONS

The USA

There is extensive doctor-patient privilege protection in many States of the USA. In 1828, the New York Privilege Statute of 1828 provided that: 'No person authorised to practise physic or surgery shall be allowed to disclose any information which he may have acquired in attending a patient in a professional character and which information was necessary for him to prescribe for such a patient as a physician or to do any act for him as a surgeon.'

Forty States in the USA now have some form of medical professional privilege protection. Apparently, the privilege was found to have an 'undesirably wide scope and as a result there was an erosion of the privilege by both judiciary and legislature' (McHale (1993), p 28). Indeed, criticism of a general doctor-patient privilege led to its exclusion from the Federal Rules of Evidence.

It would seem that there was more support for the privilege protection to be extended to the psychiatrist-patient relationship. McHale (1993) attributes this partly to the efforts of the very strong lobby of those involved in psychotherapy and psychiatry in the USA, and cites the 'first American case' which involved the psychiatrist-patient privilege, the *Grinker* case (cited by McHale, who gives no reference).

The Grinker *case*

This case involved Dr Roy Grinker, a psychiatrist, who refused to testify about his patient in an alienation of affection case brought by his patient's husband. He claimed that he was entitled to privilege because confidentiality was a prerequisite of the therapeutic relationship. The judge held that the psychiatrist-patient privilege was worthy of protection and gave judgment for Grinker.

Although not a formal legal precedent, this case was followed both in subsequent litigation and by a number of States enacting psychiatric privilege protection. However, despite the Federal Rules of Evidence incorporating a psychotherapist-patient privilege rule, the American Congress did not accept the enactment of a general privilege rule. However, Rule 501 of the Federal Rules of Evidence provides that, other than as is provided by the US Constitution, Acts of Congress or Rules of the Supreme Court, the existence of privilege shall be determined by the principles of the common law (see source cited by McHale (1993), p 28).

The Wigmore criteria

The American jurist Wigmore, who was himself avowedly opposed to a doctor-patient privilege, has been influential in arguing that confidentiality should be a vitally important consideration in determining whether a particular privilege should be enacted. He proffered a four-part test to decide whether a privilege should be granted: (a) communications must originate in confidence that they will not be disclosed; (b) the element of confidentiality must be essential to the satisfactory maintenance of the relationship between the parties; (c) the relationship must be one which should be sedulously fostered; (d) the injury caused to the relationship by the disclosure of the communication must be greater than the benefit gained by the correct disposal of litigation (see Wigmore (1983), p 818, cited and summarised in McHale (1993)).

Wigmore did not think that the doctor-patient privilege met these four criteria, and thought that in very few cases are facts communicated to a doctor really confidential, because most of the time people are willing to discuss their ailments freely with other people. He did not, therefore, subscribe to the idea that the absence of confidentiality would stop people communicating with the doctor. Other commentators have not agreed with this, and even argued that the absence of a privilege might well have deterred people from seeking medical help.

There has been 'considerable debate' over the theoretical foundation of the doctor-patient evidential privilege in the USA, criticism of the Wigmore approach and a 'movement away' from the utilitarian approach of Wigmore towards the idea of the privilege being justified on the basis of the patient's fundamental human right to privacy (McHale (1993), p 29). In effect, the constitutional right to privacy has now been extended to justify the privilege protection in the States of Pennsylvania, California and Alaska.

Disclosure in the public interest

We saw, in the corresponding chapter on English law, that apart from the general rules on medical confidentiality, its exceptions under the law and the GMC guidelines, there was an area in which the courts have allowed or disallowed disclosure depending on their interpretation of what is 'in the public interest' after a careful balancing of the public interest in maintaining medical privilege against the public interest in protecting the public from the dangers of non-disclosure (see Chapter 2). The question has also arisen in the USA whether the public interest in effective medical treatment and, therefore, of maintaining medical privilege may be outweighed by the public interest in protecting a third party (that is, not the patient) from physical harm or even death. The leading case on this, already cited in our earlier discussion, is the *Tarasoff* case, which has had an impact in jurisdictions other than the USA.

Disclosure to warn of potentially violent patient

Tarasoff et al v The Regents of the University of California (1976) 17 Cal (3d) 358, p 425

Facts

In August 1969, the patient, P, was a voluntary outpatient receiving therapy at a hospital in the University of California at Berkeley. The plaintiff's case was that P informed Doctor Moore, his therapist, that he was going to kill an unnamed girl, his former girlfriend, readily identifiable as Tatiana Tarasoff, when she returned home from spending the summer in Brazil. The therapist contacted the police, who briefly detained the patient, but released him when he appeared to be rational and promised not to harm the woman. The therapist's superior directed that no further action be taken to detain P. No further action was taken and no one warned the victim or her parents about the threat.

In October 1969, shortly after her return from Brazil, P went to see her at her home and killed her there. Her parents sued the psychologist/therapist, his superior and the university.

The Supreme Court of California held (Clark J dissenting):

(a) that there is a duty of care owed by the therapist to the woman murdered by the therapist's patient. The defendant therapist could not escape liability merely because Tatiana herself was not their patient;

(b) when a therapist determines, or pursuant to the standards of his profession should determine, that his patient presents a serious danger of violence to another, he incurs an obligation to use reasonable care to protect the intended victim against such danger. The discharge of his duty may require the therapist to take one or more various steps, depending upon the nature of the case. Thus, it may call for him to warn the intended victim or others likely to apprise the victim of the danger, to notify the police, or to take whatever steps are reasonably necessary under the circumstances;

(c) the broad rule of privilege protecting confidential communications between patient and psychotherapist does not apply if the psychotherapist has reasonable cause to believe that the patient is in such a mental or emotional condition as to be dangerous to himself or to the person or property of another, and that disclosure of the communication is necessary to prevent the threatened danger. The protective privilege ends where the public peril begins;

(d) the court accepted that there was a balance to be drawn between the public interest in effective treatment of mental illness and the consequent requirement of protecting confidentiality, and the public interest in safety from violent assault.

Clark J (dissenting) argued that:

(a) prior to this case, both legal and medical authorities agreed that confidentiality is essential to treat the mentally ill and that imposing a duty on doctors to disclose patient threats to potential victims would greatly impair treatment;

(b) overwhelming policy considerations weigh against imposing a duty on psychotherapists to warn a potential victim against harm. While offering virtually no benefit to society, such a duty will frustrate psychiatric treatment. Invade fundamental patient rights and increase violence;

(c) assurance of confidentiality is important for three reasons: (1) deterrence from treatment: without substantial assurance of confidentiality, those requiring treatment will be deterred from seeking assistance people seeking psychiatric guidance tend to be stigmatised; (2) full disclosure: the guarantee of confidentiality will is essential in eliciting the full disclosure necessary for effective treatment. The psychiatric patient approaches treatment with conscious and unconscious inhibitions against his innermost thoughts; (3) successful treatment: even if the patient fully discloses his thoughts, assurance that the confidential relationship will not be breached is necessary to maintain his trust in his psychiatrist – the very means by which treatment is effected. Many people, potentially violent – yet susceptible to treatment – will be deterred from seeking it; those seeking it will be inhibited from making revelations necessary to effective treatment; and forcing the psychiatrist to violate the patient's trust will destroy the interpersonal relationship by which treatment is effected; (4) violence and civil commitment: by imposing a duty to warn, the majority contributes to the danger to society of violence by the mentally ill and greatly increases the risk of civil commitment – the total deprivation of liberty – of those who should not be confined. The impairment of treatment and risk of improper commitment resulting from the new duty to warn will not be limited to a few patients, but will extend to a large number of the mentally ill. Although under existing psychiatric procedures only a relatively few receiving treatment will ever present a risk of violence, the number making threats is huge, and it is the latter group – not just the former – whose treatment will be impaired and whose risk of commitment will be increased.

Comment on *Tarasoff*

Evidently, Clark J's dissenting view laid great store on the perceived deterrent effect of allowing the breach of confidentiality and, in terms of the wider picture and the vast majority of patients who are potentially dangerous, but do not actually commit the threatened crimes, this is probably a justifiable view. However, it is equally sustainable to argue that, in the light of what actually happened in the *Tarasoff* case, namely, the killing of the patient's girlfriend, it would have to be a very callous court that did not allow an exception to be made to the general rule of confidentiality, because of the tragedy of the killing; also, to accept that potentially dangerous patients might sometimes carry out their threats of physical harm and, as long as there is a real and serious risk of injury to third parties, especially specified third parties, there is surely a need to protect the public at large from any realistic threats of physical harm. In other words, on its tragic facts, and the dangers from potentially dangerous patients which it exposed to third parties, the majority view appears to be, on balance, the more predictable, but also the more defensible, even on public policy grounds alone.

The *Tarasoff* case was not entirely without some sort of precedent. A case decided just two years before *Tarasoff* was *Merchants National Bank v Trust Co of Fargo v United States* (1967) 272 F Supp 409, which the court in *Tarasoff* cited and discussed. There, the Veterans Administration arranged for a patient to work on local farm, but did not inform the farmer of the man's background. The farmer consequently permitted the patient to come and go freely during non-working hours. The patient borrowed a car, drove to his wife's residence and killed her. Although there was no 'special relationship' between the Veterans Administration and the wife, the court found the Veterans Administration liable for the wrongful death of the wife.

Subsequent cases where dangerous patients were involved have interpreted the decision widely so as to impose a duty to warn whenever it is foreseeable that persons will be endangered by the patient (see, for example, the Michigan Supreme Court case of *Davis v Lhim* (1983) 335 NW 2d 481). But, other courts have given *Tarasoff* a more limited interpretation, requiring not only that a victim be foreseeable, but also that the particular victim be readily identifiable, for example, the Californian Supreme Court in *Thompson v County Alameda* (1980) 614 P 2d 728, despite a strong dissent by Tobriner J. This more limited approach was applied to cases where the patient suffered from an infectious disease, such as *Gammill* (1984) (see below, p 365) and other transmissible diseases (as in *Bradshaw v Daniel* (1993) 854 SW 2d 865 (Tenn Sup Ct)). Some jurisdictions have even refused to apply the *Tarasoff* decision at all, for example, in *Hasenai v United States* (1982) 541 F Supp 999 (D Md).

Doctor's liability to persons infected by his patient

The American courts have held that a doctor is liable to persons infected by his patient if he negligently fails to diagnose a contagious disease (*Hofmann v Blackmon* (1970) 241 So 2d 752 (Fla App), or, having diagnosed the illness, fails to warn members of the patient's family (*Wojcik v Aluminium Co of America* (1959) 18 Misc 2d 740; (1959) 183 NYS 2d 351, pp 357–58; *Davis v Rodman* (1921) 147 Ark 385; (1921) 227 SW 612; *Skillings v Allen* (1919) 143 Minn 323; (1919) 173 NW 663; and *Jones v Stanko* (1928) 118 Ohio St 147; (1928) 160 NE 456). Other courts have also held that a doctor may be liable for negligently advising the third party that there is no danger and failing to prevent the spread of the disease (see *Annotation*, 3 ALR 5th 370).

Californian and Texan legislation *permit* disclosure to the spouse of an HIV positive patient. In New York, this is extended to known sexual partners and needle-sharers, even in the face of patient objection.

The American courts have also had occasion to consider a *duty to warn* where the patient suffered from an infectious disease.

***Gammill v United States* (1984) 727 F 2d 950 (10th Cir)**

Facts

On 20 April 1978, Mrs Johnson (Mrs J) was diagnosed as having infectious hepatitis and gastroenteritis. This diagnosis was made at Fort Carson, a US military installation by Dr H, a civilian physician employed by the US. The next day, Ladonna Gammill (Mrs G), wife of plaintiff Lawrence Gammill (Mr G) and mother of plaintiff Cynthia Gammill, was told by a member of her church that Mrs J was ill with hepatitis and there was a need for someone to take care of her two small children, Christie and Stephanie. Mrs G agreed to baby-sit the children and they were consequently brought to her home for the day. Neither child showed symptoms of serious illness, although Stephanie had diarrhoea which required Mrs G and Cynthia to change her diapers (nappies). When Mr G came in from work, Mrs G informed him that Mrs J had hepatitis. At dinner that evening, Mr G sat next to Stephanie and assisted in feeding her. The children were returned to the Johnson home later that evening. Mr G was cautious in not entering their home because he knew that hepatitis was contagious. Seven days later, on 28 April 1978, Mrs J was informed by the staff at Fort Carson that her daughter Stephanie also had hepatitis. Dr H had also examined Stephanie and recommended that the whole family receive gamma globulin inoculations. Neither Dr H nor the staff at Fort Carson notified the authorities of the hepatitis in the Johnson household; such notification is required by Colorado law and regulations regarding communicable diseases at Fort Carson.

On 16 May 1978, Mr G was brought home from work because of illness. Some time after 21 May, Dr Pollard, the Gammills' family physician, tested Mr G for hepatitis and reported a suspected case of hepatitis to the county health authorities. Mr G's hepatitis tests were later confirmed and it was it was also determined that Cynthia Gammill has contracted the disease. As a result of Dr Pollard's report to the health authorities, five other cases of hepatitis were identified by epidemiological techniques. Mr G was hospitalised for a time and was ill at home for about five months.

The Gammills sued the US pursuant to the Federal Tort Claims on the basis of a common law duty running from the US to the Gammills that would require the US (that is, through Fort Carson) to notify the county health department of the hepatitis in the Johnson home.

The District Court rejected this claim.

The Gammills also made a claim at common law and claimed that the US breached a duty owing to them deriving from common law and that Dr H's duty to them arises from his professional position and relation to people who contract disease; in other words that, as a physician, Dr H owed the public the duty of ordinary care to protect them from the disease of his patients. The plaintiffs appealed to the Circuit Court.

The Circuit Court judgment

Barrett J (delivering judgment in the Circuit Court) opined that, contrary to the Gammills' contentions, they understood the authorities as expressing a much more limited duty than that urged by the Gammills. A physician may be found liable for failing to warn a patient's family, treating attendants, or other persons likely to be exposed to the patient, of the nature of the disease and the dangers of exposure. The court noted the limited persons to whom such a duty is owed, again suggesting the necessity of some special relationship between the physician and those to be warned. It would appear that, at the bare minimum, the physician must be aware of the specific risks to specific persons before a duty to warn exists. Here, Dr Hamilton did not know the Gammills, and was clearly unaware of their risk of exposure. They therefore agreed with the district court that to impose a duty on Dr H to warn the Gammills would constitute an 'unreasonable burden' upon physicians. The Gammills' claim, therefore, had no basis in law.

Liability to third party for non-disclosure

In a subsequent case, a Californian court has ruled that there may even be liability owed to the sexual partner of a patient who was foreseeably affected by the non-disclosure of the information.

The *Reisner* case (1995)

This Californian case (*Reisner v Regents of the University of California* (1995) 37 Cal Rptr 2d 518; [1997] Med LR 250) went to the California Court of Appeal and considered a doctor's liability to a patient's future partner.

Facts

A young girl, Jennifer Lawson, had been exposed to HIV infection when she was 12, through the transfusion of tainted blood. Neither she nor her parents were informed of this by the doctor who discovered the contamination the day after the transfusion. The doctor continued to treat Jennifer for the next five years but never told her of her HIV infection. Some years later, she became intimate with a boyfriend, Daniel, whom she infected with the virus. Shortly before her death, Jennifer was told she had AIDS and immediately informed Daniel, who subsequently learned of his own seropositive status. He brought an action for breach of a duty of care against the doctors for their failure to inform her, thereby subjecting him, as a foreseeable victim, to the risk of infection.

The trial court held that no duty was owed to the patient's boyfriend, Daniel, who was an unknown and unidentifiable third party with whom the defendant doctor had no special relationship. Daniel appealed to the California Court of Appeal.

Californian Supreme Court judgment

The court allowed the appeal, ruling:

(a) The duty of a defendant may extend to a person who is unknown and unidentifiable and with whom he does not have a prior special relationship when he is required to control the conduct of a person with whom he does have such a relationship in order to avoid foreseeable harm. In the instant case, there was a duty to warn Jennifer or her parents, who were likely to have warned Daniel of the risks (*Tarasoff* applied). Although not readily identifiable, Daniel, as a sexual partner of Jennifer, was a foreseeable victim, even though the injury he complained of occurred some years after the negligent act.

(b) A high standard of care is required of doctors with regard to the control and spread of infectious diseases. This exists independently of the duty to provide the best treatment possible for any given patient.

(c) Liability to fourth and fifth parties, such as other partners whom Daniel may have infected, will be limited by traditional principles of causation. There will, therefore, be little to fear from claims that the 'floodgates' will be open to a multitude of further claims.

A comment from Vogel J is noteworthy: 'Civil liability for a negligent failure to warn under the circumstances of this case may not hasten the day when AIDS can be cured or prevented, but it may, in the meantime, protect one or more persons from unnecessary exposure to this deadly virus.'

Comment

It had not been traditional for the US courts to find that the doctor owed a duty of care to anyone except a specific plaintiff and when this began to be extended, it was usually confined to the close family and sexual partners, but here the potential extension to fourth and fifth parties was certainly unusual. Of course, the rules as to remoteness and causation would come into play so as to place reasonable restrictions on how far the duty would extend. The California Court of Appeals derived the duty of care by first relying on *Tarasoff* as their main authority. Unlike *Tarasoff*, of course, the victim was neither known nor identified to the defendant doctor by his patient. The court in

Reisner noted that the *dicta* in *Tarasoff* went further than merely referring to a duty being owed only to the third party being threatened. Of course, in *Reisner* there was no need to breach any duty of confidentiality, since he did not actually tell the patient of the infection. The courts will now find it easier to extend the *Tarasoff* reasoning where there is no actual breach of confidence to justify. Indeed, a case which applied this reasoning on facts similar to *Reisner* was *Garcia v Santa Rosa Health Corp* (1996) 925 SW 2d 372 (Tex CA).

The court in *Reisner* also relied on an earlier decision of theirs in *Myers v Queensbury* (1983) 144 Cal App 3d 888. There, the plaintiff suffered a diabetic attack whilst driving a car and hit the plaintiff, who was standing by the side of the road. The patient had been told by her doctor to drive to hospital to receive treatment. The court held (pp 892–93) that the doctor owed the plaintiff a duty of care, and 'the fact that the plaintiff was a foreseeable but not readily identifiable victim of the patient's driving does not preclude him from starting an action against the doctors for negligently failing to warn her not to drive in an irrational and uncontrolled diabetic condition'. It continued: '[U]nder these circumstances, where warning the [patient] is a reasonable step to take in the exercise of the standard of care applicable to physicians ... liability is not conditioned on potential victims being readily identifiable as well as foreseeable.'

Indeed, the Court of Appeal declared that, in this case, the doctor's continuing relationship with the patient meant that 'he knew or reasonably should have known' as the plaintiff matured that she was likely to 'enter an intimate relationship'. Hence, what had happened was foreseeable to the bystander in the *Myers* case.

The court also relied upon the factually similar decision of the Pennsylvania Supreme Court in *DiMarco v Lynch Homes – Chester County* (1990) 525 Pa 558 (Pa Sup Ct). In that case, a blood technician accidentally infected herself with hepatitis. Her doctors told her that if she remained symptom-free for six weeks, it would mean that she had not been infected. She was not advised to refrain from sexual intercourse, although she did for eight weeks. She remained symptom-free, and subsequently resumed sexual relations with her boyfriend (the plaintiff), who became infected. The plaintiff sued the doctors, arguing that they should have advised the patient to refrain from sexual relations for six months, otherwise she could infect her sexual partner. By a majority (4:3) the court held that the doctors owed the plaintiff a duty of care.

The court in *Reisner* demonstrated great concern with public health policy to prevent the spread of communicable diseases; they clearly agreed that responsibility should be placed on the doctor who was, after all, the only person who was aware of the danger. In an important passage, Larsen J says (pp 561–62):

> When a physician treats a patient who has been exposed to or who has contracted a communicable and/or contagious disease, it is imperative that the physician give his or her patient the proper advice about preventing the spread of the disease. Communicable diseases ... readily spread from person to person. Physicians are the first line of defence against the spread of communicable diseases, because physicians know what measures must be taken to prevent the infection of others. The patient must be advised to take certain sanitary measures, or to remain quarantined for a period of time, or to practise sexual abstinence or what is commonly referred to as 'safe sex'. Such precautions are not taken to protect the health of the patient, whose well-being has already been compromised, rather such precautions are taken to safeguard the health of others. Thus, the duty of a physician in such circumstances extends to those 'within the foreseeable orbit of risk of harm' ... If a third person is in that class of persons whose health is likely to be threatened by the patient, and if erroneous advice is given to that patient to the ultimate detriment of the third person, the third person has a cause of action against the physician, because the physician should recognise that the services rendered to the patient are necessary for the protection of the third person.

In 1989, a California jury awarded the late Rock Hudson's former lover US$14.5 million against Hudson's estate because Hudson had not disclosed that he had AIDS. It is notable that the plaintiff remains seronegative.

Canada

Patient confidentiality is also protected in Canada, although the duty is not absolute. Hence, doctors are not generally permitted to disclose information obtained from a patient unless they are specifically authorised by (or on behalf of) the patient or required or permitted to do so by law (see, further, below, p 374). Historically, no common law medical professional privilege had developed and the legislatures of the various provinces have been unwilling to follow their neighbours, the USA. Only Quebec has a so called 'privilege statute' (see the Code of Civil Procedure Stat Quebec 1969, c 80, Medical Act s 40 stat Quebec 1973, c 46), which provides that communications made in confidence to priests, advocates, physicians and dentists cannot be disclosed unless authorised expressly or impliedly by those who confided in them (Quebec Code of Civil Procedure 1965 (Queb), c 80, s 308); Ontario also has legislation which allows medical privilege to be breached in order to protect the public from risk of harm, but this has not, until recently, covered the *Tarasoff* kind of situation, involving threatened violence by the patient to a third party.

The Canadian courts have generally been in favour of safeguarding confidential information. It is clear law that a physician owes a duty of confidence to his or her patient. This must be clearly distinguished from the tricky issue of whether patient-doctor communications are privileged when sought in court proceedings (*Halls v Mitchell* [1928] SCR 125; [1928] 2 DLR 97, p 105). This duty is recognised at common law (see *AB v CD* (1851) 14 Sess Cas (second series) 177 (Scot Ct Sess). In the words of Dubin JA (for the majority) in *Re Inquiry into the Confidentiality of Health Records in Ontario* (1979) 98 DLR (3rd) 704, p 714: 'Members of the medical profession have a duty of confidentiality with respect to their patients. They are under restraint not to volunteer information respecting the condition of their patients or any professional services performed on them ...'

As various cases, including *Tarasoff*, have held, patients must be encouraged to seek treatment without fear that their ailment, condition or treatment will be disclosed (see the Ontario case of *Carter v Carter* (1974) 53 DLR (3d) 491, p 494; *People v Calvo* (1982) 432 NE 2d 223, p 224 (Illinois Sup Ct); *Gratton v People* (1984) 477 NYS 2d 881, p 882).

At common law, it has been argued that damages for breach might be pursued through alleging a breach of a duty in contract and negligence and the equitable action in breach of confidence (see Rodgers-Magnet (1983)). Another route might be to allege a violation of the right to privacy, guaranteed either at common law or under legislation (see the Privacy Act, RSBC 1979, c 336, s 1(1)); *Wooding v Little* (1982) 24 CCLT 37 (BCSC). There is no legislation which specifically provides a remedy to a patient whose confidence has been breached, but the physician's breach of a statutory obligation of confidentiality may be evidence of negligence. If the disclosure was untruthful, a defamation action may lie against the physician. However, the patient may have difficulty in finding a cause of action that actually covers his particular case.

On the legislative front, there are three situations that exist.

Yukon Territory and the Northwest Territories

The Yukon Territory has legislation which requires a physician who 'has reason to believe or suspect' that a patient 'is infected with a communicable disease' to disclose this to any known contacts' of the patient. The Yukon Communicable Diseases Regulations, YT Reg 1961/48, s 5(1), as amended by YT Reg 1970/46, provides that: 'Every medical practitioner who has reason to believe or suspect that one of his patients is infected with a communicable disease shall advise such patient ... and any known contacts ... to adopt the specific control measures for such disease and shall give them the necessary instructions therefor.' AIDS has been declared a communicable disease (under the (Yukon Territory) Public Health Act, RSYT 1986, c 136, Sched I, as annexed by OIC 1987/214). A physician who believes or suspects that a patient has AIDS must disclose this to known contacts of the patient. Caswell argues that 'in view of the use of 'suspect' and 'infected' in the legislation and the apparent practice in at least one province ... of interpreting 'AIDS' as encompassing ARC and HIV seropositivity in addition to AIDS *per se*, it is open to question whether a physician is also required to disclose to contacts that a patient has ARC or is HIV seropositive' (Caswell (1989), p 232). Unlike the UK, in the Northwest Territories, AIDS and HIV seropositivity are listed as reportable communicable diseases; however, since HIV infection is a prerequisite to a diagnosis of ARC, in effect all cases of AIDS, ARC and HIV seropositivity are reportable. Therefore, the physician is required either to:

(a) make disclosure concerning AIDS, ARC or HIV seropositivity directly to the patient's contacts; or

(b) request the chief medical officer to do so.

A physician in the Northwest Territories who in good faith chooses to make disclosure directly to the patient's contacts rather than requesting the chief medical health officer to do so, is specifically protected by legislation from liability in respect of the breach of confidence. There is no equivalent specific provision in the Yukon; the legislation requiring the physician to make disclosure to the patient's contacts would clearly provide a good defence if the patient claimed in respect of the breach of confidence.

Prince Edward Island, Alberta, Manitoba

Prince Edward Island has legislation which *authorises*, but does not *require*, a physician to disclose to 'members of the [patient's] family' that a patient has AIDS or is HIV seropositive (see Public Health Act, SA 1984 (the 1984 Act), c P-27.1, s 63(5)(b)). The basic statutory position is contained in s 63(1) and (3) of the 1984 Act which imposes confidentiality of patient information concerning communicable diseases. AIDS is listed as a communicable disease. Hence, as an exception to this general rule, s 63(5)(b) expressly provides that confidential patient information about communicable disease may be disclosed 'to any person with the written consent of the Minister, where in his opinion it is *in the public interest* that the information be disclosed to that person'. Alberta and Manitoba have legislation which, with ministerial approval, *authorises disclosure* of confidential patient information concerning communicable or sexually transmitted diseases respectively. This includes patient information concerning AIDS, but does not cover ARC or HIV seropositivity. Hence, as Caswell (1987) points out, subject to the difficulty of interpreting what 'AIDS' includes, it is arguable that this legislation (Alberta and Manitoba) may authorise a physician to disclose AIDS-related patient information with ministerial approval. But the legislation does *not* require him to do so. So there is no mandatory duty to disclose.

British Columbia, New Brunswick, Newfoundland, Nova Scotia, Ontario, Quebec and Saskatchewan

In all the other above-named provinces, there is no legislation either requiring or authorising a physician to disclose AIDS-related patient information to a patient's partner.

Disclosure justifiable if doctor has honest and reasonable belief

In *C v D* (1925) 1 DLR 734, the plaintiff, a young girl, alleged that the defendant physician had slandered her when he advised one of his patients that she had a venereal disease and should not, therefore, continue sharing a bed with the patient's own daughter. It must be noted that the plaintiff was not a patient of the defendant and indeed, the plaintiff's doctor was another doctor. Riddell J ruled that the defendant had been under a moral, but not a legal duty to warn his patient. As he put it: 'I am of opinion that any medical man – while there is, or may be, no legal obligation cast upon him to do so – owes a moral duty to those for whom he is family physician to warn them of danger of venereal infection concerning which he has credible information.' He referred to the Ontario legislation which dealt with communicable disease reporting, and emphasised that none of the Acts specifically made it the legal duty of a physician to report communicable disease except to the health officer. Consequently, Riddell J held that the defendant had established a defence of qualified privilege since he had an honest and reasonable belief that the plaintiff was infected with a venereal disease and had acted under a sense of moral duty and without malice. Therefore, the plaintiff's action was dismissed.

Sharpe (1987) has remarked that 'It seems quite unlikely that a modern court would decide the case the same way today, given the public interest in controlling communicable diseases has probably been sufficiently addressed by additional statutory reporting provisions, and in view of the contemporary climate of respect for individual privacy' (Sharpe, p 182). Thirteen years on, with AIDS awareness even more acute than in 1987, this comment is even more feasible.

Some debate has ensued as to whether there is judicial discretion to exclude confidential information, and if there is such a discretion, what form it takes (McHale (1993), p 29). In *Dembie v Dembie* (1963) 21 RFL 46, Stewart J held that it was shocking that one profession should dictate the ethics of another and refused to order a psychiatrist to testify, thus upholding medical privilege. The Supreme Court case of *Cronkwright v Cronkwright* (1970) DLR (3a) 168 ONLR, was a case where Wright J held that a clergyman who had attempted a reconciliation of a married couple could not claim privilege. The learned judge did say that persons enjoying confidences and professional people needed special protection and that the judge had a discretion to exclude confidential professional information. Wright J relied on the Ontario Court of Appeal's decision in *R v Wray* (1970) 11 DLR (3d) 673, which had actually been overturned before his judgment had been delivered in the instant case, but the court were unaware of the more recent decision. The more recent decision held that the trial judge could exercise his discretion only if the admission of the evidence would be unfair. To admit evidence 'of probative value' would not be unfair.

This approach was followed in the case of *In Reference re Legislative Privilege* (1978) 39 CCC (2d) 226 (Ont CA), where the Ontario Court of Appeal held that 'there is no recognised discretion to exclude relevant and admissible evidence based on confidentiality alone'(p 230).

The Code of Ethics of the Canadian Medical Association (CMA)

This Code requires that a physician keep in confidence information derived from his or her patient and divulge such information only with the permission of the patient or if required to do so by law (see Rule 6). However, after some discussion at their 1987 annual meeting and again at their 1998 meeting, the CMA published a 'position' (that is, what the British Medical Association would call a Guidance document: see, further, the Introduction to this book), which stated that the Association stressed the need to respect the confidentiality of patients with HIV infection and recommended that legal and regulatory safeguards be put into place to protect such confidentiality. It advised physicians:

> The disclosure to a spouse or current sexual partner may not be unethical and, indeed, may be indicated when physicians are confronted with an HIV-infected patient who is unwilling to inform the person at risk. Such disclosure may be justified when all of the following conditions are met: the partner is at risk of infection with HIV and has no other reasonable means of knowing of the risk; the patient has refused to inform his or her sexual partner; the patient has refused an offer of assistance by the physician to do so on the patient's behalf; and the physician has informed the patient of his or her intention to disclose the information to the partner.

There has been a divergence of opinion between the Canadian Law Reform Commission – which concluded that a judicial discretion should be established by statute to give the court power to exclude certain professionals from being compelled to testify regarding the confidences of their clients – and the Federal Provincial Task Force on the Uniform Rules of Evidence, which totally rejected the introduction of a privilege for professional relationships. In their view, the 'public interest in the administration of justice outweighed the protection of confidentiality. They thought the existing law to be quite adequate' (see McHale (1993), p 30). They referred to *Slavutych v Baker* (1975) 55 DLR (3d) where the Supreme Court of Canada held that judges could examine the merits of arguments both for and against the creation of new privileges for confidential communications. The court there accorded judicial recognition to Wigmore's four-part criteria (see above, p 360) and they saw only one limited situation where a doctor-patient privilege might be justified – that of communications between a defendant and a psychiatrist when they formed part of a psychiatric examination which had been judicially ordered.

In Canada, there is now a common law duty that obliges doctors to inform the authorities, the threatened party, or both, if violence is threatened. However, the medical profession's regulations prohibit doctors from providing such information without the consent of the patient and no statutory law permits or requires disclosure in these particular circumstances. Note that all the legislation we have been reviewing pertains specifically to serious communicable diseases (such as AIDS). Until now, doctors ignoring this provision were subject to disciplinary action by their regulating college.

Under present Canadian law, provincial mental health legislation provides for confining potentially dangerous patients in psychiatric facilities if appropriate.

Ontario: changes to confidentiality laws to protect the public

Under current Ontario law, doctors are required to provide information about a patient without consent when reporting suspected child abuse, certain infectious diseases, and medical unfitness to drive; making reports related to aviation safety or to the Workplace Safety and Insurance Board; completing certificates under the Vital Statistics Act; and responding to a court subpoena.

However, in autumn 1997, an expert panel representing five medical colleges and associations in Canada recommended unprecedented changes to the Ontario Medicine Act. These changes are being implemented and will give the province's 20,000 doctors a mandatory duty to inform the authorities when a patient threatens serious harm to others and the doctor believes that violence is likely. This new duty clarifies contradictions in the law and will benefit doctors, patients, and potential victims of violence. Ferris (1998) observes that, 'By taking a proactive stance, defining the duty to inform explicitly, and making the duty mandatory, the Canadian medical profession has set an international precedent, and, in the process, made a strong statement about preventing violence in [Canadian] society'.

Patients' access to medical records

In *McInernery v MacDonald* (1992) 93 DLR (4th) 415, the Canadian Supreme Court held that, as a general rule, patients should have a right of access to their own medical records. In the words of La Forest J (p 421):

> Information about oneself revealed to a doctor acting in a professional capacity remains, in a fundamental sense, one's own. The doctor's position is one of

trust and confidence. The information conveyed is held in a fashion somewhat akin to a trust. While the doctor is the owner of the actual record, the information is to be used by the physician for the benefit of the patient. The confiding of the information to the physician for medical purposes gives rise to an expectation that the patient's interest in and control of the information will continue. The trust-like 'beneficial interest' of the patient in the information indicates that, as a general rule, he or she should have a right of access to the information and that the physician should have a corresponding obligation to provide it.

Australia

The Australian Medical Association's code of ethics directs doctors to preserve their patients' confidences. As far as legislation is concerned, the states of Victoria, Tasmania and the Northern Territory have expressly recognised the physician-patient relationship (see the Health Administration Act 1982, Evidence Act 1958, s 28(2) (Victoria); Evidence Act 1910, s 96(2) (Tasmania); Evidence Ordinance 1939–72, s 18(2) (Northern Territory)). The form and wording of these statutes are all very similar and apply only in civil proceedings. The New South Wales Health Administration Act 1982 makes it unlawful for any person to disclose any information in connection with the administration of that or any other Act conferring responsibilities on (amongst others) departmental or hospital staff except with the patient's consent or in special specified circumstances.

The Evidence Act of Victoria 1958 provides, in s 96(2), that: 'No physician or surgeon without the consent of his patient divulge in any civil action or proceeding, unless the sanity of or the testamentary capacity of the patient is the matter of dispute, any information which he has acquired in attending the patient and which was necessary to enable him to prescribe or act for the patient.'

In South Australia, the South Australian Health Commission Act 1976 makes it an offence for staff of the Commission at the hospitals or health centres to divulge personal information relating to patients.

In the Northern Territory, there is a criminal code provision that is intended to restrain breaches of confidence (see Criminal Code (NT), s 222), but as far as the existence of a duty in equity to protect confidentiality is concerned, the general law is contained in the statements of Gummow J in *Corrs Pavey v Collector of Customs* (1987) 74 ALR 428, p 437 when he said:

> It is now settled that in order to make out a case for protection in equity of allegedly confidential information ... a plaintiff (i) must be able to identify with specificity, and not merely in global terms, that which is said to be the information in question, and must be able to show that (ii) the information has the necessary quality of confidentiality (and is not, for example, common or public knowledge), (iii) the information was received by the defendant in such

circumstances as to import an obligation of confidence, and (iv) there is actual or threatened misuse of that information.

He then cited cases such as *Saltman Engineering Co Ltd v Campbell Engineering Co Ltd* (1948) 65 RPC 203 and *O'Brien v Komesaroff* (1982) 150 CLR 310. The learned judge also thought that it may be necessary, 'as Megarry J thought probably was the case (*Coco v Clark (AN) (Engineers) Ltd* (1969) RPC 41) and as Mason J accepted in the *Fairfax* decision (1980) 147 CLR 39 (at least for confidences reposed within government), that unauthorised use would be to the detriment of the plaintiff'.

Would Tarasoff *be followed in Australia?*

We have seen how the American courts coped with the situation of the risk of serious physical harm to a third party by allowing, in the admittedly unusual circumstances of *Tarasoff*, a right to breach the duty of confidence if this was necessary to protect a third party and the public from violence. Australian commentators have canvassed the possibility of a duty of disclosure and Abadee, for example, submits that 'there are strong legal and ethical grounds that would justify a medical practitioner breaching, in the strict sense, the duty of confidentiality when confronted by a situation such as *Tarasoff*. But the legal and ethical grounds for imposing an affirmative duty of disclosure are not so clearly established' (Abadee (1995), p 222).

The Australian Medical Association's Code of Ethics states that the 'overriding consideration' for doctors, in considering whether to disclose information without the patient's consent, is 'the adoption of a line of conduct that will benefit the patient or protect his interests'. This guidance may or may not present dilemmas depending on the interpretation put on it. It can be seen as clear cut if one regards the interests of the public as paramount. On the other hand, it could present a dilemma: if disclosure is found to be unjustified, doctors are liable to disciplinary proceedings for breach of the duty of confidentiality (see comments of Abadee (1995)).

On the other hand, it has to be said that other writers have contended that, given that there are statutory provisions which impose penal sanctions for breach of professional secrecy, disclosure is directed only to proper authorities. Consequently, it could also be argued that the mere failure to do an act will not ordinarily attract an action unless the defendant could establish 'a relationship of proximity'. The upshot of the current state of authorities is that 'the present state of Australian law suggests an alignment with English law; at most, a doctor will have a discretion to breach the duty of confidentiality. As has been argued, although disclosure would not be mandatory, it may be justified in the public interest' (Abadee (1995), p 225).

Disclosure required by statute

As we have seen in the corresponding chapter in Part I, a medical practitioner is required to comply with certain statutory requirements to divulge information relating to his patients, even if this means breaching the duty of confidentiality to the patient. The Road Traffic Act 1972 has its equivalent in most of the Australian jurisdictions, so the *Hunter v Mann* situation (see Chapter 2) would also apply to Australian doctors.

Documents and privilege

Under Australian law, all documents, except for certain 'privileged communications', are subject to the jurisdiction of the court, which has the power to compel their disclosure during litigation. Unlike the English law distinction between documents prepared 'in contemplation' of litigation (which would be privileged communications) and those that are not (which would not), there is no privilege against disclosure as far as medical documents are concerned.

Does a common law right of access to medical records exist in Australia?

Under English law, there is an 'innominate' common law right of access to medical records. This was laid down in the leading case of *R v Mid-Glamorgan Family Health Services ex p Martin* [1995] 1 All ER 356, where the English Court of Appeal held that a public health authority had a 'duty to administer its property in accordance with its public purposes' and that, as owner of a patient's medical records, the authority may deny a patient access to his or her records if it is in the best interests of the patient to do so.

Breen v Williams *(1995)*

In the Australian case of *Breen v Williams* [1995] 6 Med LR 385, decided by the Australian Supreme Court of New South Wales, the question arose as to whether, in the absence of a statutory provision, a patient has the right to compel a doctor to divulge that patient's medical records. The earlier High Court decision undertook a careful review of the law in various jurisdictions and held:

(a) without a contractual term, a patient's right of access to his or her medical records has no foundation in the law of Australia;

(b) the common law did not imply a term in the contract between the doctor and the plaintiff (the patient) that he would always act in her best interests or that she had a right of access to his record of her treatment. So far as advice and treatment were concerned, the only relevant contractual term implied by law was to exercise reasonable care and skill;

(c) no ground exists for implying a 'best interests' term as a matter of fact;

(d) as the law stands, the doctor-patient relationship is not an accepted fiduciary relationship, like a trustee and beneficiary, agent and principal, solicitor and client, employee and employer, etc. A doctor is not generally even primarily a representative of his patient;

(e) *Rogers v Whitaker* also rejected the notion of 'the patient's right of self-determination' as providing any real assistance in the 'balancing process that is involved in the determination of whether there has been a breach of the duty of disclosure';

(f) any change in the law must be for Parliament – the role of the common law courts is a far more modest one than to provide a solution for every social, political or economic problem.

The result of this very careful consideration by the Australian High Court of the question of a right of access to medical records resulted in the finding that the *Mid-Glamorgan Family Health Services* case does *not* apply in Australia and will, therefore, not have any persuasive effect in Australia.

On appeal, the Supreme Court of New South Wales concentrated on the question of whether medical files, records and allied documents were the property of the patient or the doctor. The Court believed that, *prima facie*, a medical file kept by a doctor is the property of the doctor. Nevertheless, some documents created for the purpose of enabling the doctor to diagnose and to determine the treatment to be recommended may be the property of the patient. Thus, a document, though held by a doctor, may be the property of the patient because it was procured by or for the patient and has been paid for by her. X-rays, pathology reports and some reports by consultant specialists may come into this category. Similarly, correspondence with consultants or with treating hospitals may, if of this kind, be the property of the patient. However, in the case of notes taken by the doctor to record the patient's medical history and her signs and symptoms, if these included comments and observations which are made and recorded for the purpose of helping the doctor form the diagnosis and opinion to be formed as to treatment, inherent in the way medical practice is conducted, the records remain the property of the doctor. As a result of these deliberations, the court upheld the lower court decision and was not in favour of disclosure.

It is pertinent to note that Kirby P dissented in this case, ruling in favour of disclosure, on the basis of a fiduciary duty owed to the patient and, on a comparative note, this was followed by the Canadian Supreme Court in

McInerney v MacDonald (1992) 93 DLR (4th) 415 (see discussion of Canada, above, p 369).

Nevertheless, under Australian common law, a patient cannot compel a medical practitioner to divulge medical records, but there is now freedom of information legislation which gives patients a right of access to the medical records held by government authorities, including hospitals. According to Devereux (1997), under this legislation, most Australian States have legislation which allows a patient access to his or her records. However, if the records contain information of a 'medical or psychiatric nature' and it is felt that disclosure of the records might have an adverse effect on the health of the patient, then the records may be disclosed to a registered medical practitioner of the patient's choice, rather than directly to the patient.

New Zealand

Despite being a common law jurisdiction, which means, *inter alia*, that it generally relies on case law rather than statutes to develop their law and respond to socio-economic needs in the country, New Zealand has, in fact, been very progressive in frequently studying English Law Commission papers and reports of areas of law reform and then implementing its own, unique *legislative* versions thereof (for example, in the field of company law and contract). Consequently, in the medical law and accident compensation field, New Zealand has been quick off the mark to introduce a 'no-fault' compensation scheme which has only recently been circumscribed. As far as medical confidentiality is concerned, New Zealand introduced a medical professional privilege for civil cases in 1968 (s 8 of the Evidence Act (NZ) 1908) but it was only in 1980 that this was extended to criminal proceedings. The privilege is tightly circumscribed because its rationale is that some illnesses, addiction and forms of behaviour should not be the subject of prosecution. In order for the statute to operate, the communications must have been within doctor and patient for (a) drug dependency, or (b) any other condition or behaviour which manifests itself in criminal conduct.

New Zealand case law has not been plentiful, but it has certainly highlighted some other aspects of this area of the law and revealed how carefully other jurisdictions have approached this difficult area of ethics.

Duncan v Medical Practitioners' Disciplinary Committee *[1986] 1 NZLR 513*

This case involved the disclosure of medical information (by a doctor, Dr D, to a third party), namely that the patient, a bus driver, who had had two heart attacks and a (successful) triple coronary artery bypass was, nevertheless, not fit to drive passenger service vehicles. The patient had been issued with the necessary certificate from the heart surgeon who had performed the bypass, enabling him to obtain a licence to drive the aforesaid vehicles, but D, the doctor in question, tried to prevent the patient from driving by, *inter alia*, seeking revocation of the patient's licence, revealing the patient's medical history to a passenger for the trip, and also attempting to organise a petition to have the patient barred from driving, by asking help from a friend of the patient, and therefore even disclosing this information to a third party who was in no danger from the patient. A complaint was made to the Medical Practitioners' Disciplinary Committee (NZ) which, having heard all the evidence, and having heard representations by counsel for the doctor and the patient, upheld the complaint and found that:

(a) although accepting Dr D had been motivated by concern for the welfare of his community, his actions and interventions were both 'unwise and unwarranted' and amounted to professional misconduct;

(b) Dr D was guilty of professional misconduct in that he breached professional confidence in informing lay people of his patient's personal medical history.

On an appeal by the doctor for judicial review of the decision, Jeffries J dismissed the appeal and made some thoughtful observations:

> (a) The disciplinary offence of breach of confidentiality is nowhere defined as we understand criminal offences are statutorily defined in New Zealand. What is required [in the case] is an examination of patient confidentiality ... to decide whether the conduct amounted to professional misconduct.
>
> (b) What is medical confidence? ... On a strict analysis of legal relationships, it is probably contractually based, as several cases have suggested. It is primarily an ethical issue and must be distinguished from medical privilege, which is an evidentiary rule whereby a patient has the right to exclude from evidence protected communications made to him by a doctor (see ss 32 and 33 of the Evidence Amendment Act (No 2) 1980. It is acknowledged privilege and confidentiality have much in common, but privilege is much more limited than confidentiality, which is an ethical obligation of a professional man to preserve the confidence and secrets of a lay person. The source of information and the fact that others might share the knowledge do not affect the ethical precept. Overall, confidentiality has recently become more prominent as an issue. Society's response has been articulate in that it seeks to break down unnecessary official secrecy, but to strengthen protection of personal confidences and secrets.
>
> (c) There rests with a doctor a strong ethical obligation to observe strict confidentiality by holding inviolate the confidences and secrets he receives in the course of his professional ministerings. If he adheres to that ethical principle, then the full scope of his ability to administer medical assistance to his patient will develop.

(d) Confidentiality is not breached by private discussions with colleagues in pursuance of treatment, but this may require full disclosure and consent. The confidentiality may be waived by the patient. The doctor may be required by law to disclose. A doctor may be in a group practice where common filing systems are used ... (various other examples were given) ... As this very case demonstrates, a doctor may reveal confidences and secrets if he is required to defend himself, or others, against accusations of wrongful conduct.

(e) There may be occasions ... fortunately rare, when a doctor receives information involving a patient that another's life is immediately endangered and urgent action is required. The doctor must then exercise his professional judgment based upon the circumstances, and if he fairly and reasonably believes such a danger exists, then he must act unhesitatingly to prevent injury or loss of life even if there is to be a breach of confidentiality. If his actions are to be scrutinised as to their correctness, he can be confident any official inquiry will be by people sympathetic about the predicament he faced. However, that qualification cannot be advanced so as to attenuate, or undermine, the immeasurably valuable concept of medical confidence ... Some might say it is line-drawing and if they do, then so be it. The line-drawing is not arbitrary, but based upon reason and experience, and is the exercise of professional judgment which is part of daily practice for the doctor.

Having considered the evidence and the facts of the case, he concluded that a doctor who has decided to communicate should discriminate and ensure the recipient is a responsible authority.

According to these comments, albeit *dicta*, the *Tarasoff* principle, although decided on the basis of unique set of circumstances, would probably be applied in New Zealand, if anything similar occurred.

Remedies for breach of confidence

Enforcement of the duty to maintain patient confidentiality may, if successfully proved, result in damages for the breach of confidence and for any consequential losses that may follow. The New Zealand High Court, in the rather unusual case of *Furniss v Fitchett* [1958] NZLR 396, appeared to give some indication of how far the doctor's duty of confidence to his patient should extend.

Furniss v Fitchett *[1958] NZLR 396*

Facts

The case involved a Mr and Mrs Furniss, whose marriage was experiencing difficulties and was extremely strained, and both were patients of Dr Fitchett. Mr Furniss requested the doctor to provide him with a letter detailing his wife's psychiatric problems, and the doctor therefore wrote a letter stating that she 'was deluded that her husband is doping her; accuses her husband of cruelty and even occasional violence; and considers her husband to be insane and states that it is a family failing'. He therefore concluded that, in his medical opinion, the wife 'exhibits symptoms of paranoia and should be given treatment for same if possible. An examination by a psychiatrist would be needed to fully diagnose her case and her requirements.'

The letter was not marked 'confidential' and the doctor did not know how it was to be used. Just over a year later, this letter was produced in the course of a court hearing for a decree of separation, an action brought by the wife; it was the first time she had known of the letter's existence and the law report states that the letter caused the plaintiff 'shock to the injury of her health'. The judge actually referred to the wife's condition as a 'physical' injury. The normal negligence criteria were applied.

Judgment

Barrowclough CJ made several points which dealt with the scope of a doctor's duty in these circumstances:

(a) The duty which [the plaintiff's counsel submitted] the doctor owed to his patient was ... a duty not to disclose to a third party in the circumstances of this case his opinion of his patient's mental condition.

(b) ... I am of the opinion that, on the principle of *Donoghue v Stevenson* [1932] AC562, there arose a duty of care on his part. I have not forgotten that the certificate was accurate and true, but I see no reason in limiting the duty of care in seeing that it is accurate. The duty must extend also to the exercise of care in deciding whether it should be put in circulation in such a way that it is likely to cause harm to another. In the present case, I think the doctor was under a general duty to take care that the certificate which he issued would not cause physical harm to his patient.

(c) ... The [defendant] doctor knew – he admitted he knew – that the disclosure to his patient of his opinion as to her mental condition would be harmful to her. He was careful not to tell her directly what that opinion was. Nevertheless, he wrote out and gave to Mrs Furniss's husband a certificate (the letter) expressing that opinion.

(d) ... On the facts, it is clear that, if Mrs Furniss were to be confronted by this certificate, it was likely to do her harm. In giving the certificate to Mr Furniss,

> the doctor placed no restrictions on its use. It was not even marked 'confidential''' I find also that in the circumstances in which he issued that certificate – handing it to the patient's husband to be given to his solicitor, knowing that the husband and wife were estranged, and without marking it 'confidential' or otherwise restricting its use ... I can only conclude that the doctor ought reasonably to have foreseen that the contents of the certificate were likely to come to his patient's knowledge, and he knew that if they did, they would be likely to injure her in her health.

He concluded, therefore, that in the circumstances to which he referred, the doctor owed to his patient at common law a duty to take care to ensure that no expression of his opinion as to her mental condition should come to her knowledge. The doctor did not take any precautions in that respect.

Stauch *et al* (1998) consider this last point to be 'odd', because if this letter had been disclosed to a number of people, but in circumstances which Mrs Furniss would not know about, the implication is that the doctor would not be in breach of confidence. 'Indeed, the judge seemed to doubt whether the ethical duty of confidentiality was reflected in the law at all' (Stauch (1998), p 260). It does appear that the court in *Furniss* concentrated on the existence and scope of the doctor's duty of care in the circumstances and seemed to be basing his conclusions on the 'neighbour principle' of *Donoghue v Stevenson*, and on the principle of being justified on the basis of the 'public interest' and on the notion of foreseeability. The learned judge did not really frame his ratio or his legal reasoning in terms of a duty of confidentiality, but in broader terms of a duty of care – and this case suggests that, under common law in New Zealand, in healthcare law terms, at any rate, the health practitioner's duty of care includes an obligation not to do his patient any harm by disclosing confidential information to a third party. In the *Furniss* case itself, Mrs Furniss was awarded the sum of A$3,250 despite the fact that there did not seem to be any real evidence of actual loss. On the other hand, damages for shock and distress are no longer unique at common law, provided the injury suffered is sufficiently foreseeable.

A SCOTTISH LAW EXCURSUS

Scotland

As we have said elsewhere in this book, despite being strongly influenced by English common law, Scotland's legal heritage is much closer to that of a civil law country than a common law one. Many of its laws and standard legal textbooks are based on Romanistic models and Scottish courts place considerable store on their 'institutional writers' (who are the equivalent of the doctrinal writers in typical civil law jurisdictions), but Scotland is not dominated by legislation, has frequent recourse to English decisions and textbooks and has adopted the English doctrine of precedent, with some limitations. Scottish cases are, therefore, instructive for comparative purposes.

The matter of whether the doctor has a duty not to reveal confidential information about his patient arose in Scotland in two cases, both named *AB v CD*. In the first case, *AB v CD* (1851) 14 D 177, the Court of Session was asked to consider an action for damages brought against a doctor who had disclosed to a church minister that the pursuer's (plaintiff's) wife had given birth to a full term child six months after her marriage. The court held that there was a duty on the part of the doctor *not* to reveal confidential information about his patient unless he was required to do so in court or on the grounds that disclosure was 'conducive to the ends of science', but, in that case, it would be improper to identify the patient.

The second case was heard in the early 19th century (see *AB v CD* (1904) 7 F 72). Here, the pursuer was seeking a separation from her husband. Having been examined by the defendant doctor at the suggestion of her lawyers, she was later examined by the same doctor, who was then acting on behalf of her husband. The doctor disclosed to the husband certain information he had obtained in the course of his first examination, and the wife contended that this disclosure constituted a breach of confidence. The court again held that there was a duty on behalf of the doctor not to disclose confidential information about his patient, but stressed that not every disclosure would be actionable. Lord Trayner made some notable distinctions: some statements may be indiscreet, but were not actionable; for example, there might be an actionable breach if the disclosure revealed that the patient was suffering from a disease which was the result of misconduct on his part. Indeed, it might well be the background to the illness that is greater significance than the disclosure of the illness *per se* (see Mason and McCall Smith (1999), p 212).

THE EUROPEAN CONVENTION ON HUMAN RIGHTS AND HEALTHCARE LAW

Confidentiality and the right to private life under Art 8 of the ECHR

In the international sphere, in *Chare née Jullien v France* (1991) 71 DR 143, the European Commission on Human Rights found that the collection of medical data and the maintenance of medical records fell within the sphere of private life protected by Art 8 of the European Convention of Human Rights and Fundamental Freedoms 1950.

Art 8 provides:

> 1 Everyone has the right to respect for his private and family life, his home and his correspondence.
>
> 2 There shall be no interference by a public authority with the exercise of this right except such as is in accordance with the law and is necessary in a democratic society in the interests of national security, public safety or the economic well-being of the country, for the prevention of disorder or crime, for the protection of the rights and freedoms of others.

The case of *Z v Finland*, decided in 1997, has become the *locus classicus* on Art 8 and medical confidentiality and again involved disclosure of HIV seropostivism.

Z v Finland *(1997) 45 BMLR 107; [1999] Med LR 339*

Z was a Finnish national who at all material times was married to X, who was not Finnish. Z was diagnosed as HIV positive in 1990 and X was diagnosed as HIV positive in 1992. In 1992, X was charged with various sexual assaults and attempted manslaughter. One of the issues at the criminal trial was the point when X had become aware of, or had reason to suspect, his HIV infection. X refused to answer questions on this. The police attempted to interview Z, but, as she was married to X, she relied on her right under Finnish law not to give evidence against her spouse. Z's doctors and psychiatrists were ordered to give evidence and to produce Z's medical records. Police searched the hospital where both Z and X had been treated and seized all their medical records relating to them. The hearings were held in camera and, in 1993, X was convicted of several offences, including attempted manslaughter, and sentenced to seven years' imprisonment. The City Court ordered that the case documents be kept confidential for 10 years, although both Z and the complainants in the criminal prosecution had requested a longer period of confidentiality.

On appeal, the Court of Appeal upheld X's convictions, convicted him on two other counts of attempted manslaughter, and also increased his sentence to 11 years. It also upheld the City Court's decision that the case documents should remain confidential for a period of 10 years. In its judgment, the Court of Appeal disclosed Z's identity and medical condition. A copy of this was faxed to a Finnish national newspaper.

Z applied to the Supreme Court for an order quashing the Court of Appeal's judgment in so far as it permitted the case documents to become available to the public after 10 years on the basis that it would infringe her right to privacy. Her application was dismissed.

In May 1993, Z applied to the European Commission on Human Rights complaining that there had been violations of her right to respect for private and family life as guaranteed by Art 8(1) of the European Convention on Human Rights by reason of: (a) the orders imposed on her doctors and psychiatrist to give evidence and disclose information about her in the criminal proceedings against her husband; (b) the seizure of her medical records at the hospital where she had been treated and their inclusion, in their entirety, in the investigation file; (c) the decisions of the competent courts to limit the confidentiality of the trial record to a period of 10 years; and (d) the disclosure of her identity and medical data in the Court of Appeal's judgment.

In 1995, the Commission declared the application admissible. Before the Court, it was common ground that these measures were interferences with Z's right to respect for her private and family life, the only question being whether the measures were justified under Art 8(2) of the Convention.

The eight-man European Court of Human Rights held that there was nothing to suggest that the measures complained of by Z did not comply with the domestic law or that the effects of the relevant law were not sufficiently foreseeable to be 'in accordance with the law' for the purposes of Art 8(2).

On the question of whether the measures were 'necessary in a democratic society':

(a) The interference with Z's private and family life entailed by the orders imposed on Z's doctors and psychiatrist, to give evidence and disclose information about her, was subjected to important limitations and was accompanied by effective and adequate safeguards against abuse. The orders were supported by relevant and sufficient reasons which corresponded to an overriding requirement in the interest of the legitimate aim pursued and there was a reasonable relationship of proportionality between those measures and aims. Accordingly (de Meyer J dissenting), there had been no violation of Art 8 on this point.

(b) The seizure of Z's medical records and their inclusion, in their entirety, in the investigation file were complementary to the orders compelling the medical advisors to give evidence and were based on the same weighty public interests and subject to similar limitations and safeguards against abuse. Accordingly (de Meyer J dissenting), there had been no violation of Art 8 on this point.

(c) In deciding to limit the confidentiality of the trial record to a period of 10 years, the domestic courts did not attach sufficient weight to Z's interests. The order to make the material accessible after 10 years would, if implemented, amount to a disproportionate interference with her right to respect for private and family life in violation of Art 8.

(d) Similarly, the disclosure of Z's identity and ethical data in the Court of Appeal's judgment was not supported by any cogent reasons and thus constituted a violation of Art 8.

(e) It was not necessary to examine the applicant's complaints under Art 13 of the Convention.

(f) The respondent State was ordered to pay to the applicant within three months, 100,000 Finnish marks in compensation for non-pecuniary damage.

(g) The remainder of the claim of the claim for just satisfaction was dismissed.

This case emphasises the importance of medical confidentiality. Paragraphs 95–96 of the judgment state:

> Without such protection, those in need of medical assistance may be deterred from revealing such information of a personal and intimate nature as may be necessary in order to receive appropriate treatment and, even, from seeking such assistance thereby endangering their own health and, in the case of transmissible diseases, that of the community.
>
> Consequently, adequate safeguards have to be contained in domestic law so that there is no communication or disclosure of personal health data which is inconsistent with the guarantees in Art 8 of the Convention.

The Court laid particular stress on the importance of these considerations in relation to HIV positive status.

Article 8(1) applies where information normally covered by an obligation of medical confidentiality is divulged to third parties. However, Art 8(2) allows for interference with the right of privacy and family life where it is in accordance with the law and necessary in a democratic society in the interests of one or more of the following:

(a) national security;

(b) public safety;

(c) the economic well being of the country;

(d) the prevention of disorder or crime;

(e) the protection of health or morals;

(f) the protection of the rights and freedoms of others.

In weighing the right of confidentiality against the public interest in the prosecution of crime was the 'margin of appreciation' doctrine as enunciated by the Strasbourg Court. In *R v DPP ex p Kebeline* [1999] 4 All ER 801, pp 843–44, Lord Hope described the doctrine as representing the European Court's recognition that, by reason of their direct and continuous contact with the vital forces of their countries, the national authorities are better placed to evaluate local needs and conditions than an international court. Thus, the 'machinery of protection' established by the Convention is subsidiary to the national systems safeguarding human rights; it is supposed to work in conjunction with a European supervision. The extent of the supervision will vary 'according to the nature of the Convention Right in issue, the importance of that right for the individual and the nature of the activities involved in the case'. By acknowledging a margin of appreciation to each national system, 'the court has recognised that the Convention, as a living system, does not need to be applied uniformly by all States but may vary in its application according to local needs and conditions' ('Comment' [1999] Med LR 345).

The dissenting judge, de Meyer J, argued that the margin of appreciation should be abolished, or at least restricted in its use. He was only prepared to concede such a concept in the realm of sentencing, but not for human rights, in which he believed States should not be allowed any margin of appreciation to decide what might and might not be acceptable.

The subsequent decision of the European Court of Human Rights, in *MS v Sweden* (1998) 45 BMLR 1, suggests that the concept of margin of appreciation will permit Signatory States to impose significant limitations on the right to confidentiality of medical information which reflects the majority view in the *Z* case rather than that of de Meyer.

MS v Sweden *(1998) 45 BMLR 1; [1999] Med LR 346*

The applicant, MS, was a Swedish citizen. At the age of 14, she was diagnosed as having spondylolisthesis, a condition affecting the spine which can cause chronic back pain. In 1981, she fell at work, injuring her back. As she was pregnant at the time and had been seeing a doctor at a clinic at the hospital, she consulted the same clinic about the injury. Subsequently, she was unable to work for any sustained period of time because of severe back pain. She was granted a temporary disability pension and, from 1994, a disability pension. In 1991 she made a claim for compensation under the Industrial Injury Insurance Act 1976 from the Social Insurance Office (SIO). During the proceedings, MS discovered that the SIO had requested, and received from the clinic, details from her medical records containing information on treatment she had received in 1981, 1982 and between October 1985 and February 1986. MS had not been consulted about the disclosure. The medical records showed that, in 1985, MS had requested an abortion because pregnancy exacerbated her back complaint, but there was no indication that she had alleged that she had injured herself at work. In 1992, the SIO rejected her claim for compensation on the ground that her sick leave had not been caused by an industrial injury. All her domestic appeals were rejected and, in September 1992, she lodged a complaint with the European Commission of Human Rights, complaining that the submission of her medical records to the SIO constituted a violation of her right to respect for private and family life as guaranteed by Art 8 of the European Convention on Human Rights 1950. In 1995, the Commission declared the application admissible.

Before the Court, the Swedish Government disputed that Art 8(1) was applicable to the matter complained of by the applicant and maintained that, in any event, there had been no interference with any of her rights guaranteed by that provision. In the alternative, it was argued that the measure had been justified under Art 8(2).

The European Court of Human Rights held:

(a) The medical records of MS held at the clinic were governed by confidentiality and their disclosure depended on a number of factors beyond her control. It could not, therefore, be inferred from her request for compensation that she had waived in an unequivocal manner her right to respect for private life under Art 8. Accordingly, Art 8 applied to the matters under consideration.

(b) The medical records contained highly personal and sensitive data and had been disclosed to a wider circle of public servants for a purpose not connected with medical treatment. The disclosure to the SIO therefore entailed an interference with the applicant's right to respect for private life under Art 8(1).

(c) Although the clinic had disclosed medical records that exceeded the SIO's request, the decisive factor in determining the scope of the clinic's duty to provide information was the relevance of the information, rather than the precise wording of the request. In this case, the interference had a legal basis and was foreseeable and was, therefore, 'in accordance with the law'.

(d) The protection of personal data, particularly medical data, was of fundamental importance to a person's enjoyment of his or her right to respect for family life as guaranteed by Art 8. However, the SIO had a legitimate need to check information received from the applicant against data in the possession of the clinic. The SIO was under a duty to treat the data as confidential. In the circumstances, the disclosure of medical records was subject to important limitations and was accompanied by effective and adequate safeguards against abuse. The disclosure was not disproportionate to the legitimate aim pursued and, accordingly, there had been no violation of Art 8.

The Court observed that there was a right of secrecy under the Swedish Secrecy Act but that Act stated that the rule of confidentiality did not apply where a statutory obligation required the disclosure of information to another authority. The Act gave the clinic a very wide discretion to assess what data would be of importance to the application of the Insurance Act, and there was no duty to hear the applicant's views before passing information to the SIO. The legislation did not enshrine a 'right' to prevent communication of this type of data as a right recognisable by national law.

Contrary to their usual 'teleological' approach, which would give fundamental freedoms a wide interpretation and exceptions a narrow scope, this case did just the opposite, since the exceptions were given a wide interpretation and discretion was given to disclose information of a highly personal and sensitive nature (the information relating to the abortion) to be passed between government departments.

Despite some concessions to the need to respect the applicant's right to private life, the European Court held that the SIO did have a legitimate need to check information received from the applicant against data held by the clinic.

SELECTIVE BIBLIOGRAPHY

Abadee, A, 'The medical duty of confidentiality and the duty to disclose: can they co-exist?' (1995) 3 JL Med 75

Caswell, DG, 'Disclosure by a physician of AIDS-related patient information: an ethical and legal dilemma' (1989) 68 Canadian Bar Review 225

Devereux, J, *Medical Law: Text, Cases and Materials*, 1997, Cavendish Publishing, Chapter 5. See, also, 2nd edn, 2001

Ferris, L, 'Protecting the public from risk of harm' (1998) 316 BMJ 1033

Hermann, D, 'AIDS and the law', in Reamer, FG (ed), *AIDS and Ethics*, 1991, Columbia UP, p 277

Kennedy, I and Grubb, A, *Medical Law: Text with Materials*, 2nd edn, 1994, Butterworths. See, also, 3rd edn, 2000

Mason, JK and McCall Smith, RA, *Law and Medical Ethics*, 5th edn, 1999, Butterworths, Chapter 8

McHale, JV, *Medical Confidentiality and Legal Privilege*, 1993, Routledge

Peirris, G, 'Medical professional privilege' (1984) 33 ICLQ 301

Reamer, FG, *AIDS and Ethics*, 1991, Columbia UP

Rodgers-Magnet, S, 'Common law remedies for disclosure of confidential information', in Steel, F and Rodgers-Magnet, S (eds), *Issues in Tort Law*, 1983

Sharpe, G, *The Law and Medicine in Canada*, 1987, Butterworths

Siegler, M, 'Confidentiality in medicine – a decrepit concept', in Beauchamp, T and Walters, L (eds), *Contemporary Issues in Bioethics*, 1999, Wadsworth

Stauch, M and Wheat, K, with Tingle, J, *Sourcebook on Medical Law*, 1998, Cavendish Publishing

CHAPTER 12

THE MEDICAL TREATMENT OF DISABLED NEWBORNS: A COMPARATIVE PERSPECTIVE

INTRODUCTION

As the Royal College of Paediatrics and Child Health has put it 'The management of babies with serious incurable medical conditions is our most difficult area of paediatric practice' (RCPCH (1997) and see McHaffie (1999)). We have seen in Chapter 4 how the English courts have dealt, and continue to deal, with controversial and often heart-rending cases which involve the difficult question for parents and physicians about whether to decline or withdraw treatment for handicapped newborns.

How do other jurisdictions deal with this question? Responses to bioethical questions vary between European countries, but what has been the American experience? Do ethical codes provide definitive guidance?

THE ETHICAL FRAMEWORK

The Hippocratic Oath, the Declaration of Geneva and the International Code of Medical Ethics are all quite clear that the duty of a doctor is to put the welfare of the patient first.

Several ethical questions have to be answered in this often emotive area of law and ethics because the disabled newborn child is unable to speak for herself, or give her consent or refusal and express her intentions and wishes with regard to medical treatment or withdrawal thereof. This broaches the acts and omissions doctrine – the difference between killing and letting die, which also arises in euthanasia and physician-assisted cases – but with even more difficult questions: who should decide whether the baby lives or is allowed to die? Whose interests should the doctor consider when taking the decision – the patient, the family or society at large? How does the doctor measure the quality of life of the baby's future life? Should the parental wishes be determinative? Does the sanctity of life principle (preservation of life at all costs) or the quality of life principle prevail? How does the doctor decide whether the child's life will be so awful that preservation of its life will not be granting that baby any sort of life that could be called 'normal' or, at least, containing sufficient pleasurable sensations that arguably make life worth living? Who decides what is a 'minimum' standard of quality of life?

Letting 'nature take its course' has been one approach – if the child's prognosis is that it is dying within a short time anyway, somehow this is seen by some as less of a dilemma, since death is imminent. Apart from the 'obvious' cases, what about cases where there is severe abnormality, but imminent death is not the prognosis? There are cases where the child suffers from Down's syndrome which, just 20 years ago, would have been considered an irreversible or impossible situation on a par with the anencephalic baby.

Yet, this dilemma is another situation which, in harsher times, was called infanticide and later neonaticide, and which has a very long worldwide history, as the following historical excursus will show.

This chapter will look at the approach taken by eight European countries on the withdrawal of treatment from neonates, but will look, in particular, at the USA, Canada and New Zealand.

MEDICAL PRACTICE IN COMMON LAW AND CIVIL LAW COUNTRIES

During 1994–97, participants from eight European countries met as part of a European biomedical project, EURONIC, which was designed to study the relevant issues arising from the management of babies with serious medical conditions. The countries were France, Germany, Italy, Luxembourg, the Netherlands, Spain, Sweden, and the UK. It will be noticed that these are all civil law countries except for the UK. A sub-section of the project explored the legal and ethical limits to what may and may not be done. The work of the sub-group is reported in the article by McHaffie *et al* (1999) and, in gathering data, they confined themselves to the law governing practice and guidelines from official bodies, such as government committees and professional associations. The following discussion is based on the McHaffie article analysing the report.

It made the following preliminary findings under two headings:

(a) the issue of withholding/withdrawing treatment;

(b) active intervention to end life.

Withholding and withdrawing treatment

The group found that, when it comes to limiting treatment, the laws of individual countries vary. Infants for whom aggressive treatment might not be desirable fall into two groups: those who invariably die whether or not there is medical intervention (what they called the *no hope* situation), and those who might live if treatment is given but whose future outlook is extremely poor (the *no purpose* situation). All countries permit non-treatment decisions to be made for the first group, but there is much more debate about withholding treatment from a child on the basis of future quality of life (McHaffie *et al* (1999)).

Yet, the position of parents is the same in all countries that were examined in this research. They have the authority to make decisions on behalf of their children, and their consent should be sought to treatment except in cases of emergency. Where parental decisions are contrary to the best interests of the child, doctors are instructed to be the child's advocate and to apply to the courts for permission to overrule that decision.

France

There are no rules or guidelines in France relating to the cessation of treatment but, until recently, doctors feared that they would be prosecuted if they did not provide all necessary care. In the last few years, however, the Deontological Code (1995) has emphasised doctors' obligation to relieve pain and included a caution against inappropriate aggressive treatment. To date, no cases have come to the courts, so no doctor has been prosecuted for taking a non-treatment decision.

Luxembourg

In cases of incurable illness, doctors in Luxembourg have a stated duty to relieve pain and distress and maintain as good a quality of life as possible (Art 45 of the Deontological Code and Art 43 of the Law of 28 August 1998), enhancing the quality of life rather than providing hopeless treatment. A law passed in 1992 (Art 7 of the Law of 10 August 1992) entitles a doctor to give a minor appropriate treatment, in spite of parental opposition, in cases where not to do so jeopardises the child's life or health, but such action has to be reported to the public prosecutor within three days. At present, the law does not address a situation where parents want medically futile treatment to continue, but discussions are currently going on to clarify the legal position.

Italy

In Italian law, a doctor always has an obligation to treat a patient. Apart from emergencies, however, such obligation is conditional upon the consent of the patient (Art 32 of the Italian Constitution), a principle that is supported by the Code of Professional Medical Ethics (Art 32), and the Italian National Ethics Committee (*Informazione e consenso all'atta medico*, 1992, CNB). The explicit refusal of consent by a competent adult, therefore, justifies non-treatment decisions (Art 50 of the Penal Code). In other circumstances, limiting treatment may be seen as a refusal to provide the essential duty of care (Art 328 of the Penal Code). If the patient dies, it may become homicide.

The latest Italian Code of Professional Medical Practice warns against therapeutic aggressiveness, defined as 'persisting with a treatment for which one cannot, with good reason, expect a benefit for the patient or any improvement in his/her quality of life' (Art 14 of the *Codice di Deontologia Medica* 1998). This document, however, has no legal status and the law neither makes mention of this issue nor does it differentiate between ordinary and extraordinary treatment. The clinical position remains uncertain.

In Italian law, there is a very protective stance taken towards newborns. Non-treatment for such conditions as severe malformation or poor neurological prognosis is considered a form of discrimination which violates Art 3 of the Constitution, relating to the equality of all human beings. One court case in particular has served to clarify the situation.

In that case, a child in the course of an appendectomy suffered a cardiac arrest. One of the surgeons massaged his heart for about 10 minutes to no effect. The team were subsequently sued for manslaughter. The defence offered was that more prolonged resuscitation might have saved his life, but would have left him with irreversible brain damage. The judge would not accept the legal foundation for this claim and ruled that the principle of the inalienability of human life has to be respected.

Germany

German doctors have, until very recently, been obliged to do everything medically possible to preserve life. Within the last decade, however, limitation of treatment has become accepted as an integral part of medical care for neonates when treatment is simply delaying an inevitable death. Neither in jurisprudence nor in the literature have the limits of a doctor's obligation to treat a damaged neonate been specifically addressed. However, the German Medical Association Guidelines on Euthanasia relating to the support of dying patients are applicable in as much as they emphasise the need for dignity and good palliative care.

Sweden

Medical matters are rarely subjected to public scrutiny in Sweden, and there is little available information about the rules governing practice. However, the National Board of Health makes it plain that it is the doctor's responsibility to make the definitive decision about treating, and though the opinion of close relatives should be sought, they should not be burdened by the final responsibility of choosing whether to treat or not to treat. Furthermore, it states expressly that, under certain circumstances, a doctor has the right to limit treatment on humanitarian grounds. In May 1997, the first case relating to the management of a premature infant was brought before the Board.

A doctor was said not to have fulfilled his basic obligations following the death of an infant whose transfer to an intensive care unit was delayed. An appeal is currently with the Administrative Court of Stockholm.

United Kingdom

The Report states that 'British doctors are obliged to preserve the life of severely abnormal children' and cites a landmark case (*Re R (A Minor) (Wardship: Medical Treatment)* [1992] Fam 11) where the Master of the Rolls remarked: 'No doctor can be required to treat a child, whether by the court in the exercise of its wardship jurisdiction, by the parents, by the child or anyone else.' It goes on to say that 'decisions are based on judgments about the best interests of the child and his future quality of life and mentions a series of court cases which has tested the limits of what is permissible. The three cases cited are *Re B* [1981] 1 WLR 1421; *Re C (A Minor) (Wardship)* in 1989 ([1990] Fam 26); *Re J* in 1990 (see [1990] Fam 33 and another *Re J* in 1992 ([1992] 2 FLR 165). All these cases have been discussed in Chapter 4. The report points out that 'although these cases have clarified the acceptability of limiting treatment where the quality of life is "demonstrably awful", uncertainty remains about exactly what constitutes an intolerable quality of life and who should define this'. Its authors state that 'the circumstances of these tragic cases are ... infinitely various', but it goes on to say that 'the official legal position is governed by the *Bolam* decision, namely, that a doctor is not negligent if he would be supported by a responsible body of medical opinion' (see McHaffie *et al* (1999), p 442).

The present author would say that the situation was indeed rendered somewhat uncertain by the courts appearing to take different stances according to the crucially different medical conditions of the neonates involved. However, it seems clear that, at present, English courts are not bound in *every* case to preserve life at all costs, so that if a neonate's future quality of life is perceived as 'demonstrably awful', *and* the neonate is dying, the courts may allow the child to die with 'decency and dignity' (*Re C* and see Chapter 4 for the English law on this subject). On the other hand, the court appears to be allowed to make judgments about the future quality of life of a child who is very severely handicapped and authorise withdrawal of treatment even if the child is not diagnosed as expected to die imminently or very shortly (see, further, Chapter 4).

The Netherlands

There were two cases involving minors which have established that doctors in the Netherlands are not obliged to give medically futile or inappropriate treatment. The report says that, although the concept has proved 'elusive', the ruling of the Dutch Central Medical Disciplinary Board made it clear that it is a matter of medical judgment.

Two Dutch cases

In *TGR 1989/51*, 28 April (Supreme Court, the Netherlands), the parents of a child with Down's syndrome, and the Child Welfare Council, decided against an operation for a life threatening intestinal obstruction. The paediatric surgeon, after consulting the hospital medical ethics committee, complied with their wishes, but was subsequently prosecuted for failing to provide life saving treatment. The Supreme Court ruled that, even if an operation had been performed, both the child and the parents ran the considerable risk of a life of severe suffering and criminal proceedings were not instituted.

In *TGR 1991/28*, 11 January (Court of Utrecht), the parents of a one year old child with severe brain damage appealed a decision made by the paediatrician not to resuscitate if complications should occur. The Court of Utrecht held that doctors are not obliged to give medically futile treatment and that any decision as to futility should be based on clinical judgment.

In the Netherlands (as in the UK), ultimate responsibility for deciding the best course of action lies with the medical team caring for the child in both the Netherlands and the UK, but expert consultation is widely practised. The report stresses that, in the Netherlands, a medical ethics committee may also be consulted for advice, in contrast to the UK, where there are few established clinical, as opposed to research, ethics committees. It is a requirement that Dutch clinicians consult colleagues when actively terminating a life.

In the Netherlands, it is a criminal offence not to provide ordinary compassionate care for a baby for whom aggressive management is not the best option since, in such cases, there is a need to give good quality care.

Active intervention to end life

We now turn to the second area of inquiry, which the research revealed is an issue 'fraught with semantic, legal and ethical problems'. The authors of the paper discussing the report (McHaffie *et al* (1999), p 443) take active intervention to mean *the considered intentional termination of life* such as giving a patient a lethal injection designed to kill. However, the researchers were aware of other practices which were intended to relieve symptoms, but had the effect of shortening life (such as administration of pain relieving drugs in high doses; or paralytic agents before withdrawal of life sustaining treatment) or which are a response to the child's medically futile condition (for instance, failure to adjust ventilator settings or to respond to worsening body chemistry; withholding of feeding). The report concludes that 'persuasive arguments find no moral or legal distinction between acts of commission or of omission at the end of life, but clinicians recognise a powerful psychological distinction' (McHaffie *et al* (1999), p 443).

The consenting adult and euthanasia – the ability to state a preference

A brief mention of the position with regard to consenting adults is then made by the authors of the report. They found that in no European country is euthanasia *per se* legal. However, in the Netherlands, this prohibition is seen as inconsistent with the patient's right to self-determination. Indeed, both euthanasia and assisted suicide are criminal offences, but the acts will be 'legally pardoned' provided certain specific criteria are met. A physician can claim *force majeure* where there is a conflict of duties between preserving life and relieving suffering. However, recent Dutch recommendations specifically state that 'a decision deliberately to end a patient's life cannot be regarded as a normal part of medical practice' and 'should accordingly be carefully regulated and, most importantly, be subject to special scrutiny'.

In France, the UK and Italy, the intentional termination of life, whether or not requested by the patient, is regarded as homicide and is, therefore, illegal. There are no exceptions. In Germany, however, assisted suicide, where the act itself is *not* performed by the doctor although he may have prescribed the means, *is* legal, but this does *not* apply to the active ending of someone's life. In Luxembourg and Sweden, assisted suicide is not illegal, but is generally regarded as incompatible with the obligations of doctors.

Since neonates cannot express a view, the situation requires proxy consent in order for any sort of preference to be stated.

Germany

There are very strict guidelines under German law regarding the sick neonate which are even more stringent than for other patients. The Einbecker Recommendations of the German Society for Medical Law state that even a severely damaged newborn infant's life should be safeguarded, so that any deliberate shortening of that life constitutes killing.

France, Italy, Luxembourg and Sweden

In these four countries, all actions which terminate a life, whether adult or neonatal, are prohibited.

The United Kingdom

In the UK, a high dose of the drug DF 118 was given to a newborn with Down's syndrome, in the now famous *Arthur* case (*R v Arthur* (1981), reported in (1991) BMLR 1 (discussed fully in de Cruz and McNaughten, *By What Right?*, 1987, p 1 *et seq*; for a further discussion of the English position see Chapter 4). The doctor was acquitted of murder when it emerged that the child had additional abnormalities and it could not be proved conclusively that his death from pneumonia was due to the DF 118. A crucial distinction has been drawn in Britain between not prolonging and terminating a life. The article on the report cites Taylor LJ (in [1991] Fam 33), who said: 'The court never sanctions steps to terminate life ... There is no question of approving, even in a case of the most horrendous disability, a course aimed at terminating life or accelerating death. The court is concerned only with the circumstances in which steps should not be taken to prolong life.'

The Netherlands

The adult criteria do not apply to neonates in the Netherlands, but the researchers found that babies' lives are sometimes actively ended there. The practice is subject to the same rules of notification, namely, a statement of natural death cannot be issued and the case must be reported to the coroner.

In 1992, the Dutch Paediatric Association published a report of their deliberations on this subject. There was recognition of the concept of an intolerable life, which they attempted to define using 'parameters' such as 'life expectancy, extent of suffering, the capacity to communicate, and degree of independence' (reported in McHaffie *et al* (1999), p 444).

The Dutch discussion group considered the issues further and suggested ways in which practice might be scrutinised. They felt that the best safeguard is 'retrospective assessment of each case by a multidisciplinary committee' (McHaffie *et al* (1999), p 444). A detailed list of essential requirements was also drawn up which includes: intolerable suffering; no viable alternatives; parental agreement; team discussion; independent consultation; and responsible practice. They concluded that 'the existing framework of criminal law should largely remain unchanged, but recommended an examination of the framework towards reformulation of the legal definition of criminal action in this area' (McHaffie *et al* (1999)).

The Netherlands is the only country which has openly tested the courts on the subject of doctors actively terminating the life of a child. Two recent cases highlighted the competing duties of doctors to preserve life and to limit suffering and distress.

The Prins *case*

In *TGR 1995/41*, 26 April, a gynaecologist, Dr Prins, gave a lethal injection to a 3 day old baby girl born in 1993 with hydrocephaly, spina bifida and brain damage. A district court initially found him guilty of murder, but he escaped punishment because of the way he carefully treated the patient. In 1995, the Amsterdam Appeal Court (see *TGR 1996/1*, 7 November 1995) dismissed the charges on the grounds that he had made a 'justified choice' between his two conflicting duties. The doctor was acquitted.

The Kadijk *case*

The second case, *TGR 1996/2*, 13 November 1995, was heard just one week later in Groningen, where a district court ruled that the action of Dr Kadijk, who, as the report puts it, 'ended the life of a baby with Trisomy 13' was justifiable in law. Even though the charge of murder had been legally proven, the court found that he had acted responsibly and in accordance with accepted medical ethics. The Leeuwarden Appeal Court (see 1996/35, 4 April 1996) subsequently came to the same decision. The doctor was also acquitted.

Comparative observations in the report

The article on the report makes several further comparative points:

(a) In practice, they claim that doctors are unclear about their legal position. In Italy, the Code of Professional Medical Ethics warns against therapeutic over-aggressiveness, the State is strongly protective of infant life, and any discrimination on the basis of malformation or poor prognosis violates constitutional law. France has no rules or guidelines on the subject of cessation of treatment and no case has been heard, so clinicians are operating in a legal vacuum. No legal clarification has been forthcoming in Sweden or Germany. In the UK and the Netherlands, where stopping treatment is an accepted part of medical practice, some degree of uncertainty remains about the precise limits. Legal and professional debate continues, currently focusing in the Netherlands on when lives may be actively ended.

(b) The principle of double effect is recognised in all countries covered by the survey except Italy. It is generally considered acceptable to give drugs in sufficient quantity to relieve suffering even when to do so may shorten life.

(c) On the question of active intervention to end life, however, although every country prohibits it, the research found that practice varies. In the Netherlands, a notification procedure for physician-assisted death has been operating since 1991, but doubts have been expressed about 'the effectiveness of control' in view of the low rates of actual reporting. Adult criteria are inappropriate for infants, but it was found that Dutch doctors sometimes do actively end the life of a child with the specific consent of the parents; a recent survey revealed that as many as 45% of neotologists and intensivists had intentionally done so. It is only in the last three years that such cases have come before the courts, and there is still no clarification about the legality of active intervention. However, recommendations for the monitoring of such practices have already been issued.

(d) Apart from the Netherlands, however, the researchers found that other countries have strongly resisted a move to legalise the deliberate termination of life. British paediatricians have officially rejected it and in Germany, although the practice of physician-assisted suicide is legal, and occurs on a much larger scale than in the Netherlands, when it comes to babies, specific recommendations expressly disapprove the practice of ending the life of even a severely damaged newborn. The authors of the project warn against assuming that even with clear rules or laws, practice necessarily follows the law. As the authors of the article on the project say 'Provided clinicians are discreet, actions do not necessarily come to public attention' (McHaffie *et al* (1999), p 445).

(e) Across Europe, rules and practice vary so widely that it is difficult for groups to compose any universally acceptable guidelines. The research group felt that it was clear from their investigation that 'different cultures, religious contexts and historical antecedents influence practice within Europe'. They report that 'attempts have been made to try to harmonise practice, but as international links grow, it is important to understand our diversity as well as our similarities' (McHaffie *et al* (1999), p 445).

The USA

The history of such cases in the USA has been called 'turbulent' (Mason and McCall Smith (1999)). Three cases in the 1970s suggested that there was a strong legal bias in favour of the infant's right to a sanctity of life approach. The 1980s saw different judicial attitudes and then one seminal case that led to presidential intervention and an attempt to formulate special rules to deal with the disabled newborns.

A leading case in this controversial area has been the case called the *Baby Jane Doe* case, which took place against a background of several cases which had prompted the *Baby Doe* rules, which were in effect during the case: the *Johns Hopkins* cases (1971), and the *Mueller* and *Infant Doe* cases.

Down's syndrome (discovered by Langdon Down in 1866) is a chromosomal abnormality in which infants have 47 rather than 46 chromosomes in each cell, the extra chromosome being attached to chromosome 21. Down's syndrome is a genetic condition, always causing retardation and characteristic facial appearance; it is often accompanied by cardiac problems.

The 1971 Johns Hopkins *cases*

In 1971, in an intensive care unit (ICU) at Johns Hopkins Hospital in Baltimore, some Down's syndrome babies were born with defects incompatible with life. During this time, few such units existed and few defective infants were treated aggressively. The same baby born today in an ICU would be treated very differently.

There were several cases involving these babies.

In one case, the baby's mother was a nurse who had worked previously with Down's syndrome children; her 35 year old husband was a lawyer. Her baby had duodenal atresia – a blockage between the higher duodenum and the lower stomach – which prevented passage of food and water. She was told that the baby had Down's syndrome and that it would die if she did not consent to surgery to open the atresia. She immediately refused to sign and the husband agreed. Paediatric surgeons and administrator honoured the parents' refusal and did not go to court.

In other cases, the mothers of these babies made 'anguished' decisions. In one case, one of the mothers allowed the baby to die because it would be 'unfair to the other children of the household to raise them with a mongoloid'. Another indicated she did not want the child as soon as she heard her child had Down's syndrome. One baby took 11 and another, 15 days to die. Such a death would normally take four days, but some hospital staff members, in sympathy with the baby, surreptitiously hydrated the babies. The babies were allowed to die because it was thought that this approach was more morally acceptable and less likely to be open to prosecution.

In the 1980s, as mentioned above, public and judicial opinions swung in different directions. In a case like *Weber v Stony Brook Hospital* (1983) (the *Baby Jane Doe* case) 456 NE 2d 1186 (NY), the New York Court of Appeal refused to overturn a judgment which allowed parents to refuse permission for surgery because such a decision was within accepted medical standards. But, earlier, there was the controversial *Infant Doe* case, where the handicapped child was born in Indiana, the only State in America, at the time, which had laws which protected the life of a newborn. The *Mueller* cases preceded these other difficult cases.

The Mueller and Infant Doe *cases*

The Danville Siamese twins

On 5 May 1981, Siamese twins joined at the trunk and sharing three legs were born in Danville, Illinois to physician Robert Mueller and his wife, Pamela. Robert was in the delivery room with family physician Petra Warren, who delivered the babies. When Jeff and Scott Mueller were born, the Muellers and Warren together decided not to treat the twins aggressively so that they could die. An anonymous caller alerted Protective Child Services, which obtained a court order giving it temporary custody of the children.

Danville physicians were deeply divided over the ethics of the Muellers' decision. The Muellers were charged with neglect, but a later hearing dismissed these charges while denying custody to the Muellers. In September, they regained custody after paediatric surgeons testified that the prognosis was bleak for successful separating.

After one year, confounding their dismal prognosis, these twins survived and weighed 30 pounds. Shortly after that, a long operation separated the weaker twin, who died. Jeff, the stronger twin, lived and later entered an ordinary school.

Comparative observation – the conjoined (Siamese) twins case in Britain

The case of the Siamese twins brought to Britain for treatment in August 2000, who have been the subject of two court hearings in British courts, will no doubt be discussed by ethicists and lawyers. A judgment was handed down by the English Court of Appeal upholding the first instance judge's ruling that the twins should be separated so that the stronger one, who had a heart and lungs, might live ((2000) *The Times*, 10 October). The earlier decision, also to this effect, by Johnson J, had been opposed by the twins' parents who said they wanted nature to take its course if both twins could not be saved. The twins' parents eventually decided not wish to take the matter any further and no further appeal was lodged (for the details of this case, see Chapter 4). The operation went ahead in England and the twin with her own heart and lungs has, so far, survived.

The case of the American Danville twins preceded the *Infant Doe* case, which occurred a year later.

The Baby Jane Doe *case (1982)*

A baby who later became widely known only as 'Infant Doe' was born in Bloomington, Indiana on 9 April 1982. He had Down's syndrome, plus esophageal atresia with associated tracheosophagaeal fistula. Over the course of the next six days, he became the centre of an intensive medical, legal and ethical debate.

The physicians in charge of his case were divided regarding treatment or non-treatment. Some of them wanted to have the baby flown to Riley Children's Hospital in Indianapolis for surgery; others wanted the baby to remain in Bloomington and be given nothing but oxygen and antibiotics. Much of the medical debate had to do with the operation's chance of success, with some of the physicians arguing that 85–90% of such surgical attempts succeed, and others giving the operation only a 50:50 chance of success.

The parents remained anonymous throughout the case, which was highly publicised, and were presented with the two medical options. They chose to have Infant Doe remain in Bloomington without surgery and without intravenous feeding.

The administrators at Bloomington Hospital sought legal advice on the possibility of intervening in the case with court-mandated surgery. Special Circuit Judge John Baker, in an emergency hearing on a Saturday night, ruled that the parents had the right to withhold medical treatment in order that the baby would die.

On Monday, the Monroe County Welfare Department, which Judge Baker had appointed as the baby's guardian *ad litem*, decided not to appeal the judge's ruling. The following day – the fourth day of Infant Doe's life – Monroe County Prosecutors Barry Brown and Philip Hill intervened in the case. Judge Baker encouraged an appeal of his own ruling by appointing Hill as guardian *ad litem* in place of the welfare department. Hill, in turn, responded by filing an emergency petition with the Monroe County Circuit Court, seeking to have the court take custody of the child. When that was rejected, the prosecutors appealed to the Indiana Supreme Court to overrule the lower court judges by ordering intravenous feeding and the potentially life saving surgery. On Wednesday, the Indiana Supreme Court gave the case an informal hearing. The justices voted three to one not to intervene in the case, because they were concerned about second-guessing physicians on medical matters.

One last effort was made by the prosecutors. The Deputy Prosecutor, who had been appointed guardian *ad litem*, was going to appeal to Justice Paul Stevens for an emergency stay of the Indiana court orders on the grounds that Infant Doe had been denied due process. However, Infant Doe died while the prosecutor was travelling to Washington.

A public outcry over the case caused the prosecutors to consider bringing criminal charges against the parents and physicians, but eventually did not do so because, as Prosecutor Brown put it:

> The parents and physician were proceeding under a ruling of the Monroe Circuit Court and therefore under the colour of law. None of the traditional purposes for invoking the criminal sanction – deterrence, punishment,

> rehabilitation – are applicable in this case. We can find no theory of criminal law which would justify placing the parents or the physician in criminal jeopardy. We also believe that the pursuit of criminal action in this case would only compound the tragedy.

The Baby Doe *rules*

The case prompted President Reagan to direct the Justice Department and Department of Health and Human Services (HHS) to require compulsory treatment in similar cases. Reagan opposed abortion and had appointed C Everett Koop as his surgeon general – a paediatrician who had condemned abortion and non-treatment of impaired newborns.

In the USA, since crimes such as homicide and gross negligence are defined by State law, the federal government could not say that non-treatment was illegal. Thus, an indirect rule was utilised: the so called Baby Doe rules were implemented. These rules required treatment of all defective newborns and defined non-treatment as a violation of s 504 of the Rehabilitation Act of 1973, which forbade discrimination solely on the basis of handicap. In essence, imperilled newborns were said to be handicapped citizens who could suffer discrimination.

As Pence points out, these rules were widely misunderstood: 'they did not assert that handicapped infants had a right to life, but rather that denying them treatment violated their civil rights. Violators of such rules faced civil, not criminal, charges. The real pressure of the rules was that institutions violating the *Baby Doe* rules were threatened with loss of funds' (Pence (1990), p 141). Using these rules, the executive can make social policy by re-interpreting prior congressional legislation.

A year after Infant Doe died, HHS sent to intensive care units notice of an 'Interim Final Rule' which angered many paediatricians. Large posters were to be displayed by 23 March 1983, outside intensive care units, saying: 'Discriminatory failure to feed and care for handicapped infants in this facility is prohibited by Federal law.' A telephone 'hotline' was set up and so called *Baby Doe* squads, composed of lawyers, government administrators and physicians, investigated complaints. In the last nine months of 1983, 49 of 1,633 calls were investigated.

Briefly, it got to the stage when these squads were operating like FBI 'hit squads' or 'spot checks'. Federal auditors would suddenly arrive at a clinic and seize records and charts from attending physicians in response to calls from those who suspected neonaticide was taking place. During the time the rule was in force, no violation was discovered by this '*Baby Doe* Gestapo', as some paediatricians called them, at the time. The American Academy of Paediatricians went to court to fight these squads. The rules were eventually declared invalid by the court in 1983 and revised *Baby Doe* rules were formulated. Just before they were to take effect, another case, the *Baby Jane Doe* case, took place.

Baby Jane Doe (Weber v Stony Brook *(1983) 456 NE 2d 1186)*

Baby Jane Doe was born on 11 October 1983 in Long Island, New York, with several major defects and was transferred to an intensive care unit at another hospital. The baby had spina bifida, hydrocephalus, a damaged kidney and an alleged microcephaly. The paediatric neurologist advocated immediate surgery to drain the hydrocephalus and minimise the retardation. It was altogether a highly traumatic decision for the parents, since initially, the child's spine was protruding, and after intense disagreement between the various medical specialists over what should be done for the child, the parents decided not to authorise the operation, thinking the child would be dead in four days anyway. However, it survived and the spinal wound closed up. The guardian *ad litem*, Weber, authorised surgery but, the very next day, an appeals court overturned this decision. Another appeal was lodged.

The case was eventually decided by the New York Court of Appeal, which held that the parents of the handicapped baby in question were justified in refusing permission for surgery on their baby girl because the treatment they opted for was *within accepted medical standards*. Since the guardian *ad litem* had authorised surgery, the court held that the law left decisions up to parents when choice was available between two 'medically reasonable options'. The court also decided that the guardian *ad litem* should never have been empowered to make decisions for the baby over the wishes of her parents.

At this point, the Justice Department filed suit against the hospital in federal court, charging possible discrimination against the handicapped. The Justice Department wished to see the medical records, but a federal judge ruled that they could not have them. The case finally reached the Federal Court of Appeals for the Second Circuit which ruled that Congress had never intended s 504 of the Rehabilitation Act of 1973, which protects the rights of the handicapped, to apply to imperilled newborns, or to be applied blindly and without any consideration of the burdens and intrusions which might result. The Federal Regulations were thus revised again, but were subsequently struck down once again.

The Child Abuse Act Amendments of 1984

Following strong calls for legislation in the USA, amendments were made to the Federal Child Abuse Prevention and Treatment Act 1974, and the basic approach is that the amendments list the circumstances in which the withholding of medically indicated treatment would not amount to medical neglect. These include the presence of irreversible coma, when treatment would merely prolong dying and when treatment would be futile or inhumane. However, correction of a simple complication of Down's syndrome is not included as an exception, hence presumably this *would* come under medical neglect if not performed.

Baby K *(1994)*

This was again a case of an anencephalic baby who had no cognitive abilities or awareness. She was, nevertheless, placed on a ventilator because of respiratory distress. The prognosis was death within a few days, so the hospital prescribed supportive care only. Treatment was considered futile and both medically and ethically inappropriate. However, the baby's mother, who had already refused a termination, had a firm belief in God's unique responsibility for human life and insisted on mechanical ventilation when required.

The court supported the mother's view but, it seems, primarily because the case turned on the interpretation of a statute – the Emergency Medical Treatment and Labour Act 1992, which requires hospitals to provide 'stabilising' treatment in an emergency situation to any person who comes to hospital and requests treatment. The court's decision was, therefore, based on the narrow ground that the statute applied, but this was again only because the treatment requested was for respiratory distress rather than for anencephaly.

Several other points were made:

(a) The court held that the parents have a constitutional right to make medical decisions on behalf of their children. Clayton argues that such a right cannot, however, be absolute (see Clayton, 'What is really at stake in *Baby K*?' (1995) 23 Law Med and Ethics 13). The court also stated that no such right is available to physicians in their choice of treatment. This is clearly at odds with the British position in *Re B* [1981] 1 WLR 1421, although *Re T* (1997) did suggest that in certain circumstances, parental wishes will carry considerable weight and might even be determinative (for discussion, see Chapter 5). This approach also conflicts with the *Weber* case (*Baby Jane Doe*) which held that the parents' refusal of authorisation for surgery, when in line with standard medical practice, was justifiable, and the law allowed parents to decide for their children if the parents' choice was between two medically acceptable options.

(b) The courts who heard the case rejected the hospital's position to offer supportive care only on the grounds that their proposals were based on the ground of the child's disability, not its respiratory position.

Mason and McCall Smith (1999) argue that, in this case, the American courts were not concerned with the child's best interests, but only with the applicability of the statute. Their decision, they argue, was ultimately 'policy-based' and they were not prepared to undermine a particular statute in order to resolve this agonising dilemma (Mason and McCall Smith (1999), p 384). It does seem, on the weight of English authorities such as *Re B* (1981), that the Baby K situation would be a 'demonstrably awful' future life which would be covered under *Re B*. In Canada, the case of *Re Superintendent of Family and Child Services and Dawson* (1983) 145 DLR (3rd) 610 indicated that the court would not be obliged to abide by the refusal of parents to consent to an operation to replace a shunt for the alleviation of hydrocephalus, because non-replacement might cause increasing disability and pain for the baby. So, in Canadian law, as in English law, parents are not generally allowed, ultimately, to decide their disabled baby's fate.

Australia

Re F – *is the sanctity of life principle determinative?*

The case of *Re F, F v F* (1986), decided by the Supreme Court of Victoria, indicates that the sanctity of life principle may well prevail in all cases involving disabled children. Vincent J stated, in that case: 'No parent, no doctor, no court, has any power to determine that the life of any child, however disabled that child may be, will be deliberately taken from it ... [the law] does not permit decisions to be made concerning the quality of life, nor does it enable any assessment to be made as to the value of any human being.'

New Zealand

As another common law jurisdiction, New Zealand generally follows the English common law approach in these sorts of case. A recent case is illustrative.

The Baby L *case (*Auckland Health Services v L *[1998] NZFLR 998)*

Facts

In *Auckland Health Services v L* [1998] NZFLR 998, Baby L had been born with severe neurological abnormalities. She was unable to control the muscles on her face, which were paralysed, she was deaf, could not breathe effectively on her own, could not swallow or clear secretions from her mouth and was developing signs of severe cerebral palsy. She had been carefully monitored for eight weeks, was on a ventilator in intensive care, and her condition was deteriorating. The medical prognosis was that Baby L's outlook was hopeless and that treatment was futile. The treatment was also causing her suffering.

The Clinical Ethics Committee accepted the expert judgment of the clinicians that continued treatment was futile.

Auckland Healthcare Services therefore sought leave of the court to apply to place the baby under the guardianship of the High Court for the purposes of obtaining consent to the withdrawal of life support facilities.

Judgment

The court noted that, while there is no authority directly on point, there was authority both in New Zealand and overseas which satisfied the court that *in extreme circumstances, the welfare of the child required the discontinuance of life support* (emphasis added). They referred to *Auckland Area Health Board v AG* [1993] 1 NZLR 235, where Thomas J was required to consider whether a doctor was legally justified in withdrawing life support by discontinuing the use of a ventilator. In that case, the learned judge determined that a doctor was under no legal duty to prolong life, or to defer death, in the circumstances which existed. After a comprehensive review of the principles, Thomas J concluded that a doctor acting in good faith and in accordance with good medical practice was not under a duty to render life support necessary to prolong life if that was, in his or her judgment, contrary to the best interests of the patient. Although the patient in that case was not a child, the court saw no reason to differentiate between adults and child patients. Thomas J set out various criteria which should be applied in such cases and these criteria were recently considered by the (NZ) Court of Appeal in *Shortland v Northland Health Ltd* [1998] 1 NZLR 433. One of the criteria considered in the *Auckland Area Health Board* case was the fully informed consent of the patient's family.

The court then referred to a number of English cases, particularly *Re T (A Minor) (Wardship: Medical Treatment)* [1997] 1 WLR 242, and *Re J (A Minor) (Wardship: Medical Treatment)* [1991] Fam 33, where Lord Donaldson MR recognised, in somewhat different circumstances, that to prolong life is not the sole objective of the court and to require it to at the expense of other considerations may not be in a child's best interests. He also referred to the *Tony Bland* case (*Airedale NHS Trust v Bland* [1995] 2 WLR 316), where the House of Lords applied the best interests test to enable the withdrawal of life support from Tony Bland, a 17 year old victim of the Hillsborough Stadium disaster. In effect, Lord Goff also argued that, if it was justifiable to treat a patient who lacked the capacity to consent (as in the case of Tony Bland, who was lying in a persistent vegetative state (PVS)) because treatment was being provided in that patient's best interests, then that treatment could, and should, be discontinued if it was no longer in the patient's best interests to provide it. The court also referred to an English Practice Note [1996] 4 All ER 766 (reproduced in Chapter 10) which mentioned the need for the prior sanction of a High Court judge before certain medical procedures could be carried out on PVS patients.

Having come to the view that in was in Baby L's best interests that the application be granted, the court thought it necessary to consider the parents' wishes. Neither was prepared to give their consent, but as the present court said, 'Sadly, this was a case in which we had to make the decision, notwithstanding the wishes of the parents' and the court's view was that to have abided by their wishes would have been contrary to the best interests of Baby L.

The Auckland High Court held:

(a) It was in Baby L's best interests that the orders sought should be made. The court was satisfied, after considering Baby L's right to life, when contrasted with her right to be free from discomfort and pain, when considering her parents' deeply felt wish for her life to be prolonged as long as possible, that Baby L's best interests would be promoted by granting the application.

(b) In all but the most exceptional case, the court was required to take the necessary steps to preserve human life. An exceptional case did not involve a decision on whether to end life, but whether to prolong it by giving or maintaining treatment without which death would not ensue from natural causes. The decision had to be taken in the best interests of the patient having regard to established medical practice. The continued suffering of the patient would often be a relevant factor. Further, when the medical evidence acceptable to the court indicated that it was in the best interests of the child that a certain course be taken, the court would not lightly require the medical staff to depart from that course.

(c) Consent was given to Baby L undergoing medical investigations and medical treatment and management, acting on the advice of the appropriate specialist doctors at the hospital, and this 'may include a decision not to actively intervene to resuscitate in the event of a life threatening episode and/or the withdrawal of ventilatory support'.

THE ALLOCATION OF SCARCE RESOURCES

The question of whether to spend and utilise scarce, or at least finite/limited resources to sustain and maintain a severely handicapped child instead of on kidney dialysis or other equipment and staff to care for and treat non-terminally patients remains a difficult, delicate question and in some jurisdictions, a highly charged political one. The media always seem very interested in such cases where decisions are made to allow a severely handicapped, terminally ill child to die and such cases tend to make the headlines, usually provoking outrage from pro-life groups and the like. There is also the concern that continuing to provide intensive (and invariably expensive) care to a relatively small number of infants might also be detrimental to the resources available for older children. Hard choices will have to be made and, in a sense, the healthcare professionals cannot win: if they continue to sustain terminally ill babies, the criticism is that this is wasteful where treatment is seen as futile. On the other hand, if they do not continue to treat such children, even more strictures are often made to the effect that the sanctity of human life is being undermined or ignored on the altar of cost-effectiveness.

CONCLUDING OBSERVATIONS

Scientific advances have made it possible for severely handicapped newborn children to be kept alive where, in the past, they would have died very shortly, and nature would have 'taken its course'. This has created a new problem for doctors: should they follow the principle of preserving human life whenever they can, or should they refrain from using their new power to preserve life in cases where the quality of life will be far below the 'norm'? The problem is a serious one, because whereas a terminally ill adult may express a choice on the matter (where conscious and sensate), for the seriously or terminally ill newborn, the choice has to be made by others and this seems all the more tragic because of the newness of the baby's life and its stultified potential. The strength of feeling cannot be underestimated since a new law was passed in the USA, when it was thought that the existing legislation did not provide sufficient protection to such children. No universally acceptable formula for dealing with this problem has yet been found, and it is unlikely that the various moral, religious, ethical and pragmatic viewpoints can all be reconciled in any given judgment.

SELECTIVE BIBLIOGRAPHY

de Cruz, P and McNaughten, D, *By What Right? Studies in Medicine, Ethics and the Law*, 1987, Penrhos

Kuhse, H and Singer, P, *Should the Baby Live? The Problem of Handicapped Infants*, 1985, OUP

Mason, JK and McCall Smith, RA, *Law and Medical Ethics*, 5th edn, 1999, Butterworths, Chapter 15

Mason, KK and Meyers, DW, 'Parental choice and selective non-treatment of deformed newborns: a view from mid-Atlantic' (1986) 12 JME 67

McHaffie, H, Cuttini, M, Brolz-Voit, G, Randag, L, Mousty, R, Duguet, A-M, Wennergren, B and Benciolini, P, 'Withholding/withdrawing treatment from neonates: legislation and official guidelines across Europe' (1999) 25 JME 440

Pence, GE, 'The Baby Jane Doe case', in *Classic Cases in Medical Ethics*, 1990, McGraw-Hill

Royal College of Paediatrics and Child Health, *Witholding or Withdrawing Life Saving Treatment in Children: A Framework for Practice*, 1997, RCPCH

Weir, R, *Selective Nontreatment of Handicapped Newborns*, 1984, OUP

Wells, C, '"Otherwise kill me": marginal children and ethics at the edges of existence', in Lee, R and Morgan, D (eds), *Birthrights*, 1990, Routledge

CHAPTER 13

ABORTION: A GLOBAL OVERVIEW AND COMPARATIVE STUDY

INTRODUCTION

In Part I, we looked at the evolution of the law on abortion under English law and considered matters such as the English law dealing with the protection of the fetus as well as the moral, ethical, and political issues surrounding this controversial topic. Some might argue that it can no longer be called 'controversial' in the light of its apparently universal acceptance in countries like England and Wales. However, this would be to ignore the continuing debates that rage in the USA, Italy and, on occasion, those that surface in Ireland and other, non-European countries. This chapter commences with a global overview of the laws on abortion, before focusing on the American developments, not least the impact of the leading case of *Roe v Wade* in 1973 ((1973) 410 US 133), moving on to post-*Roe* cases, and then examining abortion laws in France and Germany, while noting abortion laws in other jurisdictions at both extremes of the spectrum – those that are very liberal, and laws which are highly restrictive or ban abortion altogether. The list of grounds surveyed on a global basis gives some idea of the range of variations between the various countries, but also highlights the similarities between the various nations. The emerging global trend towards greater recognition of women's right to reproductive autonomy will be examined, assessed and placed in historical context.

GLOBAL SURVEY

Currently, 62% of the world's population live in countries where induced abortion is permitted either for a wide range of reasons (and/or on broad social and economic grounds) or without restriction as to reason. In contrast, 25% of all people reside in 54 nations where abortion is generally prohibited or permitted only to save a woman's life. In addition, 13% of the global population live in 42 countries which permit abortion on physical or mental grounds. Put another way, 64 countries now permit abortion at the woman's request or with the approval of medical practitioners on broad social and economic grounds. The following broad categories may be identified:

(a) Outright bans on abortion – countries in this category define abortion as a criminal offence with penalties for the provider and often even for the women who have undergone the abortion.

(b) To save the woman's life – countries under this heading allow abortions to save the life of the pregnant woman. Many of the laws explicitly exempt from punishment providers who perform or women who undergo abortions when the woman's life is in danger. Other nations in this category permit providers and patients to raise a 'defence of necessity' at the time of trial.

(c) Physical health grounds – these countries have laws which authorise abortions to protect the pregnant woman's physical health. They sometimes require that the threatened injury to health be either serious or permanent. All nations under this heading also permit abortions to save the life of the pregnant woman.

(d) Mental health grounds – laws in this category permit abortion to protect the woman's mental health. In most of these countries, legislation explicitly recognises mental health grounds for abortion. The interpretation of 'mental health' varies around the world. It can encompass the psychological distress suffered by a woman who is raped, the mental distress caused by socio-economic circumstances, or a woman's psychological anguish over a medical opinion that a fetus is at risk of being impaired. Countries in this category also authorise abortions on grounds of physical health, including the need to save the woman's life.

(e) Socio-economic grounds – this category permits consideration of a woman's economic resources, her age, her marital status, and the number of her living children. These laws are generally interpreted liberally.

(f) Abortion without restrictions – the least restrictive abortion laws are those that allow abortion without restriction as to grounds. In countries with such laws, access may be limited by gestational age restrictions and by the additional requirement that third parties authorise an abortion.

The list of categories below includes only a selection of jurisdictions, generally opting for the main or better-known jurisdictions, except where the group of jurisdictions within a category is a small one.

Absolute prohibitions on abortion

The two countries in this category (as at early 2000), are Chile and El Salvador.

These two nations make up 0.4% of the world's population.

To save the woman's life

Afghanistan, Angola, Bangladesh, Benin, Brazil (which allows abortion in the case of rape), Central African Republic, Chad, Colombia, Congo, Egypt, Indonesia, Ireland, Kenya, Laos, Lebanon, Lesotho, Libya, Madagascar, Mauritius, Mexico, Nepal, Nigeria, Oman, Papua, New Guinea, Paraguay, Philippines, Senegal, Somalia, Sri Lanka, Sudan, Syria, Tanzania, Venezuela, Uganda, United Arab Emirates.

Physical health grounds

Also to save the woman's life: Argentina, Bolivia, Burundi, Cameroon, Costa Rica, Ecuador, Ethiopia, Guinea, Kuwait, Morocco, Mozambique, Pakistan, Peru, Poland, Korea, Rwanda, Saudi Arabia, Thailand, Uruguay, Zimbabwe.

Mental health grounds

Also to save the woman's life and health: Australia, Botswana, Gambia, Ghana, Israel, Jamaica, Jordan, Liberia, Malaysia, Namibia, New Zealand, Northern Ireland, Portugal, Trinidad and Tobago, Sierra Leone, Spain, Switzerland.

Socio-economic grounds

Also to save the woman's life, physical health and mental health: Finland*, Great Britain*, India†, Japan§, Taiwan*†‡, Zambia.

* abortion allowed on grounds of fetal impairment

§ spousal authorisation required

† parental authorisation required

‡ abortion allowed in cases of incest.

Without restrictions/no reasons required

Albania, Armenia, Austria, Azerbaijan, Belarus, Belgium, Bosnia-Herzegovina, Bulgaria, Cambodia, Canada, China, Croatia, Cuba, Czech Republic, Denmark, Estonia, France, Georgia, Germany, Greece, Hungary, Italy, Latvia, Lithuania, Moldova, Mongolia, Netherlands, North Korea, Norway, Puerto

Rico, Romania, Puerto Rico, Romania, Russian Federation, Singapore, Slovenia, South Africa, Sweden, Tunisia, Turkey†, Ukraine, USA§, Vietnam.

§ parental authorisation and notification in 31 States

† with certain restrictions (see discussion in text).

COUNTRIES WHICH BAN ABORTION IN ALL CIRCUMSTANCES

Some countries continue to maintain and enforce laws that criminalise abortion. El Salvador has a complete ban on abortion. The other country is Chile.

Chile

The law on abortion in Chile (18 Act No 18.826, 24 August 1989) is now among the world's most restrictive. Abortion is prohibited under all circumstances with no exception being made for procedures performed to save a woman's life. Women who have undergone abortions, especially low income women, have been prosecuted.

United Nations conferences on unsafe abortions

At various UN conferences, both governmental and non-governmental agencies have recognised the need to address the issue of unsafe abortion. The International Conference on Population and Development held in Cairo in 1994 and the Fourth World Conference on Women held in Beijing in 1995 specifically addressed reproductive rights and reproductive health, including unsafe abortion. The Cairo Programme of Action recognises unsafe abortion as a public health issue and calls for greater safety and compassion for women seeking abortions (see Programme of Action of the International Conference on Population and Development, Cairo, Egypt, September 1994 in Report of the International Conference on Population and Development, 8.25, UN Doc A/CONF 171/13/Rev 1, UN Sales No 95.XII.18 (1995). The Cairo policies on abortion were reaffirmed at a five year review by the UN in 1999, despite efforts of reactionary governments to block them.

The Beijing Platform for Action goes further by urging governments to consider removing criminal penalties for women who have undergone illegal abortions and to take affirmative steps towards understanding and addressing the causes and consequences of illegal abortion (the Beijing Declaration and

Platform for Action, Fourth World Conference on Women, Beijing, China, September 1995, UN Doc DPI/1766/Wom (1996)).

Western European countries

Writing in 1987 about abortion in Western law, Professor Mary Ann Glendon observed that 'The first striking finding of a comparative survey of abortion regulation is that fundamental change has occurred in this area all over the Western world in a relatively short period of time' (Glendon (1987), p 11).

United States of America

Overview of the American legal system in relation to American abortion laws

To fully appreciate the operation and effect of American abortion laws, it is necessary to keep in mind the American court system, particularly the system of federalism, and the theory of the separation of powers and the doctrine of judicial review (which does not refer to the same principle of judicial review utilised in English law, where it is a method of questioning administrative decisions on the basis of unreasonableness, irrationality and illegality).

In the USA, the sources of abortion law are: (a) the legislatures of the several States and territories and (b) the US Federal Supreme Court. The State legislatures are responsible for the production of most of the criminal laws and are the traditional source of regulations on abortion. Hence, from the decline of common law crimes (that is, which were judicially created) in the early 19th century to the intervention of the US Federal Supreme Court in the 1970s, State legislatures widely criminalised abortion.

In 1973, the landmark decision of *Roe v Wade* (1973) 410 US 133 was handed down by the US Supreme Court which ruled that the 14th Amendment to the United States Constitution, dealing with the right to privacy, provided a fundamental right for women to obtain abortions. The Supreme Court held that the 'right to privacy', established by the court's precedents in the contraception cases of the 1960s and early 1970s, assured the freedom of a person to abort unless the State had a 'compelling interest' in preventing the abortion. The court then held that, although the State had an interest in protecting fetal life, this interest did not become 'compelling' (that is, adequate to allow banning abortion) until fetal viability occurred in the third trimester of pregnancy. Thus, all the State abortion laws that regulated abortion during the first six months of pregnancy (except for the purpose of protecting maternal health during the second trimester) were invalidated. In fact, 46 of the 50 States' abortion laws were overturned.

Consequently, before *Roe v Wade*, the legality of abortion rested with the legislatures of the several States, but in 1973, the Supreme Court made it an issue of federal constitutional law by holding that abortion was a *constitutional* right, or at least a right that comes within the constitutional right to privacy. This means that, from then on, whether abortion was legal or not depended on the Supreme Court's decisions as to how broad the *Roe* 'right' to abortion actually was. State legislatures still have some discretion in abortion cases, but have little room for manoeuvre left outside the scope of the 'right' to abortion. In 1989, however, the *Webster* case (1989) 492 US 490 allowed further inroads into the 'right' and, in 1992, the *Casey* case gave States that wished to regulate abortion substantially, more scope to do so. From that time, elective abortions can be banned after actual viability (around 20–22 weeks), and pre-viability regulations only have to meet the new 'undue burden' standard, which means that a 'compelling State interest' is not required so long as the law does not present a 'substantial obstacle' to obtaining an abortion.

The central point that should be noted from this Supreme Court litigation, therefore, is the conflict between various States that want to make laws either protecting women or the unborn, and advocates of abortion rights who want as little governmental restraint upon the abortion option as possible. The classic scenario that frequently occurs is that the State will argue that there is no constitutional right to abortion or if there is a right, that is not violated by the law that the State wants to enforce. The abortion rights advocates argue that *Roe v Wade* rightly protects a fundamental human right and that it must not be eroded by politics.

In addition, the US Congress can pass at least some abortion regulations, but hardly ever does so. Its legislation is subject to the same constitutional scrutiny as State laws. Each State has its own State constitution and set of State constitutional rights. Though these rights cannot operate in derogation of federal constitutional rights, they can provide rights that are *not* in the federal constitution. It is possible, therefore, for a State to have its *own* version of *Roe v Wade*, which upholds an independent right to abortion in that State's own constitution.

Procedural background to abortion actions in the USA

A few procedural points may be made to illustrate the process of bringing suits dealing with abortion since 1973. Cases usually begin when someone, or an interested organisation, brings a lawsuit in federal court to challenge a particular State law, claiming it violates some provision of the US Federal Constitution. They sue the State, through an official like the State District Attorney or Governor, and the case will first be heard in a US federal district court in the State in question, where a decision will be made giving judgment to one side and the other usually appeals. The case then goes on to the US Circuit Court of Appeals for the particular federal circuit the State is in. A panel of judges will affirm or reverse the decision of the district court below and the losing side will then petition the US Supreme Court to hear the case. If the court refuses, then the district court decision will stand, and that law will be binding within that circuit (that is, that particular area/region). However, if the court agrees to hear the case (by a vote of four), then the nine member court will decide whether it agrees with the circuit ruling. However, whether the US Supreme Court strikes down the disputed law or not, its decision as to what the Constitution says and means will bind every other court in the country, whether State or federal.

Yet, *Roe* was unusual it that it came directly from the district court; some cases come out of State courts after a party lost in their State Supreme Court. The federal appellate system has also changed, so that very few cases now come to the US Supreme Court through the conventional appeal process any more. Instead, more are brought as petitions for a writ of certiorari, which are purely discretionary, so that the Supreme Court can take only those few cases which they regard as important.

Historical background to American abortion laws

In 1993, Professor Ronald Dworkin wrote that 'Abortion is tearing America apart. It is also distorting its politics and confounding its constitutional law' (Dworkin (1993)). Since then, as we have entered the 21st century, the situation in the USA remains one of contrasts and contradictions and, indeed, the passion and occasional hysteria surrounding abortion has continued to surface from time to time in various parts of America. It is always important to remember that it is potentially misleading to generalise about 'the American legal position' except in relation to its leading cases like *Roe* and *Webster*. Dwyer has observed that 'The problem of abortion is as much a public policy issue as it is a moral issue ...' (Dwyer (1997)), and this certainly reflects the situation then and in more recent times.

Before 1821, in the absence of statutory legislation on the subject, English common law applied (as incorporated into the American legal system). The interruption of pregnancy before quickening (usually occurring in the fourth or fifth month of pregnancy) was not a crime. In 1821, Connecticut became the first American State to prohibit abortion by statute. The law retained the common law quickening despite the fact that it had been modified in England in 1803 when the Ellenborough Act imposed the death penalty for abortion after quickening and transportation for any attempt to produce abortion before quickening. Within the next few years, three other States followed this example: Missouri in 1825, Illinois in 1827 and New York in 1828. However, neither the Missouri nor Illinois law made any reference to quickening. Commentators appear to think that the doctrine was, nevertheless, retained. The New York law was the first American statute which clearly followed the Ellenborough Act's language. It 'criminalised for the first time in America the wilful administration to any pregnant woman any medicine, drug, substance etc, with the intent of procuring a miscarriage'. At the same time, the New York statute was the first legislative act providing for a 'therapeutic exception' ('unless the same shall have been necessary to preserve the life of such woman' (see Frankowski (1987), p 20, and sources cited therein). In the 1830s, several other States revised their abortion laws but, on the whole, the country was 'still committed to the basic tenets of the common law tradition' (Frankowski (1987)). Only in five of the 26 States was it a crime to procure an abortion.

It was between 1840 and 1880 that the great 'upsurge of abortion legislation, promoted primarily by physicians' took place in the USA and at least 40 anti-abortion statutes were enacted. Most of the statutes were based on the notion that 'the interruption of gestation at any point of pregnancy should be considered criminal' (Frankowski (1987) and sources cited therein). By 1900, every State in the Union had an anti-abortion statute prohibition so that America became 'a nation where abortion was prohibited except in narrowly defined, extreme situations' (Frankowski (1987)).

In the 20th century, for well over 40 years, abortion was very much taboo, and a woman could obtain a legal abortion only to preserve her life, or, in some States, to preserve her health. The pro-abortion movement then started to gather momentum in the early 1960s, when many feminist activists began to press for economic issues, and this developed into a campaign for the recognition of certain inalienable social rights of women. Gradually, the right of abortion began to be considered as one of these rights. It needs to be mentioned at this point that, apart from the moral and political and even gender debates, the reality was that affluent women were able to secure 'safe' abortions which could be performed by a discreet private physician in private practice. In addition, they could also travel to those European countries where abortion was freely available (Frankowski (1987), p 21).

The abortion reform movement subsequently attracted public attention predominantly through the thalidomide cases and the outbreak of the rubella epidemic which resulted in the birth of many severely defective babies. Notably, in 1962, a pregnant American woman who had taken a tranquilliser containing thalidomide, failed to get an abortion in her home State of Arizona because Arizona law only permitted an abortion to save the life of the mother. The woman eventually managed to obtain an abortion in Sweden. It was established that, had the child been born, it would have been physically and mentally defective. This incident received very considerable publicity and two years later, in 1964, a major rubella epidemic broke out and approximately

30,000 children were born defective. This stunned the public and divided them in their views.

In 1968, the American Civil Liberties Union (ACLU) decided to promote actively the idea of repeal of all laws prohibiting abortion prior to the viability of the fetus. The ACLU was joined by another influential organisation, the Planned Parenthood Federation of America, which had previously opposed abortions and favoured contraceptives as a means of controlling family size. These two groups were strongly supported by the feminist movement of the time. It was between the mid-1960s and 1972 when 19 States relaxed their abortion laws by adopting legislation that followed the American Law Institute's Model Penal Code published in 1962. Under the Code, abortion remained criminal unless the doctor considered that the mother's physical or mental health was in danger, or that the baby was likely to be born with serious physical or mental problems, or that pregnancy was the result of 'felonious intercourse' (s 230.3 of the Model Penal Code). All these 19 States permitted abortions to preserve the life or health of the woman. There were some States that allowed termination for pregnancy resulting from rape or incest; others permitted an abortion on the grounds that the baby would be born with substantial deformities. Only four required no grounds whatsoever. Despite this liberality of laws in these States, the other 39 did not change their laws in the face of various pro-abortion pressure groups. Indeed, after various proposals to reform the laws were defeated in State legislatures, in no State was abortion made legal for up to all nine months of pregnancy. Except for four States, abortion was not permitted.

As Frankowski reminds us, 'It is an undisputed fact that duly elected State legislative bodies decided, rightly or wrongly, not to liberalise their abortion laws to the extent that it was accomplished in 1973 by the judiciary' (Frankowski (1987), p 23).

Hence, before *Roe*, the laws ranged from the very liberal, as in New York, to the comparatively restrictive, as in California. States such as Texas operated on similar principles as under the English Infant Life (Preservation) Act 1929 (that is, criminalising medical termination of a child capable of being born alive – see, further, Chapter 4), but the majority followed the line taken in the English Abortion Act 1967 (of the time, before its subsequent amendments by the Human Fertilisation and Embryology Act 1990; see Chapter 4).

Reaction in 1973 to *Roe* was notably swift – public, political and academic reaction resulted in pro-life groups beginning to organise against liberal abortion laws. The Maryland Republican representative Lawrence Hogan introduced the first of several constitutional amendments, proposing that the fetus be declared a 14th Amendment person from the moment of conception. The conflict between those who favoured the woman's right to choose and those who opposed abortion purely on religious grounds intensified. Throughout the 1980s, the abortion debate has continued, leading sometimes to violence from lobby groups. Lobbying began in the 1980s to restrict the use of public funds to support abortion services and counselling. On the political front, a candidate's stand on abortion has been a highly significant factor in recent presidential campaigns and in the selection of US Supreme Court and Surgeon General nominees.

The Medicaid programme

The US Social Security Act (Title XIX) established the Medicaid programme which enabled the States to provide federally funded medical assistance to the poor.

Dwyer (1997) observes that *Roe* was criticised from the political Right and the political Left, by feminists and non-feminists. She has reiterated that *Roe* is a controversial decision for at least two reasons. First is the complaint that the court overstepped its authority to engage in judicial review and some would argue that *Roe* engaged in judicial lawmaking. Secondly, there is concern about the implications of the fact that *Roe* grounds a woman's right to choose an abortion in the right of privacy.

The legal status of a fetus in the USA

The question of the legal status of the fetus is determined by the Federal Constitution. In particular, the 14th Amendment of the Federal Constitution covers the issue. In general, the Supreme Court of the US is not prepared to accord a fetus legal personality even though it seems prepared to afford a fetus legal protection at an advanced stage of development. Hence, Blackmun J, in *Roe*, pointed out that the word 'person', as used in the 14th Amendment, did not include the unborn. Yet, he appears to indicate that, in certain circumstances, a fetus might be 'entitled to 14th Amendment protection'. In fact, the decision in *Roe* suggests that a fetus, which has reached a viable stage of development, generally a period of about three months after a pregnancy, could be accorded the relevant constitutional protection.

In various American States, tort claims for damages in respect of injury to, or the wrongful death of, a viable fetus, resulting from the negligence or omission of another person, have usually been upheld by the judiciary. Some cases that may be cited are *White v Yup* (1969) 85 Nev 527; (1969) 458 P 2d 617, *Presley v Newport Hospital* (1976) 117 RI 177: (1976) 365 A 2d 748; *Salazar v St Vincent Hospital* (1980) 95 NM 150; (1980) 619 P 2d 826 and *O'Grady v Brown* (1983) 654 SW 2d 904.

Can a potential father prevent an abortion in American law?

As in England, a potential father has no *locus standi* to prevent an abortion on his unborn child. A married woman is seen as a person in her own right and her constitutional right to privacy entitles her to exercise such right independently of her husband. Thus, since her right to undergo a pregnancy termination is a constitutionally protected right, the exercise of that right cannot be interfered with by her husband.

In cases like *Planned Parenthood of Central Missouri v Danforth* (1976) 96 S Ct 2831, Blackmun J held that a State had no constitutional authority to grant a husband a unilateral right to prevent his pregnant wife from having the pregnancy terminated.

The leading US abortion cases

Currently, the four leading cases on abortion which have shaped the development of American law since 1973 are: *Roe v Wade* (1973) 410 US 133; *Webster v Reproductive Health Services* (1989) 492 US 490; *Ohio v Akron Centre for Reproductive Health* (1990) 4917 US 502; and *Planned Parenthood v Casey* (1992) 505 US 833.

Roe v Wade *(1973)*

The facts of this case are that in 1920, a single pregnant woman, who assumed the name of Jane Roe, filed a suit in the federal district court in Texas. She challenged the legality of the Texas statute permitting abortion only when 'procured or attempted by medical advice for the purpose of saving the life of the mother'. Jane Roe wished to have an abortion performed by a doctor, but since her life was not endangered by the pregnancy, she could not legally obtain one. She was poor and, therefore, could not afford to travel to another State where abortion laws were more liberal. She argued that there had been a constitutional violation of her right of privacy by the State. The federal district court ruled that the statute was impermissibly vague and too broad. In particular, the court held that the abortion restrictions infringed on the 'fundamental right of single women and married persons to choose whether to have children'. Both parties, Jane Roe and Wade (the local district attorney) appealed the judgment to the US Supreme Court. The case was first argued in 1971 along with *Doe v Bolton* (see below), a case involving the constitutionality of the Georgia abortion statute which was based on the Model Penal Code.

Following re-argument, Blackmun J delivered the majority opinion in *Roe v Wade*. The learned judge conceded that 'The [American] Constitution does not explicitly mention any right of privacy. In a line of decisions ... going back to 1891, the court has recognised that a right of personal privacy, or a guarantee of certain areas or zones of privacy, does exist under the Constitution.' However, in the central passage of the judgment he said:

> The right of privacy, whether it be founded in the 14th Amendment's concept of personal liberty and restrictions upon State action, as we feel it is, or, as the District Court determined, in the Ninth Amendment's reservation of rights to the people, is broad enough to encompass a woman's decision whether or not to terminate her pregnancy.

The learned judge then said that 'Appellants and some *amici* argue that the woman's right is absolute and that she is entitled to terminate her pregnancy at whatever time, in whatever way, and for whatever reason she alone chooses. With this we do not agree.'

Hence, the view of the majority, as Blackmun J made clear, is that the woman's right, although fundamental, is not absolute. He declared:

> A State may properly assert important interests in safeguarding health, in maintaining medical standards, and in protecting potential life. At some point in pregnancy, these respective interests become sufficiently compelling to sustain regulation of the factors that govern the abortion decision.

Hence, in the matter of abortion, the State was said to have only two legitimate interests – maternal health and potential (fetal) life. In providing guidance on how the point be determined at which the two distinct and separate State interests become 'compelling', the learned judge said that, on the question of the woman's maternal health, 'the "compelling" point, in the light of present medical knowledge, is at approximately the end of the first trimester'. Thus, prior to this point, said Blackmun J (p 163), 'the attending physician, in consultation with his patient, is free to determine, without regulation by the State, that in his medical judgment, the patient's pregnancy should be terminated'. In other words, the court seemed to be saying that during the first trimester, when abortion was safer than childbirth, the State could not show any interest compelling enough to impose any restrictions at all on abortion. That decision belongs solely to the woman and her doctor.

On the question of the State's interest in potential life, the court held that the 'compelling' point is viability. This is so because only then does the fetus have the capability of 'meaningful life' outside the mother's womb.

The Texas statute was invalidated as being too broad. It did not make any distinction between abortions performed early in pregnancy and those performed later, and it also limited the legal justification to a single reason – the 'saving' of the mother's life. The statute also violated the Due Process Clause of the 14th Amendment. Hence, the woman's right to be free of State controls was not, however, absolute, but it was not to be balanced against the rights of the fetus (the majority denied that the constitution recognised pre-natal life), but against the rights of the State.

In conclusion, Blackmun J enunciated (pp 164–65) what is now known as the *'trimester approach'*:

(a) for the stage prior to approximately the end of the first trimester, the abortion decision and its effectuation must be left to the medical judgment of the pregnant woman's attendant physician;

(b) for the stage subsequent to approximately the end of the first trimester, the State, in promoting its interest in the health of the mother, may, if it chooses, regulate the abortion procedure in ways that are reasonably related to maternal health.

On the question of the meaning of the 'health of the mother', this was clarified in *Doe v Bolton* (1973) 410 US 179, the case which was heard together with *Roe*. Here, the court declared (p 192) that, in any particular case, the health of the mother was a medical judgment to be:

> ... exercised in the light of all factors – physical, emotional, psychological, familial and the woman's age – relevant to the well-being of the patient. All these factors may relate to health. This allows the attending physician the room he needs to make his best medical judgment. And it is room that operates for the benefit, not the disadvantage, of the pregnant woman.

(c) For the stage subsequent to viability, the State in promoting its interest in the potentiality of human life may, if it chooses, regulate, and even proscribe, abortion except where it is necessary, in appropriate medical judgment, for the preservation of the life or health of the mother.

Blackmun J held (p 165) that this holding 'is consistent with the relative weights of the respective interests involved, with the lessons and examples of medical and legal history, with the lenity of the common law, and with the demands of the profound problems of the present day'.

The dissentients

In *Roe*, two of the justices strongly dissented. White J declared that he could find nothing in the language or history of the constitution to support the majority's decision and for him the decision was 'an exercise in raw judicial power'. Indeed, he opined (p 222) that the issue of abortion, for the most part, 'should be left with the people and to the political processes the people have devised to govern their affairs'.

An equally powerful dissenting judgment was delivered. In particular, he pointed out that adoption of the 'compelling State interest' appropriate only when fundamental rights are at stake, was unjustified in view of the fact that 'a majority of the States ... have had restrictions on abortions for at least a century'. Consequently, this should be viewed as a strong indication that the asserted right to an abortion is 'not so rooted in the traditions and conscience of our people as to be ranked as fundamental'. Thus, to reach its result he believed that (p 174) 'the [majority] ... necessarily had to find within the scope of the 14th Amendment a right that was apparently completely unknown to the drafters of the amendment'. He felt that the majority 'values the convenience, whim, or caprice of the putative mother more than the life of the fetus'.

Rehnquist J also dissented. He noted that there was no proof that Roe was in her first trimester when she filed her original suit. He said: 'While a party may vindicate his own constitutional rights, he may not seek vindication for the rights of others.' He observed that an abortion requires the services of a physician and felt that such an operation is 'not "private" in the ordinary sense of the word. Nor is the "privacy" that the court finds here even a distant relative of the freedom from searches and seizures protected by the Fourth Amendment to the Constitution.' He felt that the court was not justified in declaring the entire Texas statute to be unconstitutional. Instead, it should have been declared unconstitutional as applied 'to a particular plaintiff, but not unconstitutional as a whole'.

Burger CJ produced a three paragraph concurrence. He emphasised that he did not interpret the court's ruling as having the sweeping consequences attributed to it by the dissenting justices. He was sure, he wrote, that States could still control abortion and concluded that 'Plainly, the court today rejects any claim that the constitution requires abortion on demand'. This has been interpreted as an opinion that departed from the tenor of the main decision, but the chief justice reluctantly joined the majority only to prevent a decision even broader in scope.

Roe v Wade: *a revolutionary case?*

Frankowski (1987) maintains that Roe was revolutionary for at least four reasons:

(a) The decision invalidated virtually overnight the abortion laws of every American State, including those that followed the Model Penal Code. It was perceived that abortion on demand was suddenly a matter of constitutional right.

(b) The decision nationalised the issue of abortion, previously considered a family law matter and, as such, a matter for individual States.

(c) *Roe* meant that the judicial branch of the government took the powers from the legislature to decide matters relating to abortion.

(d) The majority of the judges discovered for the first time that the constitution did contain another fundamental right not mentioned anywhere else which had 'never been explicitly referred to' and, arguably, having no roots in the text or history of the document.

Doe v Bolton *(1973) 410 US 179*

This companion case was decided by the same vote, with the same justices concurring and dissenting. The majority held that several restrictions imposed by the Georgia statute, such as the hospital accreditation requirement, abortion review committee requirement, mandatory medical consultation requirement and residency requirement were unconstitutional because they applied throughout pregnancy and were not justified by any compelling State interest (at least before viability). The effect of this ruling was to invalidate the liberal abortion provisions of the Model Penal Code which were, therefore, held to be unconstitutional.

Webster v Reproductive Health Services *(1989) 492 US 490*

The *Webster* case arose from a 1986 Missouri law revised to update existing statutes concerning abortion and the unborn. The preamble contained a 'finding' by the legislature that the 'life of each human being at conception' and the 'unborn children have protectable interests in life, health and well being' at any stage of pregnancy. A second provision barred public employees from performing or assisting at abortions and banned the use of public facilities for abortions, even when public funds were not involved. The provisions made exceptions when the mother's life was threatened. The Act also made it unlawful to use public funds for encouraging or counselling a mother to terminate her pregnancy if her life was not endangered. A final provision required physicians to conduct certain tests to determine whether the fetus was viable if they 'have reason to believe' that the woman seeking the abortion is at least 20 weeks pregnant. An abortion clinic and a group of doctors brought a class action suit against the statute asserting violations of various rights.

The court was deeply divided and Rehnquist CJ upheld most of the Missouri provisions. The majority disposed of the Missouri preamble and the ban against abortion counselling.

Ultimately, the Supreme Court declared (by 5:4) that a Missouri law was constitutional. It stated that:

- life became human life at conception;
- that Missouri State property could not be used to conduct abortions; and
- a fetal viability assessment could be required before late term abortions are performed.

Thus, Rehnquist CJ delivered a majority opinion allowing several further State incursions into a woman's freedom of choice, while sidestepping the more overtly political implications of rejecting *Roe* altogether.

Another case was *Ohio v Akron Centre* (1990) 497 US 502, where the court ruled (by 6:3) that a State could require a parent or guardian to be notified before an under-age woman received an abortion. However, a provision must be in place for a judge to bypass this requirement if he or she regards it to be in the best interest of the woman.

Two years later, *Planned Parenthood v Casey* (1992) 505 US 833 was decided, where the court ruled (by 5:4) that Ohio could require:

- a 24 hour waiting period before an abortion is performed;
- that the woman give her informed consent to the abortion;
- that parent or guardian be notified before an abortion is performed on a minor.

However, the court struck down as unconstitutional the requirements of a Pennsylvania law which required prior spousal notification, that is, requiring wives to seek their husband's prior consent.

In this case, at issue were five provisions of the Pennsylvania Abortion Control Act 1982, as amended in 1988 and 1992. The Act requires that a woman seeking an abortion give her informed consent prior to the abortion procedure, and specifies that she be provided with certain information for at least 24 hours before the abortion is performed. For a minor to obtain an abortion, the Act requires the informed consent of one of her parents, but provides for a judicial bypass option if the minor does not wish or cannot obtain a parent's consent. Another provision of the Act requires that, unless certain exceptions apply, a married woman seeking an abortion must sign a statement indicating that she has notified her husband of her intended abortion. The Act exempts compliance with the three requirements in the event of a 'medical emergency'.

The court considered the fundamental constitutional questions resolved by *Roe*, principles of institutional integrity and the rule of *stare decisis*, and held that the essential holding of *Roe v Wade* 'should be retained and once again *affirmed*'.

This case managed to displease both pro-choice and anti-abortion lobbies. O'Connor, Kennedy and Souter JJ took a moderate line, aided and abetted by Blackmun and Stevens JJ. This majority declined to overrule *Roe*. However, Souter J delivered an additional oral statement from the Bench: 'To overrule [*Roe*] would subvert the court's legitimacy beyond any reasonable question.' The majority judgment then further diluted Roe's constraints on State autonomy; States are now prohibited only from adopting measures which provide 'an absolute obstacle or severe limitation' on a woman's choice.

However, apart from striking down the provision requiring prior spousal notification, the court upheld requirements that unmarried under 18 year olds receive parental or judicial approval for surgery; and that all women receive information about fetal development and then wait 24 hours for surgery.

State medical association regulations

Independent of the State and federal laws, physicians who perform are restricted by the regulations of their State's Medical Association. They typically do not permit abortions after 20 or 21 weeks' gestation unless the woman's health or life are seriously at risk.

COMPARATIVE OBSERVATIONS ON THE AMERICAN LAWS ON ABORTION

Commenting from a comparative point of view, Professor Mary Ann Glendon, writing in 1987, characterised abortion policy in the USA as 'singular' because 'it requires no protection of unborn life at any stage of pregnancy, in contrast to all the other countries with which we customarily compare ourselves, but also because [the US] abortion policy was not worked out in the give-and-take of the legislative process' (Glendon (1987), pp 24–25). As we have seen from our survey, the basic American approach to, and regulation of, abortion was established by the US Supreme Court 'in a series of cases that rendered the abortion legislation of all States wholly or partly unconstitutional and severely limited the scope of future State regulation of abortion' (p 25). Nowhere else in the world, emphasises Glendon, have the courts gone so far in precluding further statutory regulation. Constitutional challenges have been made in several countries, but it was only in Canada, Italy and (the former) West Germany where the legislative attempts to resolve the problem were held unconstitutional. As our survey has also shown, when the landmark case of *Roe v Wade* was decided by the US Supreme Court in 1973, it did so in such a manner that put it in a class of its own, at least in relation to other developed nations. However, the debates on abortion continue to polarise opinion, and 16 American States still have pre-1973 laws on their statute books, even though they are strictly unconstitutional and nullified after *Roe v Wade*. As we have seen, there have also been many attempts since 1973 to reduce free access to abortions and court decisions in 1989 (*Webster*), 1990 (*Akron Centre case*) and 1992 (*Casey*), for example, have all somewhat circumscribed the conditions under which an abortion may be legally performed.

Frankowski (1989) points out (p 32) that Roe's trimester approach was based on the state of medical knowledge and practice in existence at the beginning of the 1970s. However, where infants were not considered viable before 28 weeks of gestational age and if they weighed under 1,000 grams of fetal weight, today, technological and other advances in neonatal care mean that infants become viable much earlier, occasionally at 23 weeks. Survival rates for infants weighing even less than 750 grams are increasing and some experts are even arguing that a lower limit of viability might eventually become inappropriate. As viability is possible earlier and earlier, abortions may be prohibited at earlier and earlier stages of pregnancy. As Rhoden (1983) observes, 'By this ironic twist of events, *Roe v Wade* may one day become a "right to life" decision' (see Rhoden, N, 'The new neonatal dilemma: live births from late abortions' (1983) 72 Geo LJ 1451). However, in the late 1980s, second trimester abortions became safer than they were in the early 1970s, hence, as Frankowski says, 'if the same trend continues, at some time in the future, maternal health interest will become compelling much later than the court decreed *in Roe v Wade*. In other words, abortions become safer and the line drawn by the *Roe* majority at the end of the second trimester must be moved back toward the conception' (Frankowski (1987)). It is probable that, in future, the lines will pass each other 'creating an overlap and (constitutionally) a hopeless contradiction within *Roe*' (Wolfe, *The Rise of Modern Judicial Review*, 1986, cited by Frankowski (1987)).

Canada

The extent to which abortions are available in Canada vary greatly (McConnell (1989), p 906). This is partly a function of the division of legislative responsibility under the Canadian Constitution, which allocates criminal jurisdiction to the federal government while the provincial government has responsibility for health matters – which includes funding for medical services. One of the leading cases on abortion in Canada is the *Morgentaler* case (*Morgentaler, Smoling and Scott v The Queen* (1988) 44 DLR (4th) 385).

Section 251 of the Criminal Code limits a pregnant woman's access to abortion by requiring her to obtain a certificate from a therapeutic abortion committee of an accredited or approved hospital.

One of the constitutional questions which arose was whether s 251 infringed or denied the rights and freedoms guaranteed by s 7 of the Canadian Charter of Rights and Freedoms which states that:

> Everyone has the right to life, liberty and security of the person and the right not to be deprived thereof except in accordance with the principles of fundamental justice.

Five out of seven judges of the Canadian Supreme Court concluded that s 251, which made procuring or acting upon an intention to procure a miscarriage an indictable offence, infringed a woman's constitutionally guaranteed right to liberty and security of her person in a manner that could not be justified in a free and democratic society. As the court put it: 'Forcing a woman, by threat of criminal sanction, to carry a fetus to term unless she met certain criteria unrelated to her own priorities and aspirations, was a profound interference with a woman's body and an infringement of the security of the person.' The mandatory procedure by s 251 also led to a second breach of the right to security of the person which occurred independently in consequence of the delay in obtaining therapeutic abortions resulting in a higher probability of complications and greater risk. Since the harm to the psychological integrity of women seeking abortions was also established, it was said that the right to security of the person protected both the physical and psychological integrity of the individual.

However, the court also established that not all restrictions on abortion would constitute an infringement of a woman's security of the person. Justice Bertha Wilson, for example, said that s 1 of the Charter (which reads: 'The Canadian Charter of Rights and Freedoms guarantees the rights and freedoms set out in it subject to reasonable limits prescribed by law as can be demonstrably justified in a free and democratic society') allows for the imposition of reasonable limits on a woman's s 7 right. In particular, she suggested that abortion legislation that is sensitive to the developmental facts of pregnancy, for instance, which adopts a permissive attitude towards early term abortions and a more restrictive attitude towards late term abortions, would probably be constitutional.

This Supreme Court ruling invalidated the only abortion law in Canada and subsequent attempts by the Canadian Parliament to implement new legislation have not been successful. There now does not seem to be *any* legislation regulating abortion in Canada, so that such decisions are left to the women, their doctors and medical associations. Abortions are readily available for up to 20 weeks in hospitals of most large cities and in a few free standing clinics. Abortions are not available in Prince Edward Island, or in many rural areas. Section 223 of the Criminal Code states that 'a person commits homicide when he causes injury to a child before or during its birth as a result of which the child dies after becoming a human being'. Thus, for a person to be charged with murder, the fetus would have to be intentionally injured before or during birth, would have to be born alive and the child later die.

As Dwyer remarks: 'The [Canadian] Charter does appear to embody the resources to launch a sex-equality defence of liberal abortion laws, so it will be interesting to see how the Canadian Supreme Court addresses the question of abortion on future occasions.'

Australia

Under Australian law, unlike American law, there is no constitutionally protected right of woman to seek an abortion. State criminal statutes regulate Australian abortion law and specify the circumstances under which a woman may undergo an abortion, and for which a doctor may perform a lawful operation. Australian law on abortion basically followed English law, and the well known English case of *R v Bourne* (1938) (see [1938] 3 All ER 615) was the leading authority in Australia for many years. In 1969, two important developments occurred which are summarised by Fisse (in his edition of *Howard's Criminal Law* (1990)):

(a) In Victoria, in *R v Davidson* [1969] VR 667, Menhennitt J directed a jury at common law 'to establish that the use of an instrument with intent to procure a miscarriage was unlawful, the Crown must establish either (a) that the accused did not honestly believe on reasonable grounds that the act done by him was necessary to preserve the woman from a serious danger to her life or her physical or mental health (not being merely the normal dangers of pregnancy and childbirth) which the continuance of the pregnancy would entail; or (b) that the accused did not honestly believe on reasonable grounds that the act done by him was in the circumstances proportionate to the need to preserve the woman from a serious danger to her life or her physical or mental health (not being merely the normal dangers of pregnancy and childbirth) which the continuance of the pregnancy would entail. In short [the accused] must believe that the abortion is both necessary and proportionate when measured against the danger to the mother if his act is to be lawful' (see Fisse, B, *Howard's Criminal Law* (1990), p 153). As Mason and McCall Smith put it, 'The Australian courts ... used the word "unlawful" as indicating that there must be a "lawful" reason for termination of pregnancy' (see Mason and McCall Smith (1999), p 114).

(b) The second development was a statutory amendment in South Australia. Here, an abortion is lawful, in addition to the common law, if it is either performed in a hospital and in the opinion of two doctors 'the continuance of the pregnancy would involve greater risk to the life of the pregnant woman or greater risk of injury to the physical or mental health of the pregnant woman than if the pregnancy were terminated', or alternatively, in their opinion, 'there is a substantial risk that if the pregnancy were not terminated and the child were born to the pregnant woman, the child would suffer from such physical or mental abnormalities as to be seriously handicapped', or, if it is not performed in a hospital, the pregnancy is terminated by a doctor in whose opinion termination is immediately necessary to save the life, or to prevent injury to the physical or mental health, of the pregnant woman'. The operation of the Act is limited to women who have resided in Western Australia for at least two months before the abortion' (see Fisse (1990), p 167).

Australian law has also dealt with the means used to effect an abortion, with words like 'poison' and 'instrument' and the courts have held that a 'noxious thing', in this context, is limited to something likely to harm a pregnant woman. All the statutes include a reference to 'other means', which Devereux argues 'might be understood as bringing within the offence any attempt to induce abortion, however ridiculous the method used'. On this point, the South Australian Court has 'declined to accept the view that the legislature intended to catch people who might believe in the efficacy of prayer or witchcraft and limited the word "means" to "something that is, in the common experience of mankind and in some reasonable degree, capable of producing the result"' (see Fisse (1990), p 168).

Criticisms of the Australian law on abortion

In recent years, abortion law has been subjected to sustained criticism. The main criticisms are summarised by Cica (1991), who highlights several areas of inadequacies. The purported deficiencies identified are:

(a) variation between jurisdictions;

(b) uncertainty of the law from jurisdiction to jurisdiction;

(c) use of outdated medical/medico-legal concepts in legal interpretation.

In addition, she claims that, even where there are abortion laws, they are effectively 'dead letter' laws because they are simply not enforced in some jurisdictions.

Variation between jurisdictions

Cica points out that the 'most obvious' weakness of Australian law on abortion is its variation between jurisdictions. Each Australian State and Territory uses different criteria to determine the legality of an abortion and the lack of uniformity has two main practical consequences: (a) a woman resident in a jurisdiction with more restrictive laws may seek a legal abortion in a more liberal jurisdiction. She believes such a practice is undesirable because 90% of pregnant Australian Capital Territory residents seeking termination travel to Sydney clinics for their abortions and this means that they can avoid a legal prohibition in their resident jurisdiction; (b) the variations:

> ... impact differently upon women of different socio-economic backgrounds. A poorer woman seeking a legal abortion within her resident jurisdiction has her financial disadvantage minimised by the Medicare rebate for abortion. The rebate is paid from Commonwealth funds and is available to all Australian women in all jurisdictions for all lawful abortions. The option of seeking a legal abortion in a woman's non-resident jurisdiction is, however, open only to women who can afford the time and financial costs of interstate travel. These costs are most significant for women from geographically isolated jurisdictions such as Tasmania [Cica (1991), p 45].

Uncertainty of the law

Cica also submits that it is not clear exactly what the law on abortion is in each jurisdiction. 'The only jurisdictions which have offered any statutory clarification of the provisions dealing with unlawful abortion are those in South Australia and the Northern Territory'. In addition, she points out that the case law in this area is neither extensive nor authoritative. The High Court has not had any occasion to examine the relevant criminal provisions of any State or Territory and there has not been any authoritative interpretation of local provisions dealing with unlawful abortion from the courts in the Australian Capital Territory, Western Australia, Tasmania, South Australia and the Northern Territory.

The case law for Victoria comprises the ground-breaking case of *R v Davidson*, but it was made by a single judge of the Supreme Court. Another related criticism which Cica makes is that there is a 'significant gap' between the letter and practice of the law, a disparity between situations where, according to the law, an abortion would be lawful, and situations where such an abortion is actually available to a woman seeking termination of her pregnancy. The point she makes is that there are occasions when the discrepancy 'denies women abortions'.

Use of outdated medical/medico-legal concepts

Another 'major weakness', according to Cica, is the use of concepts which are based on the state of medical knowledge in the 19th and early 20th centuries. There are now doubts surrounding the meaning of key statutory phrases like 'procuring a miscarriage' in abortion provisions and 'a child capable of being born alive' in child destruction provisions.

Non-enforcement of abortion laws?

Another point that Cica makes which she calls 'liberalising' is that there has been the 'non-enforcement of the criminal law affecting abortion'. In fact, she claims that 'Prosecutions for unlawful abortion effectively ceased in Australia in the early 1970s, which is one reason why the case law is so undeveloped'. There is also an unwillingness of governments and law enforcement agencies to be seen to be adopting a policy on the controversial and newsworthy issue of abortion. Prosecuting doctors, let alone the women, in this context, is seen as 'politically unwise'. There is also the 'unlikelihood of successful prosecutions [for unlawful abortions] under the current law'. The tests in *R v Davidson* and *R v Wald* (1971) 3 DLR (NSW) 25 cast a very heavy burden of proof upon the prosecution; proof beyond reasonable doubt that a qualified doctor lacked the required honesty and reasonable belief would be 'very difficult'. *A fortiori*, Cica claims that, in some jurisdictions, 'the non-enforcement of the law has led to a situation where abortion is available virtually on demand'.

Attempted abortion statutes

There are several statutes dealing with attempted abortion and here is just one example of such a statute.

Victoria: Crimes Act 1958

> Section 65: Whosoever with intent to procure the miscarriage of any woman whether or not she is with child unlawfully administers to her or causes to be taken by her any poison or other noxious thing, or unlawfully uses any instrument or other means, and whosoever with intent to procure the miscarriage of any woman whether she is or is not with child unlawfully administers to her or causes to be taken by her any poison or other noxious thing, or unlawfully uses any instrument or other means with the like intent, shall be guilty of an indictable offence, and shall be liable to imprisonment for a term of not more than 15 years.

Comment on Australian abortion laws

If there is even some justification in Cica's comments on the defects in Australian abortion laws, then those laws could fall into disrepute and, should more of these laws fall into desuetude, this cannot be desirable for the law, doctors, social workers, or most of all, the women who think they might need abortions. Variations between jurisdictions, uncertainty and outdated laws would not, *ipso facto*, create problems with laws that have little social impact, but with a situation such as abortion, it is inevitable that a case will arise which requires clarification of the law; given the circumstances, the courts might have to decide in unseemly haste and, unfortunately, hard cases do tend to make bad law. Unfortunately, given the common law structure and ideology of the Australian system, the courts would have to wait for a dispute or case to come to the courts which required resolution or clarification of the law and even the legislature could only act if there was a perceived injustice which could mobilise public opinion. It has to be said, however, that there is certainly no shortage of abortion laws in the various Australian jurisdictions. The task facing the courts and, eventually, the legislature, if they are so minded, will be to mete out justice with humanity and also strive to achieve some measure of consistency between jurisdictions, if only so that like cases are treated alike.

Civil law countries

Scotland – Kelly v Kelly

Despite its proximity to England, and its undoubted English influences, Scotland is *not* a common law jurisdiction, but owes its legal heritage to Roman law and is, therefore, much more a civil law jurisdiction than anything else, for example, in its reliance on doctrinal writers. It has, however, adopted a limited version of the English doctrine of precedent, hence its case law is instructive and significant from a comparative point of view. The Scots legal approach to the unborn fetus is contained in cases such as *Kelly v Kelly* (1997) *The Times*, 5 June. In this case, the Second Division of the Inner House of the Scottish Court of Session held that *the fetus has no independent legal existence or actionable rights in Scots law*. Therefore, Scots law did not confer on the fetus a right to continue to exist in the mother's womb. The court was prepared to accept that, in criminal law, abortion was a distinct crime and not subsumed in the crime of murder.

France

A brief legislative history of abortion laws

The history of legislation relating to abortion in France is, in the words of Pradel, 'extremely turbulent' (Pradel (1987), p 213). 'Abortion has had its legal elements and its sanctioned punishments modified more frequently than almost any other crime [in France]'. Numerous countries with a French colonial history continue to rely on early French laws which penalise abortion except when undertaken to save a woman's life, or when the pregnancy constitutes a grave danger to her health. This has resulted in many Franco-African countries (African countries colonised by the French) having abortions which have been clandestine and unhygienic and which have resulted in the infertility or death of the woman (see Knoppers *et al* (1990), p 892, who cite the French law of 31 July 1920, which prohibited the publicity of contraceptives and their distribution: *Lois et politiques affectant la fécondité: une décennie de changements*: Serie E, No 7, Population Reports, E-20, 1985, as having been incorporated when those colonies attained independence). Only four of the francophone colonies (Mali, Cameroon, Senegal and the Ivory Coast) have repealed this law. The point that is made by Knoppers *et al* is that 'The legislative history of France has played a significant role in the development of the law of many of the Francophone countries in the world' (p 893).

As France is, *prima facie*, a Catholic country, and at least operated as such in the years leading up to the 18th century, abortion was initially prohibited as being contrary to the moral laws of the church. In 1556, King Henry II made abortion a crime, labelling it a homicide and making its performance punishable by death. This effectively meant that he had made a religious principle a legal one. In the Penal Code of 1791, the abortionist was punishable by up to 20 years' imprisonment, while the mother was not liable to any sanction and had immunity under the law. But the Napoleonic Penal Code of 1810 (Art 317) contained punishments in the form of jail sentences for the mother and the abortionist. The text of Art 317 reads:

> Whosoever, by food, drink, medicine, violence, or by any other means has procured an abortion of a pregnant woman, whether or not with her consent, will be punished with imprisonment. The same punishment will be given to a woman who procures her own abortion, or who had consented to the use of means administered for that purpose, if abortion follows. Doctors, surgeons, and other health officers, as well as pharmacists who have given advice as to the appropriate means, will be condemned to hard labour in the case where abortion has taken place [translation: Knoppers *et al* (1990), p 894].

A serious decline in the birth rate in France then transpired in 1920 and, in response, a law was passed in 1920 which, despite maintaining the criminal status of abortion, aimed to suppress incitement to abortion and propaganda for contraception. In 1923, a law was passed on 23 May which made abortion a minor offence under civil law (a delict). Pradel's view is that this did not necessarily decrease the severity of an abortion in the eyes of the law, because 'by removing it from the consideration of the jurors of the Assize Court, whose discriminatory attitudes and leniency is well known, abortion ended up being more severely punished' (Pradel (1987), p 213). Indeed, for the first time, attempted abortion was also covered by the law.

The law reform of 1939 was the next important milestone because, while the public prosecutor was exempted from proving the state of pregnancy, the exception of therapeutic abortion was established for cases where the mother's life was in danger, and Pradel sees this as a 'first step towards liberalisation' (Pradel (1987)). However, this 1939 legislation confirmed the sanction against attempted abortion and the punishment against 'professional abortionists' was increased. This legislation also contained a qualification of the term 'pregnant woman', which was used in the 1810 legislation. According to this amendment, the punishment for abortion extended to 'whosoever procured an abortion or attempted to procure an abortion on a pregnant woman or a woman who is presumed to be pregnant'. Hence, a woman could be charged if she tried to have an abortion, whether or not she was actually pregnant and whether or not she succeeded (see *Decret-loi de 1939 relatif à la famille et à la française* (DP 1939.4.369), Art 84). Presumably, it did not matter under this legislation if it was discovered that the woman was not actually pregnant, only that she *believed* she was and attempted an abortion.

Self-induced abortion was also punished by the law, although without quite such severe penalties. This was the era when 'therapeutic abortions' received formal authorisation on the grounds of saving a woman whose life was in serious danger (see Art 87 of the *Loi* of 1939). This later became Art 161.1 of the *Code de la santé publique* which was brought into force by *Decret* No 55-512 of 11 May 1955. Before yet another law passed in 1955, the law was again changed in the wake of the Second World War. Abortion was again made a crime with the punishment being as severe as death and, under the Vichy regime, a woman was executed under this provision (see Knoppers *et al* (1990)). Once liberation came, however, abortion was made an offence under civil law, thus becoming a delictual rather than a criminal act. Considerable public debate then took place in France, stimulated by an increase in convictions and in the number of clandestine abortions. There was a substantial rise in the number of abortions, and criticisms began to grow focusing on three areas, as identified by Pradel: (a) the health implications, because 400 women were dying every year from these abortions; (b) the social issue because, given the inequality between women, many could afford to obtain an abortion abroad while others, for lack of means, had to resort to the most difficult measures, even to performing abortions on themselves; and (c) the inadequacy of the legal system, since the legal norm was being openly violated with some doctors even 'bragging about operations' (see Pradel (1987), p 214).

It became clear that reform was urgently required, but:

> ... reform was long and difficult: long because the country was deeply divided, and there were several obstacles to liberalisation; difficult because liberalisation implicated both moral concerns, such as respect for life, and demographic concerns - ie, a partial permissiveness could cause the birth rate to drop as had happened in Rumania after the permissive law of 1957 [Pradel (1987)].

This led to Mrs Veil, the Minister of Health, to lead the campaign for reform and the legislature eventually voted to enact the law of 17 January 1975 (renewed in 1979) which permitted voluntary termination within the first 10 weeks of the pregnancy. According to the text, 'the crime of abortion was formally defined as the voluntary interruption of pregnancy; in effect, however, abortion became permissible under circumstances other than when the mother's life was threatened. The law of 31 December 1979 later confirmed the text of the 1975 law.

Hence, in 1975, abortion became available in France for (up to the end of the 10th week of pregnancy) any woman 'whose condition places her in a situation of distress' (see Law No 75-17 of 17 January 1975, relating to the voluntary termination of pregnancy, under Art L 162-1, which has been re-enacted and amended by Law No 79–1204 of 31 December 1979). 'Distress' is not defined and the statutory provision (Art L 162-4) allows the woman to be the sole judge of whether she is in distress or not, at least for the first 10 weeks of her pregnancy. Under the 1975 law, abortion is available in cases of 'necessity' and this is satisfied if, in the first 10 weeks, the woman considers herself to be 'in distress'. However, she must undergo counselling and (except in cases of emergency) wait one week from the date of her original request and two days from the date of her counselling before the abortion can be performed. After 10 weeks, abortion is only permitted for 'therapeutic' abortions which means that two physicians must certify that:

- 'continuation of the pregnancy is seriously endangering the woman's health; or
- there is a strong possibility that the unborn child is suffering from a particularly serious disease or condition considered incurable at the time of diagnosis': see Art L 162-12.

One of the experts must be chosen from an official list of experts.

As far as unmarried female minors are concerned, there is a need for parental consent or a judge's approval before such a person can obtain a legal abortion.

Germany

History of German abortion laws

In Germany, as in France, the Catholic Church did not want abortion to be legally recognised. In fact, the majority of lawyers in general, and criminal law experts in particular, strongly supported proposals to justify abortion not only on medical, but also on other grounds, such as averting the birth of a seriously handicapped child; or in cases of pregnancy caused by sexual assault. There was serious discussion of the justification of averting any grave social and financial consequences of a child's birth and allowing abortion during the first few weeks up to three months of pregnancy (see Gossel (1987), p 130).

Historically, para 218 of the German Penal Code (*Strafgesetzbuch*: StGB) remained nearly unchanged from 1871 to 1974. That paragraph, and paras 219 and 220 thereof, have governed the criminal law relating to the termination of pregnancy since 1871. In its original form, para 218 criminalised all forms of artificially induced abortions of a human fetus. All abortions were made punishable as 'killing the fetus'. Having been a felony since 1871, abortion was then made a misdemeanour in 1926 if perpetrated by the pregnant woman, who could be imprisoned from one day to five years. If perpetrated by anyone else, para 218 stated that killing the fetus was a felony to be punished by imprisonment from one to 15 years.

The German Penal Code punished abortion with no allowance being made for exceptional circumstances, but it was always accepted that the existence of specific reasons would justify a criminal act which would exclude it from punishment. Indeed, in practice, from the end of the 19th century onwards, abortion conducted on medical grounds was tolerated and the same informal toleration was later extended during the First World War to rape victims who wanted to have their pregnancies terminated (van Zyl Smit (1994) and authorities cited therein). It was after the First World War, during the time of the Weimar Republic, that abortion became an issue which divided the political parties of the time. However, despite several comprehensive reform proposals being made by the Social Democrats and the Communists, none managed to attract sufficient support to allow it to pass into legislation (van Zyl Smit (1994)). It was in 1926 that a less controversial amendment to para 218 began a move towards 'partial decriminalisation' by declaring that an abortion conducted by the mother, or by a third party with the consent of the mother, would in future not be a felony, but only a misdemeanour, which meant that the punishment could only be a fine, not imprisonment. In 1927, the Supreme Court of the German Reich (*Reichsgericht*: RGH) by its decision of 11 March, held that killing the fetus is not unlawful if it is the only way to avert a present danger or grave injury to the pregnant woman (RGSt, Vol 61, pp 242–56). Through the courts, therefore, and not the application of a Code provision, which was in itself an unusual development in Germany, a general reason of justification was introduced, namely, the 'state of necessity'. Even though this had not been specifically provided for by the Code, it was made applicable to abortion as well. This meant that abortion could now be justified because of the 'state of necessity', but only if this was to preserve the mother's life or her physical and mental health. From 1933 onwards, the issue of the termination of pregnancy was charged with the ideology of Nazism. Provision was made by the so called Act for the Prevention of Congenitally Defective Future Generations 1933 (*Erbgesundheitgesetz*) (full title: *Gesetz zur Änderung des Gesetzes zur Verhutung erbranken Nachwuchses*: RGB1 1933 I, p 59) for mass sterilisation and abortion for eugenic purposes (for a comparative discussion on sterilisation, see Chapter 15). At the same time, further restrictions were placed on the termination of pregnancy of healthy German mothers. In 1943, the provision for certain terminations to be treated as misdemeanours was removed, and the culmination of the movement to protect the unborn fetus was reached with the addition to para 218 of the provision that, if the actions of the abortionist had 'prejudiced the vitality of the German people', the death penalty could be imposed (see the *Verördnung zum Schütz von Ehe, Familie und Mutterschaft* RGB1 1943 I, p 140).

Immediately after the Second World War, the status of the amendments introduced during the Nazi regime was unclear but, in 1953, as part of the purge of the Penal Code in the Federal Republic of Germany (West Germany) para 218 was amended by omitting the provision relating to prejudice to the vitality of the German people. However, the old Weimar distinction between felonies and misdemeanours was not reintroduced, and the law relating to medical grounds for abortion was not clarified by the legislation (Koch). There emerged a stage where reaction to the Second World War and Nazism seemed to require a change in the law to reflect a change in German society, which wished to enact laws which were different from the Nazi laws, and in West

Germany, demands for law reform were linked with increased awareness of the rights of women and the general liberalisation of society in the wake of the student movement of the late 1960s. However, a conservative grouping with strong ties to Roman Catholicism continued to wield a powerful influence in national life, and maintained its political influence in some federal States, especially Bavaria and Baden-Württemberg. It was only in 1974, after a 'long and acrimonious public and parliamentary debate' (van Zyl Smit (1994), p 305), that the coalition of the Social Democratic and Liberal Parties managed to push through a radically revised version of para 218 and its related provisions. This 1974 version never came into force, as its constitutionality was immediately challenged by the government of the Baden-Württemberg and a qualified fraction of Members of Parliament. The Federal Constitutional Court responded by ruling that the Act should not come into force until its constitutionality had been established (see BverfGE 37, 324 *et seq*; and van Zyl Smit (1994)). In 1975, the Federal Constitutional Court, by a majority, upheld the challenge on the ground that the constitutional protection of the right to life (together with its guarantee of inviolability of human dignity (see Art 1(1) read together with Art 2(2) of the *Grundgesetz)* did not allow an undifferentiated decriminalisation of all abortions conducted in the first trimester of pregnancy (BverfGE 39, 1 *et seq*).

The 1976 legislation

In 1976, the legislature responded with a new amendment to the Penal Code which formally criminalised all terminations of pregnancy, but which also created wide exceptions to the general rule. Although abortion was still a punishable criminal offence, the 1976 version of para 218a of the Penal Code provided that termination of a pregnancy performed by a physician would *not* be punishable if the pregnant woman consented *and* any one of four exceptions or 'indications' could be established. This meant that the abortion was 'not punishable' (*nicht strafbar*) if performed by a medical practitioner at the request of the pregnant woman *and* there were also (a) *medical* (para 218(1)); (b) *embryopathological* or *embryopathic* (para 218(1)1 read with para 218a(2)1); or (c) *criminological/criminal-ethical* (para 218(1)1 read with para 218(2)2); or (d) *social* grounds for intervention. Let us further clarify each of these exceptions.

In essence, provided the abortion was performed by a medical practitioner at the request of the woman, the abortion would not be unlawful:

(a) at any stage of the pregnancy if the 'medical' exception applied: that is, taking into account the woman's present or future circumstances, the indication was that her life was in danger or there was a danger or grave danger to the physical or mental health of the pregnant woman and this danger could not be averted by other means which the woman could reasonably be expected to accept. In other words, there was no time limit in these circumstances;

(b) within the first 22 weeks if the embryopathological/embryopathic exception applied: that is, if it was very probable that, for genetic reasons, or in consequence of prenatal damage, the child would suffer from such an incurable abnormality as to be so seriously handicapped that the pregnant woman should not be obliged to carry the child to full term;

(c) within the first 12 weeks, if the criminological or criminal/ethical grounds applied: if the pregnancy resulted from an unlawful sexual act (such as rape) under paras 1176–79 of the Penal Code;

(d) the social grounds exception.

This last indication or exception meant that, within the first 12 weeks of the pregnancy, the abortion could be performed, that is, termination of the pregnancy with the consent of the woman would not be unlawful where the termination of the pregnancy is otherwise indicated in order to protect the woman from the danger of a predicament which:

(a) is so serious that it would be unreasonable to demand that the pregnant woman continue with the pregnancy; and

(b) cannot be averted in any way which can reasonably be expected of the pregnant woman.

In addition, there were further provisions introduced in 1976 which specified that a pregnant woman had to receive medical counselling on the termination of the pregnancy – that is, the woman had to be told about all the relevant aspects of the abortion; and social counselling – the woman had to be informed about public and private financial and social assistance which was available to pregnant women and to mothers and children; and about assistance which would make it easier for her to continue with the pregnancy and to care for a child in the future. The social counselling would have to take place at least three days before the termination of pregnancy and the medical counselling would have to conducted by a specialist service or by a physician, but not by the physician who performed the actual termination. In addition to the counselling, the woman also had to be advised by a physician about the 'medically significant aspects of her case' (para 218(b)(1)2). Another requirement was that, before the pregnancy could be terminated, a physician *other than* the physician performing the abortion had to certify the existence of the substantive conditions which made the termination permissible (para 219) and a physician who performed an abortion without all these requirements having been met, would be guilty of a criminal offence. However, the pregnant woman herself was not punishable, even if there was no indication or exception established, if she had undergone counselling and a medical practitioner had performed the abortion within the first 22 weeks (para 218(3)).

The 1976 laws were not challenged in the first instance and remained in force in West Germany throughout the 1980s, with social grounds dominating the indications which were invoked. However, the laws were still subjected to continuing criticism, with the result that there was a considerable traffic of women seeking abortions travelling to other States where abortion laws were not so strictly enforced. Conservative criticisms of the 1976 laws remained and, in 1990, the State of Bavaria formally submitted to the Federal Constitutional Court a challenge to the constitutionality of the 1976 amendments. However, these events were then overtaken by even more dramatic events, with the opening of the Berlin Wall on 10 November 1989. On 3 October 1990, the old German Democratic Republic (GDR) was incorporated into an enlarged Federal Republic of Germany.

The East German abortion law and the Treaty of Unification

In East Germany, the history of abortion law would necessarily be different. One reason for this would be the great numbers of the population fleeing to West Germany, resulting in a rapid decline of the population, so there would almost inevitably be strict rules on terminating pregnancies. Once the Berlin Wall had been constructed, from 1972 onwards, a woman had a statutory right to have her pregnancy terminated within the first 12 weeks after conception. The preamble to this law began with the proposition that equal treatment for women in education and occupation, and in marriage and family life, required that women be able to decide for themselves about their fertility and about whether they continue with their pregnancy. There was also extensive provision for support services in the GDR in the form of nursery schools and crèches where working mothers could leave their children. Consequently, there were clearly differences in approach and legislation between the two parts of Germany which the Treaty of Unification recognised; it provided for the key provisions of the East German law to continue to operate in the States which had constituted the former GDR. The Treaty also instructed the legislature of the united Germany to pass a new Federal law which would protect the unborn life and would allow pregnant women, by means of legally guaranteed entitlements to counselling and social assistance, to cope with conflict situations in a way which would be in conformity with the constitution (see van Zyl Smit (1994), p 308).

The 1992 law

On 27 July 1992, responding to the Treaty, the Federal President signed new legislation which had been approved by an absolute majority of both Houses of Parliament. The new legislation, despite opposition from more conservative members of the Lower House and the Bavarian Government in the Upper House, appeared to have attracted support from all parties represented in the German Parliament. The new Act for Assistance to Pregnant Women and

Families 'sought to place the whole issue of the termination of pregnancy in the context of a wider policy of population development' (van Zyl Smit (1994), p 309). The new legislation:

- provided for sexual education for the public and counselling;
- created rights to advice and assistance for pregnant women;
- allowed women over 20 years old to claim the means for birth control when these were prescribed by a physician.

Various social provisions were introduced to ensure that a woman would not be prejudiced in her education or professional career by having to spend time caring for her child. From the beginning of 1996, every child over four would have a right to be provided by the State with a place in the nursery school. Additional day-care facilities were also created to assist working mothers. Hence, the new Act was intended to be viewed in the light of this concomitant panoply of social support for pregnant women and mothers of young children. The most important innovation appeared to be the provision that, when a woman who had been counselled in accordance with the statutory provision, nevertheless decided to have the pregnancy terminated, such termination would be legal when carried out by a physician within the first 12 weeks of pregnancy. In these cases, the physician did not have to make a positive finding that there were conditions present which would justify the termination of the pregnancy. One key difference between the 1976 and 1992 versions is that this latter version intended to allow the mother's choice to prevail during the first trimester of her pregnancy, provided that she had gone for the counselling. This counselling process was not to be recorded in writing, and the woman had a choice as to whether she wished to remain anonymous.

As with the 1974 version, the 1992 Act did not come into force, because it was immediately challenged by the Bavarian Government and by Members of Parliament who had voted against it. As van Zyl Smit (1994) puts it, 'The essence of the challenge to the 1992 Federal legislation was that it did not meet the minimum standard which the constitution had set for the protection of unborn life', arguing, *inter alia*, that the standard was an absolute requirement which had not been changed in any fundamental respect by the unification of Germany because the substantive provisions of the West German *Grundgesetz* had continued to operate unchanged after unification.

The Federal Constitutional Court decision of 1993

The Federal Constitutional Court upheld the principled objection to the new legislation in its judgment of 28 May 1993. Six of the eight judges, including the only woman member of the court, Grasshof J, supported the ruling, which reaffirmed that the State had a primary duty to protect human life, even before birth. They stressed that this duty, which began at conception, related to every individual life and included a duty also to protect the unborn child against the mother. This latter protection, the court held, was only possible when the State fundamentally prohibited a termination of pregnancy and placed on the woman a fundamental legal duty to carry the fetus to term (BverfGE D 1.2 JZ, p 17). It therefore emphasised that developing, pre-natal life in a woman's womb is human life. Termination of pregnancy had to be seen as fundamentally illegal throughout the pregnancy. The court thus based their decision on three basic rights which are guaranteed under the German Federal Constitution (*Grundgesetz*): (a) Art 1(1), which protects human dignity; (b) Art 2(1), which guarantees the free development of personality, namely self-determination on all aspects of life; (c) Art 2(2), which guarantees the right to life. On the other hand, the court also recognised that this 'duty to protect unborn human life' could 'clash with the right of the pregnant woman to recognition and protection of her human dignity, and particularly with her right to bodily integrity and the development of her personality'. However, there were clear minimum constitutional standards of protection for the unborn fetus which the State always had to meet, even if these clashed with the rights of the pregnant woman.

The formal effect of the judgment was that key parts of the 1992 Act were rendered null and void: these related to the legalisation of abortion following the fulfilment of the mandatory counselling and other procedures.

The 1995 law reform: a German compromise

The 1995 law reform is the legislative response to the May 1993 Federal Constitutional Court decision.

Its three core provisions centre on a mixture of (a) the time limit; (b) the counselling; and (c) the indication concepts (for a full discussion of the specific events leading to the 1995 reform and a comparison with the English law of abortion, see Schlegel (1997)). The new Act is called the Pregnant Women's and Families' Aid Amendment Act (*Schwangeren- und Familienhilfeänderungsgesetz*) was passed by the Federal Parliament in July 1995 and came into force partially on 1 October 1995, and partially on 1 January 1996. The new Act incorporates the 1993 decision of the Federal Constitutional Court and presents an even more restricted version than the court required. In fact, para 218(1) of the Penal Code has not been modified, hence a person performing an abortion on a woman shall be sentenced to imprisonment for up to three years or fined. In aggravated cases, imprisonment for up to five years is possible, and the woman herself shall be sentenced to imprisonment for up to one year or fined.

However, para 218a of the Penal Code has several compromise provisions: the time limit model, the pro-child counselling model and the indication model. Paragraph 218a(1) has the time limit version of the 1992 law which focuses on counselling (to take place at least three days before the abortion), but an abortion performed purely on this basis is now considered unlawful.

The words stating that an abortion at the request of the pregnant woman fulfilling the counselling requirements was 'not unlawful' in the 1992 version have been deleted and replaced by a new para 218a which states that an abortion does not constitute a punishable offence under para 218 provided the three conditions of para 218a are satisfied:

(a) the abortion has to be performed at the request of the pregnant woman with whom a mandatory counselling session has taken place at least three days before the abortion; to prove this counselling has taken place, the woman has to present the operating doctor with a counselling certificate as laid down in para 219(2)2 of the Penal Code. This is not an indication certificate, which the woman does not require under para 218a(1) or 219 of the Penal Code;

(b) a medical practitioner has to perform the abortion;

(c) the pregnancy must not have lasted longer than 12 weeks.

Furthermore, two 'indications' (exceptions) are listed: 'medical' grounds and 'criminal ethical' ones.

An abortion can be performed on medical grounds without a time limit (s 218a(2)) and on criminal-ethical grounds within the first 12 weeks of a pregnancy (para 218a(3)). An abortion performed within these indication rules is 'not unlawful' if a medical practitioner decides that such an indication is present, and it is performed by a medical practitioner at the request of the pregnant woman. If the indications apply, counselling is not mandatory for the woman, but para 218c requires the doctor to inform the woman about the possible medical risks and implications of an abortion and to give the woman the opportunity to explain her reasons for wanting an abortion.

Under para 218b(1) of the Penal Code, the operating doctor shall be sentenced to imprisonment or fined if he or she performs the abortion in the case of para 218a(2) or (3) without an indication certificate issued by a colleague.

In addition, under this new law, the embryopathological or embryopathic indication from the 1976 and 1992 models has not been included, as Schlegel puts it, because of 'the vehement veto of the Catholic Church and the disabled lobby; but it is thought to be covered in most cases by the medical indication' (Schlegel (1997), p 46). The social indication (the social grounds exception) of the 1976 model has not been retained, and so an abortion purely on 'social grounds' would not now be lawful under the present law.

The provision dealing with mandatory counselling has also been re-worded so that para 219(1) now states that counselling has to 'encourage' the woman to carry the child to full term and 'to show her perspectives for a life with the child'; para 219(1) also postulates that the woman must be aware of the fact that the unborn life has an autonomous right to life at any stage of the pregnancy and that an abortion can only be accepted by the legal order in exceptional cases, namely, if a continuation of her pregnancy would be an extraordinary burden exceeding the extent of sacrifice that can reasonably be expected. Counselling is supposed to be directed at resolving the woman's inner conflict and supporting her in distress (Schlegel (1997)).

The Pregnancy Conflict Act 1995

On the question of counselling, details are now laid down in a special Federal statute, the Pregnancy Conflict Act (*Schwangersschaftskonfliktgesetz*) (PCA) which was passed as part of the main Pregnant Women's and Families' Aid Amendment Act. Paragraph 219(2) of the Penal Code states that counselling has to be conducted by an authorised person and a counselling certificate has to be issued confirming that counselling has taken place. Under para 219(2),the operating doctor may not act as such a counsellor, and where there used to regional variations in the authorisation conditions and procedure of the counselling sessions, there is now a uniform set of such conditions and procedures, applicable to *all* the German Federal States, in the PCA. The PCA requires the counselling to be neutral as to the outcome and it must include a confidential talk about the woman's motivation for the termination, but the woman is not obliged to reveal her reasons. Medical, social and legal information must be given to the woman, particularly relating to mothers and children, as well as about available financial and practical assistance. In addition, the woman is to be given help in finding a flat, a place in a kindergarten or a training place, if she wishes to continue her training. Under para 8 of the PCA, the Federal States are also under an obligation to provide a network of counselling centres within the reach of any woman and under para 9 of the PCA, such centres may be authorised only where competent counselling is assured, especially in terms of qualified staff and the necessary co-operation with public and private institutions which provide help for mothers and children. To negate any financial interest in abortions, a counselling centre must not be closely linked with institutions where abortions are performed. The centre has to be assessed at least every three years to ascertain whether it complies with the conditions for the authorisation (para 10 of the PCA).

Post-abortion treatment

An abortion can only be performed in an institution where the necessary aftercare or follow up treatment is provided (para 13(1)). The various German Federal States have to ensure that there is a sufficient network of out-patient and in-patient institutions for abortions (para 13(2)). Although the operating doctor is not permitted to be the counsellor for these purposes, para 218c(1) of the Penal Code requires the operating doctor to give the woman the opportunity to explain her motivation for the abortion, if she so wishes. The woman also has to be informed by the operating doctor about the medical implications, possible physical and psychological consequences and risks of the abortion.

Financial considerations and abortion services

Paragraph 218a of the Penal Code has been re-worded to meet the requirements of the 1993 Constitutional Court decision. The main consequences are:

- insurers under the mandatory health insurance scheme have to provide services where an abortion is 'not unlawful' and performed by a medical practitioner in an authorised institution (under para 13(1) of the Pregnancy Conflict Act;
- these services include: medical counselling; medical treatment including the abortion itself; abortion-related services like the provision of anaesthetics; medicine, remedies, dressing material and hospital treatment.

Since an abortion performed within the first 12 weeks of a pregnancy under para 218a(1) of the Penal Code is 'unlawful', there will now be no sustainable claim against the insurers for an abortion induced by social reasons because the social grounds 'indication'/exception or the embryopathic indication, both of which have been abolished and an abortion based on such grounds will be unlawful, even if performed according to para 218a. Of course, it might be possible to invoke the medical grounds or the criminal-ethical grounds, for which services will be available.

For abortions performed which are unlawful under the law, the woman may be entitled to the provision of medicine, remedies, dressing material and hospital treatment in order:

(a) to protect the health of the unborn child in case the abortion fails;

(b) to protect the health of any future children;

(c) to protect the health of the pregnant woman, especially to prevent probable complications resulting from the abortion or to cure them, provided the abortion is performed according to para 218a(1) of the Penal Code.

The Women's Aid Act concerning Abortions in Special Cases came into force on 1 January 1996 and deals with women in financial need, and was passed as part of the Pregnant Women's and Families' Aid Amendment Act to cover all costs of an unlawful abortion performed under para 218a(1) of the Penal Code. This is clearly a social welfare provision, and to minimise the stigma of making an application for a social welfare allowance, a woman can apply to the mandatory health insurers who will have their costs reimbursed by the German Federal States. As far as private insurers are concerned, the woman's costs will be reimbursed so long as the abortion was based on an exception/indication, but most of them appear to accept only the medical indication.

The Bavarian Abortion Counselling Act was passed in 1996, under which a woman will only obtain a counselling certificate if she reveals her reasons for wanting the abortion. But this clearly contradicts para 5(2) of the Pregnancy Conflict Act. However, as *Bundesrecht* (Federal law) overrides *Landesrecht* (regional or State law), this Bavarian statute has been held to be unconstitutional (see *Süddeutsche Zeitung*, 8 June 1996 and 31 August 1996).

Spain

Moving on to another Catholic country, in Spain, abortion is permitted in three situations: on grounds of (a) serious physical and psychological risk for the woman; (b) risk of serious fetal malformation; and (c) rape or incest. A second medical opinion certifying the woman's circumstances must be obtained even in early pregnancy. Widespread conscientious objection to abortion by health personnel means that in practice, 75% of abortions are performed privately. In the last few years, there have been several attempts to expand the grounds on which abortion is available, but all of these have not come to anything concrete. Indeed, in October 1998, Spain's House of Commons approved a motion to allow the abortifacient mifepristone (RU 486) to be used in public and private hospitals. This drug will be used to terminate pregnancies up to seven weeks. It was in 1978 when contraceptive methods were legalised in Spain and they then became more easily available. Opposition from the Roman Catholic Church and 'pro-life' opposition is a constant factor and explains the governmental ambivalence on sex education and family planning matters.

ROE ERA REFORMS

These countries enacted abortion laws in the *Roe* era, that is, after 1973.

Denmark

The Pregnancy Act of 1973 (Law No 350 of 13 June 1973) made abortion legal at the woman's request during the first 12 weeks of pregnancy. With approval by a hospital committee, a woman may have an abortion after 12 weeks on limited grounds, including 'socio-economic' reasons, rape and likelihood of fetal impairment. Abortion is available at any time without authorisation when the pregnancy poses a risk of 'serious deterioration' to the woman's physical or mental health.

Sweden

Sweden is usually seen as having the most liberal laws on abortion. In 1974, it enacted the Swedish Abortion Act, which made abortion legal at the woman's request up to the 18th week of pregnancy. Abortions after the 18th week of pregnancy are permitted for medical, socio-economic, and legal reasons when approved by the National Board of Health and Welfare. Approval for abortions after viability of the fetus will be granted only when the pregnancy gravely threatens the woman's life or health or in the case of severe fetal impairment.

Turkey

Before Turkey's abortion law came into force, it is estimated that about 400–500,000 women annually attempted abortion and about 10,000 women lost their lives each year. In practice, this sort of abortion is implicitly accepted in Turkish society (see Parliamentary debates on population planning: Parliamentary Debates 1984, Vol 16:1–4, cited in Aydin (1999), p 406). Turkey's so called abortion law – actually called the Law on Population Planning – came into force in 1983 on 27 May (Law No 2827: Official Gazette No 18059). The law in question is actually on population planning and 'the law regards the causes of abortion as part of population planning. Abortion is legal until the 10th week of pregnancy, as a matter of right. For later abortions, medical rationales are demanded. For abortion, the consent of the pregnant woman is required and, if she is married, that of her husband is required. For pregnant women who are not yet adult, the consent of both the pregnant woman and the guardian is required. If the woman is under guardianship and not legally mature, a justice of the peace as well as her guardian must give consent. It should be noted that, in the case of women who are mentally disabled, no consent is required for a hysterectomy. Consent is also not required in emergencies.

The law also includes penal clauses; thus, if someone performs an abortion on a woman without her consent, he can be sentenced to seven to 12 years' imprisonment. In pregnancies of longer than 10 weeks' duration, the woman and the person who performs the abortion, even with her consent, have a mandatory penalty of two to five years. The physician must have the consent form signed by the woman and the other relevant individual(s) in order to be able to perform an abortion (source: Aydin (1999)).

COUNTRIES WITH RECENT ABORTION LAW REFORMS

Albania

In 1996, Albania liberalised its national law on the lines of a Directive which was issued by the Albanian Ministry of Health in 1991. Abortion is now permitted without restriction as to reason during the first 12 weeks of pregnancy.

Guyana

In 1995, Guyana liberalised its abortion laws so that abortion is now permitted without restriction as to reason during the first eight weeks of pregnancy. After eight weeks, but before 12 weeks have elapsed, a woman may obtain an abortion on broad grounds, including socio-economic considerations.

Seychelles

In 1994, it enacted the Termination of Pregnancy Act which permits abortion during the first 12 weeks of pregnancy when the continuance of pregnancy would involve risk to the pregnant woman's life or physical or mental health greater than if the pregnancy were terminated. The law also permits abortion in cases of 'rape, incest, defilement or mental disorder' and in the case of fetal impairment.

Turkey

Turkey's Population Planning Law (15 Law No 2827 of 1983) permits abortion during the first 12 weeks of pregnancy. If the woman is married, her husband must consent to the termination of the pregnancy. After 12 weeks, an abortion may be performed with the approval of a medical specialist and a gynaecologist when the woman's life is in danger or if there is a risk of severe fetal impairment. When an abortion is immediately necessary to save a woman's life, the attending physician may authorise the procedure.

Romania

One of the first measures implemented by the new Romanian government in 1989 was to reverse the restrictive abortion laws of the Ceaucescu regime, enacting Decree Law No 1, 26 December 1989. Abortion is now permitted at the woman's request during the first 14 weeks of pregnancy. After 14 weeks, an abortion may be performed only on therapeutic grounds.

South Africa

In 1996, the Choice of Termination of Pregnancy Act (17 Act No 92 of 1996) was enacted. This is the most liberal abortion law enacted, so far, in Africa. Abortion is available at the woman's request during the first 12 weeks of pregnancy. Before 12 weeks, but before the 20th week, an abortion may be obtained if a medical practitioner is of the opinion that:

- the pregnancy poses a risk of injury to the woman's physical or mental health; or
- there is a substantial risk that the fetus would suffer from a severe physical or mental impairment; or
- the pregnancy results from rape or incest; or
- the continued pregnancy would significantly affect the social or economic circumstances of the woman.

Abortion is available at any time if the continued pregnancy poses a threat to the woman's life or there is a risk of fetal impairment or injury.

EASTERN LEGAL PERSPECTIVES

Let us look briefly at some of the Eastern countries which enacted abortion laws before the 1973 *Roe* case.

China

Since 1953, China's abortion policy has reflected the national objective of curbing population growth. Abortion is generally available at the woman's request during the first six months of pregnancy. Provincial regulations further the national population policy, referred to as the 'one-child policy', by penalising those who do not comply with family planning regulations and providing incentives for the termination of pregnancies. Furthermore, pursuant to a 1994 national law, physicians are legally obliged to 'give a medical opinion on terminating pregnancy' in cases where the fetus is diagnosed with a serious hereditary disease or impairment or where the pregnancy endangers the woman's life (see the Maternal and Infant Health Care Law 1994, translated in Law on Maternal and Infant Health Care Reporter, FBIS-CHI-94-211, 1 November 1994, pp 29–31).

India

In 1971, India enacted its Medical Termination of Pregnancy Act (No 34 of 1971, ss 3 and 4) (the 1971 Act). The 1971 Act lists four grounds for obtaining an abortion. Women in India may not obtain an abortion merely at their request. Abortion is legal within the first 12 weeks of pregnancy when one registered medical practitioner determines in good faith that the pregnancy poses a threat to a woman's physical or mental health or that the fetus is likely to suffer a serious physical or mental disability. The law recognises contraceptive failure, rape, and the woman's actual or reasonably foreseeable environment as considerations affecting a woman's mental health. After 12 weeks, a woman may obtain an abortion if two registered practitioners agree that one of the above conditions has been met. When an immediate abortion is necessary to save a woman's life, the approval of a single registered practitioner is sufficient.

Cambodia

In November, 1997, Cambodia modified its highly restrictive national law on abortion. Abortion is now available during the first 14 weeks of pregnancy without restriction as to reason.

CONCLUDING COMPARATIVE OBSERVATIONS

This selective global survey, which has focused on certain common law and civil law countries has shown that abortion is, in the first year of the 21st century, very much established as a 'right' – a constitutional right grounded in 'privacy' in the case of the USA, and a legislative right in many countries throughout the world, although the qualifications and restrictions are as multifarious as the countries themselves. Certain countries, like Sweden and South Africa, have liberal laws, but in the USA, the moves to curtail *Roe v Wade* continue apace. Even 'Catholic' countries like France and Spain have enacted laws to permit abortion at an early stage of pregnancy, in order to protect the woman from life threatening situations; or where she is in a 'situation of distress' (France) or in tightly defined situations, as in Spain, where conscientious objection by healthcare staff means that 75% of abortions are performed by private practitioners. English law remains consistent in maintaining that the unborn fetus has no legal personality, but English judges continue to place a great deal of importance on preserving the unborn fetus's life whenever the so called conflict between fetal rights and maternal rights arises in, for instance, cases involving Caesarean sections (see Chapter 1, p 13).

Indeed, as Pope John Paul II says of abortion, 'The perception of its gravity has become progressively obscured' in many parts of the world and many pro-choice organisations and, indeed, charitable organisations seek to provide support and assistance to the many women in third world and underdeveloped countries who are at the mercy of the 'backstreet abortion' (see Pope John Paul II in Beauchamp and Walters (1999)). Many countries have, therefore, come to a compromise in which the woman's autonomy is given precedence up to the point where some notion of recognition of the fetus's 'right' to life begins to operate to curtail the completely unfettered right to an abortion. This is very often the 12 weeks parameter, though variations abound. Very few countries still prohibit it altogether, like Chile, El Salvador and Nepal, and the question nowadays seems to be not 'whether' but 'to what extent' abortion is permitted. It remains a highly controversial moral question which has acquired political, social, economic and, in many jurisdictions, almost utilitarian overtones. It will doubtless continue to be debated well into the 21st century.

SELECTIVE BIBLIOGRAPHY

Aydin, E, 'Bioethics regulations in Turkey' (1999) 25 JME 404

Beauchamp, TL and Walters, L (eds), *Contemporary Issues in Ethics*, 1999, Wadsworth

Belling, W and Eberl, C, 'Teenage abortion in Germany: with reference to the legal system in the United States' (1996) J Contemporary Health Law & Policy 475

Bentil, JK, 'US and Anglo-Australian decisions on a husband's right to prevent abortion' (1989) Law and Justice 68

de Cruz, SP 'Abortion, *C v S* and the law' [1987] Fam Law 319

Cica, N, 'The inadequacies of Australian law on abortion' (1991) 5 AJFL 37

Devereux, J, *Medical Law: Text, Cases and Materials*, 1997, Cavendish Publishing, pp 152–67

Douglas, G, *Law, Fertility and Reproduction*, 1991, Sweet & Maxwell, Chapters 3 and 5

Dworkin, R, *Life's Dominion*, 1993, HarperCollins

Dwyer, S, 'A short legal history of abortion in the US and Canada', in Dwyer, S and Feinberg, J (eds), *The Problem of Abortion*, 3rd edn, 1997, Wadsworth

Fisse, B, *Howard's Criminal Law*, 1990, LBC

Frankowski, S and Cole, G (eds), *Abortion and Protection of the Human Foetus*, 1987, Nijhoff

Freeman, MDA, 'Abortion – what do other countries do?' (1988) 138 NLJ 233

Glendon, M, *Abortion and Divorce in Western Law*, 1987, Harvard UP, Chapter 1; Appendices A and B

Goggin, M, 'Understanding the new politics of abortion' (1993) 21 American Politics Quarterly 4

Gossel, KH, 'Federal Republic of Germany', in Frankowski, S and Cole, G (eds), *Abortion and Protection of the Human Foetus*, 1987, Nijhoff

Kenyon, E, *The Dilemma of Abortion*, 1986, Faber & Faber

Knoppers, BM, Brault, I and Sloss, E, 'Abortion law in Francophone countries' (1990) 38 Am J Comp Law 889

Koch, HG, 'Bundesrepublik Deutschland', in Eser, A and Koch, HG (eds), *Schwangerschaftsabbruch im Internationalen Vergleich Teil 1: Europa*, 1988

Mason, J and McCall Smith, R, *Law and Medical Ethics*, 5th edn, 1999, Butterworths

McConnell, ML, 'Abortion and human rights: an important Canadian decision' (1989) 38 ICLQ 905

Pradel, J, 'France', in Frankowski, S and Cole, G (eds), *Abortion and Protection of the Human Foetus*, 1987, Nijhoff

Schlegel, C, 'Landmark in German abortion law: the German 1995 compromise compared with English law' (1997) 11 International J Law, Policy & the Family 36

Smith, P, 'Abortion: from *Roe* to *Webster*' (1989) Law & Justice 6

van Zyl Smit, D, 'Reconciling the irreconcilable? Recent developments in the German law on abortion' (1994) 5 Med L Rev 302

CHAPTER 14

SURROGACY AND REPRODUCTIVE TECHNOLOGY

INTRODUCTION

In the earlier chapter on assisted reproduction, the 'new' reproductive technology and surrogacy, a range of legal and ethical issues surrounding the 'new' reproductive technology or reproductive medicine, with special emphasis on the law and practice of surrogacy in the UK, were examined. Apart from looking at the main English cases, we alluded to the leading American case of *Re M* (1988) 109 NJ 396; (1988) 537 NJ 396 (*Baby M*) and the legislative responses to the problem of surrogacy in the UK. Professor Margaret Brazier comments that Europeans have, for the most part, 'firmly rejected trade in body parts or bodily services' because they adhere wholeheartedly to Art 21 of the Bioethics Convention (the Convention for the Protection of Human Rights and Dignity of the Human Being with the Application of Medicine and Biology (Council of Europe, 1997) (see Brazier (1999), p 346). Hence, it is really the American and Australian jurisdictions that currently present examples of noteworthy legal developments in the area of surrogacy, and countries like France which provide examples of rejection of the commercial surrogacy model.

This chapter revisits the American developments in this area and considers cases from non-English jurisdictions. In essence, we undertake a more detailed examination of the American legal position, looking at cases like *Doe v Kelly* [1980] FLR (BNA) 3011 which pre-date *Baby M*, and those which post-date it, like *Johnson v Calvert* (1993) 851 P 2d 776; and, for a contrasting common law country, we examine Australian developments. For a civil law example, we look at French surrogacy cases. After a review of developments in reproductive technology and assisted reproduction, we then conclude with a look at Cloning in the international context (for a discussion of the ethical issues in cloning and UK developments, see Chapter 19).

SURROGACY

Comparative overview

The practice of a woman bearing a child for another is as old as childbirth itself (Downie (1988), p 113) but, as we noted in Chapter 5, it was in the 1980s that surrogacy became one of the most controversial forms of 'babymaking' (Downie (1988)). It was from the 1980s that the term 'surrogate mother' was used to describe a woman 'who deliberately becomes pregnant with the intention of delivering a baby that she will then hand over to someone else' (Downie (1988)). The people entering into an arrangement with the surrogate mother (the 'commissioning couple') was usually (but not always) an infertile couple who was unable to carry a child to term and bear that child. There are different types of surrogacy, but one of the controversial aspects of the practice is that the surrogate is paid for her 'services' – namely, to bear the child and then to hand it over to the couple. The most well known cases have been in Britain and the USA, but, in modern times, surrogacy is practised in Canada, the rest of Europe, Australia, Asia, South Africa and the Middle East. It is currently still prohibited in Austria, Germany and Sweden. Payments for gametes are prohibited in Germany, Switzerland, Italy, Denmark, France and Spain.

A number of developments have taken place in the USA and it is probably true to say that it is an area of law that is in a state of flux, where more traditional family approaches are being challenged by the new reproductive technology and its procedures and by the decision of infertile couples to act upon them. Artificial insemination is not of recent vintage, but what has changed is the gender of the infertile party within the marriage. Long established statutes, in existence for decades in numerous States, envisage an infertile husband who, together with his wife, chooses to utilise donated semen to impregnate his fertile wife or use this process to increase the chances of a husband (who has a marginally fertile sperm) impregnating his wife.

The relatively recent development is that couples have now discovered that a third party may agree to become impregnated with the semen of the fertile husband and ultimately allow the infertile wife to treat the child to be born as her own offspring. But, this was not always the case. Two so called surrogacy arrangements are frequently cited in the Old Testament. Sarah, wife of Abraham, was infertile and enlisted her maid, Hagar, to bear Abraham's child (Genesis, 16). Isaac and his barren wife, Rachel, relied upon Rachel's servant, Bilbah, to bear Isaac's child (Genesis, 30). Of course, some commentators do not regard these arrangements as 'true' surrogacies, as there was no element of payment for the services. As far as payments to surrogate mothers is concerned, these are prohibited in France, Denmark and the Netherlands.

Is surrogacy immoral?

The view of the Catholic Church on surrogacy appears unequivocal. The practice is regarded as 'morally illicit'. In the Instruction on Respect for

Human Life in its Origin and on the Dignity of Procreation, Congregation for the Doctrine of the Faith, Libreria editrice Vaticana, 1987, it is stated:

> It is contrary to the unity of marriage and to the dignity of the procreation of the human person. [It] represents an objective failure to meet the obligations of maternal love, of conjugal fidelity and of responsible motherhood; it offends the dignity and the right of the child to be conceived, carried in the womb, brought into the world and brought up by his own parents; it sets up, to the detriment of families, a division between the physical, psychological and moral elements which constitute those families.

REPRODUCTIVE TECHNOLOGIES: TERMS AND PROCEDURES

(a) AID: artificial insemination by donor.

(b) IVF: *in vitro* fertilisation. This refers to the creation of embryo outside the human body. The child thus born may be related to both, one, or neither of its 'parents' (that is, the carrying mother and her husband or partner).

(c) GIFT: gamete intrafallopian transfer. This refers to insertion in the womb of eggs, sperm or both for fertilisation to take place in the womb rather than outside it.

SURROGATE MOTHERHOOD

The difficulties of adoption in the 1980s led to many childless couples turning to another woman to have a child for them. For most, it is usually a last resort after they have had no success with infertility treatments. In the USA, in the late 1980s and early 1990s, there was something like a five to seven year wait for 'healthy white babies' to adopt. The surrogate is sometimes a sister or close friend, but more often is a stranger, with arrangements made through a lawyer or agency which matches a prospective surrogate with a childless couple.

Medical reasons for entering into surrogacy arrangements

Two medical reasons why couples might want to enter into a surrogate arrangement are: first, because there is a risk that the woman may pass on a genetic disease to the child and, secondly, if the woman is infertile. Of course, if she has a healthy uterus, these can be dealt with through the use of donor eggs or embryos. If the woman has no ovaries and no uterus, so that she cannot provide the genetic (egg) or gestational (pregnancy) components of childbirth, but wants a child, she has no alternative but to engage a surrogate or adopt. Another situation where a woman may use a surrogate is where she has eggs which can be fertilised *in vitro* and transferred to a surrogate, but does not possess the gestational ability, for instance, if she has no uterus or a uterine malformation or some medical condition such as severe hypertension or diabetes which would pose a threat to her health or the baby's.

Enforceability of surrogacy arrangement

As we have seen, under English law, the Human Fertilisation and Embryology Act 1990 inserted a new section into the Surrogacy Arrangements Act 1985 so that, under s 1A: 'No surrogacy arrangement is enforceable by or against the person making it.' This applies irrespective of whether the child was created by sexual intercourse, artificial insemination or IVF. In many American jurisdictions, for example, there may be laws which state that surrogacy is illegal or prohibited, but do not actually enforce these laws, so that in a *de facto* sense, these are also 'dead letter' laws because they have practically fallen into desuetude.

United States

Since the late 1970s, several American individuals and agencies have become interested in organising surrogate transactions and have offered such services as recruiting women, screening and counselling them and arranging for their insemination on behalf of clients wishing to commission a child. Indeed, the internet, or world wide web, is replete with a number of well advertised surrogacy services on websites. Indeed, it was the establishment in the Britain of an American agency in 1984 which led to the first well publicised surrogacy case in Britain in the 1980s, the *Kim Cotton* case (or *Re C*). By the beginning of 1988, however, nearly 600 babies had been born through surrogate mothering arrangements.

Something like 11 States have now prohibited commercial surrogacy, but some states have not even addressed the surrogacy question at all. Certain States, like Kentucky, prohibit surrogate programmes and also prohibit receiving payment in exchange for termination of parental rights. However, it seems that the law largely goes unenforced. Oklahama says that, if the husband and wife consent to an egg donation, the resulting child is theirs. By having the surrogate husband deny consent, the law is effectively nullified. Arizona law criminalises all forms of surrogacy, whether paid or unpaid, but this law was held unconstitutional by the Arizona Supreme Court in 1994. Yet, other States have laws which say that surrogacy contracts are unenforceable, but they do not actually prevent people from entering into them. These laws would, in any event, only apply if both the couple and the surrogate are from that same State.

American surrogacy cases

In 1980, Elizabeth Kane became the first known commercial surrogate in the USA, saying she became a surrogate because of her 'Christian life' and 'sisterhood' and that she felt that becoming a surrogate gave childless people new hope. Several American surrogates appear to have undertaken surrogacy for money, a desire to be pregnant and through an urge to reconcile a birth-related trauma in the past.

The first publicised dispute in the USA was between Denise Thrane (also known as Nisa Bhimani) from California and a New York couple, Bjorna and James Noyes, for whom she agreed to be a surrogate. Under a contract arranged by Noel Keane, Denise, who was a 23 year old divorced mother of three, agreed to give the baby to the couple after the birth. She was inseminated with Noyes' sperm which had been frozen and flown to California, but during the pregnancy she changed her mind and decided to keep the child. A few days before the baby was born, in March 1981, the case went to the Pasadena Superior Court judge who, two months later, awarded her custody. However, it was revealed at the 11th hour that Noyes' wife was a transsexual and Noyes withdrew his paternity claim minutes before it was to be heard by the judge. He was named as the baby's father on the birth certificate, but was not given any 'visitation' (access) rights. Judge Olsen said later that he was probably going to rule in favour of the mother, because 'Californian law states that if the sperm is used by a licensed physician to inseminate a woman other than the donor's wife, he is treated in law as if he were not the natural father'.

In another dispute in Michigan, a Wayne County judge refused, in November 1981, to declare that the man who provided the sperm was the legal father because the law presumes that a woman's husband is the father of a child born to her (which is also the English common law presumption).

Status of a surrogacy arrangement

American courts have not been consistent in their rulings on the status of surrogacy contracts.

Doe v Kelly

In this Michigan case, it was alleged that Jane and John Doe (pseudonyms) were a married couple. Jane was not capable of having children and the couple arranged for Mary Roe to be their surrogate mother for the sum of US$5,000 plus medical expenses. Mary Roe was to be inseminated with John's semen and bear a child which she would surrender to Jane and John on its birth.

The Wayne County Circuit Court declared that:

> baby-selling is against the public policy of the State and the State's interest in preventing such conduct is sufficiently compelling and meets the test set forth in *Roe*. Mercenary considerations used to create a parent-child relationship and its impact upon the family unit strike at the very foundation of human society and are patently and necessarily injurious to the community. It is a fundamental principle that children should not and cannot be bought and sold. The sale of children is illegal in all States.

This court thus held that the surrogacy arrangement was void, as it contravened the baby-selling statute and was contrary to public policy.

In the Michigan Court of Appeals, it was argued that the Michigan Adoption Code, which prohibited the exchange of money or other consideration in connection with adoption, infringed the plaintiff's constitutional right of privacy. The court held that the adoption legislation did not prohibit surrogacy arrangements, but did strike at payments.

In Kentucky, the Attorney General challenged the activities of Surrogate Parenting Associates, the organisation who have a branch in the UK and were involved in the *Baby Cotton* case (see Chapter 6). The Attorney General argued that surrogacy was prohibited in the statutes forbidding baby-selling. However, following a series of appeals, the Supreme Court held that the activities of the organisation did not contravene the legislation the Attorney General was referring to.

The leading case: the Mary Beth Whitehead story

The most famous American case in modern surrogacy law is the New Jersey case called *Re M* or in the matter of *Baby M* (1988) 109 NJ 396; (1988) 537 A 2d 1227. This case was one where all the parties involved wanted the child and there were two very sharply different approaches taken to the case by the lower court, the New Jersey Superior Court, and the New Jersey Supreme Court on appeal. It is also a case where the surrogacy contract came under close judicial scrutiny, and for good reason since, on pure contract principles, it looks oppressive and highly restrictive of one party's activities. Contrastingly, the lower court held the surrogacy legal, but the Supreme Court (by 7:0) held that surrogate contracts were 'baby-selling' and were illegal.

The trial lasted three months, attracted more than 100 reporters from around the world and resulted in 7,000 pages of manuscript.

Background to the saga

In 1986, Mary Beth Whitehead gave birth to a baby girl in an arrangement for parenting through a contract (a so called surrogacy contract). She had agreed, for US$10,000 plus expenses, to be artificially inseminated with the sperm of William Stern, the commissioning father, to carry the pregnancy to term, and when the baby was born, to hand the child over to William Stern and his wife.

For more than two years, the story, known as the *Baby M* case, was front page news across the USA as Mary Beth Whitehead tried to keep the child, first absconding with her out of the State involving a car chase that was covered by national television and then going to court to oppose the Sterns in a protracted custody battle. During the public controversy that followed, the country appeared to be polarised, some wanting to enforce the contract, others wishing to ban the practice completely, to recognise a woman's right to a child she has given birth to irrespective of any contract she may have entered into, to prohibit the payment of money, and even allegations that Mary Beth had received a 'raw deal' because of her humble background (high school drop out who left school at 15, married a sanitation truck driver) and her slightly colourful past (as a sometime nightclub ('go-go') dancer). In the first trial, she lost her case and was roundly excoriated by the judge for being 'impulsive', 'domineering', 'evil' and 'manipulative' but, on appeal, she won 'visitation rights', although the court awarded custody to the Sterns. She remains the child's legal mother with visitation rights.

Baby M *(1988) 537 A 2d 1227*

Facts

In 1985, William Stern, Mrs Mary Beth Whitehead, and Richard Whitehead entered into an agreement for surrogate motherhood through the Infertility Centre of New York (ICNY), headed by leading surrogacy broker Noel Keane. The agreement was arranged by ICNY, which had recruited Mrs Whitehead, brought the parties together, provided all the contracts, and generally facilitated the arrangement for which it received US$7,500. The agreement recited that Mr Stern's wife, Elizabeth, was infertile, that they wanted a child, and that Mrs Whitehead was willing to provide that child as the mother with Mr Stern as the father. The contract provided that, through artificial insemination using Mr Stern's sperm, Mrs Whitehead would become pregnant, carry the child to term, bear it, deliver it to the Sterns, and thereafter do whatever was necessary to terminate her maternal rights so that Mrs Stern could adopt the child. Mrs Whitehead's husband was also a party to the contract, but Mrs Stern was not. Mr Stern agreed to pay Mrs Whitehead US$10,000 after the child's birth, on its delivery to him, in addition to all costs associated with the pregnancy. On 27 March 1986, Mrs Whitehead gave birth to a healthy baby girl, but decided not to give up the baby. She took the baby home, but agreed to meet the Sterns to relinquish the child.

Initially, she did let the Sterns have the baby, but the very next day went to see them to visit M. She then claimed she had been suicidal and, in view of this, the Sterns agreed to let Mrs Whitehead have the child for a week until her feelings stabilised. Eventually, she refused to hand the child over to the Sterns, and when the Sterns obtained a court order to freeze the Whitehead assets and for temporary custody, and called on them with a policeman, they spirited the child away, handing the baby out of the bedroom window while the Sterns and the authorities were in their living room. Baby M was not traced until three and a half months later, as Mrs Whitehead had the child in hiding in various parts of Florida. When finally discovered by detectives, the child was handed over to Mr Stern's temporary custody while the parties battled it out in courts.

The trial

In the course of a highly emotionally charged trial before Judge Sorkow, which involved the playing of a tape recorded conversation between Mrs Whitehead and Mr Stern where she said that, if he did not drop the case, she would accuse him of sexually abusing her daughter and said she would rather see herself and Baby M dead before Mr Stern got her, it was found that Mrs Whitehead had lied about a number of things. Judge Sorkow obviously formed a very poor impression of Mrs Whitehead, whom he called 'manipulative' and 'exploitative'.

Judge Sorkow's ruling

Four days after the baby's first birthday, Judge Harvey Sorkow of the New Jersey Superior Court, in the course of a 127 page judgment:

- held the surrogacy contract was valid and enforceable;
- declared Mr Stern the baby's father and awarded him permanent custody; and
- completely terminated all Mrs Whitehead's parental rights, including her visiting rights;
- enjoined the Whiteheads from interfering with the Sterns;
- held that M's best interests would be best served by being placed in her father's sole custody.

He then, without giving notice to the Whiteheads, called the Sterns into his chambers and immediately processed Mrs Stern's adoption, making her the legal mother of the child.

Appeal to the Supreme Court of New Jersey

The Whiteheads appealed to the Supreme Court of New Jersey and challenged virtually all parts of the lower court's decision.

The New Jersey Supreme Court decision

By a unanimous decision, the seven strong Supreme Court held that the surrogate arrangement was void.

The Supreme Court, *per* Wilentz CJ, held that:

- the surrogate contract conflicted with laws prohibiting use of money in connection with adoptions, laws requiring proof of parental unfitness or abandonment before termination of parental rights is ordered or adoption is granted, and laws making surrender of custody and consent to adoption revocable in private placement adoptions;
- the legal adoption of Baby M was disallowed;
- the surrogate contract conflicted with State public policy by assigning custody to a father without a custody hearing focusing on the best interests of the child, by guaranteeing separation of a child from its natural mother, and by giving William Stern greater rights than Mary Beth Whitehead;
- the right of procreation did not entitle the natural father and his wife to custody of the child;
- the best interests of the child justified awarding custody to the father and his wife; and
- the mother, Mrs Whitehead, was entitled to visitation rights with the child, Baby M.

It allowed Baby M to remain in custody with the Sterns because the home life of the Sterns was more 'secure' and 'nurturing'. The court appeared to be prepared to allow voluntary, unpaid surrogacy as legal provided the mother could change her mind and keep the baby. It disagreed with Judge Sorkow's judgment on every theoretical point and, as Pence puts it, 'dissected it and left it in shreds' (Pence (1990), p 112). It should be noted that each State in the USA has its own jurisdiction and laws and hence, although the case has been hailed as a landmark decision, it does not really have great significance as a precedent in national terms across the country.

Aftermath – the post-Supreme Court developments

After the Supreme Court decision, Mary Beth returned to another lower court for visitation rights; three judges of the Superior Court allowed her to have the baby brought to her for a visit one day a week up to six hours, thereafter for two days a week with overnight stay, including two weeks with Mary Beth in the summer. The baby would also have alternate holidays between the two families. This court took a very different view of Mary Beth's fitness as a mother. She later divorced her first husband and married an accountant, Dean Gould, by whom she conceived a child in the normal way, and who is clearly a member of the Gould family. She continues to have visitation rights for Melissa, the surrogate baby who was the subject of this whole dispute, and apparently spends alternate weekends with the child.

This was at least the end to a 22 month long battle that saw Baby M with two mothers.

Comment on *Baby M*

Impact of the *Baby M* case on 'the American public'

Charo (1992) argues that 'surrogacy has captured the American imagination in a way unmatched by any other bioethics issue except abortion' and suggests that:

> ... what ... truly caught the American imagination during the *Baby M* trial was the fact that surrogacy forces [Americans] to confront [their] most basic confusions concerning maternal instinct and the role of women in modern society. The *Baby M* case was quite cathartic in that it gave the American public a chance to vent its ambivalence about the women's liberation movement under the guise of bemoaning the unintended consequences of taking feminist analysis to its seemingly logical conclusion. In sum, Americans have been fascinated with surrogacy because it has let each and every American express their strong opinions on the meaning of motherhood and has let many of them express their hostility at the changes forced upon them by the feminist movement [Charo (1992), p 232].

This appeared to manifest itself in three ways as far as American commentators were concerned: (a) it enabled many of them to assert that feminism requires the adoption of a libertarian philosophy and to note the distinction between feminist principles of self-determination and feminist political strategies of communal action for the communal good; (b) other commentators asserted the sanctity of maternal instinct, thereby 'rescuing' feminism'; (c) yet many others chose to say that if feminists had not abandoned this notion of biological determinism to begin with there would be no welfare mothers or pornography, let alone surrogacy.

As a result of the many-faceted comments that *Baby M* attracted, the surrogate mother simply cannot win. Charo (1992) argues that, if these women are seen as in control of their lives, competently agreeing to give birth to a child for pay, they are 'unnatural and cannot possibly stand on equal footing with their more tender-hearted sisters when it comes to custody'. If they are seen as passive, then they are bound by the surrogacy contract they sign. If they once again assert control, she says, and dispute the contracts 'with lies, threats, flight, and any other tool available, then they are characterised as disobedient, unstable, and unfit' (p 238).

In a nutshell, many commentators in the USA have written that there is a general attitude of disapproval toward the surrogate mother, partly linked with a 'frustration at the new patterns of family life' and the choices the [new] women make and 'at the changes they have wrought in motherhood' (Charo (1992), p 239).

As Charo says:

> Before the *Baby M* case, most legislative Bills proposed to legitimise surrogacy as a 'business arrangement' to which the 'rights of motherhood do not apply'

> or at best, to regulate the procedure heavily with the emphasis on psychological screening to weed out women likely to renege on the deal. Legislation introduced after the *Baby M* case has generally invalidated surrogacy arrangements [Charo (1992), p 239].

Since 1987, Mary Beth has campaigned for the abolition of surrogacy and has publicly opposed it on many national television programmes as well as before a House sub-committee. So far, 11 States have now banned commercial surrogacy.

Would English courts ever follow the Baby M *approach?*

The question arises as to whether the English courts would ever approach the *Baby M* case like the American courts. As the law currently stands in the UK, this seems rather unlikely, not least because English law does not usually order 'visitation rights' on the lines of the arrangement in the *Baby M* case and also because, once the surrogate agrees to hand over the child, the commissioning couple would probably initiate adoption proceedings which would mean that all links would then be severed with the child, legally, and it would be rare for an English court to order contact (previously called access) with the child after an adoption had been finalised.

GESTATIONAL SURROGACY: WHO IS THE 'NATURAL' AND LEGAL MOTHER?

Gestational surrogacy is the situation where the surrogate does not provide the egg, unlike the situation in partial surrogacy, where she also provides the egg and is, therefore, both the gestational and genetic mother. Under English law, s 27 of the Human Fertilisation and Embryology Act 1990: 'the woman who is carrying or has carried a child as a result of the placing in her of an embryo or of sperm and eggs, and no other woman, is to be treated as the mother of the child.' Thus, the gestational mother is the legal mother of the child. Consequently, the Californian case of *Johnson v Kelly* is particularly important in comparative terms as an example of the law as interpreted in an American jurisdiction which, despite being a common law jurisdiction, is completely opposite to English law, since it held that the legal mother of the child in a gestational surrogacy arrangement is the *genetic* mother.

COMPARATIVE OBSERVATIONS

It should be noted that every other country which has examined this problem has concluded that the woman who gives birth is the 'natural mother' of the child in a gestational surrogacy. Apart from the UK, these countries include Germany, Switzerland, Bulgaria and South Africa.

Gestational surrogacy in California

Johnson v Calvert *(1993) 851 P 2d 776; [1994] Med LR 239*

Facts

A husband and wife, Mark and Crispina Calvert, entered into a gestational (that is, partial) surrogacy agreement with another woman, Anna Johnson. A contract between the parties provided that Anna Johnson would carry the embryo of the Calverts and thus carry the fetus to term, and that she would relinquish her parental rights over the child upon its birth. In exchange, the Calverts would pay her US$10,000. Six months into the pregnancy, the relationship between the parties broke down and Anna Johnson, the surrogate, changed her mind as to handing over the child. Both sides filed lawsuits seeking declarations or parental rights over the child when born. After the child's birth, the trial court ruled that the Calverts were the child's 'genetic, biological and natural' father and mother, that Anna Johnson had no 'parental' rights over the child, and that the surrogacy contract was legal and enforceable against Anna Johnson's claims. On appeal, the Court of Appeal affirmed the trial court's decision. Anna Johnson then appealed to the Supreme Court of California.

The Supreme Court of California judgment

The court dismissed the appeal. It held:

(a) Crispina Calvert was the child's 'natural mother' under California law. It took into account the following:

 (1) The only Californian statute defining parental rights is the Uniform Parentage Act 1975, which was enacted to eliminate the legal distinction between legitimate and illegitimate children and to replace with the concept of parentage. The legislation was never intended to govern surrogacy disputes, yet *ex facie* it applies to any parentage determination, including the rare case in which a child's maternity is in issue.

 (2) The Uniform Parentage Act recognises both genetic motherhood (as established by the results of blood tests) and gestational motherhood (as established by proof of having given birth to the child) as ways of establishing that a woman is a child's 'natural mother'. In the instant case, Crispina Calvert was the genetic mother and Anna Johnson was

the gestational mother, and each, therefore, had equal rights under the Uniform Parentage Act to be considered the child's natural mother.

(3) For each child, however, California accords the legal rights and responsibilities of parenthood to only one 'natural mother'. This is despite advances in reproductive technology which make it possible, as in the instant case, for the female biological role in reproduction to be divided between two women. It was therefore necessary for the court to make a choice between these two women.

(4) [*Per* Panelli J (Lucas CJ, Mosk, Baxter, George and Arabian JJ concurring)] when one woman is the genetic mother of a child and a different woman is its gestational mother, the issue of who is the child's 'natural mother' at law is to be resolved by *inquiring into the parties' intentions as manifested in the surrogacy agreement. The woman who intended to procreate the child – she who intended to bring about the birth of a child whom she intended to raise as her own – is the natural mother under California law* [emphasis added].

The court also held (*per* Panelli J (Lucas CJ, Mosk, Baxter, and George JJ, concurring) (*inter alia*) that:

(b) The determination that, pursuant to a gestational surrogacy agreement, Crispina Calvert was the child's natural mother, did not violate public policy.

(11) Gestational surrogacy contracts do not violate public policies embodied in adoption statutes, in particular the social policies underlying provisions prohibiting the payment for consent to adoption of a child and prohibiting prebirth waiver of parental rights. Payments to the gestational mother under a surrogacy mother under a surrogacy contract of the kind used in the instant case constitute compensation for the services of gestating the fetus and undergoing labour, not compensation for giving up 'parental' rights to the child.

(2) Gestational surrogacy contracts do not violate prohibitions on involuntary servitude, because the necessary element of coercion or duress is lacking.

(3) Gestational surrogacy contracts do not violate public policy on the ground that such contracts tend to exploit or dehumanise women, especially women of lower economic status; and tend to encourage society to view children as commodities to be traded at their parents' will. There is no evidence that surrogacy contracts exploit poor women to any greater degree than economic necessity in general exploits them by inducing them to accept lower-paid or otherwise undesirable employment. Nor is there any evidence that surrogacy contracts foster the attitude that children are mere commodities.

Comment on Johnson v Calvert

Would the English courts have decided Johnson v Calvert *in the same way?*

Under current English law, they could not have done, because under s 27 of the Human Fertilisation and Embryology Act 1990 (HFEA 1990), the surrogate mother is always the mother of the child, whether or not she is genetically related to the child. The HFEA 1990 does not place any significance on the intention of the parties, which is the approach taken by the California Supreme Court. In view of the fact that surrogacy contracts are unenforceable under English law (see s 1A of the UK Surrogacy Arrangements Act 1985), the latter approach would acknowledge the validity of a surrogacy contract and to enforce it, which, as we have just said, is not permissible under English law.

The decision by some US courts to say that the woman who gives birth to the child in a gestational surrogacy is not the 'natural' and legal mother, but that it depends on the intention of the parties and on who intended to bring up the child, was again raised in the subsequent *Moschetta* case.

In re marriage of Moschetta *(1994) 30 Cal Rep 2d 893*

In this Californian case, the parents of a one year old child, the product of a standard surrogacy arrangement, separated, and the surrogate claimed legal parentage. She had been hired as a surrogate because Mrs Moschetta was infertile. She was impregnated with Mr Moschetta's semen and had relinquished the child at birth. Mrs Moschetta cared for the baby at home for seven months, until the day that Mr Moschetta walked out on the marriage, taking the baby with him. It turned out to be a three way custody battle between Mr Moschetta, Mrs Moschetta and the surrogate mother.

The California Court rejected the application of Mrs Moschetta, who had been looking after the child, because she was not the natural mother of the child nor (up to this point of the proceedings) the adoptive parent. However, the surrogate was both the genetic and the gestational mother in this case, which meant the court was able to distinguish this case from *Johnson v Calvert*.

Australia

Surrogacy has been the source of considerable 'legal, moral, social and ethical debate in Australia' (Stuhmcke (1998)). Each Australian jurisdiction, with the exception of the Northern Territory, has commissioned independent inquiries into the practice of surrogate motherhood.

Surrogacy legislation in Australia

Legislation regulating surrogacy has been in the forefront in Australia: in Victoria (Infertility (Medical Procedures) Act 1984); South Australia (Family Relationships Act 1975 (as amended in 1988)); Queensland (Surrogate Parenthood Act 1988) and Tasmania (Surrogacy Contracts Act 1993).

Re Evelyn – *the first litigated surrogacy case in Australia*

Prior to the *Re Evelyn* decision, there had been speculation and discussion as to how custody of a child born from a surrogacy arrangement would be dealt with by an Australian Family Court. *Re Evelyn* is the first litigated surrogacy case to come before the Australian Family Court.

Re Evelyn *(1998) 23 Fam LR 53*

Facts

A surrogacy arrangement had been made between Mr and Mrs Q, who resided in Queensland, and Mr and Mrs S, who resided in South Australia. Mr and Mrs Q had an adopted son, Tom, who was almost three at the time of the trial; Mr and Mrs S had four children aged from three to seven years. The two families had been friends for many years. Mr and Mrs Q and Mr and Mrs S were of similar age and had been married for a similar amount of time. Owing to a total hysterectomy which had arisen from ovarian cancer, Mrs Q was unable to have children. The Qs were aware of Mrs Q's condition prior to marrying. In 1995, after much deliberation between Mr and Mrs S, Mrs S offered to conceive and carry a child for Mr and Mrs Q which would be given to them following its birth. The child would be the biological child of Mr Q and of Mrs S. By this time, Mr and Mrs Q had adopted Tom, but Mrs S decided to proceed with her offer to enable Mr and Mrs Q to experience child conception and birth as close as possible to conceiving their own child. Mrs S was inseminated with Mr Q's sperm and became pregnant. Following the birth of the child, Mr and Mrs Q took the child, named 'Evelyn' for the purpose of the proceedings, to Queensland. Mrs S found it difficult to cope with relinquishment and became frustrated with what she regarded as an inadequate level of communication between the couples. On 11 July 1997, she removed the child from Mr and Mrs Q's home and returned with the child to South Australia.

The applications

Mr and Mrs Q then instituted proceedings in the Family Court in Brisbane on 15 July 1997 and Mr and Mrs S instituted proceedings in the Adelaide Registry of the Family Court on 16 July 1997. The proceedings were transferred to

Brisbane. On 18 July 1997, there was a contested interim hearing before Hilton J, who made orders in terms of the Qs' application placing the child with them pending hearing and ordering that Mr and Mrs S have contact as may be agreed and that, if no agreement was reached, then as determined by the court. Mr and Mrs S lodged an appeal against the decision and proceeded with an application to stay proceedings, which Hilton J dismissed. The hearing of the substantive application was expedited as a preferred option to an appeal. In the period before the trial, the child (Evelyn) was placed with Mr and Mrs Q. Mrs S had contact with Evelyn on seven occasions in August and five occasions in September.

The trial

On 18 September 1997, the matter came before Jordan J who made an order for Mr and Mrs S to have contact with Evelyn for one day in September, four days in October and four days in November 1997. By the time the decision of Jordan J was made on 19 December 1997, Evelyn was one year old. Mrs S had contact with her daughter during a total of 39 days throughout this period, including the period of hospitalisation during her birth and the six days thereafter.

At the trial, both parties sought an order that they should be the residence providers for Evelyn and in the alternative they sought orders for contact. Jordan J determined that from 14 February 1998, Evelyn should live with Mr and Mrs S and that they should have responsibility for her day to day care and development. He also recognised the interests of Mr and Mrs Q, ordering that Evelyn should have specific contact with them and that both the Ss and Qs share responsibility for her long term care, welfare and development. Jordan J also held that:

- Evelyn would suffer problems relating to issues such as abandonment and identity during her adolescence;
- Mrs S was best equipped to deal with those problems;
- Mrs S would suffer extreme grief if Evelyn is not placed with her; and
- the loss to Evelyn of not growing up with her biological half siblings outweighs the loss of her relationship with her adopted brother, Tom.

Mr and Mrs Q appealed to the Full Court of the Family Court. The orders of Jordan J were stayed pending the outcome of the appeal.

The Family Court judgment

The Full Court agreed with the decision of the trial judge and dismissed each of the issues and grounds of appeal argued by the appellants.

The issues and grounds of appeal

Fresh expert evidence

In support of their appeal, the appellants applied to introduce fresh evidence, namely the evidence of an American expert psychologist, Mrs H, who had 15 years' experience in the area of surrogate parenting. Mrs H had expressed her criticism of the expert evidence that had been called at the trial and had said that it was wrong to rely, as some of the experts had done, on parallels to be drawn from adoptions. Instead, it was contended that it would be better to consider any long term problems for the child at being separated from its biological mother. However, the Full Court rejected the admission of this evidence.

Trial judge erred in not requiring further evidence

They alleged that the trial judge had relied on the evidence of experts who had not seen the parties.

Consequently, he relied on untested theories and he also erred in not requiring further evidence to be put before the court. This was also summarily rejected by the Full Court, who said that the judge had the reports and evidence of five experts in front of him and there was nothing to suggest that there was anything inadequate or misleading in that evidence. Further, Mrs H's evidence was available at the time as she had been found via the internet.

Long term considerations

This was the ground that the court had difficulty with, which was questioning the basis for the findings of the trial judge placing Evelyn with Mrs S, despite the fact that Evelyn was leading a happy, contented, settled life under the loving care of the Qs and although she had formed a close primary attachment to Mrs Q and a strong secondary attachment to her biological father. The appellants argued that Jordan J's findings as to the long term welfare of Evelyn were future and hypothetical and 'untested theories or guesswork in relation to the problems that may arise for Evelyn in the period from adolescence to early adulthood'. The appeal also argued that to adopt such an approach would mean that in almost all cases the biological mother would succeed in a residence approach for infant surrogate children.

The Full Court rejected all these arguments. They opined that the trial judge did not simply decide the matter on the basis that Mrs S was the biological mother, although he did regard that as a factor in her favour. Instead, the court believed that the trial had reached his conclusions on the basis of the personal qualities of the parties, their parenting capacities and the expert evidence before him which he was entitled to accept. The Full Court felt that the trial judge had, *inter alia*, concluded that placement of Evelyn with

Mr and Mrs S would be likely to raise fewer questions in her mind given her unique situation and that any questions Evelyn would have would be best answered by Mrs S.

Accordingly, the trial judge's decision was affirmed and the appeal was dismissed.

However, the Qs refused to relinquish the child and brought a further appeal to the Full Court of the Family Court seeking leave to appeal to the High Court of Australia and a stay of proceedings. The matter was eventually heard by the High Court, but the application to have the case reopened was dismissed and the Family Court ruling was upheld, so that Evelyn was to be returned to Mrs S, her biological mother, and her husband. However, pursuant to earlier orders by Jordan J, the Qs have a right of contact with the child at such reasonable times as may be agreed between the parties and, failing agreement, in accordance with any detailed court orders that may be made.

Hence, the Qs will continue to have an input into the long term decision making in respect of Baby Evelyn as they now share with the Ss the responsibility for her long term care, welfare and development.

POSTHUMOUS TAKING AND USE OF SPERM

The famous English case of *Diane Blood* (discussed in Chapter 5) made headlines around the world and the Australian version, with which it bears some similarity, occurred in 1998: *AB v Attorney General of Victoria*, a decision by the Supreme Court of Victoria, Australia.

AB v AG of Victoria [1999] Med LR 84

Upon the sudden death of her 29 year old husband, the widow sought to have semen and associated tissue removed from the body and stored with a view to undergoing artificial insemination. The deceased did not leave a will or any other written indication of his wishes that was brought to the attention of the court. An urgent application was made for permission to remove the semen while it retained its productivity, together with an application for an order suppressing publication of identifying information. Counsel for the applicant referred the court to relevant legislation, none of which expressly authorised the removal of semen in the present case.

Gillard J made the suppression order until further order of the court, holding that it was in the interests of the administration of justice to do so, taking into account the grief of the widow at the recent death of her husband, the uncertainty of the inherent jurisdiction and the effect of publication at that stage. The judge directed that the matter be returned before the court for further consideration of the relevant legal principles and jurisdiction.

The Supreme Court of Victoria held:

(a) Permission was to be given to a legally qualified medical practitioner to remove semen and associated tissue from the deceased to be stored in accordance with the provisions of the Infertility Treatment Act 1995. The semen and tissue were not to be used for any purpose without further order of the court. In any future action, the Attorney General was to represent the public interest.

(b) The applicability of certain statutory provisions, including Part IV of the Human Tissue Act 1982, s 43 of the Infertility Act 1995 (which prohibits the insemination of a woman with sperm from a man known to be dead) together with s 56 of the same Act (conferring a power on the Infertility Treatment Authority to permit the export of sperm), as well as the extent of the court's jurisdiction and the right, if any, of a personal representative to cause the removal and use of bodily tissue and fluids from a deceased relative will be among the many issues to be resolved in any future proceedings.

(c) The suppression order was to be lifted, but not until 9 am the day after the hearing. This was in the public interest, as it would allow the applicant and her family to be made aware of the decision of the court.

Comparative observations

Blood *and* AB *compared*

Although the situation was similar to the *Blood* case, in that the surviving widow wished to use her dead husband's sperm, in *AB*, the sperm provider was already dead at the time when the sperm was removed. This is important for legal purposes because, since Diane Blood's husband was still alive, although in a coma and dying, the court had to consider the legality of storage and use of the sperm in the absence of written consent, but the Australian legislation – the Infertility Treatment Act 1995 in Victoria – does not require an individual's written consent for storage of sperm. In *AB*, the issue was the legality or otherwise of removing the sperm from a dead donor. The removal of sperm in *Blood* was clearly illegal, constituting a battery, being deliberate touching without consent or some lawful justification. The leading case on treatment of incompetent adults is the English House of Lords' decision of *Re F (Mental Patient: Sterilisation)* [1990] 2 AC 1. In order for the removal of the sperm to be justified under the principle of necessity, it would have to be in the 'best interests' of the incompetent person concerned.

CIVIL LAW COUNTRIES

France

Surrogacy in France

The practice of surrogacy has not received a favourable reception in France, being first viewed as an 'eccentricity from across the Atlantic' (Rubellin-Devichi (1987), p 489) then, as the practice was more widely reported in the press (*Le Monde*, 11 June 1980 and 3 January 1986; and *'Un acte d'amour'* by M and G Libauduere, *La table ronde* (1984), cited in Rubellin-Devichi (1987)), regarded as a practice deserving condemnation, which it duly received from the French National Ethics Committee, the Ministry of Justice and the Ministry of Health. This disapproval has apparently been reflected in various opinion polls and the views of the majority of legal and medical practitioners and academics (see Steiner (1992)). The practice of surrogacy has drawn passionate reaction from many areas of public opinion. In the first phase of the debate, surrogate motherhood was said (by sociologists and lawyers) to be common to the history of humanity (Byk (1992)). This view meant that surrogacy did not question conceptions of the traditional family (Papiernik-Berkhauer (1984), cited in Rubellin-Devichi (1987)). However, these views were soon overtaken, with disapproval replacing support for the practice. The Catholic influence in a country like France can be overestimated and is sometimes practically overlooked, but while it does not determine many ethical and moral decisions in the country, Catholicism tends always to be in the background when it comes to matters of *la famille*. In 1985, a majority of opinion opposed the payment of the surrogate mother (see public opinion poll, IPSOS, *Femme pratique*, September 1985) and only 30% of women supported altruistic cases of surrogacy exposed in the media. Another French opinion poll dated 12 and 13 October 1987 shows that 56% of the French do consider that a surrogate mother who has agreed to give up her child for money to a commissioning couple should fulfil the arrangement entered into with the surrogate (*Le journal du dimanche*, 18 October 1987, cited by Byk (1992)). In 1987, the French Government implemented measures to terminate the activities of private surrogacy agencies. Those who worked in and with private agencies 'claimed that they were working on a non-profit basis in order to help infertile couples and to prevent the existence of a black market in this field' (Byk (1992), p 157), but the courts nonetheless decided that surrogacy was illegal for two main reasons: (a) the agreement concerns the human body and, as such, is prohibited by Art 1128 of the French Civil Code; and (b) any kind of contract by which prospective parents give up their future child constitutes a criminal offence. (see *Association Nationale pour l'Insémination Artificielle, Tribunal de Grande Instance de Paris,* 20 January 1988; *Association Les Cigognes, Conseil d'Etat,* 22 January 1988; *Association Sainte Sarah, Tribunal de Grande Instance de Créteil,* 23 March 1988; *Association Alma Mater, Cour d'Appel d'Aix-en-Provence,* 29 April 1988).

Surrogacy contracts in French criminal law

On the criminal front, it is arguable that, in French law, surrogacy contracts may even be a breach of the criminal law and may therefore be a crime. There is no crime committed in merely handing over a child for money. But, an offence may be committed by the surrogate and the commissioning parents because:

(a) there may be a breach of Art 345 of the Criminal Code, which states: 'Any person who substitutes one child for another or holds a child out as the offspring of a woman who is not its mother, shall be punished by imprisonment from five to 10 years.' This may be avoided by the parties to a surrogacy agreement by registering the child under the name of his natural mother and his natural father – usually the commissioning father – and then by the commissioning mother adopting the child;

(b) it is possible that an offence may be committed under Art 353(1)1 of the Criminal Code, as it provides that it is a criminal offence for any person to induce, for gain, a parent or parents to abandon their child, either born or to be born. Hence, this may be seen as achieving the same result as the criminalising of the intermediary who, for commercial purposes, initiates or takes part in any negotiations with a view to the making of a surrogacy agreement which is the intention of s 2 of the English Surrogacy Arrangements Act 1985.

In addition, if adoption is involved, as is usually the case in surrogacy, there may also be a crime committed under Art 353(1)3 by anyone who, for gain, acts or attempts to act as intermediaries for the reception or adoption of a child. However, the commissioning parents and the surrogate would not be caught by this provision.

By contrast, s 57 of the English Adoption Act 1976, which prohibits the payment or acceptance of money in connection with any placement of a child for adoption, appears to cover the parties to the surrogacy agreement and the intermediaries.

The last possible crime might be committed under Art 334 of the French Criminal Code, which makes it a criminal offence to live off immoral earnings. If, as has been argued (by writers like Rubellin-Devichi, see (1987)) that surrogacy, when paid for, can be likened to prostitution, in the sense that it is concerned with the lease of part of the body in exchange for money; hence, if one considered prostitution 'immoral', all parties involved in negotiating a surrogacy contract would be guilty of an offence, whether it be the lawyers, doctors or other professionals (for the source of these comments and information cited, see Steiner (1992), pp 873–74).

Main issues in the surrogacy debate in France

Steiner (1992) identifies three controversial aspects of surrogacy which have dominated the surrogacy debate in France. First, the nature of the relationship between mother and child has been canvassed; a relationship called 'ontological' by Professor Seriaux (see Seriaux, '*Droit naturel et procréation artificielle: quelle jurisprudence?*' D 1985, Chr 10), meaning that motherhood is an immutable state of being (the interpretation is Steiner's). Hence, the act of a woman carrying a child for the purpose of giving it away constitutes a distortion of this relationship. Under Arts 319 and 341 of the Civil Code, the woman giving birth should, for all intents and purposes, be regarded as the mother of the child. This is exactly the same legal statutory position in English law (see s 27 of the HFEA 1990 and the discussion in Chapter 6). Secondly, the serious risk of commercial exploitation has been feared, following the creation of agencies specifically set up to arrange for the services of a surrogate mother to have the baby and then to hand the child over to someone else under a surrogate agreement. There has been no equivalent legislation to the UK Surrogacy Arrangements Act 1985 which, *inter alia*, was enacted to ban commercial surrogacy. Thirdly, the absence of a legal framework has been identified. This has raised questions over the validity and enforceability of surrogate agreements. As we have already seen, the position is now clear in English law, whereby under the newly inserted s 1A of the 1990 Act, a surrogacy arrangement is not enforceable by or against any of the parties to it.

In France, the Cour de Cassation, first in the *Alma Mater Association* case in 1990 and then, two years later, in the *Madame X* case, has attempted to lay down its strong view on this subject, which is, to put it bluntly, its disapproval of the practice of surrogacy. The following account is taken from Steiner (1992).

The *Alma Mater Association* case (1989) Cass Civ 1, 13 December 1989, D 990, J 273

Facts

An agency was created in the form of an 'association' which, in accordance with the Law on Association of 1 July 1901, was non-profit making and whose aims included the recruitment of women for surrogate pregnancy and the making of arrangements for couples wishing to use the services of a carrying mother. Thus, the Alma Mater Association was involved only with the making of voluntary arrangements intended to help childless couples. Money was, therefore, paid only to reimburse the surrogate mother for expenses and to compensate her for the hardship of a surrogate pregnancy. Nevertheless, the Public Prosecutor of Marseilles applied to the Tribunal de Grande Instance to have the Association dissolved on the grounds of it having 'an illicit and immoral purpose' since, according to Art 3 of the Law of 1901, any association having an illicit and immoral purpose may be dissolved by the courts.

Hence, the Cour de Cassation had to decide whether it was lawful to establish such an agency to help childless couples to have children or whether this was unlawful under Art 3 of the 1901 Law.

The application succeeded both at first instance and at the appellate level.

The decisions

The Tribunal de Grande Instance and Court of Appeal both focused on the legality of surrogacy in French law. Guided by the arguments of the Public Prosecutor, both courts decided that making arrangements intended to effect the birth of a child with a view to giving it away was illicit and immoral.

These decisions were based on Art 1128 of the Civil Code, which prohibits transactions dealing with things which are *'hors du commerce'* (as Art 1128 puts it: 'only things which circulate in commerce may be the object of agreements'); and on Arts 311-9 and 376, which stipulate that a person cannot surrender or transfer parental rights or duties. Another appeal was made, but the Cour de Cassation upheld the view of both the earlier courts.

In a more recent case, there was no dispute about the surrogacy agreement, but the courts nevertheless decided to consider the validity or otherwise of the agreement in French law.

***Procureur Général v Madame X* (1991) (the *Madame X* case) Cass Ass Plénière, 31 May 1991, J 417**

A surrogacy agreement was entered into between a childless couple and an American woman, Mrs D, of Louisville, Kentucky. The American court had allowed, in accordance with the law of Jefferson County, the termination of the natural mother's rights and the surrender of custody. Article 311-14 of the Civil Code stipulates that 'Filiation is governed by the personal law of the mother on the day of the birth of the child'. Consequently, American law was the personal law of the mother and would apply to the relationship between mother and child. The Court of Appeal had to consider this decision before making its own. It decided that the American judgment was not in conflict with the French law view on public policy and thus, it could not have prevented the couple from applying for adoption in France.

The actual issue before the court was whether the adoption order made by the Court of Appeal in favour of the commissioning parents was consistent with the provisions of the Civil Code dealing with the welfare and best interests of the child in adoption cases.

Thus, there was no dispute between the parties about the surrogate arrangement, but the court seemed determined to consider its validity and concluded that, on this point, surrogacy, being concerned with womb leasing, ought to fit within the category of organ donations allowed in French law if not done in exchange for money. Hence, the court held that 'surrogate motherhood, when voluntary, does not conflict with the French conception of public policy'.

The judgment of the Court of Appeal was referred to the Full Assembly of the Cour de Cassation by the Procureur Général according to the principle of the *'pourvoi dans l'intérêt de la loi'* whereby, if the actual parties to the case do not challenge the Court of Appeal ruling by launching an appeal to the Cour de Cassation from the lower court decision, the Procureur Général may refer the case to the Cour if he believes that the law in that case was wrongly applied.

The Cour de Cassation did not agree with the Court of Appeal's view and roundly declared that all surrogacy arrangements, paid or voluntary, are illegal in that they constitute a sort of disposal of the human body which is not authorised by law and which is contrary to public policy.

The French law approach to assessment of the validity of surrogacy contracts

In both the above cases, the Cour de Cassation could have stuck to the precise issue that was before the court in each case, but instead, it chose to relate the actual issues to the question of surrogacy invoking the French doctrines of *'ordre public'* and *'fraude a la loi'*, and these doctrines were the grounds for holding that the surrogacy agreements were illegal in French law.

The doctrine of *ordre public*

This is not defined in French law, but it is mentioned in Arts 6 and 1128. There appear to be more examples of the doctrine in case law than any sign of an authoritative statutory definition of the concept. This principle is, therefore, very similar to the English doctrine of public policy, because it is up to the courts to determine which contracts are unenforceable. The French judges of the highest court have recourse to unwritten principles of law as a source of *ordre public*, but as Amos and Walton explain, the main contrasts with English law 'lie in the free use made by the French courts of statute law as a source of public policy and in their tendency to have greater recourse to doctrines of subjective rights such as the right of freedom of conscience' (Amos and Walton (1967), p 169). The Cour de Cassation has decided that womb leasing and the handing over of children in these circumstances – being concerned with the human body – cannot be the subject matter of an agreement being *hors du commerce* – a matter which cannot be dealt with in a transaction. Amos and Walton further explain that the French courts have used the *ordre public* concept 'to strike at transactions which in their view are prejudicial to the institution of the family' (Amos and Walton (1967), p 170). This appears to be precisely why this concept has been used. No reason is given for the Cour de Cassation's rejection of equating womb leasing with organ donation as the Court of Appeal did, but Steiner suggests that French law has always ensured that human organ donations and transplants, whether of tissues or fluids, have never been carried out for profit. In the case of surrogacy, in the absence of a legal framework, there is always the danger of commercial exploitation (see Steiner (1992), p 872).

The doctrine of *fraude de la loi*

The Cour de Cassation also considered it possible, in both the cases we have examined, to vitiate a contract on the basis of *fraude a la loi*. As Steiner (1992) explains, this concept arises 'when a person, without openly violating the law, makes specific arrangements in order to evade it'. Previous examples of the use of this doctrine have been by the legislature in contract law to forbid certain contracts being made *in fraudem legis*, with a common example being contracts to defraud the revenue (tax authorities). In the present context, the Cour de Cassation is saying that the application for adoption in this case, which follows a surrogacy arrangement, cannot succeed because 'it is the ultimate phase of a process which, by creating a state of constructive abandonment, tends to abuse the objectives of the Law on Adoption, which are to provide a family home for homeless children' (Steiner (1992), p 873). In the context of surrogacy, 'the abuse of the law [here] arises out of the arrangement between the parties to create a homeless child in order to tae advantage of the legal provisions intended for genuine homeless babies' (Steiner (1992)). This concept is used in both the cases we have considered, to invalidate the surrogacy arrangement.

Posthumous taking and use of sperm

Apart from the *Blood* case, there have been cases in France and Germany of sperm being frozen and claims to access to stored sperm after the death of the biological father. In France, the case of *Parpalaix* is noteworthy (see *Consorts Parpalaix c/le CECOS et autre*, 1 August 1984, *Gazette du Palais*, 16–18 September 1984, p 11, discussed by Latham (1998) and Atherton (2000)).

The Parpalaix *case (1984) JCP 1984.II.20321*

This was a decision of the *Tribunaux de Grande Instance* in 1984. The facts here are that, prior to undergoing chemotherapy, 24 year old Alain Parpalaix deposited sperm with the donor insemination centre, CECOS (*Centre d'Etude et de Conservation du Sperm*) without leaving any instructions as to its use. At the time of his storing the sperm, Alain was living with Corinne Richard, whom he married two days before his death. Corinne's request for the sperm was denied, so subsequently Corinne and Alain's parents sued CECOS. They argued that sperm deposited in a sperm bank formed part of the movable property of Alain's estate and was, therefore, capable of being inherited. They also argued that they were the natural heirs of the deceased and had, therefore, become the owners of the sperm upon his death, and that CECOS was a bailee obliged to deliver the sperm to them. CECOS argued that it was only obliged to the deceased donor in contract and that 'sperm was an indivisible part of the body, much like a limb or organ, and is therefore not inheritable absent express instructions' (this is taken from the judgment of *Hecht v Superior Court of Los Angeles County* (1993) 20 Cal Rptr 2d 775, p 287).

The court held that the refusal to hand over the sperm was unlawful, but not on the basis that the sperm was property in the sense that had been argued. They held that, under contract law, the contract between CECOS and the couple obliged CECOS to hand back the sperm as the couple had not been made aware of CECOS' objections to posthumous insemination. The court was influenced by the fact that the couple were married and that procreation was the main reason for marriage. The court was prepared to hold that the wishes of the dead man could be inferred by the testimony of others. It also did not accept the idea that sperm was an indivisible part of the body. It preferred to think of sperm as the 'seed of life' linked to the 'fundamental liberty of a human being to conceive or not to conceive'. It accordingly held that the fate of the sperm had to be decided by the person who produced it. However, the deceased man had not indicated expressly what he intended to be done with his sperm, but the court deduced that he would have left it to his widow to decide. Consequently, the court ruled that the sperm be delivered to the widow's doctor for her use. Corinne's attempt to conceive failed. There was never any need to consider the status of any children born as a result of the posthumous conception.

How would a Diane Blood *situation be decided in France?*

The *Parpalaix* ruling has now been superseded by Art 10 of the French statute on respect for the human body (see *'Loi No 94–653 relative au respect du corps humain'*). The consent necessary for each embryo transfer is now revoked after the end of a marriage or stable relationship, including after the death of one of the partners of the couple undergoing NRT treatments using a donor. This applies unless treatment has already begun with that donated gamete. The rationale is because treatment can only be given to a couple initiating a *'projet parental'* or parental undertaking *together*, so both are setting out to be a parent-couple of any resulting child. Hence, as Latham ((1998), p 105) points out, 'a French Diane Blood would not be able to gain access to the stored semen of her dead husband or partner' irrespective of whether it could be proved that he had given his consent to post mortem insemination, because he could not be there *in person* to consent to the insemination or embryo transfer taking place. Similarly, as Latham also observes, a French Mr Blood could not use a surrogate to gestate an embryo that had been created from his dead wife's ova, or that had been donated to the couple.

Germany

Loss of frozen sperm

In a German *Bundesgerichtshof* case reported in November 1993 (BGHZ 124.52), before undergoing an operation which would leave him sterile, the 31 year old plaintiff had some of his sperm frozen in order to have children later. Through the fault of the university clinic, this sperm was lost. The plaintiff therefore sued for damages from the clinic. Both lower courts rejected his claim. The Federal Supreme Court also rejected his claim for the following reasons:

(a) The Appeal Court had held that the plaintiff's general right of personality was not infringed. They submitted that the destruction of the sperm deprived him of his liberty to decide whether, how, and when his sperm was to be used for fertilisation; but this freedom was not covered by the general right of personality which only protects this legal position in principle. They declared that the general right of personality protects personal integrity, but not personal activities. The Federal Court did *not* agree with these findings; they held that *the Appeal Court's previous findings are legally unsound.*

(b) As a result of the negligent destruction of his sperm, the plaintiff's claim for damages is well founded.

(c) A controversial, but dominant legal opinion, which the previous Appeal Court ruling appears to follow, is that a part of the body separated from it becomes a physical object, with the result that a person's right to his own body is transformed to a right of ownership in the separate part of his body. Some authors believe that this result applies to frozen sperm, which the Appeal Court also appears to agree with. Hence, following this view, the destruction of the sperm would not amount to a physical injury to which para 847 of the BGB links a claim for damages for pain and suffering. The Federal Court holds that this view is too narrow. This court has given the concept of physical injury (as expressed in paras 823(1), 847(1) of the BGB) a wide meaning. It considers the right to one's own body as a legally formulated section of the general right of personality. It also interprets as 'physical injury' every unjustified intrusion into bodily integrity, unless the owner of the right has given his consent. 'Physical injury' is expressly mentioned in para 823(1) of the BGB and is treated separately from 'impairment to health'. It is not the physical matter as such that is protected by para 823(1) of the BGB, but rather a person's entire area of existence and self-determination, which is materially manifested in the body. The provisions of para 823(1) of the BGB protect the body as the basis of human personality.

(d) A person's right of self-determination, emanating from his right of personality, acquires additional significance in the light of modern medical possibilities and in relation to the body as object of the protected right. Medical advances allow the extraction of body parts for later re-implantation. This applies to transplants of skin or bone parts intended for transplantation to other parts of the same body. Where parts of a body are taken out, with the consent of the person affected, in order later on to be re-implanted as a means of preserving or improving bodily functions, the legal opinion that para 823(1) of the BGB comprehensively protects corporeal integrity in order to guarantee a person's right to self-determination will lead to the following result. In view of the protective purpose of para 823, these extracted parts of the body continue to form a functional unity with the remaining body even during their separation from it. It therefore seems necessary to classify the damage to or destruction of such extracted body parts as a *physical injury* in the sense of paras 823(1) and 847 of the BGB. The result is different where, according to the wishes of the person concerned, the separated parts of his body are not intended to be used or re-integrated at a later stage.

(e) For such cases of final severance, the normal legal consequence applies, that is that, at the point of separation, the severed body parts lose all links to the protected entity of the 'body' and become 'objects' in the legal sense. The reason for the latter result is the concept that, given every person's right to self-determination, the body and its now separate parts no longer form a functional unity. This outcome applies in particular to donated organs which, under the will of the donor, are intended to be implanted into another person, or to blood donated for third persons. Even in such cases, claims for damages can arise if the donation is used or destroyed in breach of the express or tacit intentions of the donor. Under these circumstances, the right of personality influences the right of ownership in these objects, although only under the specific restrictive preconditions developed for cases of injury to the right of personality.

(f) Based on these considerations, the frozen sperm, which the owner of the right of personality intended to use for future procreation, represents a special case. On the one hand, the sperm has permanently been separated from the body. On the other hand, it is intended to fulfil a bodily function, that is, that of procreation. Where, as in the present case, the preservation of sperm was meant as a substitute to the lost capability of procreation, this sperm is no less valuable than a woman's egg cell or other bodily parts in respect of (a) the corporeal integrity of the owner of the right of personality and of personal self-determination, which is part of it; and (b) due to the importance and its particular potential. Even after their separation from the body, the latter are covered by the protection of paras 823(1) and 847(1) of the BGB. As with egg cells taken from the body to be fertilised and re-implanted, the frozen sperm represents, for the owner in this particular case, the *protected right.*

This is because it is his only chance of using his bodily functions to sire children to whom he can pass on his genetic material. In view of the similarity and equal value of both bodily parts: (1) for their need to be protected against tortious acts; and (2) because of the protective purpose of the relevant tort provisions, their equal status must also be manifest in the legal consequences provided by the law of torts. Even in cases like this, where frozen sperm is not directly covered by the factual text of the tort provisions, which outline and determine the protected right of corporeal integrity, those provisions must at least be applied analogically given the above-described circumstances. The general right of personality legitimises such extensive and extended legal application of paras 823(1) and 847(1) of the BGB for a person whose right of personality is not differently or less intensely affected than a woman's right, by destruction of her egg cells, extracted from her body and intended for re-implantation. Just like the woman in that case, *the plaintiff had a claim for damages for pain and suffering* based on para 847(1) of the BGB. [Translation by Mrs Irene Snook, under the direction of Professors P Schlechtriem, B Markesinis and S Lorenz.]

Comment

Under para 847 of the BGB, claims for compensation for pain and suffering are only admissible in cases of physical injury and deprivation of liberty, but not in cases of damage to property. In order to provide a claim for damages, the court, therefore, had to treat certain parts of the body, separated from it, not as objects, but rather as remaining parts of that body. Since there was no pecuniary loss in this case, a claim for damage to property would have failed (Dannermann, Institute of European and Comparative Law, University of Oxford).

FUTURE DEVELOPMENTS IN THE REPRODUCTION REVOLUTION

Cloning

In its Conclusions in a Report to the President of the Republic of France, the French National Ethical Consultative Committee for the Life and Health Sciences in France set out a definition of cloning: 'Cloning consists of producing a population of individuals all of which possess an identical set of genes in the nucleus of their cells.' Human cloning is basically the production of genetically identical human beings and can certainly be regarded as part of the reproductive revolution that was hailed in the 1980s and 1990s. Chapter 19 distinguishes between the two distinct forms of cloning and discusses both the English law position and ethical considerations.

Cloning is very much a technique that has been the subject of debate and discussion, resulting in international agreements generally disapproving of human reproductive cloning.

The international legal position

The European Convention on Human Rights and Biomedicine, promoted by the Council of Europe, provides unequivocally in Art 1(a) that 'Any intervention seeking to create a human being genetically identical to another human being, whether living or dead, is prohibited'. The term 'genetically identical' is defined in Art 1(2) as where a human being shares 'with another the same nuclear gene set'. The prohibition appears to cover both therapeutic and reproductive cloning because Art 7 provides that prohibition on cloning human beings covers 'all nuclear transfer methods seeking to create identical human beings'. It should be noted that Germany and the UK did not sign the Protocol to the Convention; Germany submitted that it already had its own legislation dealing with this situation (the Federal Embryo Protection Act 1990) and the UK said (*per* Baroness Hayman in the debate on the subject) that, whilst the government fully supported the principle enshrined in the Protocol, it could not sign it, because to do so would also mean signing the Convention itself. This contained provisions relating to persons not able to consent, which needed to be examined in the light of forthcoming legislation to be introduced by the government. Nevertheless, the Convention has, so far, been signed in Oviedo by 21 States ((1998) 49 International Digest of Health Legislation 547).

On 11 March 1997, the World Health Organisation published a Declaration in which it considered 'the use of cloning for the replication of human individuals to be ethically unacceptable as it would violate some of the basic principles which govern medically assisted procreation. These include respect for the dignity of the human being and protection of the security of human genetic material.'

The UK has been active in a number of initiatives which call for the reproductive cloning of human beings to be banned, such as the EC draft Biotechnology Patents Directive, which forbids the issue of a patent on work leading to deliberate cloning of human cloning; a protocol forbidding the cloning of human beings has been developed under the Council of Europe Bioethics Convention and a UNESCO Declaration on the Human Genome and Human Rights, adopted on 11 November 1997, of which Art 11 states that 'Practices which are contrary to human dignity, such as reproductive cloning of human beings, shall not be permitted'.

Among the countries that have legislation forbidding research or the cloning process itself are Denmark, the Netherlands, Norway, Germany, Slovakia, Spain, Sweden and Switzerland. However, Greece and Ireland currently do not have any legislation relating to cloning.

In the USA, shortly after Dolly the sheep was born, President Clinton gave instructions that no federal funds were to be used for the cloning of human beings. He also asked the US National Bioethics Advisory Committee (NBAC) to investigate the issue of cloning and NBAC's subsequent report recommended a five year moratorium on cloning until the risks were understood better.

As we have seen, the UK is poised to approve the use of therapeutic cloning, but the matter is far from settled.

CONCLUDING COMMENTS ON SURROGACY AND THE REPRODUCTION REVOLUTION

Various questions can be posed regarding surrogacy: Whose needs are we serving in these matters? Do ethics and morals come into the picture? What is the role of choice? Is it morally defensible to create a situation where it is highly likely that the child will be the centre of moral, ethical and legal controversy?

The way forward is probably not criminalisation, with its difficulties in policing surrogacy and the invasion of privacy under the Human Rights Act 1998, but, if regulation is the solution, the question is: should this be centralised or decentralised (Brazier (1999))?

As far as surrogacy is concerned, the comments of Professor Michael Freeman in 1990, even though referring to the UK situation, are, 10 years on, as appropriate as ever with regard to its continuing popularity in countries like the USA. He observed that:

> With infertility at new high levels ... and increasing, with opportunities to adopt healthy and acceptable babies curtailed by relatively liberal abortion laws, easier access to contraception (in particular the contraceptive pill) and greater toleration of single parenthood, it is difficult to see the demand for surrogacy (and other 'new ways of making babies') diminishing [Freeman (1990), p 164].

Criminalising it would almost certainly drive it underground, which would not be desirable, not least because of the potentially damaging effects on children produced by such arrangements, who, one might argue, will already have enough to contend with. However, careful monitoring of the child's welfare and a sensible approach to the question of the amount of expenses allowable will at least ensure that a balance will be struck in this contentious area of assisted reproduction, so that the freedom allowed to persons to enter into such contracts will be matched by a supportive framework of counselling, regular monitoring of the situation and a constant regard for the welfare of the child to be paramount.

SELECTIVE BIBLIOGRAPHY

Amos, M and Walton, F, *Introduction to French Law*, Lawson, H, Anton, A and Brown, L (eds), 1967, Clarendon

Atherton, R, '*En ventre sa frigidaire*: posthumous children in the succession context' (2000) 19 LS 139

Bainham, A, *Children – The Modern Law*, 1998, Jordan, pp 75, 201 *et seq*

Barton, C and Douglas, G, *Law and Parenthood*, 1995, Butterworths, Chapter 4, esp p 81 *et seq*

Brazier, M, 'Can you buy children?' (1999) 11 Child and Fam LQ 345

Byk, C, 'France: law reform and human reproduction', in McLean, S (ed), *Law Reform and Human Reproduction*, 1992, Dartmouth

Charo, R, 'United States: surrogacy', in McLean, S (ed), *Law Reform and Human Reproduction*, 1992, Dartmouth

Cuisine, D, *New Reproductive Technologies*, 1990, Dartmouth

de Cruz, SP 'Surrogacy, adoption, and custody: a case study' (1988) 18 Fam Law 100

Dewar, J, *Law and the Family*, 1992, Butterworths, esp pp 82–101

Downie, S, *Babymaking: Technology and Ethics*, 1988, Bodley Head

Douglas, G, 'The Human Fertilisation and Embryology Act 1990' (1991) 20 Fam Law 110

Douglas, G, *Law, Fertility and Reproduction*, 1991, Sweet & Maxwell, Chapters 6 and 7

Douglas, G 'Assisted reproduction and the welfare of the child', in Freeman, M and Hepple, B (eds), *Current Legal Problems*, 1993, OUP

Douglas, G, 'The intention to be a parent and the making of mothers' (1994) 57 MLR 636

Douglas, G and Lowe, N, 'Becoming a parent in English law' (1992) 108 LQR 414

Dickens, B, 'Reproductive technology and the "new" family', in Sutherland, E and McCall Smith, A (eds), *Family Rights*, 1990, Edinburgh UP

Fennell, P, 'Commentary' (1999) 10 Med L Rev 85

Freeman, MDA, 'Is surrogacy exploitative?', in McLean, S (ed), *Legal Issues in Reproductive Medicine*, 1990, Dartmouth

Freeman, MDA, 'Does surrogacy have a future after Brazier?' (1999) 10 Med L Rev 1

Hayes, M and Williams, C, *Family Law: Principles, Policy and Practice*, 1999, Butterworths, esp pp 18–26

Hibbs, M, 'Surrogacy legislation – time for a change?' [1997] Fam Law 564

Latham, M, 'Regulating the new reproductive technologies: a cross-channel comparison' (1998) 3 Med Law International 89

Liu, A, 'The rights and wrongs of surrogacy', in *Artificial Reproduction and Reproductive Rights*, 1991, Dartmouth

Lowe, N and Douglas, G, *Bromley's Family Law*, 1998, Butterworths, Chapter 8

Morgan, D, 'Surrogacy: an introductory essay', in Lee, R and Morgan, D (eds), *Birthrights*, 1989, Dartmouth

McLean, S, 'Mothers and others', in Sutherland, E and McCall Smith, A (eds), *Family Rights*, 1990, Edinburgh UP

McHale, J and Fox, M, *Healthcare Law: Text and Materials*, 1997, Sweet & Maxwell, Chapter 11

Otlowski, M, '*Re Evelyn* – reflections on Australia's first litigated surrogacy case' [1999] Med LR 38

Pence, G, 'The *Baby M* case', in *Classic Cases in Medical Ethics*, 1990, McGraw-Hill

Roberts, S, in Byrne, P (ed), *Rights and Wrongs in Medicine*, 1986, King Edward's Hospital Fund for London/OUP, p 80

Rubellin-Devichi, J, '*Les mères porteuses*' (1987) *Revue Trimestrielle de Droit Civil* 489

Singer, P and Wells, D, *The Reproduction Revolution: New Ways of Making Babies*, 1984, OUP

Stauch, M and Wheat, K, with Tingle, J *et al*, *Sourcebook on Medical Law*, 1998, Cavendish Publishing, Chapter 7

Steiner, E, 'Surrogacy agreements in French law' (1992) 41 ICLQ 866

Stuhmcke, A, 'Surrogacy, custody and the Family Court' (1998) 12 Aust J Fam Law 297

CHAPTER 15

STERILISATION OF PERSONS WITH A MENTAL DISABILITY: A COMPARATIVE ANALYSIS

INTRODUCTION

In Part I of this book, we examined the English courts' approach to the difficult question of when a court might decide that it is in the best interests of an incompetent mentally handicapped person or intellectually disabled person to authorise sterilisation of that person. The inability of the patient to decide for herself could be the result of a lack of capacity because she is a child, in the sense of being below the age of majority, or because of a mental incapacity, such as a mental age of four or five, although biologically and physically an adult; or, as we have seen, because a child lacks the necessary maturity or '*Gillick* competence' to make a legally valid decision. As we also saw, English law can only authorise the sterilisation of an adult *ex post facto* and only if it is in the best interests of that patient. We now examine how other jurisdictions have dealt with this issue and, while noting various jurisdictions, we shall concentrate on the USA and Australia (for common law jurisdictions) and discuss the latest developments in Germany and Scotland as examples of countries with a civil (Roman) law heritage.

HISTORICAL BACKGROUND

One commentator claims that, in the 1980s, between 90 and 100 million couples worldwide chose sterilisation as a method of contraception and that, in the USA, sterilisation has been the most popular form of birth control for couples over 30, rivalling the contraceptive pill as a method of contraception (see Isaacs (1983), p 328). Indeed, sterilisation law has been present in Western societies for some time, but it has more frequently been associated with eugenics than, less controversially, as a chosen form of contraception for adults of sound mind (for a discussion of the background to eugenics, see Chapter 7). This is when it has been performed on mentally handicapped persons and has then acquired more sinister connotations. It perhaps needs to be made clear that, in contemporary times, the carers and relatives of such patients have been nothing less than completely selfless and genuine in their desire to do what they believe is in the best interests of the patient and that sterilisation of mentally handicapped children or relatives has been seen as the best option in the patient's particular circumstances. However, history suggests that, until recently, in places like the USA, involuntary sterilisation was, in the words of Elizabeth Scott, 'used as a weapon of the State in the war against mental deficiency', and she claims that 'under eugenic sterilisation laws in effect in many States, retarded persons were routinely sterilised without their consent or knowledge' (Scott (1986), p 806), examining considerable evidence of judicial decisions and statistics going back to the early 20th century.

The first statute requiring the sterilisation of 'defectives' was passed in the American State of Indiana in 1907 and, by 1915, 15 States had legislation permitting eugenic sterilisation. In 1926, the notorious case of *Buck v Bell* (1927) 274 US 200 was heard by the US Supreme Court, which upheld the constitutional validity of Virginia's eugenic sterilisation law (see below, p 494 *et seq* for a fuller discussion of this case). By 1935, there were 32 States which had passed such laws. These laws provided (as stated in their terminology) for the sterilisation of 'criminals, idiots, the feeble-minded, imbeciles, the insane, drunkards, drug fiends, epileptics, syphilitics, and moral and sexual perverts'. Many such laws were challenged, and the courts found them unconstitutional.

Another commentator has claimed that 'In the 50 years from 1907 to the end of 1957, 60,166 persons have been sterilised, of which 31,038 were mental deficients, 26,922 were suffering from mental illness, and the remaining 2,206 were epileptics, criminals and the like. Of the total, 19,998 were performed in California' (St John Stevas (1961), p 164, fn 1). Even in 1985, the American courts were still commenting on California being the State with the most sterilisations. St John Stevas also points out that, since the Second World War, there has been a decline in the number of compulsory sterilisations. The American State laws continued to be used until the late 1960s and, by 1964, 63,678 sterilisations had taken place under compulsory State sterilisation programmes (see Freeman (1988), p 58). Another writer explains that a person was more likely to be sterilised if 'young, poor, a woman and and/or black, Hispanic or Native American. This is not surprising given that social "unfitness" was often not distinguished from intellectual or mental disability' (see Cica (1993), citing Greer (1984) and Trombley (1988)). Relying on these aforementioned accounts, Cica goes on to say that, since the 1960s, 'disproportionate numbers of poor, non-white women have continued to be sterilised'. More disquieting is the fact that, although these sterilisations were not strictly compulsory, they could be 'coercive' in that they took place 'without informed consent, as a condition for receiving welfare payments; as a condition of release from prison or other State institutions; or as a condition of continued employment' (see Greer (1984) and Trombley (1988)).

In the 1930s, legislation authorising eugenic sterilisation existed in certain parts of Canada, Denmark, Switzerland, the (then) Federal Republic of Germany, Norway, Sweden, Finland, Mexico and Japan, where there were 38,000 operations alone. Indeed, Alberta in 1928 and British Columbia in 1933 were the two Canadian jurisdictions that had the dubious distinction of being pioneers in this field and this legislation was not repealed until the 1970s. Similar legislation was not enacted in England or Australia at the time, despite support for eugenic theories in both countries.

Undoubtedly, the worst eugenics-based practice was encountered in 1933, when Nazi Germany enacted the Law for the Prevention of Hereditarily Diseased Offspring, which demanded the compulsory sterilisation of those suffering from 'congenital mental deficiency, schizophrenia, manic-depressive insanity, hereditary epilepsy, Huntington's chorea, hereditary blindness or deafness, alcoholism and any severe hereditary deformity' (as described by Cica (1993)) and, according to one source, in the first year of operation, 56,244 sterilisations were ordered ((1937–38) 29 Eugenics Review 9) and the Hereditary Health Centre (*Erbgesundheitsgerichte*) would order about 400,000 people to be sterilised. According to St John Stevas, this figure was made up as follows: feeble-minded, 200,000; schizophrenics, 80,000; deaf-mutes, 18,000; chronic alcoholics, 10,000; victims of St Vitus' Dance, 6,000; and blind, 4,000. Others who were sterilised though not within the official categories were the 'antisocial', and 'Rhineland bastards', which is the term applied to children conceived after the First World War who were fathered by French North African occupation troops. After the first year of its operation, no further records were kept and estimates of the number of people sterilised under the eugenic laws are between 200,000 and 2 million (see Trombley (1988), Chapters 7 and 9).

A CONTEMPORARY OVERVIEW

Sterilisation of the mentally disabled was very much in the news in the late 1990s. The world learnt about thousands of women apparently being sterilised in Sweden in 1935 and 1976 simply because their behaviour was regarded as 'unacceptable'. However, these sterilisations took place in a social environment where, as Denekens, Nys and Stuer put it: 'it was assumed on the basis of scientific hypothesis that all forms of mental retardation were hereditary' (see Denekens *et al* (1999), p 237).

New research has progressively undermined the hereditary argument (Garber, HL, *The Milwaukee Project: Preventing Mental Retardation in Children at Risk*, 1988, American Association on Mental Retardation, Washington, DC). New developments in special education and training, such as normalisation and mainstreaming, have led to a fundamental change in the way that mental retardation is regarded. On the international front, the Declaration on the Rights of Mentally Retarded Persons in 1971, by the United Nations Assembly, declares that the mentally retarded person has, to the maximum degree of feasibility, the same rights as other human beings.

The USA

Historical background to American sterilisation laws

The practice of involuntary sterilisation was, as we have seen at the beginning of this chapter, widespread in various parts of the USA in the early part of the 20th century. Many States authorised sterilisation of mentally handicapped persons who were believed to be burdens on society, hence they could be seen to be acting under a kind of misplaced altruism – doing something that was believed to benefit 'the public' and relieve the State purse. It is believed that the practice was most prevalent in California, with 20,108 sterilisations, followed by Virginia with 7,162, then North Carolina with 6,297 (see Scott (1986), p 806, citing Robitscher, J (ed), *Eugenic Sterilization*, 1973, p 1). Indeed, in the case of *Valerie N* (1985), the California Supreme Court noted that, historically, California led the nation in eugenic sterilisation (see *Conservatorship of Valerie N* (1985) 40 Cal 3d 143, p 152, which had prompted the State to enact a law barring sterilisation of incompetents through the Cal Prob Code s 2356(d) (1981)). However, this statute was struck down in the *Valerie* case itself.

Yet, prior to *Buck v Bell* in 1927, most courts struck down sterilisation statutes as unconstitutional (see, for example, *Davis v Berry* (1914) 216 F 413 (SD Iowa); *Williams v Smith* (1921) 190 Ind 526; *Haynes v Lapeer* (1918) 201 Mich 138). In fact, the early sterilisation statutes were used to punish habitual criminals and rapists. Hence, a Washington statute authorising the sterilisation of convicted rapists was upheld in *State v Feilen* (1912) 70 Wash 65. It was 30 years later when the US Supreme Court struck down an Oklahoma statute allowing sterilisation of habitual criminals in *Skinner v Oklahoma ex rel Williamson* (1942) 316 US 535, which had clearly been previously followed.

However, some statutes had paternalistic objectives and authorised sterilisation if it was in the best interests of the individual and society. Virginia's statute of 1924 (see Act of 20 March 1924, ch 394, 1924 Va Acts 569) was enacted partly to alleviate fears that institutionalised individuals returning to society would produce children. The Mendelian theories mentioned earlier need to be borne in mind.

In 1927, the US Supreme Court in *Buck v Bell* upheld Virginia's sterilisation statute and implicitly endorsed the eugenic theory. It is instructive at this point to consider the infamous case itself at this juncture as it was the test case for Virginia's new sterilisation law.

Buck v Bell *(1927) 274 US 200*

In this case, Carrie Buck was a 17 year old girl who had been committed to a State institution for the epileptic and feeble-minded after giving birth to an illegitimate daughter. The Virginia law required that institutionalised patients be sterilised for eugenic and therapeutic reasons as a condition of release. The law report describes Carrie's daughter as an 'illegitimate feeble-minded child'. Her proposed sterilisation was challenged on 'due process' and 'cruel and unusual punishment' grounds.

The Supreme Court responded that the sterilisation was not being done as a punishment and that her sterilisation in fact enabled her to be released into the community. Due process and equal protection arguments were rejected. Consequently, the court upheld the validity of the Virginia statute authorising her sterilisation. It was said that Carrie had been born of a feeble-minded mother, was feeble-minded herself and that her daughter was feeble-minded as well. It was this ostensibly atavistic fact that prompted the infamous remark from Holmes J that 'society can prevent those who are manifestly unfit from continuing their kind. The principle that sustains compulsory vaccination is broad enough to cover cutting the Fallopian tubes. Three generations of imbeciles are enough.'

Yet, subsequent historical research has now suggested that neither Carrie, her mother, nor Carrie's daughter were 'imbeciles' as labelled by Holmes J. On the contrary, it was subsequently reported by Lombardo that Carrie's daughter was above average intelligence, and that she was on the second grade honour roll before dying at the age of eight (see Lombardo (1985), p 61).

Yet, even at this time, the scientific merit of the theory was controversial and, as Scott points out, 'researchers in genetics increasingly dissociated themselves from the eugenic movement as scientific understanding of genetics became more sophisticated in the 1920s and 1930s' (Scott (1986), p 811). Indeed, in 1936, the American Neurological Association Committee for the Investigation of Eugenic Sterilisation issued a statement opposing eugenic sterilisation and challenging its scientific premises (see Ferster (1966) 27 Ohio St LJ 591). Such theories have now been largely discredited. By the 1960s, involuntary sterilisation was commonly characterised as an unjustified intrusion by the State on individual liberty and privacy. Yet, as late as 1966, 26 States had eugenic sterilisation laws, with State courts frequently upholding sterilisation laws on the basis of two police power justifications – preventing the birth of defective children and lowering the public welfare expense of supporting children whose parents could not support them (see *In re Simpson* (1962) NE 2d 206). It was during the 1960s and 1970s that many States repealed eugenic sterilisation laws without replacing them with alternative provisions; hence, courts generally rejected petitions to obtain sterilisations of mentally retarded persons because of the absence of statutory authorisation. In 1975, in *AL v GRH* (1975) 325 NE 2d 501, AL filed a complaint seeking a declaration of her right under the common law attributes of the parent-child relationship to have her son, GRH, sterilised. The boy, aged 15, had suffered brain damage as the result of a car accident during his childhood. The Court of Appeals of Indiana said: 'The facts do not bring the case within the framework of those decisions holding that the parents may consent on behalf of the child to medical services necessary for the child ... The common law does not invest parents with such power over their children even though they sincerely believe the child's adulthood would benefit therefrom.'

A seminal case, *Stump and Sparkman*, was then decided in 1978.

Stump v Sparkman *(1978) 435 US 49*

This case involved a 'somewhat retarded' 15 year old girl who was sterilised after she had been told that she was to have her appendix removed. Two years later, when she was married and unable to become pregnant, she was told that she had been sterilised. When the case came to court, the Supreme Court referred without disapproval to the opinion of the lower court with respect to parental powers of consent, in accordance with *AL v GRH* (above).

Here, the Supreme Court of the United States held that judicial immunity protected a judge who, after an *ex parte* hearing, had authorised the sterilisation of a minor on the application of her mother, in the absence of statutory authority. The court found that the judge had jurisdiction to do so under an Indiana statute which conferred general jurisdiction on the court. Hence, the judge's decision had not been 'in the clear absence of all jurisdiction'.

Effect of Stump v Sparkman

Even though *Stump* did not directly affirm judicial authority, it provided the gateway to a series of decisions recognising the *parens patriae* jurisdictions to order the sterilisation of mentally handicapped persons in the absence of statutory authority. Several States enacted statutory provisions that sanction *parens patriae* sterilisation of mentally handicapped persons.

The transformation of American sterilisation law

As Scott (1986) has observed, 'Sterilisation law has undergone a radical transformation in recent years', referring to the laws in the USA. She continues: 'Influenced by a distaste for eugenic sterilisation and a desire to redress past injustices, the emerging [American] law seeks to protect the interests of mentally disabled persons by erecting formidable barriers to sterilisation' (Scott (1986), p 807).

As recently as in the 1980s, American courts could be heard to say 'We are well aware of the sordid history of compulsory eugenic sterilisation laws in the United States' (*Re Moe* (1982) 432 NE 2d 712, p 717); 'the theoretical foundation of eugenic sterilisation as a method of improving society has been disproved' (*Re Hayes* (1980) 608 P 2d 635, p 540).

Factors shaping the reform of sterilisation law

Scott (1986) identifies three factors that have 'stimulated and shaped the reform of sterilisation law: (a) the discrediting of the eugenic theory; (b) the development of the constitutional doctrine of reproductive privacy; and (c) the changing conception of mental retardation (Scott (1986), p 809).

The development of the doctrine of reproductive privacy has cast considerable doubt on the continuing validity of involuntary sterilisation laws. A case that emphasised the need to have judicial approval before sterilisation could be authorised is *Re Grady* (1981) (this is discussed below). There is now a more widespread consensus that mentally disabled persons should, to the extent allowed by their disability, enjoy the same right of reproductive capacity. This view represents an application of cognitive developmental theory and a changing conception of mental retardation. The sterilisation law reform movement is largely illustrated by a series of judicial opinions beginning in 1980 with the Washington Supreme Court case of *In re Guardianship of Hayes.*

The current law

The current law in the USA is, therefore, a mixture of different criteria and different approaches to the question of when involuntary sterilisation may be permitted in the various States and, indeed, the social and legal history of the USA is a very good example of how a common law jurisdiction has been influenced by its history. Somewhat untypically for a common law jurisdiction, it enacted several pieces of legislation to deal with what was, at least initially, perceived as a social problem – 'society' having to bear the burden of looking after mentally handicapped people.

Guidelines from a leading case – Re Hayes (1980)

Re Hayes (1980)

The leading case on involuntary sterilisation in the USA is a Washington Supreme Court decision called *Re Hayes* (*In re Guardianship of Hayes* (1980) 608 P 2d 635), which laid down criteria for the judiciary in cases involving sterilisation of mentally incompetent persons. The guidelines (as summarised by Ogbourne and Ward (1989), p 237) are:

(a) it must be clearly established that the incompetent person is unable to consent – that is, make a reasoned decision – and is unlikely to develop sufficiently to make an informed judgment about sterilisation in the foreseeable future;

(b) the incompetent person must be represented by a disinterested guardian ad litem in order to protect the incompetent's interests;

(c) the court should receive independent advice on the psychological and social evaluation of the incompetent person;

(d) the judge must be satisfied on the evidence that the incompetent person is capable of procreation and is engaging in sexual activity or is likely to in the foreseeable future, so that there is need for contraception.

(e) it must be established that there is no alternative to sterilisation, in that the judge must find all other forms of contraception to be unworkable or inappropriate.

Thus, *Re Hayes* appears to create another 'best interests' test.

Yet another criterion can be found in the other leading case of *Re Grady* (1981) 85 NJ 235, decided slightly after *Re Hayes*. There, it was held that there is a need to balance the trauma of psychological damage from sterilisation against that of pregnancy and birth.

The right to procreate and the right to constitutional privacy

***Re Grady* (1981)**

This case has also been notable for a number of other guidelines. To begin with, the Supreme Court of New Jersey held that the court could, within its *parens patriae* jurisdictions, decide whether to authorise sterilisation of a legally incompetent person and that the decision should, ultimately, be made by a court, not by the guardian of the person concerned. The court canvassed the idea of a fundamental right to procreate. It said (pp 471–72): 'Any legal discussion of sterilisation must begin with an acknowledgment that the right to procreate is fundamental to the very existence and survival of the race [citing *Skinner v Oklahoma* (1942) 316 US 535, p 541] ... this right is a "basic liberty" of which the individual is "forever deprived" through unwanted sterilisation.'

The court then considered the constitutional right of privacy which involved the right to choose among procreation, sterilisation and other methods of contraception. This is based on the American constitutional principles, but is also apparently allied with another, derived from the common law principle of bodily inviolability, as well as under constitutional principles. The New Jersey Supreme Court suggested (p 475) that the only way to adequately protect the right to procreate and the right to privacy was to ensure that the decision to sterilise was the subject of independent judicial decision making, and declared:

> We need not determine here the full range of persons who may assert such a right on behalf of the incompetent. The parents are unquestionably eligible to do so. The question of who besides the parents has standing to represent the interests of the incompetent can await future determination. Nevertheless, we believe that an appropriate court must make the final determination whether consent to sterilisation should be given on behalf of an incompetent individual. It must be the court's judgment, and not just the parents' good faith decision, that substitutes for the incompetent's consent.

Two further tests have been followed by the American courts, namely, the 'ability to parent' test and the 'substituted judgment' test.

Another test – the 'ability to parent' test

This test was laid down in two other cases in the USA. The first is *North Carolina Association for Retarded Children v State of Carolina* (1976) 420 F Supp 451, where the statute authorised both voluntary and involuntary sterilisation. The court applied the ability to parent test and ordered the sterilisation of a mentally retarded girl who 'probably' would have been unable to care for a child. However, the language of Holmes J in the *Buck v Bell* case was rejected. The court noted that medical and genetical experts are no longer sold on sterilisation to benefit either retarded patients or the future of the Republic.

The court further held that, in rare and unusual cases, it can be medically determined that involuntary sterilisation is in the best interests of either the mentally retarded persons, or the State, or both.

The second case is *Re Johnson* (1980) 45 NC App, where the court again utilised this test by asking if the incompetent person could provide minimum care for a child. The English courts have not adopted this test; *Re F* did not consider the ability to rear a child, although it was mentioned in *Re B* and in *T v T*. Certainly, *Re F* has no mention of balancing of different kinds of psychological trauma.

The substituted judgment test – *Re Grady*

This test, which was first proposed by the New Jersey Supreme Court in *Re Grady*, has been used by other American courts. As Scott explains, the purpose of the substituted judgment approach 'is for the decision maker to "step into the shoes" of the incompetent' in order to make a decision that 'subjectively reflects' what the patient's values and preferences would be if *were she competent* (Scott (1986), p 823, fn 56). The effect of *Re Grady* is that 'it directs the court to consider the *Hayes* criteria and any other relevant factors in order to make the decision that the incompetent person would have made for herself if she had been competent' (Scott (1986), p 823). It has been used for cases involving medical decisions where the individual has become incompetent and many decisions involved attempts to withdraw life sustaining treatment from terminally ill patients. The approach allows the court to take several factors into account, such as the family's moral and religious views, and preserves to some extent the incompetent person's choice. As far as it is able to, the court tries to ascertain the incompetent's views. This test was used earlier in *Re Quinlan* (1976) 70 NJ 10; (1976) 429 US 522 and *Re Parham* (1979) (*Parham v JR* (1979) 442 US 584). In *Re Quinlan*, the court considered the incompetent's past beliefs and opinions before she became legally incompetent. The New Jersey Supreme Court held that, in the case of a 21 year old woman in a persistent vegetative state, her father as her appointed guardian could exercise the decision on her behalf to withdraw life-sustaining treatment.

American courts have also applied this test to cases where the patients have never been legally competent (for instance, in *Superintendent of Belchertown State School v Saikewicz* (1977) 373 Mass 728, where chemotherapy was withheld from a severely retarded 67 year old man).

Ogbourne and Ward (1989) rightly point out that this test is not practical in the majority of cases because, in cases like *Re F* (see Chapter 6), there would be no period of competence upon which to base opinions as to the patient's beliefs and the mental age of the patient would make it difficult to ascertain valid views, indeed of any views that would be of any value in this form of speculative assessment. It is submitted that, for patients who had not been originally incompetent, unless there was very clear evidence of what their views towards the proposed medical treatment might have been, this seems like a highly speculative approach to adopt.

President's commission recommendations

A presidential commission, reporting in 1983, recommended that courts apply an objective best interest standard to carers' decisions for from persons who had never been competent, although the commission endorsed the substituted judgment approach for persons who had once expressed competent preferences (President's Commission for the Study of Ethical Problems in Medicine and Biomedical and Behavioural Research, *Substantive and Procedural principles of Decision Making for Incapacitated Patients* (1983), pp 179–88).

Canada

The case of *Re Eve* (1986) 31 DLR (4th) 1, decided in 1986, attracted considerable publicity, not least because it was cited as a leading overseas authority in the House of Lords' case of *Re B* (the *Jeanette* case), which was being decided after the *Eve* decision had been handed down. The brief facts and outcome have been mentioned in Chapter 6, but we now take a more detailed look at this case.

Re Eve *(1986) 31 DLR (4th) 1*

Facts

'Eve' was 24 years of age, suffering from extreme expressive aphasia. She was described as 'mildly to moderately retarded'. She had some learning skills, but only to a limited level. She was also described as being a pleasant and affectionate person who, physically, is an adult, quite capable of being attracted to, as well as attractive to, the opposite sex. Expressive aphasia was a described as a condition in which the patient is unable to communicate outwardly thoughts or concepts which she might have perceived. In the case of a person suffering from a degree of retardation, it was said that even an expert such as a psychiatrist is unable to determine with any degree of certainty if, in fact, those thoughts or concepts have actually been perceived, or whether understanding of them does exist. In the case of Eve, this condition has been diagnosed as extreme. When Eve was a child, she lived with her mother and attended various local schools, but when she reached 21, her mother sent her to a school for retarded adults in another community. Eve eventually struck up a close friendship with a male student who was also retarded, but somewhat less so than Eve. They even talked about marriage.

Eve's mother applied for permission to consent to the sterilisation of her mentally disabled daughter. One of the main arguments which the mother put forward was that, if Eve became pregnant, neither she nor Eve could look after the baby.

The trial judge concluded that Eve is not capable of informed consent, that her moderate retardation is generally stable, that her condition is probably non-inheritable, that she is incapable of effective alternative means of contraception, that the psychological or emotional effect of the proposed operation would probably be minimal, and that the probable incidence of pregnancy is impossible to predict.

The case therefore went on an appeal by the guardian *ad litem* to the Supreme Court of Prince Edward Island, which held that they were:

> ... unanimously of the opinion that the court has, in proper circumstances, the authority and jurisdiction to authorise the sterilisation of a mentally

> incompetent person for non-therapeutic reasons. The jurisdiction of the court originates from its *parens patriae* powers towards individuals who are unable to look after themselves and gives the court authority to make the individual a ward of the court.

MacDonald J took a different view of the facts and dissented in part. He also gave a more detailed account of the steps to be taken before reaching a conclusion one way or the other. There were 14 steps (summarised and turned into questions listed by Lee (1988) as follows: is the person mentally incompetent to give consent? Is the real object to protect the child (rather than the mother)? Is there evidence that the child is probably fertile? Is there any overriding public interest? Is there evidence that the child is of child bearing age and sexually active? Is there evidence that other forms of contraceptive have proved unworkable or inapplicable? Is there a real danger of pregnancy? Is there more compelling evidence than mental handicap itself that childbearing would have a psychologically damaging effect? Is there a likelihood of substantial injury to the individual if she becomes pregnant? Is there a danger that sterilisation will cause greater damage than it will bring beneficial effects? Does the parent or guardian agree with the sterilisation? Has there been presented to the court a comprehensive medical, psychological and social evaluation of the individual? Has the individual been represented in court by a specialist lawyer? Have the method and manner of the sterilisation been set forth? (See Lee (1988), p 16.)

However, the court differed on the evidence (by 2:1), but nevertheless ordered the sterilisation of Eve by a competent medical practitioner. Leave was then granted to the guardian *ad litem* to appeal to the Supreme Court of Canada.

The Supreme Court of Canada's judgment

The Supreme Court of Canada, comprising nine judges, held (*per* La Forest J, delivering the main judgment:

> The courts should never authorise a non-therapeutic sterilisation of a mentally retarded person under its *parens patriae* jurisdiction. The grave intrusion on the retarded person's rights and the certain physical damage that ensues from non-therapeutic sterilisation without consent, when compared to the highly questionable advantages that can result from it, lead to the conclusion that it can never safely be determined that such a procedure is for the benefit of that person.

The court agreed that, on occasion, sterilisation may be lawful as 'treatment of a serious malady'. However, they drew a vital distinction between 'therapeutic sterilisation' and 'non-therapeutic sterilisation'. In the course of the judgment, La Forest J discussed the English case of *Re D* [1976] 1 All ER 326, where Heilbron J made the crucial therapeutic/non-therapeutic distinction (see Chapter 6) and *Re B* (the *Baby Alexandra* case) [1982] 3 FLR 117, dealing with the Down's syndrome baby, where the English Court of Appeal had authorised the operation to clear an intestinal blockage despite the fact that the baby would have a life expectancy of only 20 to 30 years. This indicates the willingness of overseas common law courts to cite and apply principles and approaches from English courts and it offers an illuminating example of comparative law in the making. Somewhat tellingly, La Forest opined (p 29):

> There are ... reasons for approaching an application for sterilisation of a mentally incompetent person with the utmost caution. To begin with, the decision involves values in an area where our social history clouds our vision and encourages many to perceive the mentally handicapped as somewhat less than human. This attitude has been aided and abetted by now discredited eugenic theories whose influence was felt in this country [Canada] as well.

He also remarked that judges are generally ill informed about many of the factors relevant to reaching a wise decision in this difficult area. He believed that such judges may generally know little of mental illness, of techniques of contraception or their efficacy. Thus, however well presented a case may be, it could not give all the facts. Notably, he then opined that, 'If sterilisation of the mentally incompetent is to be adopted as desirable for general social purposes, the legislature is the appropriate body to do so'.

Comment

Despite having at their disposal a thorough, well considered, and painstaking review of the law in Canada as well as American and English jurisdictions, carried out over nearly seven years, and a comprehensive judgment in *Re Eve*, the House of Lords could not agree with the *Eve* approach and, indeed, said that the therapeutic/non-therapeutic distinction was *not* a helpful one, and that the welfare principle (in the way the court was applying it) was the only criterion to resolve these kinds of cases in English law. *Re Eve* itself remains an extremely useful case in terms of its approach and its guidelines from the provincial court stage, namely, the 14 steps suggested by MacDonald J. It is important to note that the Supreme Court of Canada confirmed that, under their *parens patriae* jurisdiction, they may authorise a sterilisation, but it has to be for a 'therapeutic' reason and must be exercised in the best interests of the child. A case that was also mentioned by the *Re Eve* court as germane to the issues before them was *Re K and Public Trustee.*

Re K and Public Trustee *(1985) 4 WWR 724*

In this case, the Court of Appeal of British Columbia ordered that a hysterectomy be performed on a seriously retarded child on the ground that the operation was therapeutic. The most serious factor considered by the court was the child's alleged phobic aversion to blood, which it was feared would seriously affect her when her menstrual period began. Notably, Anderson JA (p 275) declared: 'I say now, as forcefully as I can, this case cannot and must not be regarded as a precedent to be followed in cases involving sterilisation of mentally disabled persons for contraceptive purposes.'

Australia

Petersen (1996) reminds us that the issue of sterilising mentally incompetent women under 18 years of age became public when proceedings were initiated in the English courts in the mid 1970s and the Family Court of Australia more than a decade later. The legal framework for sterilisation of mentally handicapped girls in Australia was laid down in *Marion's* case (see below, p 507). This established that court or tribunal authorisation is required before any child can lawfully be sterilised unless sterilisation occurs as a by-product of surgery appropriately carried out to treat some malfunction or disease; and authorisation can be given only if sterilisation is in the child's best interests after alternative and less invasive procedures have all failed, or it is certain that no other procedure or treatment will work.

In the early cases, the major question for the Family Court of Australia was whether parents, as guardians, had the authority to authorise sterilisation operations without court involvement. Petersen (1996) selects four first instance cases of the Family Court as illustrations of the approach that has been adopted. *Re A Teenager* (1989) FLC 92-006; (1989) 94 Aust FLR 181; and *Re S* (1989) 98 Aust FLR 41 held that parents, as guardians, did not need court authorisation. In *Re S*, for example, Simpson J stated that parents, as guardians, did not have to seek the court's consent to carry out any medical procedure on a child, even if that entailed interfering with a basic human right and the main aim of the operation was non-therapeutic. He placed considerable emphasis on the rights of parents as carers and the fact that an application to court would involve additional financial strain.

However, *Re Jane* (1988) 94 Aust FLR 1 and *Re Elizabeth* (1989) FLC 92-023 held that court authorisation was required. The facts were very similar in these cases, but although the courts decided to allow the sterilisation to go ahead in each case, the judicial approaches were quite different. This conflict was resolved in the *Marion* case, but let us first look at these earlier cases before turning to *Marion*.

Re A Teenager *(1989)*

Facts

Here, an application was made by a 14 year old girl through her 'next friend' to restrain her parents from permitting a hysterectomy operation to be performed on her. She lived at home with her family and was assessed as having the mental ability of a two to three year old child. Since the brain damage had been caused by birth trauma, there was no concern about the transmission of disability. Although severely disabled intellectually, the girl's physical health and development were 'normal', but her mental ability was unlikely to improve in any significant way. She had a phobic reaction to blood and it was argued that menstruation would be likely to affect her development and her quality of life. It was assumed that she would never marry or enter into a relationship which would involve parenting and could not understand the process of conception and birth. It was also assumed that, if a sterilisation was authorised and she became pregnant, an abortion would be indicated. Non-medical witnesses (teaching professionals) claimed that the operation was premature and that other options had not been properly explored.

Her parents and her GP made the decision after a number of medical specialists had been consulted. The operation was to be performed by the GP, who had been caring for the family for about 10 years and who was familiar with the girl's health and well being. Shortly before the operation, the father discussed the procedure with a staff member at the government centre for the care of disabled people. He believed the decision was confidential. However, the staff member was vehemently opposed to the operation and it was assumed that the staff member was responsible for the initiation of proceedings.

The judgment

Before Cook J, evidence was given about a number of menstrual management and desensitisation programmes, but at the time of the hearing the child had not commenced menstruating. Her mother believed that it would be too stressful for her daughter to learn menstrual management skills and that her limited capacities would be better used learning basic hygiene, toileting and social skills.

Cook J concluded that authority for the procedure *could* be provided by the parents of a child and that judicial sanction was not required. He examined the rights of a family to make these kinds of decisions and the point at which a court should be allowed to intrude into the family unit. He recognised the point, made in *Gillick v West Norfolk and Wisbech AHA* [1986] AC 112, that parental authority was a dwindling right; however, he considered that, in most cases, including where decisions were made as to important medical treatment, the parents were the best judges of a child's welfare. Despite the evidence of various witnesses to the effect that other options had not been properly considered, Cook J was more inclined to follow the GP's recommendations based on the girl's phobic reaction to blood; the difficulties associated with attempts to give the child medication and injections; a full consideration of the effects of the hysterectomy on the girl's body compared to the unknown long term effects of hormonal pills and injections.

It would seem that the elimination of menstruation was the primary motive for the operation and Petersen argues that 'presumably this is why Cook J said this was not a sterilisation case – even though the removal of the uterus would have the effect of sterilisation' (Petersen (1996), p 62).

Re Jane *(1988) 94 Aust FLR 1*

This case was decided shortly after *Re A Teenager*; the facts were essentially the same, but the judgment does not mention the cause of the disability. The purpose of the operation was to prevent menstruation and the risk of pregnancy, even though Jane had not commenced menstruating. Here, the restraining order had been sought by the acting public prosecutor. Evidence was given by teachers, psychologists and social workers. It was again argued on behalf of the child that the operation was premature and that alternatives had not been adequately considered. However, the medical evidence was overwhelmingly in favour of a hysterectomy.

Nicholson CJ criticised the previous decision in *Re Jane*. He believed that the child's welfare should be paramount and disagreed with the emphasis that Cook J had placed upon the rights of parents. He was opposed to leaving these sorts of decisions to medical advisers and parents. In addition, he did not share Cook J's confidence that the medical profession would be able to protect the child by acting as a safeguard, recognising that there are members of the profession who might have misguided, albeit sincere views. As he said, 'Not all parents are wise and caring and not all medical practitioners are ethical and reasonable'. Indeed, he regarded parental consent as sufficient when the medical procedure involves interference with a basic human right such as procreation. Consequently, the court had to apply the best interests test. Section 60D of the Family Law Act 1975 provides: 'In proceedings ... in relation to a child, the court shall regard the welfare of the child as the paramount consideration.'

The reasons submitted for the operation were that Jane would experience difficulties in coping with menstruation, although she had not started menstruating at that point, and she was also at risk of sexual assault and of an unwanted pregnancy.

The chief justice conceded that it is sometimes difficult to distinguish between a therapeutic and non-therapeutic medical procedure, assuming that therapeutic procedures suggest treating a malfunction or disease, and acknowledged that a procedure can be performed for a mixture of reasons. He suggested that one way of overcoming this problem would be to ask whether the principal or major aim of the procedure has a non-therapeutic purpose, and if so, then the court's consent would be required.

The proposed hysterectomy was, nevertheless, approved because it was held to be in the child's best interests.

Marion's *case* (Department of Health v JWB and SMB) *(1992) Aust HC*

In 1992, the High Court of Australia considered the issue of non-consensual sterilisation of the intellectually disabled for the first time in the now well known *Marion* case (*Department of Health v JWB and SMB* (1992) 66 ALJR 300; (1992) 106 ALR 385).

Facts

The subject of this case was Marion, a pseudonym for a 14 year old intellectually disabled girl who suffered from severe deafness and epilepsy and an ataxic gait and 'behavioural problems'. She was not able to care for herself, nor to consent to being sterilised. Her parents applied for an order authorising a hysterectomy and ovariectomy; or alternatively a declaration that it would be lawful for them to consent to the performance of these procedures. A hysterectomy was proposed for the purpose of preventing pregnancy and menstruation with its psychological and behavioural consequences; an ovariectomy was proposed in order to stabilise hormonal fluxes with the aim of helping to eliminate consequential stress and behavioural responses.

The court had to consider:

(a) whether the parents themselves could consent to the sterilisation procedures; but if not

(b) whether the Family Court possessed jurisdiction to authorise the carrying out of the procedures.

A majority of the court answered the first question in the negative, but the second in the affirmative.

The dissenting views

Deane J, while broadly in agreement with the majority, identified certain rare cases where parental consent would suffice. There could be cases where the operation would be 'according to general community standards obviously necessary for the welfare of the child', where recourse to the courts would be unnecessary so as to reduce cost and delays of litigation. Brennan and McHugh JJ dissented from slightly different stances. Brennan J would have allowed parents to consent to a therapeutic sterilisation, but would otherwise have denied them the power to consent or the Family Court to authorise such a procedure. McHugh J was prepared to let parents have the jurisdiction to consent only if there was no possibility that the young person would acquire the capacity and maturity to choose whether she could be sterilised. He identified three situations where the circumstances would be sufficiently compelling to justify sterilisation of an intellectually disabled person: (a) where failure to perform the procedure 'is likely to result in the child's physical or mental health being seriously jeopardised'; (b) where failure to perform the procedure 'is likely to result in the suffering of pain, fear or discomfort of such severity and duration or regularity that it is not reasonable to expect the child to suffer that pain, fear or discomfort'; (c) where failure to perform the procedure 'is likely to result in a real risk that an intellectually disabled child will become pregnant' and where 'she does not, and never will, have any real understanding of sexual relationships or pregnancy'.

The Family Court would only have jurisdiction if there was a conflict of their own with their daughter's interests.

Deane J, in his minority judgment, suggested two categories in which surgery involving irreversible sterilisation will be, according to general community standards, obviously necessary for the welfare of the child. The first category was where surgery 'is immediately necessary for conventional medical purposes, that is to say, the preservation of the life or the treatment or prevention of grave physical illness'. The removal of cancerous ovaries or testicles would come within this category.

The second category he mentioned was that of the facts of *Re X* [1991] 2 NZLR 365. The 15 year old girl here was severely intellectually disabled. She had a mental age of about three months, could not speak, and was not toilet trained despite intensive efforts by both her family and the staff of the special school which she attended. She had 'no control whatever over her bodily functions'; she wore large napkins and had a habit of smearing urine and faeces around the house. She was, and would always remain, incapable of understanding menstruation, sexual intercourse and reproduction. The only indications that she gave of suffering pain were non-specific reactions, including fits of irritability, which could last for an entire day and involved threatening conduct and violence towards others and a degree of self-mutilation. Her reaction to menstrual pain was therefore likely to be uncomprehending irritability, violence and self-mutilation. Her parents sought the performance of a hysterectomy upon X to prevent the imminent onset of menstruation.

In this case, the court found that it was in the best interests of the girl to have an operation.

The majority opinions

A majority of the High Court (Mason CJ, Dawson, Toohey and Gaudron JJ) stated: 'The function of a court when asked to authorise sterilisation is to decide, whether, in the circumstances of the case, that it is in the best interests of the child. We have already said that it is not possible to formulate a rule which will identify cases where sterilisation is in his or her best interests.'

A therapeutic or non-therapeutic sterilisation – an important legal distinction

Six of the seven judges accepted that the distinction between a therapeutic and non-therapeutic sterilisation is, at the very least, a useful starting point for analysis. In their majority joint judgment, the majority judges hesitated to use the terms therapeutic and non-therapeutic because of their uncertainty (p 310), but remarked that it was 'necessary to make the distinction, however unclear the dividing line might be' (p 310). They accepted the distinction in *Re Eve*, the Canadian case (discussed *in extenso* in conjunction with *Re B* (the English case of *Jeanette*) in Chapter 6), that there is a legally relevant difference between performing a therapeutic and non-therapeutic sterilisation on an intellectually disabled person.

However, they did *not* agree (with La Forest J's view in *Re Eve*) that the non-therapeutic sterilisation of an intellectually disabled person is always legally impermissible.

The majority of the High Court held:

(a) It is always necessary to obtain court authorisation before a proposed non-therapeutic sterilisation may be lawfully performed upon a child.

(b) If the sterilisation is non-therapeutic, court authorisation is a necessary procedural safeguard of the interests of the child. That authorisation may only be given if it is in the child's 'best interests', in the sense that sterilisation is 'necessary to enable her to lead a life in keeping with her needs and capacities'.

(c) Sterilisation must always be viewed as a 'step of last resort' so that it may only be authorised if she is 'so disabled that other procedures or treatments are or have proved inadequate, in the sense that they have failed or will not alleviate the situation so that the child can lead a life in keeping with [her] needs and capacities.'

Incidence of sterilisation in Australia since the Marion case

According to figures collected from the Health Insurance Commission of Australia, since 1987, there have been about 1,358 girls sterilised and since *Marion's* case in 1992, 1,045 girls sterilised. The authors of the report, Susan Brady and Dr Sonia Grover, claim that these figures are probably an underestimate because they cover only sterilisations for which a Medicare claim has been processed. The figures therefore exclude:

- sterilisations other than by hysterectomy, tubal ligation and endometrial oblation;
- sterilisation by hospital doctors on girls who were public patients in public hospitals.

Effect of Marion's *case*

Since 1992, when *Marion's* case was decided, the Australian courts have authorised 17 sterilisations.

Re Marion (No 2) *(1994) FLC 92-448*

In this case, the Australian High Court had to decide on a highly dependent 14 year old girl suffering from severe intellectual and physical disabilities. In common with many of the other young women in these cases, she did not understand reproduction, nor could she cope with pregnancy or child rearing. However, this case differed from the other cases we have discussed in that the hysterectomy and ovariectomy were ordered for medical reasons, namely, to minimise her seizures and reduce the possibility of further brain damage.

Nicholson J held that the procedure was in the best interests of the child after considering strong medical evidence and overwhelming non-medical evidence in favour of the operation. He believed that the case probably fell into the category where the court's consent is unnecessary, since, on the facts, 'the procedure was required for medical and therapeutic reasons'. Petersen suggests that this poses a dilemma – 'how does a medical practitioner know if his or her diagnosis will be accepted as lawful until the diagnosis is validated by a court? Doctors may well be reluctant to go ahead with any non-therapeutic sterilisation in the absence of court authorisation – which of course can place great emotional and financial strain on all those involved' (Petersen (1996), pp 69–70).

Re L and M (Sarah's *case) (1993) 17 Aust FLR 357; (1994) 5 Med L Rev 94*

This case involved Sarah, another intellectually disabled 17 year old girl, whose parents sought authorisation from the Family Court of Australia to consent to a hysterectomy and ovariectomy on their daughter. The disability had been caused by birth trauma, so there was no question of eugenics in this instance. Sarah was dependent on her carers for all her basic needs and was doubly incontinent. She wore nappies at all times, was epileptic and her condition was not expected to improve. She had commenced menstruating and fertility was assumed. She had been in permanent care from a young age and her parents visited her four times a year. At the time of the hearing, she lived in a disabled persons' ward in a country hospital. However, future plans included moving to shared accommodation for disabled people where other residents and carers could be male. Her parents applied for authorisation to consent to Sarah's undergoing an abdominal hysterectomy to remove her uterus and cervix to help maintain hygiene, to control Sarah's epilepsy and to prevent pregnancy. They argued it was in Sarah's best interests to undergo the procedure and placed strong reliance on parental wishes and the 'weight' to which those wishes were entitled.

Warnick J refused the application, because:

(a) The court was *not* satisfied on the balance of probabilities, to a firm degree, that there was clear and convincing proof that sterilisation was in Sarah's best interests.

(b) The paramount principle with which the court was concerned was the best interests of the child.

(c) To say that a concept was the first and paramount consideration did not exclude other considerations, but merely subordinated them (*Storie v Storie* (1945) 80 CLR 597). In trying to apply such an observation to cases to be decided by the paramountcy principle, it was important to avoid treating the 'best interests of the child' as if that concept was of the same nature as the other values. The 'best interests of the child' was the perspective from which all other facts and values must be viewed. It was the legal principle which provided the focus of deliberation.

(d) There was no room in the final deliberation for the application of some other principle of law, for such a subordinate principle would always be subsumed into the paramount principle, and could only be properly applied when its application coincided with that of the paramount principle. The subordinate principle had no independent validity. Thus, there could be no 'legal presumption' attaching in these cases to the wishes of the parents. In this case, the parents were not involved in Sarah's daily care and there was no suggestion that their attitudes to, or interaction with, Sarah would change in any way depending upon the outcome of their application.

(e) The proposed procedure would not with any certainty (subject to the removal of the risk of pregnancy) increase Sarah's capacity to enjoy life or meet a presently unmet need. Expected improvements to hygiene would be minimal. Sterilisation would not improve Sarah's health. It was unnecessary to enable Sarah to move to residential style accommodation.

> It would not demonstrably improve the attitude towards Sarah of her carers. Whether the parents' wishes were met or not would not affect Sarah. Sterilisation may increase the risk of sexual abuse. With regard to pregnancy, to make a decision in this case in favour of sterilisation would be virtually equivalent to establishing a policy that all females with profound disabilities resembling those afflicting Sarah should be sterilised. There was nothing substantial about the risk, nor clearly detrimental to Sarah about pregnancy, which justified the interference with personal inviolability.

Thus, Warnick J found that there was insufficient medical evidence to justify authorisation of the sterilisation and he also remarked that some of the medical evidence was emotive. On balance, he found that the surgical risks and possible long term harmful effects of the procedure outweighed the benefits. A notable comment from the learned judge is his comment ((1993) 17 Fam LR 374) that '[p]regnancy itself is a number of steps removed from probability'. Fears that Sarah could be sexually abused by a male carer or fellow resident were also expressed in evidence. However, Mrs T, a qualified occupational therapist who was one of Sarah's teachers and had known Sarah for more than 10 years, advised that Sarah's problems with menstruation would not prevent her from being moved to residential accommodation if the opportunity arose and that there were sufficient safeguards built into the selection and monitoring of carers to provide adequate protection against sexual abuse. On broad policy grounds, he opined that 'To make a decision in this case, in favour of sterilisation, would be virtually equivalent to establishing a policy that all females, with profound disabilities resembling those afflicting Sarah, should be sterilised' ((1992) 17 Fam L Rep 374).

Following this case, in *P v P* (1994) 120 ALR 545; (1994) 19 Fam Law 1, the Full Court of the Australian High Court heard another case involving sterilisation and distinguished *Sarah's* case and *Marion's* case from their own. In addition, it clarified a constitutional issue that had been foreseen but not resolved in *Marion's* case.

P v P *(1994) 120 ALR 545*

Facts

L, aged 16, was intellectually disabled. Her mother sought an order permitting L to be sterilised, arguing that it was in L's best interests. They lived in New South Wales where sterilisations of girls of 16 or above, who were incapable of giving their own consent to sterilisation, was governed by conditions laid down in Part 5 of the Guardianship Act 1987 (NSW). Under the Act, the Guardianship Board (the Board) had authority to consent to sterilisation only where the Board was satisfied that it was treatment necessary to save the patient's life or prevent serious damage to the patient's health. The Act forbade the Board from giving consent to sterilisation in any other circumstances. In the event, Mr and Mrs P had not applied to the Board, but relied on the jurisdiction of the Family Court by virtue of Part VII of the Family Law Act 1975.

The case was in the nature of a case stated requiring five questions to be resolved by the Full Court. Most of the issues are procedural points of greater relevance to practitioners. The response to these questions was as follows:

(a) The Family Law Act 1975 (Cth) confers on the Family Court of Australia the power to make an order authorising a person to carry out on a child of a marriage medical treatment in New South Wales that was intended, or was reasonably likely, to have the effect of rendering the child permanently infertile, in circumstances where the carrying out of the treatment would otherwise be contrary to the Guardianship Act 1987 (NSW).

(b) Such purported conferral of power is consistent with Chapter III of the Commonwealth Constitution.

(c) Such conferral of power is a valid exercise of the legislative power of the Commonwealth Constitution.

(d) The Family Law Act 1975, by virtue of s 109 of the Constitution, invalidates the Guardianship Act 1987 (NSW) but only to the extent that s 35(1) of the Guardianship Act 1987 (NSW) would prohibit medical or dental treatment authorised by a competent order of the Family Court of Australia.

(e) Orders by the Family Court, as sought by the applicant in this case, provides a valid authority to a medical practitioner in New South Wales to carry out the procedure referred to.

The jurisdiction of the Family Court corresponded with the traditional *parens patriae* jurisdiction. It was not the Family Court's order which overrode the Constitution, but s 109 of the Constitution. The Board had no power to make a determination that would prevent or frustrate or interfere with an order of the Family Court.

The effect of this case is that the law on non-consensual, non-therapeutic sterilisation as stated in *Marion's* case is law throughout Australia. The Family Court in the exercise of its welfare jurisdiction may, therefore, authorise such sterilisations in accordance with the guidance laid down in *Marion's* case.

Australian legislation

The incapacitated minor

New South Wales and South Australia are the only two Australian States which have passed legislation relevant to the incompetent minor.

New South Wales

In New South Wales, the age of the child will determine which statute governs the possible sterilisation procedure. If the child is under 16, the appropriate Act will be the Children (Care and Protection) Act 1987 (NSW). Section 20B of the Act provides that a registered medical practitioner can only perform 'special medical treatment' on a child under 16 if that practitioner believes that it is necessary, as a matter of urgency, to carry out the treatment to save the child's life or to prevent serious damage to the child's health. Alternatively, the Australian Supreme Court can consent to the carrying out of the treatment, but only if it is satisfied that the treatment is necessary to save the child's life or prevent serious damage to health.

The words 'special medical treatment' are defined to include any medical treatment that is intended, or is reasonably likely, to have the effect of rendering permanently infertile the person on whom it is carried out. The Act concerning those under 16 appears to offer the most stringent of safeguards for the mentally incapacitated minor.

The Guardianship Act 1987 (NSW) concerns the mentally incapacitated person who is 16 or above. The carrying out of 'special treatment' is dealt with in ss 33(1) and 45(2) which provide that 'special treatment' can only be carried out with the consent of the Guardianship Board. The Board must be satisfied that the treatment is necessary to save the individual's life or prevent serious damage to health.

The exception to the requirement of the Board's consent is in s 37(1), where a medical practitioner who is carrying out or supervising the treatment believes that the sterilisation is necessary as a matter of urgency to save the individual's life or to prevent serious damage to health. Otherwise, sterilisation of children of 16 or above is prohibited. Up to January 1994, the Board had approved only one sterilisation for an applicant between 16 and 18. The wider 'best interests' test is not used by the Board and it does not examine the child's capacity to reproduce or other issues such as the quality of life expected for the child, as the main emphasis has to be on whether a sterilisation would be required to avoid serious damage to health.

South Australia

Part 5 of the South Australian Guardianship and Administration Act 1993 regulates the sterilisation of the mentally incapacitated person (both minors and adults). This provides that 'prescribed treatment' (which includes a sterilisation) can only be carried out on individuals incapable of providing effective consent if the South Australian Guardianship Board grants consent, otherwise any such sterilisation is an offence. Section 62 provides an exception, dealing with the situation where there are imminent risks to life or health. Section 61(2) states that the Board cannot consent to the sterilisation unless it is therapeutically necessary for the sterilisation to be carried out on the person. There is no definition of 'therapeutic'.

However, alternatively, the Board has to be satisfied that the person is unlikely to acquire at any time the capacity to give an effective consent, that the person is physically incapable of procreation, and that the person is, or is likely to be, sexually active. It would also have to be established that there was no method of contraception that could be applied successfully in those circumstances. If the woman is having social, sanitary or other problems relating to her menstruation, it would have to be shown that cessation of her menstrual cycle would be in her best interests and would be the only reasonably practicable way to deal with these problems. The Board must have no knowledge of any refusal to consent by the person concerned.

Germany

In the light of its history and experience of sterilisation under the Nazis, postwar Germany has regarded non-consensual sterilisation as a serious issue. Various attempts have been made by the legislature and courts to deal with this situation, from draft Bills to judicial pronouncements. After the unification of East and West Germany at the end of the 1980s, momentum has slowly begun to grow for the need to deal with several controversial situations such as sterilisation. Following the typical civil law country style, the preferred method of lawmaking is through legislation, usually via the enactment of comprehensive, authoritative and succinct codes. Hence, from 1 January 1992, the legal status of non-consensual sterilisation was clarified with the coming into force on that date of the new Carership Law 1990.

In an article published in 1990, Josephine Shaw submitted that there were three main lessons to be learned from the German experience in this controversial field:

(a) that open public debate culminating in a legislative measure can assist in raising public awareness and lead to more informed consideration of the issues;

(b) that a legislative measure, informed by the values of a written constitution containing guarantees of fundamental human rights, is likely to provide a more secure method of regulating sterilisation practice than a judicial law making process;

(c) that Parliament, if it were asked to consider these questions, may well be persuaded to enact stricter conditions than those now contained in *Re F* and *Re B* (see Shaw (1990), p 106).

The Carership Law – a new guardian in German law

In January 1992, the German legislature enacted the Carership Law (*Betreuungsgesetz: Gesetz zur Reform des Rechts der Vormundschaft und Pflegschaft für Volljährige* 12.9.90 (BGB) (the BtG)). This law amended paras 1896–1908 of the German Civil Code (*Burgerlischesgesetzbuch*) (BGB) by creating a new kind of guardian for physically and mentally disabled adults. This guardian will be known as a *Betreuer* or carer. The sterilisation of incompetent adults is now regulated by para 1905 of the BGB and is subject to the general principles of carership. The following discussion is based on a detailed analysis of this Law by Little (see Little (1997)).

The key duty of carership

The main duty of a carer as set out in para 1901(1) is that *a carer must act in a manner which promotes the best interests of the ward* (the term used for the patient, since the carer is the patient's guardian), whatever the scope of his duties to the ward might be. This duty applies to all carers. But, the duty under this law is not one that exists in the abstract, unlike English law, where the best interests test is always governed by the particular circumstances of the case and whose content, although guided by precedent, will change from case to case. At a number of points in the BtG, the welfare principle is actually 'fleshed out' into objective requirements, such as a specific duty being spelt out in para 1901(3) 'to act in a way which alleviates the illness or handicap the ward suffers from or to minimise its consequences or to prevent its deterioration'.

On the specific situation of sterilisation, para 1905 stipulates a procedure for authorising the sterilisation of mentally incompetent individuals without their consent. Proxy consent in a sterilisation case can only be justified on the basis that it facilitates the best interests of the individual. Unlike English law, it specifies criteria for determining when a non-consensual sterilisation is in the best interests of the individual. The requirements are cumulative and the proxy is bound by them.

The main objectives of the Carership Law

(a) There is to be no compulsory sterilisation (*Zwangsterilisation*) in Germany. If the individual is competent, compulsory sterilisation is defined as sterilisation carried out without the person's consent; if the person is incompetent, it can be defined as sterilisation carried out against that person's will.

(b) Non-consensual sterilisation is to be confined only to situations where the operation is 'medically indicated' – what common law writers would understand to be a therapeutic sterilisation. Under the legislation, this rules out sterilisation in the public interest, in the interests of relatives or carers and sterilisation in the interests of the unborn child (see Bt-Ds 11/4528, pp 73–79 and 142–45).

(c) If an individual is mentally incompetent, sterilisation must be the option of last resort only. This is the principle of proportionality. As a key objective, this rules out, *a priori*, sterilisation where the individual is (1) temporarily incompetent; (2) where less invasive forms of contraception are feasible; (3) the sterilisation of minors; and finally (4) the requirement of proportionality 'must presuppose a definite expectation of pregnancy before proxy consent can be justified' (Little (1997), p 272). The German courts have indicated that this is not merely a general requirement, but a prerequisite of sterilisation under para 1905. With the exception of the rule against sterilisation of minors, which is regulated under para 1631c of the BGB, all these other objectives are given effect under para 1905.

Paragraph 1905 reads as follows:

> (1) Where the medical intervention consists of a sterilisation of the ward in which the ward is unable to consent, the carer may only consent if:
>
> 1 the sterilisation does not contradict the will of the ward;
>
> 2 the ward will remain permanently incapable of giving consent;
>
> 3 it is to be expected that without a sterilisation a pregnancy will occur;
>
> 4 as a result of the pregnancy, a risk of danger to the life, or a risk of serious harm to the physical or mental health of the pregnant woman is to be expected, which cannot be reasonably prevented by any other means; and
>
> 5 the pregnancy cannot be prevented by any other reasonable means.

A serious risk to the mental health of the pregnant woman also includes the danger of serious and lasting distress which may threaten her, if Guardianship Court measures associated with the removal of her child, would have to be taken against her.

Consent requires the authorisation of the Guardianship Court. The sterilisation may only be carried out two weeks after the authorisation becomes effective. The preferred method of sterilisation is always that which allows for re-fertilisation.

It should be noted that para 1905 comes into play only if the ward is unable to consent to a sterilisation. Paragraph 1905 does not mention who is incapable of consenting, but the whole scheme of carership is that a carer will only be appointed to 'assist the ward' where it is strictly necessary to do so (see para 1901 of the BGB). As long as the ward (patient) is competent to consent to a sterilisation, she may do whatever her status is as a ward. The sterilisation would then be regarded as *freiwillig* (voluntary). Capacity to consent to a sterilisation requires that the ward is fully able to appreciate the nature and implications (*Art und Tragweit*) of the planned operation. This would be a matter for the doctor treating the ward to decide.

Paragraph 1905 applies only to contraceptive sterilisation. Hence, a hysterectomy would be classed as medical treatment of a type the carer is not ordinarily entitled to consent to, without first obtaining the court's authorisation under para 1904. This is because para 1904 prohibits the carer from consenting to medical treatment which could endanger the life of the ward or involve a risk of serious and permanent damage to her health unless the matter has been reviewed by the court. Authorisation would be given if the operation was necessary to remove a cancerous womb, in other words, if the operation was medically indicated. Under these circumstances, even a hysterectomy for the purpose of menstrual hygiene, as has been the case in England (see *Re E (A Minor) (Medical Treatment)* [1991] 2 FLR 585 and *Re GF (A Patient)* [1991] 1 FLR 293) is yet to be determined. Little (1997) suggests that it seems 'unlikely' that a hysterectomy 'purely on the grounds of menstrual hygiene would be authorised under para 1904' (Little (1997), p 274).

Two carers – the ordinary carer and the sterilisation carer

An innovation implemented by this new Law is to have two types of guardian or carer: the ordinary carer and the 'sterilisation carer'. The position is that, if a sterilisation is desired, an additional and separate carer must be appointed under para 1899(4) of the BGB. It is this 'sterilisation carer' who undertakes the arrangements for the sterilisation, informs the Guardianship Court and obtains specialist reports. He provides the proxy consent which creates a contract for the operation between the ward and the physician under para 164 *et seq* of the BGB, and also the proxy consent to what could otherwise be an aggravated assault under para 224 of the German Criminal Code. This separation of powers between the ordinary carer and the sterilisation carer is designed to prevent a conflict arising between the interests of the ward and the interests of immediate carers. However, in a case known as the *OLG Düsseldorf* decision (1995) (cited in Little (1997)), the ordinary carer was the mother of the ward and the sterilisation carer was the mother's sister. This latter appointment has been criticised (see Seitz, 1996, FGPrax, p 23, cited in Little (1997), p 274). Such carers are likely to be the parents of the ward, but research carried out by the Federal Ministry of Justice has shown that the majority of carers are attorneys. Little stresses that it is particularly important to note that local authorities, health authorities or any association acting as the carer of the ward, are not allowed to consent to a sterilisation (para 1900(5) of the BGB).

The grounds for sterilisation under the Carership Law

The grounds for sterilisation under the Carership Law are highly restricted. They are contained in para 1905(1)4 and para 1905(1)2. The grounds are confined to situations where the operation is necessary to safeguard the life or health of the pregnant woman and these are the only grounds upon which a proxy can consent to a sterilisation. Hence, no other reason will justify third party intervention in the bodily integrity, privacy and lifestyle of the ward.

Two requirements must be established:

(a) there must be a pregnancy;

(b) as a result of this pregnancy, there must be a risk to the life of the woman or a risk of serious harm to her mental or physical health.

Little (1997) points out that the wording in para 1905(1)4 is that of 'harm to the pregnant woman' and not 'pregnant ward', as the two need not be the same. It appears that the wording was deliberately made gender neutral so that the law allowed for the possibility of a mentally handicapped male to be sterilised. Little regards this as 'more theoretical than practical' because it is 'hard to see how a vasectomy can ever be in the best interests of the ward' (Little (1997), p 275). His argument is that, if the woman is competent herself, she should take her own contraceptive precautions before non-consensual invasive surgery is performed on her partner, but if she herself is incompetent and at risk of pregnancy, Little argues that 'surely it is in *her* best interests to be sterilised'. With respect, it must surely depend on the circumstances of the particular case. In the controversial English case of *Re B* (*Jeanette's* case (see Chapter 7)), the House of Lords decided that it would be in the 17 year old girl's best interests to be sterilised as she had been found in a 'compromising position' with a carer, but had a mental age of about five or six, and was perceived as in danger of becoming pregnant, a condition with which the court thought she could not cope. As the present author (and other commentators) argued, sterilisation would not protect her from rape or sexual exploitation. In the present context, surely *only* a therapeutic sterilisation should be justifiable.

Little (1997) observes that the danger of serious and lasting distress the woman might suffer if she had to be separated from her child would count as a risk to the mental health of the woman. The Law is clear, however, that if further medical treatment or counselling would remove this risk of danger to the woman's health, the carer may not consent to the sterilisation (Bt-Ds 11/4528, p 144). Of course, it may be that the potential mother has no maternal instincts and would not, therefore, bond with the child; here, the carer would not be able to establish any risk of serious or lasting harm to the ward. In other words, it does look as if non-consensual sterilisation in Germany is only possible if carried out on a therapeutic basis.

The wording of para 1905(1)4 and para 1905(1)2 suggests that this therapeutic intervention will invariably be prophylactic in nature. German law, in Little's view, therefore 'avoids the pitfalls of trying to categorise sterilisation into therapeutic and non-therapeutic treatment which has bedevilled English law' (Little (1997), p 276).

The role of the Guardianship Court

The 'sterilisation carer' will consent to the operation if the requirements of para 1905(1)1–5 are established, but under para 1905(2), the sterilisation carer's consent requires the authority of the Guardianship Court (*Genehmigung*). The procedural regulations of the court's involvement are regulated in the Non-Contentious Proceedings Law (*Gesetz über die Angelegenheiten der Freiwilligen Gerichtsbarkeit*) (FGG). There is a hearing to appoint a sterilisation carer, when an application is received. There, where feasible, the court must hear the ward personally in order to obtain an immediate impression of him or her. This would normally be held in the ward's usual surroundings (para 68(1) of the FGG). Before the court approves the sterilisation, it must receive reports on the ward's condition and prognosis from two independent specialists. The physician who performs the operation must not be involved in the authorship of these reports. Paragraph 69d (3) of the FGG also stipulates that the two reports must refer to 'medical, psychological, social, special-educational and sex-educational' needs of the ward.

The court must appoint an independent guardian *ad litem* (*Verfahrenspfleger*) to represent the ward in the sense of looking after her best interests, unless the ward has her own attorney. This is the duty of the court, but it will be someone independent and with experience of carership matters, such as a social worker, attorney or retired social worker. This appointee will defend the ward's interests in a very similar manner to the Official Solicitor in the High Court in England.

Once authorised, the sterilisation operation cannot take place until two weeks have elapsed from the date of approval. The court will also specify the type of operative technique which offers the best chance of re-fertilisation.

Comment on the German Carership Law

Under the scheme, the court must adhere to the five requirements of the Carership law and, in Germany, the legality of the doctor's non-consensual intervention depends on the strict adherence to legal rules and not on anything like a *Bolam* test ([1957] 1 WLR 582) in English law, namely, whether a responsible body of clinical opinion would have supported the doctor's medical intervention as being in the ward's best interests (see Chapter 8). Another noteworthy point is that, despite the issue of a new Practice Note or Practice Direction in England in 1996 in response to the latest case decided there, the German Carership is, on balance, more protective than the latest English position because the mere likelihood of sexual activity in the future would *not* be sufficient to justify non-consensual sterilisation in Germany.

Incidence of sterilisations in Germany and England

According to figures released by the German Federal Ministry of Justice to the German Parliament for the years 1992–94, there are still a very large number of sterilisations being carried out in Germany. Taking the last two years for which full returns are available, in 1993, the Guardianship Courts made 87 sterilisation orders, 22 refusals and 25 other actions were disposed of in some way; in 1994, there were 87 sterilisation orders, 12 refusals and 23 other disposals. According to the English Official Solicitor's Department, between 1986 and 1997, the Department has advised in 32 cases, without further action being taken, and has joined proceedings or sought applications in 57 cases. Since 1986, only 48 sterilisation orders have been made. Despite the difference in population – 80 million in the new unified Germany and about 55 million in England, there is still a notable number of sterilisations still being carried out in Germany.

Little (1997) speculates that one reason why there is a disparity in the figures is that in Germany, the Guardianship Court filters out the various applications so the figures will reflect the total number of applications, whereas in England, the Official Solicitor vets the applications, and if this department does not support the application, the parties will not start proceedings or simply terminate the action. Hence, by the time the case comes to court in England, sterilisation might almost be expected to take place. This might explain the total figures but, with respect, does not explain the high number of sterilisations that have been carried out in Germany.

COMPARATIVE OBSERVATIONS ON STERILISATION

While consensual sterilisation remains popular among competent adults, particularly, but not exclusively, females, as a form of contraception or as a symbol of their independence, non-consensual sterilisation retains the potential for controversy despite enhanced protection in England in the form of a Practice Note and the judicial exhortation that court approval should usually be sought before carrying out this sort of procedure. However, other countries have taken great strides in exorcising the spectre and history of eugenic sterilisation and this is surely a positive tendency, although the laws themselves are, as ever, open to interpretation. In this area, the USA, Germany and Australia have certainly shown the way forward to other countries of the world. The price of protection of the vulnerable, however, is constant vigilance and mechanisms must be in place to ensure that, as long as there are mentally incapacitated persons, they will, particularly in these sorts of situation, continue to receive the protection of the law.

SELECTIVE BIBLIOGRAPHY

Brazier, M, 'Sterilisation: down the slippery slope?' (1990) 6 Professional Negligence 25

Bryan, M, 'Two cheers for welfare: the *Marion* case and sterilisation in Australia' (1993) 5 J Child Law 40

Cica, N, 'Sterilising the intellectually disabled: the approach of the High Court of Australia in *Department of Health v JWB and SMB*' (1993) 4 Med L Rev 186

Cynkar, R, '*Buck v Bell*: felt necessities v fundamental values?' (1981) Colum L Rev 1418

de Cruz, SP 'Sterilisation, wardship and human rights' (1988) 18 Fam Law 6

Denekens, JP, Nys, H and Stuer, H, 'Sterilisation of incompetent mentally handicapped persons: a model for decision making' (1999) 25 JME 237

Devereux, J, *Medical Law: Text, Cases and Materials*, 1997, Cavendish Publishing. See, also, 2nd edn, 2001

Ford, J, 'The sterilisation of young women with an intellectual disability: a comparison between the Family Court of Australia and the Guardianship Board of New South Wales' (1996) 10 Aust J Fam Law 30

Freeman, MDA, 'Sterilising the mentally handicapped', in Freeman, MDA (ed), *Medicine, Ethics and the Law*, 1988, Stevens

Greer, G, *Sex and Destiny: The Politics of Human Fertility*, 1984, Picador

Isaacs, SL, 'Reproductive rights – 1983: an international survey' (1983) 14 Columbia Human Rights L Rev 311

Lee, S, 'From *D* to *B* to *T*: sterilising mentally handicapped teenagers' (1988) Jo Child Law 15

Little, G, 'Comparing German and English Law on non-consensual sterilisation: a difference in approach' (1997) 8 Med L Rev 269

Lombardo, P, 'Three generations, no imbeciles, new light on *Buck v Bell*' (1985) 60 NYUL Rev 30

Myers, D, *The Human Body and the Law*, 1971, Edinburgh UP

Norrie, McK K, 'Sterilisation of the mentally disabled in English and Canadian law' (1989) 38 ICLQ 387

Ogbourne, D and Ward, R, 'Sterilisation, the mentally incompetent and the courts' (1989) 18 Anglo-Am LR 230

Peterson, K, 'Private decisions and public scrutiny: sterilisation and minors in Australia and England', in McLean, S (ed), *Contemporary Issues in Law, Medicine and Ethics*, 1996, Dartmouth

Rhoades, H, 'Intellectual disability and sterilisation – an inevitable connection?' (1995) 9 AJFL 25

St John Stevas, N, *Life, Death and the Law*, 1961, Eyre

Scott, E, 'Sterilization of mentally retarded persons: reproductive rights and family privacy' (1986) Duke LJ 806

Shaw, J, 'Sterilisation of mentally handicapped people: judges rule OK?' (1990) 53 MLR 91

Shaw, J, 'Regulating sexuality: a legislative framework for non-consensual sterilisation', in McVeigh, S and Wheeler, S (eds), *Law, Health and Medical Regulation*, 1991, Dartmouth

Trombley, *The Right to Reproduce*, 1988, Weidenfeld & Nicolson

CHAPTER 16

MEDICAL MALPRACTICE IN OTHER COMMON LAW AND CIVIL LAW JURISDICTIONS

INTRODUCTION

In Part I, we looked at how English law deals with medical negligence, or medical malpractice as it is called in other jurisdictions. We turn now to consider how some other jurisdictions have dealt with this situation, giving special attention to the USA, Canada, France, Sweden and New Zealand.

In global terms, the liability of the physician (defined as generalists and specialists) may be classified as either contractual or non-contractual (see, generally, Tunc (1973)), but there is also another fundamental comparative point of distinction – the classification of negligent conduct within each country's legal structure.

MEDICAL MALPRACTICE – A PRELIMINARY COMPARATIVE POINT

It is important to realise that, although the following discussion synthesises common features from various jurisdictions – such as whether the liability owed is contractual or non-contractual, the standard of care expected from physicians, the criterion of professional negligence, and the effect of lack of consent – a key difference between the common law and continental (or civil law) legal systems is this. The common lawyer treats specific torts as independent and only slightly related to each other, although general principles apply to the establishment of a negligence action in common law countries (such as the existence of a duty of care; and a breach of that duty by the defendant which caused the injury or harm complained of); on the other hand, in continental countries, although their lawyers subdivide the cases which fall under the general clauses of para 826 of the BGB (Germany) and Art 1382 of the Civil Code (in Francophone countries), they deal in particular groups of case under a general clause. In other words, while recognising the differences in the cases, they approach the imposition of liability in damages on a reading of the same statutory text and on the fulfilment of its requirements. They will always tend to look, for example, for a causal connection between the defendant's alleged negligence and the plaintiff's injury. Under French law, Art 1382 of the Code Civil, for example, it is not enough to prove that the defendant committed a fault: it must appear that the injury was caused by that fault.

CONTRACTUAL LIABILITY – THE GENERAL POSITION

Countries with a basically contractual approach – where there is said to be a contract between physician and patient – include Central Europe (Switzerland, Germany, Austria), Greece, and the francophone countries, such as France itself, Belgium and Italy.

Central Europe and Greece

In Swiss law, the contract between physician and patient is classified as a mandate, whereas, in German and Greek law, it is seen as a contract for services. In the latter, the rules of mandate only apply to a gratuitous undertaking. When no contract exists between physician and patient, Central European laws base the physician's liability on extra-contractual rules, such as *negotiorum gestio* and tort. But, a requirement is that the physician must be treating the patient at the time, in which case the physician will be generally liable to the patient for any damage that may occur through defective performance.

Germany

The predominant view is that a contract for services is implicit in every specified surgical operation. However, a minority believe that it is a contract for work. Nevertheless, since it is not always possible to predict the outcome and results of an operation, this minority opinion concedes that 'what is owed is simply the immediate result of the work which is performance of the operation itself with proper skill and care, not a cure, nor even an improvement in the patient's health (*Tunc* (1973), p 7, and authorities cited therein). This interpretation performs the same function as the French distinction between mere obligations for prudence and diligence on the one hand and obligations for a specified result on the other hand. It needs to be remembered that the opinions of academic writers are accorded considerable weight in civil law countries and are even cited in their courts as evidence of the prevailing legal position on a given topic or issue.

France, Belgium and Italy

French and Belgian courts and the majority of legal writers acknowledge the possibility of a contract for medical services to exist between physician and patient. This contract has been recognised as the basis for the physician's claim to fees. Most legal writers believe that this is a variation of the contract for work. It is instructive to note that, whilst admitting the contractual character of the physician's liability, the French Cour de Cassation has expressly stated that this is a contract *sui generis* (*contrat innomine*) (Tunc (1973)). The classical decision of 20 May 1936 by the Cour de Cassation established the view that the relationship between the physician and his client is contractual and results in an obligation not to cure the patient, but to offer him medical help conscientiously and diligently, in conformity with the data and advances of medical science. In a decision of 28 June 1960, the same court declared that the care given must conform to the current data and advances of medical science, so that the current level of scientific progress should be taken into consideration. A breach of this contractual obligation entails liability of a contractual nature. Both French and Belgian courts have accepted this view.

Non-contractual liability is only relevant where damage is caused to a third party or where services are rendered to a patient in a hospital or clinic when the patient is not in a position to consent to the treatment.

The burden of proof (as in English law) lies on the plaintiff patient, to prove that conscientious and diligent medical care in conformity with the rules and data of science has not been provided. However, proof of this failure is sufficient to establish the physician's failure to perform his obligation.

We now look more closely at the French position.

France

Dual systems – the public/private law divide

As a civil law country, France has a public law/private law divide which does not exist in England and Wales. This means that the court system splits the civil (private) law courts from the administrative (public) law courts. In effect, the substantive law applied by the administrative law courts is an entirely separate body of law from that applied by the private law courts, hence there is no necessary similarity between the standard of care expected of medical practitioners in private practice and those employed by the State: for example, those who work in State run hospitals. Hence, the principles of public law would apply to the State hospitals, but private law rules would govern doctors in private practice.

The administrative law courts are arranged in three tiers. The administrative tribunals are the courts of first instance; between these and the *Conseil d'Etat*, which is the supreme administrative court, are the new administrative courts of appeal. This system was implemented in 1989 when the administrative courts of appeal were created. There is, therefore, now a filtering system between the administrative courts of appeal and the *Conseil d'Etat* which will only allow the more important cases to be heard by the *Conseil d'Etat*. The administrative law courts deal with matters which involve the State, including public authorities and public servants, and the civil courts deal with all other matters. The classical doctrine of separation of powers is the basis of the public/private law divide, but the executive is subject to judicial authority to be exercised by a body separate from the ordinary (civil law) courts. The ordinary courts have no jurisdiction over the executive. Hence, a vast number of matters, which would be dealt with by private law principles in the common law jurisdictions, are dealt with by the administrative law courts.

Hence, the actions of medical practitioners employed in State hospitals are dealt with under administrative law principles. As far as substantive law is concerned, the principles utilised by the administrative courts and the ordinary courts to settle a case like a negligence action are often similar. But this was not the case in relation to the standard of care required of medical practitioners employed by the State, until the 1992 case of *M et Mme V* was decided. Up until this case, the standard of care required under private law principles was simply not the same as under public law rules.

The fundamental division of non-contractual liability in French public law is between *no fault* and *fault based liability*. No fault liability is based on the risk theory and is the most expansive form of liability. Liability for fault is also divided into two: (a) liability for 'simple' fault; and (b) liability for 'gross' fault, which applied to the kinds of acts which would be considered to indicate a *complete lack of responsibility*. These categories were developed case by case by the administrative courts. The general principle which these courts followed was that a medical practitioner employed by the State would be liable for fault only when his or her actions were such as to constitute 'gross' fault, on the premise that it was necessary to preserve the autonomy of decision makers and those engaged in so called 'complex' activities. These include the running of the prison service, irrespective of whether the person who suffers damage is a prison inmate or a third party, the provision of emergency services, and certain functions of local government, such as finance. Until the *Mme V* decision, medical negligence was also included.

Rene Chapus, in *Droit administratif general*, 1987, Padfield, N (trans) (1993), p 909, fn 11) suggests three reasons why the autonomy of decision makers and those engaged in 'complex activities' is protected by this doctrine of 'gross' fault:

(a) such activities are, by definition, difficult, and so a greater degree of fault will be excusable than in simpler activities;

(b) otherwise, there would be a tendency to hesitate in the execution of public law functions; and

(c) the effective carrying out of public duties would be hindered.

Padfield (1993) points out that certain activities such as 'the day to day running of hospitals, and general nursing care, including activities such as taking blood samples, have never been within these 'gross fault/complex activities'.

The duties for a medical practitioner in private practice derive from the contract between the doctor and the patient, under which a doctor agrees to treat the patient with reasonable care and to do his best to cure the patient, according to modern medical science. Case law shows that expert evidence will be adduced at a trial to establish whether or not the treatment prescribed by the doctor accorded with modern medical knowledge. If it is established that the method of treatment has been overtaken by modern scientific developments, the medical practitioner will be liable in damages (see Padfield (1993), citing *Civ 1st 12 Nov 1985: Bull civ No 299; Rev trim dr civ 1986, 764, obs Huet*). In return, the patient agrees to pay the doctor's fee. Hence, although the doctor's duty of care towards his patient is contractual, it is not strict. Thus, a doctor will be liable for a breach of the contractual duty if he does not take reasonable care in treating a patient, or if he makes a negligently wrong diagnosis, or does not take account of modern scientific knowledge. Padfield therefore explains:

> ... in practice, this means that a mistaken diagnosis will constitute breach of contract where a reasonable and careful doctor in the doctor's situation would not have made the error. Since the duty is to use best endeavours, the standard of care demanded will vary according to the means available to the medical practitioner [Padfield (1993), p 910].

Contrary to what appeared to be settled practice, *M et Mme V* was decided in 1992 on 10 April, and illustrates a change in the jurisprudence of the *Conseil d'Etat* with regard to the standard of care expected of medical practitioners.

M et Mme V (1992)

On a preliminary note, the hospital in which the operation was carried out on Mme V was a State hospital. The liability of the anaesthetist involved is therefore classified as a public law issue which would have to be determined by administrative law principles.

Facts

On 9 May 1979, the medical opinion was that an epidural anaesthetic should be administered to Mme V, who was pregnant. It was also decided that the baby should be delivered by Caesarean section. A scan revealed that the placenta was displaced and there was, therefore, a risk of haemorrhage, with a consequent risk of heart failure. Epidural anaesthesia carries a risk of low blood pressure and, before the start of the operation, the anaesthetist administered the epidural anaesthetic and another drug which was contra-indicated, given its blood pressure-lowering effect. This produced a second drop in blood pressure, After the Caesarean, Mme V suffered a haemorrhage and, consequently, a third drop in blood pressure. She was given a transfusion of frozen plasma, which proved to have been warmed up insufficiently, and which caused a heart attack. As a result, Mme V suffered serious neurological and physical damage.

The *Conseil d'Etat* judgment

The *Conseil d'Etat* held that a doctor or surgeon will be liable for 'fault' where his or her actions constitute 'medical fault of such a kind as to engage the liability of the hospital' (see Padfield (1993), p 911). Padfield argues that this is a somewhat circular definition and of little use in itself. The line of cases before this case suggested that there were sufficient precedents to suggest that this was not a case in which the *Conseil d'Etat* would usually have held the medical practitioner liable, because, as Padfield points out, 'the 'fault' was not serious enough to constitute 'gross' fault (Padfield (1993)). It might have been suggested that the actions of the anaesthetist were a series of 'simple' faults, and the *Conseil d'Etat* could well have decided that a series of such faults amounted to 'gross' fault. But, the court did not choose to adopt this line of reasoning.

Principle

The *Conseil d'Etat* decided that, in order to succeed in an action for negligence against a medical practitioner employed by a State hospital, it is necessary only to prove 'simple' fault by the practitioner and not 'gross' fault. In the case before it, it was therefore prepared to award damages against a surgeon in a case where previously it would have demanded 'gross' fault. Hence, the standard required has changed.

Damages were awarded to both plaintiffs, M and Mme V. Mme V had suffered serious physical and neurological damage as a result of the operation. She was 33 years old and had been a secondary school teacher. Despite a lack of evidence regarding her salary before the operation, the *Conseil d'Etat* awarded Mme V damages amounting to 1 million francs, plus interest. Her husband was awarded damages for mental suffering as a result of his wife's experiences and for the fact that his lifestyle had changed since he now had to look after the couple's three children. He was awarded 300,000 francs, plus interest.

The jurisprudential point that arises from this case is that the standard of care relating to medical negligence for a doctor employed by the State is now in greater accord with that expected of a physician in private practice.

Italy

Under the Italian Civil Code of 1942, the relationship between a physician and a client is treated as contractual and subject to the provisions of the special chapter on intellectual professions (see Arts 2229–38 of the Civil Code).

THE 'NON-CONTRACTUAL' COUNTRIES

The non-contractual approach applies in common law countries, Scandinavia, Japan and the former Socialist countries of Eastern Europe.

Scandinavia

In Scandinavian law, no consensus has been reached among doctrinal writers on whether the physician's liability is to be classified as contractual or tortious. No Scandinavian country has any legislation governing physician's liability. The case law has to be considered and this shows that the physician's profession is subject, at least in principle, to the general rules of the law of negligence. Hence, a physician is liable in damages when he has failed to maintain the safeguards of a competent and conscientious practitioner, and this has resulted in injury to the patient.

Japan

In Japan, a negligent physician is liable to the patient in tort under Art 709 of the Civil Code. A patient also has the right to sue on the ground of the doctor's breach of contract under Art 415 of the Civil Code, but, in practice, such suits are rare.

Socialist countries

In many socialist countries, where, since 1989, there has been wholesale rejection of communist principles, the majority of physicians are employed by State owned hospitals or polyclinics. This means that the hospital alone is liable to the injured person under civil law, and this will usually be a contractual liability. The physician is only liable to the hospital, under the rules of labour law.

DEGREE OF CARE OWED

In France, Switzerland, Italy, Germany, and Greece, the general principle is that physicians are not liable for 'slight negligence'. This view has been supported in the French lower courts, Swiss law (see BG 20 Feb 1940, 12 Dec 1961, BGE 87 II 372), in Italian case law in emergencies and serious cases, and in Art 2236 of the Italian Civil Code relating to intellectual professions, and in the German Civil Code. In para 680 of the said German Code, it stipulates that a person who acts in an emergency with a view to averting a hazard to another person shall be liable only for fraud or gross negligence, not for slight negligence. A similar provision is to be found in Art 732 of the Greek Civil Code. As Tunc explains, this principle takes account of the 'nature of emergency conditions under which the medical practitioner has to perform his functions and the unforeseeable circumstances and factors involved' (Tunc (1973), p 14).

The general standard – the 'reasonable medical practitioner'

In practically all countries, the general rule requires a physician to exercise his best ability, skill and care which should not lie below that care that would be shown in the circumstances by a reasonable, careful physician. As a general principle, the doctor would, therefore, be liable for any negligence in the performance of his medical functions. As a general rule, the concept of negligence makes allowances:

> ... for such specific circumstances as the urgency of the situation, the impossibility of transportation to a hospital, the scantiness or complete lack of drugs, instruments or disinfectants, and even the physician's frame of mind as affected by the pressure and other stress conditions. Only in the light of all these specific circumstances can it be determined whether or not negligence exists [Tunc (1973), p 14].

SCOPE OF THE DUTY OF CARE

The notion of 'good medical practice' or what is 'customary and usual in the profession' is the standard which is adhered to by various countries. This, of course, is somewhat broader, though not dissimilar to, the well known *Bolam* test ([1957] 1 WLR 582) in English law (see Chapter 7 on medical negligence in UK law), which requires a doctor to act as any reasonably competent practitioner skilled in that particular field or art would act. Of course, if it is alleged that an injury or death has been caused by the negligence of a physician, expert opinion will be required to ascertain the conduct and, therefore, the extent of the physician's negligence in deviating from the standard of conduct required by the diligent physician.

For over 40 years in English law, the so called *Bolam* test, decided in 1957, has been the leading case, despite it being a first instance decision. This initially found favour in non-European common law jurisdictions like Malaysia, but not in jurisdictions like Canada, although *Bolam* has recently been questioned, or at least 'clarified', by the House of Lords in *Bolitho*, which seemed to say that it has always been possible to question a particular medical opinion if it was found to be 'illogical' or 'unreasonable' even if it was supported by a responsible body of medical opinion.

CRITERION OF PROFESSIONAL NEGLIGENCE

In most modern legal systems, the criterion of negligence is objective. The standard is that of the 'prudent and competent physician'. In nearly every country, in defining this standard, account is taken not of any individual qualities of any specific physician as such, but of the typical qualities of skill and learning commonly possessed by members of the profession in good standing. In essence, a physician must not only exercise reasonable care, but also attain the standard of a reasonably competent practitioner. This principle can be discerned in Greek legislation (Art 652 of the Civil Code) and Swiss legislation. The standard is not a subjective one, as the standard is that of the prudent and competent physician, and a physician who fails to diagnose a disease will not be excused on proof that he acted to the best of his skill, if a reasonable physician would be expected to have made a correct diagnosis. However, the issue for the court will be: what would have been the conduct of a prudent and competent physician in the given specific circumstances?

EFFECT OF LACK OF CONSENT ON PHYSICIAN'S LIABILITY

Apart from malpractice, the other classical category of the physician's liability comprises cases where surgical or other treatment is applied without the consent of the patient. In brief, all legal systems generally recognise that the physician has no right to examine or treat a patient without his consent. The issue of consent has been dealt with in separate chapters; however, it is relevant in the present context simply to point out that, if a patient suffers injury or damage as a result of a poor standard of treatment, the plaintiff's lawyer may advise her to proceed on the basis of unauthorised treatment rather than negligence, which is more difficult to prove. Hence, actions for assault and battery would be brought against the doctor, where negligence might have been the more obvious cause of action.

United States

The American legal culture: background to American negligence law

In a textbook by Markesinis and Deakin, *Tort Law* (1999), p 203 *et seq*, Professor DW Robertson, a guest writer, points out that there are at least three major differences between the legal cultures of England and that of America. First, the USA has *no unified law of negligence*, but has at least 52 discrete (that is, separate and distinct) and autonomous systems, and each of the 50 States has its own tort law. Apart from the system in each State, federal maritime law is another distinct 51st system and the 52nd system is a federal common law of torts that supplements national legislation on matters such as anti-trust. Some commentators even count a 53rd system in the 'conglomerate of statutory and common law dealing with the tort liability of the federal government' (see Shapo, *Towards a Jurisprudence of Injury: The Continuing Creation of a System of Substantive Justice in American Tort Law: Report to the American Bar Association* (1984)). Further, the legislature and highest court in each State both have the power to determine the private law in that State. The federal court decisions, including the US Supreme Court, are not binding on private State law, but are merely persuasive (as stated in *State v Perry* (1992) 610 So 2d 746 (Louisiana), where the court said that it is the 'final arbiter' of the meaning of the State constitution and laws). Hence, even a US Supreme Court decision is not representative of the American law of negligence any more than a New York law by that State's highest court. However, although independent of each other, these States 'share common policy goals', declares Robertson, and 'strive for common outcomes'. Thus, these courts routinely cite one another's authorities. Robertson, therefore, calls the American law of negligence 'international comparative law'. However, Americans appear to be reconciled to the divergences between the States.

Second, Robertson highlights the *'pervasive use of juries'* in American negligence cases, applying to 49 States, so that the American trial judge has a central role in determining which issues are for the jury and how to instruct the jury on those issues. In England and Wales, the judge determines issues of fact and issues of law. Robertson therefore makes a repeated plea for consistency, solidity, clarity and firmness precisely because of the huge number of trial judges who perform these functions daily in the USA.

Thirdly, there is a difference in the way the American system compensates plaintiffs' lawyers. The American tort plaintiff almost always pays his lawyer nothing out of pocket. The client and the lawyer agree that the lawyer will take a percentage out of whatever can be recovered from the defendant. Thus, this 'contingency fee agreement' would be illegal in England, but is common practice in America. The salutary benefit of the American system is that it encourages the less fortunate and lower income-earning people to have access to the courts. However, Robertson argues that this is 'outweighed by the flood of silly, vindictive, or purely mercenary litigation' that could ensue if plaintiffs' lawyers do not exercise extremely tight discipline in deciding which cases they will accept.

Requirements of a negligence action in American law

There are five elements required to be proved by a plaintiff in a negligence action:

(a) existence of duty;

(b) breach of that duty;

(c) factual causation;

(d) legal causation; and

(e) damages are due to the plaintiff as a result of that breach of duty.

The first element is for the judge to determine, but the others are for the jury to decide.

American malpractice law

As in English law, medical negligence is a species of the tort of negligence. This is why the usual elements of the tort apply – duty, breach, causation, remoteness and damage. American courts recognise the right of an injured person to seek recovery from an incompetent or negligent doctor, upon whose services or special skill the injured party has relied. However, American courts have displayed disagreement and inconsistency regarding the theory underlying actions for malpractice. Basically, actions in medical malpractice were based both in tort and contract. Thus, some of the early decisions, made before the onset of any fully developed theory of negligence as a separate basis of action, held that a physician would be liable in *tort* for malpractice, whenever foreseeable, unreasonable risk of personal injury to the plaintiff was involved. On the other hand, more recent decisions founded the action on a *'contractual'* undertaking of a person holding himself out as belonging to a certain profession to exercise his profession with the skill commonly possessed by those engaged in it. More recent cases have said that negligence is the basis of liability, and a 1959 Circuit Court of Appeals in *Kozan v Comstock* (1959) 270 F 2d 839, p 844 described the malpractice action thus:

> It is true that usually only a consensual relationship exists and the physician agrees impliedly to treat the patient in a proper manner. Thus, a malpractice is inextricably bound with the idea of breach of implied contract. However, the patient-physician relationship, and the corresponding duty that is owed, is not one that is completely dependent upon contract theory ... On principle then, we consider a malpractice action as tortious in nature whether the duty grows out of a contractual relation or has no origin in contract.

This appears to represent the majority view. About five years later, in *Billings v Sisters of Mercy of Idaho* (1964) 86 Ida 485; (1964) 389 P 2d 224, p 230, a court in Idaho expressed the rule in the following terms:

> The gist of a malpractice action is negligence and not a breach of the contract of employment, While the contract rule is still used occasionally ... it is generally recognised as being more of a device than a valid rule of law.

However, the *mere refusal* of a physician in breach of an agreement, to treat a patient, or to perform his service in a particular manner, supports only an action in contract. In *Stewart v Rudner* (1957) 349 Mich 459; (1957) 84 NW 2d 816, a woman, having had a stillborn delivery, was permitted to recover contractual damages for a physician's failure to perform a Caesarean section which had been agreed upon by the parties. In 1969, in *Howell v Carpenter* (1969) 19 Mich App 233; (1969) 172 NW 2d 549, a surgeon was found liable for breach of contract by allowing another surgeon to operate on his patient.

From a comparative point of view, there is no right in England and Wales, or under English law, for a patient to have his or her operation performed by a specific surgeon and the consent form which patients usually sign makes no undertaking that a specific surgeon will perform the operation. Hence, American law is again different on this point, presumably because of the element of a contract and the fact that medical services are paid for within this contractual framework.

It is generally accepted that a physician does not promise or undertake to accomplish an absolute cure when he undertakes to treat a patient (see, for example, *Watterson v Conwell* (1952) 258 Ala 180; (1952) 61 So 2d 690), hence any breach of specific agreements for guaranteed results or cures or of duties which are purely contractual as well as those which impose higher standards of care are actionable on a contractual basis (*Hawkins v McGee* (1929) 84 NH 114; (1929) 146 A 641).

In general, a physician can always be sued in tort by a patient if the physician has undertaken to treat the patient and has been negligent or failed to comply with accepted standards (*Yeager v Dunnavan* (1946) 26 Wash 2d 559; (1946) 174 P 2d 755).

In Texas, in 1991, the issue of when a doctor-patient relationship comes into existence was addressed, as was the question of whether the physician in question had agreed to treat or even examine the patient in question. This case, *Fought v Solce* (1991), was a decision of the Texas Court of Appeals.

Fought v Solce *[1993] Med LR 256*

In this case, the plaintiff was brought to a hospital emergency room after being involved in a road accident. The emergency room physician who first examined him stabilised the plaintiff's condition and determined that he would need to consult an orthopaedic specialist concerning further treatment. He telephoned the defendant, who was the orthopaedic specialist on call, twice at home and asked him to come to the hospital to examine the plaintiff. The defendant refused. The plaintiff brought an action in negligence against the defendant, alleging that this refusal and resulting delay in treatment caused the eventual amputation of his leg. The trial court granted summary judgment in favour of the defendant. The plaintiff appealed.

The Texas Court of Appeals dismissed the appeal and held:

(a) a physician can be held liable for his negligence only where a physician-patient relationship exists;

(b) in the absence of an agreement between a physician and an individual, the physician has no duty to treat the individual;

(c) no prior physician-patient relationship existed between the defendant and the plaintiff. Further, no such relationship was created by the fact that the defendant had volunteered to be 'on call' at the hospital. The defendant was, therefore, under no duty to treat the injured plaintiff. In the absence of this duty, an essential element of the plaintiff's cause of action was missing and the defendant was entitled to summary judgment in his favour.

Medical malpractice law in the USA – dealing with the problems

Medical malpractice law in the USA is apparently in a state of 'crisis'. The reasons for this have been identified by Grubb (1999) as 'jury trials, huge contingency fees, absence of a developed social welfare system and a greater availability of punitive damages'. The American malpractice system has been described as a system comprising 'physician liability insurance, the use of the courts, and physician-dominated public disciplinary organisations'. Most court suits do not compensate patients. Physicians' insurance premiums are rising, yet do not appear to constitute a significant proportion of physicians' income. The crisis was sparked off by the dramatic rise in medical malpractice insurance premiums which generated forceful State lobbying on the part of medical societies, hospitals, and the insurance industry to change State laws and control court awards in medical liability cases. The number of malpractice cases has risen dramatically in the last 10–15 years in terms of the numbers of medical malpractice suits by patients.

During the 1970s and 1980s, various State legislatures in the USA attempted to reduce awards and settlements in medical liability cases by limiting specific types of damages, for instance, by limiting the amount recoverable for non-economic losses, instituting arbitration, limiting the amount on the total recovery amount that malpractice victims could receive, providing for periodic payments of damages, and trying to prevent multiple sources of compensation to injured parties.

By the autumn of 1986, 36 legislatures from Alabama to Wyoming had enacted medical malpractice reform statutes. The variety of approaches included: limiting non-economic awards, limits on total amounts of awards, prohibition of payment for punitive damages, the abolition of joint and several liability, reduction of joint liability, control over contingency fees, mandatory arbitration, risk management loss prevention, institution of pre-trial screening panels and increased regulation of the insurance industry.

Canada

The *Bolam* case never found favour in Canada. In 1949, in *Anderson v Chasney* [1949] 4 DLR 71, the Manitoba Court of Appeal held that, if the doctor's plea that he acted in conformity with general practice was to serve as a complete answer to any claim against him 'a group of operators by adopting some practice could legislate themselves out of liability for negligence ... by adopting or continuing what was obviously a negligent practice' (*per* Coyne JA). As we have already seen in *Reibl v Hughes* [1980] 114 DLR (3d) 1 (Can Sup Ct), the Supreme Court of Canada has stated that, when it comes to informing a patient so as to obtain consent to treatment, the doctor's duty is to pass on that information which a reasonable patient would wish to know, and not merely that which doctors might find appropriate.

Ireland

An Irish legal perspective

Until recently, it had been rightly observed that medical malpractice suits were a 'rarity in Ireland' (Murphy, 'No fault compensation for medical negligence' (1989) 9 ILT 216). However, between 1984 and 1994, this situation appears to have changed dramatically. Two landmark cases, *Dunne* and *Walsh*, reached the Irish Supreme Court, the latter shadowing developments in the UK on the difficult issue of 'informed consent' (see Symmons (1994)).

O'Donovan v The County Council of the County of Cork [1967] IR 173 is the Irish *Bolam*. Lavery J declared therein that the principle on the medical standard of care was 'well settled and is the same in the Courts of England, Scotland and Ireland'. However, UK precedents are only generally followed if there are no Irish precedents, and this is well illustrated by the *Dunne* case (1989), discussed below). However, in contrast, in the Irish case of *Walsh v Family Planning Services and Others* [1992] 1 IR 496, the leading English case of *Sidaway* [1985] 2 WLR 480 (discussed *in extenso* in Chapter 7) is clearly cited with approval.

Two trends have been identified in Irish law (by Symmons (1994)) on medical negligence in the past 14 years or so:

(a) Some cases suggest that the pendulum of Irish negligence has swung, even to the extent of being anti-medical. An example is the case of *Lindsay* (1993) 13 ILRM 350, where the doctrine of *res ipsa loquitur* was applied for the first time in Ireland to medical negligence which appeared initially to foreshadow a strict liability trend before being reversed by the Supreme Court. Irish law also imported strict liability by sidestepping the tort of negligence by using 'stricter liability' torts as in *Walsh*. Yet another strict liability trend is discernible in *Dunne's* case.

On the other hand, *dicta* from Finlay CJ in *Dunne's* case also suggest that the Irish judiciary do not perceive any trend towards strict liability. He commented:

> The development of medical science and the supreme importance of that particular development to humanity makes it particularly undesirable and inconsistent with the common good that doctors should be obliged to carry out their professional duties under frequent threat of unsustainable legal claims. The complete dependence of patients on the skill and the care of their medical attendants and the gravity from their point of view of a failure in such care, makes it undesirable and unjustifiable to accept as a matter of law a lax or permissive standard of care for the purpose of assessing what is and what is not medical negligence. In developing the legal principle outlined ... the courts must constantly seek to give equal regard to both of these considerations.

In addition, there has been strong reference in Irish case law on medical negligence to the general law of negligence, which was even evident in the leading case of *O'Donovan*, where Lavery J said: 'There is no real difference between the law of negligence to be applied in such a [medical] case and the general law which requires that a person ... shall discharge that duty with reasonable care, and if he is a person claiming a special knowledge or skill, he shall possess such knowledge or skill in a reasonable degree and will use it.'

The Dunne *case (*Dunne v The National Maternity Hospital and Another*) [1989] IR 91*

This landmark Irish case went to the Supreme Court in 1989. Here, an infant plaintiff (through his mother) claimed negligence against the medical defendants (the hospital and obstetrician) alleged to be responsible for the brain damage at the time of his birth. Eventually, after an abortive retrial following the appeal, a settlement was arrived at between the parties. The plaintiff's main complaint was that the defendants' practice in the hospital of monitoring one heart of twins (as they did in this case) amounted to negligence.

Finlay CJ, in the Supreme Court, mentioned the three principles on medical negligence which had been mentioned in the earlier Irish cases, namely, that a general and approved practice need not be universal; that the test also applied to diagnosis; and that the principle also applied to medical administrators. He then enunciated several principles to be applied in determining the standard of care in the medical context.

(a) *The true test for establishing negligence in diagnosis or treatment is whether a medical practitioner has been guilty of such failures, as no medical practitioner of equal specialist or general status would be guilty if acting with ordinary care.*

A clarification was added by Finlay CJ, namely, that this general and approved practice need not be universal, but should be approved of by a 'substantial number of reputable practitioners holding the relevant specialist or general qualifications'. There are problems in using the word 'substantial', for instance, in a case like *Dunne*, where it was necessary for the court to decide which expert opinion was better, which is never an easy task.

(b) *If the allegation of negligence is based on proof that the doctor deviated from general approved practice, that will not establish negligence unless the course taken was one which no practitioner of like specialisation and skill would have followed had he been taking the ordinary care required from a person of his qualifications.*

Symmons (1994) points out that this is a variant of the 'general practice' test, but also emphasises that this sub-test implies that a 'deviating' medical practitioner is more likely to be found to be negligent.

(c) *Even if a medical practitioner establishes that he followed a general practice which is approved by his colleagues of similar specialisation and skill, he cannot escape liability if the plaintiff establishes that the practice has inherent defects which ought to be obvious to any person giving the matter due consideration.*

This particular 'proviso' to the first *Dunne* principle and the *Bolam* test reflects earlier Irish cases like *O'Donovan*, where Walsh J stated (in [1967] IR 173, pp 184–85) that a practice which is shown 'to have been widely and generally adopted over a period of time does not make the practice any less negligent'.

Irish commentators Byrne and Binchy comment on Walsh J's views (as cited above) as representing a:

> ... compromise between absolute deference to customary professional practice and what might be considered to be undue intrusion by the courts ... If customary practice has inherent defects which ought to be obvious to any person giving the matter due consideration, then the courts consider that they can no longer stand idly by [see Byrne, R and Binchy, W, *Annual Review of Irish Law* 1992, Round Hall, p 423].

Symmons (1994) says there is no example of this proviso being applied in practice in Irish law.

(d) *An honest difference of opinion between medical practitioners as to the better of two ways of treating a patient does not necessarily speak of negligence where a doctor has followed one course rather than another.*

This principle appears to have been applied in the earlier leading case of *Daniels v Heskin* [1952] IR 73 and, more recently, in *Dunleavy v McDevitt and the North Western Health Board* (1992) (SC) 19 February. There, the defendant surgeon had performed one of two possible kinds of operation on a lump on the paratoid gland near to the plaintiff's left ear; this was the so called 'limited' rather than 'wider' option. The latter option would have exposed a facial nerve, so lessening the likelihood of contact with it. The operation resulted in the plaintiff's facial nerve being damaged. Strong evidence was presented which indicated that, for surgeons working in small Irish hospitals, the limited option was the safer option and accordingly, the plaintiff's action failed.

Res ipsa loquitur *in Irish law*

The doctrine of *res ipsa loquitur* has been successfully invoked at first instance, in the 1993 case of *Lindsay v The Mid-Western Health Board* [1993] 13 ILRM 550 (SC). In this case, the (then) infant plaintiff was admitted to the Regional Hospital Limerick in 1982 and was diagnosed by the senior house officer as suffering from acute appendicitis. This diagnosis was confirmed by the surgical registrar, who added a second possible diagnosis of 'mesenteric adenitis', a complaint with an unknown cause, which might have been caused by a viral or biological infection. Following an appendectomy in the hospital, the plaintiff remained unconscious, but breathing spontaneously, and appeared to be in a normal post-operative state. However, within an hour of the operation, complications developed: the plaintiff's depth of unconsciousness deepened and she suffered a 'full blown' epileptic fit which lasted for about 30 seconds. After being transferred back to the intensive care unit, she did not regain consciousness; and nine years later, at the time of the court hearing, she was still in a deep coma. The condition was predicted to be likely to last for the rest of her probable 15 year life expectancy. The plaintiff's case was, first, a claim for damages for the alleged negligence of the medical defendants, essentially on the basis that her injury had arisen as a result of hypoxia, that is, because of a deprivation of oxygen during the operation. The defendants disputed this, and after hearing the evidence on this, Morris J decided that the plaintiff had 'not established as a matter of probability that her brain damage had been caused in this way'. The second claim was based on the principle of *res ipsa loquitur*.

In explaining how the doctrine should apply in Ireland, Morris J referred to the Irish Supreme Court decision of *Mullen v Quinnsworth*, where the classic statement of the doctrine in English law was adopted in *Scott v St Katherine's Docks Co* (1865) 3 H & C 596, namely, that it applies 'where the thing is shown to be under the management of the defendant or his servants and the accident is such as in the ordinary course of things does not happen if those who have the management use proper care'. Two elements were extracted from this by the learned judge: (a) that the 'defendant was to be in total control of the event which gives rise to the occurrence'; all the personnel in the instant case were the defendants' servants or agents, so there was no problem about different employer-employee relationships; (b) the 'accident must be of such a nature as in the ordinary circumstances does not happen if those who have the control of the procedures use proper care'. Perhaps somewhat controversially, he appears to have regarded both the operation itself and the consequential administration of anaesthetics 'as a straightforward procedure carrying no inherent risks' yet, as Symmons rightly points out, 'both the type of operation and the administration of anaesthetics (in any operation) involve some small statistical risk' (Symmons (1994), p 18). Symmons thus sees this as a step toward stricter medical liability, especially since this approach appears to ignore possible difficulties arising from causation. Morris J reinforced his view by saying that, 'in a case such as this, it would be palpably unfair to require [the plaintiff] to prove something which is beyond her reach and what is peculiarly within the range of the defendants' capacity of proof'. The plaintiff succeeded in the High Court.

However, in the appeal to the Supreme Court, the first instance decision on *res ipsa loquitur* was reversed, although the court agreed that the doctrine could (and did *prima facie*) apply to such facts where a person goes in for a routine medical procedure and is subject to an anaesthetic without any special features and there is a failure to return to consciousness. The main point of divergence from the first instance case was in relation to the effect of the doctrine, namely, what onus of proof its application threw on the defendant. Symmons (1994) therefore argues that, as a result of the decision, 'All a medical defendant is required to do is to show that he had exercised all reasonable care in carrying out the operation, and is not to be forced to prove on balance of probability what did cause the plaintiff's injury'. The Supreme Court accepted that the defendants had exercised reasonable care in carrying out procedures in accordance with established practice. As in this case, the defendants had (at first instance) established that there was no negligence in the anaesthetic procedure, thus rebutting the burden of proof, which consequently displaced the maxim of *res ipsa loquitur.* Accordingly, the case therefore turned on the plaintiff having to prove negligence.

O'Flaherty J's comments are notable. He stressed that it was necessary to ensure that the rules established in the maxim 'do not put a burden on defendants which is so onerous as to produce an unjust result ... It would be an unjustifiable extension of the law to say that in the absence of an explanation that could be proved, negligence on the part of the defendants must be inferred'. The learned judge also made it clear that, where the defendants fail to prove on a balance of probabilities that the plaintiff 'met her injuries in a particular manner that caused her condition but which was connected with the administration of the anaesthetic', which they failed to do in the instant case, their 'other course' in using the maxim 'was to establish from beginning to end of this anaesthetic procedure there was no negligence on their part'. This they had managed to do before the first instance judge.

Comment on Irish medical negligence law

Despite the intermittent citation of leading English medical negligence authority such as *Sidaway,* the Irish judiciary have apparently sought to follow 'an independent line on such critical areas as the criterion of standard of care, namely, the effect of the concept of common practice in *Dunne,* where previous Irish case law is followed' (Symmons (1994), p 140) instead of *Bolam.* Even where English authority is cited, particularly in the case of the 'informed consent' concept as in *Walsh,* where strong reference was made to *Sidaway,* the Irish law that has emerged is even less clear than in the UK. However, the approach in Irish law of *res ipsa loquitur* in the area of medical negligence in the case of *Lindsay* has shown that the beneficial effect this doctrine may have in assisting a plaintiff to prove medical negligence.

Australia

In Australia, the *Bolam* test has been rejected by the High Court of Australia following earlier decisions in the Australian State Supreme Courts. The Court of Appeal of New South Wales, the Supreme Court of South Australia and the High Court of Australia all considered the case of *Rogers v Whitaker* (1992) 175 CLR 479. In the earlier case of *F v R* (1983) Victoria, King CJ opined that professions may sometimes adopt unreasonable practices and the court has the obligation to scrutinise professional practices to ensure they accord with the standard of reasonableness imposed by the law.

In *Rogers v Whitaker* itself, Kirby J suggests other reasons for the change in attitude: a general advance in the education of the population at large; decline in the awe of professionals and of all authority; termination of unquestioning acceptance of professional judgment; widespread public discussion of matters concerning health; growing recognition of receiving a full input from the patient so that the whole person is treated, not just a body part. At the heart of it, the attitude to the fundamental rights of the patient is different in Australia (or so Kirby J, writing extra-judicially, asserts).

Liability for transmission of HIV-infected blood

The AIDS crisis has certainly brought in its wake several problems connected to confidentiality, but it appears that there may be several bases of civil liability for the transfusion of HIV-infected blood.

Litigation provides only one method of obtaining compensation for recipients of HIV-infected blood. We shall consider the USA as an example of a common law jurisdiction's approach to this issue and Germany as an example of the civil law approach.

A COMMON LAW APPROACH

The USA

Three possible bases of liability are (a) breach of warranty; (b) strict liability in tort under s 402(a) of the Second Restatement of the Law of Torts; and (c) negligence (see Giesen (1994)).

It is arguable that one basis of liability in the USA is in contract for breach of warranty. In the absence of any contract between the hospital/supplier of the HIV-positive blood and the victim, this would have to be an implied warranty, that is, on the basis that the blood supplied should be of merchantable quality, safe for transfusion. However, American courts have rejected this cause of action and refused to apply the law of warranty to this sort of situation. In the 1954 case of *Perlmutter v Beth David Hospital* (1954) 308 NY 100; (1954) 123 NE 792, the Supreme Court of New York held that the supply of blood was merely an incidental aspect of the general service provided by the defendant hospital. The case concerned blood infected with serum hepatitis but the court seemed conscious of the fact that the continued and sufficient availability of blood is of great significance to society and it appeared to proceed on the basis that the imposition of civil liability upon hospitals and blood banks would endanger this availability.

A plaintiff may base his claim on strict liability in tort, pursuant to s 402(a) of the Second Restatement of the Law of Torts. According to this provision, the vendor of a product which is unreasonably dangerous to users and consumers is made strictly liable for damage which it causes. It is clear that a plaintiff infected with HIV can only succeed if blood is characterised as a product as distinct from a service.

In *Cunningham v MacNeal Memorial Hospital* (1970) 47 Il 12d 443; (1970) 266 NE 2d 897, the Illinois Supreme Court rejected the *Perlmutter* approach and held the defendant hospital liable to a patient who had been infected with serum hepatitis as a result of a blood transfusion. Indeed, the lower court in *Cunningham* had held that blood is as much a product as pharmaceuticals, which have been held to come within s 402(a) of the Second Restatement of the Law of Torts. This decision provoked consternation amongst hospitals and most of the US States enacted 'blood shield statutes', which expressly classify the supply of blood as a service 'for all purposes'. Subsequent case law has confirmed that these statutes apply to blood infected with HIV. Giesen (1994) deplores these developments, and stresses that their effect is that this legislative and judicial stance 'drastically limits the right of the infected individual to compensation on the basis of a mere supposition as to the requirements of the common good.

The final route for the infected plaintiff is to sue in negligence against the hospital or blood bank. The duty of care seems undeniable, but the standard of care is open to debate. Additionally, there are considerable evidential difficulties and, in view of the many ways in which AIDS can be transmitted and, in the present context, the large number of blood suppliers, many plaintiffs will fail at the causation stage. The danger remains that professional groups will be allowed to determine the incidence and extent of their own civil liability.

A CIVIL LAW APPROACH

Germany

Somewhat unusually for a civil law country which is usually dominated by codes, the German judiciary has been active in developing this area of law.

The Federal Court decision of 1991 – the negligence claim

In 1991, the German Federal Supreme Court (*Bundesgerichtshof*) established the essential principles of liability for HIV-infected blood. In this case (BGH, 30 April 1991, VI ZR 178/90 JZ 1991, 785 NJW 1991.1948) the defendant hospital had obtained infected blood from an HIV positive donor in the period before testing was possible. This was transfused to a patient, who subsequently infected her husband with the AIDS virus. The latter sued in negligence under para 8231(1) of the German Civil Code. Conscious of the plaintiff's evidential difficulties, the court made three findings:

(a) The defendant had breached its duty of care by its inadequate screening of blood donors. Members of high-risk groups were recommended not to give blood, but the life threatening danger of their disregarding this advice was not made clear in a sufficiently clear and forceful manner. The court rejected the defendant's claim that compliance with this requirement would have provoked criticism from interest groups and the media. The need to protect patients' lives took precedence over the personal rights of potential donors. Thus, regardless of the practice of the rest of the profession at the time, the law required that blood suppliers do all they could to exclude infected blood from the system where testing was possible.

(b) The breach of duty having been established, the court held that the burden of disproving that it resulted in the obtaining of defective blood rested upon the defendant. Notably, the German Supreme Court refused to characterise blood as either product or service, and looked instead to the basic principles of fairness which underpin these evidential rules. In essence, the burden of proof should be determined according to those areas under the organisational control of each party. The court, therefore, did not pursue the products/service distinction, but based its decision on procedural fairness.

(c) Since neither the plaintiff nor his wife belonged to a high-risk group, they would be held to have established a *prima facie* case that they had become HIV positive as a result of the blood transfusion, and not in any other way.

The Federal Supreme Court decision of 1991 – duty of disclosure

The second major German decision is that of the German Federal Supreme Court (BGH, 17 December 1991, VI ZR 40/91 BGHZ 116, 379 JR 1992, 19 (D Giesen), JZ 1992, 421 E Deutsch), which outlined a hospital's duty of disclosure in relation to the possible need for blood transfusions and the risk of HIV infection entailed thereby. The court held that the risk of infection with HIV through blood transfusion during surgery could not be classified as a generally known risk. At the time of the infection in question, the risk of infection was primarily associated with sexual contact and the sharing of needles during drug use. In addition, the hospital was required to take into account the devastating consequences of infection with the virus. The hospital was required, in accordance with the need for informed consent and the right to self-determination, to inform the patient of the risk of contamination of any blood used during the course of the operation. In addition, however, the hospital was also required to inform the patient of the possible alternatives, namely (a) of donating her own blood in advance, or (2) for example, of obtaining a directed blood donation, from a member of her family.

The court was also keen to emphasise that the patient's personal reasons for refusal must be respected. No 'generalising yardstick' is allowed, neither that of a reasonable patient, nor 'even less so' a medical judgment.

Comment

Giesen (1994) notes (p 4) that courts in the USA and Australia have also held hospitals and doctors subject to the same broad duty of disclosure in the present context. He cites the Texas case of *Knight v Department of the Army* where the plaintiff was not properly informed of the risk of becoming HIV positive as a result of a blood transfusion, but it was held that even if full disclosure had been made, a reasonable person in the plaintiff's position would not have foregone the transfusion. Giesen (1994) also submits that this objective test of causation fails to give effect to the right to self-determination and suggests that subjective test of causation (what the patient actually decides in terms of whether to consent or not), as applied in consent cases, does so. He also notes that, in almost all major jurisdictions, a patient need not be informed of those risks accompanying surgical and other procedures of which there is general knowledge among lay persons. However, in the German Federal Supreme Court case, the court was not prepared to say that the risk of HIV infection came within the category of a generally known risk.

NO-FAULT COMPENSATION SCHEMES FOR MEDICAL INJURIES

New Zealand

New Zealand, in 1974, adopted a no-fault scheme of compensation for medical injuries, whereby victims of 'medical, surgical, dental or first aid misadventure' could claim compensation. A whole generation of New Zealanders have therefore grown up knowing no other system (the Accident Compensation Scheme) of dealing with personal injury claims. The scheme has come under scrutiny because of cost increases averaging 25% per annum between 1985 and 1990 and a new National Party Government intent on abolishing the Social Welfare State. Various case law developments, such as those in *H v ACC* [1990] NZAR 289 (a case of a failed sterilisation), indicated that the concept of medical misadventure within the accident compensation legislation 'was refined to such an extent that it now encompasses all conduct which might at common law have been regarded as medical negligence' (Oliphant (1996), p 11).

Indeed, in the light of cases like the *Green* case (*Green v Matheson* [1989] 3 NZLR 564), the scheme was substantially amended by the Accident Rehabilitation and Compensation Insurance Act 1992 which came into effect on 1 July 1992. This 1992 Act now limits claims for 'medical misadventure' radically, by circumscribing the scope of its applicability. Medical negligence will always amount to misadventure, but the 1992 Act now excludes claims for 'medical errors, that is, failure to obtain consent, to provide treatment, or to make a correct diagnosis unless such failures are proven to be negligent'. Apart from this, adverse consequences of treatment will only be covered by the Act (as 'medical mishaps') if they are '*rare*' (that is, occur in less than 1% of cases) and '*severe*' (that is, cause death or require, for example, hospitalisation for more than 14 days or 'significant disability' lasting more than 28 days) (see Grubb (1999)).

These reforms seem to have been the result of a policy to exclude altogether the possibility of suit at common law for compensation for medical negligence. This is because, as Mahoney (1992) explains, to lodge a successful claim under this scheme, purportedly a 'no-fault' scheme, the patient has to prove fault. Without such proof, no claims will be possible, regardless of the degree of rarity or severity of the consequences suffered.

> In *all* cases of claims arising in a medical context, the medical profession will be protected from litigation because, whenever negligence is shown, 'medical misadventure' is automatically and the right to sue is thereby lost [Mahoney (1992), p 206].

Section 5(5) illustrates this point, as it states: '... medical misadventure does not include personal injury arising from abnormal reaction of a patient or later complications arising from treatment procedures unless medical misadventure occurred at the time of the procedure.'

The New Zealand claimant must still establish that the injury resulted from 'medical or surgical misadventure' and this requirement has caused difficulties in distinguishing between those conditions which result from the psychological progress of a medical condition and those which are genuinely the result of misadventure occurring in the course of treatment. A fairly large body of case law is devoted to determining just when a complication following upon a medical procedure is so rare as to amount to a misadventure.

Among the criticisms of the scheme have been the low levels of compensation, high cost to the taxpayer and the removal of deterrents to safety practices in the workplace. More fundamentally, however, commentators have strongly argued that the new definition of medical misadventure is both confused an impractical (Oliphant) and that 'amendment to the [1992] legislation is inevitable' because the changes 'cut deeply into both entitlement to cover under the scheme and the amount of compensation payable to a qualifying claimant ... this will increase the anomalies and injustices under the scheme' (Mahoney (1992)).

A civil law example of a no-fault compensation scheme – Sweden

The Swedish system also attempts to exclude compensation for injury which can be traced to an original disease and is not the result of a medical procedure, but it makes provision for compensation for injury resulting from medically unjustified inaction. Compensation depends on a finding that the medical procedure that led to the injury was not 'medically justified', which Grubb argues, 'can often reintroduce the issue of negligence in this debate'. The Swedish system is a no-fault system; it is a direct patient compensation scheme that also protects physicians from liability. Sweden has a system that emphasises public accountability, yet also protects professional interests. Patients are compensated for medical injury; fault is irrelevant to the compensation system; the profession is protected from liability suits; the courts are rarely used, although nothing actually prohibits this. Its disciplinary body is a public body which has extraordinarily strong public representation. Even though large numbers of complaints are processed, physicians are not severely censured and the medical profession is not dissatisfied with the system. It also uses the no-fault claims and disciplinary board hearings as feedback for valuable information for research and preventive purposes.

A recent development has been the Stockholm lawyers bringing a handful of cases alleging medical malpractice to the Swedish courts. These lawyers have argued that the compensation awards are too small in relation to awards made in the USA which they cite as the example Sweden should follow. Further developments are eagerly awaited.

SELECTIVE BIBLIOGRAPHY

Giesen, D, 'Liability for the transfusion of HIV-infected blood in comparative perspective' (1994) 10 Professional Negligence 2

Grubb, A, 'Problems of medical law', in Markesinis, B and Deakin, SF, *Tort Law*, 1999, OUP

Kirby, M, 'Patients' rights – why the Australian courts have rejected "*Bolam*"' (1995) 21 JME 5

Mahoney, R, 'New Zealand's accident compensation scheme: a reassessment' [1992] 40 Am J Comp Law 159

Markesinis, B and Deakin, SF, *Tort Law*, 1999, OUP

Oliphant, K, 'Defining "medical misadventure": lessons from New Zealand' [1996] Med LR 1

Padfield, A, 'French medical negligence: change in the standard of care required' (1993) 42 ICLQ 906

Rosenthal, M, *Dealing with Medical Negligence*, 1991, Tavistock

Shuaib, FS, '*Rogers v Whitaker*: the end of the *Bolam* saga in medical negligence cases in Malaysia?' (2000) 16 Professional Negligence 25

Symmons, C, 'Developments in Irish medical negligence law in the past ten years: signs of divergence from UK case law' (1994) 10 Professional Negligence 134

Symmons, C, 'Medical negligence and the doctrine of *res ipsa loquitur* in Ireland' (1992) 8 Professional Negligence 17

Tunc, A, 'Torts II: "physicians"', in Tunc, A (ed), *International Encyclopedia of Comparative Law (Part I)*, 1973, Nijhoff

CHAPTER 17

ORGAN DONATION AND ORGAN TRANSPLANTATION: COMPARATIVE PERSPECTIVES

A GLOBAL PERSPECTIVE

We have already seen how the donation and transplantation of human organs developed in England, the response of the common law to various 'scandals' which treated body parts as commodities for commercial exploitation, and it was noted then that several countries have responded to this phenomenon by enacting legislation. It is estimated that, annually, 300,000 people receive organ transplants worldwide (Williams (1994)); nevertheless, there remains a shortage of organs for the number of people in need, and this shortage remains the main obstacle to the further development of techniques of organ transplants.

It appears that early attempts to transplant human organs involved the skin (technically an organ) which Indian doctors transplanted as early as 600 BC (see Howard and Najarian (1978)). In the 16th century, Tagliacozzi transplanted skin tissue and noted that the immune system rejected tissue from other bodies. It is claimed that the first kidney transplant, using a cadaver, was performed in the Soviet Union in 1936 and, by 1954, doctors in the USA had accomplished this operation using a live donor (Kurnit (1994)) in Boston from one identical twin to another. In the next few decades, techniques of organ transplantation improved with surprising speed. The first successful heart transplant, which received extensive world coverage, was performed by Christian Barnard in South Africa, in December 1967, and the first larynx transplant took place in Belgium in 1969 (Kurnit (1994)). The first recipient of a heart transplant only lived 18 days but by 1992, 85% of heart transplants survived for at least one year (Kurnit (1994)). The number of organ donors per million population in the USA is around 17–19 donors per million (Suthanthiran and Strom (1994)) and in Western Europe it was 14.7 donors per million in 1993 (Cohen (1994)). The country out of step in terms of numbers of donors appears to be Spain, where the number of organ donors has risen continuously from 14.3 per million population in 1989 to 25 million in 1994; and this appears to be the highest rate reached for a medium sized country like Spain which has a population of 40 million. There are disparities, of course, since the Canary Islands and the Basque Country have 40 donors per million population but Andalucia has only 18 per million population.

ETHICAL PRINCIPLES

As we have already seen in Chapter 8 (on the English law of this area), there are several ethical principles involved in this area of medicine and law. The key principles are *consent* (which needs to be 'informed'; however, this term may be defined or interpreted), *autonomy* and *self-determination*, *confidentiality*, *beneficence* (if one takes an altruistic view of organ donation – that is, to benefit someone), and *respect for persons, whether dead or alive* (through ascertaining whether consent was obtained or would have been; making sure that relatives or persons close to the donor (if deceased) consent to the organ removal). Of course, if the donor is a child, or where the potential donor has never expressed a view on donating her organs, there is usually *proxy consent* on the part of the child's legal representative, or relevant, designated or appropriate person who has a legally meaningful relationship with the donor (such as a next-of-kin, but also including a cohabitant in certain legislation), respectively.

THE CONTRACTING OUT OR PRESUMED CONSENT POLICY

As we have already seen, the pattern in most jurisdictions that we have examined is that there are two systems dealing with the obtaining of organs from deceased persons: the 'contracting in' or 'opting in' policy, where explicit consent has to be given, so that deceased persons expressly declare before death that they approve of such removal,. or an appropriate family member expresses approval of removal in cases where the deceased left no statement or other evidence to the contrary; and the 'contracting out' or 'opting out' policy or presumed consent system. In the latter type of system, consent to removal of organs for transplantation from cadavers is presumed, unless those persons stated their objections while alive, or where others who were closely related or connected to them stated at an appropriate time that they objected to the deceased's body being so treated. For both systems, any objections that have been expressed will prevent removal of organs for transplantation.

Within the last 12 years, several European countries, such as Belgium, Spain, Italy and Greece, and one overseas common law jurisdiction (Singapore), have introduced schemes whereby organs required for transplantation may be removed automatically by surgeons and transplanted unless the deceased carries a card expressly registering her refusal of removal of organs or the relatives object to such a procedure. France actually introduced such a scheme in 1976, but it was only in 1994 that the French National Assembly approved a Bill to encourage more organ donations as the result of the sharp fall in the availability of organs for transplants. This is in marked contrast to the British Medical Association's continuing resistance to the 'contracting out' system in Britain, which was discussed earlier (see Part I, Chapter 8).

WORLD HEALTH ORGANISATION: PRINCIPLES ON HUMAN ORGAN TRANSPLANTATION

On 13 May 1991, the World Health Organisation (WHO) Assembly endorsed nine guiding principles on organ transplantation. As the report in *The Lancet* states:

> These guiding principles are intended to provide an orderly, ethical, and acceptable framework for regulating the acquisition and transplantation of human organs for therapeutic purposes. The term human organ is understood to include organs and tissues but does not relate to human reproduction, and accordingly does not extend to reproductive tissues – namely, ova, sperm, ovaries, testicles or embryos – nor is it intended to deal with blood or blood constituents for transfusion purposes. The guiding principles prohibit giving and receiving money, as well as any other commercial dealing in this field, but do not affect payment of expenditures incurred in organ recovery, preservation, and supply [see (1991) 337 The Lancet 1470].

The WHO was particularly concerned about 'the protection of minors and other vulnerable persons from coercion and improper inducement to donate organs'.

The nine World Health Organisation principles

Organs and tissues (referred in the text as 'organs') may be removed from the bodies of deceased and living persons for the purpose of transplantation only in accordance with the following guiding principles:

(1) *Organs may be removed from the bodies of deceased persons for the purpose of transplantation if: (a) any consents required by law are obtained; and (b) there is no reason to believe that the deceased person objected to such removal, in the absence of any formal consent during the person's lifetime.*

(2) *Physicians determining that the death of a potential donor has occurred should not be directly involved in organ removal from the donor and subsequent transplantation procedures, or be responsible for the care of potential recipients of such organs.*

The Lancet's comment on this principle is that this provision 'is intended to reduce the possibility of a conflict of interest that would arise if the physician(s) determining the death of a potential donor also had involvement in the organ removal or transplantation' ((1991) 337 The Lancet 1470).

(3) *Organs for transplantation should be removed preferably from the bodies of deceased persons.*

However, adult living persons may donate organs, but in general such donors should be genetically related to the recipients. Exceptions may be made in the case of transplantation of bone marrow and other acceptable regenerative tissues.

An organ may be removed from the body of an adult living donor for the purpose of transplantation if the donor gives free consent. The donor should be free of any undue influence and pressure and sufficiently informed to be able to understand and weigh the risks, benefits and consequences of consent.

The first paragraph 'is intended to emphasise the importance of developing cadaveric donation programmes in countries where this is culturally acceptable, and to discourage donations from living, genetically unrelated donors, except for transplantation, except for transplantation of bone marrow and of other acceptable regenerative tissues' ((1991) 337 The Lancet 1470).

The second paragraph 'seeks to protect potential donors from undue pressure and undue inducements from others. It emphasises the necessity for complete and objective information to be given to the donor. It also takes into account issues relating to persons (other than minors) who are legally incompetent to fulfil the requirements for 'free consent' or the other conditions specified in this paragraph ((1991) 337 The Lancet 1470).

(4) *No organ should be removed from the body of a living minor for the purpose of transplantation.*

Exceptions may be made under national law in the case of regenerative tissue.

This principle provides for 'absolute prohibition of the removal of organs for transplantation from legal minors. However, an exception concerning regenerative tissues may be allowed by national legislation.

In such cases, the protection of minors could be assured by requiring, among other conditions, the minor's comprehending consent and the consent of the parent(s) or the legal guardian. The parent(s) or the legal guardian may have a conflict of interest, [for example] where they are responsible for the welfare of an intended recipient of the donated tissues. In such a case, prior permission of an independent body, such as the court or other appropriate authority of comparable independence or status, should be required. However, an objection by the minor should take effect and prevail over any other consent' ((1991) 337 The Lancet 1470).

(5) *The human body and its parts cannot be the subject of commercial transactions. Accordingly, giving or receiving payment (including any other compensation or reward) for organs should be prohibited.*

This principle is aimed at prohibiting traffic in human organs for payment. 'The method of prohibition, including sanction, will be determined independently by each jurisdiction. The principle does not prohibit payment of reasonable expenses incurred in donation, recovery, preservation, and supply of organs for transplantation' ((1991) 337 The Lancet 1470).

(6) *Advertising the need for or availability of organs, with a view to offering or seeking payment, should be prohibited.*

The intention of this principle is 'to prohibit advertisements that have a commercial (profit-making) purpose. Promotion and encouragement of altruistic donation of human organs and tissues by means of advertisement or public appeal are not affected by this principle' ((1991) 337 The Lancet 1470).

(7) *It should be prohibited for physicians and other health professionals to engage in organ transplantation procedures if they have reason to believe that the organs concerned have been the subject of commercial transactions.*

This principle 'addresses medical, professional, and other involvement in removal, intermediate management, and implantation of organs with knowledge, actual or constructive, that commercial transactions have occurred' ((1991) 337 The Lancet 1470).

(8) *It should be prohibited for any person or facility involved in organ transplantation procedures to receive any payment that exceeds a justifiable fee for the services rendered.*

This principle 'reinforces principle 7 by restricting entrepreneurial practice in organ recovery and implantation. A medical or other health practitioner uncertain whether a fee proposed to be charged is justifiable may seek the opinion of an appropriate licensing or disciplinary authority before the fee is proposed or levied' ((1991) 337 The Lancet 1470).

(9) *In the light of the principle of distributive justice and equity, donated organs should be made available to patients on the basis of medical need and not on the basis of financial or other consideration.*

It can be seen that these well articulated principles, while clearly not binding on any jurisdictions, provide a comprehensive and balanced statement of aspirations, and many countries, particularly those less developed in their medical practices than others, would do well to use these guidelines as a basis for their professional codes and practices and indeed, as a basis for reforming or formulating new legislation.

CIVIL LAW COUNTRIES

In 2000, the BMA Ethics Committee published 'Organ donation in the 21st century', which we have already referred to in Part I of this book (see Part I, Chapter 8) as part of our discussion of the English law on this subject. The BMA guidance also referred to the approach to organ donation by various other jurisdictions, and the following discussion draws on some of this material.

Belgium

A central registration of non-donors was established in Belgium in 1987. Under this system, citizens of all ages can express their objection to organ or tissue donation, in their local town hall. Hence, this was also a system of presumed consent with the usual provision for a register of objections being made available. Parents may register their objections to transplantation for those of their children who are too young to make a decision for themselves, and a legal representative may register an objection on behalf of an adult who lacks the mental capacity to do so. The government set up a computerised system, a central health authority registry which is accessible to all transplant centres. The law itself (following its passage in 1986) reads:

> Organs and tissues for transplantation, and for the preparation of therapeutic substances ... may be removed from the body of any person recorded in the Register of the Population or any person recorded for more than six months in the Aliens Register, unless it is established that an objection to such a removal has been expressed [Law of 13 June 1986 on the Removal and Transplantation of Organs, see WHO (ed), *Legislative Responses to Organ Transplantation*, 1994, WHO, p 133].

Thus, the law requires the register to be checked before any organs are removed, but, despite the fact that Belgian law does not require the family to be consulted about donation, in practice, consultation is usually carried out (Kurnit (1994)). By the end of 1995, 1.75% of the native Belgian population and 3.23% of the foreign population had registered their objections to donation. A higher proportion of objections was found among young children whose parents had 'opted out' on their behalf and the level of objections decreased with age (that is, as the ages increased), so that only 0.5% of people over 69 years were on the register as objectors (see Roels (1997)). It has been argued by Kennedy *et al* (1998) that the lower rates of family objection, in comparison with the UK, may indicate that, while families are reluctant to take a personal decision about the removal of organs, they may find it easier in a system where failure to register an objection while alive can be understood as implicit consent to donation. If donation is seen as the norm and not the exception and where, in the absence of evidence to the contrary, consent is presumed, grieving relatives are relieved of the burden of making the decision about donation (see Kennedy *et al* (1998)).

Impact of the Belgian transplant law

There appears to have been some success in the level of organ procurement for transplantation. As far as the statistics are concerned, in 1988, Belgium had 342 kidney transplants with 803 patients waiting; 96 heart transplants with 34 patients waiting; 123 liver transplants with 35 patients waiting; four lung transplants with four patients waiting and five pancreas transplants with 12 patients waiting. This amounted to an increase in the number of organs procured.

It has been argued that the increase in organs procured might have been the result of the increased number of medical and hospital programmes participating in the transplant programme (Kurnit (1994)) as opposed to the system of presumed consent, which does not appear to have been strictly followed. Whatever the merits and demerits of the system, by 1990, total organs procured had increased by 183% (Kurnit (1994)).

In contrast, it is useful to look at Austria, where there is a similar law but somewhat different results have occurred.

Austria

In Austria, the law on transplants (Federal Law of 1 June 1982 Serial No 273) reads:

> It shall be permissible to remove organs or parts of organs from deceased persons in order, by means of their transplantation, to save the life or restore the health of another person. Such removal shall be prohibited if the physicians are in possession of a declaration in which the deceased person or, prior to his death, his legal representative, has expressly refused his consent to organ donation.

Apparently, with practically the same sort of laws as in Belgium (and, as we shall see, in France), a doctor in Austria may proceed without informing the next-of-kin where the deceased has not made known their objection. However, it seems that, even if the next-of-kin are reluctant to donate or refuse, the doctor may, and often will, ignore these objections (see Gorsline and Johnson (1991), p 8). Under the law, the objection must be in writing but, unlike in France, there is no obligation on the doctor to make a reasonable effort to find a record of these objections.

Impact of the Austrian law

It would seem that on the face of it, a presumed consent law, strictly applied, yields a harvest of organs for transplants. The rate of procurement for kidneys in Austria is twice that of the USA and most other European countries – something like 60 cadaveric kidneys are retrieved for every one million persons. However, opponents of the law argue that the system itself is not responsible for the increase. Melissa Kurnit (1994), for instance, argues that: 'If Austria's high rate of procurement were due only to its presumed consent law, one would expect it to outpace other countries in all categories of organs covered by the law. This, however, is not the case.' Indeed, Austria's harvest rates are only slightly higher when compared to France and Belgium when it comes to livers, and the rates are actually lower in relation to hearts. In 1988,

Austria had 270 kidney transplants with 1,116 patients waiting; 46 heart transplants with 15 patients waiting; 32 liver transplants with 10 patients waiting; three lung transplants with eight patients waiting and eight pancreas transplants with 12 patients waiting (Altman, J, 'Organ transplantations: the need for an international open organ market' (1994) 5 Touro Int L Rev 161, p 162).

Hence, at this stage it may be said that, while the Austrian system appears to have increased the number of organs available for transplantation, Austria still faces an overall shortage of organs for transplant purposes.

France

France has had a contracting-out system since 1976 (see Law No 76-1181 of 22 December 1976 on the removal of organs). This was known as the Caillavet Law, under which a person may 'opt out' from donating organs by simply signing some writing to that effect. The 1976 law states:

> Organs may be removed for therapeutic or scientific purposes from cadavers of persons who have not, during their lifetime, indicated their refusal to permit such a procedure. However, where the cadaver is that of a minor or of an incompetent person, organs may be removed for transplantation purposes only with the authorisation of the person's legal representative.

Hence, in strict law, potential donors have to register their objection to their organs being transplanted if they do not wish transplantation to take place upon their death. Nevertheless, by all accounts, it seems that French doctors invariably adopt the practice of obtaining the consent of the next-of-kin before carrying out any transplant operation in something like 90.7% of cases (Kurnit (1994)). This practice has now been somewhat regularised. First of all, there is now, pursuant to Decree No 97-704 of 30 May 1997, a computerised register of refusals with regard to the removal of organs, tissues, and/or cells from deceased persons. Secondly, Circular DGS/DH/EFG No 98-489 of 31 July 1998, declares that, while the entry of a deceased person on the register prohibits removal, the absence of an entry does *not* exempt a physician from the legal obligation of trying to find out the deceased's wishes and of obtaining the testimony of his family if the health authorities do not know the deceased's views on organ removal. This is noteworthy because, despite the letter of the law, the practice (that is, of consulting before transplanting) appears to be different.

The number of transplants performed in France is lower than in the UK, possibly because most of the French population do not appear to be aware of the existence of the 1976 law which created the policy (see Redmond-Cooper (1984)). The number of transplants rose steadily in the 1980s and reached a peak of 3,572 in 1991. However, the numbers have fallen since, so that there were 3,220 in 1992 and only 3,180 in 1993, with 195 people on waiting lists for a heart, lung, liver or kidney transplant died before an organ was available. In the first few months of 1994, the figure for available organs fell by more than a third when compared with the same period last year. In 1994, the French National Assembly approved a Bill that would allow doctors to remove organs from dead patients unless they had expressed specific opposition to organ donations. The opposition would have to be written, specifically in a national register so that doctors could find out through a computer system whether they could remove a particular organ (for source of figures, see Dorozynski (1994)). Christian Cabrol, heart surgeon and President of France-Transplant, the private non-profit organisation that manages transplants, has reportedly said that an increasing number of families refuse to let doctors take organs from their relatives and, as some indication of statistics, in 1993, French surgeons took 3,408 organs after the death of 977 patients, but 412 potentially usable organs were not collected because of the objections of the relatives concerned (see Dorozynski (1994)). The situation appeared to be worsening since the Head of Transplantation at the Necker Hospital in Paris said that the situation was so critical that the shortage may threaten the transplantation programme. Indeed, he also remarked that 'transplantation might become a purely marginal technique benefiting only a few privileged people with living relatives willing to donate an organ'.

Apparently, part of the reluctance to donate organs is traceable to a series of publicised events involving the unauthorised removal of a dead boy's eyes in 1992 and reports in 1993 of irregularities in the collection of organs.

The National Assembly discussed the legislation as part of a wide ranging Bioethics Bill and the text has been modified to include guarantees that the certification of brain death is not amended in any way. As from July 1998, in pursuance of the computerised register of refusals, the French Transplant Establishment (EFG) undertook to make the following documents available to the public in dispensing pharmacies: an information document on removal and transplantation and a donor card.

The French bioethics laws

After a long process of reflection which began in 1983 with the establishment of the National Ethical Consultative Committee for the Life and Health Sciences (CCNE), a lengthy public debate and several CCNE opinions, five official reports and a parliamentary discussion that lasted two years, three texts were approved by a strong majority and are known as the Bioethics Laws (for sources and discussion, see Mattei (1999), p 582 *et seq*).

The first Bioethics Law deals with respect for the human body (Law No 94-653 of 29 July 1994) and was presented by the Ministry of Justice. It introduces into the Civil Code major principles providing the necessary points of reference to reflect progress in medicine and biology. The second was presented by the Ministry of Health (Law No 94-654 of 29 July 1994) and essentially organises the donation and use of elements and products of the human body (with the exception of blood which is covered by specific texts), medically assisted procreation, and practices in the field of genetics, such as prenatal diagnosis or predictive medicine.

The third deals with the processing of nominative data with the objective of research in the health field.

Mattei (1999) highlights three problems that should be addressed with regard to organ transplantation:

(1) The *modalities of consent* to removal in each of three very distinct situations: transplantation, autopsies and research. Since the law was passed, 'ambiguous interpretations have led to a considerable reduction in the number of autopsies'. In Mattei's view, it is therefore necessary to state that, in the case of removals of organs for therapeutic purposes (transplants) and for diagnostic purposes (autopsies), it is the rule of presumed consent that is to apply. He argues that:

> ... it is therefore unacceptable, except in cases of positive refusal, to refrain from doing everything possible to obtain a better understanding of the causes of an unexplained death, to provide fuller information, and to prescribe preventive measures with respect to families.

However, he also concedes that removals for purely scientific purposes should not be performed without the explicit consent of the deceased.

(2) In relation to *living donors*, the position should be brought up to date. For instance, the framework of transplantation should be made more flexible. However, apart from certain special situations, Mattei does not think it is desirable to extend the living donor transplantation framework beyond the boundaries of clearly defined first degree family relationship. Mattei feels that to do so would give rise to a genuine risk of abuse, each patient being more or less engaged in a conscious search among his associates for a person 'to contribute to his survival through organ donation'. Other 'real difficulties' he identifies are the criterion suggested by some of 'appropriate ties' between persons, which he finds 'too vague and impossible to define'; and pressures of all kinds, particularly moral and economic, which might be exerted, as well as 'the consequences in terms of health and responsibility which would be difficult to manage'.

(3) There is probably also a case for anticipating events by providing the possible future framework for *xenotransplants*, especially in the light of the risks of infection.

Living donation by minors

Living donation by minors is limited to siblings. The donor's legal representative must give consent to organ removal. The procedure must be authorised by a committee of at least three experts, two of whom have to be doctors, and one of whom must have practised for at least 20 years. If the minor is mature enough to be consulted, and refuses to donate an organ, this must be respected without exception.

Effect of transplant law in France – an interim assessment

By the late 1990s, it was possible to say that the 1976 transplant law of France has met with some success but its impact has not been outstanding. The number of transplants in France steadily increased before beginning to fall in 1991, yet it can now claim to be one of the top six rates of post-mortem donors per million inhabitants among European countries (see Kurnit (1994)). However, these rates might arguably have been better had a stricter regime of presumed consent been operated. In 1998, 12 years after its presumed consent law was enacted, France had carried out 1,808 kidneys and had 4,075 patients on the waiting list; 555 heart transplants and 523 patients on the waiting list; 409 liver transplants and 189 patients on the waiting list; and 43 pancreas transplants and 16 patients on the waiting list. Hence, qualified success is perhaps the fairest interim verdict but it is still too early to say what its fresh initiatives will reap. Quite simply, despite its presumed consent law, France was really operating a voluntary system of consent and, when this is borne in mind, perhaps France can justly claim some measure of success in increasing the number of organs available for transplantation.

Germany

The German Transplantation Act 1997

By an Act of 5 November 1997, the Transplantation Act, dealing with the donation, removal and transplantation of organs (*Bundesgesetzblatt*, Parts I and II, November 1997, No 74), Germany enacted its latest law on human organ transplantation.

General provisions

The Act applies to the donation and removal of human organs, parts of organs or tissues (organs) for the purpose of transplanting of such organs and including the preparation of these measures. It also applies to the prohibition of trade in human organs. The Act does not apply to blood and marrow or embryological and fetal organs and tissues.

Donor cards, educational information

Among the duties created by the Act is that the Federal Authorities must have readily available cards on which the willingness to donate organs can be documented – that is, donor cards; as well as suitable educational material. The statutory health insurance funds and private health insurance companies shall make such material available to those persons insured with them who have reached the age of 16 at regular intervals, asking them to declare themselves willing to donate their organs.

Rules regulating declarations of donation

Any person who submits a declaration of donation can consent to the removal of an organ, can refuse such removal or can delegate the taking of the decision to a person in their trust (that is, whom they consider trustworthy) mentioned therein by name. The declaration may restrict the donation to specific organs. Both the consent and the delegation of the decision can be declared from the age of 16, the refusal from the age of 14. The stored personal data may only be used to determine the admissibility (*sic*) (that is, legality or validity) of the removal of an organ from the person by whom the declaration was made. The Act also set up facilities for the regulation of:

- transmission of the declaration of donation by the contact points to the organ donation agency as well as the storage of the declaration and the data it contains at the contact points and the registry;
- the automatic recording of all retrievals of data as well as other information from the organ donation registry for the purpose of verifying the admissibility (validity) of the enquiries and the information disclosed;
- the deletion of stored data; and
- the financing of the organ donation registry.

Removal of organs from deceased donors

The removal of organs is permissible where:

- the organ donor has consented to the removal;
- the death of the organ donor has been determined according to rules which comply with state-of-the-art medical standards;
- the intervention (procedure) is performed by a physician.

Equally, removal of organs is not permissible where:

- the person whose death has been determined has objected to the removal;
- the final, irreducible cessation of the cerebrum, the cerebellum and the brain stem has not been determined according to rules of procedure complying with state-of-the-art medical standards before the organ is removed from the donor.

In addition, the physician shall inform the donor's next-of-kin of the intended removal. The physician is also required to record the course and scope of the organ removal operation. The next-of-kin have the right to examine these records and have the right to consult a person who enjoys their confidence.

Removal of organs with consent of persons other than the donor

Under s 4(1), it is stated that, in cases where the doctor is supposed to remove the organ but has neither written evidence of consent by the donor or written evidence of objection by the potential donor, the latter's next-of-kin shall be asked whether she is aware of a declaration of donation on the part of the potential donor. If the next-of-kin has no knowledge of such a declaration either, removal of an organ shall only be permissible if a doctor has informed the next-of-kin about a possible removal and has obtained her consent. In making the decision, the law states further that 'the next-of-kin shall respect the presumed wishes of the potential donor'. The doctor 'shall inform the next-of-kin of this requirement'.

The law also stipulates that the next-of-kin may agree with the doctor that his or her consent may be withdrawn within a specific, agreed deadline. Such an agreement must be *in writing* (see s 4(4)).

Section 4(2) lists the scope of 'next-of-kin' under the Act, which includes:

(1) the spouse;
(2) children of full age (that is, above the age of majority);
(3) the parents, or in so far as the potential donor was a minor at the time of death and the (right to) custody for his or her person was exercised at that time by only one parent, by a guardian or curator, then the person exercising this custody (that is, with the right to this custody);
(4) sisters and brothers of full age; and
(5) grandparents.

Contact within two years of potential donor's death necessary to give next-of-kin power to consent

It is made clear under the Act that next-of-kin are only authorised to make a decision pursuant to s 4(1) (above) if personal contact between the former and the potential donor existed in the two years preceding the potential donor's death. The doctor is required to determine this fact by questioning the next-of-kin. In the case of several next-of-kin of equal rank (according to the ranking list under s 4(2), above), it will be sufficient for one of them to be consulted under the terms of s 4(1) and take a decision. However, an objection by any of the next-of-kin will be noteworthy. If a relative with a prior ranking cannot be contacted within an appropriate period of time, the consultation and decision of the next-of-kin of lower rank who can be reached next shall be sufficient. A non-relative above the age of majority (that is, an adult) who had an intimate personal relationship with the potential donor until the latter's death shall be treated as of equal rank and on a par with the next-of-kin.

Delegation of consent decision

Under s 4(3), if the potential donor had delegated the decision regarding organ removal to a specific person, that person shall take the place of the next-of-kin.

Physician's duty to keep records

Section 4(4) requires the doctor to maintain records of the course, content, and result of the consultation of the next-of-kin, as well as those persons listed in s 4(2). Persons designated under s 4(2) and (3) have the right to examine such records.

The Act also contains a range of procedural requirements and stresses, for example, that any removal must be done with respect for the donor's dignity and the body must be presented for burial in a dignified condition.

Removal of organs from living donors

Under s 8(1) of the Act, the removal of organs from a living donor shall only be permissible if:

1 The person
  (a) is of full age and capable of giving informed consent;
  (b) has been informed pursuant to para 2 and has consented to the removal;
  (c) is considered suitable as a donor according to medical judgment and is exposed to no foreseeable risk beyond that of the operation nor is likely to suffer any serious damage to his or her health other than the direct results of the organ removal.
2 The transplantation of the organ to the envisaged recipient is suited, according to medical opinion, to saving a person's life or to curing a serious disease, preventing it from worsening or alleviating the resulting complaints.
3 A suitable organ from a donor ... is not available at the time when the organ removal takes place.
4 The intervention (procedure) is performed by a physician.

Apart from this, the removal of non-regenerative organs is only permissible for the purpose of transplanting to relatives of the first or second degree, spouses, fiancé(e)s, or other persons with whom the donor obviously has a close and 'especially intimate personal relationship'.

Informed consent required

Section 8(2) stipulates that the donor shall be informed by a doctor about the type of operation, its scope and the possible repercussions (including any indirect consequences) and delayed sequelae of the intended organ removal for her health, the organ transplant's expected chances of success, as well as other facts which are clearly of importance to him or her, with respect to the organ donation.

The potential donor shall be given this information in the presence of another doctor and, where necessary, other experts. The content of the instruction and the declaration of consent by the organ donor shall be recorded in a document which is to be signed by the person providing the information, the additional doctor and the donor. The document shall also contain particulars of the insurance coverage of the health risks involved. It should be noted that consent may be withdrawn *either* orally or in writing.

Section 8(3) provides that the removal of organs from a living donor may only be performed after the organ donor and the recipient have declared themselves willing to participate in medically recommended post-operative care. A further condition is that the Commission responsible for these matters has given an expert opinion on whether there are real, substantiated grounds to suppose that the person's consent to the organ removal is not being given freely or that the organ is the object of the trade prohibited under the Act (s 17). The Commission shall consist of a doctor who is involved neither in the removal nor in the transplantation of organs, nor bound by the instructions of a doctor who is involved in such measures, a person who is qualified to exercise the functions of a judge, as well as a person who is experienced in psychological matters.

Transplantation centres

Section 9 requires that transplantation of the heart, kidneys, liver, pancreas and intestines may only be performed in *transplantation centres* authorised for this purpose. Section 10 describes in detail what these centres are: hospitals or facilities at hospitals authorised to transplant organs. If these organs have been removed from donors as organs which are subject to allocation it shall only be permissible to transplant them if they are allocated by an allocation agency acting in accordance with the Law. If organs which are subject to allocation are removed within the territorial scope of the present law, it shall only be permissible to transplant them if the removal has been performed within the provisions of s 11.

Section 11 provides that the removal of an organ subject to allocation, including the preparations for the removal, allocation, and transplanting, is the joint responsibility of the transplantation centres and the other hospitals on the basis of regional co-operation. All the central associations of the health insurance funds, the German Medical Association and the German Hospital

Federation or the federal associations of the institutions running hospitals, in conjunction, shall set up, or cause to be set up, a suitable facility – a co-ordinating agency – for the purpose of organising this task.

The Act then goes on to list various other procedural requirements connected with these transplant centres.

Penal provisions

Under s 18(1), any person who, in violation of s 17, trades in organs intended to be used for the treatment of patients, or who removes, transplants, or has an organ transplanted to him or herself, shall be liable to imprisonment for a term not exceeding five years or a fine. If the offender trades on a commercial basis, he or she shall be liable to imprisonment for one to five years. The attempt to commit such acts is also punishable. Under s 18(4), in the case of organ donors whose organs have been the object of prohibited trade and in the case of organ recipients, the court shall be entitled to forego the punishment provided for in s 18(1) or may reduce the punishment at its discretion.

Criteria for allocation of organs to patients by the Federal Medical Council

Germany's Federal Medical Council has published new criteria for the allocation of organs to patients who have transplants. The law declares that organs should be allocated to individuals rather than to transplant centres, which was the previous practice. As Annette Tuffs puts it: 'The new guidelines try to give equal chance to each patient while taking into account the urgency and prospective outcome of transplantation.' Under this new system, a number of points for each organ will be allocated to the individual patient on the waiting list, according to strict criteria (see Tuffs (2000), on which the information in this section is based). Thus, points will be given according to matching qualities, the length of time the patient has been waiting, mismatch possibility, and how long the particular organ would have to be conserved before it could be transplanted. Children would receive 'bonus points'.

The system stipulates that apart from blood group and size, hearts and livers are mainly distributed according to how long a patient has waited and the conservation time of the donor organ. Patients with high urgency will take priority but the status decision will have to be based on certain criteria and is audited by an expert committee, which has to be independent in the sense of not being involved in the particular transplantation. Those in breach of the new rules face penalties. Unlike the old guidelines, the new ones regulate the allocation of organs and specify which patients can become candidates for transplants. Should a patient be rejected for transplantation, the reasons have to be recorded and patients must also be informed about their place on the waiting list. The guidelines specify which patients will not be accepted for transplantation and includes: alcoholic patients who have not abstained for the past six months, HIV infected patients, heavy smokers, drug addicts, and patients with severe cardiovascular disease.

The Eurotransplant in Leiden, the Netherlands, will operate the guidelines and received the official contract as allocation centre for Germany. Nevertheless, Eurotransplant still has to modify its current guidelines according to the new rules and find some way of harmonising them with the allocation as in other member countries. In fact, Eurotransplant has been allocating organs in Germany for the past 30 years and also acts for the Netherlands, Belgium, Luxembourg, Austria and, more recently, for Slovenia.

The Netherlands

As with physician-assisted suicide, the Netherlands appears to have taken an innovative legislative step by passing the Dutch Organ Donation (*Wet op de Orgaandonatie*) Act 1998. This invites everyone over the age of 18 to register with a central registry. Four options are available to an individual, as far as post-mortem donation is concerned:

- a consent to donate any or specified organs;
- a refusal to donate;
- delegation of consent to the next-of-kin; or to a nominated person.

The choice may be altered at any time, before there is a need to decide on the disposition of an organ. Access to the Central Register is available 24 hours a day. The Act also covers living donation of organs and bone marrow. Mason and McCall Smith (1999) suggest that this legislation is 'fully acceptable on ethical grounds [because] a coercive element is avoided by providing an equal opportunity to consent or refuse'. They report that, by the end of 1998, about 30% of the adult population in the Netherlands had already registered with this Central Registry.

The Spanish system

In 1989, Spain introduced a national transplantation organisation, *Organizacion Nacional de Transplantes* (ONT) whose main objective is to improve organ donation rates. The next stage was to establish a nationwide transplantation co-ordination system, with regional co-ordinators in each of the 17 regions and a co-ordinator at every hospital. This has proved reasonably successful in increasing the number of organ donors. The BMA's view (see BMA, *Organ Donation in the 21st Century*, 2000) is that direct comparisons should be treated cautiously and the Spanish model would have to be modified in order to make it acceptable and effective in the UK.

Nevertheless, the number of organ donors has risen continuously from 14.3 per million population in 1989 to 25 per million in 1994 and there is as yet no sign of a serious decline.

The Swedish law on transplantation

A new Law on Transplantation (No 831 of 8 June 1995) came into force in Sweden on 1 July 1996. The first Swedish law on this subject was enacted in 1975 and, as a result of several subsequent amendments, it was felt that the time was right for a brand new law. The new law is based on presumed consent. According to this law, it is the wishes of the deceased, if they are known or can be ascertained, which decides whether surgery for transplantation or some other medical purpose may be performed on the deceased. Hence, surgery for transplantation may be performed on a deceased person if the deceased has not objected to it in writing or expressed an objection to any such procedure, and provided there is no other reason to suppose that the procedure would have been against the deceased person's wishes. Where nothing is known about the deceased person's attitude, the law presumes that it is not unjustifiable to presume that he would have been in favour of organ donation. Several surveys of the Swedish population suggested that about 65% of the population are in favour of organ donation, even if they have not stated as much in explicit terms. Other surveys indicate that only 10% of the Swedish population declared themselves utterly opposed to organ donation (for source of figures and discussion of this Law, see Johnsen (1997)). Hence, there is some evidence to suggest that the majority of the Swedish population are in favour of a contracting-out system.

A *veto* on organ donation has also been given to persons 'closely connected with the deceased'. In cases where the deceased's opinion was not known or unclear, this Law assumes that it may legitimately remove organs for transplantation provided there is no objection from the next-of-kin. In trying to ascertain the wishes of the deceased, the views of the immediate family (as those 'closely connected' to the deceased) are usually sought, and this primarily includes spouse, cohabitant, child and parent. However, if none of these can provide the information, then it is permissible to go further afield and consult others who might have been 'closely connected' to the deceased, such as siblings or grandparents or the spouse's children by another marriage or other relationship. Another reasonable provision of this Law is that a relative who would qualify as next-of-kin would be excluded if, for some considerable time, the deceased had no contact with him. If the deceased was a minor or suffered from some mental disturbance, the Law proceeds on the basis that no additional restrictions would be needed other than those that would generally apply.

Living donors

Surgery can be performed on a living donor provided that donor consents and the operation may be performed without seriously endangering the donor's life or health. Before consent is given, the donor must be informed of the hazards of the procedure and other consequences which might have a bearing on the decision the donor may have to make. The consent has to be both informed and voluntary and the basic principle is that the use of organs from living persons should be kept to a minimum. The main rule is that non-regenerative tissue may be taken from a person related to or otherwise very closely connected to the intended recipient. Special rules exist for the protection of minors and donors who were mentally disturbed.

Tissue from aborted fetuses

Tissue from aborted fetuses may only be used for medical purposes and only if there are special reasons justifying such usage. Emphasising the importance of respect for dead bodies to apply equally to dead fetuses, the Law stipulates that the case requiring fetal tissue must be of 'urgent importance'. Use of the tissue is conditional on obtaining the consent of the woman who carried the fetus and also on permission being granted by the National Board of Health and Welfare. The Law also provides that the use of tissue from aborted fetuses must be an activity that is kept 'neutral' in relation to abortion practices and must not in any way affect the manner or timing of abortion, or the reasons for carrying it out. There must also be no connection between individual donor and recipient. The person performing the abortion must be clearly dissociated from the person who will be using the tissue. It is important, therefore, that decisions on the use of fetal tissue should not be made by the person responsible for the care of the woman seeking an abortion.

Turkey

In Turkey, the first kidney transplantation from a living donor was performed in 1975 and from a cadaver in 1978. From 1975 to 1997, 3,618 kidney (from cadaver, 653), 107 liver (from cadaver, 83), 3,898 cornea and 520 bone marrow transplants were carried out. The law regulating human organ transplants came into force in 1979. As Aydin (1999) points out, the most important incentive for the introduction of this law was that doctors faced being accused of illegal acts whenever they conduct transplants.

The Turkish law

The Law relating to organ and tissue procurement, preservation, grafting and transplantation (Official Gazette No 16655, 3 June 1979) regulates the procurement of organs and tissues from living and cadaver donors for transplantation. Its main features (as identified by Aydin (1999), p 405) are:

- The donor must be at least 18 years old and must sign a document in the presence of two witnesses and must give her consent without being under any [undue] influence.
- The doctors who will remove the organ or tissue have to give information about the possible dangers and psychological, familial and social consequences of the procedure in a proper manner.
- No definition is given of 'proper' and the expression 'informed consent' is not used.
- Doctors must also inform the donor about the benefits to the recipient from the procedure.
- Organs and tissues cannot be supplied from people who are not in a sound mental and psychological state and who are unable to make decisions by themselves.
- It is illegal to procure organs and tissues for financial gain or for a reason incompatible with humanitarian ideals.
- If the donor is married, the doctor must inquire if the spouse has been informed about the situation and draw up a protocol to certify this. The names of the donor and recipient must not be disclosed except where relatives and close personal relations are involved.
- It is strictly forbidden to take any organ or tissues, the loss of which will jeopardise the donor's life.

Organs from cadavers

- An organ cannot be taken from a cadaver, unless the deceased drew up a written and signed document which was approved by a physician, or declared his wish to donate his organ in the presence of two witnesses.
- If these criteria are not fulfilled, it is still possible to take an organ from a cadaver with the consent of her spouse, mature children, parents or siblings who were with her at the moment of death.
- If he or she had openly expressed opposition to transplantation when alive, organ transplantation is not allowed.
- If someone whose life had ended due to serious injury in an accident or natural disaster is not attended by any relative or close person and if the cause of death is not directly related to the organs to be donated, the organs of this person can be taken without anyone's consent.

Clearly, this makes finding organs for transplantation easier.

- In the absence of a will or declaration opposed to organ donation, corneas may be taken from the cadaver.
- The corpses of people who willed and donated their bodies for scientific research as well as corpses not claimed by anyone will be given to universities to be used for research after being preserved for six months.

Penalties

Anyone who breaks the law on organ transplantation and those who carry out transplants for financial reward, will be fined and sentenced to between two to four years' imprisonment. There is no special charge for physicians giving mistaken diagnoses of death; the prosecution will be carried out under other laws.

COMMON LAW COUNTRIES

Australia

The Australian experience is notable for two reasons. First, despite being a common law country in the sense of its common law heritage and reliance on case law and precedent, it has not been content to simply wait and see how matters develop and leave it to the courts to resolve disputes, but has opted for a pro-active approach. Secondly, to a far greater extent than the UK, various States have passed legislation which deal in detail with the issue of organ transplantation and we shall consider these statutes presently. The usual common law methodology applies, however, in that, in view of its historical and contemporary reliance on case law, it will be the judiciary who will give substance to these laws when they begin to interpret them, rather than more legislative guidance that will emerge unless, as with all common law countries, there is a perceived need to enact clarifying or consolidatory legislation to respond to a crisis or to deal with possible injustice which results from the existing law.

Background

Treatment of patients with terminal renal failure by dialysis and transplantation has been available in Australia since the early 1960s and, according to the Australian National Health and Medical Council (NHMC), in 1991 some 5,000 patients were being supported by dialysis or kidney transplantation, some of whom have pancreas transplants because of diabetes associated with the original renal failure. The NHMC also claims that dialysis or kidney transplants increase by 10–16% each year but after dialysis some patients have to wait for between two to three years before a kidney becomes available.

Heart, heart-lung transplants and transplants of heart valves are being carried out in several Australian centres, the NHMC informing us that there is a five year actuarial survival rate of better than 80% for the heart transplant recipients. Transplantation of heart valves is becoming a more popular procedure for patients with major valvular disorders of the heart.

Liver transplantation in Australia began early in 1985 and the NHMC figures indicate that it is now a well established procedure in many States. Again, in 1991, the actuarial survival figure of 72% compared favourably with established overseas units. There is a now a procedure that is able to reduce adult donor livers to a size which is suitable for infants which has resulted in the saving of the lives of many more children, since approximately one-third of children waiting for a liver transplant died while the search for a suitable donor continued. The NHMC suggests that one of the reasons for the shortage of donors and delays in offering lifesaving procedures to those in need of organ transplantation is the lack of awareness on the part of the public and the medical profession of the extent of the shortage of donors, of the high success rate which now results from organ transplantation, and of the benefit it brings to patients.

In recent years, says the NHMC, the Government has launched educational and promotional programmes which have encouraged organ donation so much so that, increasingly, medical staff are being approached by relatives who inquire whether organs from dying persons can be used for transplantation. However, there is still a serious shortage of organs available for transplantation.

One of the reasons for the shortage identified by the NHMC is the 'actual or perceived' difficulty in approaching the relatives of a potential organ donor. Consequently, many Australian hospitals have devised their own policies for approaching relatives, with an emphasis on flexibility since each situation will be different.

Australian legislation on human organ transplantation

Australia has a wide range of legislation dealing with transplantation, enacted by various States but the statutes are very similar. The statutes are: the Human Tissue Act 1983 (NSW), the Human Tissue Act 1982 (Vic), the Transplantation and Anatomy Act 1979 (Qld), the Transplantation and Anatomy Act 1983 (SA), the Human Tissue and Transplant Act 1982 (WA), the Human Tissue Act 1985 (Tas), the Human Tissue Transplant Act 1978 (NT), the Transplantation and Anatomy Act 1978 (ACT) (see CCH, *Australian Health and Medical Law Reports* and Devereux (1997), p 177 *et seq*, upon which the following section is substantially based).

General statutory principles in all Australian transplant legislation

Devereux (1997) notes that all the Australian jurisdictions prohibit and criminalise '*trading in tissue*', the term used for making any contracts or arrangements by which, in return for some form of remuneration, a person agrees to: (a) sell or supply tissue, or the right to take it, from their own or another person's body; or (b) sell the right to a post-mortem or anatomical examination of their own or another person's body. In addition, the buyer of such tissue or rights is also covered by the legislation. Further, advertising for the sale or purchase of such tissue is also prohibited and any such arrangements are void and legally unenforceable.

However, Devereux also emphasises that the prohibition does not apply where:

- the tissue has been treated or processed and the sale or supply is made so that it can be used by a medical practitioner for therapeutic, medical or scientific purposes;
- necessary expenses involved in the removal of tissue under the legislation are reimbursed; and
- ministerial authorisation has been obtained

There are several common definitions used by all the Australian legislation which help to clarify the meaning of each of the terms used. These have been summarised by Devereux (1997) as follows:

Child – a person who has not attained 18 years of age and (except in Western Australia and Queensland) is unmarried.

Regenerative tissue – Tissue which, after injury or removal, is replaced in the body of a living person by natural processes.

Next-of-kin – means 'senior next-of-kin'.

Senior available next-of-kin

1 In connection with a deceased child means (in the following order):
   - a parent;
   - a brother or sister 18 years of age or over; or
   - a person who was a guardian of a child immediately before death.
2 In connection with a deceased adult means (in the following order):
   - a person who was a spouse of the deceased immediately before death;
   - a son or daughter 18 years of age or over;
   - a parent of the deceased; or
   - a brother or sister of the deceased who is 18 years of age or older.

The classes of the next-of-kin are arranged in a hierarchical order so, if there are members of more than one class available, consents must be sought from someone who is available who is a member of the most closely related class. Some jurisdictions have provisions which include adoptive parents/children or persons of the most closely related class.

Tissue – includes an organ or part of the body and a substance extracted from, or from a part of, the human body. It includes ova, semen and fetal tissue except where these are specifically excluded from the sections on tissue generally and dealt with separately.

Transplantation – most legislation describes this as including the transplantation of any part of tissue or substance obtained from it.

Designated officer – this is defined in most jurisdictions as the medical practitioner who has the relevant duty under the legislation. Each jurisdiction provides for the appointment, removal, and other such duties of these officers. In Queensland, Tasmania and the Northern Territory, the duties are discharged by persons described in various terms such as '[the] person in charge of the hospital'.

Donation of tissue by living persons

Adults

Regenerative tissue

A living adult may give her written consent to the removal of specified tissue. In most jurisdictions, the terms of the consent must be stated, namely, identifying which tissue is to be removed and for which of the purposes permitted under the statutes. In some jurisdictions, there is a requirement that the consent must be signed in the presence of the medical practitioner who furnished the advice. In South Australia and Western Australia, it is expressly stated that family members and/or friends must be absent when the consent is signed.

All jurisdictions except South Australia and Western Australia stipulate that an accompanying certificate is to be given by the designated officer or medical practitioner who was present when the consent was given.

Typically, this certificate must state the following:

- the terms of the consent;
- that the requisite medical advice was duly furnished;
- that the consent was given in the presence of the certifier;
- that the donor is an adult of sound mind; and
- that the donor's consent was freely given.

Non-generative tissue

The terms and conditions whereby a living adult of sound mind may consent to the removal of non-regenerative tissue are the same as for regenerative tissue. However, the legislation makes it clear that this may only be for the purpose of transplantation into the body of another living person. In addition, the tissue removal may only take place at least 24 hours after the consent was signed, which allows a 'cooling-off period'. The accompanying medical certificate (where this is required under the particular legislation) must also specify the time at which the consent was given.

All tissue donated is tested for HIV antibodies and donors are also required to make a declaration that to their knowledge they are not HIV positive.

Children

Some jurisdictions such as Victoria, Queensland, Western Australia and the Australian Capital Territory state that any reference to 'parents' in these sections must not be read to include a reference to the guardian of a child or another person standing *in loco parentis* to a child.

Regenerative tissue

Apart from the Northern Territory, all jurisdictions provide for the removal of regenerative tissue from children, but this must only be for the purpose of transplantation into the body of a parent or sibling. In Western Australia, Tasmania and the Australian Capital Territory, the scope of transplantation is extended to the body of a relative. The parent of the child must give consent in writing, following medical advice as to the nature and effect of the removal, which must be furnished to, and understood by, both parent and child. In all jurisdictions except South Australia and Western Australia, an accompanying certificate must be provided by a designated officer or medical practitioner, the typical form of which has to restate the terms of the consent and also state that:

- the requisite medical advice was duly furnished;
- the consent was given in his or her presence;
- the parent was of sound mind and freely gave the consent;
- the child understood the nature and effect of the tissue removal and transplantation;
- the child was in agreement with the proposed procedure.

In Queensland, an additionally 'cooling off' period of 24 hours is required under its legislation.

In South Australia, the tissue removal must be approved by a ministerial committee.

Victoria and Queensland are the only States which provide for a removal of regenerative tissue from a child who does not, due to his or her age, understand what is going on. These States stipulate that the relevant designated officer or medical practitioner must additionally certify that they are of the opinion that the proposed recipient family member is in danger of dying without the transplant.

Queensland legislation contains the additional proviso that further certification must be made that the risk to the donor child must be minimal.

Non-regenerative tissue

Only one jurisdiction, the Australian Capital Territory, makes provision for the removal of non-regenerative tissue from a child. All other jurisdictions simply forbid it, either expressly or impliedly. Under the Australian Capital Territory legislation, the tissue removal may only take place when a family member is in danger of dying without a transplant and both parents of the child consent to the procedure. These two requirements must be contained in a certificate given by the relevant medical practitioner, which must also contain the other declarations which have been stated above (see (a)–(e), above). The matter has to be referred to a ministerial committee for decision. The matter may be referred to the committee even if only one parent is available.

Revocation of consents or agreements

All the legislation provides that any of the consents or agreements just discussed in the preceding sections may be revoked at any time, either orally or in writing. And such revocation will be regarded as conclusive. There are more complex provisions in New South Wales, Victoria and the Northern Territory, which require that certain persons, such as the medical practitioners attending the donor (whether in or out of hospital), nurses or nurses' aids, to whom the donor has indicated his or her revocation, must inform the designated officer or equivalent. The designated officer or equivalent must then make enquiries as to whether anyone is proposing to remove tissue and inform them that consent has been withdrawn. They must also return the consent and accompanying certificate to the potential donor.

Consents and agreements: effects

All jurisdictions provide that the appropriate consents, agreements and certificates are 'sufficient authority' for the removal of the specified tissue for the specified purpose. The consent of the recipient will have been obtained under the usual procedures for surgery. It is also stipulated that the tissue removal must not be performed by the medical practitioner who gave the certificate.

The words 'sufficient authority' are important because they mean that the medical practitioner who performs the organ removal will have a statutory defence to any action for trespass by the donor and the procedure will be lawful. In other words, lack of sufficient authority will mean the practitioner will be criminally liable. Apart from South Australia and Western Australia, all jurisdictions expressly countenance situations where consents and certificates will not be sufficient authority. This will be the case where the medical practitioner is proposing to remove tissue but knows or has reasonable ground for suspecting that:

- consent has been revoked;
- a relevant certificate contains statements which are false or misleading (New South Wales adds 'in a material particular');
- a child donor is no longer in agreement with the proposed operation

Removal of tissue after death

All jurisdictions except Western Australia have a statutory definition of death (see, also, Part 1, Chapter 9, which discusses definitions of death) which states that death has occurred where there is:

- irreversible cessation of all brain function; or
- irreversible cessation of blood circulation.

All jurisdictions except Western Australia and Queensland have a provision which states that this definition applies for the purposes of the whole law of the jurisdiction. In Queensland, however, this definition applies only for the purposes of the Transplantation and Anatomy Act 1979, but cessation of brain function is the test where life support systems are being used. In Western Australia, although there is no statutory definition of death for the purposes of human tissue removal, the Human Tissue and Transplant Act 1982 provides that tissue shall not be removed until two medical practitioners have certified that all brain function has irreversibly ceased.

Coroner's consent

Under the legislation, no tissue removal can go ahead without the consent of the coroner where he or she would have jurisdiction under the various Coroners' Acts or, in the Northern Territory and Australian Capital Territory, where there is no death certificate. All jurisdictions stipulate that the coroner may make conditions with regard to his or her consent and that the consent may be oral and confirmed later in writing.

Where donor is unconscious and/or on life support systems

The legislation permits removal of tissue after death for the purposes specified therein. When a potential donor is unconscious before death, the designated officer (or equivalent) may make enquiries as to whether the person had ever expressed a consent or objection to organ donation during her lifetime. Any 'election' is conclusive but, if no election can be ascertained, then the senior available next-of-kin may be asked if she objects. Thereafter, the indication from such a next-of-kin will be acted upon unless the donor recovers consciousness. If after reasonable enquiries the existence or whereabouts of the senior available next-of-kin cannot be ascertained, then the designated officer (or equivalent) may authorise tissue removal.

Effect of authorisations

In cases where authorisations have been obtained under the requirements of the legislation, these will constitute sufficient authority for the tissue removal to proceed, with the provisos that (a) the removal may not be carried out by the medical practitioner who gave the authorisation nor a medical practitioner who carried out the examination referred to above; (b) the removal must proceed under the terms of the consent or authorisation.

Transplantation of cornea

Corneal transplantation from a deceased person has a much older pedigree than the other transplantation techniques which require long courses of immuno-suppressive therapy in order to be successful. Corneal transplantation runs fewer risks than kidney or heart transplants. However, for the cornea to be suitable for transplantation, it must be removed from the deceased within six hours of death. Four Australian jurisdictions have taken action to provide legislation to avoid the problem of not having qualified medical personnel available within the time limit to carry out a transplant or at least to prepare a cornea for such a transplant. New South Wales, Victoria, South Australia and Western Australia have passed legislation to allow suitably trained authorised personnel, other than medical practitioners, to remove the cornea so that it may be prepared for transplantation into a living person. Despite this legislation, a medical practitioner is still required to certify death and there is still the need to obtain consent from relatives to obtain the tissue for a transplant.

Tasmania

A declaration must be made by donors relating to their suitability for donation. If a person has undergone HIV testing in accordance with the

HIV/AIDS Preventive Measures Act 1993 she will not be liable in any civil or criminal proceedings if she believes on reasonable grounds that the result of the test was negative.

Northern Territory

A declaration from the donor must be obtained in the prescribed form.

Australian Capital Territory

The Australian Red Cross Society, hospital or medical practitioner is protected from liability if the Society obtains a declaration from the donor in a form approved by the Minister and a blood sample is tested and the result is negative.

Australian Code of Practice 1991

In 1991, the Australian National Health and Medical Research Council produced *An Australian Code of Practice for Transplantation of Cadaveric Organs and Tissues*, which predominantly restates the law on transplants. Some extracts under the categories listed in the code now follow (cited in Devereux (1997), pp 387–88).

> **Choice**
>
> Patients who may become suitable organ donors after death are those who have suffered severe and irreversible brain damage; such patients will be dependent on artificial ventilation or are expected shortly to become so. Other donors may be suitable for tissues such as blood vessels, bone, corneas, heart valves and skin.
>
> Patients who are unsuitable as donors are:
>
> - patients with malignant disease, excluding those with primary brain tumours and those with low-grade localised tumours of skin;
> - patients with any known disease of the donor organ;
> - patients with systemic or severe localised infection;
> - groups at high risk of being infected with or carriers of HIV or hepatitis B virus.
>
> In general, patients over the age of 65 years are not ideally suitable as organ donors. However, the specific requirements and constraints in relation to the selection of donors for different categories of transplantation are a matter for the relevant transplant group of donors.
>
> It may not be easy to determine whether a patient would be a suitable donor should she die. In general, patients who have had a sudden irreversible arrest of cardiorespiratory function (for example, myocardial infarction), and those

in the so called 'brought in dead' category, are unlikely to be suitable as donors other than for tissues listed above.

Prolonged circulatory arrest is not a contra-indication to collection of corneal donor material, so that most people who die in traffic accidents could be suitable donors. If there are any doubts about the suitability of patients in these categories, hospital staff should contact the transplant co-ordinator or experienced members of transplant teams.

When a hospital has in its care a potential organ donor, the local transplant co-ordinator should be approached as soon as possible, and it should be made clear whether or not authorisation for the removal of organs has been given.

Approach to relatives

If it is known at the time of death of the patient, without having to ask relatives, that the deceased had consented to act as donor (for example, if a patient carried a signed donor card or has otherwise recorded her wish to be considered an organ donor), there is no legal requirement in any State or Territory to establish lack of objection on the part of relatives. However, the possibility of organ donation should be discussed with the family in all cases.

If a relative objects despite the known request of the deceased person, the hospital may, in all States and Territories, legally ignore the relatives. However, in practice, the wishes of the next-of-kin, who usually will uphold the known request of the patient, are respected.

If it is not known at the time of death whether the deceased had consented or objected to act as a donor, the hospital is legally responsible to make all reasonable enquiries as to the existence of relatives, and seek the views of the most senior next-of-kin, if removal of organs or tissues is proposed or intended.

In circumstances where a hospital has legal power to take organs or tissues from a deceased patient without reference to relatives, for example, when it is understood that a patient has no relatives or none are known to be available, every reasonable effort should still be made by the designated officer to locate the next-of-kin as required under the relevant legislation. If this cannot be achieved after reasonable effort, the designated officer may give the necessary authority for removal of organs.

A hospital involved in organ or tissue transplantation should decide as a policy matter what procedure it should adopt for dealing with relatives of deceased persons. The hospital must at the same time ensure that the law of the relevant State or Territory is observed.

It is inadvisable to remove organs from a dead minor without the consent of the family, even if the minor had requested the removal.

The United States of America

As we noted at the outset of this chapter, it was in 1954 that doctors in the USA performed a kidney transplant using a live donor (see Kurnit (1994) and

Scott, R, *The Body as Property*, 1991, Viking) and, in the following years, advances in organ transplants were made with increasing rapidity. However, one estimate is that there are 20,000 usable cadavers buried each year without having any of their organs harvested (Crespi (1994)). A further estimate is that these cadavers could provide 40,000 kidneys and 20,000 hearts, livers and lung pairs (see Silver (1988)). The fact is that, with some exceptions, most people die without donating their organs. In the USA, the Centre for Disease Control suggests that about 15% of people actually become donors (see Clark (1995)) which is just not enough to meet the great demand for donors. Currently, the US system is broken up into regions and organs procured in one region are first offered to patients within that region before being offered to patients in other regions. Critics therefore say that this means that patients will often receive the organs because of where they live, not on the basis of their medical need (see McCarthy (1999); and see below on recent attempts to increase organ availability, p 588).

Pre-consent perfusion – a controversial example of presumed consent

A somewhat controversial use of a 'presumed consent' approach in certain American jurisdictions has resulted in a technique called *pre-consent perfusion*. As explained by Anderson (1995), this takes place in a situation where, immediately after a patient dies, doctors inject a cold preserving fluid into the patient's kidneys and abdominal cavity to arrest the deterioration of those organs, which normally occurs following interruption of the patient's blood supply. Medical personnel then have the time to obtain permission of the next-of-kin to transplant the kidneys. The reason why presumed consent is part of the programme is because the preserving fluid is injected into the patient without first asking consent –in other words, consent is being presumed. Younger (1993) points out that one of the centres which developed this technique adopted it only after families refused to grant permission in 35 consecutive cases (see Younger (1993), p 2770).

The organ donation system in the USA

Several criteria are used in the various States to ration access to organ transplants, on the rationale that there is a shortage of organs for transplantation. In order to increase the chances of a successful transplant, it is preferable that:

- cadavers are brain dead, but still have a beating heart;
- be younger than 55;
- have an organ free from infection or metastatic cancer.

Live kidney donors must be between 15 and 18, have two healthy, properly functioning kidneys, and be medically compatible with the recipient

(Callender (1987)). All that is required of a recipient is that they must be suffering from organ failure, be free from infection or cancer, and able to tolerate surgery. As a result of the shortage of organs, there is often only one organ available, but two patients who are medically ready for a transplant. Consequently, doctors and other medical personnel have to 'weigh the patient's social worth' (Jefferies (1998)). This means appraising the relative merits of each patient according to other criteria such as: (a) family related considerations such as marital status and number of dependants; (b) income; (c) educational background; (d) employment record; (e) relationship to authority figures; (f) past irresponsible background; and (g) intelligence (see Banks (1995)).

It must be said that this does seem to be a rather questionable system in that the criteria used could well lead to inequitable results and deprive some of the most needy (as opposed to 'deserving') patients of a donor organ. Clearly, a significant increase in the supply of organs would cure the shortage so there would be no need for a system of criteria to decide who should receive an organ for transplantation. Over the years, many ideas have been put forward in an attempt to increase the number of organs available for transplants. One of the suggestions has been the very practice that led to legislation in England, namely, the selling or organs on a commercial basis (for English law, see Part I, Chapter 8).

To allow people to sell their organs would require the law to recognise ownership or a property right in one's bodies and their component parts. This question has already been discussed in our earlier discussion on English law, but suffice it to say that the English common law recognised a right to bury one's dead, labelled as a 'quasi-right in property' and this is also the rule in the USA (see Gerike (1991)). Under existing American law, and indeed in most countries, the right to sell the 'property' in the body.

System of organ procurement in the USA

The system of organ procurement in the USA may be discerned in a number of its statutes. The first Statute for consideration is the Uniform Anatomical Gift Act 1968 (UAGA).

The Uniform Anatomical Gift Act 1968

The UAGA 1968 was approved by the National Conference on Uniform State Laws on 30 July 1968 (see Uniform Anatomical Gift Act (Final Draft) (see Hunter Manson, R (ed), *Statutory Regulation of Organ Donation in the United States*, 2nd edn, 1986, Vol 1). This Act gives anyone who is at least 18 years of age and mentally competent the right to designate whether he or she will donate his organs for transplantation after death (see 'Developments in the law: medical technology and the law' (1990) 103 Harv LR 1519). This version of the UAGA neither expressly allowed nor prohibited the sale of human organs (Gerike (1991), p 813). It did, however, restrict the recipients of organs to 'hospitals, doctors, medical and dental schools, universities, organ and tissue banks, and any specified individual in need of a transplant'. (see Kurnit (1994), p 410). Unfortunately, the impact of the UAGA was, as Jeffries put it, 'very modest'. Despite the fact that there was no requirement under the UAGA to obtain the approval of the next-of-kin, the general practice of doctors was to inquire as to the next-of-kin's preferences concerning donation and not to proceed with the removal of organs without their approval (see Anderson (1995), p 264). As we have seen, this was also the practice of French doctors, even before their latest guidelines requiring such consultation. In effect, the UAGA promoted a system of 'encouraged voluntarism' and this was 'lauded because it "encouraged socially desirable virtues such as altruism and benevolence without running the risk of abusing individual rights"' (Kurnit (1994), p 426). Fortunately, it was soon apparent that the UAGA failed adequately to deal with many of the problems concerning the organ shortage, resulting in the continued existence of this deficit. Melissa Kurnit identifies three problems which she submits prevented an increase in organ donation:

- The personal reluctance of individuals to donate organs (Kurnit (1994), p 428). The reasons for this are: denial of mortality; fear that the medical community will not use every effort to save the donor patient's life in order to harvest the patient's organs; opposition to organ donation as a result of a religious belief or the belief that the surviving family should decide the question, and disgust at the notion of organ removal (p 429). Kurnit argues that while some of these problems are largely 'intractable' in the case of religious beliefs or a denial of mortality, some can be partially solved. For instance, the fear that doctors or the medical staff will not do everything to save the life of the donor can be addressed through an educational campaign. Donors can also be informed that most nations adhere to the Guiding Principles announced by the WHO for organ transplantation, Guiding Principle 2 of which declares: 'Physicians determining that the death of a potential donor has occurred should not be directly involved in organ removal from the donor and subsequent transplantation procedures, or be responsible for the care of potential recipients of such organs.' (See Gorsline and Johnson (1991), p 8.)
- The second problem is that when a patient dies, with or without a donor card, the next-of-kin is often reluctant to authorise the donation of the deceased's organs. Kurnit observes that many reasons may be found for this, despite the deceased making it quite clear, during life (rather than, for example, merely in a document opened after death or through a representative), that she wished to donate. She lists these as: emotional or psychological trauma caused by the death; a feeling that authorising organ removal after death is symbolic of giving up hope of recovery if the patient is still alive; denial by the family that the patient is actually dead as a result

of a still functioning heart or other functioning bodily system, although the patient is brain dead (Kurnit (1994), p 429).

- The medical personnel's failure to ask the next-of-kin whether they would agree to donate the deceased's organs is the third problem. This, Kurnit argues, is a widespread problem and many doctors feel that the family should not be approached with the subject of organ removal immediately after the death, or they are inadequately trained in how to deal with such a 'delicate situation' (Kurnit (1994), p 430). The practice that was followed was that, if the doctor sought the permission of the family and it was refused, the organs would not usually be removed, even if the deceased had a valid donor's card.

As a result of the relative ineffectiveness of the UAGA, the Commissioners brought in revisions which appeared many years later in the 1987 version of the UAGA, and all 50 States and the District of Columbia have adopted these. Thirty-six States still have the 1968 version on their statute books.

The Uniform Anatomical Gift Act 1987

Two important changes were made by the 1987 revisions to the UAGA. First, the revisions *expressly prohibited the sale of human organs for transplantation purposes*. This section of the Act now reads as follows: 'A person may not knowingly, for valuable consideration, purchase or sell a part for transplantation or therapy, if removal of the part is intended to occur after the death of the decedent.' (UAGA 1987, s 10(a), see WHO (ed), *Legislative Responses to Organ Transplantation*, 1994, WHO, pp 133, 388, 409.) Under the 1987 Act, 'part' is defined as meaning 'an organ, tissue, eye, bone, artery, blood, fluid, or other portion of the human body'. This change meant that, for the first time, the sale of human organs was expressly prohibited.

Secondly, the UAGA now included provisions for *routine inquiry* (Kurnit (1994)) and part of this routine requires a physician to notify the hospital of a potential donor. The hospital, through a representative, will then inform the family of its options concerning donation of the deceased's organs ((1990) 103 Harv LR 1519).

Application of the UAGA 1987

In both the 1968 and 1987 versions, a problem has been the inefficiency of donor cards. This is because: (a) while donors must carry donor cards to show intent, only 3% of organ donors have been found to be actually carrying their cards when they die (see (1990) 103 Harv LR 1519, p 1619); (b) if the family refuse to authorise the removal of organs, doctors will not proceed, even if the donor has a signed donor card. The system of routine inquiry has generally been seen to be defective because it has simply not been applied; if the doctor decides that the family is too distraught to be confronted by an inquiry about organ removal, she may decide not to proceed. On the ethical front, it has been submitted that by creating a system that requires the family to be asked about donation, the revised version of the UAGA loses sight of the basic premise of this law which is to allow the individual to govern the disposition of his or her own body ((1990) 103 Harv LR 1519, p 1621).

Impact of the Uniform Anatomical Gift Act 1987

To date, writers like Anderson (1995) claim that 'there is as yet no evidence that practices have changed in the 15 jurisdictions that have adopted the new version of the UAGA'. As we have already noted, 36 States were slow to adopt the 1987 revisions although the 1987 version is now on the statute books of all States and the District of Columbia. American observers feel that the 'routine enquiry' approach has been effective and suggest a 'required request' alternative, which has been described thus:

> Under a required request system, an individual must indicate his wish concerning organ donation at certain designated instances, such as driver's licence renewal or submission of tax returns ... hospitals too could be required to ask about donation as part of the admissions process [see (1990) 103 Harv LR 1519, p 1620].

Advocates of this system argue that required request could institutionalise the request, requiring that the inquiry be made by trained personnel ((1990) 103 Harv LR 1519, p 1617).

In essence, the advocates of a required request system point to the large number of patients on the waiting lists to demonstrate the failure of the routine inquiry approach.

The National Organ Transplant Act 1984

The American Congress enacted the National Organ Transplant Act (NOTA) in 1984 with two premises: (a) to make the sale of human organs a federal offence; and (b) to announce that the US system for organ procurement would operate as a system of voluntary donations (Williams (1994)). The relevant provision reads:

> Under sub-section (a) of Section 301, it is unlawful for any person to knowingly acquire, receive, or otherwise transfer any human organ for valuable consideration for use in human transplantation if the transfer affects interstate commerce.

Penal provisions are laid down in sub-section (b). However, although there was an express prohibition of the recognition of property rights in human organs, Congress decided to exempt sales of replenishable tissues like blood and sperm from NOTA (Gerike (1991), p 814). It has been asserted that, because studies concluded that 'society's moral values militate against regarding the body as a commodity', Congress enacted NOTA to establish a commitment to altruism ((1990) 103 Harv LR 1519, pp 1622–23).

Assessment of the impact of the American legislation on human organ transplants

The view from the American scene of the American legislation up to the 1990s has been that all the changes, 'improvements' and modifications have failed to significantly increase the supply of organs for transplantation. Some commentators assert that, although over 60% of Americans claim that they would donate their own organs and over 85% claim they would donate the organ of a loved one, only 4% of American citizens actually carry organ donor cards (see Gorsline and Johnson (1991), p 8). A number of other 'logistical' problems have also beset the organ procurement programme and are identified by Gorsline and Johnson as follows:

> ... emergency personnel often fail to discover written directives concerning organ donation; organ procurement agencies have inefficient procedures in obtaining donor referrals; organs are wasted because they are not placed in time; death pronouncements are not communicated to the next-of-kin 'in a timely manner' [(1991), pp 31–32].

Another commentator makes the point that these problems continue because the system currently in place offers no incentive for people to donate their organs prior to death but the system is 'triggered by the moment of death – the moment of grief – when authorities seek to discover whether the deceased had the intent to donate or whether the families feel that donation would or would not be objectionable' (Jefferies (1998)) and, 'for a system to efficiently encourage donation, it needs to create incentives to make a rational choice well before death' (Jefferies (1998)). Among the suggestions made to improve or replace the system have been ideas that range from 'a system of mandated choice, the required request system, to a system where the surviving family is required to consent to the decedent's pre-death wishes' (Anderson (1995)).

Organ donation and the 'best interests' test in American case law

The best interests test has been interpreted in the specific context of tissues donation in several American cases. The earliest reported kidney donors were all identical twin siblings of the recipients; the courts permitted these donations, relying on the principle that the transplant would be in the donor's 'psychological best interests' (see Mumford (1998)).

In *Hart v Brown* (1972) 289 A 2d 386, the parents and two appointed guardians *ad litem* agreed to the use of a seven year old girl as a kidney donor for her identical twin sister. The court held that transplantation would be acceptable under the circumstances given that there was parental consent and a 'strong identification' between the donor and her sister. The view seemed to be that the donor would be happier in a family that was happy than one that was distressed.

In *Strunk v Strunk* (1969) 445 SW 2d 145, the same concepts were used to justify using a 27 year old mentally incapacitated man as a donor for his brother and the case of *Little v Little* (1979) 576 SW 2d 493 also utilised similar reasoning to a proposed kidney donation by a 14 year old who was mentally incompetent, ruling that there was strong evidence to the effect that she will receive substantial psychological benefits from such participation. In *Strunk*, the 'extremely traumatic effect' the death would have had on the donor was given great weight.

Three further American cases indicate that the American courts have ruled against a proposed donation and suggested limits on the application of the welfare test. In *Re Guardianship of Pescinski* (1975) 226 NW 2d 180, the court actually did not authorise the proposed kidney donation of a 39 year old catatonic schizophrenic with the mental capacity of a 12 year old. He was living in an institution and the recipient was to have been his sister. The court found itself without any authority to approve the operation because there could not be any real consent on his part and no benefit to him had been established. The third case is *Re Richardson* (1973) 284 So 2d 185, where the court distinguished *Strunk*, where the parents of a 17 year old with the mental age of three or four consented to his acting as a kidney donor for his sister, saying that there was no clear-cut case of best interests made out here, unlike *Strunk*.

The third case, reported in 1990, is the Illinois case of *Curran v Bosze* (1990) 566 NE 2d 1319, where bone marrow rather than kidney transplantation was involved. Here, the children's mother opposed the testing of three year old twins as potential bone marrow donors for their 12 year old half-brother who was their father's child by a previous relationship. The 12 year old was dying from leukaemia and the father had brought a petition requiring the mother to submit the twins to a blood test to establish compatibility with the 12 year old. The father had left both mothers and the twins had only met the prospective recipient twice. The court refused permission for the testing to go ahead. It held that, in the previous cases, the sibling relationship had been close and in each of these cases (*Strunk*, *Hart* and *Little*), *both* parents had given their consent; also, if there was to be any benefit in child donor cases, it would necessarily be a psychological benefit. It explained:

> Only where there is an *existing relationship* between a healthy child and his or her ill sister or brother may a psychological benefit to the child from donating bone marrow to a sibling realistically be found to exist [emphasis added].

This was certainly a very tragic case and, without the transplant, the 12 year old would die. However, despite the sympathy felt by the courts and all those who learned of the boy's condition, 'tragic situations cannot obscure the fact that under the circumstances presented in the case ... it neither would be proper nor in the best interests of the three and a half year old twins for the twins to participate in the bone marrow harvesting procedure. Hence, 'individual altruism in an abstract theoretical sense' was an insufficient basis for regarding a non-therapeutic procedure as being in a child's best interests

Recent attempts to increase organ availability

In mid-1999, an expert panel convened by the Institute of Medicine (Washington, DC) to review the US system of organ procurement concluded that organs should be allocated over wider geographical areas than they are at present so that organs could go to those most in need (see McCarthy (1999)). The review was commissioned by the US Congress after the Clinton Administration announced plans to revise the US organ procurement system so that organs would be distributed nationwide. The panel found that 'there was no evidence that broader sharing of organs would lead to a decline in organ donations or would make it difficult for patients from racial and ethnic minorities or who lived in remote regions to receive transplants as some had changed' (McCarthy (1999)). However, as McCarthy (1999) reports, the proposal was met with strong opposition from the United Network for Organ Sharing, which is a private agency contracted by the government to administer the country's organ transplant system. 'Intense lobbying' led the US Congress to block implementation of the proposed revisions and 'further study' of the situation was called for (see McCarthy (1999)).

In November, 1999, Republican James Greenwood proposed legislation that would establish a five year $125 million pilot programme to offer life insurance to individuals choosing to donate their organs after death. Under the proposal, the donor's beneficiaries would receive the insurance payments. So far, however, this proposal has been met with criticism from the Executive Director of the organ procurement organisation Gift of Life, who said it 'was not well thought out' and there needed to be more discussion about this type of proposal by 'ethicists, philosophers and some experts in the field'. Similarly, the Director of the Centre for Organ Research and Education said that any financial incentive-based programme was 'doomed to fail'. Instead, he suggested a presumed consent programme would be preferable. The Director of the Centre for Bioethics at the University of Pennsylvania also called the proposal a bad idea that would not work. In addition, some commentators have said that the proposed law might infringe a 1984 federal law which prohibits any 'valuable consideration' for human organs. Greenwood himself has argued that there is no time for prolonged discussion and that 'five years of discussion will generate a lot of dead bodies, people waiting for transplant'.

Conclusions on the American position on organ donation

Overall, there are clearly flaws and deficiencies in the American legislation and certain medical practices relating to the organ allocation. It must be at least debatable whether potential recipients must be judged according to some sort of social hierarchy. Anderson (1995) comments perceptively on these difficult, and it is submitted, practically impossible decisions on how to choose between donors when he writes:

> I would not try to decide whether it is more appropriate to save the rocket scientist or the unemployed welder. While it may make utilitarian sense to save the lives of only the most worthy citizens, others have pointed out the difficulty of making the necessary choices. What attributes should we (do we) value most highly – science or philosophy, art or economy, poetry or accountancy? Should we focus on past contributions, which are easier to measure, or future potential, which is more important to societal welfare? At the extremes (choosing to save the President of the United States, instead of a mass murderer), the decisions may appear relatively easy, but in the vast majority of cases, it would be impossible to reach consensus and impossible to justify whatever decisions were made.

Anderson further argues that that a possible exception might be patients who have been adjudged less worthy by society at large, because of their conduct, such as those convicted of serious criminal offences who he believes 'should automatically forfeit their ability to receive a transplant' but that there is room for debate on the nature of the offence that would be serious enough to warrant this forfeiture (only violent crimes? Only recidivists?) and the duration of the ban. He points out that a conviction for committing certain criminal acts will, in any event, remove a potential participant from consideration altogether for an appropriate period of time, but these considerations apart, the basic principle remains the same, that is, 'when deciding eligibility for transplants, the relative worth of candidates should ordinarily neither be calculated nor considered' (see Anderson (1995)).

FAR EASTERN AND ASIAN PERSPECTIVES

As a preliminary point, it needs to be noted that in most of Asia, conceptions of respect for elders had led to practically an elimination of organ transplantation as a common medical practice. Japan has a very small programme, largely devoted to transplanting kidneys from living related donors and the same attitude prevails in China. Furthermore, many Asian countries do not legally recognise the standard of brain death that Western countries tend to follow. Consequently, cadaveric donation is a relatively rare phenomenon in Hong Kong, Japan, Singapore and Korea, with Hong Kong performing about 55 kidney transplants a year with organs donated by living relatives and having a waiting list of about 600.

India

In the light of its history of British colonisation and heritage, India may still be regarded as a common law country and indeed does employ common law techniques in its judicial processes. However, while in India, the British, somewhat atypically, enacted the Indian Penal Code, which is very much in the style of the civil law codes. Of course, Indian courts interpret the Code and, unlike the European courts, cases are cited in accordance with a system of judicial precedent. Cases will therefore be significant. If federal laws are passed, they are not automatically applicable to the individual Indian States.

The Transplantation of Human Organs Act 1994

Historical background

The sale of human organs was reputedly rife in places like Bombay and Madras before the Indian government decided to set up a committee with the task of defining the problems that needed addressing before liver and heart transplants could be performed in India. The problems identified (see Nundy (1996)) were apparently twofold:

- 'Indian law did not recognise brain stem death and it was uncertain that the concept would be acceptable to the Indian population.' In the Indian Penal Code, s 46 defines death as: 'Death of a human being unless the contrary appears from the context.' This obviously does not explain what the criteria for death are. However, in s 29(B) of the Registration of Births and Deaths Act 1969, it is defined as: '... the permanent disappearance of all evidence of life at any time after live birth has taken place.' This, Nundy (1996) explains, meant that the definitions of death were inadequate and potentially confusing. Significantly, they 'did not allow scope for transplantation of organs such as the heart and liver, which require a heart-beating, brain stem dead donor'. On the other hand, the Union Territory of Delhi had enacted the Ear Drums and Ear Bones (Authority for Use for Therapeutic Purposes) Act 1982. In Maharashtra State, the Kidney Transplantation Act 1983 and the Corneal Graft Act 1986 were in force.
- In addition, Nundy explains,'[t]rade in human organs, especially kidneys, had been the subject of many parliamentary debates but there was widespread repugnance to this blatant exploitation of the poor by the rich, to the idea that parts of the body were being treated as commodities, to the risk to recipients from unnotified diseases in donors, and to reports of

criminal activities involving middlemen and even physicians' (Nundy (1996)). It should be noted that, in India, only the rich have been the position to afford organ transplants. The Committee recognised that the best way to proceed was to establish a legal framework for the concept of brain death, and prohibit the sale of organs which made it extremely difficult to develop a cadaver organ donation scheme. If conferences are anything to go by, the many held in the major cities with the aim of informing people about the government's policies seemed to suggest that public opinion was strongly in favour of such legislative changes. On 5 May, 1993, the Transplantation of Human Organs Bill was submitted to the Upper House of the Indian Parliament (*Rajya Sabha*) where there was unanimous support. However, the Lower House (*Lok Sabha*) referred it to a Select Committee which recommended minor amendments which were not accepted by the Union Cabinet. Eventually, the Bill was passed by the Lower House and it received presidential assent on 8 July 1994. The new Act repealed the Ear Drums and Ear Bones Act. The first successful heart transplant in India was performed on 3 August 1994.

Some key provisions

The Act provides for the regulation of the removal, storage and transplantation of human organs for therapeutic purposes and for the prevention of commercial dealings in human organs.

Definitions

Brain stem death – the stage at which all functions of the brain stem have permanently and irreversibly ceased and are so certified.

Human organ – any part of a human body consisting of a structured arrangement of tissues which, if wholly removed, cannot be replicated by the body.

Near relative – spouse, son, daughter, father, mother, brother or sister.

Deceased person – a person, in whom permanent disappearance of all evidence of life occurs, by reason of brain stem death or in a cardio-pulmonary sense, at any time after live birth has taken place.

Transplantation – the grafting of any human organ from any living person or deceased person to some other living person for therapeutic purposes.

Therapeutic purposes – systematic treatment of any disease or the measures to improve health according to any particular method or modality.

Payment – means payment in money or money's worth but does not include any payment for defraying or reimbursing: (a) the cost of removing, transporting or preserving the human organs to be supplied; (b) any expenses or loss of earnings incurred by a person so far as reasonably and directly attributable to his supplying any human organ from his body.

Authority for removal of human organs

Any donor over 18 years of age may grant authorisation in writing before his or her death in the presence of two witnesses, one of whom must be a near relative. In the event of brain stem death (which has to be certified by a board of four medical experts consisting of the registered medical practitioner in charge of the hospital concerned, an independent registered medical practitioner, who is a specialist approved by the appropriate authority, a neurologist or neurosurgeon, and the registered medical practitioner treating the person). Permission to remove an organ may be given by a near relative. No organ donations are to be permitted from living donors unless they are near relatives (as defined, see above) or if there is 'affection or attachment' between the donor and recipient, in which case there must be prior approval of the Authorisation Committee.

Regulation of hospitals

Hospitals carrying out organ transplantation must be registered by the appropriate authority.

Appropriate authority

Officers are to be appointed by the central or State government for the purposes of granting or cancelling the registration of hospitals, enforcing standards, investigating breaches of the Act, and inspecting hospitals periodically.

Registration of hospitals

A hospital may not be registered to carry out transplantation procedures unless the appropriate authority is satisfied that it is adequately equipped and able to maintain the necessary standards.

Offences and penalties

Unauthorised removal of human organs is punishable with imprisonment for up to five years and a fine of up to the equivalent of US$300. Physicians involved in organ trading may be struck off for the medical register for two years for a first offence and permanently struck off for subsequent offences. Penalties are also incurred for soliciting or offering organs for payment.

Impact of the Transplantation of Human Organs Act 1994

The Act has been adopted by six States (Goa, Himalchal Pradesh, Maharashtra, Andhra Pradesh, Karnataka and Tamil Nadu) and all the Union Territories. However, it is only under consideration in West Bengal and Uttar Pradesh. In its first two years of existence, Nundy (1996) reports that three heart transplants and more than 20 renal transplants were performed using organs obtained from brain stem dead, heart-beating cadavers. However, the law has not had the success in regulating and regularising organ transplants in India, particularly in relation to commercial practices using human organs. There are a number of problems with the Act. To begin with, it is a federal law, which means it has to be extended to individual States, such as Uttar Pradesh, where the Noida Medical Centre is situated. This Centre is a large private hospital which provides, *inter alia*, live kidney donors, but since the law does not apply to it, it has no need to follow any guidelines. Police action has been taken since the inception of the Act against physicians or middlemen who have breached the Act. But news reports continue to filter through about organs being removed form donors who claim they have been duped into consenting to such operations. The Secretary General of the Indian Medical Association has said that allegations of having kidneys 'stolen' are not true and that it is more likely that the donor/seller felt he did not receive adequate compensation for the organ donation. Irrespective of the real situation, there is clearly more that needs to be done about the human organ transplantation situation in India, despite its legislation and efforts to respect the autonomy of donors and to demonstrate respect for persons, whether dead or alive.

People's Republic of China

At the outset, it needs to be borne in mind that all our comments on the Chinese situation regarding human organ transplantation are based on journal articles or internet sources, and the Chinese government has categorically denied any questionable practices as to the source of these transplants. Consequently, we merely note any 'facts' and statistics that are available regarding organ transplants from the Congressional Testimony given by David J Rothman, Professor of Social Medicine, Columbia College of Physicians and Surgeons to the Committee on Government Reform and Oversight, given on 16 June 1998 (more details of the testimony may be found on www.patientsupport.net/news). The organisation Human Rights Watch estimates that more than 2,000 organs, most of them kidneys, are transplanted in China every year; the Worldwide Transplant Directory, based at the University of California, Los Angeles, say that the Chinese have reported performing 6,900 kidney transplants in the three year period 1994–96, and this is regarded as a 'vast under-representation'.

Readers may access the world wide web address to judge for themselves the full extent of alleged practices which have elicited the condemnation of the World Medical Association.

Japan

Since 1968, there has not been a single heart operation in Japan (Wise (1997)). The reason appears to be that, in that year, a Japanese surgeon performed a transplant operation and the donor died. Consequently, the doctor was investigated and charged with murdering the donor. A long case ensued but, despite the doctor's acquittal, 'the long court case put a stop to all further operations'. The Lower House of the Japanese Parliament has now voted to officially recognise the concept of brain death, which will make it easier for heart transplants to take place for the first time in the country (Wise (1997)). Japan's main law making body voted by 329 to 148 to allow a person to be declared dead when her brain stops functioning. Under their previous law, a person's heart had to stop for death to be declared, which made the heart transplants impossible. Apparently, the subject was, for many years considered too controversial to bring to Parliament. Despite the fact that Buddhism and Shinto, its two main religions, do not have ethical objections to the concept of brain death, there has been 'cultural resistance' (Wise (1997)) to donating or receiving organs. There are many Japanese people who believe that a person's body and soul are linked and thus, by giving up an organ, one is also surrendering one's soul. Other beliefs are rooted in the idea that a body should not be 'defiled' before it reaches the next world. It appears that Japanese doctors are saying that the objections to organ transplantation have 'cost thousands of lives that could have been saved' (Wise (1997)). Many critically ill patients have had to be flown to the USA and elsewhere for a medical procedure that has become far more straightforward than before. The Upper House of Parliament has not yet approved the Bill, but the signs are that it will, particularly because of the Lower House's endorsement of it, a decision which 'could have enormous effects on Japanese medicine' (Wise (1997)). Poland and Pakistan are now the only other major countries that still do not designate brain death as actual death in law and practice. The recognition of a concept of brain death will mean that 'thousands of patients [in Japan] could be taken off artificial life support and the Health and Welfare Ministry estimates that, annually, more than 8,000 people in Japan will now be declared brain dead and this means that an increase in brain transplants will be facilitated' (Wise (1997)).

COMPARATIVE OBSERVATIONS ON ORGAN TRANSPLANTATION

Having surveyed the common law, civil law and *sui generis* jurisdictional approaches to the subject of human organ or tissue transplantation, it is possible to make a number of observations in the comparative context. First of all, all jurisdictions which have passed laws or regulations dealing with this area, adopt a basic policy of respecting the intentions of the organ donor, whether dead or alive and this reflects the 'respect for persons' principle which was identified at the outset of this book (see Introduction). Indeed, criminal sanctions follow from serious breaches of this principle. Secondly, jurisdictions have frequently adopted a 'contracting out' policy (presumed consent), but sometimes a 'contracting in' policy (for instance, in the case of Germany) with variations. Even where there is a *prima facie* contracting out policy, as in France and Belgium, the practice of doctors has always been to consult the relatives of a donor before carrying out transplants of any sort (which was also the practice in 1960s America despite their earlier legislation) and, as we have seen, this has now been regularised with the passing of new guidelines. However, when the system is followed strictly, as in Austria, the country seems to do better in organ procurement than other countries, but such a simplistic equation is seriously questioned by commentators because, despite the increase in the availability of organs in Austria, there is still an overall shortage in that country. Thirdly, all the jurisdictions we surveyed require written consent to organ donations/transplants and, in the case of Germany and Sweden, have gone to some lengths to specify exactly who could qualify as 'next-of-kin' and could therefore be consulted in the absence of an indication or evidence of the donor's intentions. An interesting innovation has been the consulting of a person who is not a relative but is either 'closely connected' to the donor (Sweden) or even 'especially close' (Germany) to the donor. A common feature is a hierarchy in order of seniority for next-of-kin, so that, in Australia and Germany, one works one's way down the list to contact persons who might cast some light on whether the donor had a view on transplanting of his organs, although Australia has an interesting notion of 'senior available next-of-kin'. Fourthly, a shortage of organs for transplants to save lives appears to be a fairly universal problem with the possible exception of countries like Spain, and limited success for France and Austria. All the jurisdictions which were surveyed have been making strenuous efforts to educate the population and continue to strive to increase the number of organs that will be available for life-saving purposes. As we have seen in early 2000, however, the latest campaign by the BMA to introduce a contracting out system in Britain has, so far, not met with any success.

The very least the comparative survey in this chapter has done is to highlight how much further down the road than Britain other countries with a similar cultural, religious and economic make-up have proceeded in their efforts to make human transplants the norm rather than the exception. The approaches taken by non-European countries must, however, be treated with caution because it is not *prima facie* justifiable simply to argue that, if smaller countries than Britain have decided to move to presumed consent regimes, then Britain should necessarily follow. However, the developing trends and imaginative legislation in the various jurisdictions are certainly worth examining as pointers to possible future legal reforms in this field of activity.

SELECTIVE BIBLIOGRAPHY

Anderson, M, 'The future of organs transplantation: from where will new donors come, to whom will their organs go?' (1995) 5 Health Matrix 249

National Health and Medical Research Council, *An Australian Code of Practice for Transplantation of Cadaveric Organs and Tissues*, 1991, National Health and Medical Research Council, Canberra

Aydin, E, 'Bioethics: regulations in Turkey' (1999) 25 JME 404

Banks, G, 'Legal and ethical safeguards: protection of society's most vulnerable participants in a commercialised organ transplantation system' (1995) 21 Am J Law & Med 45

BMA, 'Organ donation in the 21st century: time for a consolidated approach' (2000) www.bma.org.uk

Callender, C, 'Legal and ethical issues surrounding transplantation: the Transplant Team perspective', in Cowan, D *et al* (eds), *Human Organ Transplantation: Societal, Medical-Legal, Regulatory, and Reimbursement Issues*, 1987

Clark, M, 'Solving the kidney shortage through the use of non-heart-beating cadaveric donors: legal endorsement of perfusion as a standard procedure' (1995) 70 Ind LJ 929

Cohen, B (1994) 121 Eurotransplant Newsletter 1

Crespi, GS, 'Overcoming the legal obstacles to the creation of a futures market in bodily organs' (1988) 55 Ohio St LJ 1

Devereux, J, *Medical Law: Text, Cases and Materials*, 1997, Cavendish Publishing. See, also, 2nd edn, 2001

Dorozynski, A, 'France approves Bill to encourage organ donations' [1994] BMJ 1119

Gerike, P, 'Human biological material: a proprietary interest or part of the monistic being?' (1991) 17 Ohio NUL Rev 805

Gorsline, C and Johnson, R, 'The United States system of organ donation – the international solution and the cadaveric organ donor act: "... and the winner is ..."' (1995) 20 J Corp Law 32

Gorsline, C and Johnson, R, *Human Organ Transplantation: A Report on Developments under the Auspices of WHO (1987–1991)*, 1991, WHO

Howard, R and Najarian, J, 'Organ transplantation: medical perspective', in *Encyclopedia of Bioethics*, 1978, Free Press, Vol 3, p 1160

Jefferies, D, 'The body as commodity: the use of markets to cure the organ deficit' (1998) www.law.indiana.edu/glsj/vol5/no2/13jeffer.html

Johnson, L, 'The Swedish transplantation law' (1997) 48 Int Digest of Health Legislation 237

Kennedy, I *et al*, 'The case for "presumed consent" in organ donation' (1998) The Lancet 1650

Kurnit, M, 'Organ donation in the United States: can we learn from successes abroad?' (1994) BC Int & Comp L Rev 405

Mattei, J-F, 'The French bioethics laws: five years on' (1999) 50 Int Digest of Health Legislation 582

McCarthy, M, 'US panel suggest changes in organ allocation' (1999) 354 The Lancet 405

Mumford, S, 'Bone marrow donation – the law in context' (1998) 10 CFLQ 135

Norrie, McK K, 'Human tissue transplants: legal liability in different jurisdictions' (1985) 34 ICLQ 442

Nundy, S, 'Origin and genesis of the Transplantation of Human Organs Act 1994' (1996) 47 Int Digest of Health Legislation 88

Redmond-Cooper, R, 'Transplants opting out or in – the implications' (1984) 134 NLJ 648

Roels, L *et al*, 'The relative impact of legislative incentives on multi-organ donation rates in Europe' (1995) 27 Transplant Proceedings 795

Silver, T, 'The case for a post-mortem organ draft and a proposed model organ draft' (1988) 68 BUL Rev 681

Suthanthiran, M and Strom, TB, 'Medical progress: renal transplantation' (1994) 365 New England J Med 365

Tuffs, A, 'Germany introduces new criteria for organ allocation' [2000] BMJ 10

Younger *et al*, 'Ethical, psychosocial and public policy implications of procuring organs from non-heart-beating cadaver organs' (1993) 269 J Am Med Assoc 2769

Williams, C, 'Combating the problems of human rights abuses and inadequate organ supply through presumed donative consent' (1994) 26 Case W Res J In Law 315

CHAPTER 18

EUTHANASIA, DEATH AND DYING: A COMPARATIVE OVERVIEW

INTRODUCTION

Euthanasia, death and dying give rise to similar dilemmas and problems throughout the world. Indeed, in the past 50 years, several Western countries have wrestled with the dilemmas associated with the rapid advances in technology. We have already seen how English law has tried to deal with the problem. In comparative terms, there appears to be only one State, the Northern Territory of Australia, which once passed a statute, in the autumn of 1996, allowing a doctor to assist a terminally ill patient to die, although this law contained several safeguards and prior consultations. This statute has now been repealed, and was law for only six months. However, in the Netherlands, Switzerland and Germany, it has been claimed that both voluntary euthanasia and assisted suicide are openly practised, even though neither practice is legal in these countries (see Vickers (1997)). As we have already mentioned in Part I, there is a voluminous amount of literature, academic, medico-legal, and informational on the subject of euthanasia generally. Indeed, there is major research continuing in Scotland, which produced the first ever book on 'self-deliverance'. In Europe, North America and Australia, changes in policy have attracted a great deal of global interest. Several American jurisdictions have, on occasion, also challenged the constitutionality of laws against assisted suicide. However, it is to the Netherlands that we first turn as, over the years, it has become the most cited jurisdiction for euthanasia whenever any comparisons are made with non-common law countries.

CIVIL LAW COUNTRIES

The Netherlands

Over the years, the Netherlands has acquired a reputation, not always justifiable, for being the country where euthanasia is both legal and widely practised. Yet, euthanasia is not *ex facie* allowed by statute in the Netherlands, but Dutch law accepts a standard defence from doctors who have facilitated a death provided they have complied with official guidelines dealing with 'physician assisted suicide'. However, the patient does not have to be terminally ill or suffering from a physical illness, so a mental illness would suffice. The other point worth noting is that, although 'euthanasia' might be taken to be wide enough to be any form of termination of life by a doctor, the Dutch definition is a *narrower* one than in other jurisdictions. Thus, any termination of life by a doctor at the request of a patient qualifies as a legal termination of life, provided the other Dutch guidelines have been satisfied. The other point that should be borne in mind is that the phrase 'voluntary euthanasia', as opposed to involuntary euthanasia, is not used in the Netherlands, because if the termination of life was not voluntary, it does not qualify as euthanasia in that jurisdiction, since lawful termination has to be at the request of the patient. The Ministries of Justice and of Health, Welfare and Sport and the Royal Dutch Medical Association agreed on rules for reporting all deaths 'as a result of termination of life on request, assisting a patient to take his or her own life or the active termination of life without express request'.

All this has come about as a result of several landmark cases in 1971, 1984, 1994 and 1995.

The Dutch medical infrastructure and proportion of euthanasia terminations

The Netherlands has a high standard of medical care which ranks as among the best in the world. Over 95% of the population are covered by private medical insurance, guaranteeing a large core of basic healthcare, including long term care. Indeed, 100% of the population are insured against protracted illness and there are no financial incentives for hospitals, physicians, or family members to stop the care of patients. Further, the legal right of patients to healthcare on the basis of their insurance will override budgetary and other financial agreements (see Wal and Dillman (1994), p 1346). There are pain and palliation centres (to provide a high level of palliative care) attached to all hospitals. The equivalent centres in other countries are costly and are called hospices. It is often recounted that, at the time of the Nazi occupation, Dutch doctors went to concentration camps rather than divulge the names of their patients. This is said to have led to an unusually close relationship between doctors and patients in the Netherlands. According to Wal and Dillman (1994) (p 1347), euthanasia occurs at home in one out of about 25 deaths, in hospitals in one out of 75, and in nursing homes in one out of 800. They point out that about 40% of patients die at home, especially patients with cancer, which is about 48% of all deaths.

A study commissioned by the Dutch Government suggests that there is serious underreporting of euthanasia (see Vickers (1997)), but the study also indicates that reporting of such deaths increased from 18% to 41% over five years and that decisions about terminating life were taken with increasing care. Hence, according to Vickers (1997), the 59% of doctors who did not report 'either feared conviction, were concerned that families should not have to face criminal investigation, or did not regard the death as unnatural'.

The Dutch Government Commission on Euthanasia (1985), under the generic heading of 'Medical Decisions to End Life', defines euthanasia as:

> A deliberate termination of an individual's life at that individual's request, by another. Or, in medical practice, the active and deliberate termination of a patient's life, on [*sic*] that patient's request, by a doctor.

Statutory provisions regulating euthanasia under the Dutch Penal Code

> Art 289: A person who intentionally and with premeditation takes the life of another is guilty of murder and is punishable by a maximum of life imprisonment.
>
> Art 293: Anyone who deliberately incites anyone to commit suicide, assists in him doing so or provides the means for him to so do will, if suicide follows, be published with a prison sentence of a maximum of 3 years or a category 4 fine.

Art 40 provides that a person who commits an offence as a result of 'irresistible compulsion or necessity (*force majeure* or duress) is not criminally liable'.

Guidelines

Doctors will not be prosecuted if they comply with the requirements published by the Royal Dutch Medical Association (RDMA) in 1984, which have been confirmed by court decisions. The requirements are:

(a) the patient must make a voluntary request ('entirely free and voluntary');

(b) the request must be well considered, durable and persistent;

(c) the patient must be experiencing intolerable (not necessarily physical) suffering, with no prospect of improvement;

(d) euthanasia must be a last resort. Other alternatives to alleviate the patient's situation must have been considered and found wanting;

(e) euthanasia must be performed by a physician;

(f) the physician must consult with an independent physician, or colleague who has experience in the field and agrees with the proposed course of action.

Notification

The Dutch Burial Act of 1994 lays down a notification procedure in its regulations to the effect that:

(a) the physician performing the euthanasia or assisted suicide should not issue a declaration of natural death but informs the local medical examiner of the circumstances by filling in an extensive questionnaire;
(b) the medical examiner reports to the district attorney; and
(c) the district attorney (public prosecutor) then decides whether or not a prosecution should be instituted.

The public prosecutor decides whether or not to prosecute according to the RDMA guidelines set out above (see the guidelines, above).

Administration

The practice in Holland is to use an injection to render the patient comatose, followed by a second injection to stop the heart. The official guidelines actually encourage the doctor to allow the patient to take the lethal dosage, under supervision, provided this is a practical alternative.

Dutch case law

Several Dutch cases have been instrumental in changing the Dutch guidelines on 'assisted suicide'.

The *Dr Postma* case (1973)

In 1971, Dr Geertruida Postma injected a patient with morphine and curare, which resulted in that patient's death. The patient was her mother, who had earlier suffered a brain haemorrhage, was partly deaf, had difficulty speaking, and had to be tied to a chair to avoid falling. On occasions, she had asked her daughter, Dr Postma, to end her life. Dr Postma was charged under Art 293 of the Dutch Penal Code. In 1973, the Leeuwarden criminal court found Dr Postma guilty, but merely gave a one week suspended sentence and one year's probation. The court indicated that it was possible (that is, legal) to administer pain relieving drugs leading to the death of the patient in certain circumstances provided the goal of treatment was the relief of physical or psychological pain arising from an incurable terminal illness. In this case, however, Dr Postma's primary goal was seen to be to cause the death of the patient.

In 1973, in the wake of the *Postma* decision, the RDMA issued a statement supporting the retention of Art 293, but arguing that the administration of pain relieving drugs and the withholding or withdrawal of futile treatment could be justified even if death resulted.

The *Alkmaar* Case (1984)

The *Alkmaar* decision was the next landmark decision, a case that came before the Dutch Supreme Court. The facts of this case are that there was a 95 year old patient who was unable to eat or drink and had temporarily lost consciousness shortly before her death. After regaining consciousness, she requested her physician to assist her to die. He consulted another doctor, who agreed that the patient was unlikely to regain her health. However, it should be noted that the patient's illness was chronic, but not terminal. The doctor carried out the patient's request and was convicted by a lower court of an offence under Art 293 of the Dutch Penal Code, although no punishment was imposed. On appeal, the Supreme Court overturned the conviction, holding that the doctor was entitled to succeed in the defence of necessity under Art 40. The court agreed with the doctor's defence, that he faced a conflict of responsibilities between preserving the patient's life on the one hand and alleviating suffering on the other. The doctor could also face a conflict over whether to obey the law or relieve suffering. The court decided that the conflict must be resolved on the basis of the doctor's responsible medical opinion measured by the prevailing standards of medical ethics. In this case, the doctor was found to have properly resolved that conflict.

In a subsequent case decided in 1986 (see NJ 1989, Nr 391) the court rejected the argument that the defence of necessity was to be determined solely in accordance with medical rules of art (*lege artis*).

The defence of necessity in Dutch law

The criteria relating to the defence of necessity need to be culled from a number of Dutch decisions, as they are not contained in any statute or code. It is, therefore, difficult to specify definitively what these criteria are. The Dutch defence of necessity *prima facie* is similar to the English law of necessity, but there is apparently an ambiguity depending on how the Dutch concept of *noodtoestand* is translated. According to Griffiths (1995), the technically correct translation is 'situation of necessity', and the Dutch defence of necessity should be the same as English law. However, in the case of euthanasia, the 'necessity' that the Dutch courts have recognised does not appear to refer to a general necessity, but a specific medical necessity, measured in terms of the state of medical knowledge and the professional norms of doctors and, Griffiths argues, it seems that no one but a doctor can successfully invoke it. Hence, there is an argument for translating the term merely to refer to medical necessity. It should also be noted that the Dutch Penal Code and the defence of necessity only become relevant where there is prosecution of a doctor. The main criteria for establishing a defence of necessity have been stated above.

The *Chabot* case (1994)

The patient was Mrs Hilly Boscher, a 50 year old, who had an unhappy marriage, and one of her two sons committed suicide while in military service in Germany. Her marital problems intensified after the suicide and she began to manifest suicidal tendencies herself. She only kept herself alive to look after her other son. Her problems were purely psychological, she had spent a little time in institutionalised psychiatric care, and had a long history of depression, spanning nearly two decades. Upon the death of her second son, she attempted suicide, but was unsuccessful and was determined to try again. She approached the Dutch Federation for Voluntary Euthanasia, who referred her to Dr Chabot, the defendant in this case. Dr Chabot diagnosed her as suffering from severe and intractable mental suffering. He came to the conclusion that Mrs Boscher's case satisfied the guidelines. He consulted a number of colleagues but none, apart from Dr Chabot, had examined her. In September, 1991, in the presence of her family doctor, and a friend of hers, Dr Chabot supplied her with lethal drugs which she consumed in their presence. She died half an hour later and Dr Chabot reported her death the same day, as one in which he had assisted, to the coroner.

Dr Chabot was prosecuted under Art 294 of the Dutch Penal Code. He invoked the defence of necessity. The Supreme Court held that there was no reason in principle why the defence of necessity could not apply where a patient's suffering was purely psychological and not in the terminal phase. For the defence to apply, however, the patient must be examined by an independent medical expert. Dr Chabot had sought medical opinions from seven colleagues, but none had actually seen Mrs Boscher. Accordingly, the defence of necessity failed. The court did also hold that the request of a person suffering from a psychiatric illness could legally be considered to be the result of an autonomous judgment, but such cases must be approached 'with extreme caution'. Dr Chabot was found guilty of an offence under Art 294, but the court declined to impose a sentence; in February 1995, he received an official reprimand from a Medical Disciplinary Tribunal which concluded that his behaviour had 'undermined confidence in the medical profession' (see Griffiths (1995)).

The aftermath of *Chabot*

This case has given rise to criticism which, generally, raises the spectre of the 'slippery slope' argument – if this sort of case is considered as justifying the defence of necessity provided there was independent consultation, how far will the courts be prepared to go in tolerating requests for physician assisted suicides?

Commentators like Griffiths (1995) dismiss such criticism by saying that anecdotal evidence suggests that psychiatrists have long engaged in practices which amount to assisted suicide and there is no evidence to suggest that this increases the incidence of such deaths. Further, he argues that, so long as it is all happening underground, there appears to be very little prospect of legal or other control of such practices.

On the political front, the new Dutch Government responded positively to the *Chabot* case by announcing a revision of its prosecutorial guidelines to fall in line with the principles the *Chabot* court laid down, and withdrew prosecutions for 11 out of 15 pending prosecutions, involving patients who were not terminally ill and suffering form non-physical illnesses.

In 1995, the Royal Dutch Medical Association's guidelines were revised as follows:

(a) assisted suicide is to be preferred to euthanasia where possible;

(b) the primary doctor's consultations should be with an experienced doctor who has no professional or family relationship with either the primary doctor or the patient;

(c) if a doctor is opposed to euthanasia, the doctor must make his or her views known to the patient and help the patient find a doctor who is willing to assist.

In late 1997, the Dutch Government responded to a study of deaths carried out during 1995 which showed an increase in the incidence of active voluntary euthanasia. It announced proposals to enhance care services and foreshadowed further regulation, but not the decriminalisation of euthanasia in Holland.

Euthanasia and handicapped neonates in the Netherlands

The Kadijk *case (1995)*

In November 1995, the Groningen District Court heard a case where a doctor was charged with offences under the Dutch Penal Code after causing the death of a 25 day old neonate girl by lethal injection at the 'explicit and earnest desire of the parents'. The child was suffering from Pateau Syndrome, the symptoms of which are cleft lip and palate, overlapping fingers, micropthalmia, serious mental retardation, multiple neurological convulsions and motor retardation. The child had suffered one cardio-respiratory arrest and there was evidence of renal failure. One of the scalp defects had become ulcerated and infected. Upper limb convulsions could not be controlled with analgesia or sedation without risking kidney failure. There was also evidence that 90% of Trisomy children had died within the first year of life. The Groningen Court upheld the doctor's defence of necessity. Both parties have lodged an appeal.

The Prins *case (1995)*

This Amsterdam Court of Appeal case was also heard in November 1995 and concerned a doctor who administered a lethal injection to a three day old neonate suffering from hycephalus spina bifida. The baby was in severe pain and was expected to live a maximum of six months. Its parents were informed of the condition and prognosis and gave a 'considered and earnest request' for the baby to be killed by lethal injection. Again, the defence of necessity was upheld by the court. This matter has also gone on appeal.

COMPARATIVE OBSERVATIONS

As we have seen, in English law there has not been any rule that required the courts to pay heed to the views of parents of handicapped neonates as regards their medical treatment until the controversial case of *Re T (A Minor) (Wardship: Medical Treatment)* [1997] 1 All ER 906 (the liver transplant case), where an English appeal court appeared to break with precedent (embodied in the 1981 Court of Appeal case of *Re B (A Minor) (Wardship: Medical Treatment)* [1981] 1 WLR 1421) and decided not to follow the medical opinion and clinical factors, but overturned the lower court's ruling because it had failed to give adequate weight to the parent's views and objections to the proposed transplant. This case has been questioned by several academics and its trend was not followed in a subsequent case which reverted to clinical factors (for a full discussion of this, see Chapters 4 and 12, which deal with the selective non-treatment of the newborn). For the common lawyer, it should be noted that English law has no equivalent of a parent's 'considered and earnest request' for a handicapped baby to have its life terminated by lethal injection.

The *ethical point* to note here is that most common law jurisdictions adhere, one way or another, to the *sanctity of life doctrine* as a general principle, but when certain non-English jurisdictions deviate from this approach, they usually do so on the ground of statutory interpretation or constitutional rights.

Germany

The German Penal Code deals with murder, and also mentions 'assisting' another in a deliberate and illegal act. Under para 211, murder is punishable with imprisonment for life. Paragraph 212 deals with manslaughter and prescribes imprisonment for a minimum of five years up to a maximum of life imprisonment for particularly severe cases falling short of murder. Paragraph 226 stipulates that injuring another with his or her consent is a crime only if indecent. Paragraph 27 states that to willingly assist another in a deliberate and illegal act is a crime. There is then para 216, which declares that, if a person is persuaded to kill another after having been expressly and earnestly requested to do so by the person killed, the punishment is imprisonment for between six months and five years, which is less than manslaughter. Any attempt to kill another in these circumstances will also be punishable.

German law also requires the request to be clear and unambiguous and, if the person assisting in the death will thereby benefit financially from the patient's death, will not necessarily exclude para 216. However, active assistance under this paragraph, for instance, by administration of a fatal drug dose, will amount to 'causing death' and is a crime with a minimum of six months' imprisonment, even if it is done as a result of an 'earnest request' for death from the patient. It should be noted that giving less direct help to die would remain legal. So suicide and attempted suicide are not against the law, and neither is acquiescence in the death of persons wishing to take full responsibility for their dying. The German Medical Chamber declares that it is unprofessional for a doctor to take part in a patient's suicide. However, assistance is provided by laymen.

Switzerland

Under Art 114 of the Swiss Penal Code, active euthanasia is illegal, but the Code provides for differential penalties depending upon the motive of the person perpetrating the death. There is a judicial power to mitigate the penalty if the actor's motives were honourable, in the sense of the killing being motivated by mercy and at the request of the individual concerned. Under Art 115 of the same Code, 'aiding and abetting suicide' is defined, and in order for the offence to be established, a selfish motive is required. Hence, if such a motive cannot be proved, a physician-assisted suicide will not be punishable under Swiss law. Since 1982, a right to die organisation in Switzerland, called EXIT, has been providing assistance with dying in accordance with the law and adheres to its own set of additional requirements. These are that the individual must be (a) 18 years of age or over; (b) a Swiss resident; (c) mentally competent; and (d) suffering from intolerable health problems. The application will be considered by a doctor working with EXIT, and will consult with the expertise of lawyers, psychiatrists or other doctors if necessary, and a member of the EXIT team will provide lethal medication to the patient. The police are informed after a death, and appropriate officials are supposed to be notified: they then visit the scene to establish whether or not the death was within the law. It is estimated that about one to two hundred patients die with the assistance of EXIT every year.

The USA

In the US Supreme Court decision of *Washington v Glucksberg* (1997) 117 S Ct 2258; (1997) 138 L Ed 2d (discussed below, p 615), Rehnquist CJ examined the history, legal tradition and practices relating to assisted suicide in the Anglo-American common law tradition. In his judgment, he stressed that, for over 700 years, this tradition has punished or otherwise disapproved of both suicide and assisting suicide. In Chapter 9, we looked at the history of English law on this area, which basically regarded suicide as one of the most serious crimes. For the most part, American colonies adopted the English common law approach, in places like Rhode Island and Virginia, but gradually, over time, the American colonies abolished the harsh common law penalties. States like Pennsylvania, in 1701, abandoned the criminal sanction and other colonies followed suit; but the State's movement away from the common law's harsh treatment did not signify an acceptance of suicide, but only a growing groundswell of opinion that it was unfair to penalise the suicide's family for his actions. However, the American courts continued to express their grave disapproval of suicide as a serious public wrong. The first American statute expressly to criminalise assisting suicide was enacted in New York in 1828 (see Act of 10 December 1828, ch 20, s 4, 1828 NY Laws 19) and many of the new States and Territories followed New York's example. By the time the 14th Amendment was ratified, it was a crime in most States to assist a suicide. In the 20th century, the Model Penal Code also prohibited 'aiding' suicide, which encouraged other States to enact or revise their assisted suicide prohibitions. In more recent times, the States' prohibitions on such assisted deaths have been re-appraised, but generally re-affirmed. The Model Penal Code states that 'A person who purposely aids or solicits another to commit suicide, is guilty of a felony in the second degree if his conduct causes such suicide or an attempted suicide, and otherwise of a misdemeanour'.

Survey of assisted suicide laws in the USA

As of July 1998 (see (1998) *USA Today*, 6 July) this appears to be the current position in the USA with regard to assisted suicide laws.

Legalised under State legislation

Oregon.

Criminalised under State common law

Alabama, Idaho, Maryland, Massachusetts, Michigan, Nevada, Ohio, South Carolina, Vermont, West Virginia.

States with no existing law on physician-assisted suicide which have also abolished common law 'criminalisation'

North Carolina, Utah, Wyoming.

Criminalised under State legislation

Alaska, Arizona, Arkansas, California, Colorado, Connecticut, Delaware, Florida, Georgia, Hawaii, Illinois, Indiana, Iowa, Kansas, Kentucky, Louisiana, Maine, Minnesota, Mississippi, Missouri, Montana, Nebraska, New Hampshire, New Jersey, New Mexico, New York, North Dakota, Oklahoma, Pennsylvania, Rhode Island, South Dakota, Tennessee, Texas, Virginia, Washington, Wisconsin, District of Columbia.

There is also the US Uniform Rights of the Terminally Ill Act 1989 which establishes the legal validity of 'living wills' or advance directives'. This Act even recognises revocation of an advance directive at any time by the declarant, regardless of the declarant's mental or physical condition.

Oregon: the Death with Dignity Act

Oregon is a US State which has a statute making assistance in suicide a criminal offence. Under ORS 163.125(b) 'Criminal homicide constitutes manslaughter in the second degree when ... [a] person intentionally causes or aids another person to commit suicide'. It also has a statute that makes assisted suicide a defence to murder when the conduct at issue 'consisted of ... aiding ... without duress or deception, another person to commit suicide'. That statute codified *State v Bouse* (1953) 199 Or 676; (1953) 264 P 2d 800, in which the court interpreted the prior assisted suicide statute to cover participation such as 'furnishing the means for bringing about death'. The case created a situation where Oregon physicians who wrote a prescription for drugs to end the life of a dying person were at risk of prosecution.

A new law was required to protect physicians who were writing prescriptions for lethal medications at their patients' request and to provide an opportunity for physicians who wished to provide such assistance to their terminally ill patients.

The Death with Dignity Act came into force in October 1997. This statute legalised 'physician-assisted suicide' and specifically prohibits euthanasia where a physician or other person directly administers a medication to end another's life. Under the Act, the patient must be (a) aged 18 or over; (b) a resident of Oregon; (c) capable (defined as able to make and communicate healthcare decisions); and (d) be diagnosed with a terminal, incurable and irreversible illness that will lead to death within six months. Patients who satisfy these requirements are eligible to request a prescription for lethal medication from a licensed Oregon physician. There are several further conditions necessary for receipt of the prescription, including: repeated requests; a consulting physician must confirm diagnosis and capacity; the patient must be advised of palliative care and pain control; and the patient must be requested, but not required, to notify their next of kin of the prescription request.

A notable feature of the Act is that physicians and health care organisations are under no obligation to participate in the implementation of the Act. It also requires that the Oregon Health Division collects information about the use of its provisions, and publishes an annual report. The first of these reports, published in December 1990, showed that 23 people received prescriptions for lethal medication in 1998, of which 15 died after taking these. Six of these people died of their underlying illness, and the remaining two were still alive at the beginning of 1999.

American case law dealing with PVS patients and physician-assisted suicide

PVS patients: cases

We look first at cases where the patients lay in a persistent vegetative state (PVS) for several years.

The *Karen Quinlan* case (1976) 429 US 922; (1976) 355 A 2d 647

In American law, two high profile cases in 1976 and 1990 have made their impact on the euthanasia or physician-assisted landscape. The first case is the *Karen Quinlan* case, which arguably represents one of America's most famous cases of medical ethics. The case attracted media attention in 1975 when Karen's parents were fighting for legal guardianship of her with the intent of removing a respirator so that she could die. She has since become a symbol of a tragic death. Karen Quinlan was a 21 year old who seemed to have the world at her feet, popular, and much loved by her parents and peers. Although the precise details are a matter of some dispute, Karen had just moved out of her family home and rented a room with two male friends. A few nights after moving out, Karen suddenly appeared faint, was taken home by her friends and put to bed. She stopped breathing at one point, which her friends discovered, and called an ambulance. However, a policeman got her heart going again, but she did not regain consciousness. Dispute also exists over what was in her bloodstream and one explanation is that there was a certain quantity of alcohol and, at the very least, some tranquillisers, although some reports suggest that there were barbiturates. Her friends confirmed she had three alcoholic drinks, and she had been dieting (or even fasting). If she had taken barbiturates and Valium followed by alcohol, the cumulative effects probably suppressed her breathing and caused loss of oxygen to her brain, followed by irreversible brain damage. Karen was taken to the intensive care unit in a New Jersey hospital.

Her condition remained unchanged and a she was kept breathing by a black respirator. She was moved to another respirator when her breathing improved, but not sufficiently, so she was put on another special respirator. She was technically in a persistent vegetative state (PVS). She had a feeding tube inserted, she gasped as the oxygen entered her windpipe and her hands were emaciated as her weight continued to drop. There was very little possibility of her ever regaining consciousness. The question arose as to what should be done. After many months, Karen's family took the decision that she was beyond hope, with her mind gone, and she would never have wanted her body to continue like this. Legal wrangles followed, the New Jersey Attorney General opposed letting Karen die on the basis that this would 'open the door to euthanasia', saying that there is no stated right to die in the federal constitution and, even if there were such a right, it would be likely to be for voluntary, adult, competent patients. When the case came to court, the lower court decision was that Karen's wishes were unknown, she was not brain dead and that physicians, not courts, should make such decisions in the future. This was certainly not the view taken in previous or subsequent cases. On appeal, the New Jersey Supreme Court unanimously held that, *inter alia*, the respirator could be turned off and other support withdrawn, legal immunity would be granted to the physicians and Karen's right to privacy could be asserted by her father to allow her to die. Nearly 14 months after falling unconscious, Karen was transferred to a nursing home where she would be maintained for over 10 years. On 13 June 1986, more than 10 years after being placed in the nursing home, Karen Quinlan was declared dead from pneumonia, from months of increasing respiratory congestion.

The case decided that there was the right under certain circumstances to refuse or to reject life sustaining medical treatment or the right to die a natural death. It also distinguished between suicide and the passive withdrawal of life support.

Cruzan v Missouri Department of Health (1990) 110 S Ct 2841; (1990) 497 US 261

In 1989, in the first 'right-to-die case' it had ever had, the US Supreme Court announced that it would hear a Missouri Supreme Court decision rejecting a family's decision to remove a feeding tube from a woman named Nancy Beth Cruzan. She had been in a PVS since an accident on 11 January 1983, when she was 25, in which she sustained a head injury. She was oblivious to her surroundings and the prognosis was that there was no prospect of an improvement in her condition. Her body twitched only reflexively, without consciousness. Her brain felt sensations, but it had degenerated badly and was continuing to deteriorate. The cavities remaining were filling with cerebrospinal fluid and the cerebral cortical atrophy was irreversible, permanent, progressive and ongoing. There was no prospect of Nancy interacting with her environment in any meaningful way. She would have remained in a PVS until her death. Since she could not swallow, her nutrition and hydration were delivered through a tube surgically implanted in her stomach.

In 1987, Nancy Cruzan's parents applied to the Missouri courts for an order permitting the withdrawal of hydration and nutrition. By a majority of 4:3, the Supreme Court of Missouri held that no such order should be made. The reasoning proceeds along three layers of constitutional law: argument was joined about the common law of Missouri; the constitutional rights guaranteed by the State constitution; and on the rights contained in the US Constitution.

The majority of the Missouri court held that: (a) under the common law of Missouri, for there to be a withdrawal of medical treatment, there had to be 'clear and convincing evidence' to the effect that the patient would not wish, under the circumstances which obtain, to be treated. Without such clear and convincing evidence, hydration and nutrition had to continue; (b) under the State Constitution of Missouri, the rights to liberty and equal protection of the laws (protected both under Art 1, ss 2 and 10 of the State Constitution and the 14th Amendment of the US Constitution) do not operate in such a way as to grant a right to have nutrition and hydration terminated. The Missouri courts do not regard the Missouri Constitution as conferring a right of privacy; (c) under the US Constitution, the right of privacy which had been developed by the Supreme Court to protect the right to contraception within marriage, and then used to provide a constitutionally protected right to abortion, did not apply. There were serious doubts about whether the privacy decisions could be applied in cases such as this.

The Cruzan parents therefore appealed to the US Supreme Court.

Given the constitutional position in the USA, the US Supreme Court had to decide only whether the law of Missouri, as determined by the Supreme Court of the State, was consistent with the US Constitution. The US Supreme Court had neither the right nor the duty to determine the law of Missouri provided that the law was consistent with the US Constitution. Hence, the question for the US Supreme Court was whether the State could, consistently with the US Constitution, require clear and convincing evidence of the wishes of the patient to be produced before it could act upon them; and whether it could, consistently with the equal protection clause in the 14th Amendment (to refuse treatment) permit rights to competent patients which were not permitted to incompetent patients.

By a 5:4 majority, the US Supreme Court held that the State of Missouri was within its powers to adopt the law laid down in Missouri on *Cruzan*.

Thus, the court authorised the removal of nasogastric nutrition and hydration from Nancy Cruzan based on evidence of her previously expressed wishes. In view of the gravity of the decision and the difficulties of establishing the necessary evidence, the court required that the evidence as to her previously expressed wishes met the raised standard of 'clear and convincing evidence'.

The majority, *per* Rehnquist CJ, 'assumed for purposes of this case' that a competent person has 'a constitutionally protected right to refuse lifesaving hydration and nutrition'. Yet, the court did not call the liberty a 'fundamental right', but a '14th Amendment liberty interest'. However, the court did not suggest that there was a '14th Amendment liberty interest' in assisted suicide. The court stressed that the State has an interest 'in the protection and preservation of human life' and supported this by declaring that the majority of States in the USA have laws imposing criminal penalties on one who assists another to commit suicide, but they 'did not think that a State is required to remain neutral in the face of an informed and voluntary decision by a physically able adult to starve to death'.

Following further evidence coming to light, no opposition was made to a further application for disconnection of nutrition and hydration. Nutrition and hydration were disconnected in 1990, and Nancy Cruzan died 12 days later, on 26 December 1990, having been eight years in a PVS.

This judgment therefore appeared to utilise the 'substituted judgment' test; this means that an attempt is made to reach a decision based on what the person would have chosen had they been able to do so. This is generally inferred from previous statements made on more than one occasion by the person who is now incompetent. The US Supreme Court had, therefore, upheld the right of a competent patient to refuse treatment, albeit through her parents, who has petitioned various courts on eight occasions that she be allowed to die.

Re Fiori (1995) 652 A 2d 1350

In this case, a man had been in a PVS for some 15 years and was tube-fed, but not ventilated. His mother requested the withdrawal of the gastronomic feeding. The Supreme Court of Pennsylvania granted the mother's request, and categorically stated that there was no necessity for a prior express statement by the patient as the test. The court went further, by saying that the surrogate decision maker can consider the 'patient's personal value system for guidance' where there was no expressed view as to the use of life support. This appears to be a confirmation of an 'objective' approach, and the court went even further by saying that there was no need for a court to intervene in the decision making process unless there was disagreement between the interested parties. The court, making clear it was referring specifically to the PVS patient who had never clearly expressed a preference for termination, held that the surrogate or proxy consent of a close family member, reinforced by the written approval of two physicians, protects the patient's interests sufficiently.

As Mason and McCall Smith (1999) observe, *Fiori* seems to represent 'a major step towards accepting the family's ultimate responsibility for taking treatment withdrawal decisions in the United States'. However, they also highlight two provisos: (a) the decision was strictly limited to the patient satisfying the PVS criteria; and (b) despite the importance attached to the family, it is 'at least arguable that the concept of family decision making is illusory, given the overwhelming power of the medical advisers. Indeed, the procedure outlined by the Pennsylvanian Superior Court will probably only work where there is complete agreement. A suggested alternative by Mason and McCall Smith (1999) is to *assume* that no one would wish to be maintained in the PVS and that, once the diagnosis is made, we could act on that assumption. It would then be up to families seeking to continue treatment to justify their stance. However, even these two authors admit that this would re-introduce the image of unrestrained medicalisation, which is always open to criticism. The present author would submit that, while a present prognosis of a given case would seem to suggest that the patient might never recover, there have certainly been instances where people have done so, rare though such cases are. In other words, although some would argue that there has to be a point where one has to 'let go', it is always going to extremely agonising and heart-rending to make that decision – to simply 'let nature take its course' – because (as in *Bland*) it is now seen as the only thing left to do which is in the patient's best interests.

Physician-assisted suicide cases

Washington and *Vacco*

In mid-1997, the US Supreme Court decided two cases on 26 June, *Washington v Glucksberg* and *Vacco v Quill* (1997) 117 S Ct 2293 (US Sup Ct), which considered, *inter alia*, the 'right to die' issue in the context of the right of a terminally ill patient to commit suicide with the aid of a physician. In *Washington v Glucksberg*, the issue was whether Washington's prohibition against 'causing' or 'aiding' a suicide offended the Due Process and Equal Protection Clause of the 14th Amendment to the American Constitution. In *Vacco v Quill*, the issue was whether New York's prohibition on assisting suicide violated the Equal Protection of the 14th Amendment. The court unanimously upheld both these State laws which made it a crime to assist a suicide. Both these laws prevent physicians from prescribing drugs for terminally ill patients to self-administer to commit suicide. The Supreme Court reversed decisions from two lower federal courts, including an *en banc* decision of the United States Court of Appeals for the Ninth Circuit.

The 14th Amendment, adopted in 1868, states that 'No State shall make or enforce any law which shall abridge the privileges or immunities of citizens of the United States, nor shall any State deprive any person of life, liberty or property without due process of law ...'

The Equal Protection Clause of the 14th Amendment of the US Constitution commands that no State shall 'deny to any person within its jurisdiction the equal protection of the laws.'

Washington v Glucksberg (1997)

In Washington, as in other States, it is a crime to aid another to commit or aid suicide. The plaintiffs included terminally ill patients and physicians who routinely treated the terminally ill. The plaintiffs sought a declaration that the Washington Code (Wash, Rev Code 9A.36.060(1) 1994) is, on its face, unconstitutional, because its ban on assisted suicide 'places an undue burden on the exercise of that constitutionally protected liberty interest. The District Code agreed with this, and also decided that the Washington statute violated the Equal Protection Clause's requirement that 'all persons similarly situated ... be treated alike'. Chief District Judge Barbara Rothstein held that 'a competent, terminally ill adult has a constitutionally guaranteed right under the 14th Amendment to commit physician-assisted suicide'. However, a panel of the Court of Appeals of the Ninth Circuit reversed this ruling, emphasising that 'in the two hundred and five years of our existence, no constitutional right to aid in killing oneself has ever been upheld by a court of final jurisdiction'. Judge Rheinhardt (for the majority) argued that historical attitudes on suicide were more ambiguous than first recognised. In essence, although American law had incorporated English law in the first instance, by 1798, it had begun to undergo a transformation, and by the time of the adoption of the 14th Amendment, suicide generally was not punishable. The judge reviewed prior Supreme Court decisions, particularly the abortion case of *Planned Parenthood of Southeastern Pennsylvania v Casey* (1992) 112 S Ct 2791 and *Cruzan v Missouri Department of Health* (1990) 497 US 261, which was thought to provide evidence that the US Constitution encompassed a due process liberty interest in controlling the time and manner of one's death and, in short, found there was a constitutional 'right to die'. The State of Washington appealed from the *en banc* Ninth Court decision.

The US Supreme Court reversed the Ninth Circuit ruling. Rehnquist CJ interpreted historical antecedents differently from Judge Rheinhardt, upholding the Washington State law, stressing that, having looked at the historical evidence, 'colonial and early State legislatures and courts did not retreat from prohibiting assisted suicide'. Nor did the prohibition against assisted suicide include an exception for the terminally ill.

Vacco v Quill (1997)

All the patients in this case testified that were in the final stages of terminal illnesses and they wanted their doctors to assist them to end their lives. By the time the case came to court, the three gravely ill patients had died. The plaintiff doctors asserted that, although it would be 'consistent with the standards of their medical practices' to prescribe lethal medication for 'mentally competent, terminally ill patients' who are suffering great pain and desire a doctor's help in taking their own lives, they were deterred from doing so by New York's ban on assisting suicide. The plaintiffs sued the State's Attorney General in the US District Court and urged that, because New York permits a competent person to refuse life sustaining medical treatment, the refusal of such treatment is 'essentially the same thing' as physician-assisted suicide. The District Court disagreed. The Court of Appeals for the Second Circuit reversed this opinion. In a separate opinion by Rehnquist CJ, the decision of the Second Circuit was unanimously reversed by the US Supreme Court. Rehnquist CJ drew a fine distinction between withdrawal of life sustaining medical treatment and physician-assisted suicide. He concluded that New York was justified in treating the two differently and regarded the distinction between them as 'important, logical and ... rational' and gave three reasons for making the distinction:

(a) When a patient refuses life sustaining medical treatment, and dies, he does so from an underlying fatal disease or medical condition; but if a patient ingests lethal medication prescribed by a physician, he is killed by that medication.

(b) A physician who withdraws, or honours a patient's refusal to begin or continue, life sustaining treatment, is only respecting his patient's wishes, ceasing doing futile things to the patient when the patient no longer stands to benefit from them. Similarly, a doctor who provides aggressive palliative care, and the pain killing drugs then hasten the patient's death, the doctor's purpose is to ease his patient's pain. However, a doctor who assists a suicide, 'must, necessarily and indubitably' intend the patient's death. The law has long distinguished between two acts that may have the same result, and made a distinction between a person who knows that another person will be killed as the result of his conduct and a person who acts with the specific purpose of killing someone. The main point was the actor's intent.

(c) The overwhelming majority of States, in durable powers of attorney in healthcare situations and enacting 'living will' statutes, have drawn a clear line between assisting suicide and withdrawing or permitting the refusal of unwanted life saving medical treatment by prohibiting the former and permitting the latter. The State has recognised the distinction between killing and letting die and of forgoing medical treatment and assisted suicide (or letting a patient die and making a patient die), for example, in *Cruzan* (1990) (above).

Accordingly, New York may permit everyone to refuse medical treatment while prohibiting anyone from assisting a suicide. It agreed that, in some cases, 'the line between the two may not be clear, but certainty is not required, even if it were possible'. Hence, the distinction between life saving medical treatment and assisted suicide was not 'arbitrary' or 'irrational' as the defendants alleged. Indeed, the Michigan Supreme Court had also accepted the distinction between acts that artificially sustain life and acts that artificially curtail life. But, many other courts had also accepted this distinction (see, for example, *Kervorkian v Thomson* (1997) 947 F Supp 1152, p 1178).

It is perhaps significant that the court in this case recognised a right to refuse treatment, but nowhere equated this right with suicide. The famous case of *Schloendorff v Society of New York Hospital* (1914), which contained Cardozo J's famous statement that 'every human being of adult years and sound mind has a right to determine what shall be done with his body', was simply an informed consent case.

These two cases have recently been followed by the Florida Supreme Court, in 1998, which ruled that there is no right to physician-assisted suicide under the Florida State Constitution. It is anticipated that there will be many further challenges of this nature in the near future.

The American Medical Association emphasises the 'fundamental difference between refusing life sustaining treatment and demanding a life ending treatment' (see American Medical Association, Council on Ethical and Judicial Affairs, Physician-Assisted Suicide).

Australia

Northern Territory of Australia

In 1995, the Legislative Assembly of the Northern Territory of Australia passed the Rights of the Terminally Ill Act 1995 (the 1995 Act). This has been called 'the world's first experiment with legalised active voluntary euthanasia' (Chesterman (1998)). It was introduced as a Private Member's Bill; legislation was tabled on 21 February 1995 and referred to a parliamentary select committee. This committee held public hearings throughout the Northern Territory and eventually published a report that did not make a recommendation on the desirability of a euthanasia law. Instead, it suggested amendments to the Bill and raised the issue of public education and the improvement of palliative care (for an account of the passage of the Act and its ultimate invalidation, see Chesterman (1998), pp 382 *et seq*, from which the material in this section is based). Eventually, 50 amendments were made to the Bill, which changed it quite considerably. The 1995 Act entered into force on 1 July 1996, but was invalidated less than a year later when, on 24 March 1997, Australia's Federal Parliament enacted legislation, in the form of the Euthanasia Laws Act 1997 (Cth), which removed the Territory's power to make laws permitting euthanasia. Nevertheless, it is useful to review the 1995 Act to assess its impact, despite its short existence.

The Rights of the Terminally Ill Act 1995

The purpose of the 1995 Act, as contained in the long title, was to 'confirm the right of a terminally ill person to request assistance from a medically qualified person to voluntarily terminate his or her life in a humane manner'. The Act provided that an adult patient who, 'in the course of a terminal illness, is experiencing pain, suffering and/or distress to an extent unacceptable to the patient, may request the patient's doctor to assist the patient to terminate the patient's life'. There was no obligation on the doctor to comply with a request under the Act, but he could do so provided he fulfilled certain detailed conditions. The Act exempted a doctor from civil or criminal liability if he did assist a patient to commit suicide within the terms of the Act, and he was also immune from professional disciplinary action.

The word 'assist' included prescribing, preparing and giving a substance to a patient for self-administration as well as the administration of a substance to a patient. Hence, the Act appeared to cover both involuntary euthanasia and physician-assisted suicide. Under the Act, 'terminal illness' was defined as 'an illness which, in reasonable medical judgment will, in the normal course, without the application of extraordinary measures or of treatment unacceptable to the patient, result in the death of the patient'.

The Euthanasia Laws Act 1997

This Act invalidated the Territory legislation by amending the Northern Territory (Self-Government) Act 1978 (Cth) to provide that the law making power of the Territory's legislative Assembly 'does not extend to the making of laws which permit or have the effect of permitting (whether subject to conditions or not) the form of intentional killing of another called euthanasia (which includes mercy killing) or the assisting of a person to terminate his or her life'. The Legislative Assembly retained the power to make laws with respect to the withdrawal or withholding of treatment and the provision of palliative care to a dying patient, but not so as to permit the intentional killing of the patient. It also retained the power to make laws with respect to the appointment of an agent authorised to make decisions about the withdrawal or withholding of treatment. In addition, the 1997 Act affirmed that the Legislative Assembly retains the power to repeal legal sanctions against attempted suicide which remains illegal under the Criminal Code. The fact that this federal law was passed subsequent to the coming into force of the 1995 Rights of the Terminally Ill Act did not affect the legality of any acts performed under the 1995 Act, as the latter law was not retrospective. As there were two patients affected by the 1995 law, attempts were made to persuade the Governor General to delay the giving of the Royal Assent to the Bill until the two patients had completed the procedural requirements under the Act and were given the opportunity to receive assistance under the 1995 Act. However, these attempts were not successful.

Self-destructing in 30 seconds: the death machine

The first person to die under the 1995 Act was Bob Dent, a 66 year old man from Darwin who had been suffering from prostate cancer for seven years. He died in September 1996 after triggering a lethal injection administered by a 'death machine' invented by Darwin doctor Philip Nitschke. This required the patient to move through three computer screens, the final one having the words: 'If you press 'Yes' you will cause a lethal injection to be given within 30 seconds and will die. Do you wish to proceed? YES/NO' (see Alcorn, G, 'Press "Yes" to die now' (1996) *The Age* (Melbourne), 17 April, p A13 and Alcorn, G, 'First death under NT mercy law' (1996) *The Age* (Melbourne), 26 September, p A1, cited in Chesterman (1998)). The second patient to die under the 1995 Act was Janet Mills, who suffered from the rare cancer mycosis fungoides (see Alcorn, G, 'So ends a mother's difficult years' (1997) *The Age* (Melbourne), 18 January, cited in Chesterman (1998)). By the time the 1995 Act was invalidated, four people had been assisted to terminate their lives and two others had completed the procedural conditions for assistance (see Middleton, K, ' NT doctor digs in as death law vote nears' (1997) *The Age* (Melbourne), 24 March, cited in Chesterman (1998)).

Impact of the Rights of the Terminally Ill Act 1995

Despite its short life, the 1995 Act appears to have had an 'approval rating' comparable to the 70–80% public support for euthanasia prior to its enactment (see Dow, S, 'Euthanasia law unsettles medics' (1997) *The Age* (Melbourne), 22 February). The survey published in the *Lancet*, however, found that doctors and, to a lesser extent, nurses, had a far lower approval rating for the legislation (see Chesterman (1998)). As Chesterman observes, the 1995 Act provided a useful example of how legislation could be used to regulate the practice of euthanasia 'in a more interventionist way' than the Dutch guidelines allow. He argues that, whereas the Dutch guidelines appear to give doctors more discretion in terms of any investigation of their areas, the Australian legislation, requiring a written record of patient consent, witnessed by a second doctor, provided greater security against abuse. Further, the legislation provided a better safeguard in relation to the possible extension of the right to include non-voluntary or involuntary euthanasia, for instance, in the case of neonates. However, the most positive benefit of the 1995 legislation appears to be that by explicitly demanding consideration of palliative care options, the Act may have highlighted the quality of palliative care in this particular Australian jurisdiction. However, the amendments to the 1995 legislation have left it to the courts and the medical profession. In the Netherlands, the device of modifying a Penal Code defence has been used, but here it has been said (see Chesterman (1998)) that the Dutch approach still leaves great power in the hands of doctors 'with inadequate supervision and regulation'.

FUTURE DECISION MAKING FOR DEATH AND DYING – ADVANCE DIRECTIVES

A Far Eastern example of an advance directive law

In Chapter 9, we looked at advance directives and noted that, in the UK, no legal framework exists which regulates such directives, or 'living wills', as they are called in Britain, and there is uncertainty about the precise legal status of advance directives in the UK. However, in a Far Eastern common law jurisdiction, Singapore, legislation was recently passed which deals with such directives.

Singapore

Singapore is a common law country situated in the Far East, a British colony until 1959, currently the fourth richest country in the world and best known for its 'economic miracle', high per capita income and worldwide reputation for banking and technology. It has also passed the Advance Medical Directive Act 1996 (for a full account of the Act and its operation and its ethical, medical and legal context, see Ter and Leong (1997) Med LR 63, on which this section is based). In Singapore, the person making the decision for a terminally ill person will usually be the physician having the care of that patient in consultation with that patient's family members. As the Singapore National Medical Ethics Committee explained, distraught family members will have to make an emotional decision which may seem 'unfilial or socially unacceptable especially in our Asian culture' (see *Advance Medical Directives: A Report by the National Medical Ethics Committee*, July 1995, p 2) and the Singapore Minister of Health stated that 'Over time, we will evolve a consensus which is moral and humane ... Advance directives will help some of us make those choices. It is only right that medical technology should be subordinated to the free will of human beings; and not the other way around.'

In 1996, Singapore enacted its first Advance Medical Directive Act 1996 (the Act) to give effect to a person's right to decide in advance that he does not wish to receive extraordinary life sustaining treatment in the event of terminal illness and to 'be allowed to die naturally, in peace and with dignity'. The advance medical directive (AMD) will give effect to the patient's wishes when he is no longer competent. The Act gives effect to patient autonomy, but also 'achieves some measure of clarity and certainty in the law in the absence of judicial precedents' (Ter and Leong (1997), p 63). Hence, the need for judicial intervention will be removed each time the issue of life sustaining treatment arises.

Ethical and religious issues

Legislation for advance directives has been a controversial and global issue, and the situation in Singapore was no different. The main reason cited for AMDs by the 24 groups consulted by the National Medical Ethics Committee (NMEC) was patient autonomy. Of the numerous groups consulted, the Muslim, Hindu, Sikh and Jewish groups explained that AMDs did not go against their religious teachings. The Catholic Church in Singapore stated that, in the light of the NMEC's assurance that they were strongly against euthanasia, the Church did not oppose AMDs. The Singapore Taoist Association said that, as Taoists, they advocated nature and the natural path, and they preferred to die natural deaths. Taoists and Buddhists make up the largest religious group in Singapore, comprising 54% of the population. The Singapore Council of Churches declared that legislation was contrary to the sanctity of life, would weaken the sanctity of life, weaken the family bond and undermine the doctor-patient relationship.

Safeguards

Sections 9, 14, 16 and 17 provide safeguards. The patient has to be terminally ill, incompetent and require extraordinary life sustaining treatment before an AMD can come into operation. Anyone coercing or compelling another person to make an AMD is criminally liable. Euthanasia or abetment of suicide is unlawful; the abetment of suicide and an attempt to commit suicide are crimes under Singapore law. There is a prohibition on the making of an AMD as a requirement for medical treatment or insurance.

Time stipulation

Once made, an AMD is valid indefinitely until revoked. There is no time stipulation, unlike Californian legislation which provides for the period of validity of a directive to be five years from the date of execution. Upon the expiry of the five year period, the directive will cease to be effective unless the declarant re-executes it. There was a waiting period of 14 days before the doctor is allowed to act on the directive after the patient is diagnosed to be in either a terminal condition or a permanent unconscious condition. All these provisions are absent in the Singapore Act.

Preservation of existing rights

Sections 11, 12 and 13 ensure the preservation of existing rights. Thus, where the patient is conscious and able to exercise rational judgment, he has (a) the right to make an informed decision on the various forms of treatment offered; (b) the right to decide on the use of extraordinary life sustaining treatment; and (c) the right to refuse medical or surgical treatment. These rights are preserved even when an AMD has been made, because it comes into effect only when the patient is both terminally ill and incompetent.

Interpretation of key terms

The legislation defines some terms, but not others.

'Incompetent' – there is no statutory definition and the doctor will determine the competence of a patient who is terminally ill before implementing an AMD. There will be no problems in most cases, except where the competence of the patient is disputed.

'Terminal illness' – defined as an incurable condition caused by injury or disease from which there is no reasonable prospect of a temporary or permanent recovery where death would, within reasonable medical judgment, be imminent regardless of the application of extraordinary life sustaining treatment and the application of such treatment would only serve to postpone the moment of death of the patient.

This definition follows the formula used by many American States and statutes, such as the California Natural Death Act 1976 and the Uniform Rights of the Terminally Ill Act 1989. It is notable that, unlike the Singapore Act, under the California Natural Death Act 1976, a declaration will also become operative when the patient is in a permanent unconscious condition, which refers (under s 1 thereof) to 'an incurable and irreversible condition that, within reasonable medical judgment, renders the patient in an irreversible coma or persistent state'.

'Recovery' in relation to a terminal illness includes, under the Act, a remission of symptoms or effects of the illness.

Ter and Leong (1997) point out (p 72) that the Singapore definition of terminal illness is different in one significant respect from the South Australian Natural Death Act 1983. The Australian Act defines terminal illness in s 3 as 'any illness, injury or degeneration of mental or physical faculties (a) such that death would, if extraordinary measures were not undertaken, be imminent, and (b) from which there is no reasonable prospect of a temporary or permanent recovery *even if extraordinary measures were undertaken*'. Hence, on the assumption that extraordinary measures are *not* undertaken, the Australian definition would permit the withdrawal of treatment from the comatose and those in a persistent vegetative state. However, the Singapore and American formulation requires death to be imminent, *irrespective of extraordinary measures* and would not permit the withdrawal of treatment from those in a persistent vegetative state because such patients can live on with artificial aids, such as being fed through nasogastric tubes. Hence, diabetic patients who need insulin and patients with renal failure who require dialysis would not come within the legislative scheme, because there would be a reasonable prospect of recovery. Ter and Leong (1997) argue that even AIDS sufferers might be excluded, since death usually results from secondary infection or other complication. Those who would be clearly excluded from the implementation of an AMD are patients who are not diagnosed as terminally ill, but are aged, in a coma and suffering from senile dementia.

'Imminent' – this is not defined in the Act, but the definition of terminal illness refers to the imminence of death according to reasonable medical judgment. No guidelines are given, because it is the legislative intent to leave the judgment of imminent death to the medical profession. The House of Lords' Select Committee defined terminal illness as resulting in death within a few months at most.

'Extraordinary life sustaining treatment' – the South Australian and the Northern Territory Natural Death Act 1988 have been followed in restricting the scope of AMDs to the refusal of extraordinary life sustaining measures in terminal cases. Extraordinary life sustaining treatment is defined as any medical procedure or measure which, when administered to a terminally ill patient, will only prolong the process of dying when death is imminent, but excludes palliative care. Examples suggested by Ter and Leong are:

> ... ventilators to take over natural breathing or cardiopulmonary resuscitation to keep the heart beating where such treatment would only serve to postpone the moment of death ... dialysis, resuscitation, blood transfusion or tube feeding will not normally fall within the definition, but, as pointed out in Quinlan, measures which could be considered ordinary in the case of a curable patient could be considered extraordinary in the context of a terminally ill patient.

The direction to withhold extraordinary life sustaining treatment has raised much concern in Singapore with questions as to whether this will lead to euthanasia. Ter and Leong emphasise that 'implementing an AMD does not amount to killing a patient because an AMD allows nature to take its course thereby permitting a natural death'.

'Palliative care' – includes the provision of reasonable medical procedures for the relief of pain, suffering or discomfort and the reasonable provision of food and water. Section 11 expressly provides that the Act shall not apply to palliative care and that nothing in the Act shall affect any right, power or duty which a medical practitioner or any person has in relation to palliative care. This is intended to dispel fears about a dying patient being denied palliative care. Consequently, a patient should continue to be provided with food and water through a nasogastric or gastrostomy tube even after an AMD takes effect. In other words, the provision of palliative care will not amount to non-compliance with an AMD.

Ter and Leong observe that the California Natural Death Act 1976 says nothing about palliative care, but the US Uniform Rights of the Terminally Ill Act 1989 provides that the Act 'does not affect the responsibility of the attending physician or other healthcare provider to provide treatment, including nutrition and hydration for a patient's comfort, care or alleviation of pain'. They also note that the World Health Organisation describes palliative care as a 'form of care that recognises that cure or long term control is not possible; is concerned with the quality rather than the quantity of life; and cloaks troublesome and distressing symptoms with treatments whose primary or sole aim is the highest possible measure of patient comfort' (WHO, *Palliative Cancer Care*, 1989, WHO). The UK Department of Health's description of palliative care is 'active total care provided to a patient when it is recognised that the illness is no longer curable. Palliative care concentrates on the quality of life and on alleviating pain and other distressing symptoms and is intended neither to hasten nor postpone death'.

Formalities

Under the 1996 Act, the following formalities must be complied with:

- a person making the directive must be of full age (21) and of sound mind;
- the directive must be made on a prescribed form which is in simple language. Making the AMD is free of charge;
- two witnesses are required to be present at the same time, one of whom must be a doctor, preferably a family doctor. Witnesses cannot be family members or interested parties who may stand to gain, including those who may benefit under any policy of insurance;
- doctors and nurses who object to AMDs should not be witnesses;
- the AMD must be filed in a central registry.

Revocation

An AMD may be revoked:

- at any time, orally or in writing;
- one witness is required;
- the central registry must be informed of the revocation.

Possible impact of the Act

Ter and Leong remark that the Singapore Act might well be amended to respond to or deal with new situations and, although AMDs represent a positive development, it is unlikely that they will affect more than a small percentage of the population. As they conclude: 'If the education of doctors, patients and the public is not enhanced to keep pace with legislative advancements, then the Advance Medical Directive Act may well become a dead letter and AMDs be allowed to die a natural death' (Ter and Leong (1997), p 88).

OBSERVATIONS ON REVOCATIONS

Californian legislation and the US Uniform Rights of the Terminally Ill Act provide only minimal formalities for revocation. All that is required is for the declarant to communicate his revocation to the attending physician or any other healthcare provider. On the other hand, the Uniform Rights of the Terminally Ill Act 1989 recognises revocation regardless of the declarant's mental or physical condition.

Indeed, s 4 of the 1989 Act provides that 'a declarant may revoke a declaration at any time in any manner, without regard to the declarant's mental or physical condition. A revocation is effective upon its communication to the attending physician or other healthcare provider by the declarant or a witness to the revocation.' The Law Reform Commission of Saskatchewan recommended that an advance directive should be revocable without formality and without consideration of capacity (*Proposals for an Advance Health Care Directives Act*, December 1991, p 27).

CONCLUDING COMPARATIVE OBSERVATIONS

It is, therefore, clear that both so called developed countries, such as the USA and Australia, as well as highly Westernised countries (in the sense of technological and educational advancement), like Singapore in the Far East, have implemented legislation dealing with physician-assisted suicides and advance directives.

Both the American and Australian legislation focus on the terminally ill patient and the American courts have concentrated on distinguishing between withdrawal of life sustaining treatment of a terminally ill patient, which is permissible, and the active termination of a terminally ill patient, which is not.

In the Netherlands, however, the patient does *not* have to be terminally ill or suffering from a physical illness to request a physician-assisted suicide, hence a mental illness would suffice. Although 'euthanasia' might be taken to be wide enough to be any form of termination of life by a doctor, the Dutch definition is a narrower one than in other jurisdictions. Thus, any termination of life by a doctor at the request of the patient qualifies as a legal termination of life, provided the other Dutch guidelines have been satisfied – that is, the patient must be experiencing intolerable suffering, the request must have been made over a period of time ('durable and persistent') and there is no prospect of improvement in the patient's condition. The phrase 'voluntary euthanasia' as opposed to involuntary euthanasia is not used in the Netherlands, because if the termination of life was not voluntary, it does not qualify as euthanasia in that jurisdiction, because lawful termination has to be at the request of the patient. To some, the slide down the 'slippery slope' has already begun .

As ever, courts and legislatures in all jurisdictions tread the line between upholding the sanctity of human life and the recognition of self-determination or autonomy in an adult competent patient who finds life, as it is currently lived, intolerable, either because of physical or mental anguish or both. In other words, the extremely poor quality of life, present and future, appears to provide a justification for intervention which invariably claims to act out of compassion for the suffering patient. History will judge whether we have become more humane towards people who have simply found it harder over the years to cope with suffering and have availed themselves of the opportunity to shorten their period of suffering through the use of drugs, or whether we have begun to pay less significance to the principle of the sanctity of human life.

SELECTIVE BIBLIOGRAPHY

Admiraal, P, 'Voluntary euthanasia: the Dutch Way' in McLean, S (ed), *Death, Dying and the Law*, 1996, Dartmouth

Alldridge, P, 'Who wants to live forever?', in Lee, R and Morgan, D (eds), *Death Rites*, 1994, Routledge, p 11

Carolan, B, 'US Supreme Court confronts right to die' (1998) 66 Medico-Legal Journal 65

Chesterman, S, 'Last rights: euthanasia, the sanctity of life, and the law in the Netherlands and the Northern Territory of Australia' (1998) 47 ICLQ 362

Giesen, D, 'Dilemmas at life's end: a comparative legal perspective', in Keown, J (ed), *Euthanasia Examined*, 1995, CUP

Griffiths, J, 'The regulation of euthanasia and related medical procedures that shorten life in the Netherlands' (1994) 1 Med Law International 137

Griffiths, J, 'Recent developments in the Netherlands concerning euthanasia and other medical behaviour that shortens life' (1994) 1 Med Law International 347

Griffiths, J, 'Assisted suicide in the Netherlands: the *Chabot* case' (1995) 58 MLR 232

Helme, T and Padfield, N, 'Safeguarding euthanasia' (1992) 142 NLJ 1335

Kamisar, Y, ' Physician-assisted suicide: the last bridge to active voluntary euthanasia', in Keown, J (ed), *Euthanasia Examined*, 1992, CUP

Keown, J, 'The law and practice of euthanasia in the Netherlands' (1992) 108 LQR 51

Korek, S, 'Following Dolly' (1997) 147 NLJ 428

Preston, 'Professional norms and physician attitudes towards euthanasia' (1994) J Law, Medicine and Ethics 36

Ter, KL and Leong, HS, 'Advance medical directives in Singapore' [1997] Med LR 63

Sluyters, 'Euthanasia in the Netherlands' (1989) 57 Medico-Legal Journal 34

Vickers, L, 'Assisted dying and the laws of three European countries' (1997) 147 NLJ 610

Wal, G and Dillman, R, 'Euthanasia in the Netherlands' (1994) 308 BMJ 1346

Wood, P, 'To what extent can law control human cloning?' (1999) 39 Medicine, Science and Journal of British Academy of Forensic Sciences 5

CHAPTER 19

A COMPARATIVE OVERVIEW OF HEALTHCARE LAW THEMES AND PRINCIPLES

We have now surveyed a range of common law and civil law jurisdictions and their responses to healthcare issues, concentrating on key areas such as abortion, consent, euthanasia, reproductive medicine and surrogacy in particular, sterilisation of intellectually disabled persons, healthcare and children, human organ transplantation and donation, and the principles relating to medical malpractice or medical negligence. As far as possible, we have concentrated on using English law as the basis for comparison in Part I, before focusing on other common law countries with the English common law heritage, such as the USA and Australia, and also Germany and France as examples of civil law countries, or countries with a Roman law heritage (the 'civil law' label deriving from *jus civilis* or 'civil law' that was created and followed in early Roman times). However, where particularly relevant, or of special comparative interest for their sheer uniqueness, we also looked at countries like the Netherlands, now well known for its 'euthanasia' laws, countries like Sweden, India, Japan and Turkey for their human organ transplantation laws, China for its new 'paying for consent' scheme, and Singapore for its advance directives legislative scheme.

A global view of abortion has been presented in Chapter 13, and we shall presently return to some of the themes that have transformed the legal and medical landscape in common law and civil jurisdictions. It has not been possible to undertake a survey of every area of healthcare law, and any attempt to cast our net very wide for every topic would have resulted in an excessively fragmented survey and more truncated coverage of the more controversial topics, such as abortion and non-consensual sterilisation. However, the basis for selection has been to include topics which represent vignettes from the beginning to the end of life. Topics such as consent, confidentiality, abortion, surrogacy, euthanasia and PVS patients, were considered to be essential, but other areas, such as sterilisation of the handicapped, the medical treatment of neonates and organ transplantation were also considered important, as there have been notable developments in various common law and civil law jurisdictions. Cloning has been included in this survey because of its growing importance and its ethical implications, and there has been reference to the human rights aspects of healthcare law (such as Art 8 and confidentiality). There is also a discussion of current developments in the field, and a speculative view of the shape of things to come.

The purpose of this final chapter is to summarise some of the main findings of our survey and to tie the threads that run through all the topics which have been reviewed, noting similarities and differences and their ethical bases. The main ethical concepts will be reviewed, in relation to the various jurisdictions, so that autonomy, respect for persons, the quality of life v sanctity of life debates, killing v letting die distinctions, beneficence, truth telling and confidentiality, and the 'best interests' test will be revisited, dissecting the latter's variable content in relation to the many situations where it has been and continues to be used. It also offers a further opportunity to note the views of commentators on these medico-legal topics, so that a panoramic overview of some academic, legal and ethical components of healthcare may be presented. Finally, we discuss some of the more recent developments in healthcare law.

COMPARATIVE METHODOLOGY

As was stated in the Introduction to this book, it is important, whenever undertaking comparisons between countries, to place the particular jurisdiction within its unique environment, culture, and particular socio-legal setting, and, where appropriate, in the context of its historical heritage. Our discussion has attempted to make comparisons within the major 'families of law' – hence, countries with a common law background were generally considered together, as were civil law countries like France and Germany. However, differences and distinguishing features were also identified within the same group, the most obvious example being between the USA and England in, for instance, the context of medical malpractice.

Applying this philosophy, it is immediately possible to see how the more developed countries of the world have not merely made advances in technology, but also that this has led to different sorts of dilemma. If technology can now keep a handicapped baby alive for much longer than in the pre-technological times, then parents and doctors are faced with the dilemma of whether or not to sustain such a child who is born with severe impairments which can never be alleviated, whose prognosis might not be imminent death, but even a life of up to two decades, coping with several expensive and emotionally draining procedures to ensure the child has even minimal nutrition and hydration. This is where the sanctity of life doctrine comes up against the quality of life principle. It needs to be said that, in the case of people living in the more remote corners of the world without 'modern' facilities and resources, when it comes to contraception, the treatment of disabled newborns and abortion regimes, for example, the immediacy of either of these principles might not always be in the forefront of their minds and medical treatment there will focus on essential services, immunisation and urgent medical cases.

ABORTION

The global survey we have undertaken of abortion laws across the world indicates that, according to current statistics, only Chile and El Salvador have an absolute prohibition on abortion, in that it is not permitted in those countries under *any* circumstances. A survey of the literature on abortion and a reading of the various websites on it give the impression that abortion is now perceived as an accepted medical procedure in many countries, provided it is performed under clear legislative conditions, with the sanction of the State and in many countries, for the welfare and well being of the woman. The sheer number of deaths of women from botched abortions (from 'backstreet', non-official abortions), and the victimisation of women, are strongly emphasised as major justifications for legalising or liberalising abortion law. In the USA, the 1973 case of *Roe v Wade* (1973) 410 US 113 remains the landmark case which established that a woman in the USA had a constitutional right to terminate a pregnancy within the parameters of the judgment and as a result of the right to privacy under the 14th Amendment to the US Constitution, although subsequent cases have begun to erode this right. In the late 1980s, legal terminations were controlled by hospital abortion committees and the saga of *Morgentaler* comes to mind, where the Canadian Supreme Court held that their criminal code statute (s 251) violated the security and liberty of the pregnant woman.

In England and Wales, the 1938 case of *R v Bourne* [1983] 3 All ER 615 managed to find a way to bypass the existing laws on abortion and create an exception, so that an abortion was not illegal if it was performed because a woman's physical and mental health were in jeopardy. However, the 1967 Abortion Act was then passed in the 'swinging '60s', possibly as part of a general liberalising trend that was sweeping the country in other matters such as fashion, the relaxing of the rules on censorship of plays, divorce, lowering of the voting age, the limited decriminalising of homosexuality and the abolition of the death penalty. A clear purpose of the Act was to eliminate the horrors of 'backstreet abortions'. But the implementation or liberalising of abortion has become a global phenomenon and our surveys indicate the pre-*Roe* and post-*Roe* abortion reforms. An important distinction between the English and American abortion laws is that the American law is based on a constitutional right to privacy, as interpreted by *Roe v Wade*, whereas the English right to abortion is statute-based.

In the USA, in the 'post-Monica' (Lewinski) era, abortion remains a controversial issue and protest marches and campaigns on both sides – pro-life and pro-choice – continue to campaign passionately: they have got out of control from time to time. In Britain, it is no longer seen as a major bone of contention and is regarded as widely accepted by the majority of the population. Since 1990, through the Human Fertilisation and Embryology Act

1990, Britain has had an official 24 week limit on abortion, but some Family Planning clinics say that 19–20 weeks is their limit for most practical purposes. There is now no limit where there is a 'substantial risk' of serious fetal handicap under s 1(1)(d), and this is arguably the most controversial of the innovations introduced by the 1990 Act. In 1996, Britain experienced a sharp rise in abortions for resident women – 167,916 – but the numbers have evened out since then.

Globally, the first trimester appears to be a fairly universal watershed, beyond which many jurisdictions require more stringent requirements to allow abortions.

CONSENT TO TREATMENT

In nearly all societies, consent to treatment is, at least in theory, an absolute prerequisite to medical treatment and is a fundamental principle in English law, which is necessary to protect a doctor from an action in battery. As we have seen, the notion of consent has very often been dubbed 'informed consent' in England and Wales, but the origins of any such 'doctrine' in English law in more modern times appear to be American, although its more ancient origins might well be English (see *Slater v Baker and Stapleton* (1767) 2 Wils KB 358; (1767) 95 ER 560). However, there is little doubt that Cardozo J's comment in the now famous American case of *Schloendorff v Society of New York Hospital* (1914) 105 NE 92, that 'Every human being of adult years and sound mind has a right to determine what shall be done with his own body', takes pride of place in the pantheon of memorable and seminal pronouncements. Although emanating from an American judge, the comment has been consistently cited in more recent English law, where the principle has been explicitly and categorically recognised only relatively recently. However, if one considers the case law on both sides of the Atlantic, there appears to be the 'prudent doctor' approach (in England and Wales) and the 'prudent patient' test, which seems to be followed in most of the American jurisdictions. If one equates 'informed consent' with the 'right to know' any or all information relating to proposed medical treatment, then English law appears to part company with the law in many American jurisdictions.

On the ethical front, no less than five ethical principles may be identified as underpinning the notion of informed consent: the principles of autonomy, justice, veracity (truth-telling), beneficence and non-maleficence (Beauchamp and Childress (1989)). Its ethical foundations are certainly extremely well established, but most clearly on the American scene rather than the British. In Britain, the 'best interests' test continues to dominate the scene (see below, p 652) and the rules on consent are very much determined by a court at any one time, although the general principles are reasonably well established (under *Re C (Adult: Refusal of Medical Treatment)* [1994] 1 WLR 290 (the gangrene case)). However, they are very much open to interpretation, and there do not appear to be adequate safeguards for mentally incompetent women when it comes to proposed *abortions*, as opposed to hysterectomies, as these are generally classified as 'therapeutic' and therefore not requiring court approval. Consent is clearly by proxy in these cases, so the best interests test looms even larger, as does *Bolam* [1957] 1 WLR 582. Fortunately, a recent case (*Re S*), heard in May 2000, suggests that at least the English Court of Appeal is prepared to veto invasive procedures if there are safe alternatives and it requires stronger justifications for performing invasive operations on mentally disabled women in this context, even if it does not involve the more highly emotive cases of contraceptive sterilisation. One can hope that, with the coming into force of the Human Rights Act 1998 in October 2000, applications on the basis of human rights will become more common, and provide greater opportunities to challenge more easily decisions regarding mentally disabled persons, if these are seen to be unduly invasive from a civil libertarian viewpoint and not in the best interests of such patients.

DISCLOSURE OF INFORMATION

The allied issue to consent is whether the *Bolam* principle applies equally to both diagnosis and treatment, as well as to the giving of information during a doctor-patient consultation. The leading case on the area, *Sidaway*, produced judgments from the House of Lords that appeared inconsistent and Lord Scarman seriously questioned the proposition that the law left it to the doctors to determine in what circumstances a duty to warn of risks arose. Lord Scarman indeed called the doctrine of informed consent 'the right to know' as developed in the USA and Canada. Two key matters on disclosure were affirmed by *Sidaway*, first, the necessity to disclose all material risks, subject only to therapeutic privilege where a doctor may hold back some information if its disclosure is thought to be harmful to the patient. A material risk is one which, as in *Canterbury v Spence*, a reasonable person in the patient's position would be likely to disclose, because of its significance. Secondly, *Sidaway* also confirmed the existence of therapeutic privilege – where there is non-disclosure of certain information which the doctor thinks may be psychologically injurious to the patient. The more significant part of the *Sidaway* ruling is that the exception to this principle is that there must be particularly good medical reasons, which the doctor would have to justify, for a doctor to fail to answer truthfully any question which the patient actually asks him.

In Canada, it has been declared by their courts that the scope of the duty of disclosure is not simply the preserve of medical experts, but that the patient has a right to know what risks are involved in undergoing certain treatment or procedures (see *Reibl v Hughes*). In similar vein, the South Australian Supreme *Court* (in *F v R*) has said that the ultimate question in these sorts of case is whether the doctor's conduct 'conforms to the standard of reasonable care demanded by the law'. The strongest assault on *Bolam* has come from the High Court of Australia in the leading case of *Rogers v Whitaker*, where the judges made it plain that, when it came to the provision of advice or information to the patient, since the patient needed to make a decision based on that information, it was simply not logical to say that the amount of information provided to the patient could be determined from the perspective of the medical profession.

Rogers appears to have made an impact as far afield as South Africa, in *Castell v De Greef* (1994) (4) SA 408, and Malaysia in *Chelliah a/l Manickam v Kerajaan Malaysia* (1997) 2 AMR 1856 and especially in *Kamalam a/p Raman v Eastern Plantation Agency (Johore) Sdn Bhd Ulu Tiram Estate, Ulu Tiram, Johore* (1996), where *Rogers v Whitaker* was seen as representing the law. The way in which the law develops in this area will have implications for the basic doctor-patient relationship and there appears to be a general movement towards increased recognition of the patient's right to know in many jurisdictions of the world.

MEDICAL MALPRACTICE AND THE STANDARD OF CARE

The *Bolam* principle has dominated this area of medicine in the UK since the 1980s, but there has been some doubt sown about its durability in the light of the House of Lords' decision in *Bolitho*, where it was said that a medical practice that was not 'logical' was open to question, even if it was in accordance with what would have been carried out by a responsible body of opinion. The general standard expected across most jurisdictions is an objective one, in that it requires a standard that a reasonably competent doctor would satisfy rather than that of an individual doctor.

The American approach is unique in that there are at least three major differences between the legal cultures of England and that of America. First, the USA has no unified law of negligence, but has at least 52 discrete (that is, separate and distinct) and autonomous systems, and each of the 50 States has its own tort law. Apart from the system in each State, federal maritime law is another distinct 51st system, and the 52nd is a federal common law of torts that supplements national legislation on matters such as anti-trust. Further, the legislature and highest court in each State both have the power to determine the private law in that State. The federal court decisions, including the US Supreme Court, are not binding on private State law, but are merely persuasive (as stated in *State v Perry* (1992) 610 So 2d 746 (Louisiana), where the court said that it is the 'final arbiter' of the meaning of the State

Constitution and laws). Hence, even a US Supreme Court decision is not representative of the American law of negligence, any more than a New York law by that State's highest court. However, although independent of each other, these States 'share common policy goals' and 'strive for common outcomes'. Thus, these courts routinely cite one another's authorities. Robertson calls the American law of negligence 'international comparative law'. However, Americans appear to be reconciled to the divergences between the States.

Secondly, there is the 'pervasive use of juries' in American negligence cases, applying to 49 States, so that the American trial judge has a central role in determining which issues are for the jury and how to instruct the jury on those issues. In England and Wales, the judge determines issues of fact and issues of law.

Thirdly, there is a difference in the way the American system compensates plaintiffs' lawyers. The American tort plaintiff almost always pays his lawyer nothing out of pocket. The client and the lawyer agree that the lawyer will take a percentage out of whatever can be recovered from the defendant. Thus, this 'contingency fee agreement' would be illegal in England, but is common practice in America. The salutary benefit of the American system is that it encourages the less fortunate and lower income earning people to have access to the courts. However, Robertson argues that this is 'outweighed by the flood of silly, vindictive, or purely mercenary litigation' that could ensue if plaintiffs' lawyers do not exercise extremely tight discipline in deciding which cases they will accept.

American law has founded its medical malpractice cases in tort or contract and, where it has been contractual, the patient can insist on a specific physician carrying out a procedure, unlike the English position.

CONFIDENTIALITY

The two areas which have caused the most controversy under this heading have been (a) the issue of how far should the duty of confidentiality be preserved where there appears to be potential danger posed to innocent third parties by the state of mind or state of health of the patient, if disclosure is not made (the *Tarasoff* case in America; the *Egdell* case in Britain); and (b) the same question of the limits to confidentiality where doctors who are HIV positive are allowed to continue treating patients without disclosure of their identities. AIDS is not a notifiable disease in the UK, but it is in many States of the USA and certain Canadian jurisdictions.

DOCTOR'S LIABILITY TO PERSONS INFECTED BY HIS PATIENT

The American courts have held that a doctor is liable to persons infected by his patient if he negligently fails to diagnose a contagious disease (*Hofmann v Blackmon* (1970) 241 So 2d 752 (Fla App), or, having diagnosed the illness, fails to warn members of the patient's family (*Wojcik v Aluminium Co of America* (1959) 18 Misc 2d 740; (1959) 183 NYS 2d 351, pp 357–58; *Davis v Rodman* (1921) 147 Ark 385; (1921) 227 SW 612; *Skillings v Allen* (1919) 143 Minn 323; (1919) 173 NW 663 and *Jones v Stanko* (1928) 118 Ohio St 147; (1928) 160 NE 456). Other courts have also held that a doctor may be liable for negligently advising the third party that there is no danger and failing to prevent the spread of the disease (see Annotation, 3 ALR 5th 370).

Californian and Texan legislation permit disclosure to the spouse of an HIV positive patient. In New York, this is extended to known sexual partners and needle-sharers, even in the face of patient objection.

The American courts have also had occasion to consider a duty to warn where the patient suffered from an infectious disease.

In Canada, in the Northwest Territories, unlike the UK, AIDS and HIV seropositivity are listed as reportable communicable diseases; however, since HIV infection is a prerequisite to a diagnosis of ARC, in effect all of AIDS, ARC and HIV seropositivity are reportable. Therefore, the physician is required either to:

- make disclosure concerning AIDS, ARC or HIV seropositivity directly to the patient's contacts; or
- request the Chief Medical Officer to do so.

ASSISTED REPRODUCTION

Some memorable events have taken place since the late 1970s in relation to modern 'reproductive technology': (a) in 1978, Louise Brown, the first 'test-tube baby', was born in Oldham, Lancashire, England; (b) in 1983, the *Rios* case occurred – Mario and Elsa Rios died in a plane crash leaving two frozen embryos at a medical centre in Melbourne, Australia; (c) in December 1998, Diane Blood gave birth to a son, Liam, who had been conceived by using semen obtained from her comatose husband, who has now been dead for more than three years; (d) about the same time as Diane Blood fell pregnant, a woman in Melbourne, Australia, obtained judicial approval for the extraction of sperm from the husband's corpse.

The German *Bundesgerichtshof* case reported in November 1993 (BGHZ 124,52) recounts how, before undergoing an operation which would leave him sterile, the 31 year old plaintiff had some of his sperm frozen in order to have children later and where, through the fault of the university clinic, this sperm was lost. The plaintiff was unsuccessful in suing for damages from the clinic in both lower courts and in the Federal Supreme Court, which also rejected his claim.

Margaret Brazier (1999) has remarked (p 191) that 'The most profound change in regulating reproductive medicine since Warnock is ... the dramatically increased role of commerce'. In the post-Warnock era, research has moved from an 'academic' exercise to an enterprise with enormous commercial potential. As Brazier says: 'A fertility "industry" has developed to provide treatment on a profit making basis both to British citizens and "procreative tourists" escaping more prohibitive regimes elsewhere in Europe. Pressure to pay gamete donors and surrogates continues.'

SURROGACY

There is little doubt that the case which caught the imagination of the media worldwide, occurred in the USA in the mid 1980s – the *Baby M* case ((1988) 109 NJ 396; (1988) 537 A 2d 1227), which had all the elements of a soap opera or 'B' movie. This was the 'rich, educated couple' who hired a 'poor' woman as a surrogate mother, Mary Beth Whitehead, who gave birth to the baby, and then changed her mind and refused to hand the baby back. The resulting car chase across State lines was the stuff which television stations can only dream about. The court case that followed also produced drama, with the New Jersey judge castigating the surrogate mother for being manipulative and noting her colourful past (as a 'go-go' dancer in a nightclub) and awarding custody to the commissioning parents. However, the sequel to this was the overturning of the original decision, when the mother appealed the decision, being awarded joint custody and extensive rights of visitation (contact).

Mary Beth has subsequently campaigned vigorously for the criminalisation of surrogate arrangements and, so far, about 11 American jurisdictions have banned commercial surrogacy. It should be noted that many American States have not invalidated surrogacy contracts. In contrast, the position in England and Wales is that a surrogacy contract is unenforceable under the Surrogacy Arrangements Act 1985 (as amended by the Human Fertilisation and Embryology Act 1990) and commercial surrogacy is prohibited.

The leading case in England, the *Baby Cotton* case, attracted media attention and was reputedly the fastest wardship hearing ever heard in an English court. Latey J approved the commissioning parent's application to take the baby out of the jurisdiction, while technically remaining a ward of court. This means that the English court would retain the right to order the return of the child back to England, if, for example, there was evidence that the child's welfare was being threatened. Kim Cotton, the surrogate mother, has since become a surrogate mother again, but now claims that she is winding up the surrogate agency she has been actively involved with for several years.

A discernible trend in surrogacy and the law in more global terms is that there is far more widespread acceptance of surrogacy as a method of assisted reproduction. In the 1970s, an English judge was heard to label a surrogate arrangement as 'pernicious', yet both the tone and the approach had become more conciliatory in the 1980s by the time other surrogacy cases reached the English courts, when they were not prepared to enforce a surrogacy arrangement when the surrogate mother had become too emotionally attached to the child and did not wish to hand the child over to the commissioning parents. Another example of the English courts' change of attitude is that they were even prepared to sanction payment of 'expenses' by a couple prior to adopting the child produced by the surrogacy arrangement, being careful to interpret this as money that was not handed over in pursuance of adoption, which would otherwise be illegal. There is an argument for saying that infertility needs to be addressed and dealt with on a State-wide level, but as long as surrogacy offers the chance to infertile couples of having a child, the practice will doubtless continue between private individuals and, in places like the USA, between private individuals and agencies. After all, it has survived, in one form or another, since Biblical times.

PATERNALISM – MEDICAL OR JUDICIAL?

The strongest evidence of judicial paternalism is in the field of child consent and the *Gillick* arena, where the English courts, at any rate, continue to overrule teenagers' refusal of medical treatment in cases where the teenagers in question have been psychotically ill, anorexic or suffering from some mental illness. The courts have deemed them not to be *Gillick* competent. However, as far as medical paternalism is concerned, the *Bolam* principle may arguably be said to have been a strongly pro-doctor approach, in that the professional procedures which may be supported by at least one responsible professional body of opinion suffices to confirm a doctor's legal compliance with the standard of care expected of him in his particular professional field of expertise. In other words, the courts have, at least up to the *Bolitho* case, tended to allow the doctors to determine the standards of diagnosis and treatment in any case where a patient has complained of negligence in either or both.

STERILISATION OF PERSONS WITH MENTAL DISABILITIES

Having surveyed the international history of non-consensual sterilisation, it transpires that the American history of compulsory sterilisation is not something that any modern American court would be particularly proud of, especially of Holmes J's somewhat blunt statements in *Buck v Bell*, which appear to reflect the eugenic overtones of the early law. However, of far more culpability, carried out with explicit eugenic content, and with 'ethnic cleansing' in mind is the Nazi programme of compulsory sterilisation in Germany, which still forms a rather large blot on this particular landscape. However, there has been a radical transformation of sterilisation laws in the USA in the 1980s, and a new Carership Law in the new unified Germany in the 1990s.

Australia has had its fair share of cases dealing with sterilisation of the handicapped, and now appears to require court approval and a best interests' approach as well. *Marion's* case established that sterilisation of a mentally incapacitated person should be a step of last resort and *Marion (No 2)* requires the courts to conduct a broad and extensive inquiry into the circumstances of each case. All possibilities and alternatives must be thoroughly examined and evaluated, with reversibility being only one factor to be considered.

In England and Wales, the therapeutic and non-therapeutic distinction was enunciated in 1976 by Heilbron J in *Re D* (the Sotos syndrome child), but in 1987, the House of Lords, when dealing with Jeanette, a 17 year old epileptic girl with a mental age of five or six, held that the therapeutic/non-therapeutic distinction was not helpful to a determination of the case and, indeed, Lord Hailsham opined that it was 'not helpful to talk of reproductive rights' when dealing with a person like Jeanette, who could not appreciate such things. The only test to be used was the 'best interests' test. Several commentators, including the present writer, have found this to be a highly dubious comment because, surely, one does not have to be in a position or condition to appreciate one's rights in order to have those rights. In 1989, in *Re F*, in the case of an incapacitated adult, the House of Lords held that, although court sanction was desirable, no one could consent on behalf of an incompetent adult as a result of the inadvertent repeal of the necessary inherent jurisdiction of the court; the court could not give consent, but it could make an *ex post facto* declaration that the treatment was not unlawful; and the *Bolam* test should be used to determine the legality of the procedure. The Law Lords relied on the common law doctrine of necessity, which allows the treatment of unconscious patients in their best interests. Several Practice Notes or Practice Directions have been issued by the Official Solicitor's Department, the latest in 1996, which generally requires court approval for compulsory sterilisations of mentally handicapped persons, but still talks about 'straightforward cases' which do not require approval. What are these cases? Can there be 'straightforward cases' where the patient is incapable of giving consent to the sterilisation? The scope for discretion allowed to both doctors and judges continues to be perpetuated by the State. Writing in the context of human rights and medical practice in 1991, Ian Kennedy called non-consensual sterilisation 'the great challenge' posed between 1987 and 1989 by *Re B* and *Re F*, and he saw the challenge to the human rights lawyer as follows: 'Make it too easy to treat the patient and the danger of abuse re-emerges. Make it too difficult, and you deny the patient the right enjoyed by the competent patient: access to medical treatment' (Kennedy (1991), p 94). Bearing in mind that there do not appear to be similar safeguards for proposed abortions on mentally incapable women, some case law suggests (see Chapter 1)that vigilance is needed in the abortion arena as well. In England and Wales, the challenge to maintain adequate protection for the vulnerable remains.

CHILDREN AND HEALTHCARE

The *Gillick* case was the landmark case in England and Wales in the 1980s and arguably remains the touchstone of children's rights as we enter the 21st century, and the so called '*Gillick* principle' (often called '*Gillick* competence') has already been applied in places like Canada; it has become the torch-bearer of the mature child's right to decide on a number of important issues – contraceptive advice and treatment is just one of the areas which the *Gillick* case specifically recognises. The child of 'sufficient age and understanding' (who would be '*Gillick* competent') is now a recognised construct which is statutorily enshrined in the Children Act 1989. This statute also gives the child a right to refuse a medical assessment of any kind, provided she has 'sufficient age and understanding'. Of course, the court would have to decide whether the underage child was *Gillick* competent or not. In Britain, there has been a growing recognition of children's rights in the field of healthcare, but a series of cases in the late 1980s and the 1990s revealed that there is also a strong element of judicial paternalism when it comes to children who refuse treatment in life threatening situations. As ever, the judges make their decisions and justify them by saying that their decision was 'in the best interests of the child'.

In Scotland, in *Houston, Applicant* [1997] Med LR 237, however, the views of Sheriff McGowan contrast sharply with those of Lord Donaldson MR in *Re W* (1992), albeit in interpreting dissimilar legislation, when he held that the view of a 15 year old boy was paramount when he refused to be detained or treated despite suffering from a psychotic illness because the court felt that he 'was capable of understanding the nature and possible consequences' of the procedures and treatments being proposed. A 15 year old girl was not given the benefit of the doubt in *Re R* (the equivalent English case). It would be illuminating to see whether the Scottish courts would treat a girl suffering from a psychotic illness in the same way, on the basis that a girl might be thought to require a greater degree of protection from the uncontrollable consequences of the illness.

TREATMENT OF DISABLED NEWBORNS AND DISABLED CHILDREN

English law relating to incapacitated newborns has been relatively consistent until the late 1990s, when the English Court of Appeal appeared to give hitherto unusual prominence to parental wishes with regard to their disabled babies. With a history dating from the early 1980s with severely disabled newborns as in the *Arthur* case, the English courts have usually held that, when asked to decide on whether an operation should proceed, the guiding test should be what was in the best interests of the child? In considering the condition of the child, the courts would consider the quality of life of the child – would its future life be so 'demonstrably awful' (laid down in *Re B* (1981) by the Court of Appeal) that it would live a life of suffering and misery – but that the wishes of its parents as regards a proposed operation would not be determinative. A break with precedent appeared to occur in *Re T*, decided in 1997, where the Court of Appeal decided to abide by parental opinion and not authorise a potentially life saving liver transplant operation on an 18 month old child. The child there was not the 'classic' severely disabled newborn with a poor prognosis for survival or a very poor quality of life anticipated. However, subsequent cases appear to have reverted to the former approach, enunciated in *Re B*.

The recent case of the conjoined twins (see *Re A (Children)* (2000) *The Times*, 10 October) discussed in Chapter 4, appears to have been a particularly agonising test case presenting an apparently impossible decision requiring the wisdom of Solomon, where the particular physical condition of the twins was one of its unique features. So far, as predicted, one twin has survived the operation which separated them.

The results of a survey across eight European countries of the ways in which different jurisdictions treated handicapped newborns revealed several insights in a report (see McHaffie *et al* (1999) 25 JME 440, discussed in Chapter 12), which stated that:

(a) In practice, doctors are unclear about their legal position. In Italy, the Code of Professional Medical Ethics warns against therapeutic over-aggressiveness, the State is strongly protective of infant life, and any discrimination on the basis of malformation or poor prognosis violates constitutional law. France has no rules or guidelines on the subject of cessation of treatment and no case has been heard, so clinicians are operating in a legal vacuum. No legal clarification has been forthcoming in

Sweden or Germany. In the UK and the Netherlands, where stopping treatment is an accepted part of medical practice, some degree of uncertainty remains about the precise limits. Legal and professional debate continues, currently focusing on the Netherlands on when lives may be actively ended.

(b) The principle of double effect is recognised in all countries covered by the survey except Italy. It is generally considered acceptable to give drugs in sufficient quantity to relieve suffering even when to do so may shorten life.

(c) Every country prohibits any active intervention to end life, and the research found that practice varies. In the Netherlands, a notification procedure for physician-assisted death has been operating since 1991, but doubts have been expressed about 'the effectiveness of control' in view of the low rates of actual reporting. Adult criteria are inappropriate for infants, but it was found that Dutch doctors sometimes do actively end the life of a child with the specific consent of the parents; a recent survey revealed that as many as 45% of neotologists and intensivists had intentionally done so. It is only in the last three years that such cases have come before the courts, and there is still no clarification about the legality of active intervention. However, recommendations for the monitoring of such practices have already been issued.

(d) Across Europe, rules and practice vary so widely that it is difficult for groups to compose any universally acceptable guidelines. The research group felt that it was clear from their investigation that 'different cultures, religious contexts and historical antecedents influence practice within Europe'. They report that attempts have been made to try to harmonise practice but, as international links grow, it is important to understand diversity as well as similarities.

PHYSICIAN-ASSISTED SUICIDE, EUTHANASIA AND PVS PATIENTS

The question of physician-assisted death has arisen in the UK with a series of cases which have drawn a crucial distinction between treatment that was intended to relieve pain and suffering which incidentally shortened life (as in *Bodkin Adams*) and administering a lethal injection that had no pain relieving effects with the primary purpose of hastening death, as in *Cox*, which led to a conviction for attempted murder, since it could not be proved that it was the injection which actually killed the patient, who was apparently already about to die in a few minutes anyway. The principle of 'double effect' therefore operates. In these difficult situations, the principle of the sanctity of human life is, for some, thrown into sharp relief against that of the quality of life.

PVS patients

The debates on euthanasia and patients in a persistent (now permanent) vegetative state (PVS) (for the Royal College of Surgeons' definition, see Chapter 9) have been based on well known moral concepts such as the 'right to life', 'personhood' and 'human dignity'. Within the medical profession, the debate centres on whether artificial forms of feeding are medical treatments which may be discontinued if they are reasonably regarded as futile, or whether they are better categorised as part of a course of care for the patient which should consequently never be withdrawn from any patient, because to do so would be tantamount to abandoning the patient and breaching the doctor's professional ethical duty to care for all his patients.

In the UK, the *Tony Bland* case remains the landmark case for PVS patients. There is little doubt that, before the *Bland* case, it was generally thought that withdrawal of life support from an insensate or PVS patient would not be legally permissible. However, the law as it currently stands is that, provided it is seen as in the patient's best interests, withdrawal of life sustaining treatment is lawful, but court authorisation is required.

John Keown (1997) offers five comments on the *Bland* decision:

(a) The ethical principle of the sanctity of life offers a middle way between the extremes of vitalism on the one hand and quality of life on the other. *Bland*, in his opinion, represented a swerve toward the quality of life extreme, accepting that certain lives are of no benefit and may lawfully be intentionally terminated by omission.

(b) Bland has left English law in a 'morally and intellectually misshapen' state, as one of the Law Lords opined, prohibiting active, intentional killing, but permitting (if not requiring) intentional killing by omission, even by those under a duty to care for the patient.

(c) To the extent that the Law Lords have embraced the quality of life principle, and effectively delegated the judgment of which lives are of no benefit to medical opinion, there is little reason to expect that judgment to be confined to patients in a PVS.

(d) The Law Lords' rejection of the sanctity principle appears to have been based on a misunderstanding of that principle. Lord Mustill observed that it was a great pity that the Attorney General had not appeared to represent the interests of the State in maintaining citizens' lives. It is to be hoped that the Attorney General will appear in an appropriate future case to 'represent, articulate and defend the traditional ethic'.

(e) The decision whether to withdraw treatment and tube-feeding from a patient in PVS should be based on an evaluation of the worthwhileness of the treatment, not the supposed worthwhileness of the patient. While there is a consensus that it is proper to withdraw treatment in such a case, there is a good argument that tube-feeding constitutes basic care and that it should, at least presumptively, be provided. Even if it were the better view that it may be withdrawn, this should be because it, and not the patient, is judged futile.

Apart from the Netherlands, however, the researchers found that other countries have strongly resisted a move to legalise the deliberate termination of life. British paediatricians have officially rejected it, as they have in Germany. Although the practice of physician-assisted suicide is legal, and occurs on a much larger scale in the Netherlands, when it comes to babies, specific recommendations expressly disapprove the practice of ending the life of even a severely damaged newborn. The authors of the project warn against assuming that, even with clear rules or laws, practice necessarily follows the law. As the authors of the article on the project say, 'Provided clinicians are discreet, actions do not necessarily come to public attention' (McHaffie (1999), p 445).

In the USA, the first 'right-to-die' case was heard in 1990 in *Cruzan* (1990) 110 S Ct 2841; (1990) 497 US 261, when the US Supreme Court upheld the right of a competent patient to refuse treatment. Since then, a consensus has developed in the USA that it is ethically and legally appropriate to discontinue life sustaining treatment for vegetative patients. Professor Jennet, who coined the term 'persistent vegetative state' with Professor Plum in 1972, writes that the American approach is 'probably related to the strength in that country of the informed consent movement, which aims to protect the rights of competent patients to refuse treatment, including that which may save or sustain life' (Jennett (1993), p 140). The 1993 Kentucky case of *DeGrella v Elston* (1993) 858 SW 2d 698 confirms the American approach that 'a person in a PVS has a right to withdrawal of further medical treatment, including artificial nutrition and hydration. This right exists within the framework and the individual's common law rights of self-determination and informed consent in obtaining medical treatment.'

The Netherlands situation

Doctors in the Netherlands are not prosecuted for carrying out euthanasia, provided they follow guidelines issued by the Royal Dutch Medical Association. These are that:

- the request must be voluntary, durable, well considered and persistent;
- the patient must be experiencing intolerable (unacceptable) suffering with no prospect for improvement;
- euthanasia must be a last resort;
- euthanasia must be performed by a surgeon who must consult with an independent medical colleague who has experience in the field.

The research into practice in the Netherlands suggests that a substantial number of the most prominent advocates of voluntary euthanasia in fact support non-voluntary euthanasia. The basis of their case is respect for self-determination, so there is little or no ground for judging wrongful the euthanasia of those who do not possess autonomy whether because they are infants, senile, mentally handicapped or comatose. The widespread condonation (that is, acceptance) of euthanasia in the case of the comatose reveals that respecting the right of self-determination is an incomplete explanation for the case for euthanasia. The basic approach seems to be that lives which fall below a certain quality are not worth living. Dutch opponents of the euthanasia principle argue that there is a real danger of falling down the 'slippery slope', because this has already taken place in the 20th century and because many of its supporters have historically shared this attitude. So, once euthanasia is permitted, even with guidelines, it is argued that there could be a tendency that it will be permitted in broader and broader circumstances.

Surveys carried out among general practitioners in 1990 in the Netherlands suggest that there are problems with these requirements, and the requirement of consultation was seen as of little value (for a detailed discussion of the Dutch position, see Chapter 18). If one prognosticates from current trends, it is arguable that it will only be a matter of time before 'physician-assisted suicide', albeit within the strict preconditions stated above, will be more widely accepted in the Netherlands, that any taint of criminality associated with the practice will continue to wane and, eventually, may even disappear altogether.

France and Germany

In the 1990s, French jurisprudence on physician-assisted suicide has developed in such a way that the slippery slope argument carries a great deal of weight. Consequently, as Nys (1999) puts it (p 245), 'the French model in the law of physician-assisted suicide aims at preventing termination of life on request from becoming an accepted practice'; this is done 'by refusing patient and physician from taking decisions that may lead to the death of the patient'. In Germany, however, the German Federal Supreme Court 'has built up during the last decennium a jurisprudence that leaves the decisions regarding refusal of medical treatment, non-treatment and pain relief with the patient … [the German model] aims to prevent termination of life [from becoming] an accepted practice by recognising the right of the patient to refuse treatment and to participate in non-treatment and pain relief decisions' (Nys (1999)).

HUMAN ORGAN TRANSPLANTATION AND DONATION

Our common law, civil law and *sui generis* jurisdictional approaches to the subject of human organ or tissue transplantation have revealed several observations in the comparative context. First, all jurisdictions which have passed laws or regulations dealing with this area adopt a basic policy of respecting the intentions of the organ donor, whether dead or alive, and this reflects the 'respect for persons' principle and, for the living donor, respect for the autonomy of the donor. Indeed, criminal sanctions follow from serious breaches of this principle. Secondly, jurisdictions have frequently adopted a 'contracting out' policy (that is, presumed consent), but sometimes a 'contracting in' policy (for instance, in the case of Germany) with variations. Even where there is a *prima facie* contracting out policy, as in France and Belgium, the practice of doctors has always been to consult the relatives of a donor before carrying out any transplants of any sort (which was also the practice in 1960s America, despite their earlier legislation) and this has now been regularised with new guidelines. However, when the system is followed strictly, as in Austria, the country seems to do better in organ procurement than others, but such a simplistic equation is seriously questioned by commentators because, despite the increase of organs in Austria, there is still an overall shortage of organs in that country. Thirdly, all the jurisdictions we surveyed require written consent to organ donations/transplants and, in the case of Germany and Sweden, have taken pains to specify exactly who could qualify as 'next of kin', and who could therefore be consulted in the absence of an indication or evidence of the donor's intentions. One innovation is the person who may be consulted, who is not a relative but is either 'closely connected' to the donor (Sweden) or even 'especially close' (Germany) to the donor. A common feature is a hierarchy in order of seniority for next of kin, so that one works one's way down the list to contact persons who might cast some light on whether the donor had a view on transplanting of his organs, for Australia and Germany, although Australia has an interesting notion of 'senior available next of kin'. Fourthly, a shortage of organs for transplants to save lives appears to be a fairly universal problem, with the possible exception of countries like Spain, and France and Austria have had limited success. All the jurisdictions we have surveyed have been making strenuous efforts to educate the population and continue to strive to increase the number of organs that will be available for life saving purposes.

As we have seen in the early months of 2000, however, the latest campaign by the British Medical Association to introduce a contracting out system in Britain has, so far, not met with any success. Our comparative survey has highlighted how much further down the road than Britain other countries with a similar cultural, religious and economic make-up have proceeded in attempting to make human transplants the norm rather than the exception. The approaches taken by non-European countries must, however, be treated with caution, because it is not *prima facie* justifiable simply to argue that if, because even smaller countries have decided to move to presumed consent regimes, then Britain should necessarily follow. In Britain, at least, the topic will remain controversial, but the developing trends and imaginative legislation in the various jurisdictions are pointers to possible future legal reform.

CLONING

In 1996, Dolly, the sheep, the first vertebrate cloned from a cell of an adult animal, generated considerable interest on a worldwide scale. Although hailed as a remarkable scientific breakthrough, concern was raised both nationally and internationally about the future of this technology, especially in the context of the cloning of human beings. Dolly was followed by Polly, a transgenic sheep produced by transfer of the nucleus of a cultured fetal fibroblast. She carries a human gene for blood clotting, Factor IX, which is used for treatment of haemophilia. The etymology of the term 'cloning' is the Greek for 'twig'. The British Human Genetics Advisory Commission (HGAC), which reports to ministers on issues arising from new developments in human genetics that can be expected to have wider social, ethical and/or economic implications, are careful to distinguish between at least two main types of cloning:

(a) Reproductive cloning – where an entire animal is produced from a single cell by asexual reproduction. Dolly falls into this category. Human reproductive cloning would involve the creation of a human being who was genetically identical to another.

(b) Therapeutic cloning – which are scientific and therapeutic applications of nuclear replacement technology, which do not involve the creation of genetically identical individuals.

These applications may include therapy for human mitochondrial disease and research, which might lead to the replacement of damaged or diseased tissues or organs without the risk of rejection reactions. One example would be skin tissue to treat burn injuries.

However, cloning is not, *per se*, a new phenomenon. Many plants can clone themselves, and fragments of genetic material are routinely 'cloned' by polynurase chain reaction (PCR) and this has become the basis of DNA fingerprinting and other applications in biotechnology. Recently, Professor Jonathan Slack, an embryologist at Bath University, England, engineered a headless frog clone, raising the prospect that headless human clones 'could be used to grow organs and tissues for transplant surgery' (Connor and Cadbury (1997) *The Sunday Times*, 19 October).

Ethical aspects of cloning

One commentator has argued that the process of human cloning would 'empty the process of human reproduction' (Duddington (1999)). On the question of therapeutic cloning, the HGAC has stressed that it is important to make the distinction between human embryo research, which may be permitted under licence under the Human Fertilisation and Embryology Act 1990 (HFEA 1990) and reproductive cloning, where an embryo is implanted in a woman's womb. The Warnock Committee concluded, in 1984, that 'the embryo of the human species ought to have a special status', which should be enshrined in legislation. The Committee stated that this special status should not afford the human embryo the same status as a living child or adult, but did not mean that human embryos should be used frivolously or unnecessarily. The Committee went on to conclude that the special status of the embryo would permit some embryo research up to the 14th day of development provided the research was strictly controlled and monitored. The recommendations of the Warnock Committee were included in the provisions of the 1990 Act, which allows research to be carried out on embryos up to 14 days' development under licence from the HFEA within certain restrictions.

On the question of human reproductive cloning, the HGAC submits that 'the use of either embryo splitting or nuclear replacement deliberately for the purposes of human reproductive cloning, to produce genetically identical human beings, raises serious ethical issues, concerned with human responsibility and instrumentalisation of human beings'. There are moral arguments to support the claim that human dignity forbids the use of human beings only as a 'means', holding that they are to be treated as an 'end' in their own right. What limits are there on the role of prior choice of characteristics in offspring, where this is scientifically made possible? These arguably apply equally to cloning, and include the obvious need for safety issues to be addressed fully.

Legal aspects of cloning

The first thing that should be considered is that there is doubt as to whether English law at present even deals with human cloning. Cloning can denote several processes and, at present, although the HFEA 1990 appears to ban cloning, there is sufficient ambiguity in the wording of the relevant provision for one to argue (as Duddington (1999) does, pp 30, 40) that cloning as we now use the term is not covered.

Section 1(1)(a) of the HFEA 1990 provides that 'embryo' means a live human embryo where fertilisation is complete. Section 1(1)(b) also uses the term fertilisation by stating that reference to an embryo includes an egg in process of fertilisation. As Wood and Korek point out, the problem here is that what Wood calls 'the reconstituted cell' which grew into Dolly, was never fertilised (see Wood, 'To what extent can the law control human cloning?' (1999) 39(1) Medicine, Science and Journal of the British Academy of Forensic Sciences 5). There was no fusion of egg and sperm and it was artificially created.

Section 3(3)(d) of the 1990 Act contains a prohibition on cloning by providing that a licence granted by the HFEA cannot authorise 'replacing a nucleus taken from the cell of any person, embryo or subsequent development of an embryo'. Again, the difficulty is that, although those words appear to prohibit nuclear transfer cloning, which is what was used in the case of Dolly, once more what precisely happened in Dolly's case is not covered, because of the use of the word 'embryo'. Hence, as Duddington (1999) points out, the 1990 Act uses the terms 'fertilisation' and 'embryo' which do not cover what is now understood by cloning. As explained, the Act allows certain activities under a licence, among which is the storing of gametes.

Section 4(2) of the Act provides that 'a licence cannot authorise storing or using gametes in any circumstances in which regulations prohibit their storage or use but, as Korek (1997) points out, this may not cover what happened in Dolly's case. A gamete is a sperm or egg cell, but only the cell membrane was used to create Dolly, and so it could be argued that this is not a gamete. As Wood says, 'to submit otherwise would be analogous to arguing that an egg devoid of its yolk is still an egg'.

Paragraphs 3 and 4 of Sched 2 provide that 'a licence under this paragraph cannot authorise altering the genetic structure of any cell while it forms part of an embryo ...' Again, the word 'embryo' is problematical.

Hence, the present legal position, based on the current legislation, is, as Duddington (1999) submits, that the 1990 Act does not cover human cloning. Any argument that the 1990 Act does cover cloning would have to interpret the term 'embryo' as having a meaning that it presently does not have. Consequently, as things stand, any decision on whether to grant a licence to permit reproductive cloning rests entirely with a statutory body, which, admittedly, is subject to judicial review. There is no other scrutiny or monitoring of the situation on any systematic or independent basis.

Britain to authorise 'spare-part' cloning

In a somewhat surprising development, it was reported, in early August 2000, that the British Government is taking steps to legalise 'spare part' human cloning. This seemed to be the thrust of comments made by Science Minister Lord Sainsbury, on the Report by the Donaldson Committee on human cloning, entitled *Stem Cell Research: Medical Progress with Responsibility* (the Report), which has been submitted to the government but not yet published for general consumption. Hence, all further comments stated hereafter come from newspaper reports. The Committee is believed to have recommended lifting the ban on 'spare part' or 'therapeutic' human cloning, with Lord Sainsbury saying that, in his view, 'the potential medical benefits (of the practice) outweigh any other considerations one might have'. Liberal Democrat MP Evan Harris announced that he intended to introduce a Bill to amend the HFEA 1990 to legalise cloning.

The Report therefore recommends (source: (2000) *The Observer*, 20 August):

(a) that British scientists be allowed, under strictly controlled conditions, to begin extracting stem cells from embryos which are a few days old and to study them to find out how they go on to develop into our brains or spines, etc.

(b) that British scientists be allowed to perform, under strict controls, 'therapeutic cloning' – the creation of human life not through fertilisation of an egg with a sperm, but through insertion of a donor nucleus, either from an embryo or, eventually, from an adult patient – into an egg, thus creating a simulacrum, something like a 'child' of the original.

The advantages of the latter are: (a) embryos can be cloned, thus allowing more stem cell research; and (b) if this is successful, then adult patients can, briefly, be cloned to allow their own undamaged stem cells to be extracted, or 'twitched' into growing into a new heart or brain or nerve cells, then reinserted into the damaged tissue. This could cure Parkinson's disease, heart disease, and spinal injury. It could possibly cure cancer. The information about this report was derived from a published interview with Sir Liam Donaldson, where he apparently confirmed the content of the Report to a reporter, who published the interview in the *Observer* newspaper. Apparently, the rest of Europe and the USA have greeted the announcement with surprise and interest and have indicated that they will probably wait and see what develops.

There remains considerable doubt about whether it would even be possible to clone humans using the techniques used to produce Dolly the sheep. The nuclear replacement technology used to produce Dolly is in its early stages. Any attempt to develop the existing technology in humans would be expensive and require a considerable amount of human experimentation.

Cloning has become the buzzword and the topic of the moment, and the story of Dolly and Polly (the sheep) has certainly had an international impact. The Chair of the Human Fertilisation and Embryology Authority, Ruth Deech, notes in an article published in 1997 that, until recently, there were only two kinds of cloning:

(a) s 3(3)(d) of the 1990 Act prohibits replacing the nucleus of an embryo with the nucleus taken from the cell of any person or embryo; and
(b) embryo splitting, whereby one could separate the embryos at the two, four or eight cell stage and develop them as normal. To do this would require a licence from the HFEA. The HFEA decided that it would not issue treatment licences for this after a report was received of research being done in the USA in 1993.

However, as Deech reminds us ((1997), p 343), the method used to create Dolly the sheep is different, involving the use of an unfertilised enucleated egg to receive the nucleus of another cell, and so is *not* covered by s 3 of the 1990 Act; and its applicability depends on whether it comes within the Act's definition of an 'embryo'. An embryo is defined by the Act as 'fertilised', and it is not clear if the Dolly-type cloning is included in that category, although fertilisation occurs after a cloned embryo becomes fused.

Deech points out that the HFEA is against cloning, because it considers it ethically unacceptable and risks devaluing the potential child as an individual in his or her own right. She reiterates that there are other reasons against cloning which she lists as:
(a) an instinctive revulsion against creating genetically identical individuals;
(b) fear of eugenics and attempts to clone particular embryos because of their particular characteristics;
(c) difficult family relationship, which is a factor relevant to the need to take into account the welfare of the child, one of the interests protected by the HFEA 1990.

Deech further clarifies (p 344) that the cloning techniques now being developed may help research into certain 'crippling, inherited diseases such as encephalomyopathy, cardiovascular disease and a type of diabetes'. If the definition of embryo were widened, the HFEA could retain its power to license research project by project. As things currently stand, the HFEA may license for five purposes only:
(a) promoting advances in the treatment of fertility;
(b) increasing knowledge about the causes of congenital disease;
(c) increasing knowledge about the causes of miscarriages;
(d) developing more effective techniques of contraception; or
(e) developing methods for detecting the presence of gene or chromosome abnormalities in embryos before implantation.

The HFEA and the HGAC endorse therapeutic cloning. In effect, people suffering from injury or degenerative disease could provide their own nuclei which would be replaced in eggs and stem cells would be developed. The resulting tissue (or organ) could be transplanted into the patient with no risk of rejection.

Although the British Government is apparently set to approve therapeutic cloning, the majority of other countries worldwide are not in favour of cloning *per se*.

In June 2000, Swedish scientists found that stem cells taken from adults could be programmed to generate heart, liver, muscle, intestine and other tissue. In the last week of July 2000, it was reported that British scientists had taken the first steps towards the possibility of growing new livers for patients from their own bone marrow.

THE 'BEST INTERESTS' TEST – SLOGAN OR *AD HOC* SOCIAL POLICY?

It is apparent that whether it is dealing with a proposed non-consensual sterilisation of a mentally incapacitated person, or deciding whether to detain a child who is anorexic and refuses to eat, or deciding in what circumstances it might be lawful to withdraw life sustaining treatment either to a handicapped newborn or to a PVS patient, the English courts apply the 'best interests' test.

The best feature of the best interests test is its universality and consistency of citation, but it remains a symbol of indeterminacy, and an *ad hoc* assessment of the patient's condition and situation have to be made in every case without any really consistent or clear guidance from the law or the medical profession. It remains a slogan in search of substance, where the only certainty is that it will be cited to justify whatever course of action the court decides upon. Commenting on the best interests test in English law, Ian Kennedy (1991) argues (pp 90–91) that the best interests formula is not really a test at all, but a 'somewhat crude conclusion of social policy' which 'allows lawyers and courts to persuade themselves and others that theirs is a principled approach to law'. Having said that, this is clearly 'ad hocery'. He then says there is no such general principle as the best interests formula 'other than the empty rhetoric of best interests; or rather, there is some principle, but the court is not telling'. Kennedy submits that the best interests approach of family law allows the courts to 'atomise' the law, to claim that each case depends on its own facts. 'The court can then respond intuitively to each case while seeking to legitimise its conclusion by asserting that it is derived from the general principle contained in the best interests formula (see Kennedy (1991)).

There is certainly a great deal of truth in Professor Kennedy's observations, and the case law applying the best interests' test which we have reviewed in relation to the English courts may be synthesised under the following headings.

TEENAGERS

If the patient is an underage teenage girl, the English courts are likely to rule in favour of treatment if the outcome of non-treatment is death or serious organic damage being suffered by the girl (*Re W; Re C*); or if the child concerned has a history of bizarre behaviour (the *South Glamorgan* case) or going berserk (*Re R*). Similarly, if there is refusal of treatment in the case of a heart transplant, the English court will also probably rule in favour of the operation to save the life of the teenager. It would seem that there is, therefore, no 'right to die' as far as these kinds of teenagers are concerned. In addition, if there is an application to sustain the life of a handicapped newborn, the courts will probably decide to let the child die with dignity, depending on the severity of the handicap and the perceived quality of life that the child would have in being kept alive. This will be seen as acting in the best interests of the child in these circumstances.

NON-CONSENSUAL STERILISATION OF INCAPACITATED PATIENTS

On the question of a proposed non-consensual sterilisation of intellectually disabled patients, again, the best interests test here suggests that court approval would usually have to be sought to authorise the sterilisation, but the ultimate decision will depend on the particular circumstances of the case. In the most recent case, heard on 18 May 2000 (*Re S*), the Court of Appeal held that, where a declaration was sought as to the lawfulness of proposed medical treatment for a patient unable to consent for herself, it was for the court to decide whether such treatment was in the patent's best interests. The court then continued: 'Once the judge was satisfied that the range of options were within the range of acceptable opinion among competent and responsible practitioners, the *Bolam* test was irrelevant to his decision as to whether the proposed treatment was in S's best interests.' This may suggest that *Bolam* may not be the over-arching all-encompassing test for all purposes that it has been, or that, in this particularly sensitive area of healthcare law, the courts are beginning to be a little more cautious about when to approve sterilisation of mentally disabled patients unless it is patently in their 'best interests' in the sense of protecting and promoting their welfare.

THE *TONY BLAND* CASE AND 'BEST INTERESTS'

The 'best interests' test has also been used in the *Tony Bland* case, and here it is important to note that, leaving aside the 'rights' and 'wrongs' of the judgment, the case undoubtedly represents a crossing of the Rubicon, in its acceptance of the legality of withdrawal of treatment from a patient who had been lying in a comatose persistent (now often called 'permanent' where appropriate) vegetative state for several years, who was not 'brain dead', but insensate. However, the Law Lords were careful to stress that there was no positive act undertaken to actually terminate Bland's life – merely an omission to act, in basically allowing nature to take its course and to allow him to die with dignity. In effect, it was also said that Tony Bland had no interests left to protect, since he was unaware of his environment or of anything that was going on around him. The eventual decision was, nevertheless, stated as being taken 'in his best interests'. The distinction between an act and an omission was recognised in the *Bland* case, in law, but the case for saying there is any *moral* difference between killing through a positive act and killing by omission or a failure to treat remains unconvincing.

ALLOCATION OF SCARCE RESOURCES

The role of resources in determining the availability and extent of medical provision is sometimes alluded to, but rarely discussed openly by healthcare administrators. There is little doubt that, given the relative scarcity of resources in the UK, there has to be some account taken of the high cost of caring for irreversibly vegetative patients which would otherwise be spent on the care and treatment of other patients. The present Labour Government has promised to earmark £19 billion for the NHS but although this will provide a much-needed boost, some budgetary and economic experts maintain that even more investment needs to be made in recruitment, training and rebuilding of the infrastructure the NHS desperately requires to provide a truly modern, dependable service.

In the much publicised case of *R v Cambridge HA ex p B* [1995] WLR 898, the patient was a 10 year old girl suffering from leukaemia. The health authority decided that treatment, which could be provided privately and might give a 20% chance of success, was not in the child's best interests and scarce resources could not be allocated to allocated to it. The decision was challenged by judicial review and the judge upheld the application, holding that the authority reconsider its decision not to allocate the resources, but the Court of Appeal overruled the lower court decision. The Master of the Rolls (Sir Thomas Bingham) said that difficult and agonising judgments have to be made about how a limited budget is best allocated to the maximum advantage of the maximum number of patients, but that it was not up to a court to make such judgments.

As far as the treatment of newborns who are severely handicapped is concerned, the position for many years has been that the provision of resources has not kept pace with the increased demand for newborn care; this appears to be the case in the USA and other Western countries. As Michael Freeman (1987–88) has said, 'Rights without services are meaningless; no law can be better than its implementation and implementation can be no better than resources permit'.

HUMAN RIGHTS AND MEDICAL TREATMENT

On the question of rights, Sheila McLean, writing in 1986, remarked that 'the rhetoric of rights has limited practical value' and 'It is as a method of highlighting the problems of removing existing capacities that the language of rights has been most functional, demanding rationalisation and justification. However, in other aspects of freedom of choice, the rhetoric of rights may have had less impact on reality.' However, with the Human Rights Act having come into force in October 2000 in Britain, thus incorporating the European Convention on Human Rights, the process of having a case heard has, at least in theory, been shortened considerably, since the Convention articles can now be enforced in the domestic courts. There is already some evidence that the English courts are beginning to take account of the potential for breach of the 1998 Act, for example, in the recent case of a handicapped baby, *A National Health Service Trust v D* (2000). The court in this case was careful to emphasise that the operation was not in breach of any articles of the European Convention on Human Rights. Because the judgment to allow non-resuscitation if the severely disabled child suffered respiratory failure was based on the best interests test, to allow the child to die with dignity, there was therefore no breach of Art 2 (the right to life) or Art 3 (the right not to be subjected to inhuman or degrading treatment, including the right to die with dignity) of the European Convention: see Sched 1 to the Human Rights Act 1998.

In her book, *Old Law, New Medicine* (1999), Professor Sheila McLean argues (p 11) that 'Medicine knows what it can do, but it may not know why it does it or whether doing it is right'. She continues, 'Failure to conceptualise what is going on in terms of human rights leads to individual disempowerment'. The question arises as to whether, now that the Human Rights Act 1998 has come into force in Britain, a health authority's blanket policy of excluding certain applicants on the basis of their 'unsuitable' past, their criminal record, their gender or lifestyle would infringe various articles under the Human Rights Act. In his Long Fox lecture, delivered in 1998 and published in 1999 (see

(1999) 10 Med L Rev 255), Lord Irvine reviews, *inter alia*, the provisions of the Convention which the 1998 Act has incorporated. Here are some of the articles he has highlighted.

Articles which might be relevant to medical treatment or to the medical field generally

Article 2 – 'everyone's right to life shall be protected by law': Lord Irvine believes that both advocates and opponents of abortion and euthanasia would be looking to the case law of the European Commission and Court of Human Rights to support their views. He cites *Paton v UK* (1980) 19 DR 244, where the Commission held that the fetus had no absolute right to life. In *H v Norway* (1992) No 17004/90, the Commission held that the abortion of a 14 week old fetus for social reasons was not contrary to Art 2. This is a 'delicate area', in which Contracting States must have greater discretion to determine what the law should be than they have where some of the other Convention rights are concerned. In the Strasbourg jargon, States are allowed a wide margin of appreciation.

Lord Irvine emphasises that, like most articles, Art 2 must not be considered in isolation. It has been argued that the right to privacy conferred by *Art 8* confers a right to an abortion. Any programme of compulsory abortion or sterilisation could be challenged under *Art 12*, which provides for the right to found a family.

Article 3 provides that 'no one shall be subjected to torture or to inhuman or degrading treatment or punishment'. This article has proved to be relevant to prisoners and mental patients. Lord Irvine suggests that it could also be relevant to the treatment given to mental patients for their medical, as opposed to their mental, conditions. In *Herczegfalvy v Austria* [1993] 15 ECHR 437, the European Court of Human Rights held that there was no breach of Art 3 where a violent, mentally ill patient who was incapable of taking decisions for himself was given food and drugs forcibly. They also held, contrary to the Commission, that keeping the applicant handcuffed to his bed for a week was also justified, since it was in accord with 'the psychiatric principles generally accepted at the time'. Article 8 also came into play because the applicant complained that the treatment amounted to an interference with his private life under Art 8. But the Court again held there was no breach under this article either.

Article 5 is relevant to prisoners and mental patients, since it secures the right to 'liberty and security of the person' as the case of *Johnson v UK* [1998] 2 EHRLR 224 illustrates.

The right to refuse medical treatment may also be reinforced, in some cases, by *Art 9*: 'everyone has the right to freedom of thought, conscience and religion [and] to manifest his religion or belief, in worship, teaching, practice and observance.' Lord Irvine also cautions that a 'balancing exercise may have to be carried out here because of the need to protect the rights and freedoms of others'.

Three days after the Human Rights Act 1998 came into force in Britain, a case went before the High Court (*NHS Trust A v Mrs M; NHS Trust B v Mrs H* (2000) 25/10/00, Lawtel) which heard the views of relatives of 'permanent vegetative state' (PVS) patients to stop the tube feeding of these patients. One of these is in full PVS, and the other is not. However, under the current guidelines, the withdrawal of feeding should not normally be considered until a patient has been in PVS for 12 months, to rule out any chance of recovery, and it is thought that at least one of these patients has only been in PVS for nine months. The court's decision was to grant declarations to withdraw treatment in both cases and held that, although Art 2 of the Convention contained a positive obligation on the State to take adequate and appropriate steps to safeguard life, it could not be correct to interpret Art 2 to mean that a decision to cease treatment in a patient's best interests was intentional deprivation of life. 'Deprivation of life' had to import a deliberate act, as opposed to an omission by someone on behalf of the State to act, resulting in death. Hence, the principles laid down in the *Bland* case were entirely in accordance with the Convention case law and, therefore, did not violate the Human Rights Convention (as implemented by the Human Rights Act 1998) (see, also, earlier discussion of this case in Chapter 9).

MEDICAL ETHICS AND THE LAW IN THE 21ST CENTURY

Old ethical problems in the new millennium?

Ethics, rights and reproduction look set to continue to be buzzwords well into the 21st century. In 1999, there appeared to be an increasing number of medico-legal cases emerging with contentious ethical issues. For instance, there was the couple mounting a legal battle for the right to have a grandchild using the sperm of their dead son and a surrogate mother. The problem here was that, although the sperm donor had written a letter saying he wanted his sperm to be taken from his body so that his fiancée could have his child, and sperm was removed while he was alive, when he was subsequently killed in a road accident, his girlfriend of 10 years decided she did not want to become the mother of the child. Hence, the clinic that stored the deceased's sperm was advised by the English Human Fertilisation and Embryology Authority

(HFEA) not to release the sperm for surrogacy, as the intended mother was not prepared to consent to motherhood in accordance with the wishes and terms of consent stipulated by the deceased. Any surrogate arrangement that was subsequently undertaken would be deliberately creating a fatherless *and* motherless child, which would therefore not be in the child's best interests or promote its welfare. It was also reported in late 1999 that almost 50 women whose eggs were frozen were attempting to overturn a ruling by the HFEA that they could not have them fertilised. However, in January 2000, the HFEA announced that the ban on thawing frozen human eggs would be lifted. This appears to be the direct consequence of technological advances. Women in Britain have been allowed to freeze their human eggs for the past two years, but the HFEA has not allowed clinics to thaw them, because very few live babies were born from IVF in the early days of this technique and scientists believed that the defrosting technique could damage the baby's genes. However, American and Japanese scientists have recently achieved 25 pregnancies from thawed eggs, which have apparently produced healthy babies. Hence, the first millennial change in policy has taken place as a result of technological advances. However, frozen embryos, which are used in about 5,000 IVF treatments each year in Britain, have only about a 12% chance of producing a baby, so women still have a poor chance of conceiving from thawed eggs.

The genetically selected test-tube baby

Another area that is currently hitting the headlines is the practice of genetic screening and the case of the first American test-tube baby to be genetically selected so that his cells could be used to save his critically ill sister created a sensation when it was reported that the six year old sister received a transplant of stem cells from the baby's umbilical cord, an operation that could offer a 90% chance of a cure for Fanconi anaemia. This has provoked debate among British doctors about the ethics of 'designer babies' ((2000) *The Times*, 4 October).

Damages and failed sterilisations

In two contrasting stories, it was reported that a mother who bore a mentally disabled son after a failed sterilisation operation had been awarded £1.3 million for 'wrongful birth' after a seven year court battle while the parents of a seven year old girl, who was conceived after her father had a vasectomy, lost their medical negligence claim, the House of Lords ruling that they could not pursue their claim for damages because a baby 'is a blessing, not a detriment'.

It would appear that failed sterilisations resulting in giving birth to a disabled child is recognised by the court as warranting compensation (not least for the costs of caring for the child) whereas, if a normal child (who would not necessarily be so costly) resulted, this would not.

Circumcision veto upheld

Finally, there was the case of the mother who won a landmark legal victory to stop her five year old son undergoing ritual circumcision at the wishes of his Muslim father. This was the first time a court had to make a decision on the circumcision of a child when one parent was opposed to it. The appeal court ruled, in a unanimous decision, that the Christian mother was entitled to veto the operation.

Ethics and fertility

At the heart of these decisions is the vexed question of 'rights' over one's body, the 'best interests' of the patient and the welfare of children. Yet, these cases are raising the same ethical issues which have faced the English courts since the mid-1970s and courts in other countries since the 1980s. In cases involving infertility treatment, the fundamental ethical consideration is the welfare of the resulting children, but where donated eggs or sperm are involved, various other issues arise: for the recipients, sperm donation requires extraordinary commitment by the man to the child, who is not his genetic offspring. For the woman, egg donation is not quite so traumatic, because she is biologically involved by carrying her pregnancy and giving birth to the child.

Autonomy, teenagers and pregnant women

The 1990s saw a spate of cases demonstrating a trend towards greater judicial recognition of autonomy in principle, but not always in practice – for example, overriding the wishes of teenagers who refused to eat because they were suffering from anorexia nervosa or authorising Caesarean sections on women despite their refusal of the operation, because the courts deemed them to be legally incapable of making a rational decision at the relevant time, for instance, because of a needle phobia. The English Court of Appeal has nevertheless reaffirmed, in 1997 (in *Re MB*), that adults of sound mind do have the right to make an autonomous decision and refuse medical treatment and that they may do so even if the decision appears to others to be irrational at the time.

FEMINIST PERSPECTIVES?

One perspective that has not been addressed in the present volume is a 'feminist perspective'. It is undeniable that only women have a uniquely individual perspective on events such as child-bearing, abortion, sterilisation and, indeed, enforced Caesarean sections (which have been very much in the news over the last four years). Yet although, statistically, women use the NHS more than men, there is scant recognition of their unique role in healthcare cases or, indeed, the way in which they have been perceived in certain medical contexts (for example, 'irrational' while in the 'throes of labour'). A man's assertion of autonomy and refusal of treatment is more likely to be respected in certain cases (as in *Re C (Adult: Refusal of Medical Treatment)* [1994] 1 WLR 290, which involved the 68 year old male schizophrenic patient who was prepared to risk death through gangrene setting in). The interested reader is strongly urged to read the excellent collection of essays edited by Sheldon and Thomson (see Sheldon, S and Thomson, M (eds), *Feminist Perspectives on Healthcare Law*, 1998, Cavendish Publishing), which offer a much-needed insight into this very topic. Including feminist perspectives into the present comparative study would have necessitated writing a different and longer book, in the light of the volume of substantive material that required dissection and synthesis. Women feature in nearly all of the leading cases we have examined, and will no doubt continue to do so.

LAW AND ETHICS IN THE 21ST CENTURY

Undoubtedly, the early years of the new millennium will see an expansion of even more difficult dilemmas involving ethical and legal issues, and a clearer code of ethics, taking into account more technological advancements, may soon be required. However, in the field of reproductive technology, for example, whether the courts will succeed in maintaining the delicate balance between respecting the rights of adults and safeguarding the welfare of children will remain as difficult a decision as ever.

On the issue of decision making, we return to Sheila McLean in her book, *Old Law, New Medicine* (1999), who says (p 180) that, when dealing with dilemmas posed by technological advances, 'by categorising dilemmas as medical, society as a whole, and the law in particular, has shuffled off responsibility and has endangered human rights'. She then cites with approval Diana Brahams, who has written that 'Society will expect the law to protect its wider ideals and, in particular, the individual citizen, from the excesses of over-enthusiastic doctors and scientists, greedy corporations and immoral profiteers and manipulators. The law will have to balance the need for future research against the need to protect society from its dangers and evils' (Brahams, D, 'Human genetic information: the legal implications', CIBA Foundation Symposium 11, p 117). However, as McLean puts it (1999): 'It is not the mechanics of the law's response which are so important as its content – a content informed by concern for liberty, for the protection of the vulnerable and for the reinforcement of ideals ... [t]he collusion of the professions [legal and medical] has minimised their capacity to respect and safeguard those whose lives they affect, sometimes invade. Their fundamental ethics are open to challenge as never before.' This is clearly a plea for continued recognition of autonomy, but also for humanity and protection of the vulnerable.

It may be expected that the law and legal concepts would continue to play a significant part in ordering the complex interaction of medicine, reproductive technology, ethics and social interaction. As McVeigh and Wheeler expressed it: 'Law and legal concepts still have a powerful ordering role in almost all regulation' ((1991), Introduction). But to what extent can the law do so, and how effective can it be when the sheer pace of the technological revolution tends to leave the law several steps behind in trying to grapple with new challenges, while it still uses 'old' legal concepts, hewn from decades of the 'old world order'? There is no doubt that new law needs to be made and, in some cases, will have to be made. But laws, new and old, at home and abroad, must not lose sight of the fundamental principles of respect for persons and their right to self-determination, seeking to do no harm and, wherever possible, doing good to the greatest number, and to continue to strike a balance between applying the principle of the sanctity of human life against the quality of life. This should be the norm, whether a case is being heard in Britain, Belgium, California or Calcutta. If the UK Human Rights Act 1998 can help in this endeavour by allowing the domestic courts to hear cases speedily and efficaciously, then it will already have justified its implementation in Britain. Comparative perspectives offer different insights, and may offer fresh ideas in dealing with medico-legal issues. They also inform us about how other jurisdictions are coping with common problems ranging from abortion to cloning to euthanasia and physician-assisted suicide. It is hoped that this book will provide several contrasting perspectives on how other parts of the world deal with some of the most challenging medico-legal dilemmas of our time. In dealing with these complex dilemmas, the common difficulty in all jurisdictions will be to formulate and maintain a consistent set of ethical values and moral standards which will reflect a core of humanity and respect for human life, while serving the needs of each individual – from the beginning of life (however that may be defined) and, where necessary, at the point of death. The maintenance of these moral and ethical values to underpin difficult medico-legal decisions, often against a background of rapidly changing technological advances, will pose the greatest challenge to healthcare professionals and the courts around the world, in the 21st century and beyond.

SELECT BIBLIOGRAPHY

Beauchamp, TL, 'The beginning and end of life' in Beauchamp, T and Walters, L (eds), *Contemporary Issues in Ethics*, 1999, Wadsworth

Beauchamp, TL and Childress, *Principles of Biomedical Ethics*, 1989, OUP

Brazier, M, 'Regulating the reproduction business?' [1999] 7 Med LR 166

Campbell, T *et al*, *Human Rights: From Rhetoric to Reality*, 1986, Blackwell

Deech, R, 'Infertility and ethics' (1997) 9 CFLQ 337

Duddington, J, 'The legal and ethical aspects of cloning: Parts 1 and 2' (1999) Law and Justice 26; 100

Fletcher, N, Holt, S, Brazier, M and Harris, J (eds), *Ethics, Law and Nursing*, 1995, Manchester UP

Irvine (Lord), 'The patient, the doctor, their lawyers and the judge: rights and duties' [1999] 7 Med LR 255

Jennett, B, 'The persistent vegetative state: medical, ethical and legal issues' in Grubb, A (ed), *Choices and Decisions in Health Care*, 1993, Wiley

Kass, L, 'The meaning of life – in the laboratory', in Alpert, K (ed), *The Ethics of Reproductive Technology*, 1995, OUP

Kass, L, 'Is there a right to die?' (1993) 38 Hastings Centre Report 41

Kennedy, I, 'Patients, doctors and human rights', in Blackburn, R and Taylor, T (eds), *Human Rights for the 1990s*, 1991, Mansell

Keown, J, 'Restoring moral and intellectual shape to the law after *Bland*' (1997) 113 LQR 481

Korek, S, 'Following Dolly' (1997) 147 NLJ 428

Mason, J and McCall Smith, A, *Law and Medical Ethics*, 5th edn, 1995, Butterworths

McHaffie, H *et al*, 'Witholding/withdrawing treatment from neonates: legislation and official guidelines across Europe' (1999) 25 JME 440

McLean, S, *Old Law, New Medicine*, 1999, Pandora

McVeigh, S and Wheeler, S (eds), *Law, Health and Medical Regulation*, 1991, Dartmouth

Nys, H, 'Physician involvement in a patient's death: a Continental perspective' (1999) 10 Med L Rev 208

Sedley, S (Sir), 'Human rights: a 21st century agenda', in Blackburn, R and Busuttil, J (eds), *Human Rights for the 21st Century*, 1997, Pinter

INDEX

Abortion . . . 77–115
abortion pills . . . 95–96
access to services . . . 103
Albania . . . 451
arguments against . . . 79–80
arguments for . . . 79–81
attempted . . . 435
Australia . . . 431–35
autonomy . . . 113
bans . . . 414, 416–19
Beijing conference . . . 416–17
BMA guidance . . . 79, 81
'born alive, capable of being' . . . 93–95
Cairo conference . . . 416
Cambodia . . . 453
Canada . . . 105–07, 430–31, 631
child destruction . . . 84, 93, 102, 112–13
children and young persons . . . 90–92
Chile . . . 416
China . . . 452
choice . . . 79
civil law countries . . . 436–49
common law . . . 83, 84, 96–97, 100–09
comparative study of . . . 413–55, 629, 631–32
conscientious objection . . . 89–90
consent to medical treatment . . . 26, 38–39, 44, 90–92, 428, 633
counselling . . . 442, 444–47
criminal offences . . . 83, 89–90, 93, 108, 413, 421, 431–32, 434, 437–40, 450
Denmark . . . 442, 446, 448
detention . . . 105
DHSS memorandum . . . 90
double effect doctrine . . . 82
Eastern legal perspectives . . . 452–53
embryo research . . . 109–12
emergencies . . . 89
England, in . . . 83–89, 97–100, 108–09, 112, 413, 431–32
ethics . . . 78–81
European Convention on Human Rights . . . 93, 656
family, right to found a . . . 656
fetal pain . . . 81
financial considerations . . . 448–49
France . . . 436–39, 453
Germany . . . 439–48, 569
Gillick case . . . 91
global survey . . . 413–14
GMC guidance . . . 92
grounds for . . . 88–89, 414–16
Guyana . . . 451
handicapped babies . . . 442
health grounds . . . 414, 415, 424–25, 631
health insurance . . . 448–49
historical background . . . 81–82
England, in . . . 83–89
homicide, as . . . 81–82, 97–100, 431
India . . . 453
injunctions . . . 92–93, 104
Ireland . . . 100–05, 112–13
jurisdiction . . . 88
legal status of fetus . . . 96–100
liberalisation . . . 86–89, 427, 631
mental disabilities . . . 39, 103–05, 414, 415, 633
multiple pregnancy, selective reduction of . . . 95
Nazi laws . . . 440–41
necessity . . . 440
New Zealand . . . 107–09
Northern Ireland . . . 100–05, 112–13
offences against the person . . . 83–85, 97–99, 101–02

organ transplantation 569
origins of life 109–12
People's Republic
of China 452
philosophical
principles 78–81, 110–11
pills 95–96
preventing 92–95
privacy 417, 422–24, 426, 453, 656
prohibitions on 414, 416–19
proportionality 432
protection of fetus 96–100
psychological harm 414, 415, 431
reform 86–89
relatives 427–28
research 109–12
restrictions, without 414, 415–16
right to 90–92
right to life 102–03, 656
Romania 451–52
saving women's lives 414, 415
Scotland 88, 90, 436
self-determination 113
self-induced 437–38
sentencing 83
Seychelles 451
socio-economic grounds 414, 415
South Africa 452
Spain 449, 453
spousal consent 92
statistics 77–78, 102, 413–14
Sweden 450
time limits 429–30, 632
tissue from
aborted fetuses 569
Turkey 450, 451
UK, in 83–96
United Nations
conferences on unsafe 416–17
United States 77, 82, 417–31, 453, 631–32
unsafe 416–17
victimisation 631
Warnock Committee 110–12
Western Europe 417
women's rights 79

Abuse 405–06

Access to medical records
applications for 69–70
Australia 377–79
Canada 374–75
common law 377–78
confidentiality 49, 69–70
Australia 377–79
Canada 374–75
contracts 377–78
data protection 69–70
death, following 70
English law, in 377
fiduciary duties 378–79
freedom of
information 379
property, as 378
self-determination 378

Accountability 233–68

Adoption
France 477, 479–81
surrogacy 172, 176–81, 465, 467, 477, 479–81

Advance directives . . . . .
assisted suicide 621
Australia 622–23
Canada 625
ethics 621
formalities 624
mental disabilities 315–17
palliative care 624
preservation of
existing rights 622
refusal of medical
treatment 315–17
relatives 620–21
religion 621
revocation 625
safeguards 621

Singapore 620–25
'terminal illnesses' 622–23
time stipulation 622
United States 616–17, 625
withdrawal of
medical treatment 616–17
withholding
of treatment 623

Advertising
organ transplantation 555
surrogacy 177

Age
assisted reproduction 191–93
children and
young persons 118–24
consent to
medical treatment 118–24
organ transplantation 579

AIDS/HIV
Australia 544, 575
Canada 370–74, 636
causation 547
children and
young persons 129–31
confidentiality 59–62, 65, 67, 70–74, 366–67, 369–74, 385, 387, 635
contacts, giving
information to 72–73
defamation 65
disclosure to others 71–72
ethics 70–71
European Convention
on Human Rights 385, 387
Germany 545–47
GMC guidance 71–74
healthcare professionals,
informing other 71
medical malpractice 544–47
organ transplantation 575
prisoners 72–73
public interest 59–62, 371
refusal of consent 129–31
United States 366–67, 369, 544–45, 636
warnings 366–67, 369, 635

Albania 451

Alder Hey hospital 287–88

Anencephalic babies 298, 406–07

Animals and
organ transplantation 275

Antenatal care 9–11

Artificial feeding 643–44

Artificial insemination 163, 165, 167, 459, 474–75

Assault 326

Assisted reproduction 163–68, 187–94
See, also, Surrogacy
access to 191–93
age 191–93
artificial insemination 163, 165, 167, 459, 474–75
best interests
of the child 191
birth registration,
changes to law on 191
Children Act 1989 164
codes of practice 192, 193
comparative law 459
consent 188
damages 483–85
deceased person,
donation from 187–91, 474–75, 481–83
EC law 189
ethics 164–68, 190, 657–58
Europe, in 193–94
fathers 166
non-recognition of 166–67
France 481–83
gamete intrafallopian
transfer 163, 168, 459
Germany 483–85
Human Fertilisation
and Embryology
Act 1990 165

Human Fertilisation
and Embryology
Authority 165–68, 188–90
in vitro fertilisation. 163, 165, 168, 184, 187–93, 459
legal framework 164–68
marriage,
presumptions
based on 164
'mothers'. 166
parenthood, types of 164
register of donors 165–66
resources. 191–92
social parenthood 164
sperm donation
after death 187–91, 474–75, 481–83
status provisions. 166–67
statistics 193–94
unborn children's
rights 26
United States 166
Warnock Committee 165

Assisted suicide 291–94, 302, 397
See, also, Euthanasia
advance directives 621
comparative law 642–45
criminal offences. 291–92
double effect doctrine. 642
homicide 291–93, 302, 397, 642
Netherlands 600, 605, 644–45
physician. 293–94, 315, 600, 607, 609–19, 642–45
refusal of medical
treatment 617
United States 599, 608–17
Singapore 621
Switzerland 607

Audit Committee 266–67

Australia
abortion 431–35
attempted 435
criticisms of 433–35
jurisdictions,
variation between 433
non-enforcement
of laws on. 434–35
outdated medical/
medico-legal
concepts 434
uncertainty
of the law on 434
access to
medical records. 377–79
advance directives 622–23
AIDS/HIV 544, 575
assisted reproduction. 474–75
autonomy. 338
best interests
of the patient 506–14
Bolam test 345–46, 543
case law. 340–41
children 573, 574–75
codes of practice 375–76, 579–80
common law 337
confidentiality 375–79
statute, disclosure
required by. 377
consent. 337–48, 514–15, 576–77, 620
cornea transplants. 578–79
costs. 347
criminal offences 375–76, 431–32, 434
dangerous patients 376
death
definition 577
posthumous taking
of sperm after. 474–75
documents 377
euthanasia 617–20, 625–26
administration. 618
consent 620
'terminal illnesses' 618

withholding or withdrawing medical treatment 618–19
experts 473
fiduciary duties 378–79
freedom of information 379
guidelines 337–38
handicapped babies 407
information 337–47
medical malpractice 262, 340–47, 543–44
organ donation 571–80, 646
privilege 377
proportionality 432
relatives 505–08, 573–74, 578, 580
sanctity of life 407
self-determination 338, 341, 344, 378
standard of care 345–46
sterilisation 504–16, 639
surrogacy 470–74
'terminal illnesses' 618, 622–23
United States 338, 340, 341, 344, 348
violent patients 376
warnings 346–47
withholding or withdrawing medical treatment 618

Austria 557–58, 646

Autonomy
abortion 113
Australia 338
confidentiality 53
consent to medical treatment 6, 12, 338, 355
euthanasia 298–99, 599
medical malpractice 260
Netherlands 645
organ transplantation 274
persistent vegetative state 309, 645
sterilisation 197
surrogacy 170

Battery
Canada 333–35
consent to medical treatment 7, 9, 32, 326–27, 331, 333–35, 632
United States 326–27, 331

Beijing Platform for Action 416–17

Belgium 526–27, 556–57

Best interests of the patient 652–54
Australia 506–14
children and young persons 117, 132, 133, 138, 140–41, 144–51, 156–61, 653
confidentiality 50
consent to medical treatment 38–39, 42, 44
criticism of 652
death 306
English law and 652
European Convention on Human Rights 655
Germany 516, 521, 639
handicapped babies . . 133, 138, 140–41, 144–51, 156–61, 391, 393, 407–09, 641, 653
mental disabilities 653
necessity 42
New Zealand 408
omissions 654
organ transplantation 279, 586–88
persistent vegetative state 306, 308, 309, 408, 643, 653–54, 657
refusal of medical treatment 653
Scotland 227–30

sterilisation 133, 197–98, 201, 208, 213–14, 218–19, 224–25, 653
Australia 506–14
Germany 516, 521, 639
Scotland 227–30
United States 498
surrogacy 172, 175–76, 180–82, 185, 187
United States 498, 586–88
withdrawal of treatment 654

Birth registration 191

Bland case 304–13

Blood transfusions 295–96

BMA
See British Medical Council

Bolam test
Australia 345–46, 543
causation 257
children and young persons 139, 638
comparative law 638
consent to medical treatment 7, 335, 345–46
handicapped babies 139
information, disclosure of 634
interpretation 243–47
medical malpractice 236, 238–41, 249–50, 255–60, 263–67, 533, 543, 634
persistent vegetative state 305, 306, 308
sterilisation 218, 639

Bolitho case 255–57, 259–61, 264, 267–68, 533, 634

Bone marrow transplantation 280–81

Brazier Report 179, 184–86, 187

British Medical Council
abortion 79, 81
confidentiality 49–50
euthanasia 317–18
organ transplantation 283–84, 286, 552–53
persistent vegetative state 309–11
surrogacy 184, 186

Cadaveric organ transplantation 275,

Caesarean section
consent to medical treatment
refusal of 13–31, 36–37, 44
declarations 14
guidelines 13, 18–19, 21–22
mental disabilities 13, 15–20
unborn children, rights of 13, 21, 24, 29–30, 37

Cairo conference 416–17

Cambodia 453

Canada
abortion 105, 430–31, 631
advance directives 625
AIDS/HIV 370–74, 636
battery 334–35
Charter of Rights 430–31
code of ethics 373–74
confidentiality 369–75, 636
honest and reasonable belief 372–73
consent 333–37, 538
damages 370
diseases 370–74
homicide 431
information 333–37, 633–34
medical malpractice 336, 538
mental disabilities 105, 374
privacy 370

privilege 369–70
psychiatrists 374
psychological harm 431
public interest 371–73
refusal of consent 333–34
research 333
standard of care 335
sterilisation 198, 205, 207–08, 212, 230, 501–04
violent patients 374
warnings 335–36, 372, 374
Wigmore criteria 373–74

Capacity
adults, incompetent 32–34
assessment 27
consent to medical treatment 11–12, 15–20, 23–43
guardians *ad litem* 28
hearings 28
legal 11, 31–32
level of understanding 11
mental disabilities 11–12, 15–20, 23–43
test for 31–32

Carers 515–21

Causation
AIDS/HIV 547
antenatal tests 11
Bolam test 257
consent to medical treatment 11
medical malpractice 236, 250–52
multiple causes 252–53

Central Europe 526

Cervical smear tests 263–66

Child destruction 84, 93, 102, 112–13

Children Act proceedings 120, 131
parental responsibility 164
prohibited steps order 132
s 8 orders 131, 132
specific issue orders 132, 150
sterilisation 222–24
wardship 132

Children and young persons 117–62
See, also, Handicapped babies, Unborn children
abortion 90–92
abuse 405–06
age 118–24
AIDS/HIV 129–31
Australia 573, 575–76
best interests of the child/patient 117, 132, 133, 138, 140–41, 144–51, 156–61, 653
Bolam test 139, 638
Children Act proceedings 120, 131
children's rights 132–34
comparative law 640–41
confidentiality 53–55, 119
consent to medical treatment 32–33, 117–31
contraception 54–55, 118–20
criminal law 158–59
'demonstrably awful' test 140
detention 123–24
disabled children 133, 135–61
ethics 136–38
European Convention on Human Rights 138, 153, 159–60
France 560–61
Gillick competence 117, 118–24, 133–34, 161, 638, 640
handicapped babies 135–61
cases on 139–61
heart transplants 125–27
homicide 139, 158–59

infanticide 135–36
inhuman and
degrading treatment. 153
international
perspectives 134
Jehovah's Witnesses 124, 126
judicial review 150–51
jurisdiction of the court 132
meaning 117, 134
mental disabilities 121–24, 638, 640–41
necessity 126, 159
'no chance' situations 148–49
'nursing care only' 139
organ transplantation 280–82, 287–88, 554
Australia 573, 574–75
France 560–61
parental responsibility . . 121–22, 127–31
parents 117, 121–22, 127–31, 138, 144–47, 155–60
pregnancy 133
prohibited
steps orders 132
quality adjusted
life years 151–52
quality of life 137–38, 142, 151–52
refusal of treatment 117–18, 120–33, 155–60, 638, 640, 653
religion 124, 126, 148–49, 155, 160
resources, allocation of 151–60
right to life 153, 159
sanctity of life 137–38, 147
Scotland 640–41
s 8 orders 131, 132
specific issue orders 132, 150
sterilisation 133, 201–15, 223, 225–26
'treatment' 118
UN Convention
on the Rights
of the Child. 134
wardship. 132

Chile 416

China. 452, 593–94

Clinical negligence
See Medical malpractice

Cloning
comparative law 486–87, 648–52
definition 486
diseases 650–51
EC law 487
embryo research 648
embryos . . . .
meaning 648–49
splitting 651
ethics 648
European Convention 486
France 486
gametes, storage
or usage of 649
Germany 486
international
legal position 486–87
legal aspects 648–49
licences 649
reproductive 648
spare part 649–52
therapeutic 648, 650–52
UK, in 486–87
United States 487
Warnock Committee 648
World Health
Organisation
declaration on 486–87

Codes of practice
assisted reproduction 192–93
Australia 375–76
Canada 373–74
confidentiality 47–51, 373–76
consent to medical
treatment 36–37

handicapped adults 393–94, 399
Italy 393–94, 399
surrogacy 186

Comparative law 629–62
abortion 413–55, 629, 631–32
assisted reproduction 459, 636–37, 659
assisted suicide 642–45
autonomy 659–60
best interests of the patient 652–54
Bolam test 638
children or young persons 638, 640–41, 653, 659–60
circumcision 659
civil law 629
cloning 629, 647–52
common law 629
confidentiality 635–36
consent to medical treatment 355–56, 632–33
English law 629
ethics 630, 657–59
euthanasia 599–627, 642–45
feminism 660–62
genetic screening 658
Gillick competence 638
handicapped babies 391–412, 641–42
human rights 655–57
information, disclosure of 633–34
medical malpractice 525–50, 634–35
mental disabilities 491–523, 639–40, 653
methodology 630
organ transplantation .. 551–97, 645–47
paternalism 638
persistent vegetative state 642–45, 653–54
pregnancy 659–60
refusal of medical treatment 638
resources, allocation of scarce 654–55
standard of care 634–35
sterilisation 491–523, 639–40, 653, 658–59
surrogacy 457–90, 637–38
United States abortion law 429–30

Compensation
See, also, Damages
confidentiality 379
New Zealand 379, 547–49
no-fault 379, 547–49
Sweden 549

Conditional fees 332

Confidentiality 47–75, 359–90
access to medical records 49, 69–70, 374–75, 377–79
AIDS/HIV 59–62, 65, 67, 70–74, 635–36
Canada 370–74
European Convention on Human Rights 385, 387
United States 364, 366–67, 369
Australia 375–79
autonomy 53
best interests of the patient 50
BMA guidance 49
breach of 56–58
British Medical Association 48
Canada 369–75, 636
children and young persons 53–55, 119
codes of practice 47–51, 373–76
common law jurisdictions 359–83
comparative law 635–36
compensation 379
competency 53

consent 50, 57
medical
treatment, to 53
consequential
arguments 52–53
contraception 54–55
crime 60–64, 375–76, 380
damages 370, 384
dangerous patients 361–64, 374, 376, 381, 635
data protection 69–70
death, following 47, 50–51, 53, 70
Declaration of Geneva 47
defamation 65–66
definition 48–49
diseases, notifiable 58, 364–74, 635–36
documents 377
employers 50
ethics 48, 52–55, 380
European Convention
on Human Rights 384–90
example of
where a duty arises 49
exceptions 48, 49–51
family life, right
to respect for 386
GMC guidance 49–51, 53–54, 56
guidance 49–51, 66
Hippocratic Oath 47
historical basis for 47–48
honest and
reasonable belief 372–73
hospital reports 66–67
identity of informant 67–68
informants 67–68
insurance companies 50
judicial discretion 372
justification for 48, 51–55
breach of 56–58
Law Commission 55
legal bases 55
legal professional
privilege 66–67
medical records 384–89
access to 49, 69–70
mental disabilities 362–63, 374, 382–83
New Zealand 379–83
no-fault compensation 379
police, volunteering
information to 58
precedent 384
privacy 53, 73, 361, 370, 384–90
privilege 58, 66–67, 69
Canada 369–70, 377
New Zealand 379, 380
United States 359–62
proportionality 386
protection of
the public 374
psychiatrists 360, 363, 374
psychologists 361–63
public interest 48, 52, 56, 59–64, 68, 74
Australia 376
Canada 371, 373
European
Convention on
Human Rights 387
United States 359, 361
public policy 67–68
quasi-legislation 66
remedies 65–66, 381–83
research 51
Scotland 383–84
sexual conduct 64–65
16, persons under 53–55
sources of the
legal obligation of 55
standard of care 367
statute, required by 377
statutory
requirements 50, 57–59
teams, disclosure
within 50

terrorism 58
therapists 362–63
third parties. 62–65, 363–64, 367
liability for non-disclosure. 366–69, 635–36
UKCC code of practice. 51
United States. 62–63, 359–69, 636
utilitarianism 52
violent patients, warning of potentially 361–64, 374, 376, 381, 635
waiver 381
warnings 361–69, 372, 374, 376, 381, 635
Wigmore criteria. 360–61, 373–74

Conjoined twins 155–60, 402, 641

Conscientious objections 89–90

Consent to medical treatment 3–45
See, also, Refusal of consent to medical treatment
abortion 26, 38–39, 44, 428, 633
adults, incompetent 32–34
age 118–24
ancillary treatments and 35–36
antenatal tests 9–11
assault 326
Australia 337–48, 514–15, 576–77, 620
Austria 557
autonomy 6, 12, 338, 355
battery 7, 9, 32, 326–27, 331, 334–35, 632
best interests of the patient 38–39, 42, 44
Bolam test 6, 345–47
Caesarean section 13–31, 36–37, 44
Canada 333–37, 538
capacity 11–12, 15–20, 23–43
causation. 11, 352
children 32–33, 117–33, 155–60
civil law countries. 348–52
codes of practice 36–37
common law 8–14
comparative observations. 355–56, 652–53
confidentiality 53
costs. 331, 347
Council of Europe Convention 323
damages 10, 331
declarations 14, 27, 42
diagnostic interventions 350–51
detention 34–36, 40–43, 123–24
disabled persons 37–38
emergencies 28
English law and 4–6, 8–44, 340–41
ethical framework. 3–7, 632–33
euthanasia 397–402, 620
experiments 324, 333, 349–50
express 325
forced feeding 35–36
France 348–49, 355, 560
Germany 349–52, 355, 516–18, 520, 563–65
Gillick competence 118–19
guidelines 21–22, 26–29, 337–38
handicapped adults 393, 397–402
high risk cases 351
historical background 8–14
Human Rights Act 1998 . . . . . 4, 633
'incompetence' 43–44

'incompetent patients' 43–44
information 339–55
disclosure 326–30, 333–38
level of required 9–11, 339
informed 3, 244–45, 247–50, 278, 632–33
Australia 337–48
Canada 333–37
civil law countries 348–52
definition 339–40
English law and 4–6, 8–14, 43
evolution of 324–31
Germany 350, 352
Ireland 538–39
Japan 352–56
New Zealand 408
non-UK jurisdictions, in 323–24
United States and 3, 8–14, 324–31, 340–41, 344, 355
Ireland 538–39
Italy 393
Japan 352–56
legal consequences of proceeding without 7
litigation 331
low risk cases 351
medical malpractice 7, 244–45, 247–50, 283, 355–56, 533
Australia 340–47
Canada 331, 335, 538
United States 326–27
mental disabilities 11–12, 15–20, 23–43, 633
Nazi Germany 349–50
necessity 37, 39–43
New Zealand 355, 408–09
non-European perspectives 352–56
non-UK jurisdictions, evolution and development in 323–57
Nuremberg Code 324, 349–50
organ transplantation 275–78, 287, 552–53, 595, 646–47
Australia 576–77
Austria 557
France 560
Germany 563–65
United States 581–89
payment for informed consent 353–56
precedent 330
pregnancy 13–31, 36–37, 44
Presidential Statement on 331
presumed 283, 289, 552–53, 581–89, 646–47
privilege 325, 327, 330, 351–52
real 9, 12–13, 32
reasonableness 6
refusal of 11–12, 14–36
res ipsa loquitur 325
research 324, 333, 349–50
right to life 4
rules of 9–12
self-determination 3, 6, 12, 329, 338, 341, 344, 349, 397
Sidaway case 6, 28, 43
standard of care 327–30, 335, 345
sterilisation 38–39, 44, 216–19, 228–30, 633, 639–40
Australia 514–15
Germany 516–18, 520

Switzerland 355
therapeutic
interventions 350–51
trespass to the person. 8–9
unborn children,
interests of. 13, 21, 24–26,
29–31, 37
understanding,
level of. 11–12
United States. 3, 8–14,
323–24, 355,
581–89, 632
valid. 5
voluntary 323–24
warnings 7, 335–36,
346–47

Contingency fees. 332, 635

Contraception
children and
young persons. 54–55, 118–20
confidentiality 54–55
Gillick competence 118–19
sterilisation 212–13, 217,
226, 491, 518

Cornea transplants 578–79

Costs
Australia 347
conditional fees 332
consent 331, 347
NHS litigation 332
United States 331

Council of Europe. 323

Crime
See, also, Homicide
abortion 83, 413, 421,
431–32, 434,
437–40, 442,
446, 448, 450
assisted suicide 291–92
Australia 375–76,
431–32, 434
confidentiality. 60–64,
375–76, 380
euthanasia 293–95,
299–302
Germany. 606–07
Netherlands 601–05
Switzerland 607
United States 608–09, 615
France. 393, 437–38,
476–78
Germany 439–40, 442,
446, 448,
566, 606–07
handicapped babies 158–59, 393,
396, 403–04
India 592
medical malpractice 234
Netherlands. 396, 601–05
New Zealand 380
organ transplantation 281–82, 595
Germany. 566
India 592
Turkey. 571
United States 585–86
persistent
vegetative state 305
protection from 60–64
public interest 60–64
surrogacy. 476–78,
487–88, 637
Switzerland 607
Turkey. 450, 571
United States. 403–04,
421, 586–87,
608–09, 615

Damages
See, also, Compensation
antenatal tests 10
assisted reproduction. 483–85
Canada 370
confidentiality 370, 384
consent to
medical treatment. 10, 331
France 530
Germany. 483–85
medical malpractice 530, 534–35,
537–38

Scotland . . . 384
sperm, loss of frozen . . . 483–85
sterilisation, failed. . . . 658–59
United States. . . . 326, 331, 534–35, 537–38

Dangerous patients. . . .
Australia . . . 376
Canada . . . 374
confidentiality . . . 361–64, 374, 376, 381, 635
New Zealand . . . 381
United States . . . 361–64
warnings . . . 361–64, 374, 376, 381, 635

Data protection . . . 69–70

Death
See, also, Advance directives, Assisted suicide, Euthanasia
access to medical records. . . . 70
anencephalic babies . . . 298
assisted reproduction . . . 187–91, 474–75, 481–83
Australia . . . 474–75, 577
best interests of the patient. . . . 306
confidentiality . . . 47, 50–51, 53
definition . . . 284, 296–97, 577
elective ventilation . . . 284
France . . . 481–83
inquests. . . . 285–86
life support machines. . . . 297
organ transplantation . . . 275, 284–87, 298
right to die. . . . 294–95, 298, 611–15, 644, 655
sperm donation after. . . . 187–91, 474–75, 481–83

Decision making . . . 660–61

Defamation . . . 65–66

Denmark. . . . 449

Detention
abortion. . . . 105
children and young persons . . . 123–24
compulsory . . . 23–24, 33–37, 41, 123–24
consent to medical treatment . . . 34–36, 40–43, 123–24
force-feeding . . . 35–36
mental disabilities . . . 34–36, 40–43, 105, 123–24

Disabled persons
See, also, Handicapped babies, Mental disabilities
children and young persons . . . 133, 135–61
consent to medical treatment . . . 37–38
handicapped babies . . . 135–61

Discrimination
handicapped babies . . . 394, 404, 405
United States . . . 404, 405

Diseases
See, also, AIDS/HIV
Canada . . . 370–74
cloning . . . 650–51
confidentiality . . . 58, 364–74, 635–36
standard of care. . . . 367
third parties . . . 366–69, 635–36
United States . . . 364–69
warnings. . . . 364–69, 372

'Do not resuscitate' . . . 317

Double effect principle . . . 82, 301, 642

EC law. . . .
assisted reproduction. . . . 189
cloning . . . 487

Elective ventilation. . . . 284

Embryos . . . 109–12

Emergencies. . . . 28, 89

Ethics . . . 657–58
- abortion . . . 78–81
- advance directives . . . 621
- AIDS/HIV . . . 70–71
- assisted reproduction . . . 164–68, 190, 657–58
- children and young persons . . . 136–38
- comparative law . . . 630
- confidentiality . . . 48, 52–55, 380
- consent to medical treatment . . . 3–7, 632–33
- decision making . . . 660–61
- euthanasia . . . 298–99, 317, 606
- feminist perspectives . . . 660–62
- France . . . 476–79, 559–60
- genetic screening . . . 658
- handicapped babies . . . 136–38, 391–92, 396
- Netherlands . . . 396
- New Zealand . . . 380
- organ transplantation . . . 273, 277–78, 281, 284, 552, 559–60
- persistent vegetative state . . . 305, 306
- Singapore . . . 621
- sterilisation . . . 197–98, 658–59
- surrogacy . . . 169–71, 185, 187, 458–59, 476–79, 487, 657–58

Eugenics . . . 198–99, 208, 639, 492–97

European Convention on Human Rights
See, also, Human Rights Act 1998
- abortion . . . 93, 656
- AIDS/HIV . . . 385, 387
- best interests of the patient . . . 655, 657
- children and young persons . . . 138, 153, 159–60
- confidentiality . . . 384–90
- euthanasia . . . 294, 656
- family life, right to respect for . . . 386–87, 656
- freedom of thought, conscience or religion . . . 657
- handicapped babies . . . 138, 153, 159–60, 655
- inhuman and degrading treatment . . . 153, 655, 656
- interpretation . . . 389–90
- liberty and security of the person, right to . . . 656
- margin of appreciation . . . 388, 656
- medical records . . . 384–89
- mental disabilities . . . 656
- persistent vegetative state . . . 309, 657
- prisoners . . . 656
- private life, right to respect for . . . 384–90, 656
- proportionality . . . 386
- public interest . . . 387
- refusal of medical treatment . . . 657
- right to die . . . 655
- right to life . . . 294, 309, 656, 657
- sterilisation . . . 656

European Union . . . 189
See, also, EC law

Euthanasia . . . 292–319
See, also, Assisted suicide, Persistent vegetative state
- active . . . 293–98
- administration . . . 602, 618
- advance directives . . . 315–17, 620–25
- age discrimination . . . 317
- anencephalic babies . . . 298

Australia 617–20, 625–26
authorisation of
non-treatment 303–17
autonomy 298–99
beneficence 298
best interests
of the patient 315
blood transfusions 295–96
BMA 317–18
civil law countries 599–607
common law 608–09
comparative law 599–627, 642–45
compulsory 299
consent 397–402, 620
criminal offences 292–95, 299–302
Germany 606–07
Netherlands 601–05
Switzerland 607
United States 608–10, 615
death . . . .
anencephalic babies 298
development of
definition of 296–97
statutory 297
definition 292–93
deliberate
termination of life 299–301
'do not resuscitate' 317
double effect principle 301
ethics 298–99, 317, 606
European Convention
on Human Rights 294, 656
Germany 397, 599, 606–07
guidelines 599–605, 626
handicapped babies 300–01, 397–402, 605–06
homicide 293–94, 299–302, 397
Germany 606–07
United States 609
involuntary 293
Jehovah's witnesses 295–96
life support machines 297
mental disabilities 600, 604
necessity 601, 603–06
Netherlands 396–97, 599–606, 626
non-treatment,
authorisation of 303–17
notification 601–02
opinions 300
organ transplantation 298
pain-killing drugs
for pain relief 301–02
passive 293–98
physician-assisted
suicide 293–94, 315, 600, 607, 609–19
Prevention of
Euthanasia Bill 317–18
psychiatrists 604–05
recent developments 317–18
refusal of treatment 616–17
religion 295–96
right to die 294–95, 298, 611–12, 614–15
right to life 294, 656
sanctity of life 299, 606, 626
self-determination 298, 626
Singapore 625–26
slippery slope
argument 315
Switzerland 599, 607
'terminal illness' 618
under-reporting of 600–01
United States 608–17, 625–26
voluntary 293–95, 299, 600
withdrawal
of treatment 616–18
withholding
treatment 293, 618
Evidence
See Experts,
Medical evidence

Experts
- Australia 473
- medical malpractice 251, 256, 259–61
- surrogacy 473

False imprisonment 236–37

Family life, right to respect for 386–87

Family, right to found a 656

Feminism 466, 660–62

Fertility treatment
- *See* Assisted reproduction

Fetal transplantation 283

Fiduciary duties 378–79

Forced feeding 35–36

France
- abortion 436–39, 453
- administrative courts in 527–28
- adoption 477, 479–80
- assisted reproduction 481–82
- assisted suicide 645
- children 560–61
- cloning 486
- consent 348–49, 355, 560
- criminal offences 393, 437–38, 476–78
- damages 530
- death, sperm donation after 481–83
- ethics 476–79, 559–60
- fault 528–30
- *fraude de la loi* doctrine 481
- handicapped babies 393, 397, 399, 641–42
- information 348–49
- medical malpractice 263, 526–30
- organ transplantation 552, 558–61
- *ordre public* doctrine 480–81
- persistent vegetative state 645
- physician-assisted suicide 645
- public/private law divide 527–30
- religion 476
- surrogacy 476–81

Freedom of thought, conscience and religion 657

Gamete intrafallopian transfer 163, 168, 459

General Medical Council
- abortion 92
- AIDS/HIV 71–74
- confidentiality 48, 53–54, 56–57

Germany
- abortion 439–58
  - 1976 legislation 441–43
  - 1992 law 443–44
  - 1995 law reform 445–47
  - cases on 444–45
  - counselling 442, 444, 445–47
  - criminal offences 439–40, 442, 446, 448
  - East Germany 443
  - financial considerations 448–49
  - handicapped babies 442
  - health insurance 448–49
  - history of law on 439–41
  - Nazi laws on 440–41
  - necessity 440
  - post-abortion treatment 447–48
  - Pregnancy Conflict Act 1995 447
  - unification 443
- AIDS/HIV 545–47
- assisted reproduction 483–85

assisted suicide 645
best interests
  of the patient 516, 521
Carership Law 516–21
cloning 486–87
consent 349–52, 355, 516–18, 520, 563–65, 639
criminal offences 439–40, 442, 446, 448, 566, 606–07
damages 483–85
East Germany 443
euthanasia 397, 599, 606–07
handicapped babies 394, 397, 442, 642
health insurance 448–49
high and low risk cases 351
homicide 606–07
information 349–52, 562
medical malpractice 526, 532, 545–47
medical records 564
Nazi 349–50, 440–41, 493
Nuremberg Code 349–50
organ transplantation 561–67, 646
persistent
  vegetative state 645
physician-assisted
  suicide 645
privilege 351–52
proportionality 517
relatives 563–6
self-determination 349, 484–85
sperm, loss of frozen 483–85
sterilisation 515–21
therapeutic and
  diagnostic
  interventions 350–51
unification 443

Gillick competence
abortion 91
Children Act
  proceedings 120
children and
  young persons 117, 118–24, 133–34, 161, 638, 640
comparative law 638
consent to
  medical treatment 118–19
contraception 118–19
paternalism 649
refusal of treatment 120–21, 649

GMC
  See General
    Medical Council

Greece 526

Guyana 451

Handicapped babies,
  treatment of
abortion 442
anencephalic babies 298, 406–07
Australia 407
best interests of 133, 138, 140–41, 144–51, 156–61, 391, 393, 407–09, 641, 653
Bolam test 139
child abuse 405–06
civil law countries 392–405
codes of practice 393–94
common law
  countries 392–405, 407
comparative
  perspective 391–412, 641–42
compulsory
  treatment 404
conjoined twins 155–60, 402, 641
consent to medical
  treatment 393, 397–402, 408–09
  refusal of 402–05
criminal offences 158–59, 393, 396, 403–04
death, definition of 298

'demonstrably awful' test 140
discrimination 394, 404, 405
double effect principle 399, 642
English law 641
ethics 136–38, 391–92, 396
EURONIC 392
European Convention on Human Rights 138, 153, 159–60, 655
euthanasia 298, 300–01, 397–402, 605–06
France 393, 397, 399, 641–42
Germany 394, 397, 442, 642
homicide 139, 158–59, 393–94, 398–99
infanticide 135–36, 392
Italy 393–94, 397, 399, 641–42
life, active intervention to end 396–97, 399–400
Luxembourg 393, 397
Netherlands 395–96, 398, 399, 605–06, 642
New Zealand 407–09
'no chance' situations 148
organ transplantation 298
parents 138, 144–47, 641
quality of life 137–38, 142, 151–52
refusal of consent 402–05
religion 148–49, 155, 160
resources 151–60, 409–10, 654–55
right to life 153, 159, 404
sanctity of life 137–38, 147, 400, 407
Sweden 394–95, 397, 642
UK, in 395, 398, 399, 642
United States 400–02, 405–07
wardship 395
withdrawing medical treatment 392–97, 399, 408
withholding medical treatment 392–97

Healthcare professionals
AIDS/HIV 71
confidentiality 50
teams of 50

Hippocratic Oath 47

HIV
See AIDS/HIV

Home, persons cared for at home 312

Homicide
abortion 81–82, 97–100, 431
assisted suicide 291–92, 302, 397, 642
Canada 431
children and young persons 139, 158–59
euthanasia 293–94, 299–302, 397, 606–07
handicapped babies 139, 158–59, 393, 394, 398
Italy 393, 394
necessity 159
Netherlands 606–07
organ transplantation 278
persistent vegetative state 307

Hospital reports 66–67

Human Fertilisation and Embryology Authority 165–68, 188–90

Human organ
transplantation
See Organ
transplantation

Human rights
See, also, European
Convention on
Human Rights,
Human Rights
Act 1998
medical treatment 655–57
sterilisation 210–14

Human Rights Act 1998
Bland case 309
consent to
medical treatment 4, 633
effect of 655
exclusions from
treatment 655–56
persistent
vegetative state 309
privacy 187
right to life 4, 309
surrogacy 187

Hysterectomies 220–22

In vitro fertilisation. 163, 165,
168, 184, 459

Indemnities 235–36

India 453, 590–93

Infanticide 135–36, 392

Infections
See Diseases

Informants 67–68

Information
See, also, Confidentiality
antenatal tests 10–11
Australia 337–47, 379
Bolam test 633–34
Canada 333–37, 633–34
comparative law 633–34
consent to
medical treatment 9–11, 326–30,
333–47
France 348–49
freedom of 379
Germany 349–52, 562–63
Japan 353–55
level of 9
medical malpractice 247–50, 260–61
organ transplantation. 562–63
police 58
privilege 633
Sidaway case 633
United States 326–30, 355
warnings 633

Inhuman and
degrading treatment 153, 655, 656

Inquests 286

Insurance
companies 600
confidentiality 50
euthanasia 600
life 588
medical 600
organ transplantation 588
United States 588

Ireland
abortion 100–05, 112–13
consent 538–39
general and
approved practice 540, 543
medical malpractice 538–43
res ipsa loquitur 539, 541–43
standard of care 540, 543
strict liability 539

Italy
codes of practice 393–94, 399
consent 393
discrimination 394
handicapped babies 393–94, 397,
399, 641–42
homicide 393, 394
medical malpractice 536–27, 531

Japan
- consent 352–56
  - payment for informed 352–56
- information 353–56
- medical malpractice 531
- organ transplantation. 594

Jehovah's witnesses . . . . .
- blood transfusions 295–96
- children and young persons. 124, 126
- consent to medical treatment 124, 126
- euthanasia 295–96
- guidelines for treatment of 295–96

Judicial review. 150–51

Jurisdiction
- abortion. 88
- children and young persons. 132
- inherent. 132, 224
- sterilisation 210–11, 217, 224

Legal aid 332

Liberty and security of the person. 656

Life
- *See* Right to life

Life support treatment
- death, definition of 297
- euthanasia 293, 297
- withholding 293

Living wills
- *See* Advance directives

Luxembourg 393, 397

Malpractice
- *See* Medical malpractice

Medicaid. 422

Medical confidentiality
- *See* Confidentiality

Medical evidence
- medical malpractice 251
- sterilisation. 224–25

Medical insurance. 600

Medical malpractice. 233–68
- AIDS/HIV 544–47
- Audit Commission report. 266–67
- Australia 262, 340–47, 543–44
- autonomy 260
- Belgium. 526–27
- *Bolam* test. 236, 238–41, 249–50, 255–60, 263–67, 634
  - interpretation of 243–47
- *Bolitho* case 255–57, 259–61, 264, 267–68, 533, 634
- burden of proof 527
- Canada 538
- care, degree of 532
- causation 236, 250–53, 257
- Central Europe 526
- cervical smear tests. 263–66
- civil law 525–30, 545–47, 549
- common law. 234–35, 525, 544–45
- comparative law 525–50, 634–35
- complaints 234
- consent. 244–45, 247–50, 326, 331, 340–47, 355–56, 538
  - lack of, effect of 533
- contingency fees 635
- contractual liability. 526–27
- criminal law 234
- criterion of 533
- current developments, keeping abreast of. 239–40
- custom. 238
- damages. 267, 530, 534–35, 537–38

doctors
 junior and
  inexperienced 238
 reasonable
  doctor test 262–63
 specialist 241
 standard of care 237, 532
duty of care 234–35, 532–33
English law, in 233–34, 267–68, 533
errors of judgment 242–45
establishment of 253–57
experts 251, 256–61
false imprisonment 236–37
France 263, 526–30
Germany 526, 532, 545–47
Greece 526, 532
guidelines 268
historical perspectives 233
information,
 amount to be given 247–50, 260–62
Ireland 538–43
Italy 526–27, 531
Japan 531
juries 635
litigation in UK 266–67
medical evidence 251
multiple causes 252–53
negligence, difference
 from actions in 236
New Zealand 547–49
NHS indemnity 235–36
no-fault compensation 547–49
opinions 243, 245, 251, 256–58
persons who
 can be sued 235
pregnancy 242
privilege 248, 263
professional
 accountability 233–68
professionals, views
 of one body of 257–59
proof of 236, 527
public/private
 law divide 527–30
reasonable doctor test 262–63, 532
res ipsa loquitur 253–57, 539, 541–43
Scandinavia 531
Sidaway case 241, 244–48, 257–58, 261–62
simple 530
slight 532
socialist principles 531
specialists 241
standard of care 233–34, 239–41, 263–66, 540, 543, 634–35
 doctors, of 237, 532
sterilisation 220–22, 230
Sweden 549
Switzerland 526
UK, in 266–67
United States 326, 331, 534–38, 544–45, 634–35
usual practice 238, 241
vicarious liability 235
warnings 7, 244–45

Medical records
 See, also, Access to
  medical records
 confidentiality 384–89
 copies of 69
 European Convention
  on Human Rights 384–89
 Germany 564
 organ transplantation 564

Medical treatment
 See, also, Consent to
  medical treatment,
  Refusal of medical
  treatment,
  Withdrawing
  medical treatment
 comparative law 655–57
 compulsory 404
 exclusions from 655–56

handicapped babies 392–97
human rights 655–57
withholding 392–97, 618, 623

Mental disabilities
See, also, Handicapped babies, Persistent vegetative state, Psychological harm
abortion 39, 105, 414, 415, 633
advance directives 315–17
best interests of the patient 653
Caesarean sections 13, 15–20
Canada 105, 374
children and young persons 121–24, 638, 640–41
comparative law 491–523, 638–40
confidentiality 362–63, 374, 382–83
consent to medical treatment 11–12, 15–20, 23–43, 633
refusal of 121, 638
detention 34–36, 40–43, 105
European Convention on Human Rights 656
euthanasia 604–05
force-feeding 35–36
inhuman and degrading treatment 656
liberty and security of the person 656
Mental Health Review Tribunals 41
necessity 39–43
Netherlands 604–05
New Zealand 382–83
organ transplantation 278–80, 283, 587
refusal of treatment 121, 638
Scotland 640–41
sterilisation 197–232, 491–523, 639–40, 653
United States 362–63, 587

Minors
See Children and young persons

Murder
See Homicide

National Health Service
costs 332
indemnities 235–36
medical malpractice 235–36

Nazi Germany 349–50, 440–41, 639

Necessity
best interests of the patient 42
children and young persons 126, 159
consent to medical treatment 37, 39–43
euthanasia 601, 603, 606
homicide 159
mental disabilities 39–43
Netherlands 601, 603, 606
sterilisation 218, 639

Negligence
See Medical malpractice

Netherlands
assisted suicide 605, 644–45
autonomy 645
criminal offences 396, 601–05
ethics 396
euthanasia 396–97, 599–606, 626
administration 602
case law 602–06
criminal offences 601–05
guidelines 599–605, 626
handicapped babies 605–06
medical infrastructure 600–01

mental disabilities....... 600, 604–05
necessity............... 601, 603–06
notification................. 601–02
psychiatrists................ 604–05
handicapped babies........... 395–96, 398–400, 605–06, 642
medical insurance................ 600
mental disabilities............ 600, 604
organ transplantation............. 567
persistent vegetative state............. 644–45
physician-assisted suicide................. 600, 644–45
psychiatrists.................. 604–05
self-determination............ 397, 645

New Zealand
abortion..................... 107–09
best interests of patient........ 408–09
common law................ 379, 407
confidentiality................ 379–83
consent..................... 365, 409
informed...................... 408
refusal of.................... 348
criminal offences................. 380
dangerous patients............... 381
English law and................. 379
handicapped babies........... 407–09
medical malpractice........... 547–49
mental disabilities............. 382–83
no-fault compensation..... 379, 547–49
privilege.................... 379, 380
remedies..................... 381–83
withdrawal of treatment.......... 408

NHS
See National Health Service

Northern Ireland........ 100–05, 112–13

Nuremberg Code........... 324, 349–50

Offences against the person.............. 83–85, 97–99, 101–02

Official Solicitor......... 223–27, 313–15

Omissions
best interests of the patient.................. 654
persistent vegetative state............. 304–05, 308, 654

Opinions..................... 243, 245, 251, 256–59

Organ transplantation........... 271–89
aborted fetuses, tissue from.................... 569
advertising........................ 55
age............................. 579
AIDS/HIV....................... 575
Alder Hey hospital scandal............. 287–88
allocation criteria......... 566–67, 589
ambiguity.................... 286–87
anencephalic babies.............. 298
Asia......................... 589–94
Australia................. 571–80, 646
Austria.................. 557–58, 646
autonomy...................... 274
background to................... 272
Belgium...................... 556–57
best interests of the donor........... 279, 586–88
BMA.................. 283–84, 286, 552–53, 555
bone marrow................. 280–81
corneas...................... 578–79
cadaveric.............. 275, 284–87, 562–63, 577, 589–90
centres for transplantation............. 565–66
children............. 280–82, 287–88, 554, 560–61, 573, 575–76, 586–88
China....................... 593–94
civil law countries............. 555–71
close relationships................ 280
codes of practice................. 579
common law............ 278, 571–89

comparative law 551–97, 645–47
consent 275–78, 283, 287, 595
 Australia 576–77
 Austria 557
 coroners 577
 France 560
 Germany 563–65
 informed 565
 pre-consent perfusion 581–89
 presumed 283, 289, 552–53, 557, 568, 581–89, 646–47
 revocation 576–77
 Sweden 568
 United States 581–89
 written 646
contracting out/
 contracting in 552–53, 595, 646
criminal offences 281–82, 566, 571, 585–86, 592, 595
death, donations after 275, 284–87, 298, 562–63, 577, 589–90
declarations
 of donations 562–63
discriminatory
 conditions 288–89
donor cards 562, 584–85
education 562
elective ventilation 284
ethics 273, 277–78, 281, 284, 552, 559–60
euthanasia 298
Far East 589–94
fetal transplants 283
France 552, 558–61
Germany 646
historical background 551, 590–91
homicide 278
hospitals,
 regulation of 592
incompetent
 adults as donors 283
increase availability,
 attempts to 588–89
India 590–93
information 562
inquests 285–86
intention 595, 646
Japan 594
legal perspectives 272
life insurance 588
life support systems 578
live donations 275, 277–82, 560–61, 564–65, 569, 574–76, 586–88
medical records 564, 592
mental disabilities 278–80, 283, 587
Netherlands 567
next of kin 563–64, 568–69, 573–74, 578, 580, 583–86, 646
People's Republic
 of China 593–94
possession of
 the body 286
pre-consent
 perfusion 581–89
reasons for 271
recent developments 287–89
reform 289
regenerative tissue 573, 574–76
registration 556, 558, 567, 592
regulation 281
relatives, contacting 286–87, 557–58, 563–64, 568–69, 573–74, 578, 580, 583–86, 592, 595, 646

removal of organs 275–77
respect for persons
principle 646
Royal College of
Pathologists
guidelines 288
sale of organs 273–75, 554–55, 590–91
Scotland 286
self-mutilation,
licence for 277
shortage of organs 271–72, 581–82, 586, 646
Spain 551, 567–68
statistics 272, 551, 556–59, 561, 568–69, 571–72, 586, 593
Sweden 568–69, 646
therapeutic donations 278, 284–87
trading in tissue 573
transgenic 275
Turkey 569–71
UK, in 274–75, 283–84, 286, 646–47
UK Transplants
Support Service
Authority 274–75
ULTRA 282
unconscious donors 578
undue pressure 554
United States 278–81, 580–89
unlawful acts 275–77
unrelated persons,
between 282–84
World Health
Organisation
principles 553–55
xenotransplantation 275

Pain relief 301–02
Palliative care 624
Parents
abortion 423
assisted reproduction 164, 166
children and
young persons 117, 121–22, 127–31, 138, 144–47, 155–60
handicapped babies 138, 144–47, 641
parental responsibility 121–22, 127–31, 168
refusal of treatment 121–24, 127–31
surrogacy 173, 180–84
Paternalism 198–99, 638, 640
People's Republic
of China 452, 593–94
Persistent
vegetative state . . . .
acts and omissions 308
artificial feeding 643–44
assisted suicide 644–45
authorisation of
non-treatment 303–15
autonomy 309, 645
best interests
of the patient 306, 308, 309, 408, 643, 653–54, 657
Bland case 304–13, 643–44, 653–54
BMA guidelines 309–11
Bolam test 305–06, 308
care, ordinary
and extraordinary 308
comparative law 642–45
consent to
medical treatment 613–14
continuing
vegetative state 303
court applications 314
criminal offences 305, 307
definitions 303
diagnosis 304, 313
ethics 305–06

European
Convention on
Human Rights 309, 657
France 645
Germany 645
home, patients
cared for at 312
homicide 307
Human Rights
Act 1998 309
incompetent
adult patients 303
investigations 314–15
judges, sanction
for withdrawal by 313
Netherlands 644–45
Official Solicitor 313–15
omissions 304–05,
308, 654
parties 314
permanent
vegetative state 303–04
Practice Notes 313–15
privacy 612
quality of life 643
refusal of treatment 611–13
relatives, significance
of views of 311–12, 315,
318, 614
right to die 611–12, 644
right to life 309, 657
Royal College
of Physicians 303
sanctity of life 305, 308, 643
Scotland 312
self-determination 645
United States 304,
610–14, 644
withdrawal of
treatment 304–06,
309–13, 612,
614, 643–44,
654, 657

Police, volunteering
information to 58

Precedent 384

Pregnancy
See, also, Abortion
antenatal tests 9–11
Caesarean section 13–31,
36–37, 44
children and
young persons 133
consent to
medical treatment 13–31,
36–37, 44
errors 242–45
guidelines 26–28
medical malpractice 242–45
multiple 95
sterilisation 201–03, 206–07,
209–11, 214–15,
223, 225, 227–28

Prisoners
AIDS/HIV 72–73
European Convention
on Human Rights 656
liberty and security
of the person 656

Privacy
abortion 417, 422–24,
426, 453, 656
Canada 370
confidentiality 53, 73, 361, 370
European Convention
on Human Rights 73, 656
Human Rights
Act 1998 187
persistent
vegetative state 612
sterilisation 497–99
surrogacy 187
United States 361, 417,
422–24, 426,
497, 612

Private life
See Privacy

Privilege
Australia 377
Canada 369–70

confidentiality 58, 66–67, 69
Australia 377
Canada 369–70
New Zealand 379, 380
United States 359–62, 377
consent 327, 330
Germany 351–52
information,
disclosure of 633
legal professional
privilege 66–67
medical malpractice 248, 263
New Zealand 379, 380
reports 66–67
United States 327, 330,
359–62, 377

Professionals
See Healthcare
professionals

Prohibited steps orders 132

Proportionality
abortion 432
Australia 432
confidentiality 386
European Convention
on Human Rights 386
Germany 517
sterilisation 221, 517

Psychiatrists
Canada 374
confidentiality 360, 363, 374
United States 360, 363

Psychological harm
abortion 414, 415, 431
Canada 431
sterilisation 225

Psychologists 361–63

Public interest
AIDS/HIV 59–62, 371
Australia 376
Canada 371, 373
confidentiality 48, 52, 56,
59–64, 68, 74
Australia 376
Canada 371, 373
European Convention
on Human Rights 387
United States 359, 361
crime prevention 60–64
definition 59–63
United States 361

Public policy
confidentiality 67–68
informants 67–68
surrogacy 172, 174,
465, 469

Public/private law divide 527–30

Quality of life
children and
young persons 137–38,
142, 151–52
handicapped babies 137–38,
142, 151–52
persistent
vegetative state 643

Quasi-legislation 66

Records
See Access to medical
records, Medical
records

Refusal of consent
to medical treatment
advance directives 315–17
AIDS/HIV 129–31
assisted suicide 617
Caesarean section 13–31,
36–37, 44
Canada 333–34
children and
young persons 117–18, 120–33,
155–60,
638, 640
comparative law 638

consent to medical treatment 11–12, 14–36
European Convention on Human Rights 657
euthanasia 616–17
freedom of thought, conscience and religion 657
Gillick competence 120–21, 640
handicapped babies 402–05
heart transplants 125–27
mental disabilities 121, 638
New Zealand 348
parents 121–24, 127–31
paternalism 640
persistent vegetative state 611
religion 124, 126, 133, 148–49, 155, 160
suicide 617
United States 402–05, 611, 616–17

Relatives
See, also, Parents
abortion 427–28
advance directives 620–21
Australia 505–06, 573–74, 578, 580
India 592
next of kin 646
organ transplants 286–87, 568–69, 573–74, 578, 580, 583–86, 592, 595, 646
persistent vegetative state 311–12, 315, 318, 614
Singapore 620–21
sterilisation 505–08
Sweden 568–69
United States 427–28, 583–86, 614
views of 286–87, 311–12, 315, 318

Religion
See, also, Jehovah's witnesses
advance directives 621
children and young persons 124, 126, 148–49, 155, 160
European Convention on Human Rights 657
France 476
freedom of thought, conscience and religion 657
handicapped babies . . . 148–49, 155, 160
refusal of consent to medical treatment 124, 126, 133, 148–49, 155, 160
Singapore 621
surrogacy 476

Res ipsa loquitur
consent 325
Ireland 539, 541–43
medical malpractice 253–57, 539, 541–43
United States 325

Research
abortion 109–12
Canada 333
confidentiality 51
consent 324, 333
embryos 109–12
United States 324

Resources
allocation 151–60, 409–10
assisted reproduction 191–92
children and young persons 151–60
comparative law 654–55
handicapped babies 151–60, 409–10, 654–55

quality adjusted
life years 151–52
UK, in 654–55

Respect for
persons principle. 646

Right to die 294–95, 298, 611–15, 644, 655

Right to life
abortion 102–03, 656
children and
young persons. 153, 159
consent to medical
treatment 3
European Convention
on Human Rights. 294, 309, 656, 657
euthanasia 294, 656
handicapped babies 153, 159, 404
Human Rights
Act 1998 . . . . 3, 309
persistent
vegetative state 309, 657
United States 404

Romania 451–52

Royal College
of Pathologists. 288

Royal College
of Physicians 303

Sanctity of life . . . .
Australia. 407
children and
young persons. 137–38, 147
euthanasia 299, 606, 626
handicapped babies 137–38, 147, 400, 407
persistent
vegetative state 305, 308, 643
United States 400

Scandinavia
See Constituent countries

Scotland
abortion 88, 90, 436
best interests
of the patient 227–30
children and
young persons. 640–41
confidentiality 383–84
damages 384
mental disabilities. 640–41
organ transplantation. 286
persistent
vegetative state 312
precedent 384
sterilisation. 227–30

Section 8 orders. 132

Self-determination
abortion. 113
access to medical records. 378
Australia. 378
consent to
medical treatment 3, 12, 329, 338, 341, 344
euthanasia 298, 626
Germany. 349, 397
Netherlands 397, 645
persistent
vegetative state 645
surrogacy 466
United States. 329, 338, 341, 344, 466

Self-mutilation. 277

Seychelles. 451

Sexual conduct 64–65

Siamese twins. 155–60, 402, 641

Sidaway case
consent to medical
treatment 6, 28, 43
information,
disclosure of. 633
medical malpractice 244–48, 257–59, 261–62

Singapore 620–25

Smear tests 263–66

Socialist countries 531

South Africa 452

Spain
- abortion 449, 453
- organ transplantation 551, 567–68

Spare part cloning 649–52

Specialists 241

Specific issue orders 132, 150

Sperm donation
- after death 187–91, 474–75, 481–83

Standard of care
- Australia 345–46
- Canada 335
- cervical smear test 253–66
- confidentiality 367
- consent 327–30, 335, 345–46
- diseases 367
- doctors 237
- Ireland 540, 543
- medical malpractice 233–34, 237, 239–41, 263–66, 532, 540, 543
- United States 327–30, 367

Sterilisation
- ability to parent test 499
- adult patients 205, 215–22
- Australia 504–16, 639
  - best interests of the patient 506–14
  - consent 514–15
  - incidence of sterilisation in 510–13
  - legislation in 514–15
  - relatives 505–08
- autonomy 197
- best interests
  - of the patient 133, 197–98, 201, 208, 213–14, 218–19, 224–25, 653
    - Australia 506–14
    - Germany 516, 521, 639
    - Scotland 227–30
    - United States 498
- birth control, as 491, 518
- *Bolam* test 218, 220–22, 639
- Canada 198, 205, 207–08, 212, 230, 492–93, 501–04
- carers 515–21
- case law, key
  - principles from 200–01
- Children Act
  - proceedings 222–24
- children and
  - young persons 133, 201–15, 223, 225–26
- comparative law 491–523, 639–40
- compulsory 198–99, 517
- consent to medical
  - treatment 38–39, 44, 200, 216–19, 228–30, 533, 639–40
  - Australia 514–15
  - Germany 516–18, 520
- contraception
  - alternative
    - methods of 212–13, 217, 226
  - as 491, 518
- court applications 218, 223–24
- damages 658–59
- England, incidence in 521
- ethics 197–98, 658–59
- eugenics 198–99, 208, 492–97, 639
- European Convention
  - on Human Rights 656
- failed, liability for 220–22, 658–59
- family, right
  - to found a 656
- Germany 198–99, 493, 515–21, 639

best interests of
  the patient . . . 516, 521
Carership Law . . . 515–21
consent . . . 516–18, 520, 639
guardianship . . . 516–21
incidence of
  sterilisation . . . 521
proportionality . . . 517
historical background . . . 198–200, 491–93
human rights . . . 210–14
hysterectomies . . . 220–22
judges, sanction of . . . 200–01, 216, 218, 221, 223
jurisdiction . . . 210–11, 217, 224
last resort, as . . . 206–07
medical evidence . . . 224–25
medical malpractice . . . 220–22, 230
mental disabilities . . . 197–232, 491–523, 639–40, 653
Nazis . . . 198–99, 493, 639
necessity . . . 218, 639
non-consensual . . . 200–15
non-therapeutic . . . 199–202, 502, 506, 509–10, 513, 639
Official Solicitor . . . 223–27
parties . . . 224
paternalism . . . 198–99
Practice Directions . . . 200, 201, 222–27, 229–30
pregnancy, risk of . . . 201–03, 206–07, 209–11, 214–15, 223, 225, 227–28
privacy . . . 497–99
procedure . . . 224
procreate, right to . . . 498–99
proportionality . . . 221, 517
psychological harm . . . 225
relatives . . . 505–08
Scotland . . . 227–30
statistics . . . 200
substituted
  judgment test . . . 499–500
Sweden . . . 493
therapeutic . . . 199–202, 502–03, 506, 509–10, 517, 639
United States . . . 198–99, 491–92, 494–500, 502, 639
  ability to parent test . . . 499
  best interests of
    the patient . . . 498
  current law . . . 497–500
  eugenics . . . 492, 494–97
  guidelines . . . 497–98
  historical background . . . 494–97
  President's
    commission
    recommendations . . . 500
  privacy . . . 497
  substituted
    judgment test . . . 499–500
  transformation
    of law in . . . 496–97
wardship . . . 202, 204, 207, 214, 216

Suicide
  See, also, Assisted
    suicide, Euthanasia
  English law . . . 608
  refusal of
    medical treatment . . . 617
  United States . . . 608, 615, 617

Surrogacy . . . 163–64, 168–87, 193
  adoption . . . 172, 176–79, 465, 467, 477, 479–81
  advantages . . . 169
  advertising . . . 177

agencies . . . 186
arguments in
favour of . . . 170
Australia . . . 470–74
experts . . . 473
legislation . . . 471
autonomy . . . 170
best interests
of the child . . . 172, 175–76, 180–82, 185, 187
BMA policy . . . 184, 186
Brazier Review . . . 179, 184–86, 187
change of mind . . . 173, 174, 179–80
choice, role of . . . 187
civil law . . . 476–85
codes of practice . . . 186
commercial . . . 174–79, 185, 460, 637
Commissions
of Inquiry . . . 171
comparative law . . . 457–90, 637–38
criminalisation . . . 476–78, 487–88, 637
enforcement . . . 172, 173, 174, 460, 637
English cases on . . . 173–84, 470, 637–38
ethical and
moral issues . . . 169–71, 185, 187, 458–59, 476, 479, 487, 657–58
expenses . . . 169, 177–79, 184–86,193, 478–79
experts . . . 473
fees . . . 169, 171–72, 174–79, 183–86, 193
feminism . . . 466
France . . . 476–81
adoption . . . 477, 479–81
criminal offences . . . 476–78
disapproval of, in . . . 476–77
expenses . . . 478–79
fraude de la loi
doctrine . . . 481
immoral earnings,
living off . . . 477–78
mother and
child relationship . . . 478
ordre public doctrine . . . 480–81
religion . . . 476
validity of
contracts on
surrogacy . . . 480–81
full . . . 169
gestational . . . 467–70
Human Rights Act 1998 . . . 187
immoral earnings,
living off . . . 477–78
in vitro fertilisation . . . 184
intention . . . 469–70
male control over . . . 169–71
meaning . . . 168
medical reasons for . . . 459–60
mother and
child relationship . . . 478
natural and
legal mother,
identity of . . . 467–70
objections to . . . 170–71
parents . . . 173, 180–84
partial . . . 169, 177–78
privacy . . . 187
problems with . . . 173
public policy . . . 172, 174, 465, 469
refusal to
give up child . . . 173, 174
regulation of . . . 171–73, 186
religion . . . 476
self-determination . . . 466
UK, in . . . 169, 173–84, 487–88
United States . . . 169, 172, 185, 458, 459–75, 637
adoption . . . 465

feminism 466
gestational surrogacy 467–70
public policy 465
self-determination 466
status of arrangements 461–62
wardship 175–76, 637–38
Warnock Committee 169, 171, 185

Sweden
abortion 450, 569
handicapped babies 394–95, 397, 642
medical malpractice 549
no-fault compensation 549
organ transplantation 568–69, 646
relatives 568–69
sterilisation 493
tissues from aborted fetuses 569

Switzerland
assisted suicide 607
consent 355
criminal offences 607
euthanasia 599, 607

Teenagers
See Children and young persons

Terrorism 58

Therapists 361–63

Third parties
confidentiality 62–65, 363–64, 366–69, 635–36
diseases 366–69, 635–36
protection of 62–65
United States 62–63, 363–64, 366–69

Transgenic transplantation 275

Transplants
See Organ transplantation

Trespass to the person 8–9

Turkey 450, 451, 569–71

UK Central Council of Nursing 51

UK Transplants Support Service Authority 274–75

ULTRA 282

UN Convention on the Rights of the Child 134

Unborn children
See, also, Abortion
Caesarean sections 13, 21, 24, 29–30, 37
consent to medical treatment 13, 21, 24–26, 29–31, 37
fertility treatment 26
legal status of 96–97
organ transplantation 283
protection of 96–100
rights of 13, 21, 24–26, 29–31, 37
United States 422

United States
abortion 77, 82, 417–31, 631–32
cases on 423–29
comparative observations on 429–30
consent 428
criminal offences 421
fathers and 423
health 424–25
historical background to laws on 419–21
liberalisation 421–22, 427
Medicaid 422
privacy 417, 422–24, 426
procedural background 418–19
public employees 427

reform movement 420–22
relatives. 427–28
sources of law 417
state medical
association
regulations 429
states and 418, 429
advance directives 616–17, 625
AIDS/HIV 364, 366–67,
369, 544–45, 636
assault 326
assisted reproduction. 166–67
assisted suicide 599, 608–17
Australia 338, 340, 341,
344, 348
battery 326
best interests
of the patient 498, 586–88
bone marrow
transplants 280–81
children
abuse 405–06
organ transplantation. 586–88
cloning 487
compulsory treatment 404
confidentiality. 62–63,
359–69, 636
conjoined twins 402
consent to medical
treatment 3, 8–14
abortion. 428
Australia 338, 340,
341, 344, 348
informed 3, 8–14,
323–331,
355, 632–33
organ transplants 581–89
pre-consent
perfusion. 581–89
presumed 581–89
refusal of. 402–05
contingency fees 332, 635
contractual
undertakings 535–37
costs 331
courts. 534
criminal offences 403–04, 421,
585–86,
608–09, 615
damages. 331, 422,
534–35, 537–38
dangerous patients 361–64
discrimination 404, 405
diseases 364–69
eugenics 492, 494–97
euthanasia 599, 608–17,
625–26
criminal offences 608–09, 615
homicide 609
physician-assisted
suicide 609–17
refusal of treatment 616–17
survey of laws 608–10
right to die 611–15
withdrawal
of treatment 616–18
federalism. 417–19, 534
fetus, legal status of a 422
handicapped babies 400–07
homicide 609
information 349–52, 355
juries 534, 635
legal culture in 534
life insurance 588
litigation 331
Medicaid 422
medical malpractice 326, 331,
534–38, 544–45,
634–35
mental disabilities. 362–64, 587
organ
transplantation 278–81, 580–89
palliative care 624
parents 423
persistent
vegetative state 304, 610–14, 644
physician-assisted
suicide 609–14

precedent 330
privacy 361, 417, 422–24, 426, 497, 612
privilege 325, 327, 330, 359–62, 377
psychiatrists 360
psychologists 261–63
public interest 361
refusal of medical treatment 402–05, 611, 616–17
relatives' views 583–86, 614
res ipsa loquitur 325
research 324
right to life 404
sanctity of life 400
self-determination 329
sources of law 417
standard of care 327–30, 367
sterilisation 198–99, 494–500, 502, 639
strict liability 544–45
suicide 608, 615
surrogacy 169, 172, 185, 458, 459–75, 637
therapists 361–63
third parties 62–63, 363–64, 366–69
UN Convention on the Rights of the Child 134
violent patients 361–64
warnings 361–67
warranties, breach of 544
Wigmore criteria 360–61
withdrawal of medical treatment 612, 614, 616–18
wrongful death 422

Unrelated Live Transplants Regulatory Persons 282–84

Utilitarianism 52

Ventilation, elective 284

Vicarious liability 235

Victimisation 631

Violent patients
See Dangerous patients

Wardship
Children Act proceedings 132
handicapped adults 395
sterilisation 202, 204, 207, 214, 216
surrogacy 175, 637

Warnings
AIDS/HIV 366–67, 369, 635
Australia 346
Canada 335–36, 372
confidentiality 361–69, 372, 374, 376, 381, 635
consent to medical treatment 7, 335–36, 346–47
dangerous patients 361–64, 374, 376, 381, 735
diseases 364–69, 372
information, disclosure of 633
medical malpractice 244–45
United States 361–69

Warnock Committee
abortion 110–12
assisted reproduction 165
cloning 648
surrogacy 169, 171, 185

Welfare principle
See Best interests of the patient

Withdrawal of medical treatment
advance directives 616–17
Australia 618

best interests of
the patient.......................654
euthanasia 293, 616–18
handicapped babies.......392–97, 408
home, patients
cared for at 312
New Zealand....................408
persistent
vegetative state......304–06, 309–12,
612, 614, 643–44,
654, 657
United States.........612, 614, 616–17

Withholding of
medical treatment.....392–97, 618, 623
Women.........................660–62
World Health
Organisation 486–87, 553–55

Xenotransplantation................275

Young persons...................53–55
See, also, Children
and young persons